Economic Growth and Change

Economic Growth and Change

National and Regional Patterns of Convergence and Divergence

Edited by

John Adams

Professor of Economics, Northeastern University and Visiting Scholar, Center for South Asian Studies, University of Virginia, USA

Francesco Pigliaru

Associate Professor of Economics, University of Cagliari, Italy and Director, Centre for North–South Economic Research (CRENoS)

Edward Elgar
Cheltenham, UK • Northampton, MA, USA

Published by
Edward Elgar Publishing Limited
Glensanda House
Montpellier Parade
Cheltenham
Glos GL50 1UA
UK

Edward Elgar Publishing, Inc
6 Market Street
Northampton
Massachusetts 01060
USA

A catalogue record for this book
is available from the British Library

Library of Congress Cataloguing in Publication Data

Economic growth and change : national and regional patterns of
    convergence and divergence / edited by John Adams, Francesco
    Pigliaru.
        Includes index.
        1. Economic development. 2. Regional disparities. 3. United
    States—Economic conditions—1981—Regional disparities.
    4. Europe—Economic conditions—1945—Regional disparities.
    5. European Union countries—Economic conditions— Regional
    disparities.   I. Adams, John, 1938–   . II. Pigliaru, Francesco.
    HD82.E2845 1999
    338.9—dc21
                                                            98–33209
                                                              CIP

ISBN 1 85898 683 4

Contents

PART III   REGIONAL MOSAICS IN NATIONAL CONTEXTS

Figures

Tables

Preface

John Adams and Francesco Pigliaru

On 19–21 June 1997, the Centre for North–South Economic Research (CRENoS) of the University of Cagliari hosted a conference devoted to the theme, 'Economic Growth and Change, A Comparative Analysis'. The co-organizer of the meeting was the Department of Economics, Northeastern University, Boston. The conference was the culmination of a three-year collaboration between CRENoS and the Economic Growth Group at Northeastern University. In addition to the participants from CRENoS and Northeastern, a number of distinguished scholars were invited to make contributions. The three-way interaction was extremely fruitful and this book is its tangible product. Because the conference was open to local faculty and student attendance, the presenters benefited from a wide spectrum of challenging and helpful commentary that we are happy to acknowledge and doubtlessly improved the quality of the contributions. In addition, two of the chapters in the book do not stem directly from offerings at the conference, because of the absence of their authors, Irma Adelman and Shahid Alam, but parts of their work were included in the conference presentation of one of the editors (Adams) and formally discussed.

The editors are grateful to the contributors for the time they have spent in preparing their chapters for final publication and for their involvement in the June 1997 conference. At Northeastern, Cheryl Noakes and Patricia Logan provided logistical support for a large number of faculty exchanges and visits, assisted graduate students from the University of Cagliari, arranged faculty participation in conferences, and handled travel details. We thank them for their work and enthusiasm for all aspects of our joint collaborations. At the University of Cagliari, which provided generous financial backing for the joint work, and the final conference, a strong initial impetus was provided by the university's Rector, Pasquale Mistretta. The former president of CRENoS, Antonio Sassu, himself an economist, likewise encouraged all aspects of the cooperative relationship even during a time when he was on leave, serving as a member of the regional government of Sardinia. The completion of this book, we hope, stands as a justification of their faith in launching the Cagliari–Northeastern endeavour. Further thanks are due to Raffaele Paci, of CRENoS, who spent the academic year 1996–97 at Northeastern and played an important role in making our collaboration work efficiently. He was one of the co-organizers of the June 1997 conference. At CRENoS, Rosanna Carcangiu deserves special thanks for taking care efficiently of all details concerning the complex organization of our Sardinia meetings. Marcella Pusceddu, secretary of the Dipartimento di Ricerche Economiche e Sociali, offered her competent advice whenever needed. One of the editors (Pigliaru) spent the final stages of editing this volume at the Department of Economics, SOAS, University of London, as a Visiting Academic. The Department and the CIEE offer an environment where one is constantly reminded of how many different patterns of development exist. He wishes to thank in particular Anne Booth, Alison Johnson and Pasquale Scaramozzino for their generous hospitality. Finally, we gratefully acknowledge generous financial support from the CNR (*Contributi* no. 96.01661 CT 10 and no. 97.01392 CT 10).

The origins of the Cagliari–Northeastern collaboration were initially sparked by Professor Gustav Schachter of Northeastern, whose long-running connections with Italian universities and economists have opened many doors on both sides of the Atlantic for some four decades. His Center for European Economic Studies has been pivotal in these activities. When initial discussions began it quickly became evident that the greatest overlap of interest among the two faculties lay in the broad subject of national and regional economic growth. Not only was this the obvious common ground between the two departments, but the topic was, and is, at the forefront of research in the profession as we exit the 20th century. Here, we thought, synergy and serendipity would enable us to make a significant contribution to on-going explorations and debates. How well we succeeded can be judged by the reviewers and readers of this volume.

The pursuit of economic growth tops every nation's policy agenda at the end of the 20th century. Poor countries seek the formula that will enable them to catch up with middle and high income leaders. Within the rich countries, and in the emerging European Union, regional disparities require action because of their political valences. This book brings together state-of-the-art scholarship authored by informed and creative contributors. It was consciously intended to provide diverse but constructive analysis of the conundrum of growth in a variety of contexts, with an eye towards laying a new foundation for policy discussions. The editors believe that the time has come to move substantially beyond a narrowly based convergence model of economic growth by opening a new range of methods and questions. This is the principal theme of the collection. Contributions were consciously solicited to represent a widening of the debate in three ways.

First, there was a desire to consider global, national and regional patterns of growth in comparative perspective in one volume. As is usual in the field, it was expected that many of the authors would rely upon data sets covering samples of cases at each of these levels. A special feature, captured in the second part of the book, would be attention to the starkly contrasting cases of the European Union and the United States, with respect to their regional convergence experiences. Second, although most work in the field has been heavily empirical, we wanted the chapters to exhibit a range of techniques and to include contributions that were explicitly qualitative in their outlook. We sought to report not only new findings in the statistical sense but to bring to the table new ideas and interpretations that might in turn serve as the basis for fresh rounds of empirical labour. Third, we hoped, correctly as it turned out, that the chapters would explore a broad set of subjects only infrequently introduced in the rather narrowly focused traditional literature on economic growth: institutional conditions, the historical background to modern growth, the role of polities and policies, the impact of changing sectoral relationships, the explicit sources and functions of technological change and others so often omitted or held constant. Instead of promulgating a single point of view, or school of thought, we elected instead to combine in one volume the widest range of styles and levels of analysis.

The first part of the book, The Fabric of Global Economic Growth, examines broad worldwide processes such as the evolution of the firm, long-term implications of the loss of national sovereignty, social and political institutions and growth, international openness and the role of R&D. This widening of the scrutiny of the total context of growth seems imperative if historical and national experiences are to be fully understood.

The second part, Contrasting Patterns: The United States and Europe, opens with two chapters on patterns of regional harmonization in the United States, looking at income and earnings trends across states and the reasons for convergence. The remaining four contributions scrutinize the contrasting experience of Europe, where persistent regional disparities endure. Examined are the role of the sectoral transformation, regional spillovers, human capital formation and the macroeconomic basis for the allocation of structural funds and official loans.

In the final part, Regional Mosaics in National Contexts, individual country experiences are surveyed. Italy, the United Kingdom, Spain and Germany are the principal cases in point. The evidence discussed in this section confirms that convergence is not a pervasive phenomenon, and that episodes of convergence are rarely independent of either regional policies or the institutional context.

We conclude with appreciation to Sandy and Ed Elgar for their constant interest and encouragement, and offer thanks for the patient and skilled work of Dymphna Evans, Elgar's senior editor, on this complicated project. Our desk editor at Elgar, Barbara Slater, worked speedily and adroitly to harmonize the components of a most complex manuscript into a finished book; and we thank her heartily.

Contributors

John Adams was Professor and Chair, Department of Economics, Northeastern University, 1990–1998. He is currently affiliated with the Center for South Asian Studies, University of Virginia and Harvard University's Center for Middle Eastern Studies. He has published extensively on growth and development in India and Pakistan. His most recent book is *The Institutional Economics of the International Economy* (Kluwer, 1996), of which he was an editor and contributor. Adams is a past president of the Association for Evolutionary Economics and the Eastern Economic Association. His current research includes children's welfare in the United States, a transactions costs approach to microcredit in Asia, the economic character of the thought of America's Founding Fathers and the political economy of reform in India and Pakistan.

Irma Adelman holds the Thomas Forsyth Hunt Professorship in Agricultural Economics in the Graduate School at the University of California at Berkeley. Earlier she served on the faculties of The Johns Hopkins University, Northwestern University and the University of Maryland. Much of her work has focused on two issues: how the economic growth of nations affects and is affected by changes in economic, social and political institutions, and whether these changes have led to a more equitable distribution of income and educational opportunities and a reduction in material and spiritual poverty. With Cynthia Taft Morris, she is the author of *Society, Politics, and Economic Development* (1967) and *Comparative Patterns Economic Development, 1850–1914* (1990). In *Income Distribution Policy in Developing Countries, The Case of Korea* (1978), she and Sherman Robinson created the computable general equilibrium (CGE) model to show that the size distribution of income is very resistant to policy intervention, excepting a reorientation of strategy towards labour-intensive growth. Adelman's latest book is *Village Economies* (1996), written with Edward Taylor. They apply the CGE technique in a framework designed to ascertain which policies have poverty-reducing potential in small rural communities. In 1971, the President of South Korea awarded Adelman the nation's Order of the Bronze Tower.

M. Shahid Alam was born in Bangladesh and holds degrees in economics from Bangladesh, Pakistan and Canada. He is currently a Professor of Economics at Northeastern University, and in the past has held teaching positions at the University of Karachi, Queèn's University, Concordia University and Colgate University. He has authored a book, *Government and Markets in Economic Development* (Praeger, 1989) and his recent papers have appeared in *Kyklos*, *Weltwirtschaftliches Archiv* and *Cambridge Journal of Economics*.

Carmelina Bevilacqua is an architect specializing in EIS (Environmental Impact Statement) and Territorial Planning with economic implications. In 1995 she attained a Master's degree in EIS, in 1997 an MS in Economic Planning at Northeastern University Boston (MA) and in 1998 a Doctorate in Territorial Planning at University of Reggio Calabria, Italy. Since 1992 she has collaborated with the LUPT (Laboratorio di Urbanistica e Pianificazione Territoriale) Departement of the University of Naples, Italy, to assess the economic and environmental impact of master plans.

Andrea Boltho was educated in Italy and at the Universities of London (LSE), Paris and Oxford. From 1966 to 1977 he was at the OECD's Department of Economics and Statistics where he was, *inter alia*, editor of the Economic Outlook. For one year (1973–74) he was a Japan Foundation Fellow at the Economic Planning Agency in Tokyo. Since 1977 he has been a Fellow and Tutor in Economics at Magdalen College, University of Oxford. At various stages he was visiting Professor at the Collège d'Europe, Bruges, at the International University of Japan, at the Bologna Center of the John Hopkins University and at the Universities of Venice, Paris and Torino. He is a Member of the Academic Council of the IFO Institute in Munich. His publications include: *Foreign Trade Criteria in Socialist Economies* (Cambridge, 1971), *Japan – An Economic Survey* (Oxford, 1975), *The European Economy: Growth and Crisis* (ed.) (Oxford, 1982), as well as numerous academic articles.

Wendy Carlin teaches in the Economics Department at University College London. She has written extensively on the post-war economic development of the West German economy and on the economics of reunification and the process of transition in East Germany and Eastern Europe. With David Soskice she is author of *Macroeconomics and the Wage Bargain* published in 1990 (and in an Italian translation in 1993).

Livio Cricelli is a PhD student in Industrial Engineering at the 'Tor Vergata' University of Rome, Department of Production, Systems and

Computer Science. He graduated from the Engineering Faculty, University of Naples. His main interest is in systems analysis and its application to economic modelling, in particular, telecommunications systems, technology transfer and economic growth.

Luca Dedola works at the Research Department of the Bank of Italy. He was awarded his first degree at the Bocconi University, Milan and his PhD at the University of Rochester. His main research interests are macroeconomics and monetary economics.

Walter N. Fogg is a Senior Research Associate at the Center for Labor Market Studies (CLMS) at Northeastern University. He received his PhD in labour economics from Northeastern in 1996 and has thirteen years of full-time work experience in labour market research, employment policy and training issues. Fogg has collaborated with Andrew M. Sum on many projects that have yielded CLMS publications. Among these are 'The Labour Market Problems of the Nation's Out-of-School Youth Population' (1996), 'Out-of-School, Out of Luck? Demographic and Structural Change and the Labor Market Prospects of At-Risk Youth' (1997) and 'Trends in the Real Incomes and Earnings of Massachusetts Residents and the Comparative Per Capita Income Position of the State' (1998).

Teresa Garcia-Milà obtained her PhD in Economics at the University of Minnesota in 1987. She was Assistant Professor at the State University of New York at Stony Brook (USA) and at the Universitat Autonoma de Barcelona (Spain). She is currently Dean of the Economics Division and Professor at the Universitat Pompeu Fabra in Barcelona (Spain). Her research fields are Applied Macroeconomics, Public Economics and Regional Economics. She has studied the factors that influence regional growth and in particular the role of public infrastructure. She has analysed the fiscal decentralization process in Spain and its effects on Spain's regional governments.

Agostino La Bella is Professor of Industrial Organization at the Engineering Faculty of the 'Tor Vergata' University of Rome, Department of Production, Systems and Computer Science. He graduated from the Engineering Faculty, University of Rome 'La Sapienza'. His main interests are the modelling of economic and territorial systems, transportation planning and the economic and organizational impact of technological innovation; the relationships between production, labour and technological innovation, viewed in a multi-regional and multi-sectoral context; and the analysis of the impact of technological innovation on the processes of economic-territorial development and on urban planning.

Sergio Lodde is Assistant Professor in Political Economy at the Faculty of Political Science, University of Cagliari, Italy and member of CRENoS (the Centre for North–South Economic Research). He has published several papers on technical change, regional economics and environmental policies.

Ramon Marimon (PhD, Northwestern University, 1984) is currently at the EUI in Florence. He has been Assistant and Tenured Associate Professor at the University of Minnesota and Full Professor at the Universitat Pompeu Fabra since 1991, as well as one of its founding members. He is a Research Fellow of NBER and CEPR. He has been a Fellow of the Hoover Institution and Visiting Professor at Stanford University, the Santa Fe Institute, Federal Reserve Bank of Minneapolis, IMF and Cambridge University. His research covers macroeconomics, contract theory, political economy, learning and experimental economics. His most recent work has appeared in *Econometrica, Journal of Economic Theory, Economic Theory, Journal of Economic Dynamics and Control* and the *European Economic Review*. He co-authored a book on the Spanish economy and its prospects in the process of European integration. Jointly with Michael Artis he directed the 1996–97 European Forum on The Political Economy of an Integrated Europe.

Dennis C. Mueller is Professor of Economics at the University of Vienna. His main research interests are in public choice and industrial economics. He is the author of many articles and several books; among them being *Public Choice II* (Oxford University Press, 1989), *Profits in the Long Run* (Cambridge University Press, 1986) and *Constitutional Democracy* (Oxford University Press, 1996). Dennis Mueller is a past president of the Public Choice Society, the Southern Economic Association, the Industrial Organisation Society and EARIE.

Peter Nijkamp holds a PhD in non-linear mathematical programming from the Erasmus University. Since 1975 he has been Professor in Regional and Urban Economics at the Free University, Amsterdam. In past years he has focused his research on quantitative methods for policy analysis and on behavioural analysis of economic subjects. He has a broad expertise in the area of public policy, services planning and environmental protection. In all these fields he has published books and numerous articles. He has been an advisor to several Dutch ministers, regional councils, the Commission of European Communities, the OECD, the Asian Development Bank and the World Bank. He is doctor honoris causa at the Vrije Universiteit in Brussels and fellow of the Royal Dutch Academy of Science and of the World Academy of Arts and Sciences. He is a past president of the

Regional Science Association International and chairman of the Network on European Communications and Transport Activity Research. In 1996 he received the Netherlands Spinoza award

Raffaele Paci (M.Phil, University of Essex) is Assistant Professor in Industrial Organization at the University of Cagliari and member of CRENoS. He was Fulbright Visiting Scholar in the Department of Economics at Northeastern University in 1996–97. He has published numerous articles on regional growth and technological innovation.

Hui Pan is Chief Economist and Director of Asia Pacific with IGI Consulting (IGIC), a Boston-based market research and consulting firm on the worldwide telecommunications market. As Chief Economist, he tracks the global telecom market development and changes in telecom policy and regulations and provides overall direction to the economic analysis of IGIC. Prior to joining IGIC, Dr Pan had taught economics and business at Northeastern University and Harvard University. He has conducted economic research at Harvard Institute for International Development. He has published many articles on economics and telecommunications in both English and Chinese. Dr Pan has a bachelors degree in economics from Jersey City State College and an MA and a PhD in economics from Northeastern University, both in the USA.

Francesco Pigliaru is Associate Professor of International Economics at the University of Cagliari, Italy. He studied economics at the University of Sassari, Sardinia, at the Scuola Superiore E. Mattei in Milan and at the University of Cambridge (M.Phil. in Economics). He was visiting scholar at the University of California-Berkeley and of London (SOAS). He is currently the director of the Centre for North–South Economic Research (CRENoS) of the University of Cagliari. His main research interests are in endogenous growth and international trade and in the mechanisms of convergence/divergence across regional economies. Recent papers on these topics have appeared in *Open Economies Review*, *Structural Change and Economic Dynamics* and *Journal of International Trade & Economic Development*.

Pasquale Scaramozzino is a Reader in Economics in the Department of Economics at SOAS, University of London. He holds Laurea (Università di Roma), MSc and PhD (LSE) degrees. He has previously taught in Bristol, University College London and at Università di Roma 'Tor Vergata'. He has published numerous articles in macroeconomics and applied econometrics.

Gustav Schachter is a Professor of Economics and Director of the Center for European Economic Studies at Northeastern University. He has taught at City College of New York, and in Italian universities at Rome, Bari and Reggio Calabria. In 1994, Schachter was appointed Fulbright Distinguished Chair at the University of Siena, with a parallel appointment as Senior Visiting Scholar at the United Nations in Geneva. In 1975, the University of Massachusetts at Lowell awarded him a D.H.C. in Science. He has been a consultant for the OECD in Turkey and worked with many public and private agencies in the United States and Europe. Schachter has published several books, presented numerous papers at professional societies and published extensively in professional journals in the United States and abroad on the European economy and on the application of regional input–output methodology. He holds PhD and Master's degrees from New York University.

Levanto Schachter graduated from the University of Massachusetts at Amherst in physics. He has worked as a programmer analyst at the Center for European Economic Studies at Northeastern University. During 1995 and 1996, he worked as a market trader and programmer in Turin, Italy. Schachter has collaborated on several research papers on Europe and Italy and has presented research results at the European Regional Science Association Congresses.

Andrew M. Sum is a Professor in the Department of Economics and Director of the Center for Labor Market Studies (CLMS) at Northeastern University. He has nearly 30 years of academic and applied policy, research and evaluation experience in the fields of applied labour market analysis and economic development planning. Sum is an authority in designing and assessing employment and training programmes at the local, state and national levels in the United States. With Neil Fogg he is a co-author of many CLMS publications including 'The State of the American Dream in New England' (1996), 'From Dreams to Dust: The Deteriorating Labor Market Fortunes of At-Risk Youths' (1997) and 'Turbulence in the American Workplace' (1991)

Stefano Usai is Assistant Professor at the Faculty of Political Science of the University of Sassari, Italy. He obtained his first degree in Political Science at the University of Cagliari, an MA in economics at the University of Warwick and a PhD in economics at the University of Naples. His research interests include regional economic growth in relation to the development of institutions and transfer of technology.

Jeroen C.J.M. van den Bergh is Professor of Environmental Economics in the Department of Spatial Economics at the Free University in Amsterdam. He holds an MA in economics from the University of Tilburg and a PhD in economics from the Free University. Among his interests are spatial aspects of environmental economics, integrated modelling for sustainable development, international trade and the environment and the economics of wetland ecosystems. He has written and edited seven books and published numerous articles on these and related topics.

Marco Vannini is an Associate Professor at the Faculty of Political Science of the University of Sassari, Italy. He obtained his first degree in political science at the University of Sassari, an MSc in economics at the London School of Economics and a PhD at the University of Naples. He has studied the economics of crime at the regional level in Italy and the role of financial institutions in economic growth.

Bart Verspagen is Professor of Economics and Technology at the Eindhoven University of Technology and at MERIT (University of Maastricht). He obtained a PhD from the University of Maastricht. During the period 1993–1998, he held a fellowship from the Royal Netherlands Academy of Arts and Sciences. His research interests include economic growth, regional growth, international trade and evolutionary modelling, all in relation to the interaction between economics and technology.

Introduction: economic growth and change

John Adams and Francesco Pigliaru

In the long march of human affairs, economic growth is a new idea and a new reality. Only in the past 200 years has the possibility of cumulative secular gains in output been convincingly established by such leader countries as England and the United States and such follower states as Germany, Japan, Korea and Brazil. After World War II, the judgement that the people of every nation are entitled to experience rising standards of living has pervaded all corners of the globe. The quest to discover exactly what combinations of conditions and policies will ignite growth in varied contexts has become the search for the holy grail in modern aggregate economics. On a practical basis, governments that fail to motivate and steer amplifying economic capacities, in order to meet their citizens' rising expectations, are questioned, challenged and more than occasionally pulled down. The global community has scant patience with backsliders in the modern integrated international economy. First-aid teams from international agencies and major commercial partners show up in capital cities just as soon as macroeconomic and financial indicators point downwards. Fellow trade-association participants prod laggards impatiently when their growth momentum stalls, in recognition of the linkages and spillovers that bind together nations' economic fortunes.

David Landes titles his new study of long-term growth in economic history, *The Wealth and Poverty of Nations, Why Some Are So Rich and Some So Poor* (1998). His explanation for comparative growth trajectories is complex and incorporates geography and initial resource endowments, the importance of innovation-friendly cultures and incentives, education and knowledge and a conducive environment of stable government and strong personal rights. Mancur Olson, Jr headed a recent essay, 'Big Bills Left on the Sidewalk: Why Some Nations are Rich, and Others Poor' (1996). Olson summarized the thesis of his lustrous essay by remarking, 'Since neither differences in endowments of any of the three classical aggregate factors of production nor differential access to technology explain much of the great variation in per capita incomes

1

we are left with the . . . [possibility] . . . that much the most important explanation of the differences in incomes across countries is the difference in their economic policies and institutions' (p. 7).

If economic growth were easily attained, or compatible with a wide range of resource profiles, social attitudes and cultural institutions, it would certainly have been more common in human experience than it has been. Likewise, if the capital, knowledge and technology spillovers from already growing nations, to those only starting down the road to affluence, were frictionless and instantaneous, then catching-up would be swift and convergence the norm. Understanding why spontaneous growth has been such a rare event, perhaps even a singular one, devolving from the British case and ascertaining why the derivative follower cases are still fairly few in number, are the tasks that lie at the heart of growth economics.

PART I: THE FABRIC OF GLOBAL ECONOMIC GROWTH

The authors of the five chapters that comprise Part I do not flinch from confronting the challenges inherent in deciphering the complexities inherent in the multiple paths of economic growth. Although strikingly different in their chosen methodologies, their contributions fall within the wide theoretic orbit delineated by Landes and Olson. They examine how institutional patterns, technological progress and governmental policies shape national economic destinies.

This section opens with an essay by Dennis Mueller that stands the conventional question on its head. Rather than inquire why nations grow, Mueller wonders why advanced nations falter. His attention focuses on that peculiar institution of capitalism, the modern corporation and its managerial leadership, in effect looking underneath the traditional economic aggregates, like labour or capital, to search for microeconomic processes that shape the applications of these conventional factors at the level of the firm. Certainly, it is convincing that the rise and fall in the relative positions of the more mature economies hinge to a large degree on their corporations' performance. Economists from Adam Smith to Douglass North have emphasized the role of market institutions, but in Mueller's view we must give equal attention, following Ronald Coase's insights, to the hallmark non-market institution of capitalism, the big corporation. Mirroring Joseph Schumpeter's identification of the path-clearing entrepreneur as the prime agent of change in capitalism, Mueller looks at the motivations and incentives that managers face in the modern mixed capitalist states. Mueller argues that periods of poor economic performance are accompanied by waves of ineffective mergers and by a falling rate of return, especially among older firms, as managers engage in self-serving rent-seeking, as does society at large when the welfare state expands at the same time. In contrast to Japan and possibly Europe, the United States' individualistic values and flow of motivated immigrants may equip it to stay indefinitely at the forefront of global economic leadership.

In the late 20th century the world is experiencing an era of freer trade and burgeoning capital movements, but such globalization of economic relations is not new, for the latter part of the 19th century had parallel features. Much of the recognized upward divergence of the rich from the poor nations has occurred in the last 100 years, but why did the combination of growth in Europe and the United States, in conjunction with the open world economy of the late 1800s, not trigger catch-up processes on a wide scale? In the second chapter, Shahid Alam argues that sovereignty, defined as the capacity of a people to set its own economic agenda, apart from colonial overlordship, is crucial in explaining the pattern of global divergence in this century. He constructs an index of sovereignty and demonstrates with compelling evidence that the greater the range of its economic and political autonomy, the more rapid was a nation's progress over the time span, 1870–1950. Afterwards, the wave of national liberation movements opened the door to the adoption of independent development strategies and the showings of former colonies improved sharply.

One of the most influential and provocative early studies of the concomitants of economic growth was *Society, Politics, and Economic Development* (1967) by Cynthia Taft Morris and Irma Adelman. The authors were audacious enough to propose that about two-thirds of the differences among national growth rates could be attributed solely to social and political variables. The third chapter of Part I represents Irma Adelman's revisit to this terrain. Insofar as possible, the same cases (67 instead of 74) and variables are used, and the reference period is moved to the 1980s and 1990s. Again, factor analysis, a flexible statistical method eschewed too widely in economics, is applied. A common feature of the prior and present studies is that social and political processes have different influences on growth in the developing world at low, intermediate and higher levels of social and economic development. Adelman regards this robust finding as a serious challenge to any one-size-fits-all theorization. With this three-fold stratification, the statistical results are formidable; for example, four factors explain a full 85 per cent of the variance in growth rates in the high sample.

Although it is widely believed that the adoption of freer trade regimes and openness with respect to capital movements are policy moves that enhance a nation's growth prospects, finding robust statistical links has been elusive. A preliminary problem has been the construction of measures of openness that were credible and based on widely available, objective indicators. In Chapter 4, Hui Pan surmounts both hurdles and, using a sample of 140 national cases, establishes that trade openness and capital freedom are positively associated with growth prospects. His indexes have the merit that they are based on readily available International Monetary Fund reports and may be replicated or updated as necessary. Country per capita income levels will converge, in the conditional sense, when one controls for such variables as human capital, political stability and tropical location. In the framework of such a convergence model, Pan demonstrates that a country that is open to trade will grow 1.25 percentage points faster per year than one that is closed and 1.39 percentage points faster if it is financially knitted into the world's capital flows.

In the fifth and final chapter of the first part of this book, Livio Cricelli and Agostino La Bella parallel Mueller's opening presentation by reverting to the examination of central microfoundational processes that affect growth outcomes. Following Robert Solow's pioneering specification, most neoclassical models treat technological change as exogenous and do not try to account for what is arguably the most important source of growth. Once the R&D process is introduced into debate, societies have the option of investing resources in the advance of technologies. Because technology is largely non-rivalrous, so that others' use does not diminish one's use, its accumulation is key to economic progress (Romer, 1990). Looking at the records of 15 developed countries over the years 1973–1993, Cricelli and La Bella explore a number of possible relationships among the growth of knowledge, national conditions and total factor productivity. The picture is complicated but, broadly, a positive relationship between the nation's stock of knowledge and productivity growth is affirmed.

All in all, Part I is a merry mix of styles and methods. The papers are unified by their global perspectives and by their quest to unearth underlying processes that account for differences in long-term national economic performance. Each ranges well beyond the scope of narrow convergence studies. Mueller and Cricelli–La Bella focus on meso-processes involving the firm, incentives, innovation and the social character of governmental policies. Alam introduces the influence of power and dominance, showing that international relations, even in a period of openness, are not always benign and conducive of universal progress. This finding for the pre-1950 era does not confute Pan's conclusion that in a different international milieu benefits may be seized by strategic engagement with the global economy. Adelman again demonstrates the effectiveness of using ingenuity and persistence in devising creative proxies for difficult-to-quantify social and political parameters, and reaps a fruitful harvest. Collectively, the chapters raise issues and identify processes that are echoed in the continental and national essays contained in Parts II and III.

PART II: CONTRASTING PATTERNS: THE UNITED STATES AND EUROPE

Should the per capita incomes of regions of an economically integrated area converge? If so, are there reasons to believe that the mechanisms leading to convergence should be stronger at the regional than at the country level? In 1970, Nicholas Kaldor wrote his seminal paper on cumulative causation in which he asserted that divergence rather than convergence could prevail as the outcome of economic integration between regions at different stages of development. His analysis was based on the existence of localized dynamic increasing returns in industry, so that 'in the case of the "opening of trade" in industrial products the differences in comparative costs may be enlarged ... with the result that the industrial centre of the [initially less industrialized] region will lose its market...' (Kaldor, 1978, p. 144). As a consequence, 'trade may injure one region to the greater benefit of the other' (*ibid.*), even though such trade-induced divergence can be somehow mitigated by labour migration (p. 150).

Although this view has been influential in regional economics, the recent enormous interest in regional data sets stems from a different theoretical research project, inspired by the prediction of absolute aggregate convergence obtained for regions of a country by Robert Barro and Xavier Sala-i-Martin, who drew their inspiration from Solow's model of growth (Solow, 1956). As Barro and Sala-i-Martin put it, '[a]lthough differences in technology, preferences, and institutions do exist across regions, these differences are likely to be smaller than those across countries' (p. 382), so that 'absolute convergence is more likely to apply across regions than across countries' (*ibid.*). Barro and Sala-i-Martin therefore offer a positive answer to both of the above questions. Indeed, they have one additional reason to reach this conclusion. Because regions are more open than countries, factors are supposed to move freely across their borders. Within the neoclassical model of growth, with one final good produced under constant returns to scale, no externalities and uniform technology across all areas, such easier factor mobility simply accelerates the process of convergence. A broad analysis of the effects of factor mobility on convergence is found in Olivier Blanchard (1991). Kaldor's worries about the unequalizing consequences of economic integration find no room in this context.

It is well known that the regional income and product data for the United States show that a strong process of convergence does characterize the American experience. The two chapters by Andrew Sum and Neil Fogg that lead off Part II yield new and extremely detailed evidence from 1929 onwards showing that regional per capita income inequality across the United States has decreased constantly in all decades, with the exception of the 1980s. By 1995, statewise inequality had reached its lowest historical level. Moreover, Sum and Fogg show that the little inequality still remaining in the data was mainly due to differences in hourly earnings and labour force participation rates. Although this outcome is compatible with a range of different theoretical arguments, including some endogenous growth ones, Solow's neoclassical model is certainly a prominent candidate for affirmation, especially if one applies the criterion of simplicity or parsimony.

Does the outcome for the United States generalize to other areas marked by initial regional divergence? The evidence is mixed. Europe's case in particular turns out to be very controversial. Even if we abstract from well-documented cases of absence of convergence within some European nations, as shown in Part III of this volume, the overall picture on European regional dynamics appears unfavourable to the strong neoclassical prediction of convergence. Although some convergence characterizes the regional data during the 1960s and the 1970s, no such pattern is present during the 1980s (Fagerberg and Verspagen, 1996; Paci, 1997; Quah, 1996). It is worth noticing that convergence in Europe comes to a halt in a period still characterized by a high degree of regional heterogeneity, relative to US standards, in terms of per capita incomes, unemployment rates and sectoral mixes. Another idiosyncrasy is the persistent dualism in the productive structures of a number of Southern European regions. Moreover, the slowdown of convergence takes place in a period in which the process of European economic integration accelerates substantially and in the presence of the European Union's commitments to reduce disparities between its core and periphery.

Not surprisingly, some of Kaldor's themes play a part in a variety of explanations put forward to deal with the European case. In particular, much of the current research concentrates on how economic integration interacts with the presence of dynamic increasing returns based on endogenous and localized components of the accumulation of technological knowledge. The diffusion of technology appears to depend upon some characteristics of the local productive structures, including the regional sectoral mix, so that knowledge spillovers vary across space and sectors. In this context, openness can have complex effects. As the literature on endogenous growth and trade shows, if innovative activities are both sector- and location-specific, specialization may easily generate uneven growth (Lucas, 1988; Grossman and Helpman, 1991). Under less restrictive assumptions, such as presuming that technological spillovers spread to some extent across sectors and areas, the effects on growth of the sectoral composition translate into a less dramatic but still important level effect. Local economies with unfavourable initial conditions may lag permanently behind in terms of per capita income (Grossman and Helpman, 1990; Murat and Pigliaru, 1998). Factor mobility in the presence of this class of localized externalities may add further obstacles to the process of convergence (Bertola, 1993; Krugman, 1991), rather than reduce inequality.

Two important suggestions arise from this literature on the effects of economic integration on growth. The first is that sectoral mixes and their structural evolution are critical in understanding the relative performance of individual economies. The second is that if technological spillovers do not spread uniformly across the whole space the performance of each region is affected by those of the surrounding regions (Quah, 1996). As for the sectoral component, Chapter 8 by Raffaele Paci and Francesco Pigliaru in this section shows that sectors do indeed matter for regional growth in Europe. Using several methods, including one proposed in Bernard and Jones (1996), they show that large part of the convergence in labour productivity is associated with shifts of factors from low- to high-productivity sectors. Further, this process is more intensive in many of the lagging southern regions.

Chapter 9, contributed by Bart Verspagen, yields new evidence in favour of the idea that space is important to assess the economic prospects of each individual region. He finds that both economically and technologically advanced clusters exist, and that the former are much broader than the latter. As a consequence, there is the possibility that spillovers from high-tech regions strongly affect the surrounding areas. The policy implications of this crucial finding are clearly important, so that further research along these lines will be very valuable to help determine how technology diffusion channels may be opened and widened as a means of securing an on-going closure of economic divisions.

On a separate but related topic, Sergio Lodde's chapter offers new evidence on the rather controversial relationship between human capital accumulation and growth across European regions. His detailed empirical work shows the existence of a robust positive correlation between labour productivity growth and the share of active population allocated to those technical jobs that require formal education. Lodde's finding suggests that one hypothesis worth further investigation is that the spillovers accruing from the high-tech clusters to other regions may be related to the composition of the latter's human capital stocks.

Finally, in Chapter 11, Gustav Schachter, Carmelina Bevilacqua and Levanto Schachter produce new evidence on the economic criteria used by the European Union to allocate development funds and loans across regions. They find that a few simple macroeconomic characteristics of the regions, such as relative per capita income and unemployment rates, are important explanatory variables of this allocation process. Their exploratory work opens the portal to two exciting avenues. First, what explicit and implicit criteria have guided the EU's allocation of structural funds? Second, are those criteria consistent with regional needs and conditions, as outlined in the previous chapters, so that the impact of the massive pro-cohesion transfers and credits is weighty enough to help dispel disparities?

Taken as a whole, the chapters in this part reflect appropriately one feature of the current research on regional convergence. They underline that convergence is not always an automatic process, and that a satisfactory understanding will only be achieved when both the American and European experiences are accounted for within a common framework.

PART III: REGIONAL MOSAICS IN NATIONAL CONTEXTS

The picture emerging from the vast empirical work of Robert Barro and Xavier Sala-i-Martin on regional convergence in the United States, Europe and Japan highlights the 'surprising ... similarity of the speed of β-convergence across data sets. The estimates of the rate of β-convergence are around 2 to 3 per cent per year in various contexts' (Barro and Sala-i-Martin, 1995, p. 413). So, convergence appears to be a slow but steady and automatic process, which is unaffected by factors other than the initial levels of per capita income. Regional policy, to name one such factor, remains firmly outside the picture frame. Both the econometric robustness of that result and even its economic interpretation have been the object of much controversy, as Durlauf and Quah (1998) explain in their comprehensive survey. Regional dynamics are often not so well-behaved as is also shown by a number of in-depth studies of national cases, especially in Europe. These studies have the obvious advantage that more detailed data are available to the researcher, which makes it easier to take account of dimensions of the historical, institutional and policy context in which regional economies operate.

The chapters in Part III confirm the usefulness of the national approach. In general, they report that convergence is not a pervasive phenomenon, at least in many parts of Europe. Episodes of convergence are rarely independent of either regional policies or the institutional context. In line with a long-standing tradition, the Italian experience captures much of the attention in this section. At least since Gunnar Myrdal's work on underdevelopment and cumulative causation (Myrdal, 1957), economists have given steady attention to the impressive persistence of this country's North–South economic divide. All available data sets have consistently yielded a picture in which Southern regions on average do not catch up with the richer Northern ones. Some convergence has indeed occurred, but it involves the initially lagging regions of the centre and of the North-East, rather than the much poorer areas of the Mezzogiorno.

Raffaele Paci and Francesco Pigliaru use a new dataset as the basis for Chapter 15, which confirms that a process of absolute convergence did characterize the regional data in the 1950s and in the 1960s, but then came to a halt in 1975. From then on, economic inequality between Northern and Southern regions has increased again. In this phase, the regional distribution of per capita income takes a bimodal polarization in which most of the Northern regions are part of the richer club, and the non-Adriatic Southern regions are part of the poorer one. Further, Paci and Pigliaru use a model of the dual economy to assess the importance for convergence of structural dynamics, especially in the form of the large outflows of labour from the backward agriculture of the poorer regions. In their analysis industrialization, or its failure, appears to be the key to understand why some of the lagging regions converge and others do not.

So, as Andrea Boltho, Wendy Carlin and Pasquale Scaramozzino put it in Chapter 13, 'the North–South gap has remained stubbornly in place' (p. 329), in spite of the huge amount of resources transferred to the Southern regions over the last four decades. They offer a comprehensive analysis of why a mix of policy and institutional factors are essential to obtain a consistent story about the dynamics of the Italian regions. The lessons they draw from the 'Italian failure' are then used to assess the economic prospects of the former East Germany. First, policy matters, in both conceivable ways. The brief convergence season in Italy was linked to a sustained policy effort focused on direct investment in equipment and machinery. The subsequent period in which the absence of convergence was restored is instead characterized by 'the retrenchment in public investment ... offset by a sharp shift towards income maintenance flows and the recruitment of civil servants' (p. 332), with the associated improved opportunities for growth-damaging rent-seeking activities.

Second, factor market institutions matter as well. The halt of convergence happens in a period in which an additional problem was the sudden
abolition of regional wage differentials.

Regional policy and its controversial role as a convergence-enhancing
factor is also the main topic of Chapter 14, in which Teresa Garcia-Milà
and Ramon Marimon consider the fate of the Spanish regions. To identify
a role for policy, they first carefully decompose regional growth rates into
sectoral and regional effects and show that positive regional effects are present in some of the poorer regions. Are these positive effects due to the
redistributive nature of the public investment policy adopted by the
Spanish government? The answer is yes, but with an important qualification. Evidence at the sectoral level shows that the positive impact of such
policies stays within the semi-public sector and does not seem capable of
extending its influence to the private sector. Although some of the observed
productivity convergence is therefore associated with public investment in
poorer regions, productivity gaps in the private sectors remain largely unaffected. As the authors put it, 'if this is the ... policy's only effect, it would be
very difficult to sustain or justify it, in the long run' (p. 350).

All together, the findings of these country-based chapters point,
explicitly and implicitly, to a further component of the relationship
between regional policy and convergence. Although 'good' policies can
crucially enhance convergence by acting as a catalyst for the private
sector of the lagging regions, redistributive policies may perversely
hamper one of the market mechanisms that often spurs convergence:
labour migration. The chapter by Luca Dedola, Stefano Usai and Marco
Vannini presents some indirect but suggestive evidence on one of the
mechanisms through which redistributive policies may slow down migration flows. The authors analyse regional data on Italy and on the United
Kingdom to assess how well the changes in consumption across regions
within each country are correlated. The economies of these two countries
differ in many respects: financial markets are far more efficient in the
United Kingdom, the variability of regional product relative to national
output is much higher and labour mobility lower in Italy. In spite of all
this, the authors find that in the short run cross-region risk-sharing is
considerable in both countries; for instance, it is significantly higher than
in the United States. Given the above-mentioned differences, the Italian
result is surprising. Are Italy's redistributive policies responsible for it?
The answer is a qualified yes. First, income transfers by the government
represent a significant channel in Italy (one-fifth of the total) but not in
the United Kingdom. Second, in Italy the major market channel acting
through holdings of financial assets is also strongly influenced by actions
of the government. In particular, the need to finance a persistently high

public debt made a powerful financial channel (the bond market) available in a country where the share market is traditionally thin. This suggests, at least as a hypothesis deserving further investigation, that redistributive policies were crucial in obtaining a high degree of risk-sharing together with a low degree of interregional labour mobility.

Lastly, the chapter by Jeroen van den Bergh and Peter Nijkamp reminds us that economic integration has an often forgotten environmental dimension. Offering yet another methodological instrument, a simulation technique, they reason that production processes in a region depend in several ways on the local environment and themselves affect the environment and therefore influence the production processes of the surrounding regions. For instance, both pollution and the benefits of pollution abatement innovations may not be confined within the region which originates them and therefore may help explain the relative dynamics of adjacent regions.

ECONOMIC GROWTH AND CHANGE

Looking at the book as a whole, its chapters collectively demonstrate the diversity of approaches necessary to advance on all fronts towards a more comprehensive understanding of the complexity of growth processes, on the global, national and regional levels. Further, the contributors offer an impressive range of theoretical and quantitative skills, leavened by judicious insights and qualitative assessments. The composite list of factors that probably contribute to the spatial and temporal distribution of growth tendencies, depending on local conditions and experiences, is prodigious and we are only beginning to grasp cardinal relationships.

The determinants of a country's growth certainly include: the nature of firms' goals and their managements' rewards, the on-going interplay of dominance and subjugation within the family of nations, the strength of well-devised linkages to the international economy, congeries of social and political parameters that operate with different weight at different states of development and national capacities to sustain applied R&D efforts. The United States and the emerging European Union have much in common as high-income, industrialized conglomerations of states and regions, but contrast sharply in their experiences with spatial convergence. Labour-force participation rates, sectoral shifts, technology spillovers, local human capital and policy interventions are only a few of the decisive factors. Finally, the European nations themselves display disparate individual experiences both with spontaneous convergence over time as well as with the success or perverseness of policy interventions.

The core–periphery pattern of the European Union, and its peculiarly obdurate Italian example, serve as a constant reminder of how much remains to be learned about the dynamics of economic growth.

REFERENCES

Adelman, Irma and Cynthia Taft Morris (1967), *Society, Politics, and Economic Development*, Baltimore: The Johns Hopkins University Press.

Barro, Robert and Xavier Sala-i-Martin (1995), *Economic Growth*, New York: McGraw-Hill.

Bernard, Andrew and Charles Jones (1996), 'Productivity and convergence across U.S. states and industries', *Empirical Economics*, **21**, 113–35.

Bertola, Giuseppe (1993), 'Models of Economic Integration and Localised Growth', in: F. Torres and F. Giavazzi (eds), *Adjustment and Growth in the European Monetary Union*, New York: Cambridge University Press.

Blanchard Olivier J. (1991), 'Comment on *Convergence across States and Regions* by R.J. Barro and X. Sala-i-Martin', *Brookings Papers on Economic Activity*, **1**, 159–74.

Durlauf, Steven N. and Danny T. Quah (1998), 'The new empirics of economic growth', Centre for Economic Performance, Discussion Paper no. 384.

Fagerberg, Jan and Bert Verspagen (1996), 'Heading for divergence? Regional growth in Europe reconsidered', *Journal of Common Market Studies*, **34**, 432–48.

Grossman, Gene M. and Elhanan Helpman (1990), 'Trade, innovation and growth', *American Economic Review*, **80** (Papers and Proceedings), 86–91.

Grossman, Gene M. and Elhanan Helpman (1991), *Innovation and Growth in the Global Economy*, Cambridge, MA: The MIT Press.

Kaldor, Nicholas (1978), 'The Case for Regional Policies', in N. Kaldor, *Further Essays on Economic Theory*, London: Duckworth.

Krugman, Paul (1991), 'Increasing returns and economic geography', *Journal of Political Economy*, **99**, 113–21.

Landes, David S. (1998), *The Wealth and Poverty of Nations, Why Some Are So Rich and Some So Poor*, New York: Norton & Company.

Lucas, Robert E. (1988), 'On the mechanics of economic development', *Journal of Monetary Economics*, **22**, 3–42.

Murat, Marina and Francesco Pigliaru (1998), 'International trade and uneven growth: a model with intersectoral spillovers of knowledge', *Journal of International Trade & Economic Development*, **7**, 221–36.

Myrdal, Gunnar (1957), *Economic Theory and the Underdeveloped Regions*, London: Duckworth.

Olson, Mancur, Jr (1996), 'Big bills left on the sidewalk: why some nations are rich, and others poor', *Journal of Economic Perspectives*, **10**, 3–24.

Paci, Raffaele (1997), 'More similar and less equal: economic growth in the European regions', *Weltwirtschaftliches Archiv*, **133**, 609–34.

Quah, Danny T. (1996), 'Regional convergence clusters across Europe', *European Economic Review*, **20**, 951–8.

Romer, Paul M. (1990), 'Endogenous technological change', *Journal of Political Economy*, **98**, S71–S102.

Solow, Robert M. (1956), 'A contribution to the theory of economic growth', *Quarterly Journal of Economics*, **70**, 65–94.

PART I

The Fabric of Global Economic Growth

1. On the economic rise and decline of nations

Dennis C. Mueller

The idea that nations rise and decline calls to mind the grander hypotheses that civilizations or cultures rise and decline as put forward by Oswald Spengler (1922, 1923) and Arnold Toynbee (1946, 1957). The rise and decline of the great civilizations and empires is to a considerable degree a history of military conquest and then defeat. As Paul Kennedy (1987) has demonstrated for the last half of the millennium, a military rise and decline is inevitably also a story of economic rise and decline, but there is clearly much more involved than economics. Moreover, in some cases, as with the Ottoman Empire, the story seems to be largely one of military superiority and inferiority, of governmental efficiency in running a military state, with economic prowess clearly taking a back seat (Fernández-Armesto, 1995, pp. 239–41, 379–80).

Other factors beyond economic and military strength may also have played important roles in the fortunes of past empires. Toynbee (1946, 1957) emphasized the contribution of religious zeal and religious decay, Spengler (1922, 1923) described a process of general cultural decline. I am an economist, and my comparative advantage in the study of history does not fall in the areas of military, cultural and religious history. Indeed, most historians would probably argue that economists are particularly ill-trained and ill-suited to the study of culture and religion. I shall therefore mostly confine myself to the question of economic rise and decline, and to more recent history, where these factors have been salient. This narrow focus is perhaps even more justified if one looks forward and tries to envisage the history of the future. With the United States now having a near monopoly of effective nuclear military power, it is difficult to imagine another nation rolling over its neighbours as Rome did two millennia ago, and as Germany briefly did a half century ago, without precipitating a violent and decisive counteract. Thus, so long as the United States is willing to play world cop, and until its decline leaves it unable to carry out this role, one can probably look forward to a Pax

Americana, in which future rise and decline histories are likely to be largely accounts of economic success and failure.

The causes behind economic advancement in recent history have been well described by several writers. I shall, therefore, only briefly recount these explanations in the following section. The reasons why a leading economic power falls into decline are more difficult to explain (Section 1.2). I shall, therefore, concentrate upon these, offering first an analogy with the rise and decline of firms (Sections 1.3 and 1.4). In Section 1.5 I present five main causes for economic decline within modern capitalism. In Section 1.6, I speculate on whether these causes of decline can be offset, and a nation can enjoy perpetual growth. The concluding section speculates on whether such an optimistic scenario seems likely for today's three leading economic powers, Japan, the United States and Europe.

1.1   THE CAUSES OF ECONOMIC SUCCESS

1.1.1   The Development of Market Institutions

The idea that there are 'gains from trade' is, of course, fundamental to the discipline of economics. Indeed, Adam Smith's (1776) theory of *The Causes and Consequences of the Wealth of Nations* is largely an account of the many ways in which all members of a nation, and all nations can prosper through trade. Adam Smith's explanation for growth has been most systematically developed and documented in the work of Douglass North (1990; North and Thomas, 1973). North has emphasized the important role played by the development of property rights, markets and other institutions of capitalism in the rise of both Great Britain and the Netherlands. Our first explanation for the economic rise of nations lies, therefore, in the development of the economic institutions of capitalism, particularly as they pertain to market transactions.

1.1.2   The Development of the Modern Corporation

While Douglass North has emphasized the importance of the evolution of market institutions in Great Britain and the Netherlands during the industrial revolution in the 18th and 19th centuries, Alfred Chandler (1990, Chapters 2 and 3) has stressed the importance of the evolution of the modern corporation, particularly in Germany and the United States, over the period between 1880 and World War II. According to Chandler and Oliver Williamson (1985), the large corporations that came into existence over this period were the major source of the innovations in production, distribution and organization in these countries. The 'economies of scale and scope' that these 'giant enterprises' achieved led to the rise of the German and United States' economies to world leadership in the second half of the twentieth century. If, following Coase (1937) and Williamson (1975), we think of firms as institutions for solving 'market failures', that is hierarchical organizations that can produce and distribute certain goods and services more efficiently than the market can, then the Chandler/Williamson view of capitalism complements that of North. Successful economic growth follows the development of 'the institutions of capitalism' in both a market and a nonmarket form.

1.1.3 Other Explanations of Growth

In addition to the general theories of growth of North and Chandler, there exists a variety of narrower hypotheses that might explain the growth of a particular country, or a particular kind of growth. For example, Great Britain's economy may have benefited from its imperialism over the 18th and 19th centuries, America's during the 19th century from the development of its frontier. One of the intuitively most plausible, and empirically best supported hypotheses as to why 'follower' nations grow more slowly than leading nations is the 'catch-up' hypothesis. The technological leaders must invent new technologies to lower their costs and improve their products. Followers can achieve these gains by simply copying the technologies and designs of the leaders.[1] Although each of these hypotheses probably does account for some of the success of the countries to which it is applicable, being country or situation specific, they are obviously less appealing than the more general alternative hypotheses discussed above. All of these explanations for the economic rise in nations are similar, however, in their inability to shed light on the complementary question of why leading nations tend to decline.

1.2 THE PUZZLE

No nation can decline, unless it has first risen. Thus, an obvious place to begin an inquiry into the decline of nations is by examining their rise. The simplest of all explanations for why some nations decline might be that the factors which led to their rise are reversed. The same causal process is at work, only the signs on the inputs are changed.

The most spectacular recent example of a nation which has risen and then fallen is, of course, Great Britain. One is hard pressed, however, to adapt Douglass North's explanation for Great Britain's rise to obtain an explanation of its decline. Most observers would probably argue that Britain's decline set in toward the end of the last century. But, one searches in vain for evidence that property rights, markets and the other important institutions of capitalism were fundamentally weakened or destroyed in Great Britain at that point in time.

Similar difficulties arise when using other explanations for why nations rise to explain their decline. What events in the last generation have occurred to convert the economies of scale and scope that led to Germany and the United States' rise into diseconomies, and thus set these economies into decline? Great Britain's economy may have benefited from its imperialism, America's from the development of the frontier, and the start of Britain's decline did roughly coincide with the close of the age of imperialism. But America's frontier was closed long before the end of the 1960s, and important parts of Britain's empire, like the United States, were lost long before Britain's decline began. Other causal factors seem needed to explain the decline of nations than those that explain their rise.

Mancur Olson (1982) has offered one such causal explanation. Economic growth is strangled by the rentseeking avarice of interest groups. I think Olson has identified an important determinant of economic decline, and will come back to it. But I do not think that it is the *sole* explanation for Great Britain's sustained slide, and America's and Europe's more recent troubles. If the activities of interest groups alone could reduce a country's growth in income per capita from 2 or 3 per cent per year, to zero or 1 per cent, all members of society could benefit from emasculating the interest groups, and somehow compensating them in other ways. To some extent, that was part of the Reagan and Thatcher revolutions, with their emphasis on deregulation, privatization and attacks on organized labour, and to some extent they succeeded. But they have not fully succeeded, and I shall argue that more is needed to return these and other mature economies to permanently higher levels of economic growth.[2]

The 'catch-up' hypothesis has, as noted, received considerable empirical support.[3] But this hypothesis predicts that followers *catch-up* to the leaders, not that they zoom right by them. As a follower catches a leader, it must take over the costly activity of developing new products and technologies, and its growth should slow down. To explain how a one-time leader falls behind other countries, one needs more than the catch-up hypothesis. Indeed, the question of why leaders become followers becomes even more perplexing, once one takes into account the considerable advantages of being the leader.

The industrial organization literature contains several hypotheses as to the advantages of first movers, and considerable empirical evidence regarding the longevity of market leadership positions.[4] The learning-by-doing hypothesis, for example, predicts falling costs over time with increasing output. While one might expect the *rate of decline* in costs to slow down after a point, there is no reason to expect it to reverse. There is no reason to expect *forgetting-by-doing* to set in after a while. Indeed, so strong are the first-mover advantages at the micro level, that a micro-based theory might predict that the leading nation would simply 'take over the world' economically.[5] Thus, the task of explaining how and why a nation which is once a leading economic power loses this position, is not an easy one. I am a microeconomist, and shall begin to try to answer this question by examining the rise and decline of leading firms.

1.3 THE RISE AND DECLINE OF FIRMS

If nations rise and decline this suggests that they go through a sort of life cycle and, to a microeconomist, this in turn calls to mind a life cycle of firms. The classic discussion of firm and product life cycles is undoubtedly that of Joseph Schumpeter (1934). Schumpeter saw firms coming into existence due to an innovative idea of their entrepreneurial founder. When this innovation was a radical departure from existing products or technologies it led to the founding of a new market. Innovation was followed by imitation by other producers until the initial market advantage of the innovator was eliminated, above normal profits disappeared, and competitive equilibrium returned.

1.3.1 Motivation

Entrepreneurs

The typical entrepreneur's ideas are not such as to launch an industry, and lead to no flood of imitators. The typical new-born firm dies within a few years of its birth (Dunne, Roberts and Samuelson, 1988; Geroski, 1991, Chapter 2). Given the high probabilities of failure, one wonders what it is that motivates some individuals to take the entrepreneurial leap, to bet their time and probably all of their money on the belief that they can do something so different or so much better than every other firm that they can succeed, where most fail? Schumpeter described the entrepreneur's motives as follows:

First of all, there is a dream and the will to found a private kingdom, usually, though not necessarily, also a dynasty. The modern world really does not know any such positions, but what may be attained by industrial or commercial success is still the nearest approach to medieval lordship possible to modern man. Its fascination is specially strong for people who have no other chance of achieving social distinction. The sensation of power and independence loses nothing by the fact that both are largely illusions. Closer analysis would lead to discovering an endless variety within this group of motives, from spiritual ambition down to mere snobbery. But this need not detain us. Let it suffice to point out that motives of this kind, although they stand nearer to consumers' satisfaction, do not coincide with it.

Then there is the will to conquer: the impulse to fight, to prove oneself superior to others, to succeed for the sake, not of the fruits of success, but of success itself. From this aspect, economic action becomes akin to sport – there are financial races, or rather boxing-matches. The financial result is a secondary consideration, or, at all events, mainly valued as an index of success and as a symptom of victory, the displaying of which very often is more important as a motive of large expenditure than the wish for the consumers' goods themselves. Again we should find countless nuances, some of which, like social ambition, shade into the first group of motives. And again we are faced with a motivation characteristically different from that of 'satisfaction of wants' in the sense defined above, or from, to put the same thing into other words, 'hedonistic adaption.'

Finally, there is the joy of creating, of getting things done, or simply of exercising one's energy and ingenuity. This is akin to a ubiquitous motive, but nowhere else does it stand out as an independent factor of behaviour with anything like the clearness with which it obtrudes itself in our case. Our type seeks out difficulties, changes in order to change, delights in ventures. This group of motives is the most distinctly anti-hedonist of the three. (Schumpeter, 1934, pp. 93–4)

Thus, Schumpeter did not simply repeat the assumption about entrepreneurial motivation that was already standard when he wrote, 'the entrepreneur maximizes the profits of the firm.' Schumpeter, observing entrepreneurs at the beginning of the 20th century, saw reincarnated medieval knights striving to build empires and to found dynasties.

Over 50 years ago, Tibor Scitovsky (1943) demonstrated that even the familiar profits maximization assumption, if single mindedly pursued, implied that the owner entrepreneur was a rather unusual fellow who was ever ready to take on a fair gamble, a workaholic who would never consume additional leisure, no matter how wealthy he became.[6] Frank Knight (1965, p. 319) saw the businessman motivated to 'produce wealth to be used in producing more wealth with no view to any use beyond the increase of wealth itself.'

Each of these descriptions sees industry's captains driven to achieve goals beyond the reach and desires of normal persons. When placed alongside the actual behaviour of the Krupps and Fords and Maritoes, they do not seem like exaggerations. The entrepreneurial founders of the industrial giants in Germany, the United States and Japan were empire-builders of extraordinary talent and drive.

Managers

Many people have observed, what Thomas Mann so brilliantly depicted in *Buddenbrooks*, that the third generation dissipates the fortune and destroys the business that the grandfather founded. Like all such observations it is not always accurate, but it is true enough often enough to indicate a danger all family businesses face. Not only are they threatened by the forces of competition from without, they are threatened by decay from within. For this reason, perhaps, most business empires come at some point in time to be governed not by members of the family that started them, but by professional managers, technocrats with no emotional attachments to the firm, and often with little financial stake in it.

Robin Marris (1964, Chapter 2) demonstrated that the pecuniary and nonpecuniary rewards of managers tend to be tied to the growth of their firms, and thus that professional managers also tend to be empire builders of sorts, more concerned with their company's growth rate than its profitability. Where the owner-manager wishes to see the firm survive and prosper indefinitely, the professional manager's horizons extend only to his expected retirement or departure to another firm. What is important is not the course of the empire over the next generation, but its course over the next five years. For this reason empire building in the managerially controlled firm frequently takes the form of mergers. Mergers are the quickest and surest way to grow, and the most popular route among professional managers (Mueller, 1969, 1972).

1.3.2 The Life Cycle of the Managerial Corporation

Although most new firms do not survive, and many that do remain small, family enterprises, in the exceptional case of a truly radical and important innovation, something like the Schumpeterian scenario does take place (Mueller and Tilton, 1969; Gort and Klepper, 1982; Graddy and Klepper, 1990). The firm that grows to be large goes through an initial phase in which it is either an innovator or an early, successful imitator (Klepper and Simons, 1993). But, first-mover advantages, barriers to entry, government protection in the form of trade restraints or other regulations, often combine to reduce 'the perennial gale of creative destruction' to a gentle breeze. Thus, many firms earn persistently high profits and seem capable of surviving almost indefinitely (Mueller, 1986, 1990).

At some point in the large, successful firm's life, it comes to be managed by professionals who, when the opportunities arise, take actions to advance their interests over those of the company's owners. Very often these actions turn out to be mergers.[7] Thus, we find Borg-Warner responding in the 1950s to Ford's cancellation of its contract for automatic transmissions by undertaking 17 acquisitions over a period of a couple of years; *all* US tobacco companies responding in the 1960s to the first serious 'tobacco scare' that suggested falling future demand for their products with a raft of mergers that reduced their dependence on cigarettes for sales to less than 50 per cent; the petroleum companies responding in the 1970s to the windfall profit increases generated by the OPEC price increase by undertaking a series of disastrous mergers;[8] and most recently, defence firms responding to budget cuts following the collapse of the Soviet Union by engaging in a series of mergers.[9] More generally, *every* period of economic and stock market expansion in the United States over the past century, except during World War II, has been accompanied by a merger wave.[10]

Did the Surgeon General's report linking cigarette smoking to cancer suddenly reveal hidden talents that cigarette company managers had for managing assets in other industries, and thus induce a rash of mergers, or did it frighten these managers into believing that their firms would soon begin to decline and thereby induced them to avoid this decline through mergers? Did the OPEC price increases reveal hidden managerial talents in the petroleum industry, or did they simply provide petroleum firms with the cash to make both their shareholders and their managers significantly better off? Do managerial abilities to manage the assets of larger companies expand with stock prices, or just the resources and discretion to do so?[11]

If the only consequence of managerial pursuit of growth through merger was that some companies grew much larger, and their shareholders somewhat poorer, it would not be a topic of much interest, or at least not of much interest with respect to the question addressed in this paper. But, the pursuit of growth through merger in the mature phases of firm life cycles is one of the factors that contributes to the decline of nations.

1.4   THE LIFE CYCLE OF MANAGERIAL CAPITALISM

Joseph Schumpeter first described the goals of the entrepreneur and the dynamics of capitalist development at the beginning of the 20th century, when he was in Vienna. The empire-building entrepreneurs, whom he would have observed close at hand, would therefore have been those from Germany, Austria and perhaps other parts of continental Europe. As Chandler (1990) has documented, the German firms that grew to be large during the first part of the 20th century quickly shifted from being family controlled to being manager controlled. In this respect the development of German and American capitalism over the course of the 20th century has been very similar.

The end of the 19th and early part of the 20th centuries was a period in which technological change and the introduction of mass production techniques led to significant economies of scale and scope, to use Chandler's term. The firms that were able to shape their organizations and raise the capital needed to take advantage of these economies grew to giant size, while remaining in the confines of their core industrial strengths. The empire building proclivities of corporate managers could be satisfied through internal expansion and horizontal or vertical acquisitions. The result was a transformation of German and American industry from the end of the 19th century to the middle of the 20th from one characterized by small family firms to one dominated by large managerially controlled corporations. The cycle of innovation, growth and monopoly that Schumpeter used to describe the life of a single innovating firm, became a cycle of innovation, growth and oligopoly across the entire economies.

Great Britain's economic development over the half century following 1880 was different from that of both the United States and Germany. To a much greater extent British firms remained in the hands of their founding families. Professional managers were hired, but were not able to rise to the highest levels in the managerial hierarchy (Chandler, 1990, pp. 292–4). Thus, ironically, as the first century of corporate capitalism evolved, the Buddenbrook's scenario became repeated much more often in the United Kingdom than in Mann's Germany, and Britain's economic development looked much more like that of the family firm than of the modern corporation. Thus, if we accept Chandler's explanation for the relative performances of the US, German and British economies up until World War II, the superior performance of the former two countries would be attributable to the institutional innovation of the large, managerially controlled joint stock company.

By the end of the 1920s corporate growth in metals, machinery, transportation equipment, rubber, chemicals, petroleum – all of the major industries in which scale economies are significant – had reached a stage of some maturity. These major industries were oligopolies dominated by large, fairly mature corporations. Already a great merger wave had taken place in the United States at the end of the 1920s. Had major US firms tried to continue to grow as they had over the 50 previous years, they would have had to resort increasingly to growth through mergers. But the Depression came, and then World War II. Corporate growth in America was arrested, except for the war build up.

The result was that when World War II ended nearly a generation had gone by since US businesses were able to invest and grow under normal demand conditions. The depression and war had left a large, pent-up demand for consumer goods, and a large pent-up supply of would-be entrepreneurs hungry to get rich. Large mature firms were able to expand rapidly within their existing markets, and many new firms came into existence and began to grow large.

The end of World War II was followed by a period of extreme shortages in Germany as people began to rebuild their war torn cities and economy. Thus, the post-war boom in Germany got started later than in the United States and with even more pent-up consumer demand and entrepreneurial supply. The major corporate giants from before the war came back to life, and many small and medium-sized firms began to thrive. There were big profits to be earned in both the United States and Germany, and many talented people were drawn into businesses both large and small.

By the end of the 1960s, many firms in the United States found themselves in much the same position as they were at the end of the 1920s. The potential for continued high internal growth was limited. But profits were currently high and the stock market was booming. The result was the United States' third major merger wave. It differed from the first two only in so far as during this wave the antitrust authorities did not sit back and idly watch. They intervened to prevent all mergers that might possibly have resulted in a substantial increase in market power, erring usually on the side of caution. Thus the third merger wave, unlike its two predecessors, was dominated by conglomerate mergers, mergers with the smallest likelihood of increasing market power, and the smallest likelihood of increasing efficiency.

Not only did the mergers of the 1960s not increase the efficiency of the merging firms, they almost certainly reduced it. Considerable evidence exists indicating that the mergers of the 1960s reduced the profits of the merging firms, reduced the market shares of the acquired firms, reduced the productivity of the acquired firms, and reduced the wealth of the acquiring companies' shareholders.[12] Perhaps no better evidence exists of the inefficiencies caused by the merger wave of the 1960s than that it led to a spin-off wave in the 1970s, as firms tried to undo the damage.[13]

Most economists do not give much thought to mergers, and when they do, presume that they must be harmless if not beneficial for the economy. This belief stems from the fact that most economists assume that all managers maximize profits, and that all, or at least most, markets are fairly competitive. If managers maximize profits, then any merger that does not seem likely to increase market power must be presumed to increase efficiency. If managers do not maximize profits, then an efficient market for corporate control will remove them. Thus, the first reaction of many economists to the conglomerate merger wave of the 1960s was to assume that these mergers *must* be creating some sort of efficiency, and many articles appeared with new hypotheses as to what these efficiencies might be. A new word was even invented – synergy – to describe these efficiencies that had never before been known to exist.

In an efficient market for corporate control an EXXON Corporation will be acquired and its management replaced as soon as it deviates from shareholder-wealth-maximizing behaviour. But buying the EXXON Corporation and throwing its management out because they have made a bad merger is not as easy as filling up at one of its stations. This fact allows EXXON's managers to pursue their own goals, even when they do not enhance the profits of the firm, as when they undertake an unprofitable merger.

Mergers do more than just reshuffle corporate assets, and transfer wealth from the shareholders of acquiring companies to shareholders of the acquired companies. Many examples exist of mergers which have destroyed healthy, efficient companies.[14] On average the efficiency of the acquired companies is reduced. The energies of the managers of the acquiring companies are diverted from making investments that create assets to investments that merely transfer them. The cash flows of companies get used to buy existing plants rather than build new ones. A whole industry grows up of investment bankers, stock analysts, lawyers and even economists engaged in the process of transferring ownership of assets, rather than producing them.

The great merger waves of the 1920s and 1960s in the United States were followed by decades of poor economic performance. We know at the micro level that the mergers tended to reduce efficiency. Could the poor economic performance of the 1930s and 1970s be *in part* a consequence of the merger waves that preceded them? The United States and Great Britain have had, proportionate to the sizes of their economies, far more mergers than any other countries. They have also had the worst post-World War II economic performances among the highly developed countries. On average Japan has one merger for every 10 in the United States. Italy has one of the lowest merger rates and highest productivity levels of all European countries. Coincidences perhaps, but I think not. If we accept Chandler's argument that the economic rise of the United States and Germany through the first half of the 20th century was to an important extent due to the rise of the giant, managerially controlled corporation, we must at least allow for the possibility that their seeming decline over the last quarter or third of this century is due to a decline in the performance of these ageing organizations. Mergers are characteristic of corporations in the mature phase of their life cycle. They are both bellwethers for and important contributors to the economic decline of nations.

1.5 THE CAUSES OF ECONOMIC DECLINE

1.5.1 Life-Cycle Effects of Corporate Capitalism

We are now ready to list the main causes of economic decline. The first of these I have discussed at length, because it is fundamental to understanding why a highly developed capitalist nation might decline. Firms and corporations are the major sources of productive investments and innovative activity. If a nation enters into decline it must in part be because these institutions have entered into decline.

Lawrence Yun and I (1995) have recently tested this life-cycle hypothesis regarding capitalism using data on large US corporations. Table 1.1 reports results for regressions of annual changes in the market values of firms on their annual investments. The coefficient on investment

Table 1.1 Estimates of c *with* δ *and year-effects the same for all firms*

$$\frac{M_t - M_{t-1}}{M_{t-1}} = -\delta + c \, \frac{I_t}{M_{t-1}} + \mu_k$$

$c_o = c$ for old firms $c_y = c$ for young firms

Time period	$-\delta$	c_o	c_y	n	$\bar{R}^2$
1951–1960	−0.0004	1.15	1.00	1493	0.420
	0.04	28.08	7.42		
1961–1970	−0.032	1.14	1.60	2403	0.370
	3.15	23.14	22.60		
1971–1980	−0.064	0.53	0.87	3692	0.396
	10.39	21.36	31.86		
1981–1990	−0.042	0.69	1.00	4008	0.661
	9.16	41.49	76.47		

Note: *t*-values below coefficients.

measures the ratio of the return on that year's investment to the firm's cost of capital.[15] A dollar invested at a return equal to the firm's cost of capital raises the market value of the firm by one dollar. Thus, if all firms invested in projects which on average had returns equal to their costs of capital, the coefficient on investment would be 1.0.

The data on firm investments and market value changes have been pooled by decade with separate coefficients estimated for old and young firms, with young firms defined as those that were incorporated after 1940. On average young firms earned significantly higher returns relative to their costs of capital than old ones in three of the four decades. In the 1950s and 1960s, American capitalism's golden age, investment opportunities were sufficiently attractive that even mature companies could on average earn returns greater than their costs of capital. Neither group had an average return on investment in the 1970s that equalled its costs of capital, with the typical mature firm earning a return only slightly greater than one half of its costs of capital.

The economic rebound of the 1980s raised the returns on investment of the by now somewhat mature young firms back to equality with their costs of capital, but the returns of the mature companies remained significantly below their costs of capital. Each dollar invested by a large, mature firm in our sample produced only 69 cents of new assets during the 1980s. This figure is very close to what Elizabeth Reardon and I (1993) estimated for a much larger sample of firms (699) from the end of 1969 to the end of 1988. These 699 firms invested a total of $3670 billion over this 19 year period. These investments produced only $2587 billion in new assets, however. Thus, more than a trillion dollars in potential wealth was lost because large US corporations invested in projects which on average had rates of return significantly below their costs of capital.

The life-cycle problems of corporate capitalism reflect the principal/agent relationship that exists between managers and shareholders. Shareholders would like to see managers invest in only those projects that promise returns greater than the cost of capital. Managers wish to see the firm grow faster (or decline more slowly) than this investment policy implies. Note that a form of rentseeking, or rent dissipation is involved here. In a perfectly competitive world, managers could not invest in projects with returns less than the cost of capital. Some markets – the product market, capital market, market for corporate control – would prevent such investments. But when the market process creates large economic rents, as it often does, those individuals who gain control over those rents are free to use them or dissipate them as their interests dictate.

1.5.2   Motivation

At the end of the 1960s I undertook several case studies of how companies grow. I looked at marketing innovations, technological innovations
and mergers. For my case study of a technological innovation I chose the
Xerox company.

Xerox was a classic example of a Schumpeterian firm. In 1950 it was
a small photographic paper manufacturer in Rochester, New York
struggling to survive competition with its giant neighbour Kodak. Its
managers decided they would need to develop a new product. The director of research read an article describing some early experiments with a
photocopying process, and he convinced the President of the company to
buy up the patents on the process and start to develop it. To bring out the
first machine in 1960, the management had literally 'to bet the company',
a phrase I often heard used at Xerox. To finance the R&D the top managers invested all of their savings, took out additional mortgages on their
homes and the like. Needless to say they were handsomely rewarded for
the risks they took.

I was particularly impressed by some remarks of Chester Carlson, the
photocopying process inventor, during my interview of him. He had
graduated in physics from the California Institute of Technology in 1930,
but could not get a job as a physicist during the Great Depression. He
worked as a sort of errand boy in a patent office, and had the idea that it
would be useful if there were a box that you could stick a document into
and out would come clean copies, rather than have to make the many
messy carbon copies that law firms required. He spent his evenings and
weekends in a garage trying to construct such a box. Thirty years after he
graduated from Caltech, the first commercially successful photocopier
was produced, and Carlson began to reap the rewards from his persever-
ance. By the time I interviewed him in the late 1960s. he had earned more
than $20 million in royalties and stock appreciation. What I remember
most from the interview, however, was Carlson's observation that he
would undoubtedly *not* have pursued his invention, if he had graduated
from Caltech in the late 1960s. At that point in time there were plenty of
good paying jobs for physicists and he would simply have taken a job
with a large firm and been content to earn his regular salary.

Carlson was driven to invest the time and take the risks to invent a
photocopying process by the economic hardships in the Depression.
The managers of Haloid, who developed the process to commercial success, were driven by the hardship of having to try to compete with a
progressive first mover like Kodak. Under less difficult circumstances
neither might have been willing to undertake the risks. Indeed, Carlson

approached over 20 large firms including Kodak and IBM and tried to interest them in picking up the development of his process before he agreed to give it to Haloid. They were less desperate for a new product, however, and refused to take up the opportunity.[16]

Although difficult to quantify, motivation is of central importance in the innovation and development process. According to Chandler (1990) corporate capitalism's development was more successful in the United States and Germany from 1880 to the end of World War II than it was in Great Britain, because the rising corporations in the first two countries were led by professional managers, while leadership in major UK corporations remained in the hands of members of the firms' founding families. This difference is important not only because it allowed US and German firms to recruit more competent managers, but it also meant corporate leadership in these countries continually went to those individuals who were most strongly driven to get to the top of the corporate ladder, who were hungriest for success. In Great Britain corporations were run by descendants of the founders, 'gentleman' who were less concerned with the growth of their firms than were their professional counterparts in Germany and the US (Chandler, 1990, pp. 291–4). Professional managers in the UK were prevented by a 'glass ceiling' from moving into the highest management ranks. Top managers in the UK did not have to work to get to the top, they inherited their positions.

In a low income family parents pressure their children to study hard, get an education and choose a job that pays well. Those children that seek a better life style than their parents follow their advice. In a well-to-do family, children do not necessarily seek a better life style than their parents. The pressure 'to get ahead' is less intense. Education and career choices take on the form more of consumption goods than of investment goods, with smaller consequent payoffs for society. In the UK careers in business were of low status relative to those in government, science or even academia throughout the last century.[17] The most talented individuals were simply not drawn into business (Chandler, 1990; Porter, 1990, pp. 115–22, 409).

In contrast business occupations have been of relatively high status in the US and Germany for the past century, and became so in Japan immediately after World War II. Akio Morito (1988, pp. 64–5), cofounder of the SONY Corporation, has succinctly expressed the motivation of entrepreneurs in post-World War II Japan. 'We were engineers and we had a big dream of success. We thought that in making a unique product we would surely make a fortune.'

To take great risks one must be truly driven to 'make a fortune', or found a dynasty. Such hunger is less likely in those born to a fortune, to those who are nth in the line of an existing dynasty. It is most likely in those who inherit neither wealth nor status, or in some other way are outsiders. The importance of motivation is also illustrated in the disproportionate role immigrants and members of religious or ethnic minorities have played in starting new firms. Many major UK companies were founded by entrepreneurs, who were *not* university graduates (Porter, 1990, pp. 496–8). Bill Gates, the founder of Microsoft, is one of Harvard's most celebrated dropouts.[18] On a much grander scale, Toynbee (1946, pp. 48–163, 209–16, 276) has emphasized the necessity of the proper 'challenge' to launch a civilization's rise, and the crucial role certain individuals and minorities play in leading a civilization's response to these challenges.

Thus, one reason that successful nations decline is that their very success, and the wealth it produces, dulls the incentives of the population to create new wealth, and to make the investments and take the risks that new wealth creation requires.[19]

Before discussing an additional reason for decline, it is perhaps worth pausing to contrast the argument presented here with those recently put forward by Manfred Neumann (1991).

Neumann seeks to explain not the secular decline of nations, but the kinds of cyclic variations first observed by Kondratieff. Neumann argues that the prosperity generated by long economic upswings changes individual rates of time preference thereby resulting in a fall in the saving rate, decline in investment and an economic contraction. My argument is complementary to Neumann's, but somewhat different. It is not the relative attraction of present and future consumption that changes with prosperity that I am emphasizing, but the relative attraction of work and leisure, of different types of work, and of risktaking.

The difference is illustrated by the history of Akio Morito's (1988, Chapter 1) family firm, a history which by the way contradicts the third generation law of family firm decline. This firm's decline set in several centuries after its founding. Morito's great-grandfather and grandfather chose not to manage the firm themselves, but to hire managers and devote their own time and money to acquiring precious antiques. The hired managers behaved exactly as Adam Smith (1776, p. 700) and John Stuart Mill (1885, pp. 138–9) predicted that they would, and in two generations the firm was nearly bankrupt. Here the problem was not so much the consumption pattern of Morito's great-grandfather and grandfather, but their substitution of leisure/consumption for work. Indeed, since their consumption was a sort of investment, Morito's father was able to save the firm, by selling some of the antiques, firing the hired managers and resuming the managerial role himself.

1.5.3 Managerial Rentseeking

Chandler (1990) depicts the professional managers, who built the giant enterprises of Germany and the United States, as growth maximizers continually reinvesting their companies' cash flows to expand their empires. Hiroyuki Odagiri (1982, 1991) has argued that since World War II Japanese managers have also behaved like Marris-growth-maximizers, and that this behaviour helps explain the Japanese miracle. Porter (1990, p. 471) claims that Korean firms, whose managers exhibit an 'awesome willingness to take risk, ... are [also] managed less for profitability than for growth.'

When Schumpeter first described the motives of the entrepreneur at the start of this century, it was only possible to rule an industrial empire, if one founded and created one. The same was true in Japan after World War II had destroyed the *zaibatsu* (Morito, 1988, p. 149), and today in Korea. It is not true today in North America and much of Western Europe. Someone set on ruling a corporate empire can do so either by creating one, or by rising to the top of an existing empire. For many the latter alternative must seem the most attractive. Very few people will be able to start a company and build it into a Coca Cola or Daimler-Benz in their lifetime. If they try and fail, they may find after 20 years that they are no richer than when they began. If one tries instead to reach the top of the managerial ladder at a giant firm, one does so with the knowledge that *some* of one's peer group will certainly succeed, and even if you do not reach the very top, you are almost certainly not going to find yourself no wealthier after 20 years than when you began the climb.

If the highest paid CEO in the United States in 1994, Charles Locke of Morton International,[20] is asked whether he has earned his $25.9 million compensation and other perks associated with his position, he could respond in the affirmative by pointing out that he attained this lofty position by beating out a hundred or more rivals that entered the CEO tournament at the same time that he did, and that due in part to his efforts Morton Salt, the company's most famous product, for yet another year remained the country's leading brand of table salt. No mean feats, but arguably the value of his efforts to society would have been better if he had helped launch a new firm and created a new market.

When corporate empires already exist, any rents tied to them go to those who gain control of the empire. The tournaments that ultimately select these individuals are classic rentseeking contests that award the prize to the person who has made the highest bid, in this case the bids taking the form of investments in effort, in human capital accumulation, etc. to get to the top of the managerial hierarchy. Such rentseeking contests are prone to generate aggregate investments that exceed the value of the prize won. Of course, the profits that large corporations make are not pure rents in the sense that they are forthcoming regardless of the efforts and talents of the managers. But there is a rent element to them, and to the extent there is, the familiar costs of rentseeking exist.

1.5.4 The Welfare State

The poor are more apt to enter risky occupations, and buy little insurance. The rich buy most of the insurance sold. The same is true of societies. The welfare state is the ultimate form of this sort of collective luxury good, an attempt to protect the individual against every sort of economic risk.

The institutions of the welfare state first began to be introduced in Europe at the end of the 19th century. At that time, taxation levels in the United Kingdom, France and Germany were low and roughly comparable to those in the United States.[21] By the mid-1920s taxes in the UK and France were more than double the figure for the US, almost triple in Germany.[22] Since then the institutions of the welfare state have grown on both sides of the Atlantic, but the government sector remains anywhere from 50 per cent to 100 per cent larger in European countries than in the United States, with the important exception of Switzerland.

The welfare state grew large in virtually all European countries, of course. But because of the great potential gains from rebuilding after the war, or the potential gains from 'catch-up', or the gains from introducing the Common Market, or the salutary effects of corporatism, most other European countries seemed to be more engaged in positive-sum-game activities than the UK, at least during the first generation after World War II. Their economies have only fairly recently exhibited signs of the 'British disease'.

One reason why the harmful effects on growth of the welfare state have only recently become significant is that its disincentive effects evolve slowly over time (Lindbeck, 1995a,b). Habits of upbringing and peer group pressures initially deter individuals from abusing the system. But the example of some individuals taking advantage of its generous benefits leads others to do the same, and eventually peer group pressure against abusing the system disappears – or perhaps reverses. Only 'a sucker' fails to take all of his sick leave, quickly finds a new job, and retires at the maximum age. Of particular importance to the growth of the economy are the welfare state's effects on individual savings rates and willingness to take risks. We return to the latter point in Subsection 1.5.6.

Recent papers by Alesina and Rodrik (1994) and Persson and Tabellini (1994) have modelled and estimated the effect of vertical redistribution on macro growth. They reason that the pressures on government to redistribute will be greater, the greater is the exogenous inequality of income. When redistributive taxes affect savings and investment, governmental vertical redistribution will reduce growth. Both studies find an inverse relationship between the extent of income inequality at the beginning of a time period and the growth of the economy during the period. Persson and Tabellini find that the inverse relationship only holds in democracies, and link the effect to governmental transfers. Alesina and Rodrik find that it holds in all countries regardless of form of government.

1.5.5 Collective Rentseeking

The existence of wealth provides an incentive to redistribute it, not only to those who are poor, but to any group in a position to use the government to their advantage. Mancur Olson (1982) argues that the ability of interest groups to organize and effectively engage in rentseeking develops slowly. Thus, as with the detrimental effects of the welfare state, the adverse effects of interest group rentseeking appear only after long periods of stability and prosperity.

Olson is careful *not* to merge his interest-group-decline thesis with a government-size-decline hypothesis. Peter Murrell and I (1986), however, have found that the number of interest groups in a country *is positively,* and it would seem causally, linked to the size of government. Interest group rentseeking through government activities should be a central part of the Olsonian thesis, also.[23]

The classic zero/negative sum activity of government is, of course, war. Defence expenditures are also the quintessential pure public good. Although a country may be significantly better off making large defence expenditures and experiencing zero economic growth than to make zero defence expenditures and be defeated in war, still better would be to make zero (low) defence expenditures, invest the money that would be spent on defence on growth, and not to be defeated in war. The relatively slow growth of the United States since World War II must be attributed in part to the wasteful dissipation on defence of potentially productive government outlays on other public goods. Particularly costly for economic growth has been the large diversion of scientific personnel and research and development activity to defence. Conversely, the growth of Japan and European countries has been helped by their opportunity to free ride on US defence expenditures, and thereby to avoid this wasteful diversion of resources.[24]

1.5.6 Interactions

Unfortunately, some of the causes of decline listed above reinforce one another thereby strengthening their adverse effects on growth. The growth of the giant corporation and the control over its rents that the principal/agent problem gives managers, converts managers into a rentseeking interest group. A possibly effective constraint on managerial discretion is the threat of take-over and expulsion. When this constraint began to be invoked in the United States in the late 1980s, managers approached the legislatures of the states in which they were incorporated and pressured them to pass legislation to protect them from hostile takeovers (Roe, 1993). When President Bush made his ill-fated trip to Japan to promote American economic interests, it was the managers of the giant, mature uninnovative companies who were most heavily represented in his entourage. When the United States risked a costly trade war with Japan in 1995, it was to advance the fortunes of its declining automobile industry.

The goal of the welfare state is to protect individuals from economic risks. Economic success and failure are no longer viewed as the responsibility of the individual, but become the responsibility of the state. State initiatives replace individual initiative (Taylor, 1987). Social solidarity reinforces social conformity. The social culture becomes increasingly hostile to the kinds of risk-taking, nonconformist attitudes that characterize innovators and entrepreneurs. No employee benefits are more generous in the welfare state than those of the government employee. No employee's life is more secure. As the state grows so too does the number of talented people drawn into government. Why take a chance building one's own empire, when one is asked to help run the nation's biggest one. Not surprisingly, new firm starts are proportionately much higher in the United States and Japan than in Sweden, Germany and the UK (Porter, 1990, pp. 327, 351, 413, 504). Within Europe, new firm start-ups are much greater in Italy with its individualistic, independent, risk-taking culture, than in its Teutonic neighbours (Porter, 1990, pp. 445–7).

1.6 THE POSSIBILITY OF PERPETUAL GROWTH

Schumpeter's (1934) description of capitalistic economic development at the beginning of this century suggested the possibility of perpetual growth. Entrepreneurial innovations would create profits and consumers' surplus. Imitation and the 'gale of perennial destruction' would eliminate these profits and reconstitute incentives to innovate. But the rise of large, managerially controlled corporations, and the growth of democratic governments bent on redistribution made obsolete Schumpeter's image of entrepreneurial capitalism.

Despite these events, Schumpeter (1950), writing at the middle of the 20th century, somewhat surprisingly was still able to paint a rather cheerful picture of economic development. Innovations would now pour forth from the R&D laboratory of the large corporation, and the whole process could be sufficiently routinized to be taken over by the state, when democracy's egalitarian tendencies eventually led to socialism's triumph. Once launched, capitalistic economies might innovate and grow indefinitely, even if transformed into some form of democratic socialism.

It is difficult from a post-1989 vantage point to give Schumpeter high marks for the predictive content of his last major work. Small firms have accounted for a disproportionate share of major innovations throughout the 20th century (Jewkes, Sawyer and Stillerman, 1969; Pavit *et al.,* 1987). The most dramatic economic failure of the Communist economies was undoubtedly their inability to introduce innovations. Even the most successful of the quasi-socialistic economies, like Sweden, have been better at maintaining employment and productivity by shifting workers around between existing firms than by generating new ones (Porter, 1990, p. 351).

The best examples of Schumpeterian corporations have been the pharmaceuticals, which have continually reinvested profits from existing drugs to develop new ones. More typical, however, have been companies like Polaroid, which despite strenuous efforts to create innovative environments and heavy expenditures on R&D have failed to duplicate their initial success.[25] Most mature companies eventually give up trying to develop new major products and switch to mergers as their route to perpetual life. Even the largest pharmaceutical companies appear to have switched to this strategy in the last few years.

That no country has found the formula for perpetual growth so far does not mean of course that no country ever will or ever could. Since all citizens can be better off if a country's wealth grows, agreement on policies to achieve this end should in principle be possible. We have identified three categories of impediments to perpetual growth: rentseeking and dissipation in the private (corporate) sector, rentseeking through government and motivation.

The inefficiencies that arise because of the principal/agent problem between stockholders and managers can be reduced by strengthening the hand of shareholders. Requiring managers to provide shareholders with more information, so that they can monitor managers better; prohibiting managers from owning *voting* shares; and taxing undistributed profits are just some examples. To the extent that wealth destroying mergers are the managers most egregious use of discretion, they could be prevented simply by prohibiting all acquisitions by large firms, subject to an efficiency defence.[26]

A prohibition on large firm acquisitions would also mitigate the costs of managerial rentseeking by reducing the magnitudes of the rents sought. Both managerial compensation and the nonpecuniary advantages of management are related to company size. Smaller firms are also easier for shareholders to monitor and control. A vigorous competition policy will limit corporate rents and thus the competition to control them.

Most directly, tax, competition and regulation policies might be adopted to encourage the formation of new companies. For example in Italy, where small and medium-sized firms have been an important source of growth, small firms are exempted from certain taxes and regulations of employment practices.

The welfare state can be dismantled and rentseeking made more difficult. Reforms to prevent collective rentseeking would most likely be of a constitutional nature. Switzerland has the smallest governmental sector in Western Europe, because its decentralized federalist structure and heavy reliance on direct democracy allow its citizens to keep government in check. Swiss institutions can be copied and supplemented by requiring supramajorities to pass some (all) legislation in the parliament, constitutional constraints placed on the nature of issues that can be adopted, and the like (Mueller, 1996).

Although policies such as these can be conceptualized, they are obviously not easy to adopt. To the extent that economic decline is the result of rentseeking, those who currently receive the highest rents will resist the reforms. For example, the potential benefits from privatizing state-owned enterprises in Europe have been undermined by placing ownership shares in the hands of groups 'friendly' to incumbent managements (*Economist*, 15 July 1995, p. 14). More generally, in countries like Sweden the number of people employed by or directly dependent on the government has grown so large that measures to contract government are now almost politically impossible (Lindbeck, 1995a,b).

The most difficult of all of the causes of decline to avoid, however, is the motivational factor. Mancur Olson (1982, pp. 252–53, n.10) demonstrated the fallacy in the argument that Germany, Italy and Japan's economic success relative to that of the US and the UK was due to *an advantage* the two defeated countries had because their capital stocks had been destroyed by the war, by pointing out that the US and UK could and would then have improved their economic performance by destroying their industrial capital.

A similar point cannot be made, however, against the argument that prosperity reduces the incentives to start businesses, take risks and to innovate. Since the goal of these activities, and the desirability of economic growth in general, is that it produces prosperity, it would be self-defeating to *manufacture* scarcity to create prosperity. The challenge to perpetual growth is to induce a well-fed society to behave as if it was hungry, while remaining well fed.[27]

1.7 SPECULATIONS

Which if any of the leading economic powers in the world today will be able to meet this challenge? We close with some speculative thoughts regarding this question. Let us start with Japan. Although it is difficult to view Japan as a socialist economy, it does have a fairly egalitarian structure, and many might cite it as an example of managed innovation and growth of the type Schumpeter described in *Capitalism, Socialism and Democracy*, with Japan's giant industrial groups and MITI working hand in hand to sustain economic growth. Who is to say that this will not go on indefinitely?

Perhaps it will, but there is reason to think otherwise. Throughout the post-World-War-II era, Japan was governed by a single party. This helped prevent Japan from engaging in the kind of governmental rentseeking that more competitive politics and majority rule tend to produce. The result is that Japan has a much smaller governmental sector than any other country with a similar standard of living. Japan's politics seems to be becoming more competitive, however. One expects more efforts to use government to redistribute Japan's immense wealth, with the inevitable consequences for growth.

It also seems likely that Japan's military budget will grow dramatically, as it assumes the place in world politics that its economic status allows, and that this too will have negative consequences for Japan's economic growth. Although they continue to eschew domestic mergers, Japanese firms have begun to show signs of maturity in shifting to growth through (foreign) acquisitions.

Finally one must wonder whether Japanese families will continue to place great pressure on their children to succeed in school, and Japanese workers will continue to work longer hours and take shorter vacations than workers in other developed countries, now that they are the richest country in the world?

During its economic rise over the 19th and 20th centuries, the United States was a large, competitive market. Over much of this period the government sector was small and did not interfere with the private sector except to ensure the competitiveness of its markets. Wave upon wave of immigrants entered the labour market, started new firms, and contributed to the country's economic dynamism through their drive and ambition. New waves of immigrants now press to get in. Why cannot America's development strategy of the past be applied again in the future?

Again the answer is that it possibly can, but again there is also reason for doubt. The immigrants from Europe in the 19th and 20th centuries went in search of 'the American Dream'. They left their homelands for good, they forced their children to learn English, they *became* Americans, legally and psychologically. Many immigrants today do not seem willing to make the same commitments. Sometimes they come seeking only work, with their families remaining in their homelands. Often they wish not to adopt the language of their community, but to retain their native language and culture, and have the community accommodate this 'diversity'.[28] A danger exists today in the United States that the same kind of linguistic divisions will develop as exist in Canada and Belgium, and that they will produce the same type of economically costly frictions. Not surprisingly, the United States seems likely to adopt ever more restrictive policies against new immigrants, thereby mitigating one problem, but eliminating a historically important source of economic dynamism.[29] America's protectionist immigration policies might also easily spill over into protectionist economic policies. We gave recent examples of this above.

On the other hand, the individualist, antigovernment ideology of the Americans seems much more likely to allow them to rein in governmental rentseeking than the Europeans will be able to achieve with their sense of social solidarity and deference to the state. Despite the much smaller share of GNP going to government in the US than in all European Union countries, politicians from Ronald Reagan to Newt Gingrich have scored major political victories by promising to reduce significantly the scale of the US welfare state and government intervention more generally. In stark contrast, even the modest recent proposals to cut back welfare spending in France, Germany and Austria have met with public protests and strikes. The US deficit and inflation rates as of June 1997 would have qualified it for membership in the European Monetary Union. Among the Union's countries, only Luxembourg qualified. At the end of 1998, by which time the major EU powers had imposed harsh monetary and fiscal restraints to meet the Maastricht targets, electoral processes had brought to power new left-of-centre governments.

The integrative steps that began in 1992 might have initiated in Western Europe the kind of disruptions that Olson (1982) feels are necessary to overcome interest group power, and initiate economic growth. Add to these the events of 1989 and 1991 in East Europe and the Soviet Union, and one might have envisaged the birth of a new Europe, whose growth and prosperity would be facilitated by its large common market, and stimulated by both demand and supply side pressures from the east.[30]

Had such an era dawned one would have expected Europeans to have recognized the critical juncture in history at which they stood, and have responded by writing a constitution *for Europe* that would integrate Europe politically as well as economically, and introduced the kind of safeguards to individual rights and to the market process that are necessary in such a large, heterogeneous community; introduced a new European language that in the long run would facilitate communication and cooperation among its diverse peoples, without giving an existing linguistic group an advantage over any other; introduced a single currency to facilitate economic transactions, and so on.

Some of these measures, like the common currency, are coming to pass. But Europe seems much more interested in protecting its institutions and rents of the past than in creating new ones. Many European corporations today, like their American counterparts in the 1970s and 1980s, respond to the pressures from increased competition not by developing new or less costly products, but by merging. Instead of developing a new language that all Europeans would use, existing languages are defended by forcing their use on individuals, and prohibiting the use of competing languages. How symbolic an intersection of Spenglerian cultural decline and economic decline is the effort led by France to protect the European film industry by *forbidding* the showing of non-European, that is, American, films. Could one imagine Holland in the 17th century prohibiting foreign artists from competing with Rembrandt or Hals? Could one imagine even France as recently as a century ago forbidding the showing of Van Gogh in Paris for fear that then no one would buy Monet and Manet?

Mere mention of the term 'European Federalism' puts large numbers of Europeans in a state of apoplexy. Yet, some form of truly federalist structure seems to be needed, if the European Union is ever going to assume a role in world politics that matches its economic position (see Mueller, 1997). Symbolically, the biggest item in the European Union's budget is not defence or some other pan-European public good but, as it has always been, subsidies for its most important industry, from *before* the Industrial Revolution.

NOTES

1. For discussions of the catch-up hypothesis in the context of Olson's hypothesis about the decline of nations, see Abramowitz (1983) and Pryor (1983).
2. Part of the reason that the Reagan and Thatcher revolutions were only partially successful is that they did not take on all interest groups with equal zeal. Business group rentseeking was virtually ignored.
3. For discussions of the catch-up hypothesis in the context of Olson's hypothesis about the decline of nations, see Abramowitz (1983) and Pryor (1983).
4. On the historical side see Chandler (1990, pp. 34–6, 227–8, 597–605), on the empirical side, Shepherd (1975) and Mueller (1986).
5. Such was the fear of the United States in Europe at one point in time, as expressed by Jean-Jacques Servan-Shreiber (1968). Akio Morito (1988), a founder of Sony, seemed in similar awe of America early on in his career.
6. For profits maximization always to be equivalent to utility maximization regardless of the rate of transformation of effort into profits, the owner-entrepreneur must have a constant marginal utility of income.
7. For reviews of the evidence that mergers reduce shareholder wealth see Mueller (1987, 1995). Firth (1980) presents evidence directly linking growth through merger and above normal increases in managerial salaries.
8. Petroleum mergers dominated *Fortune Magazine's* list of the 'Decades Worst Mergers' (Fisher, 1984).
9. An important exception to this pattern was General Dynamics, which simply used its existing cash flows to buy up its own shares and thereby handsomely increased the wealth of its shareholders.
10. Merger activity and stock market prices have also been strongly correlated in the United Kingdom, see Nelson (1959, 1966) and Geroski (1984).
11. Not only do most mergers occur when stock prices are rising, but the companies who make the acquisitions significantly outperform the market on average *prior* to their making the acquisitions. These companies' managers are most likely to have the resources and discretion to undertake mergers, even when these mergers reduce the profits and efficiency of the merging firms (Magenheim and Mueller, 1987; Mueller, 1995).
12. See surveys by Caves (1989), Jensen and Ruback (1983), Mueller (1987, 1995).
13. See Ravenscraft and Scherer (1987, Chapters 5 and 6) and Porter (1987). Some individual examples are striking. Heublein acquired Theodore Hamm Brewing Co. in 1965 for $62 million, and sold it in 1973 for $6 million. Murray bought Easy Washer in the mid-1950s for $9.4 million and sold it in 1963 for $0.77 million (Mueller, 1986, p. 204). American Safety Razor had sales of $27.3 million when Philip Morris acquired it in 1960, and sales of $17.8 million when it was spun-off in 1977 (Ravenscraft and Scherer, 1987, Chapter 5).
14. Many examples are given by Davidson (1985).
15. Let I_t be a firm's investment in period t, C_{t+j} the cash flow this investment generates in $t + j$, and i_t the firm's discount rate in t, then the present value of this investment is

$$PV_t = \sum_{j=1}^{\infty} \frac{c_{t+j}}{(1+i_t)^j} \tag{1}$$

If we take PV_t from (1) and place it into (2), we can define for any i_t, a permanent return, r_t, on the investment I_t, which creates an equivalent present value to that defined by (1):

$$PV_t = \frac{I_t r_t}{i_t} \tag{2}$$

The market value of the firm at the end of period t can be defined as

$$M_t = M_{t-1} + PV_t - \delta_t M_{t-1} + \mu_t \tag{3}$$

where PV_t is the present value of the investment made during t, δ_t the depreciation rate for the firm's total capital, and μ_t the market's error in evaluating M_t.

The assumption of capital market efficiency implies that the error term in (3) has the usual properties assumed in regression analysis. In a cross-section of firms of varying sizes, however, μ_t is likely to be heteroscedastic. To remove heteroscedasticity we deflate (3) by M_{t-1}. Replacing PV_t in (3) with $c_t I_t$, $c_t = r_t / i_t$

$$\frac{M_t - M_{t-1}}{M_{t-1}} = -\delta + c \frac{I_t}{M_{t-1}} + \frac{\mu_t}{M_{t-1}} \tag{4}$$

and rearranging yields equation (4) under the assumption that δ_t and c_t are constant across firms and time.

16. Kenneth Arrow (1962) was the first to show formally that the possession of monopoly power can act as a deterrent to innovation.

17. The low status of business occupations relative to the military, was also an important contributing factor to the decline of the Ottoman Empire, once its military expansionism had reached its limits, and wealth could no longer be acquired through conquest.

18. Porter (1990, p. 114) stresses the role immigrants have played in developing new products in the US, UK and Switzerland.

19. On success breeding failure, see Toynbee (1946, pp. 307–10). Results of a recent survey of 18-year-old Austrians by an institute in Linz are typical for both Europe and the United States, today. When asked what their greatest concerns for the future were, less than half mentioned uncertainties about their careers or employment. Nor were environmental dangers or crime a cause for much concern. The question that troubled the largest fraction of Austrian youths was how they would best be able to use their future leisure and vacation time (*Der Standard*, 5/6 August 1995, p. 1).

20. As reported in *The Economist*, 3 June 1995, p. 77.

21. Seligman (1925, Chapter 1), also reported in Tanzi (1986, p. 5), and Mueller (1989, p. 323).

22. *Ibid.*

23. For an analysis of the 'British disease', that links rentseeking, majority rule and government activity together, see Samuel Brittan (1975).

24. 'Offensive' governmental outlays have been a popular means to growth throughout the ages. All empires built through military conquest have eventually perished by the sword, however. The heavy burden of continually having to support armies to fend off the barbarians and resolve leadership disputes appears to have contributed to the fall of the Roman Empire (Gibbon, 1985). Paul Kennedy (1987, p. 539) notes that a 'great power' must have both manufacturing and military strength, but that the high cost of the latter undermines the former.

25. Polaroid's average return on investment over the 1969–88 period was *negative* (Mueller and Reardon, 1993, p. 440).

26. For further discussion of these and other proposals, see Mueller (1993, 1995).

27. Neumann's (1991) thesis would allow for perpetual growth, albeit with periodic depressions to regenerate the incentives to save and invest, and in the context of my thesis to innovate and take risks.

28. In part this change may reflect a shift in the composition of the immigrant population in the United States. Since the mid-1960s changes in immigration laws, a far greater fraction of US immigrants have come from the Western Hemisphere, so that returning home has been a more realistic option than was returning to Europe in the 19th or early 20th centuries (Borjas, 1994). In part this change reflects changes in the actual and perceived rights of immigrants (Soysal, 1995).

29.　The changing composition of the immigrant population also appears to have been accompanied by a decline in their education and skill levels compared to earlier immigants, so that even if the flow of immigrants is not cut off, immigrants may not be as important a source of entrepreneurial talent in the US in the future as they were in the past. See Borjas (1994), and references therein.

30.　More pessimistically, one might interpret the Great Depression sandwiched between the two world wars as Europe's 'Time of Troubles', and the European Union as Europe's 'Universal State'. Following Toynbee's life-cycle scenario, creation of the Universal State would provide only an interregnum in Europe's decline, which would be followed by the complete disintegration of its civilization as it is invaded by barbarians (from east and south?). All that is missing from Toynbee's saga is a Universal Religion (consumerism?).

REFERENCES

Abramovitz, Moses (1983), 'Notes on International Differences in Growth Rates', in Dennis C. Mueller (ed.), *The Political Economy of Growth*, New Haven and London: Yale University Press, pp. 79–89.

Alesina, Alberto and Dani Rodrik (1994), 'Distributive politics and economic growth', *Quarterly Journal of Economics,* **109,** 465–90.

Arrow, Kenneth (1962), 'Economic Welfare and the Allocation of Resources for Invention', *NBER, The Rate and Direction of Inventive Activity,* Princeton: Princeton University Press, pp. 609–25.

Borjas, George J. (1994), 'The economics of immigration' , *Journal of Economic Literature,* **32,** 1667–718.

Brittan, Samuel (1975), 'The economic contradictions of democracy', *British Journal of Political Science,* **5,** 129–59.

Caves, Richard E. (1989), 'Mergers, takeovers and economic efficiency: foresight vs. hindsight', *International Journal of Industrial Organization,* **7,** 151–74.

Chandler, Alfred D. Jr (1990), *Scale and Scope,* Cambridge, MA: Belknap Press.

Coase, Ronald H. (1937), 'The nature of the firm', *Economica,* **4,** 233–61.

Davidson, Kenneth M. (1985), *Megamergers,* Cambridge, MA: Ballinger.

Der Standard, 5/6 August 1995, p. 1.

Dunne, Timothy, Mark Roberts and Larry Samuelson (1988), 'Patterns of firm entry and exit in U.S. manufacturing industries', *Rand Journal of Economics,* **19,** 495–515.

Fernández-Armesto, Felipe (1995), *Millennium,* New York and London: Scribner.

Firth, Michael (1980), 'Takeovers, shareholder returns, and the theory of the firm', *Quarterly Journal of Economics,* **94,** 315–47.

Fisher, Anne B. (1984), 'The decade's worst mergers', *Fortune,* 30 April, 262 ff.

Geroski, Paul A. (1984), 'On the relationship between aggregate merger activity and the stock market', *European Economic Review,* **25,** 223–33.

Geroski, Paul A. (1991), *Market Dynamics and Entry,* Oxford: Basil Blackwell.

Gibbon, Edward, (1985), *The Decline and Fall of the Roman Empire,* London: Penguin Classics (first published in 6 volumes from 1776 to 1788).

Gort, Michael and Steven Klepper (1982), 'Time paths in the diffusion of product innovations', *Economic Journal,* **92,** 630–53.

Graddy, Elizabeth and Steven Klepper (1990), 'The evolution of new industries and the determinants of market structure', *Rand Journal of Economics,* **21,** 27–44.

Jensen, Michael C. and Richard S. Ruback (1983), 'The market for corporate control', *Journal of Financial Economics,* **11,** 5–50.

Jewkes, John, John Sawyer and Richard Stillerman (1969), *The Sources of Invention,* 2nd edn, New York: Norton.

Kennedy, Paul (1987), *The Rise and Fall of the Great Powers,* New York: Random House.

Knight, Frank H. (1965), *Risk, Uncertainty and Profit,* New York: Harper and Row (first published in 1921).

Klepper, Steven and Kenneth L. Simons (1993), 'Technological change and industry shakeouts', mimeo, Carnegie Mellon University.

Lindbeck, Assar (1995a), 'Hazardous welfare-state dynamics', *American Economic Review,* **85,** 9–15.

Lindbeck, Assar (1995b), 'Welfare state disincentives with endogenous habits and norms', *Scandinavian Journal of Economics,* **97,** 477–94.

Magenheim, Ellen and Dennis C. Mueller (1987), 'On Measuring the Effect of Mergers on Acquiring Firm Shareholders', in Jack Coffee, Louis Lowenstein and Susan Rose-Ackerman (eds), *Knights, Raiders and Targets,* Oxford: Oxford University Press, pp. 171–93.

Marris, Robin (1964), *The Economic Theory of Managerial Capitalism,* Glencoe: Free Press.

Meeks, Geoffrey (1977), *Disappointing Marriage: A Study of the Gains from Merger,* Cambridge: Cambridge University Press.

Mill, John Stuart (1885), *Principles of Political Economy,* 9th edn, London: Longmans, Green & Co.

Morito, Akio, with Edwin M. Reingold and Mitsuko Shimomuna (1988), *Made in Japan,* New York: Signet.

Mueller, Dennis C. (1969), 'A theory of conglomerate mergers', *Quarterly Journal of Economics,* **LXXXIII,** 643–59, reprinted in G. Marchildon (ed.) (1991), *Mergers and Acquisitions,* Cheltenham: Edward Elgar.

Mueller, Dennis C. (1972), 'A life cycle theory of the firm', *Journal of Industrial Economics,* **20,** 199–219.

Mueller, Dennis C. (1986), *Profits in the Long Run,* Cambridge: Cambridge University Press.

Mueller, Dennis C. (1987), *The Corporation: Growth, Diversification, and Mergers,* London: Harwood Academic Publishers.

Mueller, Dennis C. (1989), *Public Choice II,* Cambridge: Cambridge University Press.

Mueller, Dennis C. (1990), *The Dynamics of Company Profits* (editor and contributor), Cambridge: Cambridge University Press.

Mueller, Dennis C. (1993), 'U.S. merger policy and the 1992 merger guidelines', *Review of Industrial Organization,* **8,** 151–62.

Mueller, Dennis C. (1995), 'Mergers: Theory and Evidence', in Giuliano Mussatti (ed.), *Mergers, Markets, and Public Policy,* Dordrecht: Kluwer, pp. 9–43.

Mueller, Dennis C. (1996), *Constitutional Democracy,* New York: Oxford University Press.

Mueller, Dennis C. (1997), 'Federalism and the European Union: a constitutional perspective', *Public Choice,* **90,** 255–80.

Mueller, Dennis C. and Peter Murrell (1986), 'Interest groups and the size of government', *Public Choice,* **48**(2), 125–45.

Mueller, Dennis C. and Elizabeth Reardon (1993), 'Rates of return on investment', *Southern Economic Journal,* **60,** 430–53.

Mueller, Dennis C. and John E. Tilton (1969), 'Research and development costs as a barrier to entry', *Canadian Journal of Economics,* **II**(4), 570–79.

Mueller, Dennis C. and Lawrence Yun (1995), 'Rates of return over the firm's life cycle', mimeo, University of Vienna.

Nelson, Ralph L. (1959), *Merger Movements in American Industry 1895–1956,* Princeton: Princeton University Press.

Nelson, Ralph L. (1966), 'Business Cycle Factors in the Choice Between Internal and External Growth', in W. Alberts and J. Segall (eds), *The Corporate Merger,* Chicago: University of Chicago Press.

Neumann, Manfred (1991), 'Das Buddenbrook-Syndrom und lange Wellen in Wirtschaft und Politik', *Bayerische Akademie der Wissenschaften, Philosophisch–Historische Klasse,* **2,** 3–21.

North, Douglass C. (1990), *Institutions, Institutional Change, and Economic Performance,* Cambridge: Cambridge University Press.

North, Douglass C. and Robert P. Thomas (1973), *The Rise of the Western World: A New Economic History,* Cambridge: Cambridge University Press.

Odagiri, Hiroyuki (1982), 'Antineoclassical management motivation in a neoclassical economy: a model of economic growth and Japan's experience, *Kyklos,* **35,** 223–43.

Odagiri, Hiroyuki (1991), *Growth Through Competition, Competition Through Growth: Strategic Management and the Economy in Japan,* Oxford: Oxford University Press.

Olson, Mancur (1982), *The Rise and Decline of Nations,* New Haven: Yale University Press.

Pavit, K., M. Robson and J. Townsend (1987), 'The size distribution of innovating firms in the U.K.: 1945–1983', *Journal of Industrial Economics,* **35,** 297–316.

Persson, Torsten and Guido Tabellini (1994), 'Is inequality harmful for growth?', *American Economic Review,* **84,** 600–621.

Porter, Michael A. (1987), 'From competitive advantage to corporate strategy', *Harvard Business Review,* May–June, 43–59.

Porter, Michael A. (1990), *The Competitive Advantage of Nations,* New York: Free Press.

Pryor, Frederic L. (1983) , 'A Quasi-Test of Olson's Hypotheses' , in Dennis C. Mueller (ed.), *The Political Economy of Growth,* New Haven and London: Yale University Press, pp. 90–105.

Ravenscraft, David J. and F.M. Scherer (1987), *Mergers, Sell-Offs, & Economic Efficiency,* Washington, DC: Brookings Institution.

Roe, Mark J. (1993), 'Takeover Politics', in Margaret M. Blair (ed.), *The Deal Decade,* Washington, DC: Brookings Institution, pp. 321–53.

Schumpeter, Joseph A. (1934), *The Theory of Economic Development,* Cambridge, MA: Harvard University Press (first published in German, 1911).

Schumpeter, Joseph A. (1950), *Capitalism, Socialism and Democracy,* 3rd edn, New York: Harper and Row.

Scitovsky, T. (1943), 'A note on profit maximization and its implications', *Review of Economic Studies,* **11,** 57–60.

Seligman, E.R.A. (1925), *Studies in Public Finance,* New York: Macmillan.

Servan-Schreiber, Jean-Jacques (1968), *The American Challenge,* New York: Atheneum.

Shepherd, William G. (1975), *The Treatment of Market Power,* New York: Columbia University Press.

Smith, Adam (1937), *The Wealth of Nations,* New York: Random House (first published in 1776).

Soysal, Yasemin Nuhoglu (1995), *Limits of Citizenship: Migrants and Postnational Membership in Europe,* Chicago: University of Chicago Press.

Spengler, Oswald (1923), *Der Untergang des Abendlandes,* I, Munich: Oskar Beck.

Spengler, Oswald (1922), *Der Untergang des Abendlandes,* II, Munich: Oskar Beck.

Tanzi, Vito (1986), *The Growth of Government Expenditures in Industrial Countries: An International and Historical Perspective,* Washington DC: International Monetary Fund.

Taylor, Michael J. (1987), *Anarchy and Cooperation,* 2nd edn, Cambridge: Cambridge University Press.

The Economist, 3 June 1995, p. 77.

The Economist, 15 July 1995, p. 14.

Toynbee, Arnold J. (1946, 1957), *A Study of History* (D.C. Somervill, abridgement), 2 volumes, Oxford: Oxford University Press (unabridged version published in 10 volumes, 1933, 1939).

Williamson, Oliver (1975), *Markets and Hierarchies: Analysis and Antitrust Implications,* New York: Free Press.

Williamson, Oliver (1985), *The Economic Institutions of Capitalism,* New York: Free Press.

2. Does sovereignty matter for economic growth? An analysis of growth rates between 1870 and 1950

M. Shahid Alam

INTRODUCTION*

This chapter explores the connections between sovereignty and the growth record of lagging countries over the two centuries leading up to the 1950s. It combines theory and empirics to show that sovereignty was a powerful force driving the polarization of the global economy during this period.

The first phase of the industrial epoch ending in the 1950s was characterized by (i) international integration of markets, (ii) concentration of manufactures in a small number of advanced countries, (iii) rising global disparities and (iv) centralization of power in the advanced countries.[1] Although these stylized facts are not controversial, not all of them are acknowledged by orthodox or dissenting accounts of the global economy. Orthodox analyses of the global economy accommodate only the first and second stylized facts; their prediction that integration will lead to all round growth being at variance with the third. Dissenting economists incorporate the first, second and third stylized facts but leave out the fourth; they generally claim that rising disparities were caused by integration of markets. This chapter takes explicit account of all four stylized facts. It argues that the patterns of global integration and growth during phase one of the industrial epoch were intimately connected to the spatial concentration of manufactures *and* power. When two economies at unequal levels of development were freely integrated, they moved further apart in terms of levels of development. Sovereign countries had greater success in structuring their integration into world markets – they could decide when, how fast and how far to integrate, what markets to integrate, and with whom to integrate – and, therefore, experienced more rapid industrialization and growth. The reverse was true for countries that lost their sovereignty.

This connection between sovereignty and growth is also explored empirically. The first step is to construct a four-fold taxonomy of sovereignty, consisting of sovereign countries, dependencies, quasi-colonies and colonies.[2] The impact of sovereignty on growth is then estimated by incorporating these sovereignty dummies into regressions explaining variations in growth rates across countries.[3] The results of these exercises show that sovereign countries and dependencies grew faster than quasi-colonies and colonies (QCC) over the period 1900 to 1950, when differences in sovereignty across countries were both large and sustained. This inverse relation between loss of sovereignty and growth is not weakened when we control for several economic and institutional influences on growth rates. The concern that our taxonomy of sovereignty may be a proxy for differences in initial conditions is also examined and found to be lacking in sound theory and not supported by evidence.

A final segment of this chapter draws attention to shifts in the global economy which advanced the industrial epoch into its second phase characterized by a dramatic decentralization of power and a growing dispersion of manufactures to lagging countries. Over the past two decades, however, primarily in response to the industrial challenge mounted by several lagging countries, a *re*-centralization of power in the advanced countries has been underway since the 1980s. Once again, this has curtailed the sovereignty of most lagging countries and their ability to formulate indigenous responses to the challenges of international integration.

A THEORY OF THE GLOBAL ECONOMY, 1760–1960

The Industrial Revolution inaugurated a new period in world history, an industrial epoch, which at first concentrated the world's industries in a small number of advanced countries, but is now, in its second phase, dispersing them to a growing number of lagging countries.[4]

The evolution of the global economy in the first phase of the industrial epoch – roughly the period between 1760 and 1960 – was attended by growing disparities in development even as integration between the advanced and lagging countries continued to grow. This paradox of inequality, the issue at the heart of this chapter, contradicts much of what we have been taught for more than two hundred years about international integration. Ever since Adam Smith (1776) formulated his critique of mercantilist policies, economists have believed that free markets, and their extension across national boundaries, offer the best chances for growth. Starting with Ricardo (1817), generations of economists have worked to translate this vision into theories of the international economy that have

remained unassailable in their eminence. In time, with a little mathematical teasing, economists pulled out theorems and lemmas about
international trade whose rigour is only matched by their irrelevance. One
of these theorems, the factor-price equalization theorem, proclaims that
free trade alone may push all trading countries to the same absolute level
of factor rewards.[5] Even in a world of nation states, each jealously guard-
ing its frontiers against the movements of capital and labour, free trade
would create the Valhalla of absolute global equality.

In fact, so deeply impressed were the early economists by the potential
gains from international integration, they counted it perverse if any country chose to erect barriers to integration. Not surprisingly, this perversity
was not to be tolerated. Throughout the 19th century, Western arms
worked overtime to bring the black sheep into the fold of the global economy. Some quickly saw the light and acquiesced to the opening of their
markets, in order to avoid worse consequences. Many more had to be
conquered and colonized for a more thorough makeover of their
economies and institutions. This global 'social work' was, of course, well
worth the trouble. Nearly always, a party of obstreperous traders followed hard upon the heels of the 'social workers'.

This vision of the global economy was deeply flawed. Starting in the
16th century, many countries were forcibly integrated into the global
economy, their markets flung open to the free movement of goods, capital, labour and enterprises. Yet, these primary-producing economies
languished while their exports multiplied, so that after decades, and
sometimes centuries, of assimilation into the global economy, they had
very little to show for their unqualified devotion to free markets. In
contrast, lagging countries which were free and chose to structure the
terms of their integration into the global economy – to save, shore up and
modernize their manufactures, enterprises and skills – continued to
industrialize, to grow and to narrow their economic distance behind the
advanced countries. Quaintly, free countries with unfree markets nearly
always outperformed unfree countries with free markets.

This discrepancy between theory and facts was scarcely noticed by
mainstream economists for nearly two hundred years. The failure of
some three-quarters of mankind to derive any advantage from their
incorporation into global markets did not surprise, much less disturb,
anyone. This was part of the Darwinian struggle for survival to which
many are called but few are chosen. This equanimity was breached only
in the 1950s when a changing world order had elevated the 'wretched of
the earth' to the centre stage of global conflicts. After a long regress into
abstractions, a few economists were now constructing theories of global
markets that did not flinch in the face of facts. Perhaps the two most

notable contributions to this new theoretical literature came from Myrdal (1957) and Myint (1954). Markets, they argued, set up disequalizing forces between advanced and lagging countries. An initial advantage, even a small one, can be compounded several times by the free play of market forces; conversely, those who are drafted into markets with handicaps get the short end of the bargain. Their arguments rested on the recognition of differences in the technologies of manufacturing and primary sectors *and* the presence of monopoly power that worked against lagging countries.

Writers of the dependency school in Latin America also blamed global markets for their backwardness. But they told a different story. Capitalist development failed in lagging countries because it was not homegrown; it was transplanted by foreign capitalists who used their monopoly power to siphon off surpluses from lagging countries. Much worse, the foreign capitalists found allies in the indigenous landowning classes, and together they perpetuated a social system based on primary production, inequities and repression. Some neo-Marxists offered a more esoteric explanation of underdevelopment. Trade between countries with unequal wages, they argued, results in exchange of unequal amounts of labour, and it is this unequal exchange that is at the root of underdevelopment. To free themselves from this unequal exchange, lagging countries would have to disengage from the world economy.

While the unorthodox writers drew attention to the disequalizing tendencies in global markets, they were much less interested in how these tendencies were enhanced and structured by unequal power between states and classes. Missing from their discussions are the uses of state power in shaping both market and non-market outcomes in lagging countries. Even when they invoke imperialism, it is not treated as a determining factor in the evolution of the global economy. One looks in vain for a systematic analysis of how advanced countries deployed their superior power to disequalize the terms under which lagging countries were integrated into the global economy. These unequal relations are treated as integral to the functioning of global markets, and not outcomes enforced by inequalities of power between advanced and lagging countries. As a result, imperialism – as the deployment of real force – rarely becomes a factor comparable in importance to market forces in the ordering of economic relations between advanced and lagging countries.

The central task of this chapter is to bring the state back into the global economy. The Industrial Revolution endowed the advanced countries with a comparative advantage in manufactures and, later, a military superiority over most lagging countries. The free operation of market forces deepened both asymmetries. Manufacturing costs declined as trade expanded, and this set into motion cumulative rounds of growth and trade expansion which concentrated manufactures, commerce, capital and power in advanced countries. At the same time, the advanced countries exploited their growing military superiority to gain uninhibited access to lagging countries, to establish monopoly control over their markets and resources, and take what else they could by force. This deepened the polarization between advanced and lagging countries. Naturally, lagging countries tried to resist the forces of polarization, but success depended on sovereignty, measured as the power of indigenous factor-owners to shape government policies in opposition to *foreign* factor-owners. In the long run, sovereignty improved a lagging country's chances of developing manufactures and an indigenous capitalist base, thus creating the conditions for sustained economic growth. This is the central thesis of this chapter.

Although our interest in the global economy begins with the Industrial Revolution, a brief digression as to its origins may be useful. The maritime ascendancy of Western nations, signalled by the voyages of 'discovery', produced results that were momentous for the evolution of the global economy. It led to the dominance of Western mercantile capital over the major circuits of international trade; conversely, it produced a retreat of mercantile capital based in other regions of the world. This growth in Western mercantile capital led to cumulative advances in shipping, financial markets, property rights and urbanization – developments which eventually produced, in countries where they were most advanced, the ascendancy of markets over states in the spheres of production and exchange. In time, these changes culminated in the Industrial Revolution – a stream of innovations in energy use, production technology and organization – which gave to advanced countries a growing comparative advantage in manufactures and placed manufactures in the driver's seat of the global economy.

The Industrial Revolution created another asymmetry. The military superiority that Europeans had enjoyed for two centuries on the high seas was extended to the land in the first decades of the 19th century. Even the most powerful Asian empires were now unable to match the superior arms, organization and fighting tactics of the great European powers. The die was now cast. The spread and consolidation of Western Europe's dominance was now mostly a matter of time and opportunity. The only remaining hindrances were distance, difficulty of access and tropical diseases. Advances in steam navigation and railways removed the first two, quinine and vaccinations took care of the third.[6]

Although these developments created conditions that would lead to growing polarization, the disparities between advanced and lagging countries at the time of the Industrial Revolution were still quite small. In

1760, or even as late as 1800, these disparities were within a range that was not uncommon by historical standards. Although estimates of these disparities vary, they were nearly always smaller than two to one, and upon excluding the polar cases, the differences often favour some of today's lagging countries. Similarly, notwithstanding the catalytic role it had played in the two preceding centuries, international trade was still a sideshow. Even as late as 1820, global trade amounted to a modest two per cent of global output.[7] On the whole, the global economy had changed very little.

All this would change over the next century and a half. The eight decades preceding 1800 recorded a doubling of global trade; in the next eight decades it had expanded 13-fold, and in 1913 it was more than 43 times its level in 1800.[8] A global capital market, centred in London, had also been established, with the capacity for moving vast sums of capital between advanced and lagging countries. This dramatic acceleration in the integration of global markets produced sustained growth in the advanced countries but stagnation or worse in most lagging countries. In consequence, the income gap between them in 1950 had widened to more than five to one.[9] Paradoxically, the development gap between advanced and lagging countries had widened even as their economies were pulled together by global markets.

The dissenting economists explained this paradox in terms of global markets. Integration created polarization when it joined countries at unequal levels of development. The sources of this polarization were to be found in technological asymmetries between the manufacturing and primary sectors. Not only were economies of scale stronger in manufacturing, this sector also generated important externalities for primary activities, transportation, and labour and financial markets. These asymmetries ensured that integration would deepen the advanced country's comparative advantage in manufactures, reduce costs in primary activities, increase the efficiency of capital markets and augment their organizational skills. Armed with these growing advantages, manufactures, enterprises, capital and skills in advanced countries would displace their counterparts in lagging countries. In addition, attracted by higher returns, savings of lagging countries would gravitate to advanced countries.[10]

This analysis of international integration, however, tells less than half the story about the evolution of the global economy. Polarization was not caused by market forces *per se* – nor by market forces alone. The global economy was not a spontaneous order created by the free play of market forces; it was a politically constructed reality, often shaped by bitterly fought contests between states and, within countries, between classes. It

was the relative power of states and classes – as mediated by many fortu-
itous factors and events – which determined whether a lagging country
could and would structure its integration, and whether its markets and
resources would be monopolized and appropriated by foreign factor-
owners.[11] In order to unveil the political construction of the global
economy, it may be helpful if we begin by examining the asymmetric
impact of integration on states and classes in advanced and lagging
countries presented in Table 2.1.

Capital, manufacturing labour and the state gain – landowners and
primary-sector labour lose – from integration in advanced countries.
Since capital and the state were already strong in advanced countries, this
explains why they moved towards greater integration, even though this
passage was delayed in deference to the interests of powerful landowners.
While landowners had the power to prevent or delay the free import of
food and raw materials which competed with their own produce, they
could not stifle the expansion of capital abroad. Manufactures, enterprises and skills from advanced countries could thus mobilize official
support in gaining free access to the markets in lagging countries. Thus,
well before they had adopted a policy of free trade for their own
economies, the advanced countries were advocating and pushing for free
trade in the lagging countries. It is not too difficult to see why the lagging
countries generally were not enthusiastic about such a policy.

The gains and losses from integration are reversed in lagging countries.
Capital, manufacturing labour and the state *lose* – landowners and
primary-sector labour *gain* – from integration. Although landowners were
the dominant class in many lagging countries, they still had to contend
with the combined interests of the state, capital and labour. This contest
could go either way, though most likely, the size, power and symbolism of
the state were the determining factors. Not surprisingly, at the beginning
of the 19th century, we encounter a variety of solutions to this contest.
Some countries chose to structure their integration, others integrated

Table 2.1 Gains and losses from international integration

	The state	Capital	Landowners	Labour manufacturing	Labour primary
Advanced countries	Gain	Gain	Lose	Gain	Lose
Lagging countries	Lose	Lose	Gain	Lose	Gain

more freely, and a few opted for complete isolation. A fourth group had no choices to make: they had already been integrated into the global economy by their colonial masters.

There was no *ex ante* complementarity of interests between advanced and lagging countries. The advanced countries sought to gain unconditional access to markets and resources in lagging countries; in most cases, no *quid pro quo* was contemplated. It was unlikely that any lagging country would acquiesce to these demands. Even when the balance of their class forces pushed them towards integration, they would move forward gingerly; there were industries they wanted to protect for reasons of security and domestic politics, and almost certainly they would seek to protect indigenous enterprises, capital and skills from foreign competition. Moreover, at some later date, when political and economic conditions were more favourable to manufactures, they may want to reverse their present policy of integration. Those wishing to industrialize, or to isolate their economies from foreign contacts, would erect stronger barriers to deter entry into their markets. These conflicts were fundamental and defined the first and minimal task of imperialism: the advanced countries would have to use force to open up the economies of lagging countries.

Imperialism had other aims too. The advanced countries would not be content with the gains that free markets offered; surely they had the power to extract more. This could be assured only if rivals could be kept out of the lagging countries. Therefore, whenever they could, advanced countries would claim free *and* exclusive access to the markets and resources of lagging countries. But even monopoly control could carry them only as far as markets generally go; and they wanted to go farther. And so they would use their superior power over lagging countries to seize their assets, lands, mineral resources and savings; to draft their labour for use on public works and on plantations and farms owned by settlers; to use their tax revenues for foreign conquests, to attract settlers, or guarantee minimum returns on investments in infrastructure. While monopoly control over lagging countries may have restricted their integration, direct appropriation moved them in the opposite direction. Whenever expropriation exerted the stronger effect, we would encounter *hyper*integration, that is, integration beyond what would be possible under free markets.

Since advanced countries sought exclusive access to lagging countries, to use them as they wanted, the logic of imperialism pointed inexorably in the direction of colonization. But while colonies were eagerly sought – and often fiercely fought over – colonization of all lagging countries was not inevitable. Although the advanced countries wielded great power, they were also up against obstacles set up by geography, diseases, distance, obstinate devotion to freedom and, most importantly, they came in each other's way. Most countries in Asia and Africa were colonized because they were not shielded by these obstacles. A few were luckier and managed to preserve their own governments while giving up various degrees of control over their policies. Many more in Europe and South America had even greater luck and succeeded in keeping their undivided sovereignty.

The classical economists, Karl Marx included, have maintained that colonialism was the *deus ex machina* that would revive the backward countries from their ancient somnolescence. The superior rule of Europeans, together with free trade and some white settlers, would eventually elevate the colonies into the ranks of civilized nations. Though somewhat tattered, this prognosis still has many loyal followers.[12] Only the neo-Marxists rejected it openly, but their rejection did not go far enough. They argued that independence of lagging countries did not matter; advanced countries could always, or nearly always, threaten, cajole, or bribe their way around independent governments in lagging countries. We examine a neglected third possibility, claiming that sovereignty did matter. The more lagging countries had of it, the more likely they were to experience sustained growth. In essence, the logic of it is simple. Free integration into world markets was bad for economic growth in lagging countries; monopolization and direct appropriation of their resources were worse. The economic losses from integration, monopolization and direct appropriation varied directly with loss of sovereignty. Therefore, loss of sovereignty was detrimental to economic growth in lagging countries.

SOVEREIGNTY DIFFERENTIALS IN THE GROWTH RECORD

The central thesis of this chapter is now tested by estimating sovereignty differentials in the growth record of lagging countries, defined as differences in growth rates between two countries that may be attributed to differences in their sovereignty once allowance is made for other factors affecting growth rates.

In order to estimate these sovereignty differentials, first we need to construct a taxonomy of sovereignty. This is quite straightforward once we have defined sovereignty as the power of the state to advance, in the long run, the interests of *indigenous* factors in opposition to the interests of *foreign* factors.[13] Three criteria were employed in judging a country's sovereignty: whether it had an indigenous government, whether it was subject to open-door treaties that limited their policy autonomy, and whether foreign capital had established a position of dominance in key sectors of the economy. This led to a four-fold taxonomy of sovereignty.

In declining order, these four categories are sovereign countries, dependencies, quasi-colonies and colonies. Sovereign countries (*SOV*) had indigenous governments were free from open-door treaties, and generally foreign capital did not dominate their economies.[14] Dependencies (*DEP*) had indigenous or mostly indigenous governments, were free from open-door treaties, but foreign capital had a dominating presence in their modern sectors. Quasi-colonies (*QC*) had mostly indigenous governments, were subject to open-door treaties limiting their policy autonomy, and their exchange sectors were dominated by foreign capital. Colonies (*COL*) had governments consisting of expatriates appointed from and by a foreign country; foreign capital and, often, expatriates, dominated the exchange sectors in their economies. For the countries in our sample, determination of where they belong in our taxonomy is quite straightforward.[15]

Systematic variations in the content of economic policies across these four categories are easily verified. We have shown in earlier papers that for the century preceding 1950, the extent of a country's resistance to international integration and monopoly control by foreigners was directly correlated with its sovereignty.[16] Sovereign countries and, to a lesser degree, dependencies employed a variety of policies to support domestic manufactures and indigenous capital, including generally high tariffs, overvalued exchange rates, repudiation of foreign debts, creation of public enterprises and industrial investment banks, tax-breaks, monopoly of indigenous firms over state procurements, state subsidies for schooling and training, various restrictions on entry of foreign enterprises and an infrastructure which integrated internal markets. Not only were these policy supports generally unavailable to domestic manufactures and indigenous factors in quasi-colonies and especially the colonies often they faced policy regimes which discriminated in favour of foreign factors. In the period before 1950, the Listian thrust of policies in the sovereign countries was matched by Ricardian policies in the colonies.

Once a taxonomy of sovereignty has been established, we can proceed to estimate sovereignty differentials relating to growth rates of per capita income (*GY*). This involves estimating an equation of the form: $GY = \alpha + \beta U + \delta V + \varepsilon$, where *U* is a set of sovereignty dummies, *V* is a set of *other* social and economic factors affecting growth rates, and ε is a random error term. We introduce two sovereignty dummies amongst the independent variables – sovereign countries (*SOV* = 1) and dependencies (*DEP* = 1), with quasi-colonies and colonies (*QCC*) as the base category; the estimated coefficients of *SOV* and *DEP* measure the sovereignty differentials between sovereign countries and dependencies relative to the *QCC*. The quasi-colonies and colonies were merged into a single category because of the small number of observations in each of the two categories taken individually.

Before turning to estimates of sovereignty differentials, however, let us first see what we can learn from a more direct examination of growth rates for lagging countries. Thanks to the work of a generation of economic historians, now integrated into a common framework by Maddison (1995), we can compare growth rates of per capita income between 1870 and 1950 for lagging countries with different levels of sovereignty.[17] Table 2.2 presents data on weighted average annual growth rates of per capita income for three categories of lagging countries – sovereign countries, dependencies and quasi-colonies-*cum*-colonies (*QCC*) – over one or more of three periods, 1870–1900, 1900–1913 and 1913–1950.[18] A country was identified as lagging if it had a per capita income of 66 per cent or less of US per capita income in 1900. The growth rates for the sovereign countries and the *QCC* were available for each of the three periods, while growth rates for the dependencies were only available for the last period. In each of the three periods, the sovereign countries grew faster than the *QCC*, and the differentials in growth rates between them widen significantly over successive periods, rising from 0.41 per cent over the first period, to 1.11 and 1.61 per cent over the next two periods. Over the third period, the sovereign countries grew at an average annual rate of 1.34 per cent, ahead of the dependencies that grew at 0.96 per cent, and both outpaced the *QCC* which were falling back at the rate of 0.27 per cent per annum.

Table 2.2 Sovereignty and growth rates of per capita income, 1870–1992

	1870– 1900	1900– 1913	1913– 1950	1900– 1950	1950– 1992
Weighted growth rates:					
Sovereign countries	1.00	1.61	1.34	1.43	2.58
Dependencies	(.)	(.)	0.96	(.)	0.95
Q-colonies and colonies	0.59	0.50	–0.27	–0.08	2.96
Percentage of world population:	1870	1900	1913	1900	1950
Sovereign countries	17.0	19.9	22.5	19.9	22.1
Dependencies	(.)	(.)	0.22	(.)	0.32
Q-colonies and colonies	48	50	49	50	48

Notes:
Growth rates are weighted averages for countries in each category: the weights are populations in initial year of growth period.
Growth rates for dependencies are for 1920–1950 and 1950–1990.
Based on all lagging countries with per capita income in 1900 equal to, or less than, US per capita income in 1900.

It would be an error to suppose that these results are not representative because of the relatively small number of *QCC* in our sample: the growth rates for the *QCC* in the three periods are based on four, 12 and 13 countries, respectively.[19] First, the global impact of imperialism should be evaluated by counting people, not countries. Although the samples of *QCC* are relatively small, they include the largest countries in this category, ensuring that their total populations in each of the three periods were only slightly less than three-quarters of the total population of all *QCC,* or nearly half of the world's total population at the beginning of each of the three periods.[20] In addition, with the possible exception of a few countries in West Africa which experienced rapid export growth during this period, it is unlikely that growth rates of the missing *QCC* were much different from the growth record of the *QCC* included in our sample.

A comparison of the mean growth rates of the sovereign countries, dependencies and *QCC* yields similar results. The average annual growth rates for the sovereign countries over 1870–1900, 1900–1913 and 1913–1950 are 1.07, 1.67 and 1.34 per cent respectively; the corresponding growth rates for the *QCC* are 0.49, 0.81 and –0.02 per cent.[21] Over the first period, only one of the 14 sovereign countries grew at rates below the mean for the *QCC*; in the second period, only three of the 18 sovereign countries grew at rates below the mean for the *QCC*; in the third period, there was no sovereign country with growth rates below the mean for the *QCC.* Similarly, none of the dependencies grew at rates below the mean for the *QCC* over the relevant time period. Once again, the disparity in mean annual growth rates between sovereign countries and the *QCC* increased progressively over the three periods.

The results of these simple comparisons carry over to the estimates of sovereignty differentials relating to growth rates of per capita income from 1900 to 1950.[22] The sovereignty differentials were estimated with three control variables, namely initial per capita income, adult literacy rates in 1930 and a dummy variable (*EUR* = 1) for countries in Europe.[23] We expect the growth rates to vary inversely with initial per capita income, a prediction that may be derived from the neoclassical as well as productivity-gap theories of growth.[24] Adult literacy rates are included as proxies for human capital, and are expected by recent theories of endogenous growth to have a positive impact on growth rates.[25] It has been argued that European countries may have grown faster because of institutional and locational advantages over other lagging countries. The evidence on institutional advantages is quite weak for our sample of countries.[26] Further, had these advantages been strong and instrumental, we may expect that they would be reflected, via higher growth rates, in higher levels of initial incomes, making it unnecessary to add a European dummy. The matter must be resolved by the empirical evidence.

The sovereignty differentials are estimated for four different samples of lagging countries obtained by increasing the restrictiveness of our definition of lagging countries. The largest sample of 40 lagging countries consists of all countries with a per capita income in 1900 (1913 for some sovereign countries and 1920 for the dependencies) equal to or less than 66 per cent of the per capita in United States in 1900. Three more samples were defined by moving the cutoff points successively to 50, 40 and 30 per cent; this reduced the sample of lagging countries from 40 to 37, 34 and 27, respectively. It may be noted that the number of *QCC* remains unchanged across all the four samples, while the number of dependencies remains unchanged for all but the last sample which includes four dependencies, down from five in the larger samples. Four sovereignty differentials are estimated for each of these samples corresponding to the three alternative taxonomies of sovereignty, namely sovereign countries, dependencies and *QCC;* sovereign countries-*plus*-dependencies and *QCC*; and sovereign countries and dependencies-*plus*-*QCC*. In order to conserve space, we only report the estimated values of the sovereignty differentials together with the corresponding adjusted R^2s, *F*-statistics and mean growth rates of per capita income for the base category.

An examination of the results on sovereignty differentials in Table 2.3 provides strong confirmation of the thesis that sovereignty had a large positive impact on growth rates in lagging countries. The sovereignty dummies for each of the three taxonomies have positive coefficients for all four samples of lagging countries, and all but two of them are statistically significant at the 1 per cent level, with the remaining two significant at the 5 per cent level.[27] The size of these coefficients show that sovereignty made a large difference to growth rates. This may be illustrated with respect to the results for the largest sample of lagging countries: sovereign countries grew faster than comparable *QCC* by 1.60 percentage points; sovereign countries grew faster than comparable *DEP-QCC* by 1.37 percentage points; *SOV-DEP* grew faster than comparable *QCC* by 1.19 percentage points; and even the dependencies grew faster than comparable *QCC* by 0.64 percentage points. In addition, each of the four sovereignty differentials became larger as the sample size became more restrictive, implying that the efficacy of sovereignty in generating growth increased at lower levels of development. Thus, the sovereignty differential between sovereign countries and *QCC* was 1.60 percentage points for the largest sample, but increased progressively to 1.80, 1.96 and 2.18 percentage points as the sample was reduced successively to 37, 34 and 27 countries. The same pattern may be observed for the sovereignty

Table 2.3 Sovereignty differentials (SD) in growth rates of per capita income, 1900–1950

Category I	Category II	SD: I over II (% points)	Mean growth rates in II (%)	R^2	F
(PCI<$2703 in 1900: Sample size = 40)					
SOV	QCC	1.60**	0.20	0.29	4.21**
DEP	QCC	0.64*	0.20	0.29	4.21**
SOV	DEP-QCC	1.37**	0.38	0.26	4.57**
SOV-DEP	QCC	1.19**	0.20	0.23	3.89*
(PCI<$2408 in 1900: Sample size = 37)					
SOV	QCC	1.80**	0.20	0.32	4.38**
DEP	QCC	0.87**	0.20	0.32	4.38**
SOV	DEP-QCC	1.45**	0.38	0.26	4.24**
SOV-DEP	QCC	1.41**	0.20	0.25	4.07**
(PCI<$1638 in 1900: Sample size = 34)					
SOV	QCC	1.96**	0.20	0.36	4.71**
DEP	QCC	1.02**	0.20	0.36	4.71**
SOV	DEP-QCC	1.56**	0.38	0.28	4.28**
SOV-DEP	QCC	1.61**	0.20	0.29	4.41**
(PCI<$1229 in 1900: Sample size = 27)					
SOV	QCC	2.18**	0.20	0.43	4.88**
DEP	QCC	0.83*	0.20	0.43	4.88**
SOV	DEP-QCC	1.90**	0.34	0.40	5.24**
SOV-DEP	QCC	1.69**	0.20	0.31	3.89*

Notes:
** and * denote statistical significance at the 1, 5 and 10 per cent levels.
The samples of lagging countries are defined with respect to US PCI in 1900; the four samples have PCI in 1900 equal to, or less than, 66, 50, 40 and 30 per cent of US PCI in 1900.

differentials between *SOV* and *DEP-QCC* and *SOV-DEP* and *QCC* for every reduction in sample size. The sovereignty differential between *DEP* and *QCC* increased over the second and third samples, but declined between the third and fourth samples.

The estimated sovereignty differentials were checked for robustness using Leamer's extreme bounds analysis.[28] The independent variables in the regressions were disaggregated into three subsets, as follows:

$Y = \alpha + \beta_i \, I + \beta_m \, M + \beta_z \, Z + \varepsilon$, where I is a vector of always-included variables, M is a vector of sovereignty dummies, and Z is a subset of other explanatory variables. For one set of estimations, the I-variable is per capita income and the Z-variables are adult literacy rates and the European dummy; alternatively, the adult literacy rates were defined as the I-variable with per capita income and the European dummy as the Z-variables. In order to check the sensitivity of our results to changes in specifications, all the previous regressions were estimated with all linear combinations of the Z-variables. A comparison of the high and low estimates for each of the sovereignty differentials (alternatively, with per capita income and adult literacy rates as the I-variable) showed that the sovereignty differentials between *SOV* and *QCC, SOV* and *DEP-QCC* and *SOV-DEP* and *QCC* were robust at the 1 per cent level in all the samples, while the sovereignty differentials between *DEP* and *QCC* were robust at the 1 per cent or 5 per cent levels in all the samples.

It now remains to show that our taxonomies of sovereignty are not proxies for some other factors affecting growth. It may be argued that only the most backward lagging countries were converted into *QCC,* and that those adverse factors which retarded their growth before colonization continued to produce the same effect in the subsequent period. This argument is based on two premises. The first premise equates economic backwardness with military weakness and, therefore, with vulnerability to foreign conquest. The second premise assumes that the institutional factors which caused the backwardness of the *QCC* before their colonization persisted throughout the period of colonial domination, thus ensuring their poor growth record during this period. The flaws in these premises are quickly addressed. If colonization was not a charitable activity, it is hard to see why the most backward countries would become the preferred targets for colonization. Further, vulnerability to conquest does not follow ineluctably from backwardness; it depends on a host of other factors, including distance from the colonizing powers, presence of incurable diseases, barriers set up by terrain, the presence of fierce tribes, a politically cohesive population and, most importantly, the rivalry of colonial powers. As for the second premise, it is hard to see – even if we were to concede that only the most backward countries were colonized – how the structural factors that held back development before colonization could survive all the traumatic changes in governance, classes, institutions and laws that generally attended colonization.

This conjecture is tested empirically by re-estimating all the previous sovereignty differentials for growth rates between 1950 and 1992, but with the original country samples and taxonomies of sovereignty. All the *QCC* in our sample had gained sovereignty by 1950, so that large and sustained differences in sovereignty had ceased to be a factor affecting growth during the period after 1950. If the taxonomies of sovereignty are proxies for structural obstacles to growth during the colonial period, we may confidently predict that the sovereignty differentials for post-1950 growth rates will also be positive and statistically significant. This is convincingly refuted by the evidence.[29] The estimation results in Table 2.4 show that each of the four sovereignty differentials for growth rates over 1950 to

Table 2.4   Sovereignty differentials (SD) in growth rates of per capita income, 1950–1992

Category I	Category II	SD: I over II (% points)	Mean growth rates in II (%)	R^2	F
(PCI<$2703 in 1900: Sample size = 40)					
SOV	*QCC*	−0.95	2.75	0.26	3.74*
DEP	*QCC*	−1.79**	2.75	0.26	3.74
SOV	*DEP-QCC*	−0.29	2.27	0.14	2.53*
SOV-DEP	*QCC*	−1.38**	2.75	0.26	4.36*
(PCI<$2048 in 1900: Sample size = 37)					
SOV	*QCC*	−0.86	2.75	0.25	3.43*
DEP	*QCC*	−1.77**	2.75	0.25	3.43*
SOV	*DEP-QCC*	−0.13	2.27	0.13	2.39+
SOV-DEP	*QCC*	−1.38*	2.75	0.25	3.97*
(PCI<$1638 in 1900: Sample size = 34)					
SOV	*QCC*	−0.68	2.75	0.25	3.19*
DEP	*QCC*	−1.75**	2.75	0.25	3.19*
SOV	*DEP-QCC*	0.07	2.27	0.13	2.25
SOV-DEP	*QCC*	−1.31*	2.75	0.23	3.55*
(PCI<$1229 in 1900: Sample size = 27)					
SOV	QCC	−0.59	2.75	0.24	2.61+
DEP	*QCC*	−0.62**	2.75	0.24	2.61+
SOV	*DEP-QCC*	−0.06	2.30	0.15	2.11
SOV-DEP	*QCC*	−1.22*	2.75	0.24	3.08*

Notes:
**, * and + denote statistical significance at the 1, 5 and 10 per cent levels.
The samples of lagging countries are defined with respect to US PCI in 1900; the four samples have PCI in 1900 equal to, or less than, 66, 50, 40 and 30 per cent of US PCI in 1900.

1992 are negative for all four samples of lagging countries. Moreover, these differentials are far from negligible. The sovereignty differentials between *SOV* and *QCC* range from –0.59 to –0.95 percentage points over the four samples; the differentials between *DEP* and *QCC* range from –1.62 to 1.79 percentage points and are statistically significant at the 1 per cent level; and the differentials between *SOV-DEP* and *QCC* range from –1.22 to –1.38 percentage points and are significant at the 1 or 5 per cent levels. This dramatic reversal in the sign of the sovereignty differentials before and after 1950 – by which time all the *QCC* in our sample had gained sovereignty – implies that absence of sovereignty before 1950 was the operative factor retarding growth rates in the *QCC*. In order to disavow this interpretation of our results, one would have to maintain that all the long-surviving obstacles to growth that had pulled down the growth rates of the *QCC* over the period leading up to the 1940s, disappeared abruptly and simultaneously in all the *QCC* at around the time that these countries gained their sovereignty.

CONCLUDING REMARKS

A few closing words are now in order on how the global economy, and the connections between sovereignty and growth within this economy, have evolved since 1950.

This requires that we step back and examine the economic and political forces which brought the old global economy to a closure. This closure was immanent in its internal dynamics. Since polarization between advanced and lagging countries widened the wage gap between them, at some point this gap would begin to shift the comparative advantage in labour-intensive manufactures to lagging countries. Wages in the most advanced countries began to rise towards the middle of the 19th century once their labour surpluses were exhausted and industrial labour became more effectively organized. At the same time, productivity growth in the labour-intensive manufactures was slowing down as production technologies matured, and this made it easier for some lagging countries to adapt these technologies to their own conditions. In time, these factors combined to eliminate the advanced country's comparative advantage in some manufactures. It was these conditions that permitted India and Japan, even under conditions of *laissez faire*, to begin setting up their own textile industries towards the end of the 19th century. It was the task of imperialism to delay this shift in comparative advantage to lagging countries.

Colonialism too was plagued with internal contradictions. Since advanced countries sought exclusive control over markets and resources in lagging countries, they often competed with one another for control over the same markets and resources. These rivalries were contained as long as Britain's competitive and industrial lead sustained its hegemonic role in the global economy. When new industrial powers, in particular the United States and Germany, emerged to challenge Britain's industrial preeminence and hegemony, a period of instability followed that would lead eventually to two great wars during the first half of this century. Devastating as these wars were for most of the advanced countries, they opened windows of opportunity for the lagging countries. Ineluctably, and in stages, the two wars forced a massive decentralization of power to lagging countries. World War I freed the quasi-colonies from their worst disabilities, while World War II led to the dismantling of colonial empires.

The second phase of the industrial epoch was inaugurated by the second more massive devolution of power which occurred after the second great war. Most lagging countries employed their new-found sovereignty to break out of the narrow specialization imposed on them by the international division of labour; they enforced economic and social policies to promote manufactures and to nurture a class of indigenous capitalists. The result was the emergence in many lagging countries of an industrial sector which first displaced imported consumer goods and gradually moved into the production of intermediate and capital goods. This dispersion of manufactures was pregnant with ramifications. All too soon, it would inject a new dynamic into the global economy. A clear notice of these changes was first served during the 1970s when manufactures from lagging countries, with the advantage of lower wages and rapidly improving skills, began to penetrate markets in advanced countries. The industrial genie in lagging countries was now out of the bottle.

This new industrial challenge was the cue for the advanced countries to re-centralize power: thus began the task of crafting a new imperialism to meet the challenges of the new global economy. The conditions for such a resurgence had also improved dramatically since the debacle of the last war. With minor exceptions, the global efforts to contain communism had been successful. The Soviet Union and China were openly split. Due to a quick recovery and two decades of unprecedented growth, the advanced countries had gained a wider absolute lead than before over most lagging countries. The military and economic unity created in their ranks by the threat of communism, made it easier for the great powers to contain their imperialist rivalries. The break came soon with the international debt crisis of the early 1980s, which forced several major lagging countries into a vulnerability they had not known for several decades. The new imperialism stepped into this breach, with the International Monetary Fund and the World Bank in the lead. The aim of the new imperialism was not to reverse the dispersion of manufactures that was underway, but to delay its spread to higher value-added industries and to other lagging countries and to capture the markets and investment opportunities it was creating in the lagging countries. As imperialism *II* has unfolded, lagging countries have come under growing external pressures to liberalize their trade policies, capital accounts and financial markets, to privatize their industries, adopt the labour and environmental standards of advanced countries, enforce intellectual property rights, prosecute trade in counterfeit products and eliminate preferences for domestic suppliers in state procurements. This new imperialism, codified in the 'Washington Consensus', looks eerily like its predecessor.[30]

But there are differences too. Since direct colonization was not an available option, the imperialism *II* has been forced to find new instruments of coercion. It now operates primarily through markets, although military options have not been abandoned. This is only a minor limitation since advanced countries can quickly mobilize their power to deny lagging countries access to financial markets, long-term investments and advanced technologies. This power has grown dramatically in recent years because of three factors. Since the 1980s, their growing debt liabilities have forced a growing number of lagging countries to trade their sovereignty for debt rescheduling. There is greater unity in the ranks of major advanced countries in response to the growing industrial power of some lagging countries. The most serious blow came from the demise of the Soviet Union. The advanced countries lost no time in signalling the new *re*centralization of power this had created; this message was delivered with stunning clarity by the Allied forces during the Gulf War. Imperialism *II* would now have a field day.

Imperialism *II* has narrowed the windows of opportunity that had opened up for lagging countries in the aftermath of World War II. The dispersion of manufactures to lagging countries that gained momentum in the 1960s is likely to continue but not – as in Taiwan, Korea and Japan – under the aegis of indigenous capital. The creation of new cores of indigenous industrial capital in a third tier of lagging countries will face growing difficulties. More and more, capital from advanced countries as well as the newly industrializing countries will seek to ensure that lagging countries serve as so many production platforms, whose function in the global economy will be to supply cheap labour and infrastructure, with minimal share in the value-added, ownership and control of the new industries. At the least, this image of lagging countries as production platforms is troubling. To succeed as production platforms, lagging countries will have to compete by erecting regimes that keep their infrastructure burnished, taxes low and labour cheap and disorganized.

APPENDIX

Table 2.A1 Average annual growth rates of per capita income, 1870–1992

Country	1870–1900	1900–1913	1913–1950	1900–1950	1950–1992
Sovereign					
1 Finland	1.27	1.79	1.89	1.87	3.01
2 Italy	0.50	2.78	0.84	1.35	3.70
3 Canada	1.77	3.20	1.39	1.88	2.25
4 Sweden	1.44	1.46	2.10	1.93	2.19
5 Ireland	1.14	0.70	0.68	0.69	2.86
6 Norway	1.01	1.97	2.11	2.07	3.00
7 Greece	(.)	(.)	0.05	(.)	3.96
8 Portugal	0.87	–0.30	1.23	0.83	3.93
9 Spain	1.31	0.77	0.17	0.32	3.93
10 Bulgaria	(.)	(.)	0.20	(.)	2.14
11 Czechoslovakia	1.32	1.48	1.39	1.41	1.60
12 Hungary	0.94	1.70	0.45	0.78	1.96
13 USSR	0.58	1.54	1.74	1.69	1.19
14 Yugoslavia	(.)	(.)	1.10	(.)	2.20
15 Brazil	–0.17	1.35	1.87	1.73	2.43
16 Chile	(.)	2.37	0.58	1.05	1.52
17 Columbia	(.)	2.13	1.41	1.60	2.09
18 Mexico	1.63	1.83	0.95	1.18	2.14
19 Peru	(.)	1.83	2.10	2.04	0.55
20 Venezuela	(.)	2.28	5.15	4.40	0.50
21 Japan	1.42	1.24	0.92	1.00	5.57
22 S. Africa	(.)	(.)	1.19	(.)	1.02
Wt. average	1.00	1.61	1.34	1.43	2.58
% world pop.	17.0	19.9	22.5	19.9	22.1
Dependencies			1920–1950		1950–1990
1 Costa Rica	(.)	(.)	0.90		1.72
2 El Salvador	(.)	(.)	1.70		0.63
3 Guatemala	(.)	(.)	1.07		0.96
4 Honduras	(.)	(.)	0.10		0.94
5 Nicaragua	(.)	(.)	0.40		0.90
Wt. average			0.96		0.95
% world pop.			0.22		0.32

Table 2.A1 (continued)

Country	1870–1900	1900–1913	1913–1950	1900–1950	1950–1992
Colonies and Q-Colonies	1870–1900	1900–1913	1913–1950	1900–1950	1950–1992
1 Egypt	(.)	–0.01	0.05	0.03	3.13
2 Turkey	(.)	(.)	0.76	(.)	2.92
3 Thailand	0.42	0.30	0.01	0.09	4.07
4 Ghana	(.)	2.60	1.65	1.90	–0.40
5 Bangladesh	(.)	0.46	–0.30	–0.11	0.64
6 Pakistan	(.)	0.45	–0.31	–0.11	2.21
7 India	0.38	0.45	–0.28	–0.09	1.94
8 Myanmar	(.)	–0.16	–1.30	0.99	1.53
9 Indonesia	0.42	1.60	–0.13	0.32	2.73
10 China	0.73	0.41	–0.31	–0.12	3.85
11 Phillipines	(.)	2.44	–0.25	0.45	1.28
12 South Korea	(.)	0.83	–0.21	0.06	5.80
13 Taiwan	(.)	0.34	0.40	0.39	6.03
Wt. average	0.59	0.50	–0.27	–0.08	2.96
% world pop.	48	50	49	50	48

Note: Listed countries had per capita income in 1900 less than 66 per cent of US per capita income in 1900; weights in weighted averages are populations in initial year of growth period.

NOTES

* I wish to acknowledge a special debt to John Adams and Keith Griffin who provided valuable support and encouragement over the years as I discovered that departing from the mainstream was a lonely task. I also wish to thank Irma Adelman, Amitava Dutt, Alan Dyer, G.K. Helleiner, Shahrukh Rafi Khan, Peter Kilby, David Landes, Steve Morrison, Jeffrey Nugent, Raffaele Paci, Francesco Pigliaru, Rati Ram, Salim Rashid and Andy Sum for their comments on this and other related research. I hasten to add that the inadequacies of this chapter are still only my own.

1. The industrial epoch started with the large-scale application of inanimate sources of energy to production – first water power, then coal and oil. For nearly two hundred years, this led to a growing concentration of manufactures in a small number of countries; this tendency was reversed beginning in the 1950s. Between 1750 and 1900, the share of Britain, United States, Germany, France and Russia – the five largest industrial nations – in world manufacturing output increased from 13.9 to 70.9 per cent (Bairoch, 1982, 296)

2. This taxonomy was first proposed in Alam (1994a)
3. The same method has been employed to estimate the impact of sovereignty on industrialization and levels of human capital across lagging countries (Alam, 1994b, 1995).
4. 'Advanced' and 'lagging' are relative terms; they are defined with respect to the development of markets, especially the markets for capital, labour and land.
5. Samuelson (1948).
6. Headrick (1981).
7. Maddison (1995, pp. 227, 239).
8. Rostow (1978, p. 669).
9. Bairoch (1981, p. 7).
10. Technical progress in most primary activities in lagging countries was slow because they could not gain from the presence of a growing manufacturing sector. Also, they were unable to benefit from technical progress in the agricultural sector of advanced countries because of differences in their ecologies and plant varieties.
11. The state is defined in terms of three functions – governance, production and defence – and three overlapping interests – those of its personnel, the dominant classes and national security. In addition, three classes are defined, depending on whether their primary source of income is land (primary production), capital (manufacture and commerce) or labour.
12. There have been some valiant attempts to revive Marx's original vision of imperialism (Warren, 1973, 1980).
13. Whether a factor is indigenous or foreign is determined by place of permanent residence of the factor-owners.
14. Foreign capital includes only direct foreign investments, not portfolio investments or foreign loans.
15. See Appendix A.
16. See Alam (1994a, 1994b and 1995) for evidence on policies across different categories of sovereignty.
17. A word of explanation may be necessary on why we chose 1950 as the cutoff point for our exercises. Alam (1994a, pp. 244–7, 253–5) has argued that the growing strength of liberation movements, the two great wars among the colonial powers, and the rise of communism leading up to the Cold War, combined to force the colonial powers to show greater solicitude for the interests of indigenous populations in the colonies, and by the 1950s most of them were working on an assortment of plans to promote the development of their colonies. With this narrowing in differences between colonies and sovereign countries, it would appear that this distinction had lost much of its salience after 1950.
18. A list of all the lagging countries together with their growth rates of per capita income may be found in Appendix A. The weighted growth rates for the sovereign countries and the QCC were derived from Maddison (1995), and the growth rates for dependencies are from Bulmer-Thomas (1987, p. 312). The weights in the weighted growth rates are the population of individual countries at the beginning of each growth period.
19. The growth rates for the sovereign lagging countries in the three periods are based on samples containing 14, 18 and 22 countries, respectively. These samples are larger relative to the total number of countries in this category.
20. Maddison (1995, pp. 23–4, 226).

21. The means for the sovereign countries and QCC, for each of the three periods, are different at the 1 per cent level of significance.
22. The growth rates for the dependencies are for 1920 to 1950; and the growth rates for Greece, Bulgaria, South Africa, Turkey and Yugoslavia are for 1913 to 1950. The period before 1900 was excluded because there were very few observations for the QCC.
23. Since per capita income for the dependencies were not available in Maddison (1995), we used 1950 per capita income from Maddison and growth rates in Bulmer-Thomas (1987) to derive the per capita income in 1920. Data on adult literacy rates for China, India, Pakistan, Bangladesh and Ghana are for 1950. Data on adult literacy rates were from Eisenstadt and Rokkan (1973, pp. 245–7).
24. Solow (1956) and Abramovtiz (1986).
25. Romer (1986) and Lucas (1988). See Van de Klundert and Smulders (1992) for a survey of this literature.
26. Morris and Adelman (1988) have presented data which show that in 1850 the QCC in our sample did not lag behind the sovereign countries in adult literacy rates, state of inland transportation, agricultural technology and development of market institutions. In 1850, adult literacy rates in India and Egypt (less than 10 per cent) were comparable to those in Brazil and Russia; China was in the same league as Spain, Argentina, Japan and Italy; and Burma was better placed than Spain, Brazil, Argentina, Japan and Italy. In the same year, India, Burma, China and Egypt were comparable in their inland transportation to Argentina, Brazil, Australia, Canada, Denmark, Italy, Russia, Spain, Sweden, Switzerland and Japan. Agricultural technology in China, Egypt and India in 1850 was at the same level as in Russia and Spain. Judging from the level of development of market institutions in 1850, Myanmar, China and Egypt were at the same level as Brazil, New Zealand and Russia; and India was at the same level as Argentina, Australia, Denmark and Japan (Morris and Adelman, 1988, pp. 391–2, 321–8, 283–9, 462).
27. The reported results are corrected using White's heteroskedasticity-consistent estimator. The results for the control variables may be quickly summarized. As expected, Y always appeared with a negative sign but none of the coefficients is statistically significant even at the 10 per cent level. The dummy for Europe also appears with a negative sign that is significant in three regressions at the 10 per cent level. The coefficients for adult literacy rates appear with mixed signs, but none of them is significant at the 10 per cent level. There is little evidence that these results are due to multicollinearity between these variables and the sovereignty dummies. Dropping the sovereignty dummies did not alter these results much and, in addition, produced very low adjusted R^2s.
28. Levine and Renelt (1992).
29. The data in Table 2.2 support the same conclusion. The QCC experienced not only a dramatic acceleration in growth rates during the four decades after 1950 but grew faster than the sovereign countries and the dependencies during this period. The weighted average annual growth rate of the colonies was 2.96 per cent over 1950 to 1992 compared to –0.08 per cent between 1900 and 1950; the growth rates of the sovereign countries and dependencies over 1950 to 1992 were 0.95 and 2.58 per cent respectively.
30. See Williamson (1994, 1996).

REFERENCES

Abramovitz, Moses (1986), 'Catching up, forging ahead, and falling behind', *Journal of Economic History*, **46**(2), 385–406.

Alam, M. Shahid (1994a), 'Colonialism, decolonization and growth rates: theory and empirical evidence', *Cambridge Journal of Economics*, **18**, 235–57.

Alam, M. Shahid (1994b), 'Why isn't the whole world industrialized? The contribution of imperialism', Boston: Department of Economics, Northeastern University.

Alam, M. Shahid (1995), 'Sovereignty and human capital formation: an empirical study of historical links', Boston: Department of Economics, Northeastern University.

Bairoch, Paul (1981), 'The Main Trends in National Economic Disparities Since the Industrial Revolution', in Paul Bairoch and Maurice Levy-Leboyer, (eds), *Disparities in Economic Development Since the Industrial Revolution*, New York: St. Martin's Press.

Bairoch, Paul (1982), 'International industrialization levels from 1750 to 1980', *Journal of European Economic History*, **11**(2), Spring, 269–333.

Bhagwati, Jagdish N. (1978), *Foreign Trade Regimes and Economic Development: Anatomy and Consequences of Exchange Control Regimes*, Cambridge, MA: Ballinger, for National Bureau of Economic Research.

Bulmer-Thomas, Victor (1987), *The Political Economy of Central America since 1920*, Cambridge: Cambridge University Press.

Easterlin, Richard (1981), 'Why isn't the whole world developed?', *Journal of Economic History*, **41**, 1–19.

Eisenstadt, S.N. and Stein Rokkan (eds) (1973), *Building Nations and States: Models and Data Resources, Vol. 1,* Beverly Hills, CA: Sage Publications.

Headrick, Daniel R. (1981), *The Tools of Empire: Technology and European Imperialism in the Nineteenth Century*, New York: Oxford University Press.

Levine, Ross and David Renelt (1992), 'A sensitivity analysis of cross-country growth regressions', *American Economic Review*, **82**(4), September, 942–63.

Lucas, Robert (1988), 'On the mechanics of economic development', *Journal of Monetary Economics*, **22**, 2–42.

Maddison, Angus (1995), *Monitoring the World Economy, 1820–1992,* Paris: Organization for Economic Cooperation and Development.

Morris, Cynthia Taft and Irma Adelman (1988), *Comparative Patterns of Economic Development, 1850–1914,* Baltimore, MD: The Johns Hopkins University Press.

Myint, Hla (1954), 'An interpretation of economic backwardness', *Oxford Economic Papers,* New Series, **6**(2), June, 132–63.

Myrdal, Gunnar (1957), *Economic Theory and the Underdeveloped Regions*, London: University Paperbacks [1964].

Ricardo, David (1817), *The Principles of Political Economy and Taxation*, London: Dent [1965].

Romer, Paul (1986), 'Increasing returns and long-run growth', *Journal of Political Economy*, **94**, 1002–37.

Rostow, W.W. (1978), *The World Economy: History and Prospect*, Austin, TX: University of Texas.

Samuelson, Paul A. (1948), 'International trade and the equalization of factor prices', *Economic Journal*, **58**(2), 181–97.

Smith, Adam (1965), *An Inquiry into the Nature and Causes of the Wealth of Nations*, New York: The Modern Library [1776].

Solow, Robert (1956), 'A contribution to the theory of economic growth', *Quarterly Journal of Economics*, **70**(1), February, 65–94.

Van de Klundert, Theo. C. M. J. and S. Smulders (1992), 'Reconstructing growth theory: a survey', *De Economist*, **140**(2), 177–203.

Warren, Bill (1973), 'Imperialism and capitalist industrialization', *New Left Review*, **81**, 3–44.

Warren, Bill (1980), *Imperialism: Pioneer of Capitalism*, London: New Left Books.

Williamson, John (ed.) (1994), *The Political Economy of Policy Reform*, Washington, DC: Institute for International Economics.

Williamson, John (1986), 'Lowest Common Denominator or Neoliberal Manifesto: the Polemics of the Washington Consensus', in Richard M. Auty and John Toye (eds), *Challenging Orthodoxies*, New York: St. Martin's Press.

3. *Society, Politics, and Economic Development* thirty years after

Irma Adelman[1]

In his seminal paper on time series analysis, the well known Swedish statistician, Herman Wold, proposed the hypothesis that all dynamic processes are composed of two fundamental elements: continuity and innovation. The present chapter examines how these two elements are reflected in the analysis of interactions among processes of economic and institutional change in the development of developing countries since the 1960s. Specifically, I apply the same methodology as used by Cynthia Taft Morris and myself in our 1967 book *Society, Politics, and Economic Development*[2] to data updated to describe the economic, social and political institutions and economic performance during the 1990s.

Now, as before, the focus of the analysis is on intercountry differences in rates of growth of per capita GNP. Growth rates *per se* are not good indicators of development in the broad sense. The term 'development' is used in Kuznets's sense[3] – sustained economic growth accompanied by structural change in the economy and by a wider diffusion of the economic and social benefits of growth. The results for the 1990s indicate the distinctions between the two concepts rather clearly, in that we find that, in the short run, growth and development do not necessarily coincide and that countries at similar initial levels of development must generally choose which achievements they will stress.

3.1 THE DATA

The sample of countries included in the present analysis started with the list of 74 non-communist developing countries that had been included in our earlier work. From this sample I dropped: two countries which had since become developed – Israel and Japan; four developing countries which had become communist – Cambodia, Laos, Myanmar and South Vietnam; and one developing country for which information on rates of economic growth of per capita GNP between 1990 and 1994 was unavailable – Iran. The final sample thus comprises 67 non-communist developing countries.

For comparability, the same list of variables, the same conceptualizations, and the same variable definitions were used to characterize each aspect of social, political and economic development and performance for the 1990s as were used in our previous work for 1960. A list of variables together with short definitions is given in the appendix to this chapter. The dynamic variables were defined with respect to rates of change between 1980 and 1990, rather than between 1960 and 1965, and the rate of growth of per capita GNP covers the period 1980 to 1994 rather than 1950 to 1964. The direction of scoring of the various aspects of change summarized by our variables generally associates higher variable scores with characteristics typical of higher levels of economic development. There are only five exceptions to this statement: the size of the traditional agricultural sector, the crude fertility rate, the political power of the traditional agricultural elite and the political power of the military, where it would have been confusing to do otherwise, and the degree of centralization of political power, where *a priori* theorizing did not suggest a clear direction of association.

Two departures from the 1967 definitions had to be adopted: first, due to general social progress and economic change during the generation intervening between the time of the two studies, the earlier category limits could no longer adequately differentiate among countries for most social and economic variables; the category limits for these variables were therefore redefined better to span the entire range of variation reflected in the 1990 data. Second, the operationalization of the variable describing the extent of leadership commitment to economic development had to be modified since the distinctions applied to the 1960s no longer differentiated among countries in the 1990s. During the 1960s, the two observable characteristics used to distinguish among governments that were serious about economic development and those that were not were: (1) the existence and effectiveness of their central plans and planning agencies, and (2) the extent to which governments had undertaken one unpopular, but generally acknowledged to be necessary, action to promote development, namely established family planning institutions. These characteristics could no longer distinguish among developing-country governments in 1990, since all developing countries now had a family planning apparatus and central planning has fallen into general disfavour. Instead, in the present analysis, the distinctions among countries with respect to the seriousness of their commitment to development were based on (1) the extent of policy reform they had undertaken in liberalizing trade and markets and (2) on the quality of their macroeconomic stabilization and adjustment policies. These policies reflect the extent of government success in implementing a different set of equally unpopular, but generally considered to be necessary, Washington-consensus type measures. There is also ample quantitative information (inflation rates, government-budget deficits and current-account imbalances) for assessing differential degrees of success in achieving and maintaining internal and external stability and World Bank country reports provide information on the extent to which trade-liberalization measures have been undertaken and their consistency over time.

3.2 STATISTICAL TECHNIQUE

As in our earlier study, the statistical technique used in the present paper is factor analysis.[4] This technique of multivariate analysis is no more familiar to economists now than it was in the 1960s. However, a closely related technique, principal components analysis, has become more familiar due to its use in latent and instrumental variable regressions.

Both techniques start with the correlation matrix among the variables included in the statistical analysis. Both techniques seek to represent the correlation matrix in a lower-dimensional space by translating the axes in which the correlation matrix is represented to a set of different axes. The new axes consist of linear combinations of the original dimensions of the correlation matrix. Thus, while the original dimensions of an $(m*m)$ correlation matrix are represented in an m-dimensional space consisting of the m individual variables composing the correlation matrix, the axes along which the correlation matrix is represented in both principal components and factor analyses are orthogonal linear combinations of the original variables. They are extracted from the original correlation matrix by imposing the requirements that (1) the original correlation matrix be represented as closely as possible in the new axes; and (2) the axes used to represent the correlation matrix are orthogonal to one another. Deriving the new axes involves solving an eigenvector–eigenvalue problem in which: (1) the eigenvectors (factors) represent the new dimensions of the space in which the correlation matrix is portrayed; (2) the squares of eigenvalues indicate the percentage of variance of the original correlation matrix 'explained' by the associated eigenvector (factor); and (3) each succeeding eigenvector (factor) captures a smaller percentage of the overall variance.

In principal components analysis, all eigenvectors are calculated, but only the first few, those associated with a statistically significant proportion of the variance, are considered in the interpretation (or subsequent use) of the eigenvectors. In factor analysis, the number of eigenvectors extracted is specified *a priori*. Thus, factor analysis is identical to principal components analysis except that:

1. only a subset of eigenvectors, that with the largest eigenvalues (which account for the largest proportion of the total variance among all variables), is included;
2. instead of extracting the eigenvectors of the original correlation matrix, in factor analysis the successive eigenvectors are extracted from a modified correlation matrix in which the ones along the diagonal are replaced by the multiple regression r-squares of each variable on all the eigenvectors included in the analysis; this feature of factor analysis is a direct consequence of the first;
3. the eigenvectors are normalized in length; the normalization used here is the same as that used in our 1967 study in which the length of each eigenvector was normalized to equal its eigenvalue; the successive factors are thus analogous to the dimensions of an ellipsoid; and
4. for ease of interpretation of the results, the eigenvectors are subjected to a rigid rotation.[5] The rotation principle applied in this paper was the same as that used in the 1967 study.[6]

The so extracted eigenvectors are referred to as factors.

In the tables presented in this paper, the variables are listed along the rows of the tables; the factors appear in the successive columns, and are labelled F1, F2 and so on. The numbers appearing in the body of the tables are the correlation coefficients of the variable in that row with the factor in that column.[7] Thus, variables with large coefficients in a given factor are closely associated with that factor and those with small coefficients are not. The factors constitute latent variables that are composed of the variables most closely correlated with them. More specifically, if a variable has an entry of, say, -0.50 in the column of the first factor, the first factor 'explains' 25 per cent of the overall variance of this variable in the sample. And if, say, the share of income of the poorest 20 per cent has a (statistically significant) positive correlation with the first factor, increased values of the variable in question are systematically associated with lower shares of national income accruing to the poorest 20 per cent, on the average.

The order of the rows (variables) in the tables is arbitrary, but the order of the columns (factors) is not. The columns are listed according to the percentage of overall variance in all variables that each factor 'explains',[8] with the factor explaining the largest percentage appearing first. For ease of interpretation, the variables in each table are listed in the order of the factor with which they are most closely associated. Thus, the variables most closely associated with the first factor are listed first; those most closely associated with the second factor next, and so on. The number of factors extracted is limited by both the percentage of overall variance accounted for by the included factors and by the share of variance the last factor explains. As in the 1967 analysis, the criterion used to decide on the number of factors extracted is that, provided all factors included account for at least 65 per cent of the overall variance among all variables, the last factor extracted should account for at least 10 per cent of the overall variance.[9]

In interpreting the results, five different bits of information will be used: (1) the magnitudes and signs of correlations of each variable with each factor; (2) the relationship among the signs of the variables with significant correlations within each factor; (3) the square of the correlation coefficient of the particular distributional indicator with each factor – it indicates the percentage of overall variance of this distributional feature explained by a given factor; (4) the ratio of the square of the eigenvalues associated with a particular factor to the sum of squared eigenvalues for all factors – it indicates what percentage of the overall variance in all indicators is associated with a given factor; and (5) the factor scores of individual countries on each factor – they indicate how well a particular factor captures the experience of each country. The analysis of results will therefore be based on a rich information base.

3.3   STATISTICAL ANALYSES FOR THE 1950–1965 PERIOD

3.3.1   The Setting

Our 1967 analysis studied interaction patterns among economic growth, structural change and economic, social and political institutions during the Golden Era of economic development. The end of World War II had ushered in an era of unprecedented sustained economic growth in both developed and developing countries. The Marshall Plan had helped rebuild the capital stock destroyed during World War II and generated an investment boom in Europe. Developed-country governments became committed to demand-management policies aimed primarily at maintaining high employment. There was relative peace. The international economic order became liberal, with low non-agricultural tariffs and few quantitative restrictions in the OECD countries and a fair degree of flexibility in tariff-setting in developing countries. The Bretton Woods agreement reintroduced a fixed-exchange-rate payments regime, supported by a system of international institutions designed to offer some exchange-rate flexibility and facilitate the management of international foreign exchange imbalances. The result was a stable, expansionary national and global policy framework in which the rate of growth of real per capita GDP in OECD countries[10] escalated to almost precisely double its previous peak rate during the Industrial Revolution. As a result, the import demand in developed countries and the volume of international trade expanded very rapidly.

The impetus from this unprecedented growth in developed countries was transmitted to developing countries. The combination of fast import-demand expansion from OECD countries, a liberal global trading system and a stable, but flexible, exchange rate regime generated a global environment favourable to rapid increases in exports from developing countries. Following the end of World War II, the institutions of colonialism were dismantled, giving developing countries an unprecedented degree of political control over their economic destinies. International foreign assistance institutions were established for the first time in history and bilateral foreign assistance programmes were initiated. Never before, or alas since, have developing countries experienced such a concatenation of favourable economic and global institutional circumstances.

By historical standards, the resulting growth rate of developing countries between 1950 and 1973 was nothing short of breathtaking. The average rate of growth of real *per capita* GNP for all developing countries rose to 3.3 per cent,[11] more than triple the rate of growth of the early industrializers between 1820 and 1914. Furthermore, for the first time in history, the economic expansion of developing countries was also marked by substantial structural change in their economies, societies, polities and institutions.

It is to the study of the systematic association patterns among these changes that our 1967 book was devoted.

3.3.2   Statistical Results

Our 1967 study indicated that the process of economic development was highly non-linear and highly multifaceted. We found that the interaction patterns among economic and institutional changes differed sharply among countries characterized by different institutional, social and economic initial conditions. Our initial attempts to analyse patterns of economic growth and institutional change with all countries considered to be points moving along a single multidimensional continuum failed miserably. We could not make sense of the signs of association among many economic and institutional variables; and, despite the fact that the sample included only developing countries, the coefficients and their signs were sensitive to the inclusion or exclusion of individual countries. Attempts to stratify the sample of countries by geographic region yielded more meaningful results; but the results were still not entirely satisfactory for regions, such as Latin America and Asia, which include countries at very different levels of socio-economic development. It was only after we decided to stratify our sample by levels of socio-institutional and economic development that our results became transparent, interpretable and robust.

The low sample[12]

This set of countries at the lowest end of the spectrum in socio-economic development comprised mostly sub-Saharan African countries but also included Afghanistan, Cambodia, Laos, Nepal and South Vietnam in Asia and Libya and Morocco in North Africa. In 1960, these countries were characterized by minimal degrees of development of market institutions and political systems and by a pre-eminence of social tribal influences over the economic activity of a predominantly subsistence agrarian economy.

Our statistical analysis indicated that, in this group of countries, the economic growth process entailed principally an interrelated process of economic and *social* transformations. The means by which economic growth was induced in this low-development group of countries entailed the dualistic development of a modern, export-oriented, primary sector which provoked significant transformations of social structure, the diffusion of the market economy and a reduction in the sway of traditional tribal customs over economic activity. Political influences exercised negligible impact on economic growth even though countries shared common severe political barriers to growth and development because there was so little variation in their political characteristics.

The intermediate sample[13]

In the next group of transitional economies, that were intermediate in socio-political and economic degrees of institutional development, the process of social, economic and political modernization had proceeded far enough profoundly to disturb traditional customs and institutions without progressing far enough to set them on the path of self-sustained economic development. This set of countries was geographically diverse: it included Algeria, Tunisia, Iran, Iraq, Syria and Jordan in the Middle East and North Africa; Sri Lanka, India, Pakistan, Myanmar, Thailand, Indonesia and the Philippines in Asia; Bolivia, Guatemala, Ecuador, Honduras and Surinam in Latin America; and Ghana, Rhodesia and

South Africa from Africa south of the Sahara. The countries in this group were also historically and culturally heterogeneous; characterized by rapid and unbalanced social transformations; by high degrees of social tensions and political instability; and by generally ineffective governments with weak administrative capacities.

Our statistical results for this group of countries indicated that dualistic industrialization, the buildup of economic institutions, particularly financial systems, and investment in physical infrastructure have dominated the explanation of intercountry differences in rates of economic growth. There was no longer evidence of a direct systematic impact of changes in social structure upon rates of economic progress, perhaps because the specific patterns of socio-economic progress, including specific social impediments to progress, varied substantially among clusters of countries in this transitional group. Furthermore, neither the precise form of the political system nor the extent of the leadership's commitment to economic development played an important role in influencing growth rates in this transitional group, because the states were 'soft' and the countries were beset by high degrees of social tension and political instability.

The high sample[14]

The 25 countries at the highest level of socio-economic development included in our study comprise the socio-institutionally and economically most advanced developing countries. The majority of them had a century or more of political independence and were well ahead of the intermediate group in social achievements (larger middle class, higher literacy, more secondary and tertiary education, more urbanization, more mass communication, and so on); in degrees of industrialization; and in extent of development of economic and political institutions. The sample includes: sixteen Latin American nations – Argentina, Brazil, Chile, Colombia, Costa Rica, Dominican Republic, El Salvador, Jamaica, Mexico, Nicaragua, Paraguay, Peru, Trinidad, Uruguay and Venezuela; six Mediterranean countries – Greece, Turkey, Cyprus, Lebanon, Israel and Egypt; and three East Asian countries – Japan, South Korea and Taiwan.

In this set of countries, the crucial forces accounting for intercountry differences in economic performance were the effectiveness of economic institutions and a cluster of variables indicating the extent of national mobilization for economic development. This latter cluster combined the extent of leadership commitment to development, levels of development and rates of improvement of financial and tax institutions, investment effort, rate of industrialization and the extent of technological modernization in agriculture and industry.

3.4   STATISTICAL ANALYSES FOR THE 1980–1994 PERIOD

3.4.1   The Setting

Unlike the setting of the previous analysis, which consisted of the Golden Age of economic development, the bulk of the period covered by the present analysis represents its nadir.

The seeds for the drastic economic decline of developing countries during the 1980s were sown during the 1973–81 period. Towards the end of the Golden Age, the Bretton Woods international monetary system became increasingly inadequate to the liquidity needs of the world economy. When it broke down, the stable, fixed exchange rate system was replaced with a fluctuating exchange rate regime. The resulting sharp effective devaluation of currencies against the dollar contributed to inflationary pressures in Europe and Japan. Productivity growth in developed countries slowed down and wage settlements started outrunning increases in productivity. These fundamental long-run trends were exacerbated by a series of bunched short-term price shocks: a doubling in the price of cereals in 1973; a tripling in oil prices in 1974 and another doubling in 1980. Strong upward pressures on commodity prices and strong inflationary expectations were the result. Inflation rates tripled. Balance of payments constraints became binding. As a result, the governments of OECD countries replaced the goal of full-employment growth with the twin objectives of containing inflation and restoring balance of payments equilibrium. They moderated their counter-cyclical budgetary policies; adopted cautious macroeconomic policies; espoused a stance of fiscal restraint; and engaged in protectionist policies. The result was a drastic slow-down in OECD growth. Between 1973 and 1981, the annual real rate of growth of GNP per capita declined to about one fourth of its previous rate and the growth in real world trade fell to less than one half.[15]

For the first time in peacetime history, developing countries' growth rates did not follow the rhythm set by growth rates in the OECD countries. Instead, faced with severe balance of payments pressures stemming from the drastic increase in oil prices combined with lower rates of growth of export demand for their products and with generally declining terms of trade,[16] most developing countries borrowed heavily to maintain their growth momentum. Between 1973 and 1982 the foreign debt of developing countries escalated: for the average non-oil developing country, total foreign debt increased to a third of its GDP and 152 per cent of exports. In the heavily indebted countries, the average *debt–service* ratio rose to 20 per cent of exports, and started mounting at clearly unsustainable rates.

Initially, growth and industrialization in developing countries continued to proceed apace and, while performance was mixed, in many developing countries some favourable structural change was taking place. Despite increasing protection in OECD countries, a few developing countries started penetrating the manufacturing-export markets of developed countries. But, with a few notable exceptions, overall policy reform was rather limited despite mounting pressures from international lenders.

This short period of debt-led growth in developing countries came to an abrupt end in 1981. It was followed by a decade of debt crisis, structural adjustment and policy reform. The debt crisis was brought to a head by the inability of Brazil and Turkey to meet their debt–service obligations. As a result, banks in developed countries became unwilling to extend further loans to *all* developing countries. Out of necessity, priorities in developing countries shifted from economic development to achieving external balance.

Adjustment patterns varied. Some developing countries adopted restrictive import regimes, deflationary government expenditure and macroeconomic policies and restrictive wage policies. Others attempted to export their way out of the crisis. They shifted from import-substitution to export-promotion, devalued to promote expenditure switching among imports and domestic goods and curtailed their growth rates temporarily. The latter adjustment pattern was considerably more successful. Most developing countries, however, adopted combinations of these policies and shifted among policy regimes in a stop–go fashion.

Rampant inflation, capital flight, low investment rates, drastic declines in living standards, and substantial increases in urban and rural poverty have marked the 1980s in most developing countries. The average developing country has transferred more than its entire growth of GDP abroad annually, for debt service. Overall, debt–service requirements have led to a net export of capital to the developed world. The debt of developing countries has continued to increase, as two-thirds of developing countries did not achieve a current-balance surplus sufficient to service their debts. The most underdeveloped countries, that had benefited least from previous expansionary regimes, were also the hardest hit in the 1980s.

While the growth performance of most developing countries during the 1980s was poor, the East Asian and South Asian countries have continued, if not improved, their previous developmental performance. Poverty in some of these countries has diminished substantially (China, India and Indonesia) and a few (Thailand and Indonesia) may even become semi-industrial countries in the near future. Perhaps most importantly, the 1980s and 1990s have also been an era of significant institutional adjustment and policy reform in most developing countries.

Many Latin American countries have adopted at least some features of open-trade regimes. Market institutions have generally been strengthened, especially in some African and Latin American nations. There has been some political development as well. Military or civilian dictatorships have declined and democracies have increased, although in about a third of developing countries democracy is only skin-deep and in all of them democracy is fragile. In addition, all developing country governments have become convinced of the priority of good economic policy over ideology and politics, although they may or may not adopt it.

Many of the economic and political institutions that form the core of capitalist development have thus been created in a significant number of developing countries. Partially as a result, the last few years have seen a revival of growth mostly in the more developed developing countries.

Thus, the setting of the 1990s analysis is considerably less propitious for development. Performance has been more uneven among periods, development levels and development spheres. Institutional development, social development (education, literacy, middle class, mass communication), democracy and policy reform have increased, but in terms of growth rates and poverty reduction the 1980s have been a lost decade.

3.4.2   Statistical Results

As in the 1967 study, the whole sample is subdivided into three groups which are fairly similar in their levels of socio-economic development.[17] The sample composition remained very similar.

The low sample
This sample is the same as the sample for 1967 except that it excludes Cambodia, Laos and South Vietnam, which have since become communist; and Morocco, which has become more developed and graduated to the intermediate sample. It also now includes Pakistan, which has retrogressed from the intermediate sample. The composition of the sample is thus more heavily sub-Saharan African than in the earlier analysis.

Sample characteristics   The countries in this low-development group, although remaining severely underdeveloped, have undergone substantial social development; a limited degree of industrialization has resulted from the dualistic growth that was characteristic of the 1960s; they have started to focus on agricultural development; and have experienced some minimal levels of development of market institutions. The average share of population dependent on traditional subsistence agriculture has fallen from 80 to 60 per cent and the villages in which they reside have become considerably less isolated. Geographic, informational and psychic ties with cities have expanded through better transport links with an increased number of nearby market-towns and more distant urban centres and through close personal links with village-compound members that have migrated to cities. The cash economy has grown significantly. About a third of the population is now literate; school enrolment ratios have increase dramatically from less than 15 per cent to almost 60 per cent. Urbanization has proceeded very rapidly, with residents in cities exceeding 20 000 rising from an average of less than 10 per cent to about 40 per cent. The indigenous middle class has more than doubled, rising from about 8 to about 20 per cent of the non-agricultural population, and the role of expatriates in the countries' economies and governments has declined substantially. But almost half the population is less than 15 years of age. Tribal allegiances continue to be strong and clan and village ties play a significant role in economic and political life. The sense of national unity is weak, primary loyalties are to the tribe, local and national systems are poorly integrated, and the polity has barely penetrated into the villages in which the majority of the population resides. Political systems are still very fragile and are characterized by significant instability. Social tensions among tribal and religious groups have escalated, in part as a result of previous dualistic growth; and nine out of the 25 countries in this group have been ravaged by violent coups, violent domestic outbreaks, civil war or violent insurrections during some part of the period under consideration.

The countries in this group have also been hit hard by the adverse changes in the global environment. They have become net exporters of capital; have not achieved a sufficient current account surplus to service their debts and are therefore increasing their foreign debt at an unsustainable rate. And, only seven of these countries have been able to achieve an average positive growth rate of real per capita GNP over the last 15 years.

Statistical results The results of the statistical analysis are presented in Table 3.1. The analysis explains 67 per cent of intercountry differences in rates of growth of per capita GNP. It decomposes intercountry variances in all aspects of social, economic and political change into five clusters: two mixed socio-economic clusters (F1 and F4 in Table 3.1); a politico-economic cluster, describing the extent of democracy and its consequences for the economy (F2 in Table 3.1); a socio-political one, describing the degree of centralization and its social concomitants (F3 in Table 3.1); and a social one (F5 in Table 3.1), describing the extent of social development. Thus, there is now some differentiation among socio-economic facets of development.

Table 3.1 Rotated factor matrix for change in per capita GNP 1980–1994 together with 30 political, economic and social variables[a]: low sample

Variable name	F1	F2	F3	F4	F5	R^2
Growth of GNP per capita 1980–94	.39	.16	−.14	**.68**	−.07	.67
Extent of socio-economic dualism	**.84**	.02	.20	−.10	.03	.75
Size of traditional agricultural sector	**−.65**	−.27	.02	.09	−.16	.54
Predominant farming system	**.63**	−.04	−.15	.10	.44	.64
Level of technology in agriculture	**.84**	−.15	.07	.20	−.09	.79
Rate of improvement of agricultural productivity	**.80**	.09	.22	.09	.09	.71
Degree of development of financial institutions	**.60**	−.08	.31	.00	.18	.50
Basic social organization	**.58**	.18	−.10	.41	.36	.67
Rate of improvement of human resources	**.58**	.32	.15	.49	−.04	.71
Extent of mass communication	**.60**	.00	.21	−.31	−.17	.54
Degree of democracy	.21	**.79**	.03	.06	−.17	.70
Degree of competitiveness of political party system	−.24	**.83**	.09	−.14	−.13	.69
Predominant basis of political party system	−.22	**.82**	.24	−.03	−.09	.79
Political power of the military	−.05	**−.59**	−.51	.06	−.35	.74
Degree of leadership commitment to development	.14	**.52**	.04	−.22	−.20	.38
Rate of industrialization	.33	**.55**	−.22	.35	−.02	.59
Degree of centralization	.41	.08	**.52**	.19	.14	.50
Degree of administrative efficiency	.57	.15	**.61**	.50	.41	.82
Degree of national integration	.52	.12	**.54**	.10	−.21	.63
Degree of urbanization	.39	−.30	**.59**	−.19	−.05	.62
Adequacy of infrastructure	.47	.26	**.65**	−.20	−.15	.77
Degree of social tension	.04	−.16	**−.85**	.04	−.09	.76
Degree of political stability	−.10	.12	**.87**	−.09	.08	.80
Natural resource abundance	.21	−.05	**.65**	−.39	.10	.48
Structure of foreign trade	−.15	.00	−.07	**.72**	.08	.54
Literacy rate	.34	.32	.15	**−.61**	.12	.63
Degree of modernization of outlook	.23	.19	−.10	**−.71**	.13	.62
Size of middle class	.12	.12	.10	−.03	**.70**	.53
Degree of social mobility	.40	−.11	−.22	−.39	**.65**	.79
Degree of ethnic homogeneity	.15	.34	−.08	−.03	**−.72**	.66

Notes:

[a] Bold figures indicate the factor with which each variable is most closely associated.

Variables omitted because of insignificant high correlations: crude fertility rate; political power of the traditional elite, strength of the labour movement; gross investment rate, level of technology in industry, rate of improvement in physical infrastructure, degree of development of tax system, rate of improvement of tax system, rate of improvement in financial institutions.

Percentage of overall variance explained by all factors: 65.4 per cent; percentage of variance explained by the last factor: 7.4 per cent.

The two mixed socio-economic clusters, F1 and F4, explain the lion share of intercountry differences in rates of economic growth (61 per cent for both clusters taken together). They describe two alternative paths to faster economic growth in this group of countries.

Factor F1 portrays an agricultural-development based approach to achieving faster rates of economic growth leading to reductions in socio-economic dualism[18] between rural and urban areas achieved through greater economic and social development in the countryside. Factor F1, which explains about 16 per cent of intercountry differences in growth rates of per capita GNP, associates faster economic growth with more emphasis on rural development – greater commercialization of agriculture leading to a declining traditional agricultural sector; a farming system that is moving from a primarily communal one towards a farming system consisting of primarily small, owner-operated, subsistence farms with incidental marketing of surpluses combined with a sprinkling of larger commercial farms; and which cultivates the land with more productive, but still largely traditional, agricultural technology and exhibits faster rates of improvements in agricultural productivity. This pattern of agricultural development is associated with greater responsiveness of agriculture to economic incentives, leads to a greater degree of monetization of economic transactions (more developed financial institutions), and reduces the influence of tribal customs on the economy and on its social organization (improvement in basic social organization). The rural economy is also becoming less isolated through greater penetration of mass communication media, and more investment in education (rate of improvement of human resources). The countries in our sample whose growth is best described by this rural-development-based approach to economic development are:[19] the mostly former French colonies in sub-Saharan Africa – Cameroon, Gabon, the Ivory Coast, Kenya and Senegal; Libya in North Africa and Pakistan in South Asia. The countries whose development path is most antithetic to this rural-development-based pattern[20] are the mostly war-torn basket cases of Afghanistan, Ethiopia, Niger, Somalia and Uganda, in which there is neither economic growth nor rural development.

Factor F4, the second mixed socio-economic factor, which accounts for 46.8 per cent of intercountry variance in growth rates, describes a very different approach to economic development. It depicts a trade-based approach. F4 associates higher growth rates with a less primary-dependent, more diversified export structure, on the one hand, and less literacy, and more traditional attitudes, on the other. Other aspects of change that are also significantly correlated with this factor (but which do not have the highest correlations with it) are: faster industrialization, greater decline in the influence of tribal forces, more investment in human resource development and greater administrative efficiency. The combination portrays a picture of trade-based industrialization, leading to an elite-oriented, polarizing pattern of social development in which secondary and higher education are emphasized at the expense of literacy; and in which tribal allegiances are breaking down but the educated urban elite is nevertheless becoming more traditional.[21] This factor depicts a specific kind of growth pattern, which trades off faster economic growth and more significant structural change in the economy against a wider sharing in the benefits of growth throughout society. One may venture the conjecture that this trade-based, elitist, approach to development may well be planting the seeds for internal violence and political instability in the future.

The three factors of little importance to growth rates, which are discussed below, are important for portraying intercountry differences in all aspects of economic, social and political change. The first factor in this category, F2, accounts for 13.3 per cent of variance in all facets of development but for only 2.6 per cent of variance in rates of economic growth. It describes the extent of political democracy (F2 in Table 3.1) and associates greater democracy with faster rates of economic growth.[22] It should be pointed out, however, that the degree of democracy it describes is quite limited: the average country in this group was moving from a political system with little or no effective practice of nationwide institutional democracy to one in which the institutions of democracy operated during some part of the period; and it had only one dominant national-unity political party, with other parties either banned or severely circumscribed. Faster growth was also associated with less political influence of the military and more leadership commitment to development. The greater leadership commitment to development was leading to faster industrialization partly in response to government efforts to liberalize foreign trade, expand markets and stabilize the economy. While this (limited) democracy factor explains a very small fraction of the variance in economic growth rates over the whole 15-year period under study, a separate analysis for the 1985–94 period suggests that its influence on intercountry differences in growth rates has become considerably more important during the last decade.[23]

The next factor in this category, F3, combines less political centralization and greater administrative efficiency with an enhanced degree of national integration and sense of national unity; a more urbanized society; in which villages are less isolated and the countryside is linked through a denser transport network to the cities; with declining social tensions and enhanced political stability; and with a better resource base that reduces competition for access to land and other resources. This cluster accounts for 2.1 per cent of intercountry variance in rates of economic growth and 11.3 per cent of overall variance in all aspects of societies, polities, institutions and behaviour among these low-development countries.

The last factor in this set is F5. It describes the extent to which the process of development is inducing social polarization. It combines increases in the size of the middle class and enhanced social mobility with a (fundamentalist) backlash against programmes of cultural assimilation that manifests itself in decreases in the degree of ethnic and cultural homogeneity.[24] This factor accounts for 7.4 per cent of overall variance and a negligible proportion of variance in growth rates.

Comparison with the 1960s We find both continuity and innovation in the comparison between our results for the 1960s and our results for the current period. Socio-economic forces continue to account for the lion's share of intercountry differences in rates of economic growth. Tribal allegiances continue to exert an influence on the efficacy of purely economic activities and to affect government–civil society interactions in the economic sphere. However, during the generation that has passed since our earlier study, Western education, urbanization and market forces have penetrated the tribal-subsistence sector sufficiently so that the sway of tribal cultures and customary resource allocation patterns no longer poses the overwhelming barriers to economic development that it did during the 1960s.

Now, as then, one can couch the discussion of intercountry differences in growth rates in either socio-economic or purely economic terms.[25] But, unlike during the 1960s, when growth was almost exclusively industrial-ization and trade-oriented, we now have two different paths depicted in our results: (1) a broadly-based rural-development approach; or (2) a continuation of the earlier trade-led, limited industrialization pattern of narrowly-based economic growth.

As to political forces, while there are strong signs that this is changing, progress towards democracy and nation-building in the countries in this group has yet to reach a level such that intercountry differences in democracy and national integration can have significant systematic effects on economic performance. The insignificance of these two aspects of political development for economic growth provides an element of continuity between the 1967 and the 1990 analyses. But the mild indications that less democracy was associated with faster economic growth in the 1960s has been replaced by an equally mild indication that greater democracy is associated with more rapid growth in the 1990s. Also, government policies underly the choices between the alternative paths of change depicted in our results. So the growth-orientation of governments must have become important, even if their degrees of democracy are not.

The intermediate sample

This sample is similar in composition to the 1960s sample except that it excludes Pakistan, which has moved down to the low sample, and includes Morocco, which has moved up from the low sample. It also includes El Salvador, Lebanon, Peru and Egypt which have moved down from the high sample, and excludes Iran, for which information on growth during the 1990s could not be obtained.

Country characteristics This group of countries is considerably more developed than the low sample and less developed than the high one. Its progress relative to the earlier period has been uneven along different dimensions of change as well as among countries. At one extreme, the sample includes two countries, India and Indonesia, in which mass poverty has been substantially reduced, and two countries, Indonesia and Thailand, which are likely to graduate into the high sample in the near future. At the other extreme, it includes Iraq, Jordan, Lebanon and Syria, which, despite relatively high levels of development, have performed miserably during the period under study. For the whole sample, growth performance has been much more favourable than for the low sample; there are only four countries with negative average growth over the 15-year period covered by this study.

Statistical results The results for this group of countries are summarized in Table 3.2. They indicate that the most striking differences among countries in this group have become the complexion of their political systems summarized in F1 of the table. Not only does this political complex explain 22.7 per cent of intercountry differences in all aspects of their societies, polities and economies, but it also appears to exert a strong influence on rates of growth of per capita GNP, 38.6 per cent of whose intercountry differences it explains. The pattern of associations in this group of countries relates higher growth rates to more democratic systems, with more competitive party systems based on parties that are more personalistic rather than purely tribal in nature, and with greater freedom of opposition and press. Lower centralization and less dualism are also correlated with this factor, although this is not the factor with which they are most closely correlated. However, one should not overestimate the degree of democracy typical of the transitional countries in this group. In the average country in this set, while two or more effective political par-

Table 3.2　Rotated factor matrix for change in per capita GNP 1980–1994 together with 29 political, economic and social variables[a]: intermediate sample

Variable name	F1	F2	F3	F4	F5	R^2
Growth of GNP per capita 1980–94	**−.66**	.05	.04	−.17	−.60	.83
Degree of democracy	**−.87**	−.18	−.21	.05	−.14	.86
Degree of competitiveness of political party system	**−.78**	−.14	−.25	−.08	−.32	.80
Predominant basis of political party system	**−.82**	−.18	.08	.12	.07	.73
Freedom of opposition and press	**−.92**	.19	.13	−.04	−.10	.93
Gross investment rate	.05	**−.58**	.18	−.46	−.45	.79
Degree of development of tax institutions	−.21	**−.74**	.08	−.22	.07	.73
Degree of administrative efficiency	−.18	**−.73**	.16	.05	.00	.59
Natural resource abundance	−.21	**−.73**	−.16	.16	−.20	.68
Degree of national integration	.16	−.16	**.80**	.21	−.13	.75
Extent of ethnic homogeneity	.17	.31	**.60**	−.08	.41	.62
Degree of social tension	.08	.04	**−.88**	−.03	.26	.86
Degree of political stability	−.18	−.66	**.61**	.02	.01	.84
Degree of centralization	.51	−.41	**.61**	−.01	−.21	.85
Level of agricultural technology	.21	−.27	−.10	**−.69**	.38	.76
Level of industrial technology	−.22	−.38	−.04	**−.74**	.37	.88
Rate of industrialization	−.24	.03	.49	**−.51**	.38	.67
Structure of foreign trade	−.15	.18	−.14	**−.81**	−.14	.74
Rate of improvement in infrastructure	.23	−.08	.39	**−.60**	.11	.58
Degree of development of financial institutions	.02	−.52	.13	**−.73**	.09	.83
Rate of improvement in tax institutions	−.32	−.41	.09	**.66**	−.04	.72
Crude fertility rate	.21	−.13	.12	**.73**	.35	.74
Degree of leadership commitment to development	.08	−.23	.37	.07	**−.56**	.51
Degree of socio-economic dualism	.43	.03	.29	.27	**.54**	.63
Size of traditional agricultural sector	−.31	.40	.22	−.03	**−.70**	.80
Predominant farming system	.13	.17	−.13	.05	**.69**	.54
Adequacy of infrastructure	.12	−.44	−.03	−.30	**.67**	.75
Rate of improvement in human resources	.08	.17	−.14	−.45	**.58**	.59
Degree of urbanization	.24	.00	−.14	.03	**.87**	.83
Extent of mass communication	−.13	.08	.12	−.02	**.71**	.55

Notes:
[a] Bold figures indicate the factor with which each variable is most closely associated.
Variables omitted because of insignificant high correlations: character of basic social organization, extent of literacy, degree of modernization of outlook, size of the middle class; strength of the labour movement, political strength of the military, political strength of the traditional elite; rate of improvement in agricultural productivity, rate of improvement in financial institutions.
Percentage of overall variance explained by all factors: 74.2 per cent; percentage of variance explained by the last factor: 7.7 per cent.

ties operate, there is no reasonable expectation of rotation or sharing of control at the national level. The dominant political party is still not ideological or class based. Rather, it is intensely personalistic and characterized by extensive political opportunism. And some political parties continue to represent regional, religious, cultural, or ethnic groupings of the population. Furthermore, while political parties are free to organize, they are generally limited in their political activities and in their freedom to oppose the dominant party; and the freedom of the press is restricted or intermittent. The political contrast among more and less democratic countries summarized in this factor is used by the statistical analysis to explain a major share of the distinctions in performance between the good South Asian performers in this group, India, Sri Lanka, Thailand and Indonesia, on the one hand, and the poor performers in the Middle East, Iraq, Jordan, Lebanon and Syria. But the overall explanatory power of modest democracy, its influence on growth rates, and the direction of its association with growth rates persist even when the Middle Eastern countries are excluded from the sample or when an extra variable, regional war, is included to account for the poor performance of the Middle Eastern nations.

The second most striking differences among countries, which explain 17.4 per cent of overall intercountry variance but fail to account for any systematic differences in growth rates are primarily economic (F2, in Table 3.2): more investment, greater development of financial and tax institutions, greater administrative efficiency, more abundant natural resources and more political stability. F2 summarizes a complex of institutional development that is not reflected in concurrent economic growth. The failure of these institutional influences to result in economic growth is most probably due to the longer time lags required for institutional development to exert an influence on economic growth at the levels of socio-economic and political development represented in this sample of transitional countries.

The next two factors also fail to account for much intercountry variance in growth rates. They represent, respectively, the extent of social polarization (F3 in Table 3.2) and the extent of structural change of a mostly economic variety (F4 in Table 3.2). The social polarization factor, F3, accounts for 14.6 per cent of overall variance among countries and explains a negligible proportion of intercountry differences in rates of economic growth. This factor combines greater degrees of national integration, less social tension and fewer ethnic and religious cleavages with greater political stability. It thus summarizes the extent of progress towards national unity. The transitional countries in this sample have, alas, made only very limited progress in this direction; in most of them there are periodic eruptions of bloody civil strife or more lasting internal wars in which thousands of individuals are killed. The progress of national integration is, at the very least, not helped by the dualistic growth process characteristic of the majority of countries in this transitional group. The limited progress in national integration explains the lack of impact of differences in national integration upon growth.

The fourth factor combines higher levels of agricultural and industrial technology; faster industrialization which results in a larger share of manufactured exports; more rapidly improving physical overhead capital; more developed financial systems; with drops in crude fertility rates and less rapidly improving tax collection systems. The structural changes incorporated in this cluster account for 11.5 per cent of intercountry differences in overall variance but only about 1.7 per cent of intercountry differences in rates of economic growth. Like the second factor, which included mostly institutional aspects of economic development, this fourth factor, which reflects mostly economic structural change, also represents development without much economic growth.

The final most important set of influences (F5 in Table 3.2), which accounts for 36 per cent of intercountry variance in growth rates but only 7.7 per cent of overall intercountry differences, depicts a profile of narrowly based dualistic socio-economic growth: it combines faster economic growth with greater leadership commitment to development leading to more dualistic growth characterized by *less* agricultural development (larger traditional agricultural sectors, in which the overwhelming majority of farmers engage in predominantly subsistence farming on farms that are too small to be economically viable and have fewer transport linkages with cities) and *less* social development (less improvement in the human resource base, less urbanization and less mass communication). In contrast to the previous factor, which represented development without economic growth, this factor represents growth without development. The narrow-based dualistic growth occurring in the faster growing transitional countries in this set is induced by the nature of the government-led policy reforms – the shift to greater openness of the economy and increased reliance on market mechanisms.[26]

Comparison with the 1960s The outlines of the transition processes occurring in this group of countries have become much clearer than they were during the 1960s. The analysis of intercountry differences in growth rates now succeeds in explaining 83 per cent of their variance as compared with only 48 per cent for the 1960s. In the 1960s analysis intercountry differences in rates of economic growth were accounted for exclusively by intercountry differences in extent of development of economic institutions and investment effort. Now, differences in political institutions among countries have become important to growth rates, with more democratic institutions associated with better growth performance. Furthermore, our results for this group of countries now reflect, strikingly, the differences between economic growth and economic development. The previous development of market institutions reflected in our results for this group of countries during the 1960s has enabled a subsequent bifurcation between economic growth and economic development to take place in the 1990s. Our results for the 1990s show that, on the one hand, we have narrow-based, dualistic growth without much concurrent development (the India pattern). And on the other, we have development and structural change without concurrent growth, characteristic of the low-development Latin American countries in this group. We also see that these narrow-based, dualistic, transition processes are taking their tolls in impeding greater national integration within countries, intercountry differences which have become more important to the analysis of overall change.

The high sample

Two countries that were included in the 1960s sample (Israel and Japan) are now excluded because they have since become developed. El Salvador, Lebanon, Peru and Egypt are also omitted from this sample since they have retrogressed to the intermediate level. Fourteen of the 19 remaining countries in this group are now Latin American.

Country characteristics The countries in this group have all become semi-industrial. On the average, they have industrial sectors that generate about 40 per cent of value added; 65 per cent of their exports are manufactures; and their rates of increase in industrial output average about 2 per cent per year in constant prices. Traditional subsistence agriculture provides for the livelihood of no more than 15 per cent of the economically active population; large commercial absentee farms and plantations predominate but they coexist with a significant share of small commercial owner-operated farming enterprises. Internal transport and power networks are generally adequate for more rapid economic development, though specific bottlenecks still exist. Economic institutions are moderately well developed: tax systems are reasonably effective, with a ratio of government domestic revenues to GNP of between 15 and 20 per cent and a ratio of direct tax revenues to total government-domestic revenue of at least 30 per cent. Their financial institutions are at least moderately effective in attracting private savings and providing long- and medium-term credit to industry and agriculture but their ability to operate has been significantly hobbled by hyperinflation or capital flight during a significant portion of the period. The sharp socio-economic dualism characteristic of the intermediate sample has diminished, although there are still definite contrasts between an important modern industrial sector and a mining or commercial-agricultural sector using intermediate or traditional technology. Often, the traditional subsistence sectors are confined to specific regions and limited to ethnic minorities.

Along social lines, there has been a considerable degree of social development: 60 per cent of the populations of the 'high' group reside in cities; literacy rates average 85 per cent and secondary school enrolment ratios 65 per cent; indigenous middle classes comprise about 20 per cent of the population; despite marked social stratification, social mobility is considerable by developing country standards; and crude fertility rates have dropped to around 2 per cent.

Politically, during the 1980–94 period there has been a general shift towards greater democracy and away from military regimes, although the military continue to wield considerable political influence. Nationwide democratic parliamentary institutions have operated fairly well during this period, but their effectiveness has been restricted by low voter participation, constraints upon opposition parties, instability of the party system, and/or inexperience with democratic forms. The political influence of tradition-oriented national elites has been moderate but the political influence of commercial and industrial groups, and/or modernizing bureaucrats has been growing. The 1980–94 period in the 'high' countries has been characterized by reasonable political stability without much domestic violence and by a markedly lower degree of social tension compared to that prevalent in the intermediate group. Recently, however, the political economy of adjustment has led to increased social tensions with the potential for greater political instability in the near future.

Statistical results The results of the analysis are summarized in Table 3.3. There are four explanatory clusters which, taken together, account for 85 per cent of intercountry variance in rates of economic growth. They are discussed in order of their contribution to the explanation of intercountry differences in growth rates.

First, there is a socio-economic and political factor which describes the spread effects of growth (F4 in Table 3.3). This factor associates growth rates positively with improvement of human capital, the size of the middle class, and decreases of dualism and negatively with leadership commitment to development. It describes the Latin American growth pattern during this period of adjustment, in which more vigorous internal and external stabilization efforts have resulted in more dualistic growth,

*Table 3.3 Rotated factor matrix for change in per capita GNP 1980–1994
together with 25 political, economic and social variables[a]:
high sample*

Variable name	F1	F2	F3	F4	F5	R^2
Growth of GNP per capita 1980–94	−.25	.51	−.11	.60	.38	.85
Size of traditional agricultural sector	**.85**	−.00	−.05	−.02	.20	.76
Literacy rate	**−.82**	−.08	−.08	.17	−.14	.74
Extent of mass communication	**−.81**	−.08	−.10	−.36	−.06	.80
Degree of modernization of outlook	**−.81**	.04	.32	.08	−.10	.77
Adequacy of infrastructure	**−.78**	−.00	.07	.11	.17	.66
Degree of development of tax institutions	**−.59**	.22	−.27	−.51	.12	.74
Gross investment rate	.22	**.67**	.09	−.43	−.00	.70
Level of industrial technology	−.33	**.75**	.23	.22	−.20	.82
Rate of industrialization	−.22	**.70**	−.41	.14	.21	.77
Structure of foreign trade	.16	**.85**	.13	.15	.25	.85
Predominant farming system	−.17	**.61**	−.42	−.07	−.27	.67
Political power of the traditional elite	.18	**−.75**	−.15	.18	−.09	.66
Degree of ethnic homogeneity	.29	**.64**	.00	.04	−.16	.52
Degree of democracy	−.21	.16	**.86**	−.05	−.24	.86
Degree of competitiveness of political party system	−.07	.10	**.78**	−.28	.11	.71
Freedom of opposition and press	−.20	.38	**.64**	−.00	−.38	.74
Political power of labour	−.05	−.30	**.85**	−.17	−.03	.86
Rate of improvement of agricultural productivity	−.09	−.02	**−.81**	−.20	−.04	.70
Degree of leadership commitment to development	−.00	.23	.21	**−.64**	−.10	.52
Rate of improvement of human resources	−.21	.40	−.03	**.56**	−.40	.70
Size of the middle class	−.08	−.10	.02	**.80**	−.09	.67
Degree of socio-economic dualism	−.29	.03	−.02	**.80**	−.12	.74
Degree of national integration	.03	.43	−.12	.09	**−.74**	.77
Degree of centralization	.30	−.09	−.31	−.10	**.65**	.62
Rate of improvement of financial institutions	−.02	−.24	−.06	−.10	**.64**	.77

Notes:
[a] Bold figures indicate the factor with which each variable is most closely associated.
Variables omitted because of insignificant high correlations: character of basic social organization, extent of social mobility, crude fertility rate, urbanization, social tension; predominant basis of political party system, political power of the military, degree of political stability; natural resource abundance, level of technology in agriculture and the rate of improvement in physical infrastructure.
Percentage of overall variance explained by all factors: 73.1 per cent; percentage of variance explained by the last factor: 8.6 per cent.

with smaller improvements in the quality of human capital, and led to a
policy of wage repression which has reduced the size of the middle class
and resulted in a more polarizing growth process. This cluster of influences accounts for 36 per cent of intercountry differences in rates of
economic growth.

Second, there is a mostly economic factor (F2 in Table 3.3), which
describes the extent of industrialization effort, towards which both
investment rates and the development of economic institutions are
directed. It also includes two major non-economic impediments to
economic modernization: the political sway exercised by traditional agricultural elites and the lack of ethnic homogeneity. More specifically, this
factor associates more rapid economic growth with higher investment
rates in more advanced industrial technology leading to a larger share of
manufactured exports and facilitated by more developed tax systems and
more reliance on commercial agriculture. This effort is enabled by a
decline in the political power of the traditional agricultural elites and
has a larger effect where there is greater ethnic homogeneity. This cluster
of influences accounts for another 26 per cent of intercountry differences in growth rates.

Third, there is a socio-political cluster (F5, in Table 3.3), which
describes the degree of national integration and sense of national unity.
This factor associates a more polarized nation with a more centralized
political system and with financial institutions that perform better in
mobilizing national saving due to less politically induced capital flight
that has been characteristic of many Latin American countries during
this period. This factor explains another 14 per cent of overall variance in
rates of economic growth.

Fourth, there is a socio-economic factor (F1 in Table 3.3), which
explains 21 per cent of overall variance in all included variables but adds
only 6 per cent to the explanation of rates of economic growth. It combines relatively smaller agricultural sectors with greater literacy rates,
greater mass communication, more modern attitudes, denser transportation networks linking the countryside to cities and a more effective tax
collection apparatus that relies more heavily on direct than indirect taxes.
Since the characteristics described in this cluster are already well developed in this group of countries the analysis indicates that further
increases are subject to diminishing returns in terms of growth.

Finally, there is a democracy factor (F3 in Table 3.3), which explains
15 per cent of the overall variance in all aspects of development but adds
only 1 per cent to the explanation of intercountry variance in growth
rates. It combines greater democracy with more competitive political
party systems, greater freedom of opposition and press and more politi-

cal influence of labour groups. The greater democracy gives rise to a more industry-oriented pattern of development and is therefore associated with a lower rate of improvement in agricultural productivity.[27]

Comparison with the 1960s The results for the 'high' countries are rather similar to the earlier ones. Social and political development have proceeded far enough so that the primary influences on growth rates are provided by economic policies and economic institutions. But, now some political influences other than leadership commitment to development also affect intercountry differences in growth rates. These are provided by the influence of traditional elites on economic policies, and by the concomitants of adjustment policies in Latin America, which have led to an increasingly unequal distribution of the fruits of growth, often along ethnic lines. And our redefined indicator of leadership commitment to development, which, in the present analysis, characterizes differential success in achieving trade liberalization, internal stabilization and external equilibrium, is now strongly negatively associated with economic growth while the analogous (but differently defined) indicator was the only political variable strongly positively associated with growth in this group of countries during the 1960s. Is this contrast a comment on the relative merits of Washington-consensus type policies and the development-economics of the 1960s? Or is it mainly induced by the change in the external environment? Or is the one merely a reflection of the other?

3.5 CONCLUSIONS

As expected of any historical process, we find both elements of continuity and innovation in the comparison of results for the 1990s with those for the 1960s. Perhaps the most important elements of continuity between our analyses of development in the two periods are that: (1) economic, social and political aspects of development continue to be intertwined; (2) the nature of their interactions continues to differ systematically among development levels; (3) non-economic and institutional forces continue to exert a significant impact on the content and speed of economic growth; and, last but not least, (4) the same techniques used to study interactions among economic and non-economic institutions and economic performance continue to yield fruitful insights into development processes at different levels of socio-economic and institutional development.

The difference in development setting, the passage of time, and previous domestic development have also led to some elements of innovations.

In the 1960s, we were unable to discern alternative development paths at the same initial levels of socio-economic development. In contrast, our results for the low and intermediate samples now yield clear indications that countries at similar initial development levels may and do choose to pursue different development strategies. These different strategies may yield equivalent results for economic growth but tend to contrast substantially in their implications for the spread of economic and social benefits from economic growth and in the structural changes they imply. As a result, the processes of transformation occurring within transitional countries have now come to reflect strikingly the distinctions between economic growth and economic development. Indeed, in the 1960s we were very pessimistic about the prospects of the 'low sample'. They seemed to be doomed to a narrow, dualistic, primary-export based, industrialization process that was inequitable and fraught with the potential for increased domestic violence. While the violence has, alas, materialized, our results for the low sample in the 1990s have pointed to an alternative development process, more akin to that which had been traversed historically by the current OECD countries prior to their Industrial Revolutions, that of agriculture-led, broad-based development.

Taken together, the statistical results for both periods suggest several generalizations concerning economic development. First, they indicate that institutions, economic, social and political, matter greatly in explaining which countries among those having similar initial conditions perform much better than others. Second, they show that different economic, institutional and political processes are important in countries characterized by different economic and institutional initial conditions. The nature and effectiveness of substitutions for incomplete, missing or underdeveloped domestic institutions, inadequate domestic factor supplies and deficient domestic aggregate demand tend to vary systematically with a country's development level. Third, they show that institutions affect development in a very non-linear fashion. More specifically, they suggest rather strongly that the effectiveness of individual institutions on development is subject to both thresholds, before they can have a noticeable impact, and ceilings, after which they cease having much impact on further economic development. Fourth, they indicate that, among countries similar in institutional development, economic policies with respect to trade, agriculture and investment are critical. However, they also indicate that the critical policies and governmental actions required in each of these spheres differ by development level and that their relative effectiveness is conditioned by the institutional setting in which policy interventions take place.

These lessons have yet to be incorporated into modern development economics.

APPENDIX: THE LIST OF VARIABLES

An abbreviated set of definitions of variables is given below. All rate-of-change variables refer to the period 1979/80–1989/90 and all 'level' variables refer to 1987–92. Variables for which the category limits were changed from the 1960 limits are starred*.

Economic Indicators

- *Annual Rate of Growth of Real Per capita GNP** between 1980 and 1994
- *Gross Investment Rate**: share to GNP
- *Abundance of Natural Resources*: arable land per capita and abundance of fuel and non-fuel natural resources
- *Level of Technology Industry**: use of power-driven technology and relative importance of modern, large-scale industry
- *Rate of Industrialization**: average real annual rate of change of industrial production
- *Predominant Farming System** (formerly called *Character of Agricultural Organization*): this variable ranges from communal ownership of land to viable commercial farming. Intermediate categories are: owner-operated subsistence farming and large-scale absentee or owner-operated farms or plantations combined with either subsistence farming or small-scale commercial farming
- *Level of Technology Agriculture**: use of mechanical power and fertilizer; and share of non-monetized subsistence farming
- *Degree of Improvement of Agricultural Productivity**: change in use of chemical fertilizer, mechanical power, or modern irrigation systems
- *Adequacy of Infrastructure**: transport and power networks
- *Rate of Improvement of Infrastructure**: rate of change in miles of paved road plus kilometre tons carried by rail
- *Level of Development of Tax Institutions**: share of domestic tax revenue to GNP and share of direct to indirect taxes
- *Rate of Improvement of Tax System**: rate of change of domestic tax revenue to GNP and in share of direct to indirect taxes
- *Level of Development of Financial Institutions**: effectiveness in attracting private savings and channelling them to investment
- *Rate of Improvement of Financial Institutions**: rate of increase of share of demand plus time deposits to GNP
- *Rate of Improvement of Human Resources**: weighted average of secondary plus tertiary enrolment rates
- *Structure of Foreign Trade**: share of manufactured commodities in total exports plus diversification of exports by commodity and country

Socio-Economic Indicators

- *Size of Traditional Agricultural Sector**: proportion of population engaged in traditional subsistence agriculture. Nets out proportion in commercial agriculture from the total
- *Extent of Socio-Economic Dualism*: extent of modernization of methods of production throughout sectors, regions and scale. Lowest category has very limited development of the exchange sector and preponderance of subsistence production; highest has significant modernization of production in all sectors, regions and scales of production
- *Degree of Urbanization**: percentage of population in cities over 20 000
- *Crude Fertility Rate*: per thousand population
- *Basic Social Organization*: ranges from countries in which tribal allegiances and organization predominate to ones in which the immediate family is the primary form of social organization
- *Size of Indigenous Middle Class**: percentage of indigenous male population in professional, managerial administrative or technical occupations
- *Degree of Social Mobility**: breadth of opportunities for entry into the middle class. Judged by school enrolment ratios; share of middle class occupations; and extent of ethnic, religious or cultural barriers to entry into middle class occupations
- *Literacy Rate** of adult population
- *Extent of Mass Communication**: composite index based on newspaper circulation and radio licenses per capita
- *Degree of Cultural and Ethnic Homogeneity*: composite index based on percentage of population speaking the dominant language; percentage of ethnic minorities; and religious heterogeneity
- *Degree of Social Tension*: qualitative indicator ranging from countries with no overt signs of social tension or violence to countries with marked social tensions accompanied by substantial violence and social instability
- *Degree of Modernization of Outlook*: qualitative indicator based on extent of modernization of the educated urban groups and the extent of general popular support for programmes political, social and economic modernization

Political Indicators

- *Degree of National Integration*: ranges from countries in which there is a marked absence of national integration as indicated by the absence of a common language and culture, ineffective integration of local

and central political systems and little sense of national unity to countries in which the same criteria indicate that there is a marked degree
of national integration

- *Degree of Centralization of Political Power*: ranges from countries in
  which central governments did not maintain effective control throughout important parts of the country to countries with centralized
  authoritarian governments
- *Degree of Democracy*: ranges from countries in which there was little
  or no practice of nationwide institutional democracy to ones with
  well-established nationwide democracy, with at least two effective
  political parties, freedom of opposition and at least 30 per cent of eligible voters participating in national elections
- *Freedom of Opposition and Press*: ranges from countries in which
  political parties were limited to non-political activities and political
  opposition was banned to countries in which parties were free to organize, operate and oppose the government throughout the period and in
  which the freedom of the press was restricted at most intermittently
- *Degree of Competitiveness of Political Party Systems*: ranges from
  countries in which there were no political parties effective at the
  national level to ones in which there were two or more reasonably
  effective political parties operating at the national level between at
  least two of which rotation or sharing of government control could
  be expected
- *Predominant Basis of Political Party System*: ranges from countries in
  which there were no effective political parties or all parties were
  banned to countries in which the predominant party or parties had an
  ideological or class orientation. Intermediate categories are countries
  in which the predominant parties represented regional, religious,
  ethnic or cultural groupings; and countries in which the dominant
  parties were highly personalistic
- *Political Strength of the Labour Movement*: ranges from countries with
  negligible or proscribed labour movements to ones in which labour
  movements were reasonably well established, active and had substantial popular support
- *Political Strength of the Traditional Elite*: ranges from countries in
  which tradition-oriented elites had little or no political power during
  most of the period to ones in which landed or other tradition-oriented
  elites were politically dominant during the greatest part of the period
- *Political Strength of the Military*: ranged from countries in which the
  military had little or no political influence to countries in which the
  military were in direct political control during an important part of
  the period

- *Degree of Administrative Efficiency*: ranges from countries with extreme bureaucratic inefficiency, with highly corrupt civil services and suffering from serious instability of policy at high levels to countries with a relatively well-trained civil service that did not suffer from instability of policy at high level and that did not have high levels of corruption
- *Extent of Leadership Commitment to Development*: based on extent of shift towards an open trade regime, market-oriented reforms and internal and external stabilization efforts
- *Extent of Political Stability*: ranges from countries characterized by violent coups, violent outbreaks or violent insurrections during a significant part of the period to countries characterized by relatively effective internal security, considerable continuity in the form of government and a relative consensus about the prevailing political system.

NOTES

1. I am indebted to Cynthia Taft Morris for her valuable comments. I naturally retain responsibility for any remaining errors.
2. Johns Hopkins University Press, Baltimore, 1967
3. 'Quantitative aspects of economic growth of nations', *Economic Development and Cultural Change*, 1956, 5, 5–94.
4. For a rigorous mathematical description of the technique see Adelman and Morris (1967, Chapter 3).
5. The rotation represents an angle-preserving rotation of the axes in which the eigenvectors are measured.
6. Specifically, the varimax rotation principle was used. The varimax rotation, which is applied simultaneously to all eigenvectors, makes the coefficient of the variables in each eigenvector as close to either zero (if the original coefficients are small) or unity (if the coefficients are large). The rotation does not affect the results, merely the ease of interpretation.
7. In factor analysis, these correlation coefficients are called 'loadings'.
8. That is, the factors are listed in order of the size of their eigenvalues. As indicated in the text, the square of the eigenvalue indicates the percentage of the overall variance among all variables accounted for by its associated eigenvector.
9. This is the value of R-square which is statistically significant at the 5 per cent level.
10. The numbers cited here refer to all OECD countries taken together. They exclude Greece, Iceland, Portugal, Spain and Turkey.
11. This figure is an unweighted average, based on David Morawetz (1997), *Twenty Five Years of Economic Development: 1950 to 1975*, Baltimore: Johns Hopkins University Press. It refers to 1950–1975, with per capita incomes in 1974 US dollars converted at official exchange rates, and includes the oil exporters.
12. Adelman and Morris, 1967 Chapter 5.
13. Adelman and Morris, 1967 Chapter 6.
14. Adelman and Morris, 1967 Chapter 7.
15. Nevertheless, non-oil imports of developed countries grew by 12 per cent.
16. The group of low-income Asian countries is an exception.
17. Factor scores on the first factor in a combined factor analysis describing various aspects of socio-institutional and economic development levels were used for this purpose. For a discussion see Adelman and Morris, 1967, pp. 167–71.

18. The dualism variable assigns higher scores to *less* dualistic countries.
19. These are the countries with the highest factor scores on F1.
20. These are the countries with the lowest factor scores on this factor.
21. The countries with highest positive scores on this factor are Yemen and Nepal; those with the highest negative scores on this factor are: Kenya, the Ivory Coast, Malagasy and the Sudan.
22. The countries with high positive scores on this factor are: Gabon, the Ivory Coast, Malagasy, Senegal and Yemen; those with high negative scores on this factor are: Guinea, Libya, Nepal, Nigeria and Pakistan.
23. An analogous factor analysis of growth rates for the 1985–94 period ascribes to the democracy factor a full 36 per cent of explanatory power in accounting for intercountry differences in growth rates. However, it unambiguously associates less democracy with higher growth rates.
24. The country with a high positive score on this factor is the Ivory Coast; those with high negative scores on this factor are: Libya, Malagasy and Yemen.
25. A separate run, with social and political variables only, explains 67 per cent of the variance in growth rates, with political variables accounting for a negligible share of the variance. Another separate run, with only economic variables, accounts for 70 per cent of the variance in growth rates.
26. These are the predominant elements of the 'leadership commitment to development' variable in this group of countries.
27. This factor explains the contrast between Chile, Taiwan, Panama and Surinam, which have the lowest scores on this factor, and the Dominican Republic and Jamaica, which score highest.

4. Openness, capital mobility and global convergence

Hui Pan

4.1 INTRODUCTION[1]

In recent years there has been a renewed interest in economic growth and a corresponding increase of literature on the topic. One issue that has attracted attention over the last few years is the issue of convergence (Barro and Sala-i-Martin, 1990, 1991, 1995; Barro, Mankiw and Sala-i-Martin, 1992; Sachs and Warner, 1995a). Two concepts of convergence are used in the literature: beta convergence and sigma convergence. Beta convergence refers to the phenomenon that countries with lower per capita income grow faster than countries with higher per capita income; sigma convergence means that the dispersion in per capita income across countries declines over time. The primary finding of the studies is that countries converge at a speed of about 2 per cent per year after controlling for different steady states and that the variance in per capita income across countries moves to a steady state level. When controlling the random shocks, faster beta convergence will lead to the reduction of the dispersion of per capita income across economies over time.

In a recent paper, Sachs and Warner (1995a) studied the relationship between trade openness and economic convergence. After detailed examination of trade openness for 117 countries, the authors separated these countries into two groups: the open economy group and the closed economy group. Unconditional convergence was found in the open economy group while there was no sign of convergence for the countries in the closed economy group. The authors conclude that prudent economic policies, especially opening trade, will lead to economic convergence.

While Sachs and Warner's empirical study focuses mainly on trade, Barro, Mankiw and Sala-i-Martin (1992) have developed an open economy growth model and showed that with borrowing and lending possible in the international capital market, the rate of beta convergence is faster, implying that financial integration will lead to economic convergence.

The effect of trade and financial openness on economic growth and convergence was further studied by Pan (1996) in a neoclassical framework. Based on the number of trade and capital mobility restrictions reported in the IMF's Annual Report on Exchange Arrangements and Exchange Restrictions, the author constructed indexes of trade openness and capital mobility for 71 countries. The regression results confirmed what has been found by others that there is conditional convergence among countries. More importantly the effects of trade openness and capital mobility on economic growth have been quantified.

Following the same methodology as in Pan (1996), but greatly expanding the sample, this chapter will measure the degree of trade and financial openness for a group of 140 world economies. The impact of financial integration and trade openness on economic growth and global convergence will be analysed in a neoclassical growth framework.

The chapter is organized as follows: Section 4.2 briefly reviews the literature on convergence; Section 4.3 constructs measures of trade openness and capital mobility. It uses quantitative measures to gauge a country's degree of trade openness and financial integration with the rest of the world. Information from the IMF's Annual Report on Exchange Arrangements and Exchange Restrictions will be examined and indexes of trade openness and capital mobility will be constructed. Section 4.4 examines the effects of openness on economic growth and convergence. Finally, Section 4.5 draws some conclusions and gives policy implications.

4.2 A BRIEF REVIEW OF THE LITERATURE

Beta and Sigma Convergence

One framework for analysing convergence is the neoclassical growth model. In this model, the representative infinite-horizon household, whose membership is growing at a constant rate of n, is assumed to maximize present discounted value of a future utility stream, where utility is a function of per capita income. On the production side, firms have access to the same production technology (usually assumed to be Cobb–Douglas), and will maximize current period profit. The transition path which describes the evolution of consumption and capital variables toward the steady state will form the basis for the growth equation which is used to analyse the rate of beta convergence. By log-linearizing the system, the average growth rate of per capita income is shown as a function of initial per capita income, the growth rate of technology and the steady-state income per effective unit of labour as shown by the following equation:

$$\log\left(\frac{y_{it}}{y_{i,\,t-1}}\right) = a - (1 - e^{-\beta})[\log(y_{i,t-1}) - g(t-1)] + u_{it}$$

where:

$$a = g + (1 - e^{-\beta}) \log(\hat{y}^*)$$

Here y is the per capita income, g is the growth rate of technology, $\hat{y}^*$ is the steady-state level of income per effective unit of labour, i denotes country or region, t denotes time. The coefficient of the initial income will give the speed of unconditional convergence, that is, the speed with which the poorer economies are catching up with the more advanced economies. When holding constant the differences in technology and steady-state levels of income per effective unit of labour, the coefficient of initial income will give the speed of conditional convergence. In their studies on US states and European regions and countries Barro and Sala-i-Martin (1990, 1991, 1992) found that the US states are converging unconditionally. Poor states have been growing faster than the richer ones and are catching up. This unconditional convergence is not evident for the 98 countries in their study. However when holding constant the different steady states of different countries by including such variables as school enrolment rates in the initial year, average government consumption ratio and the number of revolutions and coups per year, the countries are also converging at about 2 per cent per year. That means the countries are showing conditional convergence.

One shortcoming of the above analysis is the assumption that economies are closed. In a related paper, Barro, Mankiw and Sala-i-Martin (1992) analyse the effect of capital mobility on convergence in a neoclassical growth model. In the model, countries are allowed to borrow or lend on the international market by issuing bonds. With perfect capital mobility, they show that the speed of convergence will be infinite implying instant convergence. If a constraint is put on borrowing by assuming that only physical, not human, capital can be used as collateral for borrowing, they show the speed of convergence will be finite. The speed of convergence under limited capital mobility will be greater than for the closed economies. Capital mobility will lead to faster economic convergence.

Another concept of convergence is sigma convergence, which measures the cross-country or cross-region dispersion in the log of per capita income. Barro and Sala-i-Martin (1990) show that the cross-economy variance of log income at time t evolves in accordance with the first difference equation. The solution of the difference equation shows that the variance approaches its steady-state level as time goes to infinity. This steady-state level increases with the cross-economy disturbance but declines with the convergence coefficient beta. If the initial cross-economy variance is larger than the steady-state level, sigma will decline over time to its steady-state level. On the other hand, if the initial variance is smaller than the steady-state level, sigma will rise over time to its steady-state level. They have shown in their calculations that the dispersion in log of per capita income and product across the 48 continental states of the US has declined steadily since 1880 through the mid-1970s. However the dispersion increased in the 1980s. They attributed the increase in dispersion to the oil shocks. The dispersion in log of GDP for 20 OECD countries has also followed the steady declining trend from 1950 to 1986, confirming Dowrick and Nguyen's (1989) finding. However, the dispersions in logs of income over time in large cross-country samples do not show signs of decline over time. In Barro and Sala-i-Martin's study, this dispersion for the samples of 60 and 98 countries increased gradually after the 1950s and 1960s. This lack of sigma convergence should not come as a surprise given the evidence on the lack of unconditional beta convergence across countries. A measure of conditional sigma convergence will depend on the measure of steady-state income per effective unit of labour, and this is difficult to measure.

The Relationship between Beta and Sigma Convergence

As is shown in Barro and Sala-i-Martin (1990) cross-economy variance is a negative function of beta. Everything else equal, the larger the beta, the smaller the dispersion. Beta convergence, *ceteris paribus*, will lead to sigma convergence if the initial dispersion is larger than the steady-state level, but disturbances in the economy increase the dispersion. Dowrick and Nguyen (1989) found that the dispersion in the level of per capita income for the OECD countries has declined continually over the period 1950 to 1985. Capital mobility is shown to increase the speed of convergence and beta (Barro, Mankiw and Sala-i-Martin, 1992). Thus capital mobility, in the absence of shocks, will lead to a smaller variance of the cross-economy log of per capita income.

4.3 MEASURES OF TRADE OPENNESS AND CAPITAL MOBILITY

The Measurement of Outward Orientation

There are several measures of openness and outward orientation in the literature. The simplest measure is the ratio of sum of exports and imports over GDP. This is also called the unadjusted trade intensity ratio. This measure has the advantage of being easy to compute for a large number of countries. However, there are several problems with this straightforward measure. The most important is that it does not take into account a country's resource endowment, tastes and other natural barriers to trade, which are other major determinants of trade intensity.[2]

Leamer (1988 pp. 147–200) developed an approach to get an adjusted trade intensity ratio as a measure of trade openness, which takes into account these other major determinants of trade intensity. Using 1982 trade data desegregated at the three digit SITC (Standard International Trade Classification) level, Leamer estimated an openness measure for 53 countries. In his model, trade intensity ratio is a function of resource supplies, tastes, technologies and prices. The measure of openness is the difference between the actual trade intensity ratio and the trade intensity ratio predicted by the model. Since the model implicitly assumes that the trade barriers are the only important omitted variables and that they are uncorrelated with the included variables (both of the assumptions are doubtful), the estimated measure of openness is subject to suspicion.

The author used two models to estimate the measures of openness: a factor analytic model and a regression model. In the regression model, net export is regressed on land, labour, capital, oil and coal production, minerals, distance to markets and trade balance. The adjusted trade intensity ratio, which is used as a measure of openness, is the actual trade intensity ratio minus the trade intensity ratio predicted by the model. The larger the adjusted trade intensity ratio is, the more open is a country. The measures implicitly attribute the residuals in the model completely to the trade barriers. Even though this measure is no doubt a significant improvement over the simple unadjusted trade intensity ratio, it will be unreliable if there are omitted variables that could account for a significant portion of the unexplained variability in trade. Indeed, the estimation results have left the author 'with a feeling of scepticism regarding the usefulness of the adjusted trade intensity ratios as indicators of trade barriers' (Leamer, 1988, p. 198).

Another measure of outward orientation is based on distortion and variability of the real exchange rate. Dollar (1992, pp. 523–44) estimated an index of outward orientation for 95 developing countries[3] using data on price levels reported by Summers and Heston (1991). The Dollar distortion index gauges the extent to which a country's price level is high or low relative to its endowments. In his model with panel data for 117 countries and 10 years (1976–85), price levels were regressed on country factor endowments, which were proxied by GDPs. A large positive residual is taken as an indication of inward orientation; that is, a higher price level than can be justified by the country's endowments. A large negative residual would mean a more open country. The author also found that countries with more outward oriented trade tend to grow faster than more closed countries. Since the basic approach is the same as that of Leamer, the criticisms would also apply to the estimation of Dollar's outward orientation index.

More recently, Sachs and Warner (1995a) constructed an index to measure the openness of a country to international trade. This index is the fraction of years between 1965 and 1989 that a country was considered to be open to trade. The characterization whether a country is open or closed in a particular year is based on four dimensions of the country's trade policy. They include: average tariff rates, extent of imports governed by quotas and licensing, average export taxes, and the size of the black market premium on the exchange rate.[4] Satisfying the minimum criteria on all four aspects of trade policy will qualify the country as open. The minimum criteria include: average tariffs must be lower than 40 per cent, quotas and licensing must cover less than 40 per cent of total imports, average export taxes should be moderate, and the black market premium must be less than 20 per cent. Even though this index takes into account several aspects of trade policy, the qualification criteria for openness are quite subjective.

From the above discussions, it is clear that there are different problems with each of the existing measures of trade openness. Based on my earlier work (Pan, 1996) a new approach will be used to construct an index of trade openness for a group of 140 world economies. In addition a capital mobility index is also constructed so as to get full measure of a country's outward orientation.

My approach uses direct measures of trade barriers as instituted by official government trade and foreign exchange policies. Even though some of these official barriers can often be circumvented, the presence of them will at least give an indication of the restrictiveness of the nontariff barriers and of the openness of a country's trade and financial systems.

An Index of Trade Openness (*t-open*)

In recent years there has been a continuing trend for countries to liberalize their economies. Since the integration of the goods market of a country into the world economy requires that there be fewer trade restrictions and that its currency be convertible for current account transactions, trade and foreign exchange markets reforms are two of the most important areas in the economic reform package. Exchange rate policy is one of the major tools for exports and imports controls. The imposition or tightening of exchange restrictions will impede the free international flow of goods and services and distort relative prices and reduce economic efficiency.

There are many ways a government can restrict the free flow of goods and services. Some of the most commonly used measures are foreign exchange controls for imports and exports (such as multiple exchange rates policies), import surcharges, advance import deposits and surrender or repatriation requirement for export proceeds.

The IMF publishes an annual report on Exchange Arrangements and Exchange Restrictions, in which detailed descriptions of the exchange and trade systems of individual member countries are provided. The report contains an appendix of summary features of the exchange and trading systems in member countries. It provides information on the exchange arrangements, restrictions on payments for current and capital transactions and other information on exchange rates and foreign trade. In the IMF's Exchange Arrangements and Exchange Restrictions Annual Report, the presence of the following restrictive measures is evaluated and documented. These restrictions include:

1. more than one exchange rate for imports
2. more than one exchange rate for exports
3. import exchange rate(s) different from export rate(s)
4. restrictions on payments for current transactions
5. import surcharges
6. advance import deposits
7. surrender or repatriation requirement for export proceeds.

To measure the degree of trade openness of an economy, I have calculated the average number of restrictions per year for each country in the above seven categories for the period between 1967 and 1992. The number is normalized by dividing by seven (the maximum number per year), and one minus the normalized number gives us the index of trade openness (1 = most open, 0 = closed). The trade openness index for all the 140 countries is presented in Appendix 4.1

Among the 140 countries with observations for more than half of the years between 1967 and 1992, the average index number for trade openness (*t-open*) equals 0.6723. Of the 90 countries with *t-open* greater than the average, 26 (29 per cent) of these countries are high income countries, 40 (44 per cent) are middle income, and 24 (27 per cent) are low income according to classifications of the World Bank (1993).

An Index of Capital Mobility (*k-open*)

Even though there has been a growing trend toward liberalization of financial markets in many economies in the world since the 1980s, most IMF members have imposed some restrictions on capital account transactions throughout the post-World War II period. According to the IMF's Exchange Arrangements and Exchange Restrictions Annual Report 1990, 123 of the 153 territories and member countries had restrictions on payments for capital transactions and/or used separate exchange rates for some or all capital account transactions at the end of 1989. In addition, the speed with which additional countries eliminate capital controls has not been very fast. For example, the number of industrial countries with capital account convertibility rose from three in 1975 to nine in 1990, and only one additional developing country achieved capital account convertibility (Mathieson and Rojas-Suarez, 1993, Table 1, p. 5).

There are many ways the concept of capital mobility is defined but most stem from the different ways that capital mobility is measured. I will define capital mobility as when residents of different countries can trade financial assets with residents of other countries without impediments from the governments. I will call such economies financially open and there is a high degree of, or perfect, capital mobility.

The benefits of capital mobility and financial integration were long ago noticed (Kenen, 1976). Perfect integration implies competitive efficiency in the allocation of financial resources and the allocation of the world's real capital stock. Individuals will gain by having larger sets of investment assets available to them to diversify risk and obtain the highest returns. Capital mobility will also foster a better intertemporal allocation of resources. While the advantages of capital mobility are obvious, there are disagreements on how to measure capital mobility. There have been numerous studies attempting to measure the mobility of capital across nations (Feldstein and Horioka, 1980; Frankel, 1991, 1992; Haque and Montiel, 1990, 1991; Montiel, 1994; Obstfeld, 1986; Sinn, 1992). The methodologies in these studies differ, and the authors often reach opposite conclusions.

Most of the existing literature on the measurement of capital mobility has used indirect approaches such as the estimation of the saving and investment correlation or the estimate of the covered-interest differentials. There are interpretation difficulties associated with these indirect measures. Therefore, it is desirable to have independent measures of capital controls. Epstein and Schor (1992) used the measures from the IMF annual report to construct an index of capital controls for 16 OECD countries for the period between 1967 and 1986. Their paper, however, focused on the political economy of capital controls and used the capital controls index as the left-hand-side variable in their regression analysis.

I also use the IMF's annual report to construct an index of capital mobility which is based on (i) restrictions on capital account transactions and (ii) special exchange rates for some or all capital transactions and/or some or all invisibles. The IMF annual report has indicated if such practices are present for individual countries in a given year.

The capital mobility index (*k-open*) is constructed as follows: from the IMF Annual Report on Exchange Arrangements and Exchange Restrictions, count the number of restrictions per year between 1967 and 1992 on (1) restrictions on capital account transactions and (2) special exchange rates for some or all capital transactions and/or some or all invisibles (the maximum number of restrictions per year is two if the country maintains restrictions on both (1) and (2)). Before 1967, the IMF did not make a designation about whether a restrictive practice was in place. An annual average is calculated and is normalized by dividing by two. The capital mobility index number equals one minus the normalized number (1 = most open, 0 = closed). The capital mobility index for 140 countries which have observations for more than half of the years between 1967 and 1992 is presented in Appendix 4.1

Among these countries the average number of restrictions per year equals 0.4989. There are 92 countries with annual number of restrictions above this average. Of the 92 countries, 23 (25 per cent) are high income countries, 44 (48 per cent) middle income and 25 (27 per cent) low income countries. This indicates that many of the low and middle income countries are quite financially open.

The General Openness Index (*open*)

A general openness index (*open*) of an economy is created by averaging the trade openness and capital mobility indexes. These measures of openness are used in the next section to examine the effects of openness on economic growth and global convergence. The complete listing of the general openness measure is contained in Appendix 4.1. In addition, the 140 countries are ranked in decreasing order of openness and then are divided into four quartiles. The four groups are listed in Table 4.1. Within each group, countries are listed in decreasing order of openness.

The openness index seems to be consistent with observations and other studies. Most of the developed economies and Hong Kong, Singapore, Malaysia and Indonesia are in the most open quartile. The second quartile includes Mexico, France, Belgium, Spain, Italy and Thailand. The third quartile consists of some of the less open countries from all conti-

Table 4.1 Openness rankings for 140 countries, 1967–1992

Most open quartile	Second quartile	Third quartile	Most closed quartile
Bahrain	Benin	Tanzania	Jamaica
USA	Mexico	Tunisia	Iraq
Seychelles	Honduras	Ethiopia	Equatorial Guinea
Switzerland	Fiji	Upper Volta	Guinea
Saudi Arabia	Botswana	Central Africa Rep.	Morocco
Germany	Gabon	Cyprus	South Africa
Canada	Senegal	Uganda	Western Samoa
Qatar	Spain	Lesotho	Nepal
Kuwait	Dominica	Israel	Bahamas
Oman	France	Ireland	Algeria
Hong Kong	Belgium	Sierra Leone	Argentina
Djibouti	Cameroon	Rwanda	Mauritius
Panama	St. Vincent	Venezuela	Costa Rica
Maldives	St. Lucia	Malawi	Ecuador
Lebanon	Swaziland	Congo	Iran
Liberia	Mali	Jordan	Pakistan
Netherlands	Thailand	Gambia	Laos
UAE	Haiti	India	Chile
Malaysia	Ivory Coast	Korea, Rep.	El Salvador
Japan	Togo	Yugoslavia	Peru
Singapore	Niger	Zaire	Turkey
Australia	Chad	Burundi	Somalia
New Zealand	Malta	Philippines	Ghana
Sweden	Trinidad & Tobago	Libya	Vietnam
Austria	Cape Verde Is.	Guatemala	Paraguay
Netherlands Antilles	Guinea-Bissau	Nicaragua	Afghanistan
Indonesia	Barbados	Yemen, PDR	Grenada
Denmark	Comoros	Uruguay	Bangladesh
Solomon Is.	Sao Tome & Principal	Zambia	Sudan
Finland	Mauritania	Guyana	Brazil
UK	Suriname	Greece	Dominican Republic
Yemen	Myanmar	Nigeria	Romania
Norway	Madagascar	Iceland	Syria
Papua N. Guinea	Portugal	Sri Lanka	Colombia
Bolivia	Italy	Kenya	Egypt

Source: Author's calculations.

nents, though mostly from Africa, such as Tunisia, Cyprus, Israel, Venezuela, India, Philippines and Nigeria. The most inward group includes some of the countries well known to be highly distorted: Nepal, Pakistan, Laos, Ghana and Bangladesh.

The main anomalies are countries in the Middle East that are found to be surprisingly open: Lebanon, Yemen, Oman, Kuwait, Saudi Arabia, Bahrain and Qatar. Since oil is the single most important export in most of these countries, it may not be appropriate to use the index to measure the overall openness of these countries.

An analysis of the correlation of our general openness index with other measures of outward orientation will shed some light on the usefulness of such an index. Low correlations between the measures are an indication that our openness index contains information not in the other measures. High correlations suggest, on the other hand, that our index may add little additional information. Table 4.2 presents the results.

As Table 4.2 indicates, the correlations are relatively low. Our general openness index has a correlation coefficient of only 0.34 with the Leamer index and 0.37 with the unadjusted trade intensity ratio calculated using the Heston and Summer's data set (Summers and Heston, 1997). The correlation with the Sachs and Warner openness measure is higher, at 0.53. Noticeably, the correlation coefficient with the Dollar outward orientation index is only –0.20. This low correlation is largely due to the large number of anomalies in the Dollar index. For example, the Dollar index puts countries such as Bangladesh, Nepal, Pakistan, Colombia and Peru in the most open quartile, whereas they are in the least open quartile in my index. Overall, the correlations support the contention that the general openness index contains considerable additional information about the outward orientation that is not captured in the other measures.

Table 4.2 Correlation coefficients of different measures of outward orientation

	Number of observations	Open
Unadjusted trade intensity ratio (Summers and Heston *open* variable)	130	0.37
Leamer index	53	0.34
Dollar index	111	–0.20
Sachs and Warner index	102	0.53

Sources: PWT 5.6a (1995), Leamer (1988), Dollar (1992), Sachs and Warner (1995b) and author's calculations.

4.4 THE EFFECTS OF OPENNESS ON ECONOMIC GROWTH AND GLOBAL CONVERGENCE

Test of Unconditional Convergence

To test the existence of unconditional convergence, I regress the average annual GDP per capita growth rate between 1967 and 1992 on a constant term and the log of GDP per capita in 1967 (*LGDP67*). Average growth rates of per capita GDP are calculated from GDP per capita measures in the Summers and Heston data set (Summers and Heston, 1997). The initial GDP per capita, also from the same source, is measured in 1985 constant international dollars. The regression results are reported in Table 4.3. In regressions (1) and (2), the regressions show the absence of unconditional convergence for a sample of 143 and 122 countries. Regression (2) contains a smaller sample because countries with missing observations on real GDP values for the years 1990–92 are excluded from the sample. The coefficients on initial income are either negative but insignificant or positive in these two regressions. The low R^2s indicate very poor fit of the regressions.

Test of Conditional Convergence

As discussed earlier the standard Solow-type growth models indicate conditional convergence. That is, when controlling different steady-state income, countries will converge. Many different variables have been used by researchers as controlling variables such as initial human capital endowment, the number of revolutions and coups, investment to GDP ratios and changes in terms of trade (Barro, 1991; Sachs and Warner, 1995a). Standard growth models in general stress the importance of human capital and physical capital in the growth process. Following the convention, we include more variables in the growth regression.

Regression (3) includes the average number of years of secondary schooling in 1965 from Barro and Lee (1993) and the average ratio of gross domestic investment to GDP between 1967 and 1992 from the World Bank data. The coefficient on initial income (*LGDP67*) now becomes negative and statistically significant at the 5 per cent level. In addition, the coefficients for both the initial education level and average investment rate are positive and significant at the 1 per cent level. When using gross domestic savings rate instead of investment rate in regression (4), the basic results did not change much. The regressions (3) and (4) show that there is strong evidence of conditional convergence.

Table 4.3 Growth regression, 1967–1992: dependent variable G6792, average growth of per capita GDP (1967–1992)

Independent variable	Coefficients (t-statistics)					
	(1)	(2)	(3)	(4)	(5)	(6)
No. of obs.	143	122	91	93	90	92
LGDP67	-0.17 (-0.82)	0.42 (2.07)**	-0.55 (-1.98)**	-0.76 (-2.51)***	-1.24 (-4.42)***	-1.50 (-5.10)***
Schooling (log)			1.03 (5.12)***	0.80 (3.54)***	0.67 (3.60)***	0.52 (2.75)***
Investment			11.64 (5.75)***		7.73 (4.24)***	
Savings				5.77 (3.59)***		4.20 (2.95)***
t-open						
k-open						
open						
Tropics					-1.31 (-3.62)***	-1.79 (-5.03)***
Growth of economic active population					0.68 (2.79)***	0.76 (2.97)***
Growth of dependent population					-1.19 (-5.29)***	-1.20 (-5.13)***
Adj. R sq.	-0.002	0.03	0.41	0.29	0.59	0.54

Independent variable	(7)	(8)	(9)	(10)	(11)	(12)
				Coefficients (*t*-statistics)		
No. of obs.	88	88	88	90	90	90
LGDP67	-1.26 (-4.40)***	-1.24 (-4.42)***	-1.27 (-4.51)***	-1.57 (-5.32)***	-1.53 (-5.15)***	-1.57 (-5.34)***
Schooling (log)	0.59 (2.94)***	0.53 (2.66)***	0.56 (2.85)***	0.51 (2.53)***	0.42 (2.10)**	0.47 (2.34)**
Investment	7.03 (3.82)***	7.29 (4.08)***	6.99 (3.86)***			
Savings				4.03 (2.86)***	3.87 (2.71)***	3.85 (2.73)***
t-open	1.25 (1.66)*			1.83 (2.43)**		
k-open		1.39 (2.04)**			1.50 (2.13)**	
open			1.69 (2.11)**			2.09 (2.57)***
Tropics	-1.53 (-4.14)***	-1.59 (-4.29)***	-1.60 (-4.31)***	-2.01 (-5.63)***	-2.04 (-5.64)***	-2.05 (-5.75)***
Growth Economic Active Pop.	0.90 (3.43)***	0.83 (3.38)***	0.90 (3.56)***	1.02 (3.87)***	0.92 (3.58)***	1.00 (3.86)***
Growth of Dependent Pop.	-1.25 (-5.61)***	-1.24 (-5.63)***	-1.25 (-5.67)***	-1.25 (5.48)***	-1.26 (-5.49)***	-1.26 (-5.56)***
Adj. R sq.	0.59	0.59	0.59	0.57	0.59	0.56

Notes:
*** significant at 1% level. ** significant at 5% level. * significant at 10% level. A constant term is included in all regressions, but not reported in the table.

Recent research has shown that demographics and geographic location of a country also have significant impact on the growth rate (Radelet, Sachs and Lee, 1996). In particular the faster the growth of a country's working age population, aged 15–64, the larger the workforce, hence the higher the growth rate of the economy. On the other hand, the higher the growth of the dependent population, aged under 15 or above 64, the slower the growth rate. Tropical temperature is more susceptible to the spread of diseases and therefore lowers the productivity and life expectancy of the population. It will have a negative effect on economic growth.

Regression (5) includes the growth rates of the economically active population and the dependent population and a dummy variable for tropics. The results confirm the hypothesis about population and geography. Each percentage point increase in the growth rate of the economically active population is associated with an increase in the growth of per capita income of 0.68 percentage points. Each percentage point rise in the growth of dependent population lowers the growth rate by 1.19 percentage points. A country located in the tropical zone tends to have lower growth rate, everything else being equal. The schooling and investment variables continue to be very significant. The coefficient on the initial income is negative and significant at the 1 per cent level, indicating strong conditional convergence. When using saving rate instead of investment in regression (6), similar results remain.

Adding Openness Variables

In the last several years, there has been an interesting debate on the question of economic convergence. Will poor countries grow faster than richer countries, therefore narrowing the income gap as time progresses? While theoretical models of growth with increasing-returns-to-scale production technology à la Romer (1986) predict no convergence between the rich and the poor economies, standard Solow-type growth models indicate conditional convergence. That is, if holding constant the different steady-state income levels, there will be a tendency for countries to converge. The steady-state income levels are held constant by the structural variables such as initial human capital levels and indicators of political stability. What are the effects of openness on economic growth and, therefore, on convergence among world economies? Will poor countries catch up with the more advanced countries if the more backward economies implement good economic policies? We will examine the evidence on growth and openness across countries and try to answer the above questions.

The positive effects of openness particularly in trade on economic growth has long been recognised by economists (Lewis, 1955; Krueger,

1980; Feder, 1982; Balassa, 1985; Grossman and Helpman, 1991; Dollar, 1992). It is often argued that the developing countries that are more integrated with the rest of the world will have an advantage in absorbing technological innovations generated in the advanced countries (Lewis, 1955). In addition, foreign trade will have spillover benefits.[5] Exports will raise productivity through the positive externality on the efficiency of resource allocation and capacity utilization, as well as permitting greater economies of scale (Krueger, 1980; Feder, 1982; Balassa, 1985). Recent studies have demonstrated the positive growth effects of trade through its impact on innovation, research and development and the exchange of information and knowledge among the trading partners (Grossman and Helpman, 1991).

Many empirical studies on economic growth and trade liberalization have found that openness, usually measured by the total of exports and imports to GDP ratio, has contributed positively to the growth performance of a country. It is generally agreed that the fast economic growth of Southeast Asian countries over the last two decades is partially due to the export oriented trade policies.

In order to examine the effect of openness on economic growth,[6] we next add the index measures of openness from Section 4.3 to the growth regression.

Regression (7) includes the index of trade openness. It is positive and significant at the 10 per cent level. With a coefficient of 1.25, a country with an open trade policy will grow 1.25 percentage points faster than a closed economy, *ceteris paribus*. Regression (8) uses the capital mobility index in the regression; the coefficient of the capital mobility index is 1.39 and statistically significant at the 5 per cent level. With the general 'open' index, which is the average of two indexes in regression (9), the coefficient is 1.69 and significant at 5 per cent. This means, a country that is open in both trade and finance will grow 1.69 percentage points faster per year than a completely closed economy. The coefficients of other variables did not change much.

With a magnitude of –1.27, the coefficient on initial income suggests that each percentage point rise in per capita income in 1967 reduces subsequent annual growth by 0.013 percentage points. Each doubling of the initial (1967) income will reduce the subsequent annual growth by 0.88 percentage points. These results are about the same of what has been found by Sachs and Warner (1995a).

Regressions (10), (11) and (12) use savings rate instead of investment rate and include '*t-open*', '*k-open*' and '*open*' variables respectively. The coefficients of these openness variables are somewhat larger than before, and the savings variable is very significant. The schooling variable becomes less significant. However, in all cases, the coefficient on the initial GDP is highly significant, which indicates strong conditional convergence.

The above analysis shows that there is a strong positive effect of openness on economic growth. The estimates show that, everything else equal, a country with open trade will grow 1.25 percentage points faster than a country closed to international trade. A country will grow 1.39 percentage points faster if it is financially integrated with the international community than otherwise. (We use estimates from regressions (7), (8) and (9), using investment rather than savings rate because these regressions give a better fit and a more significant schooling variable.) Integration with the world economy both in trade and in financial market will help a country grow 1.69 percentage points faster. The evidence supports the hypothesis of conditional global convergence while there is no sign of countries converging unconditionally.

4.5   CONCLUSION AND POLICY IMPLICATIONS

This chapter has constructed indexes to measure the openness of a country both in foreign trade and financially using information from the IMF annual report on exchange agreements and exchange restrictions. The effect of openness on economic growth and convergence is studied in a neoclassical growth framework. The results confirmed what has been found by others: that there is conditional global convergence among countries. Moreover it has quantified the effects of trade openness and capital mobility on economic growth. The results, interpreted directly from the regressions, show that the sacrifice in economic growth rates when a country changes from an open economy to a closed economy is about 1.69 percentage points per year. The study shows that a more open economy will lead to faster economic growth. This conclusion lends strong support for the argument of trade and financial liberalization.[7]

However one should put less faith on the absolute magnitude of the effect of openness on growth derived from the regression model than on the direction of the impact because the robustness of the model requires more thorough examination. In addition, there may be two-way causality between openness and economic growth. Therefore, more detailed study is warranted on the timing of economic policies and the subsequent growth performance of individual countries. Further research is also warranted to examine the effect of openness on the dispersion of income across countries and over time.

APPENDIX 4.1

Table 4.A1 Indexes of trade openness and capital mobility, 1967–1992

Number	Country	t-open	k-open	open
1	Afghanistan	0.23077	0.23077	0.23077
2	Algeria	0.69231	0.15385	0.42308
3	Argentina	0.39011	0.42308	0.40659
4	Australia	0.87912	0.63462	0.75687
5	Austria	0.95604	0.51923	0.73764
6	Bahamas	0.85714	0.00000	0.42857
7	Bahrain	1.00000	1.00000	1.00000
8	Bangladesh	0.40000	0.02500	0.21250
9	Barbados	0.71429	0.50000	0.60714
10	Belgium & Lux	0.74725	0.53846	0.64286
11	Benin	0.85714	0.50000	0.67857
12	Bolivia	0.58791	0.76923	0.67857
13	Botswana	0.79167	0.52083	0.65625
14	Brazil	0.31319	0.07692	0.19505
15	Burundi	0.58333	0.50000	0.54167
16	Cameroon	0.82418	0.46154	0.64286
17	Canada	0.98352	1.00000	0.99176
18	Cape Verde	0.71429	0.50000	0.60714
19	Central African Rep.	0.71978	0.42308	0.57143
20	Chad	0.76923	0.46154	0.61538
21	Chile	0.58242	0.09615	0.33929
22	Colombia	0.05495	0.05769	0.05632
23	Comoros	0.71429	0.50000	0.60714
24	Congo	0.66429	0.44231	0.55330
25	Costa Rica	0.50549	0.28846	0.39698
26	Cote d'Ivoire	0.78571	0.46154	0.62363
27	Cyprus	0.63736	0.50000	0.56868
28	Denmark	0.87363	0.57692	0.72527
29	Djibouti	0.88776	1.00000	0.94388
30	Dominica	0.82653	0.46429	0.64541
31	Dominican Rep.	0.16484	0.21154	0.18819
32	Ecuador	0.30769	0.48077	0.39423
33	Egypt	0.08844	0.00000	0.04422
34	El Salvador	0.34066	0.30769	0.32418
35	Equatorial Guinea	0.72050	0.23913	0.47981
36	Ethiopia	0.65934	0.50000	0.57967

The fabric of global economic growth

Table 4.A1 (continued)

Number	Country	t-open	k-open	open
37	Fiji	0.82313	0.50000	0.66156
38	Finland	0.90659	0.51923	0.71291
39	France	0.84615	0.44231	0.64423
40	Gabon	0.84615	0.46154	0.65385
41	Gambia	0.70286	0.40000	0.55143
42	Germany	0.99451	1.00000	0.99725
43	Ghana	0.36264	0.23077	0.29670
44	Greece	0.51099	0.50000	0.50549
45	Grenada	0.38655	0.05882	0.22269
46	Guatemala	0.49451	0.57692	0.53571
47	Guinea	0.43407	0.50000	0.46703
48	Guinea-Bissau	0.71429	0.50000	0.60714
49	Guyana	0.60989	0.40385	0.50687
50	Haiti	0.75275	0.50000	0.62637
51	Honduras	0.65934	0.67308	0.66621
52	Hong Kong	0.96154	0.96154	0.96154
53	Iceland	0.59341	0.40385	0.49863
54	India	0.59890	0.50000	0.54945
55	Indonesia	0.58791	0.86538	0.72665
56	Iran	0.40659	0.36538	0.38599
57	Iraq	0.58242	0.38462	0.48352
58	Ireland	0.85714	0.26923	0.56319
59	Israel	0.64835	0.48077	0.56456
60	Italy	0.78571	0.38462	0.58516
61	Jamaica	0.56044	0.42308	0.49176
62	Japan	0.92857	0.75000	0.83929
63	Jordan	0.60440	0.50000	0.55220
64	Kenya	0.49451	0.50000	0.49725
65	Korea	0.59890	0.50000	0.54945
66	Kuwait	0.97802	0.96154	0.96978
67	Laos	0.46286	0.22917	0.34601
68	Lebanon	0.81319	1.00000	0.90659
69	Lesotho	0.83929	0.29167	0.56548
70	Liberia	0.90659	0.86538	0.88599
71	Libya	0.57692	0.50000	0.53846
72	Madagascar	0.70330	0.48077	0.59203
73	Malawi	0.60989	0.50000	0.55495
74	Malaysia	0.82418	0.86538	0.84478

Number	Country	t-open	k-open	open
75	Maldives	0.85714	0.96429	0.91071
76	Mali	0.82967	0.44231	0.63599
77	Malta	0.72024	0.50000	0.61012
78	Mauritania	0.74725	0.46154	0.60440
79	Mauritius	0.63095	0.16667	0.39881
80	Mexico	0.71978	0.63462	0.67720
81	Morocco	0.65934	0.25000	0.45467
82	Myanmar	0.69780	0.50000	0.59890
83	Nepal	0.35714	0.50000	0.42857
84	Netherlands	1.00000	0.73077	0.86538
85	Netherlands Antilles	0.76374	0.69231	0.72802
86	New Zealand	0.85165	0.65385	0.75275
87	Nicaragua	0.50000	0.53846	0.51923
88	Niger	0.77473	0.46154	0.61813
89	Nigeria	0.62088	0.38462	0.50275
90	Norway	0.86813	0.50000	0.68407
91	Oman	0.97959	0.95238	0.96599
92	Pakistan	0.37912	0.38462	0.38187
93	Panama	0.88462	1.00000	0.94231
94	Papua New Guinea	0.85714	0.50000	0.67857
95	Paraguay	0.24176	0.23077	0.23626
96	Peru	0.40659	0.23077	0.31868
97	Philippines	0.52198	0.55769	0.53984
98	Portugal	0.67033	0.50000	0.58516
99	Qatar	1.00000	0.97500	0.98750
100	Romania	0.30000	0.00000	0.15000
101	Rwanda	0.61538	0.50000	0.55769
102	St. Lucia	0.78022	0.50000	0.64011
103	St. Vincent & Grenadines	0.78022	0.50000	0.64011
104	Sao Tome and Principe	0.71429	0.50000	0.60714
105	Saudi Arabia	0.99451	1.00000	0.99725
106	Senegal	0.84066	0.46154	0.65110
107	Seychelles	1.00000	1.00000	1.00000
108	Sierra Leone	0.64286	0.48077	0.56181
109	Singapore	0.88462	0.76923	0.82692
110	Solomon Isl.	0.85714	0.57143	0.71429
111	Somalia	0.31319	0.28846	0.30082
112	South Africa	0.65385	0.25000	0.45192
113	Spain	0.79670	0.50000	0.64835

Table 4.A1 (continued)

Number	Country	t-open	k-open	open
114	Sri Lanka	0.62143	0.37500	0.49821
115	Sudan	0.14835	0.25000	0.19918
116	Suriname	0.70807	0.50000	0.60404
117	Swaziland	0.83851	0.43478	0.63665
118	Sweden	1.00000	0.50000	0.75000
119	Switzerland	1.00000	1.00000	1.00000
120	Syria	0.19780	0.05769	0.12775
121	Tanzania	0.67033	0.50000	0.58516
122	Thailand	0.76923	0.50000	0.63462
123	Togo	0.78022	0.46154	0.62088
124	Trinidad & Tobago	0.73626	0.48077	0.60852
125	Tunisia	0.66484	0.50000	0.58242
126	Turkey	0.31319	0.30769	0.31044
127	Uganda	0.69231	0.44231	0.56731
128	UAE	0.89143	0.80000	0.84571
129	UK	0.89011	0.50000	0.69505
130	USA	1.00000	1.00000	1.00000
131	Upper Volta	0.73810	0.41667	0.57738
132	Uruguay	0.39011	0.63462	0.51236
133	Venezuela	0.57143	0.53846	0.55495
134	Viet Nam	0.42857	0.06000	0.24429
135	Western Samoa	0.54422	0.35714	0.45068
136	Rep. Yemen	0.66234	0.71739	0.68986
137	Yemen, PDR of	0.57857	0.45000	0.51429
138	Yugoslavia	0.59341	0.50000	0.54670
139	Zaire	0.61224	0.47619	0.54422
140	Zambia	0.57692	0.44231	0.50962

Source: IMF Annual Report on Exchange Arrangements and Exchange Restrictions. Various issues.

APPENDIX 4.2: DATA SOURCES

1. World Tables (1993)

Savings and investment shares in GDP used in the estimation are from the World Tables (1993) in disk format.

2. Penn World Table (Mark 5.6)

The Penn World Tables data set is often referred to as the Summers and Heston data set named after two of the original members on the team which constructed the data set.

One variable from this data source is the real GDP per capita in 1985 international prices (the variable *RGDPL* in the Penn World Table). The *RGDPL* variable is used in the growth and convergence regressions to get the initial income and average growth rate measures from *RDGPL*. Another variable is the measure of openness.

3. IMF Exchange Arrangements and Exchange Restrictions annual report

The annual reports of the International Monetary Fund – Exchange Arrangements and Exchange Restrictions are used to construct the '*t-open*' and '*k-open*' indexes. Specifically, I mainly used the appendix of Summary Features of Exchange and Trade Systems in Member Countries in the IMF annual report.

4. Barro and Lee data on educational attainment (schooling)

The data on initial schooling are supplied by the World Bank on a diskette which contains data used in the article 'International comparisons of educational attainment' by Robert Barro and Jong-Wha Lee. The paper was published in the *Journal of Monetary Economics*, **32**(3), December 1993, 363–94.

5. World population prospects 1950–2050, United Nations

Data on working age and dependant population are from this UN publication (1994 revision) in electronic format.

NOTES

1. I would like to thank Professor Bruce Bolnick, Professor John Adams and Professor Gustav Schachter of Northeastern University for their guidance and comments on my dissertation on which this paper is based. An earlier version of this paper was presented at the 20th Annual Northeast Regional Science Association Meetings in Boston, 29 May–1 June 1997 and at the Conference on Economic Growth and Change: A Comparative Perspective, held on 19–22 June 1997 in Cagliari, Italy. I thank the participants for useful comments.
2. The government can encourage or discourage the imports or exports of types of goods and services by groups or domestic producers by affecting the cost and availability of

foreign exchange. To control imports, advance import deposits can be required. Other measures such as the surrender of export proceeds and import surcharges are also used by governments in many developing countries.

3. The number is negative because the Dollar index measures the real exchange rate distortion and variability with a higher number indicating more distortion and more closure of an economy.

4. I thank Steve Radelet of HIID for offering me the opportunity to work on the Asian Development Bank growth project at the Harvard Institute for International Development (HIID) during 1996, especially for many of the discussions on some of these variables.

5. Findlay (1984) and Smith (1984) provide excellent surveys on the relation between trade and economic growth.

6. See Edwards (1989) for a critical review of the empirical evidence on trade regimes and economic performance in developing countries.

7. If we double the income of 1967, the variable $LGDP67$ will become $\ln (2 * GDP67) = \ln 2 + \ln GDP67 = \ln 2 + LGDP67$. If the coefficient on $LGDP67 = -1.27$, the change in the dependent variable, $G6792$ as a result of doubling initial income will be $-1.27 * \ln 2 = 0.88$ percentage points. Similarly, if we increase initial income by 1%, $LGDP67$ will become $\ln [(1/100 + 1)GDP67] = \ln 1.01 + LGDP67$. With coefficient of -1.27, the growth rate will decrease by $1.27 * \ln 1.01 = 0.013$ percentage points.

REFERENCES

Balassa, Bela (1985), 'Exports, policy choices, and economic growth in developing countries after the 1973 oil shock', *Journal of Development Economics*, **18**, 23–35.

Barro, Robert J. (1991), 'Economic growth in a cross section of countries', *Quarterly Journal of Economics*, **106** (2), 407– 44.

Barro, Robert J. and Jong-Wha Lee (1993), 'International comparisons of educational attainment', *Journal of Monetary Economics*, **32** (3), 363–94.

Barro, Robert, N.G. Mankiw and X. Sala-i-Martin (1992), 'Capital mobility in neoclassical models of growth', NBER Working Paper no. 4206.

Barro, Robert and Xavier Sala-i-Martin (1990), 'Economic growth and convergence across the United States', NBER Working Paper no. 3419.

Barro, Robert and Xavier Sala-i-Martin (1991), 'Convergence across states and regions', *Brookings Papers on Economic Activity*, **1**, 107–82.

Barro, Robert and Xavier Sala-i-Martin (1992), 'Convergence', *Journal of Political Economy*, **100** (2), 223–51.

Barro, Robert and Xavier Sala-i-Martin (1995), *Economic Growth*, New York: McGraw-Hill.

Dollar, David (1992), 'Outward-oriented developing economies really do grow more rapidly: evidence from 95 LDCs, 1976–1985', *Economic Development and Cultural Change*, **40** (3), 523–44.

Dowrick, Steve and Duc-Tho Nguyen (1989), 'OECD comparative economic growth 1950–85: catch-up and convergence', *American Economic Review*, **179** (5), 1010–30.

Edwards, Sebastian (1989), 'Openness, outward orientation, trade liberalization and economic performance in developing countries', NBER Working Paper no. 2908.

Epstein, Gerald A. and Juliet B. Schor (1992), 'Structural Determinants and Economic Effects of Capital Controls in OECD Countries', in Banuri and Schor (eds), *Financial Openness and National Autonomy – Opportunities and Constraints*, Oxford: Clarendon Press, pp. 136–61.

Feder, G. (1982), 'On exports and economic growth', *Journal of Development Economics*, **12**, 59–73.

Feldstein, M. and C. Horioka (1980), 'Domestic saving and international capital flows', *The Economic Journal*, **90**, 314–29.

Findlay, R. (1984), 'Growth and Development in Trade Models', in R. Jones and P. Kenen (eds), *Handbook of International Economics*, Vol. I, Amsterdam: North-Holland.

Frankel, Jeffrey A. (1991), 'Quantifying International Capital Mobility in the 1980s', in Bernheim and Shoven (eds), *National Saving and Economic Performance*, Chicago: The University of Chicago Press, pp. 227–60.

Frankel, Jeffrey A. (1992), 'Measuring international capital mobility: a review', *American Economic Review*, **82** (2), 197–202.

Grossman, Gene M. and Elhanan Helpman (1990), 'Comparative advantage and long-run growth', *American Economic Review*, **80**, 796–815.

Grossman, Gene M. and Elhanan Helpman (1991), *Innovation and Growth in the Global Economy*, Cambridge, MA: MIT Press.

Haque, Nadeem Ul and Peter J. Montiel (1990), 'How mobile is capital in developing countries?', *Economics Letters*, **33**, 359–62.

Haque, Nadeem and Peter J. Montiel (1991), 'Capital mobility in developing countries: some empirical tests', *World Development*, **19** (10), 1391–8.

Kenen, Peter B. (1976), 'Capital Mobility and Financial Integration: A Survey', *Princeton Studies in International Finance*, no. 39, Princeton, NJ: Princeton University Press.

Krueger, Anne (1980), 'Trade policy as an input to development', *American Economic Review*, **7**, 288–92.

Leamer, Edward E. (1988), 'Measures of Openness', in Robert E. Baldwin (ed.), *Trade Policy Issues and Empirical Analysis*, Chicago and London: University of Chicago Press, pp. 147–200.

Lewis, Arthur (1955), *The Theory of Economic Growth*, London: Allen & Unwin.

Mathieson Donald J. and Liliana Rojas-Suarez (1993), 'Liberalization of the capital account experiences and issues', Occasional Paper, 103, March, Washington, DC: International Monetary Fund.

Montiel, Peter J. (1994), 'Capital mobility in developing countries: some measurement issues and empirical estimates', *The World Bank Economic Review*, **8** (3), 311–50.

Obstfeld, Maurice (1986), 'Capital mobility in the world economy: theory and measurement', *Carnegie–Rochester Conference Series on Public Policy*, **24**, Spring, 55–104.

Pan, Hui (1996), 'Openness, convergence, and the efficient allocation of capital', Ph.D. Dissertation, Boston: Northeastern University.

Radelet, Steve, Jeffrey Sachs and Jong-Wha Lee (1996), 'Economic growth in Asia', mimeo, Boston: Harvard Institute for International Development.

Romer, Paul M. (1986), 'Increasing returns and long-run growth', *Journal of Political Economy*, **94** (5), 1002–37.

Sachs, Jeffrey D. and Andrew M. Warner (1995a), 'Economic convergence and economic policies', NBER Working Paper no. 5039.

Sachs, Jeffrey D. and Andrew M. Warner (1995b), 'Economic reform and the process of global integration', *Brookings Papers on Economic Activity*, **0** (1), 1–95.

Sinn, Stefan (1992), 'Saving–investment correlations and capital mobility: on the evidence from annual data', *The Economic Journal*, **102**, September, 1162–70.

Smith, M.A. (1984), 'Capital Theory and Trade Theory', in R. Jones and P. Kenen (eds), *Handbook of International Economics*. Vol. I, Amsterdam: North-Holland.

Summers, R. and A. Heston (1991), 'The Penn World Table (Mark 5): an expanded set of international comparisons, 1950–1988', *Quarterly Journal of Economics*, **106**, 327–68.

Summers, R. and A. Heston (1997), 'The Penn World Table (Mark 5.6)', available on diskette from the National Bureau of Economic Research, Cambridge, MA.

United Nations (1994), 'World population prospects 1950–2050', 1994 revision, electronic data, New York.

World Bank (1993), *World Tables*.

5. R&D, technology and economic growth

Livio Cricelli and Agostino La Bella

5.1 INTRODUCTION

It is generally believed that economic growth in the modern era has been grounded on the exploitation of scientific knowledge. As a result, national science policies, at least in the most developed countries, have tended to become more strongly interventionist and more explicitly committed to planning and management in this field, even in a period of general retreat of government influence.

The foundations of modern growth theory were laid in the 1950s by R. Solow (1957) and M. Abramovitz (1956). They found that capital accumulation and changing labour conditions explained only a fraction of the secular growth of labour productivity; the residual is attributed to exogenous technical progress.

Solow's growth model, based on standard neoclassical assumptions (perfect competition, maximizing behaviour, no externalities, positive and decreasing marginal productivities, production functions homogeneous of degree one, and so on) describes an economy whose output grows in response to larger inputs of capital and labour.

Together, the above assumptions give to neoclassical growth models two crucial implications. First, as the stock of capital expands, growth slows and eventually halts: to keep growing, the economy must benefit from continual infusions of technological progress. Yet this is a force that the model itself makes no attempt to explain, and is left exogenous (Solow's residuals). The second implication is that poorer countries should grow faster than rich ones. The reason is diminishing returns: since poor countries start with less capital, they should get higher marginal returns on investments.

Many empirical studies (see for instance Nelson, 1981) since Solow's pioneering work have confirmed the first implication, showing that capital accumulation and changing labour conditions explained only a fraction of the rate of economic growth of developed countries. The second implication, however, has so far received only partial and contradictory empirical evidence (Fagerberg, 1987). Further attempts have therefore been made for a better understanding of the role of technical progress in preserving the potential for growth, building new growth models able to include technological innovation among the endogenous variables.

The rising importance of technology in modern growth theory (Dosi *et al.*, 1988; Nelson and Winter, 1982) originates from its nature as a non-rival and partially non-excludable good. That is, when an agent uses a given technology to produce a good or service, this action does not preclude other agents from doing so, even simultaneously: in other words, the cost of an additional user is zero. This is what distinguishes technology from other production factors such as capital equipment. Moreover, the creators or the owners of technical information, in spite of several forms of legal protection extended to patents (a patent is in itself a form of disclosure, which can lead to artful imitation in forms that make property rights not applicable), may have difficulties in preventing others from making unauthorized use of it. An invention, however protected, almost always generates additions of various importance (spillovers) to the stock of general knowledge, readily available to everybody. This attribute also differentiates technology from capital equipment, which is easily excludable. Technological spillovers have a prominent role in new growth theory.

Since the mid-1980s a good deal of research effort, both theoretical and empirical, has focused on the various issues related to economic growth. A large portion of the literature deals with the so called 'convergence problem', that is, with the attempt to interpret time series data on growth rate across many different countries to verify whether any 'catching-up' processes in terms of per capita output can be detected and explained. Another important line of research focuses on the determinants of growth. In this frame the relations between government policies and growth have been widely investigated; also, much attention has been devoted to the impact of R&D expenditure on such variables as patented inventions, trade performance, productivity and growth. It must be said that, in spite of many scholarly works, we still have contrasting empirical results and no clear-cut evidence of the prevailing mechanisms of growth. What we can be sure of does not feature the impact of any single factor of growth, but the whole package, which certainly matters a lot.

The aim of this chapter is that of contributing, with the support of some empirical data, to the analysis of one of the fundamental problems of the 'new' growth theory, that is, the relationship between technological innovation and productivity. Our discussion is based on the the results of statistical tests involving two fundamental variables. The first is a measure of the level of accumulated technical knowledge, while the second is an estimate of the total factor productivity (TFP).

The following section is devoted to a short review of the fundamental mechanisms of the 'new' models of growth. Then, in Section 5.3, we present our database, including 21-year time series from 15 developed countries, and a preliminary test on the hypothesis that R&D expenditure favours growth. As we shall see, a simple analysis is not conducive to conclusive results. In Section 5.4, we discuss along strictly neoclassical guidelines the measure of TFP for all countries of our sample, while, in Section 5.5, we formulate a model of the knowledge accumulation process and estimate a relationship between productivity and the stock of knowledge. The analysis is completed in Section 5.6, where we prove the existence of a positive correlation between the rate of knowledge accumulation and the TFP growth rate; also, we get a strong indication that increasing returns to scale govern the generation of technical knowledge.

5.2 NEOCLASSICAL VERSUS 'NEW' GROWTH MODELS

Production functions are the base of neoclassical growth models. They incorporate the two conventional factors, that is, capital and labour. To attain growth, the economy increases its capital stock by net investment, which is calculated as the difference between savings and the depreciation of the capital stock itself; as a result, we have more capital per unit of labour and therefore more aggregated output. But, as a result of capital accumulation and because of diminishing returns, at some point gross investment just covers the depreciation of capital: the system will therefore reach a steady state unless exogenous productivity gains intervene to preserve the incentives for new investment (Figure 5.1).

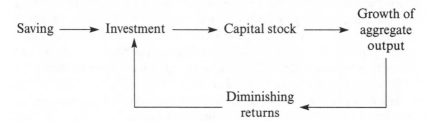

Figure 5.1 The neoclassical model of growth

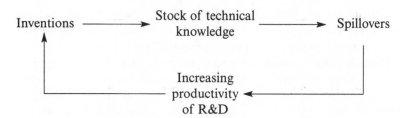

Figure 5.2 The positive feedback in the generation of technical knowledge

By contrast, in the new growth models investment incentives are endogenously maintained by technological spillovers, which allow successive generations of researchers to achieve technological breakthroughs using fewer resources than their predecessors (Figure 5.2).

The resulting decline in the real cost of invention counteracts any tendency for profits to fall: the process of knowledge accumulation generates endogenously the productivity gains that sustain growth in the long run. It should be stressed that this line of thought is strongly based on the belief that the rate of return to invention is kept sufficiently high to sustain growth. Should it fall too low, the process of innovation may grind to a halt, because the contribution of technology to capital productivity, that we have assumed to exceed the diminishing returns, may in its turn become lower and lower. However, the economic properties of technology, and in particular the non-rivalry, suggest that this need not occur.

As a matter of fact, there are many reasons to believe that resources invested in R&D will continue to yield positive and non-diminishing contributions to the stock of knowledge into the indefinite future. First, there is nothing in the history of science, technology and innovation (Singer *et al.*, 1958) to suggest that we are exhausting the potential of scientific advance. Secondly, following Schumpeter (1942, 1947), we can contrast invention with the cultivation of new plots of land. Cultivation must run into diminishing returns because it is to be expected that the more productive plots are cultivated first. Instead, from the fact that some technological possibilities have been explored before others it cannot be inferred that the former were more productive than the latter (the experience being exactly opposite). Those opportunities that are still completely unexplored may be more or less productive than any that have so far come within the range of observation.

The point above can be proved by the following thought experiment. Assume a production function having both tangible and non-tangible arguments:

$$Y = F(T, K, L, ...)$$

where K and L are the neoclassical capital and labour factors, which are rival inputs to production, while T represents the stock of knowledge, non-rival by definition. If we want to double production, we may in principle think of duplicating the process. To do that, however, we would need to double all tangible inputs, while we need not duplicate the non-rival inputs like T, obtaining:

$$2Y = F(T, 2K, 2L, ...) \quad \text{and} \quad F(\alpha T, 2K, 2L, ...) > 2Y \quad \text{for any } 1 < \alpha < 2$$

Then, if T increases, output should increase still further. Therefore the marginal product of knowledge need not decline as more knowledge is accumulated. Figure 5.3 shows the overall functioning of 'new growth' models, where the positive feedback (increasing returns) in the generation of technical knowledge overcompensates the negative feedback (diminishing returns) in the production process.

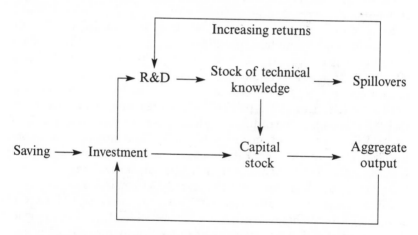

Figure 5.3 The 'new' model of growth

We can therefore conclude that:

- only technical progress can explain secular trends of economic growth;
- technology is a partial public good: it is non-rival and partially excludable; the latter property guarantees that it can be produced by the private sector (even if not in sufficient quantity for a social optimum), while the former allows some of it to 'spill over' and become available to everybody;

- the above spillovers ensure that there are no diminishing returns in the production of technological knowledge, and that economic growth based on knowledge accumulation may continue for ever; and,
- technological spillovers have two contrasting effects: from one side, reducing the appropriability of knowledge, they discourage its private production, forcing governments to intervene in the R&D sector; from the other, it is only through them that the continuous growth process mentioned above may take place.

5.3 R&D AND GDP: A FIRST EMPIRICAL ANALYSIS

Several authors have claimed that the growth rate of real per capita GDP has no secular tendency to decline (see for instance Barro and Sala-i-Martin, 1995). We accept that claim, even if our 21-year database does not allow us to support it empirically. Actually, in the short run we may even notice a slowdown of productivity.

Most of our analysis is based on data from 15 countries: the G-7, the four Scandinavian countries, plus Spain, Ireland, The Netherlands and Australia. The time series is limited because of the difficulties of obtaining reliable data on R&D expenditures on a cross-country base. Our data, taken from several OECD publications and from *The Penn World Table (Mark 5)* span from 1973 to 1993. All figures are given in real terms in 1985 US dollars. Two different deflators have been used for GDP and R&D expenditures on one side, and capital stock on the other. Comparisons among the various countries have been done using Purchasing Power Parity, rather than the official exchange rate. For Germany we use data until 1990, the year of German reunification.

Figure 5.4 shows the evolution with time of domestic GDP for the 15 countries of our sample. There is a clear overall tendency to experience growth even if with considerable oscillations. The average annual growth rates, given in Table 5.1, appear very different, ranging from 1.01 per cent for Sweden to 3.29 per cent for Ireland. Moreover, with the exception of Ireland, which shows a continuously increasing growth rate, for all other countries a tendency to decreasing rates of growth can be observed. We do not attempt here any explanation of this phenomenon, the study of which would probably require a much longer time series. Rather, we aim at verifying the existence of a relationship between a country's economic performance, measured by its per capita GDP, and the size of its effort in the internal generation and/or adoption of technological innovations, measured by its expenditure on R&D as a percentage of GDP.

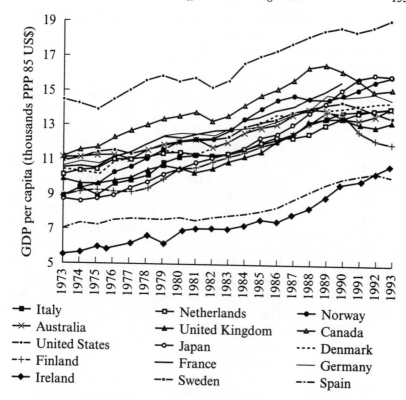

Figure 5.4 Per capita GDP in our sample countries, 1973–1993

Such a relationship is shown in Figure 5.5, as a result of a simple regression analysis, with a level of statistical significance at 5 per cent. As expected the R&D effort appears positively related to per capita GERD; however, the low level of the correlation coefficient suggests great caution in the interpretation of that result.

Actually, a closer look at the relationship in Figure 5.5 reveals that all countries with a comparatively large volume of R&D expenditures are placed below the regression line, the only exception being the US. Moreover, removing the outliers (US, Spain and Ireland), we find a substantial independence between the two variables considered: that is, all the countries in our samples fall into two clusters with similar average performance but completely different average R&D effort.

A further complication concerning any conclusions about the influence of R&D on economic performance is added by the raw data in Table 5.1, where an overall tendency to decreasing growth rates (at least within the

Table 5.1 Per capita GDP annual growth rate (A) and average GERD/ GDP% (B) in several time intervals

Country	1973–79 A	1973–79 B	1980–89 A	1980–89 B	1990–93 A	1990–93 B	1973–93 A	1973–93 B
Australia	1.06	1.06	1.62	1.14	1.56	1.59	1.18	1.20
Canada	2.81	1.14	2.25	1.35	-2.14	1.49	1.45	1.31
Denmark	1.66	0.93	2.08	1.27	0.92	1.70	1.59	1.24
Finland	1.74	0.95	3.04	1.51	-4.41	2.10	1.42	1.44
France	2.32	1.76	2.04	2.14	-0.32	2.41	1.55	2.07
Germany	2.53	2.09	2.03	2.67	–	–	2.21	2.44
Ireland	2.00	0.53	2.75	0.75	3.33	1.00	3.29	0.72
Italy	3.21	0.78	1.98	1.05	0.61	1.35	2.25	1.01
Japan	2.41	1.78	3.52	2.61	1.65	2.98	2.95	2.40
Netherlands	1.89	1.93	1.41	2.05	0.94	1.93	1.53	1.99
Norway	4.35	1.14	2.13	1.38	2.22	1.45	2.85	1.31
Spain	1.30	0.35	2.49	0.56	0.48	0.85	1.76	0.55
Sweden	1.48	1.81	1.82	2.67	-2.23	2.95	1.01	2.44
United Kingdom	1.48	2.23	2.70	2.27	-0.54	2.14	1.48	2.23
United States	1.43	2.29	1.86	2.70	0.74	2.64	1.33	2.55

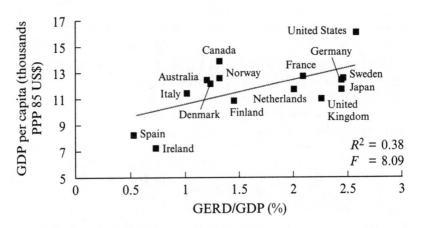

Figure 5.5 Relationship between average per capita GDP in the time interval 1973–1993 and the average expenditure on R&D as a percentage of GDP

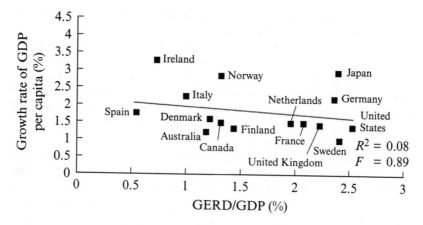

Figure 5.6 Relationship between the average GDP growth rate and the GERD/GDP ratio

time span under consideration) corresponds to increasing levels of R&D expenditure. That observation is further confirmed by the analysis of the correlation between average growth rates and the same R&D indicator used above. The results, shown in Figure 5.6, reveal an unexpected, even if weak, negative correlation. Given the statistical weakness, those results also cannot be taken as conclusive. It all amounts to saying that the hypothesis that R&D expenditure favours growth is not easy to test. Rather, from what we have seen so far, it seems that greater and richer countries tend to invest more in R&D simply because they have larger availabilities of human and financial resources. To prove the existence of a significant economic impact of R&D activities more sophisticated analyses are required.

5.4 A NEOCLASSICAL ANALYSIS

In this section we present the result of an analysis performed along standard neoclassical guidelines. We assume constant returns to scale and a Cobb–Douglas production function such as:

$$Y = A(t)K^{1-\alpha}L^{\alpha} \tag{5.1}$$

where, as usual, L and K stand for the two classical labour and capital factors. Coefficient α is the labour share, while function $A(t)$ represents the total factor productivity (TFP), that is, that portion of income not explained by capital and labour. Our goal here is to study its level of correlation with R&D. We shall start measuring TFP according to (5.1), where GDP is taken as Y, L is given by the number of workers and K is the net capital stock (thus implicitly including in our analysis the depreciation of capital). We shall also assume $\alpha=0.4$ as the average value among our sample countries over the period under consideration. This assumption, which is beyond any doubt a rough approximation, is in accordance with many cross-section studies in the literature (OECD, 1996a,b; Dougherty, 1991; Fare *et al.*, 1994).

A first assessment of the importance of TFP in the growth process can be obtained from Table 5.2 and Figure 5.7, which show the average growth rates of GDP for the various countries in our sample, decomposed according to the respective contributions of labour, capital and TFP.

We observe many different situations, ranging from countries with a high growth rate of TFP both in absolute terms and as a contribution to the GDP growth (Ireland, Norway), to countries where TFP grows at a low rate (US, The Netherlands). This result must be taken with extreme caution, given the limits of our analysis. We have assumed a constant

Table 5.2 Decomposition of GDP growth rates (annual averages) according to TFP, labour and capital contributions

Country	GDP growth rate	TFP growth rate		Labour contribution		Capital contribution	
Australia	2.55	0.76	30.57%	0.85	33.57%	0.91	35.86%
Canada	2.81	0.42	15.68%	1.03	36.49%	1.34	47.83%
Denmark	1.76	0.92	52.63%	0.20	11.56%	0.63	35.81%
Finland	1.84	0.92	50.11%	–0.18	–9.66%	1.10	59.55%
France	2.07	0.59	29.00%	0.13	6.25%	1.34	64.75%
Germany	2.34	1.14	49.44%	0.17	7.41%	1.01	43.15%
Ireland	4.03	1.99	50.51%	0.17	4.25%	1.82	45.24%
Italy	2.46	0.76	31.33%	0.18	7.14%	1.52	61.53%
Japan	3.66	0.77	21.91%	0.61	16.80%	2.24	61.29%
Netherlands	2.19	0.12	6.01%	0.68	31.21%	1.37	62.79%
Norway	3.29	1.76	54.47%	0.54	16.45%	0.96	29.08%
Spain	2.36	1.16	49.78%	–0.25	–10.57%	1.43	60.80%
Sweden	1.38	0.24	18.04%	0.07	4.73%	1.06	77.24%
United Kingdom	1.65	0.96	58.53%	0.04	2.40%	0.65	39.07%
United States	2.33	0.05	2.68%	1.02	43.69%	1.25	53.62%

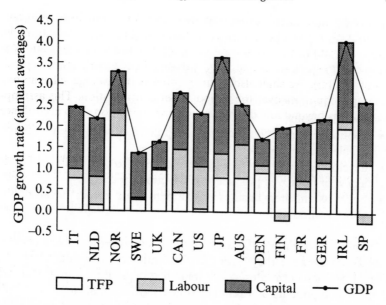

Figure 5.7 Decomposition of GDP growth rates (annual averages) according to TFP, labour and capital contributions

cross-country labour share and constant returns of scale both of which may be unrealistic in the analysis of series with a short timespan and pertinent to countries clearly in different phases of their development.

We can certainly conclude, in accordance with the literature, that on the average, TFP significantly contributes to growth. However, its low weight in some of the most developed countries, even if confirmed by several recent studies (OECD, 1996b; Jorgenson, 1988; Dougherty, 1991; Griliches, 1994), deserves further attention. A technical explanation of this interesting phenomenon goes beyond the goal of our work, which focuses on a more aggregate view. Nevertheless, we can advance the hypothesis that TFP, besides contributing directly to economic growth, has a more subtle but not less relevant correlation with other factors' productivity growth, based not on its rate of growth, but rather on its total value. In other words, the higher the TFP value, the faster would the other factors' productivity grow.

5.5 THE KNOWLEDGE ACCUMULATION PROCESS

For a more detailed analysis of the relationship between R&D and the stock of accumulated technical knowledge it is important to consider that

there are various activities that contribute to the accumulation of knowledge, and that a complete formal representation of the corresponding
processes would be overwhelming. We shall therefore limit our analysis to
data on R&D investments. The only distinction we make is among:

- fundamental research, which is not immediately oriented to any
  specific results;
- applied research, devoted to planned goals close to but not directly
  usable in any production;
- development and engineering, whose aim is to contribute directly to
  a new or improved product or production process;
- business and non-business investment (with respect to all of the
  above components).

The need to distinguish at least among the above three R&D components arises because they have different impacts on productivity and
different obsolescence rates, which must be taken into account. Data on
the above components of R&D investments are available for our sample
countries for several years. We have therefore calculated the stock of technical knowledge as the discounted cumulated investment in R&D:

$$x_t^r = \sum_{i=1}^{6} [I_{t-\delta_i}^r + (1 - \rho_i) * x_{t-1}^r] \qquad (5.2)$$

where

- $i = 1$ (business fundamental research); 2 (business applied research);
  3 (business development and engineering research); 4 (non-business
  fundamental research); 5 (non-business applied research); 6 (non-
  business development and engineering research);
- r is the country code;
- δ_i define the time lags necessary for any specific activities to produce their effects on productivity;
- ρ_i is the activity-specific obsolescence rate;
- $I_{t-\delta_i}^r$ is the activity specific expenditure of country r at time $t-\delta_i$.

The choice of the various parameters in (5.2) is certainly of critical
importance. In this chapter we present a first attempt in which some simplifications have been made in order to attain a first approximate level of
understanding of the phenomena under consideration. In particular, we
have assumed $\rho_i = \rho = 0.2 \ \forall i$, and $\delta_i = \delta = 3 \ \forall i$. These simplifying
assumptions have been made according to other studies on the estimation

of the knowledge stock, such as those of Namatame (1989), The Japan Economic Institute (1986) and Pakes and Schankerman (1984), which on the basis of the actual length of research programmes estimate $0.1 \leq \rho \leq 0.25$ and $3 \leq \rho \leq 7$. Griliches and Litchtenberg (1984) assume $0.1 \leq \rho \leq 0.20$; Adams (1990) includes in a much more complicated model values ranging in the following intervals: $0.0 \leq \rho \leq 0.25$; $0 \leq \delta \leq 5$.

Another key point is the definition of the initial state: in our case the stock of knowledge at the starting time has been chosen imposing a uniform rate of growth during the initial years. On the other hand, even large variations in the initial state, because of the depreciation factor, do not cause appreciable changes in the knowledge stock after a few years. In spite of the above simplifications, we shall see how the approach outlined above allows us to grasp the fundamental link between R&D and productivity. We have also verified that our results are robust around the chosen parameter values.

Figure 5.8 shows the relationship between the average annual value of TFP and the average stock of knowledge per worker over the period under consideration, which is restricted here to the time interval from 1976 to 1993 because of the lag of three years assumed before R&D activities produce any effects on productivity. We obtain here a stronger correlation than that in Figure 5.5. This supports the hypothesis that

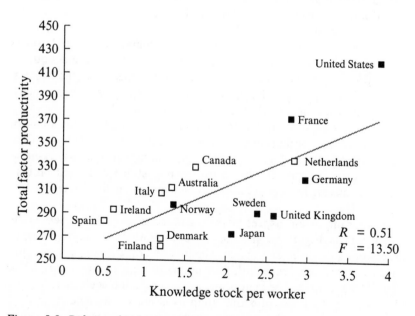

Figure 5.8 Relationship between TFP and the knowledge stock per worker

countries with a higher knowledge stock have the tendency to reach a higher level of productivity. In this case also some of the countries endowed with high stocks are located below the regression line implying that there are differences in the capabilities of transforming R&D investments into knowledge stock and, mainly, into productivity. In particular, Canada and Italy seem able to make better use than Japan and UK of their more limited R&D expenditures and knowledge stocks. Several factors, such as the organization of the scientific system, its relation with production activities, the focus of public research projects, and so on, may explain the different effectiveness of R&D in different countries. Even if we have not explored this problem here, we want to add a further remark on the different quota of stock generated by the private sector. Since the average quota of business stock is 0.55, in Figure 5.8 we have indicated with a small filled square the countries presenting a higher than average proportion, and with a small open square the others.

Summing up, we can draw the following conclusions:

- the countries where business stock prevails are also the ones with the highest absolute values of the knowledge stock;
- a clear-cut relationship between productivity and the business/non-business components of the knowledge stock does not exist; we can observe that countries where the non-business component clearly dominates (for instance Australia and Canada, with business quotas given by 0.31 and 0.43, respectively) have a better performance that some countries showing net dominance of the business component such as UK, Sweden and Japan (with business quotas of 0.63, 0.66 and 0.65 respectively). On the other hand, the two best performers, US and France, are characterized by prevailing proportions of business stock (0.67 and 0.58, respectively);
- we have also attempted to relate TFP and the business stock of knowledge, obtaining a correlation coefficient (0.43) lower than that reported in Figure 5.8, thus confirming that the business/non-business origin of the stock is not statistically relevant in determining its effectiveness in enhancing productivity rates.

Another important aspect of the phenomena investigated here is the time dynamics. Figure 5.9 attempts to capture the evolution over time of the relationship discussed above. The markers on the single curves are placed in correspondence with four points in time, namely years 1976, 1980, 1985 and 1993. The regression gives a correlation coefficient comparable with that of the previous analysis (Figure 5.8), and a level of statistical significance of 1 per cent. The tendency of the more knowledge-

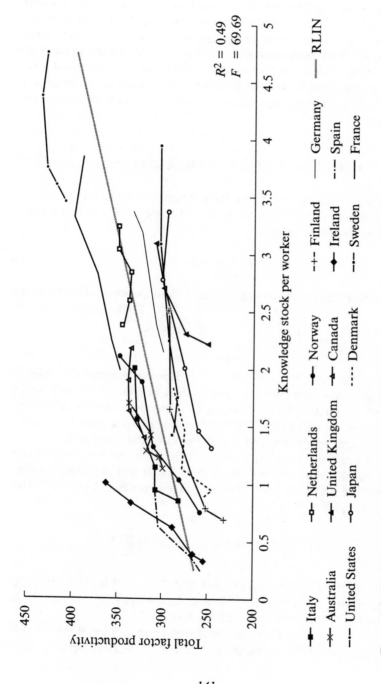

Figure 5.9 Evolution with time of the relationship between TFP and the knowledge stock per worker

endowed countries to attaining greater TFP values is therefore confirmed. The fluctuations of TFP that can be observed in Figure 5.9 are clearly due to the economic cycles in the various countries; they become more evident if we take into consideration yearly data rather than the averaged values. In spite of these fluctuations, the analysis reveals some fundamental trends which differ across the various countries, giving place to quite different growth paths. In the next section we try to assess the existence of a general relationship between the growth rate of the TFP and that of the knowledge stock.

5.6   TECHNICAL KNOWLEDGE AND PRODUCTIVITY

In this section we discuss the results of an analysis based on the rates of growth of both the TFP and the stock of knowledge. Let us first assume the following general relation:

$$TFP_t = A(t)*S_t^{\gamma}$$

where S represents the knowledge stock. With simple manipulation we get:

$$\ln\left(\frac{TFP_{T+1}}{TFP_T}\right) = \gamma_0 + \gamma*\ln\left(\frac{S_{T+1}}{S_T}\right)$$

where γ_0 and γ are regression coefficients. However, a regression analysis based on annual data gives very poor results. In order to obtain a better estimate we smooth the fluctuations in TFP growth rates by averaging their values, as well as those of the knowledge stock growth rates, on extended time spans. We have also disregarded the data for the first six years of our time series, since the stock figures at the beginning of the series are too sensitive to the choice of the initial state, which may otherwise become a critical factor. The results are presented in Figure 5.10; the estimated equation is given by:

$$\ln\left(\frac{TFP_{T+1}}{TFP_T}\right) = -0.0463 + 0.225*\ln\left(\frac{S_{T+1}}{S_T}\right)$$

with a statistical significance at 1 per cent. The result is convincing: the countries with the higher growth rate of knowledge stock are also those with higher TFP growth rate (see Table 5.3).

This result is robust to changes of the observation interval (provided it is of adequate length); again, the distribution of the stock between busi-

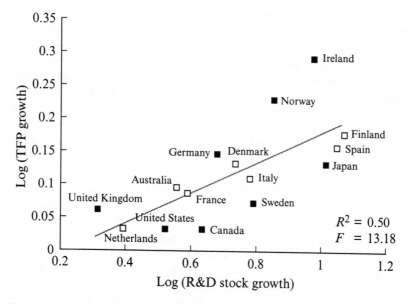

Figure 5.10 Relationship between the growth rate of TFP and the growth rate of the knowledge stock

Table 5.3 Average annual growth rates for TFP and knowledge stock

Country	Average R&D stock growth (%)	Average TFP growth (%)
Australia	4.04	0.66
Canada	4.58	0.23
Denmark	5.41	0.94
Finland	7.98	1.28
France	4.32	0.61
Germany	4.96	1.05
Ireland	7.19	2.13
Italy	5.77	0.77
Japan	7.60	0.96
Netherlands	2.82	0.21
Norway	6.27	1.65
Spain	7.80	1.12
Sweden	5.89	0.51
United Kingdom	2.23	0.44
United States	3.85	0.24

ness and non-business origins seems completely irrelevant to the result. What can be said in that respect is that for all countries but Australia the greatest contribution to the growth of the knowledge stock comes from the business sector. As earlier, filled black squares in Figure 5.10 indicate countries where the non-business sector contributes more than the average over all countries (65 per cent); all other countries are indicated by open squares. Even without strong statistical support, we remark that, at least pictorially, our data suggest, counterintuitively, that open-square countries (non-business stock above average) tend to have a better performance, in terms of TFP growth, than filled-square countries (business stock above average).

In order to further verify the robustness of our hypothesis, we present in Figure 5.11 the result of a regression made taking averaged values over the two sub-periods 1979–86 and 1987–93, respectively (see also Griliches and Litchtenberg, 1984). The regression coefficients (0.48) and the estimated parameters (–0.0078; 0.201) confirm the previous conclusions.

As a final analysis we tested the hypothesis that the stock of knowledge has a growing influence on productivity. We have therefore repeated the analysis above considering four pairs of six-year time intervals and obtained the coefficient estimates shown in Table 5.4. All estimates have a

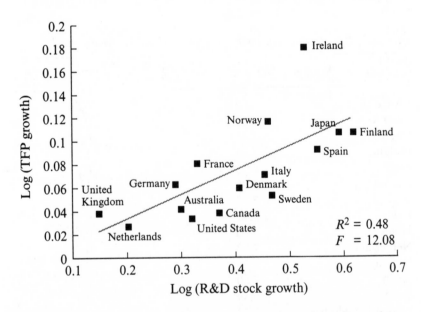

Figure 5.11 Relationship between seven-year average values of growth rates for TFP and knowledge stock

Table 5.4 Time intervals and coefficient estimates

Initial interval	Final interval	Regression coefficient γ
1979–1984	1985–1990	0.175
1980–1985	1986–1991	0.178
1981–1986	1986–1992	0.207
1982–1987	1988–1993	0.213

correlation coefficient close to 0.51 and statistical significance at 1 per cent. We take this result as a strong indication that increasing returns to scale govern the generation of technical knowledge and therefore the continuous growth of output foreseen by the new growth models.

5.7 CONCLUSIONS

We have discussed in this chapter the results of an analysis on the intricate relationships between R&D expenditure and economic growth. We have used data from 15 countries: the G-7, the four Scandinavian countries, plus Spain, Ireland, The Netherlands and Australia. The time series, limited because of the difficulties of obtaining reliable data on R&D expenditures on a cross-country basis, span from 1973 to 1993. All figures have been converted to 1985 US dollars; two different deflators have been used for GDP and R&D expenditures on one side, and capital stock on the other. Comparisons among the various countries have been done using Purchasing Power Parity, rather then the official exchange rate.

Our main conclusions can be summarized as follows:

- the countries with higher growth rate of knowledge stock are also those with higher TFP growth rate;
- the above result is robust to changes of the observation interval (provided it is of adequate length);
- a clear-cut relationship between productivity and the business/non-business components of the knowledge stock does not exist; we observe that countries where the non-business component clearly dominates have a better performance than some countries showing net dominance of the business component. On the other hand, the two best performers, US and France, are characterized by prevailing proportions of business stock;
- the countries where business stock prevails also have the highest absolute values of knowledge stock; however, even without strong

statistical support, we venture to remark that, at least pictorially, our data suggest, counterintuitively, that countries with non-business stocks above average tend to have a better performance, in terms of TFP growth, than countries with business stocks above average;

- our analyses confirm that the stock of knowledge has a growing influence on productivity; we take this result as a strong indication that increasing returns to scale govern the generation of technical knowledge and therefore the continuous growth of output foreseen by the new growth models.

We are well aware that the above conclusions should be validated by further work with extended time series and complemented with analysis at the single country level. Also, more sophisticated models are needed to deal properly with the complexity of the huge information flows generated by the knowledge accumulation process and their prominent role as a growth factor, which has been completely ignored in this discussion.

REFERENCES

Abramovitz, M. (1956), 'Resource and output trends in the United States since 1870', *American Economic Review, Papers and Proceedings*, **46**, 5–23.

Adams, J.D. (1990), 'Fundamental stocks of knowledge and productivity growth', *Journal of Political Economy*, **98** (4), 673–702.

Barro, R.J. and X. Sala-i-Martin (1995), *Economic Growth*, New York: McGraw-Hill.

Dosi, G., C. Freeman, R.R. Nelson, G. Silverberg and L. Soete (1988), *Technical Change and Economic Theory*, London: Pinter Publishers.

Dougherty, C. (1991), 'A comparison of productivity and economic growth in G-7 countries', PhD dissertation, Cambridge, MA: Harvard University.

Fagerberg, J. (1987), 'A technology gap approach to why growth rates differ', *Research Policy*, **16**, 87–99.

Fare R., S. Grosskopf, M. Norris and Z. Zhongyang (1994), 'Productivity growth, technical progress and efficiency change in industrialized countries', *American Economic Review*, **84**(1), 66–83.

Griliches, Z. (1988), 'Productivity puzzles and R&D: another nonexplanation', *Journal of Economic Perspectives*, **2**(4), 9–21.

Griliches, Z. (1994), 'Productivity, R&D and data constraint', *American Economic Review*, **84**(1), 1–23.

Griliches, Z. and F. Litchtenberg (1984), 'R&D and Productivity at the Industry Level: Is There Still a Relationship?', in Z. Griliches (ed.), *R&D Patents and Productivity*, NBER, pp. 77–88.

Japan Economic Institute (1986), 'Economic analysis of R&D and technology innovation', Research Paper no. 103.

Jorgenson, D.W. (1988), 'Productivity and economic growth in Japan and the United States', *American Economic Review, Papers and Proceedings*, **78**(2), 217–28.

Namatame A. (1989), 'Dynamic comparison of R&D innovation process structures', *International Journal of Technology Management*, **4**(3), 305–15.

Nelson, R.R. (1981), 'Research on productivity growth and productivity differences: dead ends and new departures', *Journal of Economic Literature*, **XIX**, 1029–64.

Nelson, R.R. and S. Winter (1982), *An Evolutionary Theory of Economic Change*, Cambridge, MA: Harvard University Press.

OECD (1996a), *Research and Development Expenditure in Industry*, Paris.

OECD (1996b), *Technology, Productivity and Job Creation*, Paris.

Pakes, A. and M. Schankerman (1984), 'The Rate of Obsolescence of Patents, Research Gestation Lags and the Private Rate of Return to Research Resources', in Z. Griliches (ed.), *R&D Patents and Productivity*, NBER, pp. 77–88.

Schumpeter, J.A. (1942), *Capitalism, Socialism and Democracy*, New York: Harper & Brothers.

Schumpeter, J.A. (1947), 'The creative response in economic history', *Journal of Economic History*, November, 149–59.

Singer, C., E.J. Holmyard, A.R. Hall and T.I. Williams (1958), *A History of Technology*, 4 volumes, Oxford: Clarendon Press.

Solow, R. (1957), 'Technical change and the aggregate production function', *Review of Economics and Statistics*, **38**, 312–20.

Summers, R. and A. Heston (1991), 'The Penn World Table (Mark 5): an expanded set of international comparisons, 1950–1988', *Quarterly Journal of Economics*, **106**(2), 327–68.

PART II

Contrasting Patterns: The United States and Europe

6. Inequality in regional and state per capita incomes in the United States: how much convergence has taken place?

Andrew M. Sum and Walter N. Fogg

INTRODUCTION

In recent years, there has been widespread interest in examining the comparative economic performance of countries across the world (Alam, 1992; Alam and Naseer, 1992; Barro, 1991; Barro and Sala-i-Martin, 1992, 1995; Baumol *et al.*, 1994; Leonardi, 1995; Mankiw, Romer and Weil, 1992), including analyses of the extent to which countries have been converging or diverging on real GDP per capita measures. Simultaneously, there has been growing interest in determining whether regions and states in the United States and regions in other countries are converging on key economic measures of performance, including incomes and outputs (Blomstrom and Wolff, 1994; Coulombe and Lee, 1993; Mallick and Carayannis, 1994; Paci and Pigliaru, 1997; Paci, 1997; Sum *et al.*, 1995; Vohra, 1993).

The comparative economic performance of regional and state economies in the United States can be assessed from a number of different perspectives. Use of multiple measures of economic performance, such as earnings, employment, incomes, or real output, would seem to be particularly helpful in analysing the degree to which states are converging or diverging over time on each of these key measures (Sum *et al.*, 1995). The degree of economic convergence or divergence among states or regions during any given time period may well be expected to vary by type of economic performance measure. For example, studies of output per capita and labour productivity in regions of Italy and Western Europe have shown convergence in labour productivity but not in real output per capita (Paci and Pigliaru, 1997; Paci and Saba, 1998).

Although the use of multiple measures of economic performance is clearly desirable, in this and the following chapter we will examine two measures of economic performance, namely the per capita personal incomes and per capita earnings from employment of residents of regions and states in the United States. Our analysis of per capita incomes will, however, include measures of pre-transfer, pre-tax incomes, personal incomes including transfers, and post-transfer, post-tax incomes.

We begin by examining trends in the per capita personal incomes of US residents over the 1929 to 1996 period, with particular emphasis on the period since 1969. The US Commerce Department's Bureau of Economic Analysis (BEA), the source of data on per capita personal incomes of regions and states, has recently revised its estimates of the per capita personal incomes of state residents beginning with the year 1969. Following this analysis of historical trends in per capita personal incomes, we will briefly describe three statistical measures that have been used in many previous studies to assess the existence and degree of convergence of incomes and outputs among regions and states. The next two sections examine the degree of convergence in per capita personal incomes among regions and states in the US. A brief comparison of regional and state income inequality in the US with that for Western Europe in 1980 and 1990 is then presented. This is followed by an analysis of the degree of inequality in the per capita incomes of state residents along a number of different measures of personal incomes, including pre-tax, pre-transfer income, pre-tax and post-transfer incomes and post-tax, post-transfer incomes.

TRENDS IN PER CAPITA PERSONAL INCOMES IN THE US

The most comprehensive and frequently-cited measure of the incomes of persons in states and regions is the per capita personal income data produced by the US Department of Commerce's Bureau of Economic Analysis. The Commerce Department's per capita personal income data are based on a comprehensive measure of income accruing to state residents during a calendar year, including wages and salaries, wage supplements, incomes of the self-employed, property income in the form of dividends, personal interest and rent, government cash transfer payments (including Social Security retirement, unemployment insurance and cash public assistance payments) and a variety of in-kind transfers, including the value of food stamps, Medicare and Medicaid payments.[1]

The personal income data for states and regions provided by the Bureau of Economic Analysis are reported in nominal terms, unadjusted for the effects of inflation over time. The Consumer Price Index for All Urban Consumers (the CPI-U) for the nation can be used to convert these nominal per capita income data for each region and state into their real dollar (or constant dollar) equivalents, or the available CPI-U data for major metropolitan areas in some states can be used to convert their nominal per capita income data into real dollars for those states. At present, there are no currently available official regional or state cost-of-living data that could be used to convert state per capita income data into purchasing power parity equivalents.[2] This absence of regional cost-of-living data complicates the task of determining the true degree of convergence in regional and state living standards. We will use a set of cost-of-housing adjusted poverty lines for states to convert their 1996 incomes into purchasing power parity equivalents.

Data on the personal incomes of US residents are available on an annual basis from 1929 onward. The official total personal income data are expressed in nominal terms. We have used the CPI-UX1 index of the US Bureau of Labor Statistics to convert these nominal income data into their constant dollar equivalents since this yields a more conservative measure of inflation for the time period 1959–1981 than the CPI-U index.[3] Data on the real per capita incomes of US residents are presented in Table 6.1 for the ending year of each decade and for 1996. The years 1929, 1959, 1969, 1979 and 1989 were business cycle peak years. While 1996 is not a cyclical peak year, it does represent the sixth consecutive year of economic growth following recovery from the 1990–1991 recession.[4]

Table 6.1 Total personal incomes and per capita personal incomes, US, 1929–1996 (in nominal and constant 1996 dollars)

Year	Total personal income (millions)		Per capita personal income	
	Nominal	Real (1996$)	Nominal	Real (1996$)
1929	85 800	723 765	692	5 837
1939	72 900	757 484	550	5 715
1949	208 300	1 261 864	1 378	8 348
1959	380 014	1 886 842	2 195	10 899
1969	772 027	3 074 392	3 835	15 272
1979	2 041 337	4 328 186	9 090	19 273
1989	4 474 014	5 661 071	18 127	22 937
1996	6 428 129	6 428 129	24 231	24 231

Sources: Economic Report of the President, 1964; Survey of Current Business, October 1996; BEA Press Release, 28 April 1997.

Over the entire 1929 to 1996 period, the total real personal incomes of US residents increased from $724 billion to just over $6428 billion, nearly a nine-fold increase. During that same time period, the nation's population more than doubled, rising from 122 million in 1929 to 265 million in 1996. Per capita real incomes (in constant 1996 dollars) quadrupled in size over this time period, increasing from $5837 in 1929 to $24 231 in 1996. Tests for convergence in per capita incomes across regions and states over the long 1929 to 1996 period are, thus, taking place in an economic environment characterized by a substantial rise in the affluence of the US population.

The growth rates of per capita real personal incomes in the US over the 1929–96 era varied markedly by decade. During the depression decade of the 1930s, the per capita real incomes of US residents actually declined by 2 per cent (Table 6.2). During the deep depression of the early 1930s, the degree of inequality in the state per capita income distribution widened, the last time that it would do so until the 1980s. The 1940s were characterized by explosive growth, with real per capita incomes rising by 46 per cent. This decade was marked by substantial convergence of per capita incomes across regions and states. Per capita income growth remained quite strong during the 1950s and 1960s, with a growth rate of 40 per cent prevailing during the latter decade. Growth rates of per capita incomes have slowed considerably and steadily since then, falling to 26 per cent in the 1970s, to 19 per cent in the 1980s, and to only 6 per cent during the first seven years of the 1990s. The national recession of 1990–91 and the slow growth of real GDP in the early stages of economic recovery during 1991 and 1992 have resulted in only a moderate improvement in the per capita real incomes of US residents in the past seven years.

Table 6.2 Percentage change in total real personal incomes and per capita real personal incomes, US, 1929–1996 (in constant 1996 dollars)

Period	Total personal income	Per capita personal income
1929–1939	4.7	–2.1
1939–1949	66.6	46.1
1949–1959	49.5	30.6
1959–1969	62.9	40.1
1969–1979	40.8	26.2
1979–1989	30.8	19.0
1989–1996	13.5	5.6

Sources: As for Table 6.1.

MEASURES OF REGIONAL AND STATE INCOME INEQUALITY

There are a number of alternative statistical measures of inequality that can be used in conducting analyses of the convergence of regional or state incomes over time.[5] Three of the most frequently used such measures are displayed in Table 6.3. The first of these statistical measures is the coefficient of variation, a measure of the degree of relative dispersion in the distribution of per capita incomes.[6] Use of this measure in analyses of international and intra-national outputs and incomes is often referred to as a test of sigma convergence (Barro and Sala-i-Martin, 1995; Vohra, 1993; Coughlin and Mandelbaum, 1998).[7] A second measure of inequality involves comparisons of the relative degree of dispersion between the values of per capita incomes at selected points along the per capita personal income distribution. Two such measures are the interquartile variation and interquintile variation. The value of the latter measure is obtained by subtracting the per capita personal income of the fortieth ranked state from the tenth highest ranked state and dividing the difference by the average of the two values. Since the measure deflates absolute differences by the average size of per capita incomes, it provides a relative measure of dispersion that allows comparisons of inequality among states over time.

Finally, there are those economic analyses that use simple regression models of per capita income or output growth rates to test for unconditional convergence (Barro and Sala-i-Martin, 1992; Baumol *et al.*, 1994; Keil and Vohra, 1993; Vohra, 1993; Sum *et al.*, 1995). Convergence tests based on this model are referred to as 'beta convergence'. For our analysis of trends in the convergence of *regional* per capita incomes in the United States, we will rely solely on the coefficient of variation, given the limited number of observations (9) for each time period. Our analyses of convergence in *state* per capita incomes will use all three measures of inequality.

Table 6.3 Alternative measures of regional and state income inequality

1. Coefficients of variation (sigma convergence).
2. Interquintile or interquartile variation.
3. Simple regression tests for the unconditional convergence of per capita incomes (beta convergence).

TRENDS IN REGIONAL INCOME INEQUALITY IN THE USA

Data on the per capita personal incomes of the residents of geographic regions across the United States are available from 1929 onward. We have classified all states and the District of Columbia into nine geographic regions using the regional classification system of the US Census Bureau.[8] The states comprising each of the nine Census Bureau regions are displayed in Figure 6.1,

The coefficients of variation for the regional per capita income data are characterized by a substantial downward secular trend over the 1929–96 period (Table 6.4). In 1929, the (unweighted) mean per capita income of the residents of these nine regions was $651, but varied from a low of $344 for the East South Central region to a high of $961 for the Middle Atlantic region, representing a relative difference of nearly three to one. The coefficient of variation in 1929 was 0.348. The coefficient of variation fell moderately to 0.317 in 1939 and then more markedly during the 1940s, falling to 0.189 in 1949. The coefficient of variation for regional per capita incomes continued to decline during the 1950s, 1960s and 1970s, reaching an historic low of 0.106 in 1979. Then the 1980s witnessed a sharp increase in regional income inequality. By 1989, it had increased to 0.149, a level similar to that experienced during the 1960s. Since 1989, however, the coefficient of variation has continued its historical decline, falling to 0.122 by 1996. Overall, these findings clearly indicate that substantial convergence has taken place in regional per capita incomes over the past 67 years.

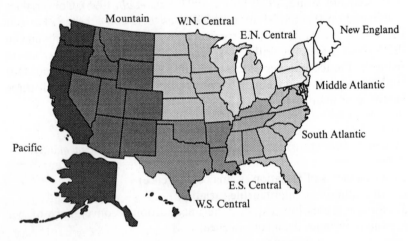

Figure 6.1 Census regions in the US

Table 6.4 Nominal per capita personal incomes, by region, selected years, 1929–1996

Census region	Year							
	1929	1939	1949	1959	1969	1979	1989	1996
New England	862	694	1440	2402	4230	9432	22084	28989
Middle Atlantic	961	723	1581	2517	4337	9697	21088	28250
E.N. Central	786	610	1501	2361	4021	9441	17818	24575
W.N. Central	565	452	1310	2034	3568	8883	16880	23414
South Atlantic	452	420	1127	1840	3440	8297	17703	23825
E.S. Central	344	268	870	1512	2791	7159	14233	20219
W.S. Central	430	361	1168	1828	3189	8436	15235	21300
Mountain	573	483	1345	2069	3429	8575	15829	22139
Pacific	888	712	1682	2604	4398	10384	19596	25141
Mean	651	525	1336	2130	3711	8923	17830	24206
Standard deviation	227	166	252	366	561	944	2656	2950
Coefficient of variation	0.348	0.317	0.189	0.172	0.151	0.106	0.149	0.122

The degree of convergence in regional incomes varied considerably by decade with an actual reversal of the trend towards reduced inequality taking place during the 1980s. The 1940s, including the war years, were characterized by the highest rate of convergence, with the coefficient of variation declining by 40 per cent. The rate of convergence was also quite high in the 1970s when the Sun Belt region and the Mountain region achieved substantially higher rates of growth than the Frost Belt, particularly the New England and Middle Atlantic regions. The 1980s, however, witnessed a substantial reversal in the trend toward income convergence among regions (Coughlin and Mandelbaum, 1998; US Congress, Joint Economic Committee, 1986). The so called 'bi-coastal boom' was accompanied by substantially higher rates of per capita income growth in New England, the Middle Atlantic region and the South Atlantic region. During the 1980s, New England moved to the top of the regional per capita income distribution followed by the Middle Atlantic region. The South Atlantic region improved its ranking from eighth in 1979 to fifth by 1989.

Since 1989, the longer historical trend toward economic convergence among regions has been renewed. The New England and Middle Atlantic regions experienced real output declines between 1989 and 1991 and have achieved only moderate growth in per capita real incomes over the

1989–96 period.[9] Over the same time period, the East South Central, West South Central, East North Central and Mountain regions experienced relatively high rates of personal income growth. Adjusting the nominal per capita income data for variations in the cost of living across regions would undoubtedly lower the coefficient of variation even further, given the estimated higher costs of living in the New England, Middle Atlantic and Pacific regions.[10]

TRENDS IN INEQUALITY IN PER CAPITA INCOMES ACROSS STATES

Our analysis of the per capita personal incomes of individual states and the District of Columbia cover the time period 1939 through 1996. The time trends in income inequality for the states as measured by the coefficient of variation are quite similar to those for the regions (Table 6.5). During 1939, the coefficient of variation stood at 0.376; however, by 1996, it had declined markedly to 0.159, representing nearly a 60 per cent drop in value over this 57-year period.

The declines in income inequality among the states were far from uniform over this period. As was the case for the regions, the most substantial rate of decline in inequality occurred during the 1940s. More moderate but steady declines in inequality occurred during the 1950s, the 1960s and the 1970s; however, income inequality began to increase in the late 1970s and continued to do so throughout the late 1980s. By 1989, the

Table 6.5 Means, standard deviations and coefficients of variation of state per capita personal incomes, selected years, 1939–1996 (in nominal dollars)

Year	Mean	Standard deviation	Coefficient of variation
1939	512	192	0.376
1949	1 313	286	0.218
1959	2 063	397	0.192
1969	3 612	622	0.172
1979	8 784	1 266	0.144
1989	17 235	3 070	0.178
1996	23 413	3 726	0.159

Note: Estimates for 1939 and 1949 exclude Alaska and Hawaii since they did not enter statehood until 1959.

coefficient of variation had slightly surpassed its level in 1969. Many states along the Atlantic seaboard, including most of the New England states, New York, New Jersey, Delaware, Maryland and many South Atlantic states, achieved substantially above average growth rates in personal incomes during the 1980s while many energy states in the Southwest and Mountain regions performed quite poorly due in large part to the drop in world oil prices (Coughlin and Mandelbaum, 1988; Sum *et al.*, 1995).

The rise in inequality in per capita incomes among states peaked in 1988, and the coefficient of variation has been declining fairly steadily since then (Table 6.6). By 1996, the coefficient of variation had declined to 0.159, coming close to the previous low of 0.144 recorded in 1979. A substantial portion of the decline in inequality over the 1989–96 period was brought about by the decline in the economic fortunes of the New England states, the Middle Atlantic states, California and Alaska.

Following a classification scheme adopted by authors of other convergence studies (Coughlin and Mandelbaum, 1998; Vohra, 1993), we have categorized each of the ten highest and ten lowest per capita income states in 1989 into one of the following four categories based on their growth rates in per capita real personal incomes between 1989 and 1996.

- *Upwardly divergent:* states that had a per capita income above the US average in 1989 and grew at a rate above the unweighted average (7.4 per cent) for all 50 states between 1989 and 1996.

Table 6.6 Means, standard deviations and coefficients of variation of state per capita personal incomes, 1988–1996 (in nominal dollars)

Year	Mean	Standard deviation	Coefficient of variation
1988	16 121	2 882	0.179
1989	17 235	3 070	0.178
1990	18 255	3 134	0.172
1991	18 821	3 138	0.167
1992	19 784	3 274	0.165
1993	20 475	3 320	0.162
1994	21 321	3 390	0.159
1995	22 389	3 595	0.161
1996	23 413	3 726	0.159

- *Downwardly convergent:* states that had a per capita income above the US average in 1989, but grew at a rate below the all state average between 1989 and 1996.
- *Upwardly convergent:* states that had a per capita income below the US average in 1989 but grew at a rate above the all state average between 1989 and 1996.
- *Downwardly divergent:* states that had a per capita income below the US average in 1989 and grew at a rate below the all state average between 1989 and 1996.

States that are downwardly convergent and those that are upwardly convergent will contribute to a decline in the coefficient of variation while the opposite will hold true for those states that were either upwardly divergent or downwardly divergent. Of the ten highest per capita income states in 1989, nine were characterized as downwardly convergent between 1989 and 1996, including two states that experienced declines in their per capita real incomes (Table 6.7). Only the District of Columbia, which has been characterized by substantial population and labour force decline since 1990, was classified as upwardly divergent over this period. The District had an above-average per capita income in 1989 and grew at an above-average rate over the 1989 to 1996 period.

Nine of the ten states with the lowest per capita incomes in 1989 achieved 1989–96 per capita income growth rates in excess of the all-state average. The real per capita incomes of these nine states increased from 9.3 per cent to 20.9 per cent. Eight of the nine states achieved double-digit growth rates, and five had growth rates that were more than twice the all-state average. Sharp differences between the per capita income growth rates of the ten highest and ten lowest states were primarily responsible for the renewed decline in income inequality among the states over the 1989–96 period.

INTERQUINTILE VARIATIONS IN STATE PER CAPITA PERSONAL INCOMES

A second measure of state income inequality involves the use of interquintile variation. The formula for this measure of state income inequality is the following:

$$\text{Interquintile Variation} = \frac{Y_{10} - Y_{41}}{\left(\dfrac{Y_{10} + Y_{41}}{2}\right)}$$

Table 6.7 Growth rates in per capita real incomes between 1989 and 1996 of the ten states with the highest and lowest per capita personal incomes in 1989 (nominal dollars)

	(A) 1989	(B) 1996	(C) Percentage change	(D) Convergence status
Ten highest states				
Connecticut	32109	33189	3.4	Downwardly convergent
New Jersey	30037	31053	3.4	Downwardly convergent
Washington, DC	29567	34932	18.1	Upwardly divergent
Massachusetts	28615	29439	2.9	Downwardly convergent
New York	27607	28782	4.3	Downwardly convergent
Maryland	27140	27221	0.3	Downwardly convergent
Delaware	26023	27622	6.1	Downwardly convergent
New Hampshire	25987	26520	2.1	Downwardly convergent
California	25481	25144	−1.3	Downwardly convergent
Alaska	25213	24558	−2.6	Downwardly convergent
Ten lowest states				
Montana	17957	19047	6.1	Downwardly divergent
South Carolina	17879	19755	10.5	Upwardly convergent
South Dakota	17794	21516	20.9	Upwardly convergent
North Dakota	17313	20710	19.6	Upwardly convergent
Louisiana	17200	19824	15.3	Upwardly convergent
New Mexico	17177	18770	9.3	Upwardly convergent
Arkansas	16876	18928	12.2	Upwardly convergent
Utah	16738	19156	14.4	Upwardly convergent
West Virginia	16638	18444	10.9	Upwardly convergent
Mississippi	15169	17471	15.2	Upwardly convergent

where

Y_{10} = the per capita income of the residents of the tenth highest ranked state; and

Y_{41} = the per capita income of the residents of the forty-first highest ranked state (since the District of Columbia is included in the analysis there are 51 states).

Findings on the estimated size of the interquintile variation for the 50 states and the District of Columbia for the 1969–1996 period are presented in Table 6.8. At the end of the 1960s, the value of the interquintile variation was equal to 0.367. The value of this inequality measure declined sharply over the next eight years, falling to 0.261 during both 1977 and 1978. From 1983 through 1989, however, the value of the interquintile variation increased continuously and sharply, peaking at a value of 0.336 in 1989. Not surprisingly, this peak occurred during the same year that the coefficient of variation peaked. Since 1989, the interquintile variation has declined quite sharply and steadily, falling to a

Table 6.8 Per capita real personal incomes of the tenth highest and forty-first highest states and interquintile variation, 1969–1996 (in 1996 dollars)

Year	Y_{10} ($)	Y_{41} ($)	Interquintile variation
1969	17402	12002	0.367
1970	17426	12214	0.352
1971	17732	12730	0.328
1972	18612	13637	0.309
1973	19516	14304	0.308
1974	18907	14160	0.287
1975	18680	13898	0.294
1976	19317	14578	0.280
1977	19608	15082	0.261
1978	20404	15695	0.261
1979	20834	15809	0.274
1980	20759	15486	0.291
1981	21008	15906	0.276
1982	20838	15679	0.283
1983	20733	15967	0.260
1984	21933	16847	0.262
1985	22524	16887	0.286
1986	23359	17278	0.299
1987	24070	17433	0.320
1988	24421	17506	0.330
1989	25213	17964	0.336
1990	25266	18396	0.315
1991	24665	18360	0.293
1992	24873	18829	0.277
1993	24758	18949	0.266
1994	25381	19210	0.277
1995	25316	19541	0.257
1996	25580	19824	0.254

value of 0.254 in 1996. By 1996, the degree of inequality in the state per capita income distribution as measured by the interquintile variation had fallen to a new historical low.

TESTING FOR BETA CONVERGENCE IN STATES' PER CAPITA INCOMES

A third approach to testing for convergence in state per capita incomes involves the use of a simple regression model in which the per capita income growth rates of each state are regressed against their initial levels of income (Baumol *et al.*, 1994; Barro and Sala-i-Martin, 1992; Paci and Pigliaru, 1997; Paci and Saba, 1998; Vohra, 1993). The first regression model simply takes on the following form:

$$PCHGINC_i = B_0 + B_1 INC_{Base,i}$$

where

$PCHGINC_i$ = The percentage growth rate in the per capita real income of state *i* over the relevant time period, for example, 1939–1949 or 1989–1996

$INC_{Base,i}$ = The per capita real income of state *i* in the base year of the analysis[11]

This type of convergence model is referred to in the economic growth literature as unconditional convergence. The coefficient B_1 represents the influence of the initial level of income on the expected growth rate of state's per capita income over each time period in question. If the sign of the coefficient B_1 is negative, the findings imply that the growth rates of states' per capita incomes are negatively related to their initial position; thus, convergence must be occurring. Regression models for states' per capita income growth rates have been estimated for seven different time periods: 1939–49, 1949–59, 1959–69, 1969–79, 1979–89, 1989–96 and 1969–96. In conducting this analysis, we transformed the variable representing the per capita real income of the state in the base year by subtracting the mean per capita real income of all 51 states from each state's estimated per capita real income in the base year. This new income variable is referred to as *PIMEAN* in the regression models displayed in Table 6.9. The advantage of this variable re-specification is that it allows the intercept term (B_0) to possess economic meaning. Its value now represents the expected growth rate of a state with a per capita income in the base year equal to that of the mean for all 50 states and the District of Columbia.

Table 6.9 State per capita personal income convergence regressions, by decade, 1939–1996

	1939–49	1949–59	1959–69	1969–79	1979–89	1989–96	1969–96
N	49	49	51	51	51	51	51
Adjusted R-square	0.773	0.262	0.228	0.357	0.020	0.282	0.193
F statistic	164.0	18.0	15.8	28.8	0.0	20.6	13.0
Significance of F	0.0000	0.0001	0.0002	0.0000	0.9435	0.0000	0.0007
Constant							
Coefficient	58.7	29.1	41.3	30.4	17.1	7.8	63.8
t-statistic	30.24	29.28	36.00	31.00	9.97	13.03	38.32
PIMEAN							
Coefficient	−0.0126	−0.0025	−0.0023	−0.0021	−0.0000	−0.0007	−0.0024
t-statistic	−12.81	−4.25	−3.97	−5.36	−0.07	−4.54	−3.60

The findings displayed in Table 6.9 provide evidence of significant beta convergence for the 1940s, 1950s, 1960s, 1970s, the 1989–96 period and the entire 1969–96 period. For the 1980s, we find no evidence of beta convergence. In fact, the estimated value of the coefficient B_1 for this period is equal to zero. This result was clearly expected given our earlier findings of rising income inequality among states and regions in the 1980s. In the models for the time periods supporting beta convergence, the coefficients (B_1) on the base year per capita real income variable were negative and statistically significant at the 0.001 level, implying that the higher the level of the state's per capita income at the beginning of the period, the lower was its expected growth rate over each of these periods. As anticipated, the relative size of this effect was considerably greater in the 1940s than in following decades.[12] Simple plots of the dependent variable (the percentage change in per capita real personal income) and the independent variable (initial level of per capita real personal income minus the mean) are displayed on Figure 6.2 providing visual support to our statistical conclusion, namely that there was convergence across states in all decades except the 1980s.

The above statistical tests for beta convergence in the per capita personal incomes of states in the US were based on regressions of decadal growth rates on initial absolute levels of state per capita incomes. The regression models used to test for beta convergence in many international studies and a growing number of regional studies use a different variant of that model. Borrowing from a Solow-type neoclassical growth model with Cobb–Douglas technology and exogenously determined aggregate savings rates and technological progress, the model used to test for unconditional convergence takes the following linear form (Barro, 1991; Mallick and Carayannis, 1994; Paci and Saba, 1998):

$$\frac{1}{T} \log \left(\frac{Y_{i,t}}{Y_{i,t-T}} \right) = B_0 + B_1 \log(Y_{i,t-T}) + \varepsilon_i$$

The left-hand side dependent variable represents the annual average growth rate in the per capita incomes of the residents of state i over a period of years (primarily a decade). The log of the per capital personal income of each state in the initial year appears as the independent variable on the right-hand side of the model. A negative, statistically significant coefficient for B_1 implies the existence of unconditional beta convergence, and the size of B_1 can be interpreted as a measure of the speed of convergence. For example, an estimated value of –0.025 for B_1 implies that state inequality in per capita incomes would be eliminated in 40 years.

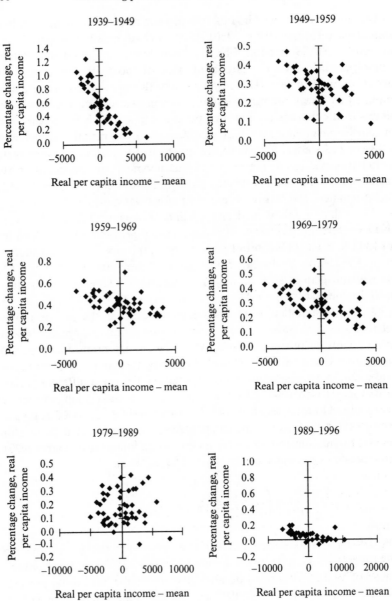

Figure 6.2 Simple plots of dependent and independent variables

Findings of our tests for beta convergence in the distribution of per capita incomes across states for the entire 1939–96 period and for individual decades are displayed in Table 6.10. For the entire time period and for each decade, except the 1980s, significant beta convergence is found to have taken place. Over the 1939–96 period, the rate of convergence was estimated to be 1.2 per cent per year. As revealed in our other analyses, the speed of convergence was greatest in the 1940s when it equalled 4.4 per cent per year. This rate of convergence was two to three times as high as that of every other decade. While beta convergence came to an end in the 1980s, it was resumed in the 1990s with a rate of convergence approximately equal to that of the 1970s.

TRENDS IN INCOME INEQUALITY AMONG STATES WITHIN REGIONS

Our preceding analyses have examined trends in the convergence of per capita incomes across regions and states in the United States over the past 60 to 70 years. The BEA personal income data can be used to examine trends in the degree of inequality of per capita incomes of states within regions. There are three key questions that can be answered with this analysis. First, has each region been characterized by long-term convergence in states' per capita incomes? Second, have more recent trends within regions (1979–89, 1989–96) been characterized by convergence or divergence? Third, how does the degree of inequality in each region during 1996 compare to that of all states throughout the nation? Our analysis of inequality will be based on the coefficients of variation in states' per capita incomes within regions.

Viewed from a long-run perspective, each of the nine geographic regions was characterized by a fairly substantial degree of convergence over the 1939–96 period. The relative sizes of the declines in the coefficients of variation for these nine geographic regions ranged from –21 per cent (New England) to –74 per cent (Pacific) (Table 6.11). Seven of the nine geographic regions reduced their coefficients of variation by 50 per cent or more over the 1939–96 time period. In more recent years, the pattern of findings has been more mixed. During the 1980s, a period characterized by rising inequality among the states, the coefficients of variation rose in six of the nine regions, including both regions in the Northeast, both in the Midwest, and most of the South. In three of these regions, the coefficient of variation rose by 50 per cent or more. In only the West and Southwest did income inequality decline during the 1980s.

Table 6.10 State per capita personal income convergence regressions, by decade, 1939-1996

	1939-49	1949-59	1959-69	1969-79	1979-89	1989-96	1969-96
N	49	49	51	51	51	51	49
Adjusted R square	0.809	0.270	0.246	0.372	-0.020	0.317	0.882
F statistic	204.2	18.8	17.3	30.6	0.0	24.2	360.4
Significance of F	0.0000	0.0001	0.0001	0.0000	0.8987	0.0000	0.0000
B_0 Coefficient	0.415	0.160	0.189	0.254	0.028	0.231	0.127
t-statistic	15.99	5.15	5.09	6.17	0.28	5.16	24.09
B_1 Coefficient	-0.044	-0.015	-0.017	-0.024	-0.001	-0.022	-0.012
t-statistic	-14.29	-4.33	-4.16	-5.54	-0.13	-4.92	-18.98

Table 6.11 Trends in the degree of inequality in the per capita personal incomes of the residents of states within the nine geographic regions, selected time periods and relative to the US in 1996

Geographic region	(A) Percentage change in CV, 1939–96	(B) Percentage change in CV, 1979–89	(C) Percentage change, in CV, 1989–96	(D) CV of region as percentage of CV among all states, 1996
New England	−20.6	+16.7	+7.6	111
Middle Atlantic	−26.4	+95.2	−12.2	72
East North Central	−50.0	+11.3	−2.6	42
West North Central	−63.9	+79.0	−35.2	42
South Atlantic	−63.0	+12.7	+5.2	126
East South Central	−52.1	+50.3	−13.0	56
West South Central	−65.3	−17.6	−18.4	44
Mountain	−54.9	−6.4	−6.8	80
Pacific	−74.0	−35.2	−48.2	27

During the 1990s, a renewed trend toward convergence in per capita incomes has taken place in most regions. Only New England (+7 per cent) and the South Atlantic regions (+5 per cent) were characterized by a moderate increase in their CVs. In New England, both Connecticut and Massachusetts, the two highest per capita income states in that region, have experienced no growth in their resident labour force and either a slow growing (Massachusetts) or declining population (Connecticut). In the South Atlantic region, the District of Columbia, which had the third highest per capita income in the nation during 1989, achieved an above average rate of growth in its per capita income over the 1989–96 period that moved it to first place among the states by 1991. The District of Columbia has retained its first place ranking since 1991 despite steep declines in its population (a 10 per cent loss since 1990) and in its labour force.

During 1996, the coefficients of variation in state per capita incomes within the nine regions ranged from a low of 0.042 (Pacific) to a high of 0.200 (South Atlantic) (Table 6.12). Seven of the nine geographic regions had achieved a lower CV than the nation, and New England was within 11 per cent of the CV for all states in the nation (Table 6.11, column D). Only the South Atlantic region had a considerably higher CV (0.200) than the nation, but all of the excess variation in this region was due to the District of Columbia, with its high per capita income in 1996.

Table 6.12 Coefficient of variation for per capita personal incomes of states within regions, selected years, 1939-1996 (number of states in parentheses)

	1939	1949	1959	1969	1979	1989	1996
New England (6)	0.223	0.146	0.172	0.159	0.141	0.164	0.177
Middle Atlantic (3)	0.156	0.101	0.099	0.101	0.067	0.131	0.115
E.N. Central (5)	0.134	0.087	0.083	0.072	0.062	0.069	0.067
W.N. Central (7)	0.186	0.066	0.115	0.091	0.058	0.104	0.067
South Atlantic (9)	0.541	0.323	0.256	0.192	0.169	0.190	0.200
E.S. Central (4)	0.187	0.129	0.112	0.097	0.068	0.103	0.089
W.S. Central (4)	0.199	0.183	0.138	0.111	0.103	0.085	0.069
Mountain (8)	0.282	0.151	0.135	0.142	0.145	0.136	0.127
Pacific (5)	0.164	0.046	0.095	0.093	0.127	0.082	0.042

Excluding the District of Columbia from the calculations for the South Atlantic region for 1996 reduced the estimated CV to only 0.130, nearly 20 per cent below the CV for all states. Thus, by 1996, nearly all regions had achieved a higher degree of convergence in their states' per capita incomes than the nation as a whole.

COMPARISONS OF REGIONAL INCOME INEQUALITY IN THE USA AND WESTERN EUROPE

Our previous estimates of the degree of inequality in the regional per capita income distribution of the US in recent years can be compared to those for regions in Western Europe and selected European nations in 1980 and 1990.[13] Paci (1997) derived estimates of the standard deviation of the relative per capita incomes of 109 European regions in 1980 and 1990 while Paci and Saba (1998) computed estimates of the standard deviation of the log levels of per capita income in purchasing power parity for six European countries in 1980 and 1990 (Table 6.13).[14] Estimates of the standard deviation of the log levels of per capita incomes in regions of the US also are displayed in Table 6.13.

Comparisons of the findings on the degree of inequality in per capita incomes among regions of the US with those for the 109 regions in Western Europe for both 1980 and 1990 reveal a considerably lower degree of income inequality in the US. In 1980, regional income inequality in the US was only about one-third as high as that of the 109 regions in Western Europe. While regional income inequality increased in the US

Table 6.13 Comparisons of the degree of inequality in per capita incomes among regions in Western Europe, the US and selected Western European nations, 1980 (standard deviation of log of per capita incomes)

Geographic region	(A) 1980	(B) 1990	(C) Change 1980–90
Western Europe, total	0.356	0.356	0.000
France	0.138	0.158	+0.020
Germany	0.203	0.201	−0.002
Greece	0.187	0.183	−0.004
Italy	0.264	0.274	+0.010
Spain	0.190	0.204	+0.014
UK	0.105	0.117	+0.012
USA	0.113	0.140	+0.027

Sources: (A) Paci and Saba (1998); Paci (1997); (B) US Department of Commerce, Bureau of Economic Analysis, tabulations by authors

during the 1980s, the degree of regional inequality in 1990 was only 39 per cent as high as that of Western Europe. Comparisons of the degree of regional income inequality in the US with that of six individual European nations reveal that the US ranked second lowest in both years, exceeded only by the United Kingdom. The degree of regional income inequality was highest in Italy, which was characterized by twice as much inequality as the US in both years. [15]

The rise in regional income inequality in the US during the 1980s clearly was not a phenomenon confined to its boundaries. For the 109 regions of Western Europe there was *no* change in overall income inequality during the 1980s, and income inequality actually increased within four of the six nations studied by Paci and Saba (France, Italy, Spain and the UK). An analysis of regional output performance in Mexico over the 1970–85 period indicated that the previous trend toward convergence in gross state product per capita came to an end in the first half of the 1980s (Mallick and Carayannis, 1994).

THE IMPACT OF GOVERNMENT TRANSFERS AND PERSONAL TAXES ON STATE INCOME INEQUALITY

The personal income data of the Bureau of Economic Analysis are capable of being disaggregated into their component sources, including labour compensation, proprietors' income, property income and government transfer payments. The latter payments include both cash and in-kind transfer payments from the government.

In this section, we will assess the impact of government transfers and personal taxes on the degree of inequality in state per capita personal incomes from 1989 through 1995. The coefficient of variation will be used to represent the degree of inequality in the per capita incomes of the residents of the 50 states and the District of Columbia.

Included in the personal incomes of the residents of any state are all cash and most in-kind transfers received by residents from federal, state and local governments. The cash transfers include social security retirement benefits; federal, state and local government pensions; unemployment insurance benefits; workers' compensation and public cash income assistance programmes. The personal income estimates also include the estimated value of many in-kind transfer programmes, the largest of which are the Medicare and Medicaid programmes providing health care for the elderly and low income families and the food stamp programme.

The values of the above cash and in-kind government transfer programmes have grown substantially in the US in recent decades, outpacing the growth of the other components of personal income. Nationally, the share of personal income accounted for by government transfers has risen from 6.8 per cent in 1959 to just under 17 per cent in 1995.[16] The above average rate of growth in government transfer incomes has continued unabated in the 1990s. The mean per capita transfer incomes of the residents of the states had risen from $2483 in 1989 to $3821 in 1995, an increase of 54 per cent in nominal dollars (Table 6.14).[17] The mean share of per capita personal incomes attributable to government transfers rose from 14.7 per cent in 1989 to 17.3 per cent in 1995, a new historical high.

A key task for state income inequality analysis is that of determining the role of these government transfers in moderating the degree of per capita personal income inequality generated by market forces.[18] To estimate the impact of government transfers on the degree of inequality in state per capita personal incomes, we calculated the annual amount of per capita transfers received by the residents of each state every year from 1989 through 1995 and the annual per capita personal incomes less transfers received by the residents of each state.

Given the nature of most government transfer programmes in the US, one might well expect that transfer incomes would only marginally impact personal income inequality across states. This is so for several different reasons. First, many transfer programmes in the US are not income conditioned. For example, the receipt of Social Security benefits and Medicare benefits by the elderly, the nation's two largest transfer pro-

Table 6.14 Mean per capita transfer incomes across states in absolute dollars and as a percentage of per capita personal incomes, 1989–1995 (in nominal dollars)

Year	(A) Mean per capita transfers	(B) Transfers as a percentage of personal incomes
1989	2483	14.7
1990	2709	15.1
1991	3002	16.2
1992	3281	16.8
1993	3454	17.1
1994	3597	17.1
1995	3821	17.3

Source: Bureau of Economic Analysis, tabulations by authors.

grammes, are not subject to income eligibility criteria.[19] Second, the value of the monthly benefits received by transfer recipients under certain income-conditioned programmes, such as AFDC benefits, vary from state to state depending on the state legislatures' generosity toward welfare recipients. Higher income states, *ceteris paribus,* tend to pay above average AFDC benefits to eligible recipients. Third, the size of the unemployment benefits received by eligible unemployed workers is also set by state law, and the formulas typically pay higher weekly benefits to workers with higher weekly earnings on the jobs from which they were laid off subject to monthly ceilings.

To illustrate the variability across states in the absolute and relative amount of government transfers received by state residents in 1995, we calculated the value of the per capita transfers of residents in those states with the ten highest and ten lowest per capita personal incomes. During 1995, per capita transfer incomes of state residents ranged from a low of $2613 in Utah to a high of $7069 in the District of Columbia. Mean per capita transfer incomes of the residents of the ten most affluent states were $4433 versus a mean of $3618 for residents of the ten least affluent states. On average, the residents of the most affluent states received higher absolute amounts of per capita transfers than the residents of the least affluent states. However, the mean per capita transfer incomes of the ten most affluent states was only 23 per cent higher than the mean per capita transfer income of the bottom ten states. In contrast, the 1995 mean per capita income of the ten most affluent states was 53 per cent higher than the bottom ten states, indicating that the provision of transfer income had a moderating influence on the degree of inequality in the state income distribution at least from the top and bottom of the distribution.

A second approach to an analysis of the role of transfer incomes in reducing state income inequality involves an examination of the shares of per capita personal income accruing to the residents of each state in the form of government transfers. In 1995, the value of these transfer shares ranged from lows of 13.7 per cent in Colorado and Connecticut to a high of 26.3 per cent in West Virginia. In 1995, within the ten most affluent states, government transfers accounted on average for 15.8 per cent of personal incomes versus nearly 20 per cent for the ten least affluent states.

Our third approach to estimating the impact of government transfers on the degree of personal income inequality across states involves the calculation of coefficients of variation for two per capita income distributions: per capita incomes including transfers and per capita incomes excluding transfers. During 1995, the coefficient of variation for per capita personal incomes excluding government transfers was 0.176 while the coefficient of variation for per capita incomes including government transfers was 0.161 (Table 6.15). The inclusion of government transfers, thus, reduced the degree of inequality in the pre-transfer state income distribution by 8.6 per cent. Findings are quite similar for the previous six years. Government transfers reduced the degree of inequality in the state per capita income distribution by 8.6 to 10.0 per cent each year from 1989 to 1995. Findings in Column (B) of Table 6.15 also clearly reveal that the degree of inequality in per capita market incomes across states declined steadily from 1989 to 1994, with the coefficient of variation for this income variable falling by 12 per cent over this time period.

Table 6.15 The degree of inequality in the state per capita income distribution including and excluding cash and in-kind government transfers, 1989–1995

Year	(A) CV including transfers	(B) CV excluding transfers	(C) Percentage change in inequality [(A − B)/B]
1989	0.178	0.198	−10.0
1990	0.172	0.190	−9.5
1991	0.167	0.184	−9.3
1992	0.165	0.182	−8.9
1993	0.162	0.179	−9.2
1994	0.159	0.174	−8.8
1995	0.161	0.176	−8.6

INEQUALITY IN STATE PER CAPITA DISPOSABLE INCOMES

Government tax policies can influence the amount of inequality in state per capita incomes by affecting the amount of personal income available to state residents after the payment of personal taxes and non-tax payments (fines, fees, donations) to national, state and local governments. The Bureau of Economic Analysis produces annual estimates of per capita disposable incomes for each state and region. The disposable income estimates are derived by subtracting all personal taxes (primarily federal and state incomes taxes) and non-tax payments from the personal income estimates. Findings on the (unweighted) mean per capita personal and disposable incomes of states for the years 1989 to 1995 are displayed in Table 6.16.

Between 1989 and 1995, mean per capita disposable incomes accounted for 87 per cent of the personal incomes of state residents.[20] Given the progressivity of the federal income tax and the fact that higher income states are more likely to rely on an income tax to raise state revenue, one would expect the ratio of personal taxes to personal incomes to vary by state, being higher for more affluent states. The ratios of personal taxes to personal incomes in 1995 ranged from a low of 8.8 per cent in Mississippi (the lowest per capita income state) to a high of 16 per cent for Connecticut, the second highest per capita income state. The ten most affluent states had an average tax ratio of 14.3 per cent with 11.8 per cent for the ten least affluent states.[21]

Table 6.16 Mean per capita personal incomes and mean per capita disposable incomes of the 50 states and the District of Columbia, 1989–1995 (in 1996 dollars)

Year	(A) Per capita income	(B) Per capita disposable income	(C) Disposable as percentage of personal income
1989	21 807	18 998	87.1
1990	21 915	19 120	87.2
1991	21 681	18 993	87.6
1992	22 125	19 421	87.8
1993	22 232	19 462	87.5
1994	22 572	19 732	87.4
1995	23 050	20 082	87.1

Table 6.17   Coefficients of variation for state per capita incomes before transfers, post-transfers and post-tax, 1989–1995

Year	(A) Pre-transfer	(B) Post-transfer	(C) Post-tax, post-transfer
1989	0.198	0.178	0.164
1990	0.190	0.172	0.159
1991	0.184	0.167	0.155
1992	0.182	0.164	0.152
1993	0.179	0.162	0.149
1994	0.174	0.159	0.145
1995	0.176	0.161	0.147

The disposable per capita personal income series for states for the years 1989–95 was used to calculate coefficients of variation for each year (Table 6.17). The CVs for per capita disposable incomes ranged from a low of 0.145 in 1994 to 0.164 in 1989 and similar to the pre-tax per capita income measures exhibit a fairly steady decline over the first half of the 1990s. The measures of inequality for the post-tax, post-transfer incomes of states can be compared to the pre-transfer, pre-tax and the post-transfer, pre-tax distributions. In 1995, the CV for disposable personal incomes was 0.147, with 0.161 for the pre-tax distribution and 0.176 for the pre-transfer, pre-tax distribution. Thus, the combined effect of government transfer and personal tax policies in the US was to reduce the degree of inequality in the per capita income distribution across states by 16–17 per cent in 1995. Similar findings apply to each other year in this time period. The reduction in income inequality across states is equally attributable to the effects of government transfers and personal tax payments.

INEQUALITY IN STATE COST-OF-LIVING ADJUSTED DISPOSABLE INCOMES

Given the absence of official cost-of-living data for regions or states in the US, our analyses of the degree of inequality in the per capita personal incomes of the residents of regions and states were based on nominal or constant dollar incomes which assumed no geographic variation in living costs across states. In their final report to the US Congress on poverty income concepts and measures, the National Research Council's Panel on

Poverty and Family Assistance provided estimates of cost-of-housing adjusted poverty indices for metropolitan areas and non-metropolitan areas in the US in 1990 based on variations in the cost of purchasing rental shelter with specified characteristics for a four-person family.[22] We have used these local area poverty indices together with weights representing their share of each state's population to calculate a set of state cost-of-living indices for use in adjusting each state's per capita disposable personal incomes in 1995 and 1996.[23]

The values of these cost-of-housing adjusted poverty indices for states ranged from a low of 84.3 in Mississippi, the lowest income state, to highs of 115 and 117 in California and Massachusetts (Table 6.18). Low income states in the more rural South and in the more rural segments of the nation's Farm Belt had the lowest rental costs of shelter, hence the lowest cost-of-housing adjusted poverty lines.

Table 6.18 Variation in the cost-of-housing adjusted poverty index for selected states, 1990 (US = 100)

State	Index
Top five	
Massachusetts	117.2
California	114.6
Rhode Island	114.0
Connecticut	113.2
New Hampshire	112.8
Bottom five	
Arkansas	88.2
Kansas	87.9
South Dakota	86.1
North Dakota	86.1
Mississippi	84.3

Source: Sum, Bahuguna and Palma (1998)

Each state's per capita disposable income in 1995 and 1996 was adjusted for the state of cost-of-living index based on this new poverty index. Adjustments for cost of living substantially reduced the degree of inequality in per capita disposable incomes across states in both years. In 1995, the CV was reduced from 0.149 before adjustment to 0.108 after adjustment, a relative decline of 28 per cent. A similar-sized reduction in the CV occurred in 1996 once cost-of-living adjustments were introduced (Table 6.19).

Table 6.19 Measures of inequality in the cost-of-housing adjusted per capita disposable incomes of states, 1995 and 1996

Variable	(A) 1995	(B) 1996
Per capita disposable income		
Mean	$19578	$20373
Standard deviation	$2916	$2994
Coefficient of variation	0.149	0.147
Per capita cost-of-living adjusted disposable income		
Mean	$19954	$20773
Standard deviation	$2162	$2266
Coefficient of variation	0.108	0.109

Note: Findings exclude the states of Alaska and Hawaii.

These findings clearly indicate that the per capita disposable incomes of states in the US adjusted for estimated differences in purchasing power had converged considerably by the mid-1990s. Reduced inequality in incomes across regions and states in recent decades was, however, simultaneously accompanied by rising inequality in the earnings of workers and the incomes of families across most regions and states in the US. Place inequality was being supplanted by worker and family inequality as a major source of public policy concern.

NOTES

1. The per capita personal income estimates of the US Department of Commerce's Bureau of Economic Analysis (BEA) are more comprehensive in coverage than the money income concepts used by the Bureau of the Census in conducting the monthly Current Population Surveys. The per capita income estimates of BEA encompass all wage supplements, including employer contributions to health and pension funds as well as in-kind payments to workers, food produced and consumed on the farm, the rental value of owner occupied homes, the value of in-kind government benefits such as food stamps and Medicaid and imputed interest income from banks for services provided without charges. For a more detailed review of conceptual differences between these two personal income series, see US Bureau of the Census (1984) and Ryscavage (1986).

2. The US Bureau of Labor Statistics stopped publishing family budget data for metropolitan areas across the nation after the fall of 1981. There are a number of private organizations, including the American Chamber of Commerce Research Association, that do produce estimates of the costs of achieving a mid-level management standard of living in many urban areas across the US.

3. The US Bureau of Labor Statistics has provided estimates of the value of the CPI-UX1 index for the years 1959–81. We have extended this index back to 1929 by applying the annual growth rates of the CPI-U index for the years 1929–59. For an explanation of the CPI-UX1 series and comparisons of its values with the CPI-U index, see US Bureau of the Census (1992).

4. The year 1949 actually was a recession year, with recovery beginning in the late fall of that year. The 1990–91 national recession officially ended in March of 1991. For the timing of business-cycle peaks and troughs in the United States since the end of World War II, see Sorkin (1988).

5. Many of these income inequality measures also are used in analysing inequalities in the incomes of households and families in countries around the world (Osberg, 1991).

6. For an example of the use of the coefficient of variation in previous state income inequality studies, see the 1988 study by Coughlin and Mandelbaum.

7. The coefficient of variation is considered to be an unbiased measure of inequality when the underlying data (in this case state per capita incomes) are normally distributed. Analyses by Coughlin and Mandelbaum for the 48 continental states and by the authors of this paper for all 50 states for the 1969–96 period reveal that the per capita incomes of states can be judged to be normally distributed using the Shapiro–Wilk (1965) test for normality.

8. This regional classification system is somewhat different from that used by BEA. For a recent example of the use of the BEA's regional classification system, see Friedenberg and Tran (1994).

9. The New England region was most adversely affected, with real Gross State Product for the region falling by 5.6 per cent between 1989 and 1991 (US Department of Commerce, 1997).

10. The National Research Council has generated estimates of cost-of-living adjusted poverty lines for metropolitan and non-metropolitan areas across regions of the country. The poverty lines for large metropolitan areas in the New England, Middle Atlantic and Pacific region are 14 to 20 per cent above the US average.

11. Many other empirical studies use the log of personal incomes due to the frequent lack of normality in the per capita income or output distribution; however, as noted earlier, the distribution of state per capita incomes in the USA has been found to be normal in nearly all years under the Shapiro–Wilk test of normality.

12. Using the standardized regression coefficient as our measure of the relative size of the effect, the size of the standardized regression coefficient was 0.88 for the 1940s, 0.53 for the 1950s, 0.49 for the 1960s and 0.60 for the 1970s.

13. The 'per capita income' measures appearing in the Paci and Saba (1998) and Paci (1997) studies actually are measures of real GDP per capita in purchasing power parity terms. The US per capita income measures reflect the personal income concepts from the national income accounts. Similar findings would apply, however, if we used per capita Gross Regional Product estimates for the US in 1980 and 1990. The coefficients of variation for Gross Regional Product in 1980 and 1990 were 0.102 and 0.107, respectively (Sum *et al.*, 1995).

14. The 109 European regions included in Paci's 1997 study of income and productivity inequality included the following countries: Belgium, Denmark, France, Germany, Greece, Ireland, Italy, Luxemburg, Netherlands, Portugal, Spain and the United Kingdom. The standard deviation of the relative incomes for the European regions in 1980 and 1990 should be statistically comparable though not identical to the standard deviation of the logs.

15. The per capita income measures for Italy in Table 6.13 actually reflect GDP per capita rather than personal incomes which include cash and in-kind transfers. A separate analysis of the distribution of family income across regions in Italy revealed much less inequality than the per capita output measures.
16. In 1995, approximately one half of all transfer payments to persons in the US went to finance Social Security retirement, disability and Medicare benefits for the elderly. See Council of Economic Advisers (1997), Table B-27, pp. 330–31.
17. The mean per capita transfer incomes represent unweighted means for the 50 states and the District of Columbia. As a result, they will differ slightly from the per capita income transfers for all residents of the USA. For example, in 1995, the per capita personal transfer payments from government for the US was $3893 versus an estimated mean per capital transfer income of $3821 for the 50 states and DC.
18. A more comprehensive analysis would take into account the impacts of these transfer payments on the labour supply, savings and investment behaviours of state residents. Such economic simulations are beyond the scope of this paper.
19. Income taxes on these social security retirement benefits are, however, dependent on the adjusted money incomes of the family receiving such benefits.
20. The unweighted mean for the 50 states and DC in 1995 was basically identical to the ratio for all 50 states combined.
21. Excluding New Hampshire, which has no state income tax, from the top ten raises the tax ratio for the remaining states to 14.6 per cent.
22. The rental base housing unit of comparison is a 'two bedroom apartment that had complete plumbing facilities, electricity, kitchen facilities and in which the occupant had moved in within the past five years'. The rent at the 45th percentile of the distribution for the above rental units was used to identify the fair market rent in each area.
23. The shares of the state's population in each metropolitan area and non-metropolitan area as of March 1996 were used as weights in deriving a cost-of-living adjusted poverty index for each state in 1996.

REFERENCES

Alam, M.S. (1992), 'Convergence in developed countries: an empirical investigation', *Welfwirtschafliches Archiv*, **128**, 189–201.

Alam, M.S. and A. Naseer (1992), 'Convergence and polarization: testing for an inverted-U-relation between growth rates and GNP per capita', *Applied Economics*, **24**, 363–6.

Barro, Robert J. (1991), 'Economic growth in a cross section of countries', *Quarterly Journal of Economics*, **196**, 407–43.

Barro, Robert J. and Xavier Sala-i-Martin (1991), 'Convergence across states and regions', *Brookings Papers on Economic Activity*, **0**(1), 107–58.

Barro, Robert J. and Xavier Sala-i-Martin (1992), 'Convergence', *Journal of Political Economy*, **100**, 223–51.

Barro, Robert J. and Xavier Sala-i-Martin (1995), *Economic Growth*, New York: McGraw-Hill.

Baumol, William J., Richard R. Nelson and Edward N. Wolff (eds) (1994), *Convergence of Productivity*, New York: Oxford University Press.

Blomstrom, Magnow and Edward N. Wolff (1994), 'Multinational Corporations and Productivity Convergence in Mexico', in William J. Baumol *et al.* (eds), *Convergence of Productivity*, New York: Oxford University Press, pp. 263–84.

Coughlin, Cletus C. and Thomas B. Mandelbaum (1988), 'Why have state per capita incomes diverged recently?', *Federal Reserve Bank of St. Louis Review*, September/October, 24–36.

Coulombe, S. and F. Lee (1993), 'Regional economic disparities in Canada', discussion paper, Department of Economics, University of Ottawa.

Council of Economic Advisers (1964), *Economic Report of the President: 1964*, Washington, DC: US Government Printing Office.

Council of Economic Advisers (1997), *Economic Report of the President: 1997*, Washington, DC: US Government Printing Office.

Friedenberg, Howard and Duke D. Tran (1994), 'Total and per capita personal income by state and region', *Survey of Current Business*, April, 117–26.

Keil, Manfred W. and Rubina Vohra (1993), 'What's Wyoming got that we don't', Working Paper, Department of Economics, Northeastern University.

Leonardi, Robert (1995), *Convergence, Cohesion, and Integration in the European Union*, New York: St. Martin's Press.

Mallick, Rajiv and Elias Carayannis (1994), 'Regional economic convergence in Mexico: an analysis by industry', *Growth and Change*, **24**, 325–34.

Mankiw, N. Gregory, David Romer and David W. Weil (1992), 'A contribution to the empirics of economic growth', *Quarterly Journal of Economics*, **107**, 407–35.

Osberg, Lars (ed.) (1991), *Economic Inequality and Poverty: International Perspectives*, Armonk, NY: M.E. Sharpe Inc., pp. 3–19.

Paci, Raffaele and Francesco Pigliaru (1997), 'Structural change and covergence: an Italian regional perspective', *Structural Change and Economic Dynamics*, **8**, 297–318.

Paci, Raffaele (1997), 'More similar and less equal: economic growth in the European regions', *Weltwirtschaftliches Archiv*, **133**, 609–34.

Paci, Raffaele and Andrea Saba (1998), 'The empirics of regional economic growth in Italy, 1951–1993', *Rivista Internazionale di Scienze Economiche e Commerciale*, **45**, 515–42.

Ryscavage, Paul (1986), 'Reconciling divergent trends in real income', *Monthly Labor Review*, **109**, 24–9.

Shapiro, S.S. and M.B. Wilk (1965), 'An analysis of variance test for normality', *Biometrika*, **52**, 591–611.

Sorkin, Alan L. (1988), *Monetary and Fiscal Policy and Business Cycles in the Modern Era*, Lexington, MA: Lexington Books.

Sum, Andrew, John Adams, Donna Desrochers, Neal Fogg and Gustav Schachter (1995), 'Trends in income and output inequality among regions and states in the United States', paper presented to the North American Regional Science Association Meetings, Cincinnati, Ohio.

Sum, Andrew, Anwiti Bahuguna and Sheila Palma (1998), 'Rethinking poverty measures: local housing costs, adjusted poverty lines and their consequences for Massachusetts', report prepared for MassINC, Center for Labor Market Studies, Northeastern University.

US Bureau of the Census (1984), Current Population Reports, Consumer Income, Series P-60, No. 142, *Money Income of Households, Families, and Persons in the United States: 1982*, Washington, DC: US Government Printing Office.

US Bureau of the Census (1992), Current Population Reports, Series P-60, No. 180, *Money Incomes of Persons, Households, and Families: 1991*, Washington, DC: US Government Printing Office.

US Bureau of Labor Statistics (1994), *Geographic Profile of Employment and Unemployment*, Washington, DC: US Government Printing Office.

US Congress, Joint Economic Committee, Staff Study by the Democratic Staff (1986), 'The bi-coastal economy: regional patterns of economic growth during the Reagan Administration', Washington, DC.

US Department of Commerce (1996), *Survey of Current Business*, Washington, DC: US Government Printing Office.

US Department of Commerce, Bureau of Economic Analysis (1997), *BEA Press Release on State Per Capita Incomes in 1996*, Washington, DC.

Vohra, Rubina (1993), 'An economic analysis of the growth path of states' real gross state product and convergence trends among states', 1969–1989, PhD dissertation, Northeastern University, Boston.

Yotopoulos, Pan A. and Jeffrey B. Nugent (1976), *Economics of Development: Empirical Investigations*, New York: Harper and Row.

7. Per capita earnings inequality across regions and states in the United States: trends, sources, determinants

Andrew M. Sum and Walter N. Fogg

INTRODUCTION

In the previous chapter, trends in inequality in per capita personal incomes across regions and states in the US were identified and assessed. Findings revealed a marked decline in inequality among regions and states over the entire 1929–96 period, a trend toward convergence in all decades except the 1980s, and a renewal of convergence trends in the 1990s. Per capita market incomes (wages, salaries, property incomes) remain more unequally distributed than per capita personal incomes which include government transfers, and national and state personal tax policies have a further moderating effect on state income inequality. Although inequalities in property income do contribute to remaining income inequalities across states, the bulk of the differences is attributable to earnings from employment.[1]

This chapter is designed to identify and analyse inequality in per capita earnings from employment across regions and states in the US over the 1979–95 period. The analysis will begin with an examination of the relative importance of earnings as a source of the personal incomes of state residents and analyse the degree of inequality in per capita earnings across states over the 1989–96 period. This will be followed by an analysis of the economic, labour market and demographic forces influencing the per capita earnings of state residents and the contribution of each of these sources to remaining inequality in per capita earnings across regions and states. The final sections will be devoted to a multivariate statistical analysis of the real hourly earnings of workers across states and changes in those real hourly earnings over time, with an emphasis on the critical role of state differences in labour productivity as measured by Gross State Product per hour of work (Sum and Fogg, 1996).

INEQUALITY IN NET EARNINGS PER CAPITA ACROSS STATES

The bulk of the personal incomes received by residents of states consists of earnings from wage and salary employment and self-employment. The US Department of Commerce's Bureau of Economic Analysis produces a set of 'net earnings' estimates for residents of each state. The net earnings estimates are derived by first summing all wages and salaries and proprietor incomes generated within the state, subtracting out employee contributions for social insurance, and then adjusting these earnings by place of residence of workers.[2] The final earnings figure is referred to as 'net earnings by place of residence'.

Estimates of the (unweighted) mean per capita net earnings of the residents of the 50 states and the District of Columbia are displayed in Table 7.1 for the years 1989 through 1995. In the latter year, mean per capita earnings were equal to $14 767, and they represented just under 66 per cent of the mean per capita personal incomes of states. Similar ratios have prevailed throughout the entire 1989–1995 period.

Table 7.1 Mean per capita net earnings of state residents in absolute dollars and as a percentage of per capita personal incomes, 1989–1995 (in nominal dollars)

Year	(A) Mean per capita net earnings ($)	(B) Net earnings as a percentage of personal incomes
1989	$11 514	66.7
1990	$12 149	66.4
1991	$12 392	65.7
1992	$13 133	66.3
1993	$13 569	66.2
1994	$14 150	66.3
1995	$14 767	65.9

Differences in per capita earnings across states have accounted for the largest share of inequality in per capita incomes in recent years. We calculated the coefficients of variation for the per capita earnings distribution for all 50 states and the District of Columbia and compared the values of the coefficients of variations for per capita earnings with those of per capita personal incomes each year over the 1989–1995 period. In 1989, the coefficient of variation for per capita net earnings was 0.197, exceeding the coefficient of variation for per capita personal incomes by 10 per cent (Table 7.2). Since 1989, the coefficient of variation for per capita net earnings has fallen fairly steadily, dropping to 0.170 in 1994, a 13 per cent reduction. In each year since 1989, the coefficient of variation for per capita net earnings has exceeded that for per capita personal incomes by 7 to 10 percentage points. The trend toward convergence of state per capita earnings clearly has been the driving force behind the renewed convergence in state per capita incomes during the 1990s.

Table 7.2 Comparisons of the degree of inequality in the state per capita personal incomes and net earnings distributions, 1989–1995

Year	(A) CV, per capita income	(B) CV, per capita net earnings	(C) Column B as a percentage of column A
1989	0.178	0.197	110
1990	0.172	0.189	110
1991	0.167	0.182	109
1992	0.165	0.180	109
1993	0.162	0.176	109
1994	0.159	0.170	107
1995	0.161	0.172	107

ANALYSING THE SOURCES OF VARIATION IN PER CAPITA EARNINGS

Ideally, the state earnings data of the Bureau of Economic Analysis would be capable of being disaggregated so that we could identify the contribution of demographic, labour force behaviour, employment and productivity variables to the remaining inequalities in the per capita earnings of residents of regions and states. Unfortunately, we cannot directly tie these data to other related data sources on the demographic characteristics of a state's population or the labour market and productivity behaviour of its working age residents.

While BEA per capita earnings data cannot be directly linked to the regional and state demographic and labour market variables producing their annual values, a second source of annual data on the personal incomes of the residents of the nation, each region and state is produced by the US Census Bureau with the March Current Population Survey, the monthly household survey used to produce the national employment and unemployment estimates.[3] The March Current Population Survey contains a work experience and income supplement that collects annual data on the labour force behaviour, employment experiences, earnings and money incomes of all persons (15+) living in sample households (US Bureau of the Census, 1997). The data collected with the March supplement pertain to the actual labour market and earnings experiences of respondents during the prior calendar year. For example, the March 1996 survey was used to collect data on 1995 labour market and earnings experiences.

THE FACTORS INFLUENCING THE PER CAPITA EARNINGS OF THE RESIDENTS OF REGIONS AND STATES

The money incomes of state residents are generated by a number of different sources, including employment, property income and cash transfers from the government. In recent years, earnings from labour income have represented just under 70 per cent of the personal incomes of national residents under the BEA personal income series and closer to 80 per cent of the money incomes of persons under the US Census Bureau's per capita money income estimates. The labour earnings' share of money incomes under the Census Bureau's per capita income series is higher than the BEA's since the money income measure excludes wage supplements, imputed rental incomes from owner-occupied homes and in-kind transfers, such as food stamps and Medicaid and Medicare health benefits (Ryscavage, 1986).

Use of the Census Bureau's per capita money income series allows us to examine the role of key demographic, labour force participation, labour supply, labour utilization, and hourly earnings variables in influencing the level of per capita earnings of state residents. The population and work experience data can be directly tied to the earnings data from the same household survey. We have used the March 1980, March 1990 and March 1996 CPS work experience data to analyse the levels and sources of the 1979, 1989 and 1995 per capita earnings of all US residents, those of the residents of each of the nine Census regions, and the residents of individual states.

Findings of our analysis will be used to identify the role of key demographic and labour market variables in generating the observed differences in the per capita earnings of the residents of regions and states over the 1979–95 period. The set of findings will help provide answers to the following questions: How do the residents of the more affluent regions and states obtain per capita earnings higher than those of their less affluent counterparts across the nation? How closely have regions and states converged on each of the variables influencing per capita earnings? What are the key sources of the remaining differences in per capita earnings across states?

Given the critical role played by labour earnings in determining the living standards of state residents, an examination of the diverse forces producing these earnings is critical to our understanding of differences across regions and states at a given point in time and changes in state residents' living standards over time. The per capita personal earnings from employment of the residents of any area will be influenced by five separate, though somewhat interrelated, sets of forces, including demographic variables, the labour force participation behaviour of the area's working-age resident population, the utilization rate of the state's labour force, the intensity of their attachment to the labour market during the year and earnings per hour of work (Sum and Fogg, 1995). These five variables are described in the following paragraphs (see the algebraic formulas underlying these relationships in Table 7.3).

The first variable (Pw/P) is a demographic variable representing the share of a state's resident civilian non-institutional population that is of working age. For our analysis, we are defining the population aged 15 years and older as a state's working-age population, a definition in close accord with the 16 and older definition used by the US Bureau of Labor Statistics in its analysis of the nation's official labour force statistics. The symbol Pw is used to represent the state's working-age population, and the symbol Pw/P represents the fraction of a state's resident population that is of working age (15+).

The second variable (L/Pw) represents the share of the state's working-age population that either worked or sought work at some point during the calendar year. Any resident (15+) who participated in the civilian labour force at some point during the year, regardless of the duration of participation or success in finding a job, will be counted in our definition of the resident labour force. The symbol L/Pw is used to represent this labour force attachment variable.

The third variable (E/L) represents the fraction of a state's active labour force participants who were able to obtain paid employment at some time during the year. Not all individuals who enter the labour force during the year succeed in obtaining employment. The value of E/L often will be found to be quite high (98 per cent) for most states in the US. Persons who mixed unemployment and employment during the year are included in our count of E. A substantial majority of a typical state's unemployed population works at some point during the year (Sum and

*Table 7.3　The role of demographic forces, residents' labour force
participation behaviour, labour utilization rates, hours of work
and hourly earnings from employment in influencing the total and
per capita personal earnings of state residents*

---

(1)　Total earnings of state residents during a calendar year are a function of the following five factors:

$$Y_e = Pw \cdot L/Pw \cdot E/L \cdot H/E \cdot Y_e/H$$

where　　Y_e　=　total personal income received by state residents in the form of earnings (wages and salaries and self-employment income)

Pw　=　size of the state's working-age population (15+)

L　=　number of individuals (15+) in the state who participated in the civilian labour force at some time during the year

E　=　number of individuals (15+) in the state who were employed for one or more weeks during the year

H/E　=　average (mean) annual hours worked by employed residents of the state

Y_e/H　=　average (mean) hourly earnings from employment among all employed state residents (15+)

(2)　Per capita earnings of state residents are influenced by the following factors:

$$Y_e/P = Pw/P \cdot L/Pw \cdot E/L \cdot H/E \cdot Y_e/H$$

where　　P　=　total resident population of the state

Pw/P　=　the fraction of the state's resident population that is 15 years of age or older

---

Fogg, 1996). Unlike many of our Western European counterparts, few of the unemployed in the US remain unemployed all year (Martin; Organization for Economic Cooperation and Development).

The fourth variable (H/E) represents the mean annual number of hours that each employed person worked. These estimates are paid hours rather than actual hours at work. They include weeks of paid vacation, holidays, and sick leave. Mean annual hours of work among a state's employed labour force are influenced by both their weeks of employment during the year and the average hours of work per week of employment. The March CPS work experience supplement collects data from each employed person (15+) on weeks of employment during the prior year and average hours of work while employed. The product of these two variables provides our estimates of annual hours of work. The symbol H/E is used to represent the mean annual hours of paid work for employed persons within the nation, a region or a state.

The fifth variable (Y_e/H) represents the gross pre-tax earnings of employed state residents (including the self-employed) per hour of paid employment. In accord with neoclassical economic theory, the hourly earnings of workers should be a good proxy for their contribution to the revenue of the firms in which they are employed. In neoclassical labour economics, the earnings of a worker (including the value of fringe benefits and other employer-financed wage supplements) should be equal to the value of the marginal revenue product; that is, the additional revenue obtained by the firm from the hiring of one more unit of labour (Smith and Ehrenberg, 1997). The symbol Y_e/H is used to represent the mean hourly, before-tax earnings of workers in the state, excluding fringe benefits and other non-cash wage supplements. Unlike most published data on hourly earnings, this variable does not simply measure the earnings of hourly paid workers, but instead reflects the earnings experiences of all wage and salary workers as well as the self-employed in each state.

TRENDS IN THE PER CAPITA REAL EARNINGS OF US RESIDENTS, 1979–95

Findings of our estimates of the levels and sources of the 1979, 1989 and 1995 per capita real earnings of residents of the US are displayed in Table 7.4. During 1979, the per capita real annual earnings of residents of the USA in constant 1995 dollars were $11 921. By 1989, US residents obtained per capita earnings of $13 388, or 12 per cent above the 1979 average, and by 1995 per capita real earnings had risen to $13 792, 16 per cent above their 1979 level. What economic and demographic developments between 1979 and 1995 help explain this growth in earnings?

Between 1979 and 1995, there were only slight changes in the relative size of the nation's working-age population, the labour force attachment of the working age population, or the utilization rate of the labour force. Not one of these three variables changed by as much as 1 per cent over the entire 1979–95 period, and the combined effect of these three variables on per capita real earnings growth over this period was less than 1 per cent. The two dominant factors contributing to the rise in the per

Table 7.4 *Per capita real earnings and their sources, US, 1979–1995 (earnings in constant 1995 dollars, CPI-UXI index)*

Year	Real earnings per capita	Percentage of population that is working age (15+)	Percentage of working-age pop. in labour force	Percentage of labour force employed	Average annual hours per worker	Average real earnings per hour
1979	$11 921	77.0	69.3	98.3	1683	$13.52
1989	$13 388	77.8	70.4	98.8	1765	$14.01
1995	$13 792	77.3	69.8	98.1	1805	$14.42
1979–1989						
Absolute change	$1 467	0.008	0.011	0.005	83	$0.50
Percentage change	12.3	1.0	1.6	0.5	4.9	3.7
1989–1995						
Absolute change	$405	−0.005	−0.006	−0.007	40	$0.41
Percentage change	3.0	−0.6	−0.8	−0.7	2.3	2.9
1979–1995						
Absolute change	$1 871	0.003	0.006	−0.002	123	$0.91
Percentage change	15.7	0.4	0.8	−0.2	7.3	6.7

Source: March 1980, March 1990 and March 1996 CPS surveys, tabulations by Center for Labor Market Studies.

capita real earnings of US residents were an increase in mean annual hours of work among the employed (+7 per cent) and a comparable, moderate gain in real hourly earnings (+7 per cent). The increase in mean annual hours of work primarily took place among non-elderly adult women who were more likely to work year-round, full-time. The absence of strong gains in labour productivity in the private non-farm business sector (slightly under 1 per cent per year) and the rising share of labour compensation accounted for by non-wage benefits and employee taxes kept real hourly wage growth at 0.4 per cent per year over this period (Council of Economic Advisers, 1997).

PER CAPITA REAL EARNINGS ACROSS REGIONS, 1979–95

Estimates of the level and sources of per capita real earnings of residents in each of the nine geographic regions in 1979, 1989 and 1995 are displayed in Table 7.5. Over the 1979–95 period, the per capita real earnings of residents in each geographic region improved; however, the rates of growth in per capita real earnings varied considerably across regions and over time within regions. Moreover, the sources of the growth in earnings varied markedly across regions. Several regions changed their relative rankings over this time period, with New England moving from third place in 1979 to first place in 1989 and remaining there in 1995 despite more adverse labour market conditions in the 1990s. The South Atlantic region improved its ranking over this period, moving from eighth in 1979 to fifth highest in 1989 before falling back to sixth in 1995.

In 1979, the Pacific region ($13 348) ranked first in terms of per capita earnings followed by the East North Central region ($12 645) and New England $12 637. The East South Central region ranked last with per capita earnings of only $9 670, or 28 per cent below that of the Pacific region. During the 1980s, the growth rates of per capita real earnings varied markedly across the regions. New England's growth rate of 32 per cent was nearly three times as high as that of the nation, and the two other Atlantic coastal regions (Middle Atlantic and South Atlantic) also experienced growth rates well above the US average.

During the 1989–95 period, the economic fates of most regions shifted markedly from their experiences in the 1980s. The regions along the Atlantic coast either experienced declines in per capita real earnings or grew at a rate below the national average. The East South Central region, which ranked last in 1989, was characterized by the highest rate of growth (+12 per cent) in per capita earnings followed by the two Midwest

Table 7.5 Real per capita earnings and their sources, US and nine census regions, 1979–1995 (earnings in constant 1995 dollars)

	Real earnings per capita ($)	Percentage of population that is working age (15+)	Percentage of working-age pop. in labour force	Percentage of labour force employed	Average annual hours per worker	Average real earnings per hour ($)
1979						
US total	11 921	77.0	69.3	98.3	1683	13.52
New England	12 637	79.4	72.5	98.9	1645	13.48
Middle Atlantic	11 949	78.3	65.1	97.8	1659	14.46
E.N. Central	12 645	76.3	70.3	98.0	1685	14.28
W.N. Central	11 945	77.7	74.9	99.0	1705	12.16
South Atlantic	10 969	77.2	67.7	98.2	1704	12.55
E.S. Central	9 670	76.2	65.3	98.0	1673	11.86
W.S. Central	11 006	75.1	69.0	98.3	1717	12.57
Mountain	12 102	74.6	73.8	98.8	1677	13.27
Pacific	13 348	77.5	70.8	98.4	1667	14.83
1989						
US total	13 388	77.8	70.4	98.8	1765	14.01
New England	16 684	80.3	75.0	99.2	1769	15.78
Middle Atlantic	14 708	79.1	67.8	98.8	1775	15.65
E.N. Central	13 284	78.1	70.8	98.5	1742	14.00
W.N. Central	12 708	77.3	75.5	99.1	1773	12.39

South Atlantic	13 193	79.4	70.0	99.0	1797	13.34
E.S. Central	10 643	78.0	66.4	98.1	1756	11.92
W.S. Central	11 513	75.6	69.3	98.3	1755	12.74
Mountain	12 170	75.2	71.5	99.1	1747	13.08
Pacific	14 420	76.3	71.0	99.0	1757	15.28
1995						
US total	13 792	77.3	69.8	98.1	1805	14.42
New England	15 822	79.0	71.4	98.3	1791	15.93
Middle Atlantic	14 499	78.4	66.4	97.2	1786	16.03
E.N. Central	14 462	77.2	72.2	98.6	1807	14.57
W.N. Central	13 684	77.3	76.4	98.7	1795	13.06
South Atlantic	13 405	79.2	67.7	98.1	1851	13.77
E.S. Central	11 952	77.0	66.4	98.2	1810	13.15
W.S. Central	12 251	75.9	69.9	98.5	1824	12.85
Mountain	13 079	75.6	72.9	98.6	1755	13.71
Pacific	14 330	75.8	69.7	97.3	1785	15.62

regions and the Mountain region, each of which lagged badly behind the nation in the 1980s.

The bulk of the 1980s per capita earnings growth was clearly confined to residents of the East Coast. The Midwest 'Rust Belt', the oil states of the Southwest, and the Mountain region, which also was adversely affected by the decline in world oil prices, experienced growth rates in per capita earnings less than half of the national average.

The exceptionally strong performance of most states in the New England economy was influenced by substantial growth in real hourly earnings of its workers (Blanchard and Katz, 1992). In 1979, the mean real hourly earnings of New England workers were $13.48, slightly below the US average of $13.52 and only fourth highest in the nation. By 1989, real hourly earnings of New England workers had risen to $15.78, a gain of 17 per cent, moving its ranking among the nine regions to first place, nearly 13 per cent above the US average. A substantial restructuring of the New England region's industrial base and a major shift in the occupational composition of its jobs toward professional, management and high level sales occupations underlie this rapid growth in the hourly earnings of its workers (Sum, Fogg and Harrington, 1991). Both of the above sets of economic forces produced a sharp rise in labour productivity in the region, facilitating these above average gains in real hourly earnings (Sum *et al.*, 1995).

Findings of an analysis of changes in the degree of inequality in the per capita earnings of residents across the nine regions are summarized in Table 7.6. In 1979, the coefficient of variation for regional per capita earnings was 0.094, quite close to the estimated CV for per capita personal incomes during that year (0.106). During the 1980s, the degree of inequality in the regional per capita earnings distribution widened considerably, rising to 0.138.[4] Since 1989, inequality in per capita earnings has been declining, falling to 0.088 in 1995. The estimated CV in 1995 was actually lower than in 1979, indicating that per capita earnings across regions in the USA likely reached a historical new low in 1995.

The findings in Table 7.6 can be used to identify the remaining sources of per capita earnings inequality across regions. By 1995, the regions had converged to near equality on labour force utilization, average annual hours of work per employee and the age structure of their populations. The coefficients of variation for each of these three variables in 1995 were in the 0.5 to 1.7 per cent range. In 1995, variations in regional per capita earnings were primarily due to differences in hourly earnings per capita (a CV equal to 0.089) and in labour force participation rates (0.047). Differences in labour productivity (GSP per hour of work) and labour force participation rates underlie the bulk of the remaining differences in the real per capita outputs of states (Sum *et al.*, 1995; Sum and Fogg,

Table 7.6 *Means, standard deviations and coefficients of variation of real earnings per capita and its sources, nine census regions, 1979–1995 (earnings in 1995 dollars)*

	Real earnings per capita ($)	Percentage of population that is working age (15+)	Percentage of working-age pop. in labour force	Percentage of labour force employed	Average annual hours per worker	Average real earnings per hour ($)
1979 Mean	11 808	76.9	69.9	98.4	1681	13.27
1989 Mean	13 258	77.7	70.8	98.8	1763	13.80
1995 Mean	13 720	77.3	70.3	98.2	1800	14.30
1979 Std. deviation	1107	1.5	3.5	0.4	24	1.07
1989 Std. deviation	1822	1.7	3.0	0.4	17	1.46
1995 Std. deviation	1212	1.4	3.3	0.6	27	1.28
1979 CV	0.0938	0.0198	0.0500	0.0042	0.0141	0.0806
1989 CV	0.1375	0.0224	0.0424	0.0040	0.0096	0.1055
1995 CV	0.0883	0.0176	0.0467	0.0057	0.0150	0.0894

1996). Since regions' rankings on these various determinants of per capita earnings do vary somewhat, the CV for per capita earnings is not markedly different from the CV for hourly earnings. Given the fact that the per capita earnings data for regions have not been adjusted for regional variations in the cost of living, the degree of convergence achieved by 1995 is quite remarkable. While New England maintained a 16 per cent per capita earnings advantage over the rest of the nation in 1995, the cost of achieving a middle class standard of living in the Greater Boston area (which contains one-half of the population of Massachusetts) in 1995 was roughly estimated to be 16 per cent higher than that for all metropolitan areas in the nation. Thus, the purchasing-power-parity-adjusted earnings of residents in New England are likely to be much closer to the US average. Similar results would hold true for the Middle Atlantic and Pacific regions, each of which is characterized by higher costs of living, particularly with respect to housing. The nation, thus, had come quite close to achieving regional parity in the per capita real earnings of residents by the middle of the 1990s.

INEQUALITY IN STATE PER CAPITA EARNINGS, 1979–1995

Similar analyses of per capita earnings can be performed for individual states. The per capita earnings (in constant 1995 dollars) of the top ten and bottom ten states in 1979 and 1995 are displayed in Table 7.7. In 1979, the per capita earnings of the top 10 states ranged from a high of $16 953 (Alaska) to $12 950 (New Jersey). The value of the unweighted mean per capita earnings for these ten states during 1979 was $14 283. In contrast, the mean per capita earnings of residents in the bottom 10 states during the same year were only $9331. The mean for the top ten states exceeded that of the bottom ten states by 53 per cent in 1979, a sizable relative difference.

Between 1979 and 1995, there was a fair degree of mobility among states in their movement into and out of the top ten and bottom ten rankings. In 1995, three new states (Massachusetts, New Hampshire and Minnesota) had joined the top ten while Wyoming, Nevada and California had fallen out of the top ten. At the bottom of the distribution there was somewhat less mobility. Eight of the bottom ten states in 1979 were in the bottom ten in 1995. The two states which moved out of the bottom ten were Maine (moving from forty-fifth to thirty-fifth) and Florida (moving from forty-seventh to thirty-seventh). In 1995, the unweighted mean value of per capita earnings for the top ten states ($16 369) was 54 per cent higher than the mean of the bottom ten states.

Table 7.7 States with the ten highest and ten lowest per capita real earnings, 1979 and 1995 (earnings in 1995 dollars)

	1979 Rankings			1995 Rankings			
	1979 Earnings per capita($)	1979 Rank	1995 Rank		1995 Earnings per capita($)	1995 Rank	1979 Rank
Ten highest							
Alaska	16953	1	4	Washington DC	17 192	1	4
Colorado	14767	2	7	Maryland	17 168	2	3
Maryland	14759	3	2	Massachusetts	16 664	3	13
Washington DC	14451	4	1	Alaska	16 646	4	1
Connecticut	14227	5	5	Connecticut	16 602	5	5
Wyoming	13926	6	33	New Jersey	16 592	6	10
Nevada	13895	7	11	Colorado	16 288	7	2
California	13549	8	18	New Hampshire	15 636	8	12
Illinois	13356	9	10	Minnesota	15 628	9	16
New Jersey	12950	10	6	Illinois	15 278	10	9
Unweighted mean	14283			Unweighted mean	16 369		

Table 7.7 (continued)

1979 Rankings					1995 Rankings		
	1979 Earnings per capita($)	1979 Rank	1995 Rank			1995 Earnings per capita($)	1995 Rank	1979 Rank

	1979 Earnings per capita($)	1979 Rank	1995 Rank		1995 Earnings per capita($)	1995 Rank	1979 Rank
Ten lowest							
New Mexico	9758	42	51	Oklahoma	11406	42	34
Louisiana	9725	43	47	S. Dakota	11393	43	44
S. Dakota	9648	44	43	S. Carolina	11196	44	49
Maine	9565	45	35	Alabama	11180	45	50
Mississippi	9248	46	50	Montana	10813	46	33
Florida	9213	47	37	Louisiana	10621	47	43
W. Virginia	9199	48	48	W. Virginia	10182	48	48
S. Carolina	9012	49	44	Arkansas	10090	49	51
Alabama	9010	50	45	Mississippi	9694	50	46
Arkansas	8931	51	49	New Mexico	9597	51	42
Unweighted mean	9331			Unweighted mean	10617		

198

Given the substantial degree of inequality in the per capita earnings of the residents of the top ten and bottom ten states in 1995, we estimated the sources of the per capita earnings for each of these states (Table 7.8). Demographic variables (Pw/P), the labour force utilization rate (E/L) and annual hours of work (H/E) played no substantive role in explaining differences in per capita earnings between the highest and lowest states. In both groups of states, the mean share of the resident population that

Table 7.8 Sources of the per capita real earnings of the ten highest and ten lowest states, US, 1995

	(A)	(B)	(C)	(D)	(E)	(F)
	Earnings per capita	Pw/P (%)	L/Pw (%)	E/L (%)	H/E	Y/H ($)
Ten highest						
Washington DC	17 192	78.2	70.4	96.2	1 859	17.44
Maryland	17 168	77.5	72.9	97.9	1 834	16.93
Massachusetts	16 664	79.8	70.7	98.2	1 798	16.75
Alaska	16 646	69.8	81.0	97.7	1 761	17.11
Connecticut	16 602	77.7	70.5	98.4	1 795	17.16
New Jersey	16 592	79.1	69.7	97.6	1 800	17.12
Colorado	16 288	77.7	79.3	98.7	1 806	17.12
New Hampshire	15 636	78.4	76.0	98.8	1 790	14.83
Minnesota	15 628	76.4	78.9	98.8	1 790	14.83
Illinois	15 278	77.8	72.4	97.9	1 799	14.67
Average	16 369	77.2	74.2	98.0	1 803	16.40
Ten lowest						
Oklahoma	11 406	78.1	65.5	99.3	1 824	12.31
S. Dakota	11 393	76.3	77.3	98.8	1 799	10.88
S. Carolina	11 196	75.9	66.0	97.5	1 865	12.28
Alabama	11 180	76.7	64.4	98.5	1 773	12.96
Montana	10 813	78.8	72.2	98.9	1 665	11.55
Louisiana	10 621	76.4	65.7	98.5	1 777	12.16
W. Virginia	10 182	82.4	60.8	97.5	1 675	12.45
Arkansas	10 090	76.7	66.5	98.5	1 819	11.04
Mississippi	9 694	77.1	63.9	98.1	1 814	11.06
New Mexico	9 597	71.3	66.5	96.8	1 705	12.27
Average	10 617	77.0	66.9	98.2	1 772	11.90

was of working age in 1995 was nearly identical (77.2 per cent versus 77.0 per cent). The mean utilization rates of the states' resident labour forces also were statistically identical (98.0 per cent versus 98.2 per cent). Mean annual hours of work among the employed population in the high earnings' states were only 2 per cent higher than in the low earning states. Thus, the above three factors combined could not account for as much as two of the 54 percentage point difference between the mean per capita earnings of the top and bottom ten states.

The dominant factor underlying the per capita earnings differences between the top and bottom ten states in 1995 was real earnings per hour of work. The mean hourly earnings of workers in the top ten states was $16.40 versus only $11.90 for the bottom ten states, a relative difference of 38 per cent (see bar chart at Figure 7.1). Over three-quarters of the total difference between the mean per capita earnings of the top ten and bottom ten states was attributable to variations in mean hourly earnings of workers. The remaining factor is a variable representing the labour force attachment of state residents. The mean participation rate of working-age residents in the top ten states was 74.2 per cent but only 66.9 per cent in the bottom ten states, a relative difference of 11 per cent. Within each of these two groups, however, there was a fair degree of variability in participation rates. For example, among the top ten states, labour force participation rates ranged from a low of 70 per cent in New Jersey to a high of 81 per cent in Alaska.[5] Among the bottom ten states, the participation rates ranged from 61 per cent in West Virginia to 77 per cent in

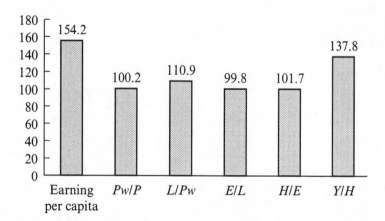

Figure 7.1   Advantages of the ten highest per capita earnings states relative to the ten lowest per capita earnings states on earnings per capita and their underlying sources, US, 1995

South Dakota. State differences in labour force participation rates have narrowed modestly over the past three decades in the US; however, the gaps between the highest earning and lowest earning states are still fairly sizable, accounting for about 20 per cent of the difference in their mean per capita earnings.

SOURCES OF INEQUALITY IN STATE PER CAPITA EARNINGS, 1979–1995

To identify trends in the degree of inequality in the per capita earnings of state residents over the 1979–95 period, we estimated the coefficients of variation for the state per capita earnings distribution for 1979, 1989 and 1995 (Table 7.9). The coefficient of variation in 1979 stood at 0.153. During the 1980s, the degree of inequality in per capita earnings increased, rising to 0.177 by 1989. This finding closely parallels that for inequality in state per capita incomes. Since 1989, inequality in per capita earnings has declined, falling to 0.149 by 1995. Since 1979 was a historical low point in per capita income inequality among the states, it is quite likely that the CV of 1995 represented a new historical low for the states.[6]

In 1995, inequality in earnings per hour of work accounted for the bulk of the variation in per capita earnings across the states. The CV for average hourly earnings was 0.126, twice as high as the CV for labour force participation and four or more times higher than the CVs for the demographic, labour force utilization and annual hours of work variables. Given the dominant role of average hourly earnings in explaining existing state differences in per capita earnings, how can we explain these remaining differences across states in hourly earnings? We have estimated a series of multiple regression models to explain variations in the average hourly earnings of workers across states in both 1979 and 1989.

A MULTIVARIATE STATISTICAL ANALYSIS OF HOURLY EARNINGS DIFFERENCES ACROSS STATES, 1979 AND 1989

Knowledge of the economic and institutional forces producing the hourly earnings differences would be helpful in explaining the variation in mean per capita earnings of residents across states. The mean hourly earnings of workers can best be thought of as an average price for an hour of labour, excluding fringe benefits and employee taxes for social

Table 7.9 *Mean, standard deviation and coefficient of variation of real earnings per capita and its sources, 50 states and the District of Columbia, 1979, 1989 and 1995 (earnings in 1995 dollars)*

	Real earnings per capita ($)	Percentage of population that is working age (15+)	Percentage of working-age pop. in labour force	Percentage of labour force employed	Average annual hours per worker	Average real earnings per hour ($)
1979 Mean	11 693	76.6	71.0	98.4	1 684.6	12.97
1989 Mean	12 989	77.7	71.8	98.9	1 759.0	13.33
1995 Mean	13 463	77.3	71.4	98.3	1 792.6	13.83
1979 Std. deviation	1 792	2.5	5.0	0.7	47.5	1.62
1989 Std. deviation	2 297	2.4	4.5	0.6	51.3	1.74
1995 Std. deviation	2 005	2.3	4.8	0.7	50.0	1.74
1979 CV	0.1532	0.0327	0.0707	0.0068	0.0282	0.1247
1989 CV	0.1769	0.0308	0.0622	0.0056	0.0292	0.1304
1995 CV	0.1489	0.0301	0.0678	0.0076	0.0279	0.1262

security, unemployment benefits, and so on. Since labour is a factor of production that is bought and sold in markets (in both external labour markets and internal labour markets), the price of labour should be determined through a combination of supply and demand forces, with some institutional effects via unions, professional associations and other employee collective bargaining arrangements. Labour, however, is a very heterogeneous factor of production that has various human capital traits, including education, occupational skills, literacy and work experience which would be expected to influence its market wage. The average hourly earnings of workers in a given state are, thus, a weighted average of a series of wages paid to different types of workers. There is no simple aggregate model of labour supply and demand that can be used to illustrate the underlying forces.

One would expect that the average real wages of workers in a state would be positively correlated with the value of labour productivity in a state. Given the high degree of geographic mobility of capital and labour in the United States, over the long run, real wages and labour productivity would have to be closely tied to one another. If wage growth outstrips labour productivity growth in a state, then unit labour costs would rise, resident firms would find themselves in a less competitive position and capital would be expected to relocate to more profitable economic locations. Similarly, if worker wages lag productivity growth, some workers will find it worthwhile to relocate to areas where their higher productivity will be matched with higher earnings.

Official state labour productivity measures are not available from the national government. We have used available data on real Gross State Product (GSP) for each state for the years 1979 and 1989 and employment data for states from the Current Population Survey to generate labour productivity estimates for each state for the years 1979 and 1989 (Beemiller and Dunbar, 1993 and 1994).[7] The labour productivity variable for each state represents the value of real Gross State Product (in constant 1987 dollars) per hour of paid employment during a given calendar year. This labour productivity variable covers all sectors of the state's economy: agricultural and nonagricultural, goods and services, private and public.

The real hourly earnings of workers are likely to be affected by factors other than productivity, at least in the short run. The existence of low unemployment rates in a state may force employers temporarily to bid up the wages of workers. To test for such effects, we have included a three-year average unemployment rate for the state as an additional explanatory variable (US Bureau of Labour Statistics, 1980 and 1990). The industrial structure of output of a state may also influence the wage–productivity relationship. In some very capital intensive sectors like mining, especially oil and gas industries, labour compensation is a relatively small share of the GSP originating from that sector.[8] For example, during 1992, employee compensation accounted for only 31 per cent of the total gross state product originating from the nation's oil and gas industries.[9] To test for the effects of the energy sector on the wage–productivity relationship, we included a variable representing the share of each state's real GSP accounted for by the energy sector. The hypothesis is that real hourly earnings, *ceteris paribus*, will be lower than expected in states with a large energy sector. After controlling for the high values of labour productivity of workers in such energy industries, we would expect workers to capture a less than proportionate share of their productivity in the form of higher wages.

Nominal and real GSP data (in constant 1987 dollars) for states and regions are available for the time period 1977–1992 from the US Commerce Department's Bureau of Economic Analysis (Beemiller and Dunbar, 1994).[10] We have used state CPS data on estimated hourly earnings, our labour productivity variables, and annual average unemployment rates for the years 1977–1979 and 1987–1989 to estimate our regression models of real hourly earnings.[11] Definitions of the variables appearing in these models are displayed in Table 7.10 while the regression results are presented in Tables 7.11 and 7.12.

Findings for the 1979 regression model of hourly earnings reveal that labour productivity significantly raised the expected real hourly earnings of workers. The regression coefficient for the log of the labour productivity variable was 0.66 (Table 7.11). For each additional percentage point rise in real output per hour, workers would obtain 0.66 per cent more per hour in hourly earnings. The coefficient of the state unemployment rate variable was negative, but was not statistically significant in the 1979 hourly earnings model. The hourly earnings of workers in states with a larger energy sector, *ceteris paribus*, were significantly lower than in states with comparable levels of labour productivity. The coefficient on this variable was statistically significant at the 0.01 level.

The overall regression model for the 1979 hourly earnings equation had a fairly high degree of explanatory power, given the cross-sectional nature of the data. The adjusted R^2 was 0.565, and the F-statistic was significant at the 0.001 level.

The regression model for the 1989 real hourly earnings of state residents performed even better (Table 7.12). The labour productivity variable was statistically significant at the 0.01 level. Each additional percentage point increase in labour productivity in the state (in constant 1987 dollars) would be expected to raise the real hourly earnings of resi-

Table 7.10 Definitions of the variables appearing in the multiple regression analysis of the real hourly earnings of state residents, 1979 and 1989 (excluding Alaska and Washington, DC)

Dependent variable	Definition
LHEARN79	The natural log of the real hourly earnings of resident workers in the state in 1979 (in 1987 dollars)
LHEARN89	The natural log of the real hourly earnings of resident workers in the state in 1989 (in 1987 dollars)
Independent variables	
LGSPHR79	The natural log of real gross state product per hour of labour in the state in 1979
LGSPHR89	The natural log of real gross state product per hour in the state in 1989
UR77-79	The average unemployment rate of the state in 1977–1979
UR87-89	The average unemployment rate of the state in 1987–1989
ENGSHARE79	A variable reflecting the intensity of energy production in the state as measured by its share of state real GSP in 1979
ENGSHARE89	A variable reflecting the intensity of energy production in the state in 1989 as measured by its share of state real GSP

dent workers by 0.76 percentage points. The lower the unemployment rate of the state over the 1987–1989 period, the higher were expected average hourly earnings; however, the coefficient fell slightly short of significance at the 0.10 level. Finally, expected hourly wages in a state with a relatively large energy sector, *ceteris paribus*, would be lower. This finding does *not* imply that workers in major energy-producing industries get paid less than in other industries. The opposite holds true. Workers in mining industries are among the best paid in the nation. Rather, the finding of a negative coefficient on the mining variable implies that wages of workers

Table 7.11 Findings of the multiple regression analysis of the log of hourly earnings of workers across states, 1979 (excluding Alaska and Washington, DC)

Variable	(A) Coefficient	(B) t-statistic	(C) Significance of coefficient
LGSPHR79	0.658	7.07	0.01
UR77-79	–0.132	0.13	Not sig. 0.10
ENGSHARE	–0.905	3.33	0.01
CONSTANT	0.373	1.53	0.10

R^2 adj. = 0.565 $F = 21.8$
Degrees of freedom = 45   Sig. of $F = 0.01$

Table 7.12 Findings of the multiple regression analysis of the hourly earnings of workers across states, 1989 (excluding Alaska and Washington, DC)

Variable	(A) Coefficient	(B) t-statistic	(C) Significance of coefficient
LGSPHR89	0.758	10.61	0.01
UR8789	–0.707	–1.09	Not sig. 0.10
ENGSHARE	–0.734	3.34	Sig. 0.01
CONSTANT	0.102	0.46	Not sig. 0.10

R^2 adj. = 0.732 $F = 44.7$
Degrees of freedom = 45   Sig. of $F = 0.01$

in such states do not rise in the same proportion to higher labour productivity as they do in other states.

The overall explanatory power of the 1989 earnings model was quite high. The value of the adjusted R^2 was 0.73, indicating that the model was able to explain 73 per cent of the overall variance in 1989 real hourly earnings across states.

A MODEL OF HOURLY EARNINGS GROWTH ACROSS STATES, 1979–89

Knowledge of the determinants of changes over time in the real hourly earnings of workers across states would be useful in accounting for observed growth in the state's per capita earnings and incomes. Over the entire 1979–95 period, the growth rates of real hourly earnings (in constant 1987 dollars) of workers across states varied quite markedly, ranging from declines of 3 to 6 per cent in major energy-producing states (Alaska, Louisiana, Wyoming and West Virginia) to increases of 18 to 27 per cent in the New England states of Connecticut, Massachusetts, and Vermont.[12] To analyse the determinants of changes in average hourly earnings across states over the 1979–89 period, we constructed a relatively simple regression model.[13]

The dependent variable in the regression model is the percentage change in the mean real hourly earnings of workers in the state between 1979 and 1989. The two independent variables in the model are the following:

- The percentage change in labour productivity in the state between 1979 and 1989 as measured by real GSP (in 1987 dollars) per hour of paid employment.
- The percentage growth in civilian wage and salary employment in the state over the 1979–89 period as measured by the establishment payroll survey.

Findings of the regression analysis are displayed in Table 7.13. The growth of labour productivity had a powerful effect on the rate of growth in the real hourly earnings of workers over the 1979–89 period. For each 1 per cent rise in labour productivity, real hourly earnings would be expected to rise by 0.62 per cent. The coefficient on labour productivity was significant at the 0.001 level. The higher the growth rate of employment in the state, *ceteris paribus*, the higher the expected rate of growth in real hourly earnings. Each additional 1 per cent rise in employment would raise expected hourly earnings by approximately 0.08 per cent. In faster growing states, employers may need to raise wages to attract a sufficient supply of workers both from within the state and outside the state. The employment growth variable was statistically significant at the 0.03 level (one-tailed test). The labour productivity and employment change variables together were able to explain nearly one-half of the total variance in the growth of real hourly earnings across states between 1979 and 1989.

Table 7.13 Findings of the multiple regression analysis of percentage changes in the real hourly earnings of workers in states between 1979 and 1989 (excluding Alaska and Washington, DC)

	(A)	(B)	(C)
Variable	Coefficient	*t*-statistic	Significance of coefficient
PCHGSPHR	0.62	6.75	0.01
PEMPCH7989	0.077	1.90	0.03
CONSTANT	−0.03	−1.68	0.10
R^2 adj. = 0.476			
Degrees of freedom = 0.46		Sig. of $F = 0.01$	

A second regression model was used to estimate changes in the mean real hourly earnings of workers in each state over the 1979-89 period. This model included the percentage change in a state's overall GSP deflator over the 1979–89 period as an additional predictor variable. The percentage change in a state's GSP deflator was used as a proxy variable for the 'terms of trade' between a state's exports of goods and services and its imports from other states (Samuelson and Nordhaus, 1995; Sum and Fogg, 1996). The Bureau of Economic Analysis uses a national price deflator for the output of each major industrial sector appearing in the GSP of a state. Since each state is assigned the same output price deflator for a given sector, a state can obtain an overall GSP deflator different from that of the nation only by having a different industrial mix. A state whose GSP deflator rose at an above average rate must contain an above average share of industries whose prices increased at an above average rate over the 1979–89 period. Those industries in which a state is relatively specialized are typically found to be export industries. Thus, a state with above average growth in its GSP deflator should be characterized by more favourable terms of trade; that is, prices of its exports rising faster than prices of its imports.

The existence of more favourable terms of trade implies that states can buy a larger volume of imports with any given physical volume of its exports.[14] The relative rise in its export prices should allow firms in such industries to pass part of the gains in this pricing power to its workers in the form of higher consumption wages; that is, nominal wages adjusted for changes in the Consumer Price Index, our measure of real wages. One would, thus, expect the real wages of a state's workers to grow more rapidly, *ceteris paribus*, in those states whose GSP deflators rose faster than average. Similar findings have been found in studies of growth in the real wages of production workers in US manufacturing industries (Galbraith, 1991; Sum and Goicoechea, 1993). Workers in manufacturing industries that have a favourable net trade position (exports exceed imports) obtain higher hourly wage gains than their counterparts in less trade competitive industries even after adjusting for productivity and employment growth rates.

Findings of the analysis are presented in Table 7.14. The coefficient on the GSP deflator variable was positive as hypothesized and statistically significant at the 0.05 level. A 1 per cent change in the GSP deflator of the state relative to that of the nation would increase the growth of real hourly earnings of workers in that state by 0.25 per cent. The coefficient on the labour productivity variable was reduced moderately in size but remained highly significant (0.001 level). On the other hand, the coefficient on the employment growth variable, while remaining positive, was reduced in size and was no longer statistically significant.

Table 7.14 Findings of the multiple regression analysis of percentage changes in the real hourly earnings of workers in states between 1979 and 1989 (excluding Alaska and Washington, DC)

	(A)	(B)	(C)
Variable	Coefficient	t-statistic	Significance of coefficient
PCHGSPHR	0.542	5.32	0.01
PEMPCH7989	0.037	0.81	0.21
PCHDEF7989	0.251	1.74	0.05
CONSTANT	0.001	0.13	0.89

R^2 adj. = 0.498   Significance of $F = 0.01$
Degrees of freedom = 45

Future research on modelling real hourly earnings growth of state workers might well consider including more sophisticated variables representing the changing terms of trade for the state's exports of goods and services, the role of unionism in the state, and the degree of slack in its labour markets as measured by average unemployment and underemployment rates over a given time period.[15] Specific output price variables reflecting a weighted average of price changes in each state's export industries might be more useful as a measure of changes in terms of trade than the state's relative GSP deflator. A greater union presence among workers in the state might create a closer link between labour productivity growth and real wage growth due to the ability of unions to secure a greater share of productivity gains for workers. States with lower unemployment and underemployment rates might be characterized by higher real wage gains via a Phillips-curve type relationship which was found to prevail in many state labour markets in the USA in the 1970s and 1980s (Hyclack and Johnes, 1992).

NOTES

1. In an earlier analysis by the authors, it was found that the exclusion of property incomes from the personal incomes of state residents reduced the estimated degree of inequality in the state per capita income distribution by 3 to 4 per cent over the 1989–96 period (Sum and Fogg, 1997).
2. These adjustments take into account commuters into the state by residents of other states and the earnings of residents from employment in other states. The net earnings adjustments can be positive or negative for any given state. For example, in Massachusetts, the net adjustments are negative while in the border state of New Hampshire they are positive.
3. For a review of the design features of the monthly CPS survey and the key labour force concepts and measures underlying the labour force statistics derived from that survey, see US Bureau of Labor Statistics (1997).
4. These per capita earnings date are not adjusted for differences in the regional cost of living due to the absence of any official recent data in this area. A regional wage study adjusting for estimated differences in the cost of living has found that the variance in regional wages in the 1980s actually declined rather than increased once wages were adjusted for local cost of living (Eberts and Schweitzer, 1994).
5. It should be noted that these labour force participation rates represent the incidence of participation over the entire calendar year (a flow measure) rather than the annual average participation measures which are based on average monthly stocks of labour force particpants (Sum and Fogg, 1995).
6. While the state per capita income series can be extended back to 1929, our data source on per capita earnings (the March CPS surveys) can only be disaggregated back to 1975.
7. For a review of findings on regional and state gross product performance for the time period 1977–92, see Sum *et al.* (1995).
8. For a review of the construction of the state GSP data series and the components of a state's GSP, see Beemiller and Dunbar (1994).
9. An analysis of the impact of the energy sector on a state's GSP per worker appears in Sum and Fogg (1996).
10. The Bureau of Economic Analysis has recently updated state GSP estimates through 1994. The new series used a chained-weight price index to convert nominal GSP data into constant 1992 dollars.
11. Due to unique factors influencing the high values of real GSP per worker in Alaska and Washington, DC, these two areas are excluded from our analysis (Sum and Fogg, 1996).
12. Part of the estimated above average increase in the real hourly earnings of New England workers was attributable to an inability to use regional CPI data for adjust-

ing the nominal earnings data. Between 1979 and 1989, the rate of inflation as measured by the CPI-U index for the Greater Boston area exceeded that for the USA by about 8 percentage points.

13. At the time of the writing of this paper, GSP data for states were not available for 1995; thus, we could not construct a labour productivity variable for 1995.

14. An improvement in terms of trade can also favourably increase the output growth rate of a state if it leads to increased employment and output. Barro (1997) has found that an improvement in a nation's terms of trade does lead to higher growth rate of real GDP.

15. Studies of the impacts of imports on the wages of workers in key manufacturing industries of the USA have found that unionized industries are better able to prevent wages from falling in the face of declining product prices (Woodbridge, 1991).

REFERENCES

American Chamber of Commerce Research Association (1997), *Cost of Living Index, Third Quarter 1996*, Washington, DC.

Barro, Robert J. (1997), *Determinants of Economic Growth: A Cross-Country Empirical Study*, Cambridge, MA: Harvard Institute for International Development.

Beemiller, Richard M. and Ann E. Dunbar (1993), 'Gross state product, 1977–90', *Survey of Current Business*, December, 28–39.

Beemiller, Richard M. and Ann E. Dunbar (1994), 'Gross state product, 1977–91', *Survey of Current Business*, August, 80–97.

Blanchard, Olivier Jean and Lawrence F. Katz (1992), 'Regional evolutions', *Brookings Papers on Economic Activity*, **1**, 1–61.

Council of Economic Advisers (1997), *Economic Report of the President, 1997*, Washington, DC: US Government Printing Office.

Eberts, Randall W. and Mark E. Schweitzer (1994), 'Regional wage convergence and divergence: adjusting wages for cost-of-living differences', *Economic Review*, **QII**, 26–37, Federal Reserve Bank of Cleveland.

Galbraith, James K. (1991), 'A new picture of the American economy', *The American Prospect*, **7**, 24–36.

Hyclak, Thomas and Geraint Johnes (1992), *Wage Flexibility and Unemployment Dynamics in Regional Labor Markets*, Kalamazoo, Michigan: W.E. Upjohn Institute for Employment Research.

Ryscavage, Paul (1986),'Reconciling divergent trends in real income', *Monthly Labor Review*, **109**, 24–9.

Samuelson, Paul A. and William D. Nordhaus (1995), *Economics* (15th edition), New York: McGraw-Hill.

Smith, Robert S. and Ronald G. Ehrenberg (1997), *Modern Labor Economics* (5th edition), New York: HarperCollins.

Sum, Andrew and Neal Fogg, 'Trends in inequality in regional and state per capita incomes in the U.S.', paper prepared for the 3rd Conference on Economic Growth and Change: A Comparative Analysis, Cagliari, Italy, 19–21 June 1997.

Sum, Andrew M. and Neal Fogg (1996), 'Analyzing the output performance of state and regional economies', report prepared for the National Labor Market Information Training Institute.

Sum, Andrew M. and Neeta Fogg (1995), 'Analyzing the labor force: the use of labor force concepts, measures, data sources, and applied research techniques', report prepared for the National Labor Market Information Training Institute.

Sum, Andrew, John Adams, Donna Desrochers, Neal Fogg and Gustav Schachter (1995), 'Trends in income and output inequality among regions and states in the United States', paper presented to the North American Regional Science Association Meetings, Cincinnati, Ohio.

Sum, Andrew and Julio Goicoechea (1993), 'Determinants of the growth and decline of the real hourly earnings of production workers in US manufacturing industries', Working Paper Series, Center for Labor Market Studies, Northeastern University, Boston.

Sum, Andrew, Neeta Fogg and Paul Harrington (1991), *New England Labor Markets During the Miracle Decade of the 1980s*, Center for Labor Market Studies, Northeastern University, Boston.

US Bureau of Census (1997), *The March CPS Survey: Technical Documentation*, Washington, DC.

US Bureau of Labor Statistics (1997), *Employment and Earnings*, Washington, DC: US Government Printing Office.

US Bureau of Labor Statistics (1990), *Geographic Profile of Employment and Unemployment, 1989*, Washington, DC: US Government Printing Office.

US Bureau of Labor Statistics (1980), *Methodology for Projections of Industry Employment to 1990*, Bulletin 2036, Washington, DC: US Government Printing Office.

Woodbridge, Graeme (1991), 'Regional wage responses in declining industries: the case of the US textiles, clothing, and motor vehicle industries', PhD dissertation, Department of Economics, UCLA.

8. European regional growth: do sectors matter?

Raffaele Paci and Francesco Pigliaru

8.1 INTRODUCTION*

The recent theoretical and empirical literature on economic growth has generally neglected the role played by the sectoral mix and structural change in aggregate growth. This shortfall is hardly surprising since most studies are based on Solow's one-sector growth model and on its prediction that initially poorer economies grow faster than richer ones, due to decreasing return to capital (Barro and Sala-i-Martin, 1991; Mankiw, Romer and Weil, 1992). In other theoretical approaches, the determinants of an economy's sectoral mix and of its changes over time are assumed to have an impact on the growth performance. The reasons for this range from the values of marginal factor productivity being not continuously equalized across the existing activities, as in Lewis (1954) and Kaldor (1966, 1968); to the existence of significant differences across sectors in terms of accumulation of technological knowledge, as in several equilibrium models of endogenous growth and trade (see Lucas, 1988; Grossman and Helpman, 1991, among many others).

Is this emphasis on sectoral composition relevant for the analysis of regional growth in Europe? In our opinion, the answer to this question is positive. The assumptions of the aggregate neoclassical growth model are perhaps more appropriate for the analysis of mature and well integrated economies. This condition is not satisfied across the European regional economies because of the still remarkable differences of some of their structural characteristics. For instance, in the 1980s several regions in southern Europe have a very large agriculture sector, which is likely to hide massive amounts of underemployed labour.

The aim of this chapter is to show that the sectoral mix and structural change do matter in determining aggregate growth and catching up across European regions.[1] A careful assessment of the impact of sectoral composition is crucial not only to get a better understanding of the observed aggregate convergence, but also to appraise how strong we should expect this process to be in the future, and to assess the role played by national and European sectoral policies at the regional level.

The chapter is organized as follows. In Section 8.2 we describe the structural specialization of European regions and their sectoral productivity and growth. In Section 8.3 we evaluate the sectoral sources of growth. In Section 8.4 the catching up process is analysed, both at aggregate and sectoral levels. Section 8.5 examines the role of sectoral specialization and structural change in determining overall convergence. Section 8.6 concludes. The datebase is described in the Appendix.

8.2   SECTORAL SPECIALIZATION IN THE EUROPEAN REGIONS

This section presents our data for the 109 European regions over the period 1980–90.[2] We first analyse output and employment shares for the three main sectors – agriculture, industry and services – and their evolution over time; we also provide a spatial description of the sectoral specialization across the European regions. Secondly, labour productivity and its growth at the aggregate and sectoral levels are considered.

Table 8.1 summarizes the data on labour and output shares in 1980 and 1990 for the European Community and for the average of the northern and southern regions.[3] We have also reported for each sector the lowest and the highest share, in order to highlight the tremendous variation in sectoral specialization that exists across regions.[4] The agriculture sector shows the largest dispersion: labour shares span from less than 1 per cent (Ile de France which includes Paris) to a maximum of 50 per cent (Kriti in Greece). The European average is decreasing (6.5 per cent in 1990), although the coefficient of variation signals an increase in the differences across regions. As expected, the southern regions are characterized by much higher agricultural labour shares. These are declining over time, but still in 1990 the average share in the south is almost four times larger than in the north. It is worth remarking that the dispersion in the south is increasing and this means that the structural change process in southern regions is proceeding at different speeds. A similar pattern, but with lower shares, is detected if we observe the value added data.

The industrial sector represents more than 30 per cent of the entire economy for both labour and output. It also shows remarkable variations; for example, in 1980 the industrial labour shares range from 17 per cent (Ionia Nisia in Greece) to 49 per cent (Baden Wuerttemberg in Germany). The dispersion tends to increase, especially for output shares.

Table 8.1 Labour and output shares in the European regions (percentage values)

| | Labour shares | | | | Output shares | | | |
| | 1980 | | 1990 | | 1980 | | 1990 | |
	value	coeff. var.	value	coeff. var.	value	coeff. var.	value	coeff. var
			Agriculture					
Min	0.8		0.4		0.6		0.2	
Max	50.9		48.3		36.3		31.2	
European average	9.4	150	6.5	181	4.3	203	3.1	221
Northern regions	6.1	86	4.3	83	3.3	86	2.6	96
Southern regions	22.2	63	15.2	90	9.6	108	5.9	153
			Industry					
Min	16.9		18.5		22.9		15.9	
Max	48.9		44.6		55.0		45.3	
European average	36.4	23	31.3	23	38.5	21	33.3	23
Northern regions	37.3	18	32.0	20	39.2	17	33.7	18
Southern regions	31.2	27	28.8	28	35.3	26	31.0	29
			Services					
Min	25.1		36.2		26.7		34.7	
Max	69.5		75.4		73.0		79.1	
European average	54.2	20	62.1	17	57.1	16	63.6	14
Northern regions	56.2	13	63.7	11	57.5	12	63.7	10
Southern regions	46.5	22	56.0	20	55.1	20	63.1	18

Although the northern regions are more specialized in the industrial activities the differences between north and south are diminishing.

Finally, services are the most relevant sector in the economy; its size is still growing and in 1990 it reached an average of 62 per cent and 63 per cent, respectively, in terms of labour and output shares. Interestingly, the dispersion in this sector is the lowest in the economy and it is also decreasing over time. However the differences across regions are still large, ranging from 36 per cent (Dytiki Makedonia in Greece) to 75 per cent (West Nederland) in terms of employment shares.

Looking at the coefficients of variation, we can see that the dispersion in the sectoral composition of the economy is considerably larger in the south, except for agriculture where regional disparities within the northern regions are greater. Agriculture shows in all areas a cross-regional dispersion that is enormously higher than in the rest of the economy.

Although the period considered is limited, it is possible to document a clear process of structural change taking place in the European regions. On average, there is a shift away from agriculture and industry towards services in terms of both labour and output shares. This process is stronger among the southern regions, which at the beginning of the period still showed a strong specialization in agriculture.

Figure 8.1 shows a spatial representation of the sectoral specialization across the European regions in 1990, based on the index of comparative advantage of labour shares computed for each region and sector.[5] Each region has been assigned to a specialization sector if its index for this sector exceeds 1.1.[6] We obtain the following portrait.

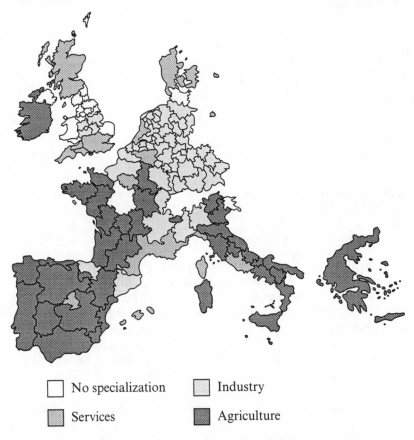

☐ No specialization   ▨ Industry

▨ Services   ■ Agriculture

Figure 8.1 Sectoral specialization across European regions, 1990

1. *High specialization in agriculture.* All Portuguese and all but one Greek region, most Spanish and Italian regions; most western regions in France; Ireland.
2. *High specialization in industry.* A cluster of regions in the north-east of Spain and in the north of Italy, most German Lander, six French northern regions.
3. *High specialization in services.* In this group are included most of the regions that host the national capitals and important cities (Ile de France, Lazio, Attiki, Bruxelles, Madrid, South East of UK, Berlin, Hamburg), a group of regions with a strong tourism sector (Baleares, Canarias, Liguria, Provence, Languedoc) and with autonomous local government (Scotland, Corse).
4. *Homogeneous sectoral distribution.* In this cluster we have regions, all in the north of Europe, that are characterized by a sectoral composition of the economy very similar to the average of the European Union. These regions do not show any specific specialization pattern.

In summary, the picture of the sectoral specialization across the European regions in 1990 shows a well defined pattern. Agriculture still prevails in the south, while industry tends to concentrate in contiguous clusters, perhaps due to the presence of local strategic complementarities (Krugman, 1991).[7]

Let us now turn to the analysis of labour productivity. In Table 8.2 the levels of labour productivity are calculated relatively to the overall productivity of the European average in order to account for sectoral and regional differences. Considering the sectoral averages in 1990, the most productive sector is industry (relative index = 106) closely followed by services (102). Labour productivity in agriculture is less than half of the aggregate level (48).

As regards the differences across regions, our results show a large degree of disparities. For example, considering the whole economy in 1990, the highest regional level of aggregate labour productivity (Ile de France, relative index equal to 148) is four times higher than the lowest one (Ipeiros in Greece, 37). In 1990 the gap between north and south is still large (the indices are, respectively, 104 and 84) although it shows a tendency to decline. The regional disparities are tremendous in agriculture, where the productivity level of Champagne (France) is fourteen times higher than in Norte (Portugal). On average northern regions display an agriculture productivity level two times higher than the southern regions. The range between the most and least productive regions is also broad in industry, while it is smaller in the service sector. The pattern of

Table 8.2 Productivity levels and growth in the European regions

		Index Europe total = 100				Growth percentage annual average 1980–90	
		1980		1990			
	value	coeff. var.	value	coeff. var.	value	coeff. var.	
Agriculture							
Min	14		12		−4.8		
Max	132		172		22.5		
European average	46	51	48	56	2.8	148	
Northern regions	56	41	63	41	3.7	95	
Southern regions	35	44	32	57	1.2	397	
Industry							
Min	51		33		−2.1		
Max	143		160		10.7		
European average	106	25	106	23	2.3	83	
Northern regions	109	19	110	15	2.4	63	
Southern regions	92	29	90	27	2.0	120	
Services							
Min	53		40		−2.1		
Max	131		145		5.4		
European average	405	23	102	22	1.9	64	
Northern regions	107	17	104	16	1.9	61	
Southern regions	96	27	94	26	2.0	66	
Total							
Min	39		37		−1.1		
Max	134		148		7.0		
European average	100	25	100	24	2.3	50	
Northern regions	105	16	104	14	2.2	45	
Southern regions	81	30	84	30	2.6	50	

productivity differentials over time shows that the degree of disparities slightly decreases at the aggregate level and in the industry and service sectors, while it considerably increases in agriculture.

The last columns of Table 8.2 document the average growth rate of labour productivity over the period 1980–90. The most remarkable result is an enormous variation across sectors and regions. At the aggregate level, the European regions are growing at an average rate of 2.3 per cent, ranging from –1.1 per cent in Noord Nederland to 7 per cent in Algarve (Portugal). Southern regions exhibit an average growth (2.6 per cent) higher than the northern ones (2.2 per cent). Since they started with lower productivity levels, it indicates that a process of aggregate catching up is occurring across the European regions.

Agriculture displays the highest rate of productivity growth (2.8 per cent), followed by industry (2.3 per cent) and services (1.9 per cent). As we have already noted, a larger intra-sector difference in growth rates is detected in agriculture, where some regions had significantly improved their productivity due to larger than average outflows of labour. For example, the fastest productivity growth in agriculture is shown by the Greek region of Notio Aigaio (22.5 per cent per year), which, over the entire period, has decreased its agriculture labour share by 12 percentage points. On average, however, the growth rate of agriculture productivity in northern regions (3.7 per cent) is higher than in the south (1.2 per cent). It seems that although labour migration out of agriculture has been higher in the southern regions, this process has not automatically led to rapid increases in productivity.

Finally, in the south the aggregate productivity growth rate is higher than that detected at the sectoral level. This result suggests that an important part of the aggregate gains enjoyed by the southern regions originates from a process of sectoral changes. This latter feature will be further analysed in Sections 8.5 and 8.6.

To sum up, the results reported in this section highlight the enormous differences in employment and output shares, productivity levels and growth rates across sectors and regions. All these differences appear to be magnified in agriculture.

8.3   SECTORAL SOURCES OF AGGREGATE GROWTH

What is the relationship between sectoral specialization and growth? What are the sectoral sources of aggregate productivity growth? These are old questions often addressed by the development literature, which has emphasized how the differences across sectors (in terms of technological change, inter-sectoral linkages and spillovers) affect their contribution to the overall growth.

A well-known attempt to investigate the relationship between sectoral and aggregate growth is represented by Kaldor's 'third law' (KTL): this states that the growth of overall labour productivity is positively correlated with the growth of manufacturing output. Interestingly, such correlation is consistent with various models. For instance, in Lewis's model of the dual economy the shift of labour from low- to high-productivity sectors is a key component of the overall growth rate of productivity. The positive impact on aggregate growth of the expansion of specific sectors is also emphasized by several endogenous growth models. For example in Lucas's learning-by-doing model, the larger the size of the high-learning sector, the higher the growth rate of overall productivity (Lucas, 1988). The same result is obtained by allowing for the possibility of intersectoral spillovers (Murat and Pigliaru, 1998).

The precise functional form of KTL has been discussed at length in the literature. Kaldor (1975) estimates a regression where the growth rate of aggregate labour productivity is a function of growth rates of industrial output (with an expected positive sign) and non-industrial employment (negative effect). McCombie (1981) has shown that there is an underlying identity in this KTL specification, so that any attempt to interpret it as causal relationships would be incorrect. An economically more meaningful specification proposed in the literature is as follows:

$$\dot{y}_i/y_i = a + b\ \dot{Y}_i^A/Y_i^A + c\ \dot{Y}_i^I/Y_i^I + d\ \dot{Y}_i^S/Y_i^S \qquad (8.1)$$

where, for each region i, $\dot{x}/x$ indicates the annual average growth rates of x between the initial year t and final year $t+T$, Y is value added for the three sectors agriculture (A), industry (I) and services (S) and y is the overall labour productivity defined as $y_i = \Sigma_j Y_{ij}/\Sigma_j L_{ij}$.

The cross-section estimates of this specification for 109 European regions are reported in Table 8.3. Our findings give support to KTL: in regression (1) the growth of industrial output is indeed positively correlated to the growth of labour productivity in the entire economy. However, the services sector also shows a positive impact and its influence appears to be even larger. On the other hand, agriculture output growth does not show any significant effect on aggregate labour productivity. The regression residuals exhibit serial correlation. In regional studies this is often a signal for the presence of spatial correlations, since regional observations are usually grouped by state. In other words, the regional growth process of the European regions seems to have followed a pattern characterized by idiosyncratic national elements. To take into account these country-specific omitted variables, we have included some national dummies in our equation (see regression 2).[8] The coefficients for industry and services output growth do not change, while the coefficient of agriculture becomes positive, although it remains insignificant. The explanatory power of the regression is now very high (R^2 adj. = 0.71) and the serial correlation disappears.

Table 8.3 Econometric estimates of sectoral sources of overall productivity growth

	Regression 1	*Regression 2 with national dummies*
Constant	0.002 (0.54)	0.007 (2.48)[b]
Agriculture	−0.003 (−0.11)	0.032 (1.31)
Industry	0.101 (2.00)[b]	0.106 (2.53)[a]
Services	0.489 (6.22)[a]	0.423 (6.14)[a]
R^2 adj.	0.33	0.71
F	18.7[a]	25.3[a]

Notes:
Estimation methods: OLS; t-statistic in parentheses; 109 observations; significant levels: [a] 1 per cent, [b] 5 per cent.
Dependent variable: growth rate of aggregate labour productivity, annual average 1980–90.
Explanatory variables: sectoral growth rate of output, annual average 1980–90.

Our analysis shows that industrial output growth is positively associated with overall productivity growth. It also shows that, in modern economies, an increasingly important role is played by the services sector. However, as noticed before there are several shortcomings in the use of KTL as a behavioural equation. Therefore to assess the effect of sectoral specialization on aggregate growth it may be more appropriate to use accurate accounting approaches. Several methods to estimate the sectoral sources of overall growth have been proposed in the literature (McCombie, 1980; Paci and Pigliaru, 1997; Bernard and Jones, 1996). Here, following the latter authors, we decompose the growth rate of aggregate labour productivity in each region into within- and between-sector components as follows:

$$\frac{\dot{y}}{y} = \underbrace{\sum_j \frac{\dot{y}_{ij}}{y_{ij}} \left(\frac{y_{ijt}}{y_{it}}\right) \bar{w}_{ij}}_{\text{Within Sector Effect (WSE)}} + \underbrace{\sum_j (w_{ij,\,t+T} - w_{ijt}) \left(\frac{\bar{y}_{ij}}{y_{it}}\right)}_{\text{Structural Change Effect (SCE)}} \qquad (8.2)$$

where, for each region i, the labour shares, $w_{jt} = L_j/\Sigma_j L_j$, $\bar{x}$ represents the average value of x over the period and the annual average growth rate is expressed in percentage values. The first component of (8.2) represents the contribution of *within*-sector labour productivity growth. It is computed using the average employment shares over the period as weights. The second component captures the effect of structural change in each sector on total productivity growth. This effect is negative in sectors with declining labour shares.

Table 8.4 reports the sources of productivity growth for the average European case and for some specific groups of regions. The dominant sectoral source of labour productivity growth is the services sector. This sector has a positive growth effect (52 per cent), together with a strong positive structural change effect (40 per cent). Therefore, in total the services sector accounts for 92 per cent of aggregate productivity growth. A total positive effect is also shown by industry (10 per cent). This weak effect is the net result of two opposite processes: the positive within-

Table 8.4 Sources of productivity growth in the European regions, 1980–1990

	Within sector		Structural change		Total effect	
	value	%	value	%	value	%
	Europe					
Agriculture	0.10	5	−0.15	−7	−0.05	−2
Industry	0.82	36	−0.60	−26	0.23	10
Services	1.19	52	0.91	40	2.10	92
Total	2.11	93	0.17	7	2.28	100
	Northern regions					
Agriculture	0.10	5	−0.12	−5	−0.01	−1
Industry	0.87	39	−0.66	−30	0.20	9
Services	1.19	53	0.85	38	2.03	91
Total	2.16	97	0.07	3	2.22	100
	Southern regions					
Agriculture	0.10	4	−0.32	−12	−0.22	−8
Industry	0.69	26	−0.30	−11	0.39	15
Services	1.23	47	1.23	47	2.46	94
Total	2.01	77	0.61	23	2.62	100

sector productivity growth (36 per cent) is partially offset by the negative share effect (–26 per cent). A similar pattern is shown by agriculture: the positive growth effect (5 per cent) is accompanied by a negative and stronger structural change effect (–7 per cent) that gives rise to a total negative result on aggregate productivity growth.

An issue worth addressing is whether the results characterizing the European regions as a whole can be found for sub-sets of regions. As we have pointed out in the previous section, the sectoral mix varies remarkably across regions, so we expect some significant differences to emerge. In Table 8.4 we have decomposed the sources of aggregate growth for the northern and southern European regions. The most relevant difference is that in the south the positive effect of structural change is much higher: it accounts for 23 per cent of the overall growth. At the sectoral level it is worth noticing the higher negative impact of agriculture in the south (–8 per cent), due to the more pronounced decrease of their labour shares. In the southern regions the industrial sector represents a more important source of growth (15 per cent compared to 9 per cent in the north). Interestingly, this effect is the combined result of the two following contrasting elements. First, in the north the within-sector productivity growth is much higher than in the south (39 per cent vs. 26 per cent) – perhaps a signal that important agglomeration economies are at work. Second, in the northern regions the growth gains are in large part offset by the vast decline of their industry shares; the negative growth impact of structural change is –30 per cent in the north as compared to only –11 per cent in the south.

8.4 AGGREGATE AND SECTORAL CATCHING UP

Let us now turn to the analysis of the convergence process across the regions of the European Union. In this section we test a simple catching up model where, for each region, the labour productivity growth gap is a function of the productivity difference in the initial year. The gap is defined as the distance between each region and the average for the whole European Union. We use this procedure because of the absence of a clear and constant leader region over the entire period considered. Moreover, using the European average the catching up process is not affected by specific shocks that may have hit the leader region over the period. The following regression has been estimated using cross-sectional data:

$$\dot{y}_i/y_i - \dot{y}_E/y_E = a + b\,[\log(y_{it}) - \log(y_{Et})] \qquad (8.3)$$

Table 8.5 Aggregate productivity catching up across European regions

	Regression 1	Regression 2 with dummy South	Regression 3** with national dummies	Regression 4 66 Northern regions	Regression 5 43 Southern regions
Constant*	-0.65	-0.42	0.72	0.00	0.94
	(-0.73)	(-0.39)	(0.99)	(0.09)	(0.65)
Productivity gap 1980	-0.011	-0.011	-0.018	-0.029	-0.005
	(-4.20)[a]	(-3.60)[a]	(-5.55)[a]	(-5.30)[a]	(-1.36)
Dummy South*		-0.84			
		(-0.40)			
R^2 adj	0.13	0.13	0.64	0.32	0.02
F-test	17.6[a]	8.81[a]	33.7[a]	31.3[a]	1.77
White heter. F-test	2.95	2.06	2.40[b]	3.78[b]	3.97[b]

Notes:

OLS; whole sample: 109 regions; t-statistics in parentheses; significant levels: [a] 1 per cent, [b] 5 per cent.

* coefficients × 1000

** Regression 3 includes only significant national dummies: F (+), E (+), N (−), I (−), G (−).

When the White F-test is significant at 1 per cent or 5 per cent the reported t-statistics are corrected for heteroskedasticity.

Dependent variable: gap of labour productivity, annual growth rate 1980–90.

where the subscript E indicates the European average.[9] A negative and significant coefficient for the initial productivity differential would signal that regions with a higher gap at the beginning of the period have grown faster, so that they have caught up the richer regions. It is a well-known fact that this equation does not allow us to identify the economic mechanism supporting the convergence process. This functional form is compatible with both the diminishing returns to capital effect emphasized by the neoclassical growth model, as well as with technological diffusion models (Sala-i-Martin, 1996a). Moreover, such an aggregate convergence equation does not allow us to assess explicitly the role of the structural change process in generating convergence. This latter point will be directly addressed in Section 8.5.

The results of the convergence equation at the aggregate are reported in Table 8.5. Our findings show that a process of catching up has taken place across the European regions over the 1980s.[10] However the initial productivity gap explains only a small fraction of the growth process (R^2 adj. = 0.13) and the speed of convergence is not very fast (1.2 per cent per year). In regression (2) we have included a dummy for the southern regions to control for differences across regions not fully explained by the initial productivity gap. However this hypothesis is not confirmed by the data and the dummy South is not significant. The existence of country-specific factors is tested in regression (3) where a set of national dummies has been included. The explanatory power of the conditional convergence equation is much higher (0.64) meaning that the national dummies are capturing crucial country-specific elements, omitted in the absolute convergence model. The coefficient of the initial productivity gap is still negative and significant, and the speed of convergence increases to 1.98 per cent. In the remaining two regressions we split our sample into two groups, northern and southern regions, to assess whether there are differences in the catching up process. Interestingly, the observed overall convergence originates mainly from the sub-sample formed by the northern regions, in which a strong and significant catching up process takes place (their convergence speed is 3.42 per cent). On the other hand, the productivity growth in the southern regions seems unaffected by the initial magnitude of the gap.

As regards the convergence process at the sectoral level (Table 8.6), in agriculture there is no evidence of absolute convergence; however, the coefficient of the initial productivity gap becomes significant in the estimates with the south and national dummies, as well as for the sub-sample of the northern regions. The industrial and services sectors display similar behaviour: there is absolute catching up across the European regions together with the presence of local convergence clubs. Moreover, in these

Table 8.6 Sectoral productivity catching up across European regions

	Regression 1	Regression 2 with dummy South	Regression 3** with national dummies	Regression 4 66 Northern regions	Regression 5 43 Southern regions
Agriculture					
Constant*	1.78 (0.61)	10.6 (2.75)[a]	22.8 (5.39)[a]	11.5 (3.14)[a]	-9.76 (-1.47)
Productivity gap 1980	-0.006 (-0.99)	-0.019 (-2.64)[a]	-0.025 (-3.81)[a]	-0.023 (-2.10)[b]	-0.013 (-0.97)
Dummy South*		-22.1 (-3.24)[a]			
R^2 adj.	0.00	0.082	0.30	0.10	0.00
F-test	0.98	5.91[a]	8.82[a]	8.35[a]	0.95
White heter. F-test	1.09	1.78	1.32	7.66[a]	0.77
Industry					
Constant*	-2.94 (-2.70)[a]	0.31 (0.25)	10.5 (5.85)[a]	1.06 (0.93)	-7.40 (-3.48)[a]
Productivity gap 1980	-0.016 (-2.19)[b]	-0.024 (-3.94)[a]	-0.021 (-3.25)[a]	-0.042 (-6.95)[a]	-0.016 (-1.54)
Dummy South*		-9.87 (-3.21)[a]			

R^2 adj.	0.09	0.16	0.45	0.42	0.06
F-test	11.9[a]	11.7[a]	13.6[a]	48.2[a]	3.79
White heter. F-test	21.9[a]	14.4[a]	2.62[a]	0.59	7.75[a]
Services					
Constant*	−0.81	−0.23	−2.28	−0.25	−0.47
	(−0.78)	(−0.19)	(−3.53)[b]	(−0.20)	(−0.34)
Productivity gap 1980	−0.011	−0.013	−0.018	−0.025	−0.007
	(−3.39)[a]	(−2.90)[a]	(−2.66)[a]	(−4.00)[a]	(−1.10)
Dummy South*		−1.81			
		(−1.12)			
R^2 adj.	0.08	0.073	0.52	0.18	0.01
F-test	9.94[a]	5.27[a]	24.5[a]	15.3[a]	1.56
White heter. F-test	4.48[b]	3.00[b]	10.1[a]	3.00[b]	4.98[a]

Notes:
OLS; whole sample: 109 regions; t-statistics in parentheses; significant levels: [a] 1 per cent, [b] 5 per cent.
* coefficients × 1000
** Regression 3 includes only significant national dummies: D (−), E (−), I (−), P (−), G (−); industry: D (−), F (−), N (−), E (−), I (−), G (−); services: F (−), N (−).
When the White F-test is significant at 1 per cent or 5 per cent the reported t-statistics are corrected for heteroskedasticity.
Dependent variable: gap of labour productivity, annual growth rate 1980–90.

227

sectors the catching up process is mainly driven by the northern regions. Finally, it is worth remarking that a high rate of convergence occurred among the industrial sectors of the northern regions (5.45 per cent).

Summing up, the aggregate catching up process arises mainly from the industrial and services sectors and from the northern European regions, while in agriculture and in the southern regions there is no clear tendency to converge to the European average.

8.5   THE SOURCES OF CONVERGENCE

Using the accounting framework of (8.2), it is interesting to calculate the contribution of each sector to overall convergence. More precisely, following again Bernard and Jones (1996), the growth gap of each region relative to the European average is decomposed into within-sector productivity growth and structural change effects as follows:

$$\frac{\dot{y}_i}{y_i} - \frac{\dot{y}_E}{y_E} = \underbrace{\sum_j [WSE_{ij} - WSE_{Ej}]}_{\text{Within Sector Effect}} + \underbrace{\sum_j [SCE_{ij} - SCE_{Ej}]}_{\text{Structural Change Effect}} \qquad (8.4)$$

The average results for the whole sample of 109 regions are reported in Table 8.7. The most interesting outcome is that the structural change effect now dominates over the within-sector growth. The catching up process, although quite small in absolute terms, is mainly induced by a mechanism of shifting employment across sectors. More specifically, migration from low- to high-productivity sectors is relatively faster in the initially poorer regions than in the richer ones. So, the total effect of structural change is an important component of aggregate convergence.

Table 8.7 Source of convergence in European regions, 1980–1990

	Within sector		Structural change		Total effect	
	value	%	value	%	value	%
Agriculture	0.11	74	−0.12	−82	−0.01	−8
Industry	−0.17	−46	0.12	79	0.05	32
Services	−0.01	−4	0.12	79	0.11	75
Total	0.04	24	0.12	76	0.15	100

As regards the contribution of each individual sector, we find a confirmation that the services sector plays the most relevant role. Almost 4/5 of the total convergence originates from the positive structural change effect of services. The industrial sector also shows a strong positive structural change effect, while the same effect is negative for agriculture. These results indicate that the shifts out of agriculture into manufacturing and services are faster than average in the initially lagging regions. Agriculture is the only sector that shows a positive within-sector growth effect (74 per cent), signalling that poorer regions have enjoyed higher growth rates of productivity in this sector. Interestingly, the contribution of productivity growth in industry is large and negative (–46 per cent). This negative within-sector effect is due to the fact that high-productivity regions obtained relatively higher growth in this sector – an outcome not favourable to convergence.[11] However, as we have already pointed out, the net effect of industry is positivity, due to a huge employment migration into this high productivity sector in the poorer regions.

The total net effect of each sector on convergence turns out to be positive in the industrial and services sectors while is negative for agriculture. This outcome is compatible with the sectoral estimates of the catching up equation presented earlier, where we found a convergence process occurring in industry and services but not in agriculture.

In short, the presence in the southern regions of a still large agriculture sector seems to be the key element in the analysis of regional growth in Europe. Indeed, in 1980 the correlation between the labour share in agriculture and the productivity level of the entire economy was negative and highly significant ($r = -0.79$). In Figure 8.2 we can see that the regions (mainly in southern Europe) with an initial high specialization in the primary sector were on average those with low values of aggregate labour productivity.

Given this sectoral characterization of the lagging regions, much potential for future convergence is likely to exist. As we have already pointed out in Section 8.2, the regions with initial higher agriculture shares are more likely to obtain large and fast flows of labour out of the primary sector in the subsequent period. This kind of structural change may accelerate convergence. As a matter of fact, over the period 1980–90 a negative relationship ($r = -0.27$) does exist between the changes in the agriculture labour shares and aggregate growth rates (see Figure 8.3).[12] Regions that show higher out-migration flows from agriculture tend to grow faster than the others. Nonetheless, our data also suggest that this is far from being an automatic process. Not all the southern regions have succeeded in transforming their migration flows out of agriculture into aggregate productivity gains of the magnitude required to generate absolute convergence. The sources of such a differentiated performance within the subgroup of the lagging (agricultural) regions is an important topic for future research.

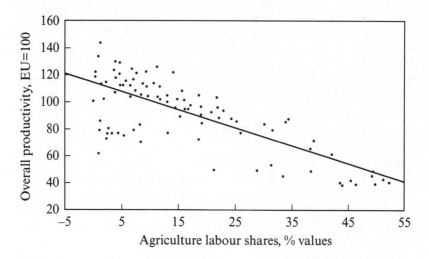

Figure 8.2 Agriculture labour shares and overall productivity level, 1980

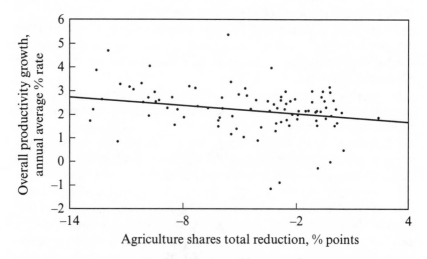

Figure 8.3 Agriculture shifts out and overall productivity growth, 1980–1990

8.6 CONCLUSIONS

The European regions are still characterized by large differences in terms of sectoral specialization, productivity levels and growth and these differences appear to play a crucial role in determining the overall growth rate of the regional economies. The key distinction seems to be between agriculture on the one side and industry and services on the other. More specifically agriculture displays an average level of labour productivity less than half of the aggregate one; moreover the degree of regional disparities in this sector are enormous. This explains the low aggregate productivity of several southern regions that are still characterized by the presence of large labour shares in agriculture. Several European regions in the south seem still to be characterized by a dualistic economic structure.

In order to analyse how aggregate growth is influenced by sectoral mix, we have used two approaches: an econometric estimate of a modified version of Kaldor's third law, and an accounting decomposition of the overall growth rate. Our results show that the major role in determining aggregate growth is played by the increase in the productivity within the services sector. This result is stronger among the more developed northern regions. In the south, a relevant contribution to overall growth is also due to inter-sectoral shifts of the labour force.

Other important issues analysed in the chapter are the existence of a catching up mechanism and the assessment of the sectoral sources of this process. We have documented the existence of a slow convergence process across the European regions, the statistical significance of which is higher when we control for national idiosyncratic elements. Moreover, convergence is stronger among the northern regions, while the southern regions tend to converge to a lower steady-state. At the sectoral level, unconditional catching up is detected in both industry and services, but not in agriculture.

Finally, the accounting decomposition of the catching up process has revealed that a large part of the convergence is induced by changes of the initial sectoral mixes. Sectoral shifts from low- to high-productivity sectors turn out to be relatively faster in southern regions. However, not all the initially backward regions have been capable of exploiting this potentially convergence-enhancing structural change. The key question to be addressed in future research is therefore what lies behind such a highly differentiated pattern.

More generally, a thorough understanding of the correlation linking sectoral mixes to aggregate growth is a crucial task, especially in a period in which the accelerating process of economic integration in Europe is likely to bring about further differentiation in the patterns of specialization across the European regions.

APPENDIX

In this chapter we have used the database *Regio-Eu* set up by CRENoS (see Paci, 1997). The 109 territorial units are:

B   BELGIUM
B1   BRUXELLES
B2   VLAAMS GEWEST
B3   REGION WALLONNE

D   GERMANY
D1   BADEN-WUERTTEMBERG
D2   BAYERN
D3   BERLIN
D4   BREMEN
D5   HAMBURG
D6   HESSEN
D7   NIEDERSACHSEN
D8   NORDRHEIN-WESTFALEN
D9   RHEINLAND-PFALZ
D10 SAARLAND
D11 SCHLESWIG-HOLSTEIN

DK   DENMARK

E   SPAIN
E1   GALICIA
E2   ASTURIAS
E3   CANTABRIA
E4   PAIS VASCO
E5   NAVARRA
E6   RIOJA
E7   ARAGON
E8   MADRID
E9   CASTILLA-LEON
E10 CASTILLA-LA MANCHA
E11 EXTREMADURA
E12 CATALUNA
E13 COMUNIDAD VALENCIANA
E14 BALEARES
E15 ANDALUCIA
E16 MURCIA
E17 CANARIAS

F   FRANCE
F1   ILE DE FRANCE
F2   CHAMPAGNE-ARDENNE
F3   PICARDIE
F4   HAUTE-NORMANDIE
F5   CENTRE
F6   BASSE-NORMANDIE
F7   BOURGOGNE
F8   NORD-PAS-DE-CALAIS
F9   LORRAINE
F10 ALSACE
F11 FRANCHE-COMTE
F12 PAYS DE LA LOIRE
F13 BRETAGNE
F14 POITOU-CHARENTES
F15 AQUITAINE
F16 MIDI-PYRENEES
F17 LIMOUSIN
F18 RHONE-ALPES
F19 AUVERGNE
F20 LANGUEDOC-ROUSSILLON
F21 PROVENCE-ALPES
     COTE D'AZUR
F22 CORSE

G   GREECE
G1   ANATOLIKI
     MAKEDONIA, THRAKI
G2   KENTRIKI MAKEDONIA
G3   DYTIKI MAKEDONIA
G4   THESSALIA
G5   IPEIROS
G6   IONIA NISIA
G7   DYTIKI ELLADA
G8   STEREA ELLADA
G9   PELOPONNISOS
G10 ATTIKI AIGAIO
G11 VOREIO AIGAIO

G12	NOTIO AIGAIO	**N**	**NETHERLANDS**
G13	KRITI	N1	NOORD-NEDERLAND
		N2	OOST-NEDERLAND
IR	**IRELAND**	N3	WEST-NEDERLAND
		N4	ZUID-NEDERLAND
I	**ITALY**		
I1	PIEMONTE	**P**	**PORTUGAL**
I2	VALLE D'AOSTA	P1	NORTE
I3	LIGURIA	P2	CENTRO
I4	LOMBARDIA	P3	LISBOA E VALE DO TEJO
I5	TRENTINO-ALTO ADIGE	P4	ALENTEJO
I6	VENETO	P5	ALGARVE
I7	FRIULI-VENEZIA GIULIA		
I8	EMILIA-ROMAGNA	**U**	**UNITED KINGDOM**
I9	TOSCANA	U1	NORTH
I10	UMBRIA	U2	YORKSHIRE AND
I11	MARCHE		HUMBERSIDE
I12	LAZIO	U3	EAST MIDLANDS
I13	CAMPANIA	U4	EAST ANGLIA
I14	ABRUZZI	U5	SOUTH EAST
I15	MOLISE	U6	SOUTH WEST
I16	PUGLIA	U7	WEST MIDLANDS
I17	BASILICATA	U8	NORTH WEST
I18	CALABRIA	U9	WALES
I19	SICILIA	U10	SCOTLAND
I20	SARDEGNA	U11	NORTHERN IRELAND

LU   LUXEMBURG

The database covers the period 1980–90 for the whole group of 109 regions. All monetary variables are expressed in purchasing power parity (PPP) terms and at constant 1985 prices.

The data sources are Eurostat's *Regio*, several statistical yearbooks and various National Statistical Offices.

NOTES

* This chapter is part of a CRENoS research project on growth across the European regions. We are grateful to Teresa Garcia-Milà and to participants at the 3rd CRENoS Conference in Cagliari and at CEPR workshop in Alghero for helpful comments. We thank Giuseppina Pira and Alessandra Amitrano for assistance in setting up the database.

1. The role of structural change in the convergence process has been analysed by Paci and Pigliaru (1997) for the case of the Italian regions. See Section 2 of that paper for a survey of the different viewpoints of the literature on structural change and growth. Other recent empirical studies relating sectoral mix and its changes with economic growth are Bernard and Jones (1994, 1996) and Garcia-Mila and Marimon (Chapter 14, this volume).

2. See Paci (1997) for a detailed description of the database. In our data, Industry includes the Manufacturing, Construction and Mining sectors; Services includes Private services and Public·Administration.

3. The southern region group includes Greece, Spain, Portugal and the eight Mezzogiorno regions in Italy.

4. The ranking does not include Brussels, because of its complete specialization in the services sector.

5. The specialization index is calculated as: $SPE_{ij} = (L_{ij}/\Sigma_j L_{ij})/(\Sigma_i L_{ij}/\Sigma_i \Sigma_j L_{ij})$, where L are units of labour in region i and sector j. The index is higher than one when the region has a relative specialization in that sector and it is less than one when it has a disadvantage.

6. Few regions show a specialization index higher than 1.1 in two sectors. In such a case the region has been included in the sector that exhibits the highest index.

7. The potential role of these local industrial clusters is strengthened by the high degree of spatial concentration of the technological activity that prevails across the European regions. See Verspagen (Chapter 9, this volume) and Paci and Usai (1997).

8. A recent analysis of the effects of spatial elements on Kaldor's laws is presented by Bernat (1996) for the states of the United States.

9. The annual average growth rates are computed as log differences between final and initial years, divided by the number of years.

10. The process of convergence across the European regions has been analysed by Barro and Sala-i-Martin (1991), Neven and Gouyette (1995), Fagerberg and Verspagen (1996), Quah (1996) and Sala-i-Martin (1996b). Most of these studies are based on per capita income growth. For a critique to the use of this variable in the convergence studies see Paci (1997) which shows how the convergence results are highly affected by the choice of the dependent variable.

11. This result is compatible with the presence of externalities such as localized spillovers and agglomeration economies.

12. In Figure 8.3, the Greek region of Voreio Aigaio (G11) has been omitted because of the out-of-range decrease of its agricultureal share.

REFERENCES

Barro, R. and X. Sala-i-Martin (1991), 'Convergence across states and regions', *Brookings Papers on Economic Activity*, **1**, 107–82.

Bernard, A. and C. Jones (1994), 'Comparing apples to oranges: productivity convergence and measurement across industries and countries', *American Economic Review*, **86**, 1216–39.

Bernard, A. and C. Jones (1996), 'Productivity and convergence across U.S. states and industries', *Empirical Economics*, **21**, 113–35.

Bernat, A. (1996), 'Does manufacturing matter? A spatial econometric view of Kaldor's laws', *Journal of Regional Science*, **36**, 463–77.

Fagerberg J. and B. Verspagen (1996), 'Heading for divergence. Regional growth in Europe reconsidered', *Journal of Common Market Studies*, **34**, 431–48.

Grossman, G.M. and E. Helpman (1991), *Innovation and Growth in the Global Economy*, Cambridge, MA: MIT Press.

Kaldor, N. (1966), *Causes of the Slow Rate of Growth in the United Kingdom*, Cambridge: Cambridge University Press.

Kaldor, N. (1968), 'Productivity and growth in manufacturing industry: a reply', *Economica*, **35**, 385–91.

Kaldor, N. (1975), 'Economic growth and the Verdoorn Law: a comment on Mr Rowthorn's article', *Economic Journal*, **85**, 891–6.

Krugman, P. (1991), 'Increasing returns and economic geography', *Journal of Political Economy*, **99**, 483–99.

Lewis, W. (1954), 'Economic development with unlimited supplies of labour', *Manchester School*, **22**, 137–91.

Lucas, R.E. (1988), 'On the mechanics of economic development', *Journal of Monetary Economics*, **22**, 3–42.

Mankiw, G., D. Romer and D. Weil (1992), 'A contribution to the empirics of economic growth', *Quarterly Journal of Economics*, **107**, 407–37.

McCombie, J. (1980), 'On the quantitative importance of Kaldor's laws', *Bulletin of Economic Research*, **32**, 102–12.

McCombie J. (1981), 'What still remains of Kaldor's laws?', *Economic Journal*, **91**, 206–16.

Murat, M. and F. Pigliaru (1998), 'International trade and uneven growth: a model with intersectoral spillovers of knowledge', *Journal of International Trade and Economic Development*, **7**, 221–36.

Neven, D. and C. Gouyette (1995), 'Regional convergence in the European Community', *Journal of Common Market Studies*, **33**, 47–65.

Paci, R. (1997), 'More similar and less equal. Economic growth in the European regions', *Weltwirtschaftliches Archiv*, **133** (4), 609–34.

Paci, R. and F. Pigliaru (1997), 'Structural change and convergence: an Italian regional perspective', *Structural Change and Economic Dynamics*, **8**, 297–318.

Paci, R. and S. Usai (1997), 'Technological enclaves and industrial districts. An analysis of the regional distribution of innovative activity in Europe', Contributi di Ricerca CRENoS, 97/8.

Quah, D. (1996), 'Regional convergence clusters across Europe', *European Economic Review*, **40**, 951–8.

Sala-i-Martin, X. (1996a), 'The classical approach to convergence analysis', *Economic Journal*, **106**, 1019–36.

Sala-i-Martin, X. (1996b), 'Regional cohesion: evidence and theories of regional growth and convergence', *European Economic Review*, **40**, 1325–52.

9. European 'regional clubs': do they exist, and where are they heading? On economic and technological differences between European regions

Bart Verspagen*

9.1 INTRODUCTION: TECHNOLOGICAL CHANGE IN REGIONS

Economists have always identified technological change as the prime factor behind economic growth. There are, however, clear differences between different ways in which economists from different theoretical perspectives have looked at the way in which technological change 'works'. In traditional growth theory (Solow, 1956, 1970), technology is supplied as an exogenous public good. Countries, regions or firms are seen as entities, which, at least in the long run, can all make use of the same technology. Not surprisingly, the prediction of this theory is that growth paths of different countries or regions will (unconditionally) converge to each other.

In the recent so-called 'new growth theory', technology becomes a partly private and partly public good. For example, in Romer (1990), technological inventions can be patented by firms, which gives them the exclusive right to produce new (intermediate) goods, but, at the same time, inventions generate new 'general knowledge', which is freely available to all firms. This approach typically leads to 'endogenization' of steady-state growth rates of countries and, hence, convergence becomes 'conditional' on the factors endogenously determining this growth rate.

In the view of a group of economists identifying themselves as 'Schumpeterians' (for example, Dosi, 1988), technological change is characterized by strong tendencies for cumulativeness, implying that not all firms (or countries, or regions) are equally well placed to make innovations. In this view, the innovation capability of firms depends on a number of tangible assets, such as knowledge embodied in people, experience with certain production processes, and so on. A number of authors in this tradition (Fagerberg, 1987; Dosi, Pavitt and Soete, 1990; Nelson and Winter, 1982), have implemented this view of technology in theories of the relation between technological progress and economic change. They argue that technology is a strong disequilibrating factor in processes of economic growth, giving rise to the opportunity of pervasive growth rate differentials between countries.

In economic geography, a similar argument about technological change is found. This body of work stresses the importance of local spillovers in technology. For example, research and development (R&D) is more efficiently carried out when other R&D-intensive firms or institutions (public research labs, universities) are close by, because this enables the R&D firm to draw on resources such as skilled personnel, and to interact with other R&D performers. Examples of this line of research are Cowan and Cowan (1997) and Jaffe, Trajtenberg and Henderson (1993).

Spatial technology spillovers combined with cumulative innovation capabilities of firms may easily lead to self-reinforcing, virtuous circle type processes of economic growth. Thus, a (small) initial advantage of one region in terms of innovation capabilities would generate a higher growth rate in this region, as well as attract new R&D-performing firms to the region. This would in turn lead to higher growth, and so on. If there are, however, at some stage also some 'negative feedback' effects, such as congestion, decreasing marginal returns to (R&D) investment, or increasing (real) wages, such a process of diverging growth rates is likely to come to a stop at some level, leading to a positive and persistent growth rate differential between regions.[1]

On the other hand, however, the idea of technology as something that may be imitated is not entirely strange. Obviously, once an innovation has been made, there is a certain potential for other firms (or regions, or countries) than the original innovator to imitate it. What is crucially stressed, however, in the above mentioned 'Schumpeterian' theories, is that this imitation process requires some learning capability as well as investment in 'learning' from the side of the imitator. Thus, for imitation, a firm needs capabilities, just as it needs capabilities for innovation. Obviously, the two capability sets differ: an innovator needs to be on the technological frontier, while an imitator can afford to be a little behind, but needs a strong absorptive capacity. From the point of view of a region or country, both types of capabilities are crucially related to institutions such as the education system (Abramovitz, 1994).

What is the driving force for this chapter is not so much the consequences that this perspective on technology and economic change has for individual regions. Instead, the idea is that spatial technology spillovers may also extend over regional borders. In other words, the basic hypothesis in this chapter is that technology spillovers between regions have a strong spatial component. This implies that on the map of European regions considered here, one may, for example, find 'clusters' of high-growth regions engaged in high-tech activities, while other, economically more backward 'clusters' are relatively blank with respect to technology. The basic aim in this chapter is to explore whether one can usefully identify such clusters, as well as to explore the consequences thereof for differences in economic performance between regions.

The idea of such 'regional clubs' in Europe is not only a theoretical one stemming from the above observations about the nature of technology. Commonly used phrases such as 'Europe at different speeds' indicate the general concern among policy-makers and 'policy-watchers' for increased heterogeneity from an economic point of view, which may bring with it a decreasing tendency for 'social cohesion'. An important element of European regional policy is indeed to enhance such social cohesion. The so-called 'structural funds' are one well-known example of a policy instrument geared at reducing the economic 'backwardness' of the European regions 'at lower speed' or in 'lower order growth clubs'.

In previous papers (Fagerberg and Verspagen, 1996; Fagerberg, Verspagen and Caniëls, 1997), the hypothesis of different 'regional clubs' in Europe was investigated applying regression analysis. Fagerberg and Verspagen (1996) identified three such growth clubs, which could (endogenously) be identified by unemployment rates, while Fagerberg, Verspagen and Caniëls (1997) used four 'quartiles' of (initial) GDP per capita. The emphasis in those papers was on explaining economic growth in regions, and the analysis of 'clubs' was limited to the attempt to come up with a number of 'stylized' explanations for differences in regional growth performance. The current chapter, in a sense, takes the possibility of 'regional clubs' much more seriously, and recognizes it as a natural outcome of the cumulativeness and the local character of technological change and its relation to economic growth.

In exploring the existence of 'regional clubs', the analysis is deliberately started from two different types of clubs. The first type of club is defined from a purely economic perspective. Here, variables such as GDP per capita and its growth, (un)employment and productivity are looked at. The second type is defined in terms of technology variables, and defines regional clubs as clusters of regions which differ in terms of investment in technology, as well as specialization in different production technologies. Obviously, the theoretical perspective sketched above points out that there would be some connection between the two types of clubs. One would, for example, expect that high-tech regions (those which are specialized in new technologies, and invest heavily in it) show relatively 'good' economic performance.

At the same time, however, it is clear that such a connection between the two types of clubs is far from simple or 'linear'. Technological investment takes many different forms (see for example the distinction between innovators and imitators, as introduced above). It is likely that these different forms have different consequences for different economic variables. For example, in Fagerberg, Verspagen and Caniëls (1997), it was confirmed that regions with relatively low GDP per capita are relatively well placed to grow rapidly due to imitation and 'catch-up', but they are not so well placed to perform R&D. A strong correlation between R&D intensity and the level of GDP per capita was found and, at the same time, an inverse correlation between initial GDP per capita and its growth rate. It is also true that growth may result from other than technological sources, such as natural resources and factor-intensive growth (rapidly growing population, inward migration, or high investment rates). When technology is embodied in people or investment goods, technology-intensive growth and factor-intensive growth are obviously interrelated.

In order not to equate technological performance and economic performance from the start, the analysis therefore proceeds by investigating the existence of regional clubs in Europe for each of the two types of clubs identified (economic and technological). After discussing the results for both types of clubs, the two different types of clubs will be combined, thus investigating the complex linkages between technology and economic performance in Europe in an exploratory way.

9.2 THE DYNAMICS OF ECONOMIC GROWTH, PRODUCTIVITY AND EMPLOYMENT IN EUROPEAN REGIONS DURING THE 1980s

It is a well-known fact that European regions show widely varying economic performance. Table 9.1 shows some of the differences with regard to some of the most commonly used statistics to evaluate regional economic performance, for the sample of regions in France, Germany, Italy, Spain and the United Kingdom. Of the three variables expressed as levels (GDP per capita, productivity and the unemployment rate), unemployment is perhaps the one with the most 'uneven' distribution. This is indicated by the coefficient of variation (standard deviation divided by the mean), as well as positive skewness. For unemployment, the coefficient of variation is higher than for either (labour) productivity or GDP per capita, and this variable also shows a (positively) skewed distribution

Table 9.1 Differences in economic performance between European regions (France, Germany, Italy, Spain, United Kingdom), 1980s

Variable	Mean	STD	CV	Skewness	SE Skewness	N
Employment growth (%, annual)	0.94	0.99	1.05	0.64	0.28	75
Labour force growth (%, annual)	1.07	0.90	0.84	0.39	0.28	74
Productivity growth (%, annual)	1.98	0.62	0.31	−0.29	0.28	74
GDP per capita growth (% annual)	2.07	0.69	0.33	0.37	0.28	74
Unemployment rate (% 1983)	10.30	4.35	0.42	0.75	0.28	75
GDP per capita (ECU PPS, 1980)	11.36	2.62	0.23	0.10	0.28	74
Productivity (ECU PPS, 1981)	29.85	4.37	0.15	0.03	0.28	74

Source: Calculations on the basis of the REGIO database of EUROSTAT.

(the other variables do not show any particularly skewed distribution, the standard errors of the skewness statistic are relatively large). The large coefficient of variation points to heterogeneity between regions. Positive skewness indicates that the unemployment observations that can be characterized as 'extreme', tend to be larger than the mean. In other words, it indicates that the distribution for unemployment rates tends to have outliers with high unemployment.

Labour productivity shows a lower coefficient of variation than GDP per capita. Naturally, this is connected to the distribution of unemployment. In the regions with high unemployment, relatively fewer workers are engaged in the production of GDP, so that the unevenness of unemployment rates leads to higher disparity in GDP per capita.

In the case of growth rates, unevenness is generally larger than for the level variables. The coefficients of variation for the growth rates of employment and the labour force are larger than any level variable; productivity and GDP per capita growth rates show larger coefficients of variation than their level counterparts. The rate of growth of employment is somewhat smaller than the rate of growth of the labour force, illustrating the tendency towards higher unemployment rates in European regions during the 1980s. Employment growth shows positive skewness, as did the rate of unemployment; the other growth rates do not show skewed distributions.

Thus, European regions are generally more heterogenous from a dynamic perspective than they were from a static perspective in the early 1980s. This conclusion alone does not imply any specific tendency for divergence or convergence in variables such as GDP per capita or labour productivity. This chapter does not present additional evidence on trends with regard to convergence or divergence, but it has been well established that during the 1980s, contrary to the period before that, there was little 'net' convergence in terms of GDP per capita. For example, Fagerberg, Verspagen and Caniëls (1997) showed that although the 'poor' regions in the sample had the potential to grow faster due to 'catching-up opportunity', this was almost completely offset by differences in variables such as R&D efforts in the 'richer' regions. The net result was that the 'poor' regions grow a few tenths of a percentage point faster over the decade, but this has little effect on the differences in levels.

In order to explore the existence of regional clubs, cluster analysis is applied to the data on regional economic performance. Relative to the earlier approaches in Fagerberg and Verspagen (1996) and Fagerberg, Verspagen and Caniëls (1997), this approach has the advantage that the grouping is based on more than just one variable. Rather than the usual 'hierarchical clustering', an iterative procedure to establish the clusters is used.[2] This has the advantage that a wider range of clusters may be achieved. Contrary to hierarchical clustering, however, the number of clusters needs to be determined *ex ante* rather than *ex post*. It was arbitrarily decided to use four clusters, although the analysis was also carried out for three clusters. Given that the procedure points to significant differences between the four clusters (p-values smaller than 1 per cent for all variables), these results are used. Clustering was done using the standardized values of all variables (so called Z-scores, obtained by subtracting the mean and dividing by the standard deviation).

Table 9.2a gives the means for each of the economic performance variables for the four clusters, while Table 9.2b describes the results of Scheffe-tests for differences with respect to each of the variables between the clusters. What the latter table shows first of all is that each cluster differs from all the others with respect to at least two variables. In other words, grouping two clusters together would indeed mean information is lost. Figure 9.1 shows the geographical distribution of the clusters.

In terms of GDP per capita, the clusters 1 to 3 do not differ significantly from each other. They are all relatively poor compared to cluster 4:

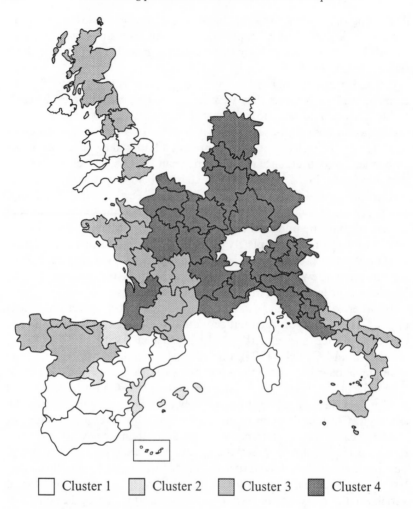

☐ Cluster 1   ▣ Cluster 2   ▦ Cluster 3   ■ Cluster 4

Figure 9.1 Economic clusters of regions in Europe

the values of GDP per capita in 1980 in clusters 1–3 are 64–73 per cent of
the value in cluster 4. The 'rich' fourth cluster consists of 31 regions,
located in three countries: seven German regions (that is, the whole of
Germany), thirteen French regions and eleven Italian regions. They are
all contingent, with the exception of one French region (Aquitaine).
Within France and Italy, the 'rich' regions form clear geographical groups
corresponding to well-known patterns: North-Italy and Central-North-
East France. The analysis thus clearly seems to confirm the idea that for

Table 9.2a Economic clusters of regions in Europe

	Clusters			
	1 (*n*=13)	2 (*n*=5)	3 (*n*=24)	4 (*n*=31)
GDP per capita, 1980	8.71	9.87	9.97	13.67
Productivity, 1981	25.21	31.40	27.23	33.55
Unemployment, 1983	15.35	14.60	11.05	7.23
Growth of GDP per capita	2.76	2.74	1.86	1.82
Growth of productivity	2.52	1.10	2.12	1.75
Growth of employment	2.03	2.71	0.47	0.59
Growth of labour force	2.17	1.55	1.08	0.52
In percentages of cluster 4				
GDP per capita, 1980	64	72	73	100
Productivity, 1981	75	94	81	100
Unemployment, 1983	212	202	153	100
Growth of GDP per capita	151	151	102	100
Growth of productivity	144	63	121	100
Growth of employment	347	464	81	100
Growth of labour force	415	296	206	100

Table 9.2b Statistically significant differences between the economic clusters

	1	2	3
2	*Y, GY*		
3	*GQ, GE, GN, UE*	*GQ, GY, GE, Y*	
4	all	*GQ, GE, GN, Q, UE*	*Q, Y, UE, GN*

Note: Q = GDP per capita (1980), Y = productivity (1981), UE = unemployment rate (1983), GQ = average annual growth of Q (1980–1990), GY = average annual growth of Y, GE = average annual growth rate of employment (1983–1990), GN = average annual growth rate of labour force (1983–1990).

the economically advanced cluster, there is some spatial dimension to an explanation of its emergence. This cluster is characterized by low or intermediate growth rates of GDP per capita and productivity. Unemployment is well below the other clusters. Employment growth is also relatively low, but this is combined with low growth of the labour force, thus not leading to major dynamics in the unemployment rate.

There are several differences between the three 'poor clusters'. First of all, they differ in terms of countries. Cluster 1 is mainly Spanish and British (six regions each, plus one Italian region). Cluster 2, a small one, is exclusively Spanish, with five regions. Cluster 3 is a 'mixed bag' of five Spanish regions, six Italian, eight French regions and five British regions. In economic terms, the five Spanish regions in cluster 2 are characterized by much higher productivity combined with relatively high unemployment. Cluster 1 is the one which is most economically depressed, with low GDP per capita and productivity, and high unemployment. GDP per capita and productivity grow relatively rapidly though, which indicates some tendency for catching up. Cluster 3 has the lowest unemployment of the three 'poor' clusters, but it also shows the lowest growth rate of GDP per capita.

Overall, these results point out that there is indeed a core–periphery distinction between European regions. The core consists of Germany, North Italy and the Central-North-East French regions that connect them. The 'periphery' consists of three separate groups, which can all in some way be characterized as 'depressed', although they show some significant differences between them. The 'peripheral' regions in Italy and France all belong to the most advanced part of the 'periphery' together with regions in Britain and Spain.

In terms of the spatial alignment of clusters 1, 2 and 3, they do not form clear homogenous groups in the sense that they are contingent. It rather seems to be the case that in each country, the regions in clusters 1 and 3 are contingent. Thus, while cluster 4, the economically advanced one, seems to stretch over country borders into one big area around the Alps,[3] the more backward clusters are confined to national borders. Within each country they are by and large contingent, indicating some degree of 'spatial auto-correlation', but this does not extend over international borders. These results generally confirm that the earlier results obtained by Fagerberg and Verspagen (1996) and Fagerberg, Verspagen and Caniëls (1997) are rather robust to changes in the variables used to group regions. There are, however, two important differences in the characterization of the clubs relative to these earlier papers. First, there seems to be a clear spatial component in the clusters identified here. The economically advanced cluster extends over international borders into one big central EU area, the more backward clusters are confined to contingent geographical space within countries. Second, although there are differences in terms of economic growth between regional clusters, the differences in terms of level variables such as GDP per capita, productivity and unemployment rates remain rather substantial and, thus, important. Although the 'poor clusters' grow somewhat more rapidly than richer regions, this difference is rather small. For example, based on the annual growth rates in Table 9.2a, it would take cluster 1 about 50 years to catch up to the GDP per capita level of cluster 4. For cluster 2 and 3, respectively, this value is 36 and 781 years. It thus seems as if the phrases 'Europe at different speeds' or 'European growth clubs' are perhaps better replaced by alternatives such as 'Europe at different unemployment levels' or 'European GDP per capita clubs'.

9.3 TECHNOLOGY IN EUROPEAN REGIONS DURING THE 1980s

Technological change is a phenomenon that can only be measured in an indirect way. Economists often use either research and development (R&D, either expenditures on, or personnel engaged in R&D), or patent counts. R&D is clearly an input indicator, and as such it does not take into account differences in research efficiency between regions. Patent counts are an indicator of technology output, but one with a number of shortcomings. For example, many patents do not lead to innovations, and of those that do, the economic impact may differ widely. Moreover, the efficiency of patents as a means of protection against imitation differs between sectors, which leads to different propensities to patent between sectors (this is, for example, high in pharmaceuticals and low in aerospace). Part of the drawbacks of using patents as technology indicators can be overcome by using them in relative measures, such as the revealed technology advantage indicator, which will be introduced below. A final note that concerns both R&D and patents as technology indicators is that they do not work well for the non-manufacturing industries. For example, in many parts of the services industry, innovation is related to the introduction of new electronic equipment and the use of this equipment in new products.

A solution for the shortcomings of R&D and patents as innovation indicators cannot be offered here. Until recently, data on R&D personnel were the only available source of information on comparative technological efforts in European regions. These data are not broken down by industry and they are only available for a limited timespan from the mid-1980s onwards. Breschi (1995) introduces patents as a regional indicator of technology, while Caniëls (1997) further extends Breschi's analysis by adding information on patenting by industries to the existing data. This chapter uses the data developed by Caniëls (1997). This patenting data set is developed from information on patent applications at the European Patent Office (EPO). The main 'technology class' of each patent application is used to assign it to one or more of 22 industries within manufacturing, according to the concordance scheme developed by Verspagen *et al.* (1994). The patent applications are assigned to regions using a concordance scheme between postal codes and NUTS-regions, kindly supplied by EUROSTAT. The postal code of the inventor(s) is used for this purpose.[4]

The patent data are used as an indicator for technological specialization. Although information on 22 industrial classes is available, the choice was made to aggregate the data into three broad classes, that is, 'high-tech' industries, 'medium-tech' industries and 'low-tech' industries. The classification of the 22 sectors into these groups is the standard one used by OECD, and is based on average R&D intensity of the sectors. High-tech consists of pharmaceuticals (ISIC 3522), computers and office machinery (ISIC 3825), electronics (ISIC 3832), aerospace (ISIC 3845) and instruments (ISIC 385). Medium tech industries are chemicals (ISIC 351+352-3522), machinery (ISIC 382-3825), electricals (ISIC 383-3832), automobiles (ISIC 3843) and other transport (including high speed trains, ISIC 384-3841-3843-3845). All other industries are classified as low-tech. The main reason for aggregating the data into these three groups is that the number of patent applications in some of the regions is quite small. This would yield very small, or even zero numbers in many of the detailed sectors. Although this problem is not completely solved in the case of the three aggregate sectoral groups, it is certainly less severe in most cases.

The data on high-tech, medium-tech and low-tech patenting is used to calculate the so-called revealed technological advantage (RTA) index, which is defined as the share of the sectoral group in total patenting of the region divided by the share of the sectoral group in total patenting of all regions. Values higher than one point to specialization of the region in that specific sectoral group, values between zero and one point to 'negative specialization'. In order to make the index symmetric, however, a transformation of the type $(X-1)/(X+1)$, where X is the revealed technology advantage index, is applied. This new indicator always lies in the interval $[-1,1]$, with positive (negative) values pointing to specialization (despecialization).

Although these different technology indicators have different shortcomings, and are aimed at measuring different aspects of the 'technological system' of a region, strong cross-regional correlations between the variables were found. For example, R&D-intensity is strongly positively correlated with high-tech specialization (RTA). This correlation points to the fact that regions which are strong in high-tech also tend to invest more in technology. The reason for this is that the technological opportunities in their production processes are higher.

Table 9.3 gives summary statistics on the technology variables. The general impression from the table is that the disparity between regions in terms of technology is higher than in terms of the economic variables considered earlier. The coefficient of variation for each of the technology variables is higher than for any variable in Table 9.1, and each of the distributions of the technology variables is skewed. For R&D intensity (interpreted as measuring differences in 'absolute' technological efforts), heterogeneity as measured by the coefficient of variation is lower than for the three specialization variables, with medium-tech specialization coming out as the indicator with most heterogeneity.[5]

Table 9.3 Differences in technological performance between European regions (France, Germany, Italy, Spain, United Kingdom), 1980s

Variable	Mean	STD	CV	Skewness	SE Skewness	N
R&D intensity, 1985	0.42	0.47	1.12	1.93	0.28	73
High-tech specialization	−0.13	0.25	−1.92	−1.53	0.28	73
Medium-tech specialization	−0.05	0.15	−3.00	−2.34	0.28	73
Low-tech specialization	0.10	0.18	1.80	−1.23	0.28	73

Source: Calculations on the regional patenting database at MERIT, developed by Caniëls (1997) and the REGIO database of EUROSTAT.

The means of the high-tech and medium-tech specialization variables are both negative, while the one for low-tech specialization is positive. By definition, however, the weighted average of these variables over regions (using the volume of patenting as weights) is zero. The non-zero means are the direct result of the uneven distribution of patenting over regions. There is only a limited number of regions (24, or about one third of all regions) with strong patenting profiles in high-tech. These regions show up with a positive specialization index for high-tech, but the majority of regions has a negative value for this indicator. The same holds, but to a lesser extent, for medium-tech patenting. Skewness for all three RTA variables is negative. This indicates that the extreme observations tend to be negative, or, in other words, that extreme specialization patterns tend to be characterized by absence of patenting in one of the three sectors, rather than by patenting in only one of the three.

The analysis proceeds by applying the same type of cluster analysis as in the case of the economic variables. However, because the number of patents on which the technology specialization variables are based is rather small in some of the regions, it was decided to enter only regions with more than 50 patents into the cluster analysis. The RTA variables for regions with less than 50 patents are considered as less reliable, because a (random) change of one or a few patents would have large consequences for the values of these variables. The 17 regions for which the number of patents is smaller than 50 were assigned to one cluster *ex ante*, that is, without any statistical analysis. The remaining regions were classified into three clusters using the same procedure as before.

The analysis points to significant differences between clusters, as in the case of economic variables (Table 9.4b). The differences in terms of technology specialization seem to be somewhat more pronounced than in terms of mere R&D intensity, however. Only the two clusters with extreme R&D intensity (that is, highest and lowest) differ significantly

Table 9.4a Technological clusters of regions in Europe

	1 (n=17)	2 (n=14)	3 (n=24)	4 (n=17)
R&D intensity	0.05	0.26	0.53	0.78
High-tech specialization		–0.31	–0.14	0.09
Medium-tech specialization		–0.02	0.04	–0.07
Low-tech specialization		0.23	0.06	–0.03
In percentages of cluster 4				
R&D intensity	6	33	68	100

Table 9.4b Statistically significant differences between the technological clusters

	2	3
3	*HT, LT, MT*	
4	*R&D, HT, LT*	*HT, LT, MT*

Note: *R&D* = business R&D as a percentage of the labour force (1985), *LT* = specialization in low-tech, *MT* = specialization in medium-tech, *HT* = specialization in high-tech.

from each other in terms of R&D intensity. With regard to high-tech specialization, all three clusters are different from each other.

As Table 9.4a shows, the cluster which was *ex ante* fixed on the basis of patent counts, also shows the lowest R&D intensity. Among the three other clusters, there is clearly one which can be characterized as 'high-tech'. This cluster shows a high value for R&D intensity and positive technology specialization in high-tech industries. Figure 9.2 shows the geographical spread of the technological clusters.

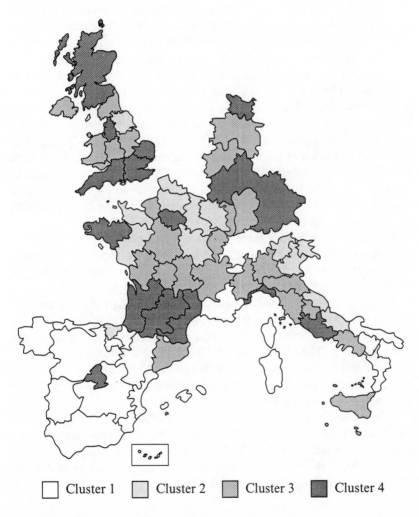

☐ Cluster 1   ▨ Cluster 2   ▨ Cluster 3   ■ Cluster 4

Figure 9.2 Technology clusters of regions in Europe

Cluster 4, the 'high-tech' cluster of Europe, has R&D-intensity about 17 (cluster 1), 3 (cluster 2) or 1.5 (cluster 3) times larger than the other clusters. Cluster 4 is thus a technologically advanced cluster. It has 17 members, which is not a very small or large group, compared to the other clusters. Germany (4), France (5) and the United Kingdom (5) are the main countries represented in this cluster. Together, these regions are specialized in high-tech, although not to an extreme degree.

In geographical terms, there is some evidence for the regions of cluster 4 to cluster together in space, but this applies within countries rather than over international borders. The degree of clustering is certainly less than was the case for the economically advanced cluster. A possible explanation for this difference is the hypothesis that technological spillovers take two different forms. First, they may have an effect on the efficiency of the R&D process itself, thus leading to geographic clustering of regions with high R&D intensity (but the evidence presented here is not very conclusive on this). Second, technology spillovers may lead to economic effects, in the sense that regions adjacent to R&D-intensive regions grow rapidly, without necessarily having high R&D intensity themselves. The interpretation of the spread of the clusters over the map of Europe would then be that the first type of spillover is more 'local' than the second, leading to high-tech clusters of regions within each country, and a broad contingent cluster of economically advanced regions encompassing and connecting the high-tech clusters across international borders.

Cluster 3 is a relatively large cluster (24 members). It is specialized in medium- and low-tech industries, and has second-ranking R&D intensity. This cluster consists of a mixed bag of nationalities: French regions (8), Italian (7), British (5), German (3) and Spanish (1).

Cluster 2 consists mainly of French (7) and Italian (5) regions. This cluster shows specialization in low-tech industries, with a neutral value for medium-tech specialization, and a negative value for high-tech specialization. Finally, Cluster 1 (fixed *ex ante*) consists mainly of Spanish and Italian regions. The mean of R&D intensity is very low in this cluster. No specialization values are given for this cluster because of the small number of patents.

Summarizing, as was the case with economic variables, one can usefully distinguish between different clusters of European regions with regard to technology efforts. There are 14 regions forming a 'high-tech core' in this respect. It thus turns out that the 'technological core' of Europe is smaller than the 'economic core'.

9.4   COMBINING ECONOMIC AND TECHNOLOGICAL CLUSTER MEMBERSHIP

Finally, membership of the four economic and technological clusters is directly compared. Table 9.5 gives the 'crosstab' of both memberships. Reasoning from a 'linear' relationship between economic performance and technology, one might expect a tendency for the observations to cluster around the diagonal of the table. However, as was stressed in the introduction, this is too simplistic, and one should not expect 'perfect association' between the two cluster dimensions.

Table 9.5   Combining economic and technological cluster membership

Economic clusters	Technology clusters				
	1	2	3	4	
1	6	0	5	2	13
2	4	0	0	1	5
3	7	5	6	6	24
4	0	9	13	8	30
	17	14	24	17	72

In terms of the distinction core–periphery, it is not so clear that being a core technology region increases the probability of being a core economic region. The probability of being a core economic region, given that the region belongs to the technology core, is 47 per cent. For a region not being part of the technology core, this probability is only 44 per cent. The other way around, there seems of being a somewhat stronger connection. The probability for a core technology region to be in the most backward economic cluster is only 11 per cent, while for regions not belonging to the technology core, this probability is 20 per cent.

However, for the non-technology core regions, the probability of being a core economic region differs strongly between the three peripheral clusters. For Technology Cluster 3, the probability of being a core economic region is 54 per cent, for Technology Cluster 2, it is 64 per cent. However, for Technology Cluster 1, the probability is zero. Although this does not say anything about causality, it is clear that being technologically backward does have economic implications.

What are the reasons for this rather fuzzy relation between technology and economic performance? First, there is the geographical factor, as already outlined above in the discussion of differences in geographical constellations of the economically and technologically advanced regions. Many of the regions in Technology Clusters 2 and 3 (with relatively high probability to be part of the economic core), are located closely to technological core regions. Thus, although their own technological capabilities are low, they may benefit from technology spillovers from the nearby high-tech regions.

The second reason for the higher probability of Technology Clusters 2 and 3 to be part of the economic core might lie in the technology dynamics of the regions themselves (contrary to the previous argument, which was based on spillovers). These regions are characterized by technological specialization in low-tech or medium-tech industries, and a negative value for high-tech specialization. These industries may benefit from catch-up driven growth, rather than depending on (own) R&D efforts.

9.5 CONCLUSIONS: PERSPECTIVES ON EUROPEAN COHESION

This chapter has shown that, during the 1980s, different European 'regional clubs' existed. In terms of variables measuring economic performance, it was found that Europe (Germany, France, Italy, Spain, the United Kingdom) can be characterized as consisting of four regional clubs. One of these is clearly the advanced club, with high productivity and GDP per capita, and relatively low unemployment. The other three clubs are less advanced, although they all have some specific characteristic that distinguishes them from the other two 'peripheral' clubs. In the technology dimension, one advanced club with high R&D intensity and patenting in high-tech activities was found. The other three 'technology clubs' are gradually less R&D intensive, and specialize more in the low- and medium-tech industries.

Comparing the geographical constellations of the advanced technology and economic clusters, several interesting points emerge. First, the advanced technological cluster is smaller in terms of the number of regions than the advanced economic cluster. Second, whereas the advanced economic cluster is an almost perfectly contingent set of regions stretching from Germany, through Central and East France to Northern Italy, the advanced technological cluster is a set of centres within individual countries, but is not geographically connected across borders.

What do these results have to say on the issue of economic policy aiming to stimulate economic development in the regions which are members of the 'peripheral' clusters (among others the 'less favoured regions', in eurospeak)? One might interpret the results here as saying that innovation and technology are successful factors in getting on to the road to economic development, but this obviously raises the important and difficult question of how to stimulate innovation in regions which are relatively backward from the economic perspective. Innovation requires resources not easily available in those backward regions, such as investment by firms, public research institutes and universities. In other words, many of the 'less favoured regions' are caught in a virtual circle of low innovation and low productivity/GDP per capita. Simply subsidizing (private or public) research in those regions would not solve the problem because one cannot develop (high-) technology from scratch.

The results here do point to another policy option, however. The fact that the economically advanced cluster is very much broader than the technologically advanced cluster, as well as the specific geographical arrangement found, points to the interpretation that 'high-tech' regions have a rather broad spillover in terms of economic growth. Thus, regions adjacent to 'high-tech' regions may not directly benefit in terms of attracting more R&D-intensive firms, but they may have important benefits in terms of higher economic growth. One may think of simple (Keynesian) multiplier effects as one causal factor explaining such a pattern.

From the policy point of view, this would mean that one would not necessarily have to concentrate on the less favoured regions themselves when implementing technology policy to stimulate development. Instead, policy makers might target one or a few central region(s), in which facilities such as public research institutes or universities would already be relatively abundant. Complementary policy measures might then focus at facilitating economic spillovers from this central region targeted for technological development to the regions around it. One might for example think about stimulating business contacts between the central and peripheral regions.

APPENDIX: REGIONS USED IN THE ANALYSIS

NUTS	NAME
DE1	Baden-Wurttemberg
DE2	Bayern
DE7	Hessen
DE9+DE5	Niedersachsen + Bremen
DEA	Nordrhein-Westfalen
DEB+DEC	Rheinland-Pfalz + Saarland
DEF+DE6	Schleswig-Holstein + Hamburg
UK1	North

UK2	Yorkshire and Humberside
UK3	East Midlands
UK4	East Anglia
UK5	South East
UK6	South West
UK7	West Midlands
UK8	North West
UK9	Wales
UKA	Scotland
UKB	Northern Ireland
IT11	Piemonte
IT12	Valle d'Aosta
IT13	Liguria
IT2	Lombardia
IT31	Trentino-Alto-Adige
IT32	Veneto
IT33	Friuli-Venezia Giulia
IT4	Emilia-Romagna
IT51	Toscana
IT52	Umbria
IT53	Marche
IT6	Lazio
IT7	Abruzzo-Molise
IT8	Campania
IT91	Puglia
IT92	Bascilicata
IT93	Calabria
ITA	Sicilia
ITB	Sardegna
FR1	Ile de France
FR21	Champagne-Ardenne
FR22	Picardie
FR23	Haute-Normandie
FR24	Centre
FR25	Basse-Normandie
FR26	Bourgogne
FR3	Nord–Pas-de-Calais
FR41	Lorraine
FR42	Alsace
FR43	Franche-Comte
FR51	Pays de la Loire
FR52	Bretagne

FR53	Poitou-Charentes
FR61	Aquitaine
FR62	Midi-Pyrenees
FR63	Limousin
FR71	Rhone-Alpes
FR72	Auvergne
FR81	Languedoc-Roussillon
FR82	Provence-Alpes-Cote d'Azur
FR83	Corse
ES11	Galicia
ES12	Principado de Asturias
ES13	Cantabria
ES21	Pais Vasco
ES22	Communidad Foral de Navarra
ES23	La Rioja
ES3	Communidad de Madrid
ES41	Castilla y Leon
ES42	Castilla–la Mancha
ES43	Extremadura
ES51	Cataluna
ES52	Comunidad Valenciana
ES53	Islas Baleares
ES61	Andalucia
ES62	Region de Murcia
ES7	Canarias

NOTES

*   My research is made possible by a fellowship of the Royal Netherlands Academy of Arts and Sciences. The paper has benefited from discussions with my colleagues Marjolein Caniëls and Ivo De Loo, as well as an ongoing research project on European regions and many discussions with Jan Fagerberg. I nevertheless take full and sole responsibility for the views expressed here.

1.   Dixon and Thirlwall (1975) provide an example of a model which has these characteristics. The model does not have, however, endogenous R&D investment, but relies on the Kaldor–Verdoorn law for productivity increases.

2.   The K-means cluster analysis algorithm in SPSS 6.0 for OSF/1 is used. This algorithm requires the user to specify the number of clusters, and starts with a random cluster configuration. In the iterative procedure, cases are re-assigned to clusters on the basis of their distance to cluster centres.

3.   One may indeed argue that Swiss regions, which are not taken into account in the analysis, are also a part of this cluster. Because there are no data available on Switzerland, however, this is a speculative argument.

4.   One could also have used the postal code of the applicant, but this may introduce a bias to the more 'central' regions, because patents are often applied for by the main offices of firms, rather than the research facility. The patent's inventors are always 'natural

persons', listed by their living address. However, given the possibility that inventors live in 'neighbouring regions' to their workplace, this introduces another possible distortion, but this seems less serious than in the case of using applicants' addresses, especially given that the regions are relatively large.

5. It should be noted that, of course, by their nature, the specialization variables measure dissimilarity instead of similarity. One would therefore expect some degree of heterogeneity between regions with regard to these indicators. Technological heterogeneity between regions is thus better illustrated using coefficients of variation in the 'absolute' indicators. Nevertheless, the statistics for the specialization indicators have some informational value, especially those for skewness.

REFERENCES

Abramovitz, M. (1994), 'The Origins of the Postwar Catch Up and Convergence Boom', in J. Fagerberg, B. Verspagen and N. Von Tunzelmann (eds), *The Dynamics of Technology, Trade and Growth*, Aldershot: Edward Elgar.

Breschi, S. (1995), 'Spatial patterns of innovation: evidence from patent data', paper presented at the workshop on 'New research findings: the economics of scientific and technological research in Europe', Urbino, Italy, 24–25 February 1995.

Caniëls, M. (1997), 'The geographic distribution of patents and value added across European regions', paper for the 37th European Congress of the European Regional Science Association, Rome, 26–29 August 1997.

Cowan, R. and W. Cowan, (1998), 'On clustering in the location of R&D: statics and dynamics', *Economics of Innovation and New Technology*, **6**, 201–29.

Dixon, R.J. and A.P. Thirlwall, (1975), 'A model of regional growth rate differences on Kaldorian lines', *Oxford Economic Papers*, **11**, 201–14.

Dosi, G. (1988), 'Sources, procedures and microeconomic effects of innovation', *Journal of Economic Literature*, **26**, 1120–71.

Dosi, G., K. Pavitt and L. Soete (1990), *The Economics of Technical Change and International Trade*, London: Harvester Wheatsheaf.

Fagerberg, J. (1987), 'A technology gap approach to why growth rates differ', *Research Policy*, **16**, 87–99.

Fagerberg, J. and B. Verspagen (1996), 'Heading for divergence? Regional growth in Europe reconsidered', *Journal of Common Market Studies*, **34**, 431–48.

Fagerberg, J., B. Verspagen and M. Caniëls (1997), 'Technology, growth and unemployment across European regions', *Regional Studies*, **31**, 457–66.

Jaffe, A., M. Trajtenberg and R. Henderson (1993), 'Geographic localization of knowledge spillovers as evidenced by patent citations', *Quarterly Journal of Economics*, **108**, 577–98.

Nelson, R.R. and S.G. Winter (1982), *An Evolutionary Theory of Economic Change*, Cambridge, MA: The Bellknap Press.

Romer, P. (1990), 'Endogenous technological change', *Journal of Political Economy*, **98**, S71–S102.

Solow, R.M. (1956), 'A contribution to the theory of economic growth', *Quarterly Journal of Economics*, **70**, 65–94.

Solow, R.M. (1970), *Growth Theory: An Exposition*, Oxford: Oxford University Press.

Verspagen, B., T. van Moergastel and M. Slabbers (1994), 'MERIT concordance table: IPC-ISIC (rev. 2)', MERIT Research Memorandum 94-004.

10. Human capital and growth in the European regions: does allocation matter?

Sergio Lodde

INTRODUCTION

The purpose of this chapter is to give a contribution to the analysis of the relationship between human capital and economic growth in a regional context. The central question is whether taking into account the allocation of human capital among different activities which may be more or less growth enhancing, helps to clarify why this factor, theoretically so relevant in the growth literature, fails to give consistent results in the empirical analysis.

The role of human capital in the growth process was extensively examined by economists in the 1960s and 1970s as an extension of the neoclassical growth model aimed at explaining the Solow residual and, more recently, within the framework of endogenous growth theory. While there is general agreement on the hypothesis that the quality of the labour force and the amount of technical knowledge embodied in it play a crucial role in the growth performance of the economy no firm conclusion has been reached on this point in the empirical analysis. Several explanations have been given for this anomaly but none of them has yet gained a general consensus among the scholars of the subject. One hypothesis suggests that not all the skills generated by education are equally growth enhancing, their contribution to economic growth depending which activities they are applied to. According to the ruling structure of pay-offs some skills may be allocated to rentseeking activities. Although they can generate high individual earnings their effects on the growth performance of the economy might be marginal or even negative.

This chapter attempts to give some empirical support to the above mentioned hypothesis testing whether the allocation of skills and knowledge embodied in the educated labour force among technical and non-technical occupations influences the rate of growth of the European regional economies and the speed of the convergence process. The test is done using data on the educational attainment of the active population and on its distribution among various occupations.

The chapter is organized as follows. The first section contains a survey of the recent empirical literature on the effects of the stock of human capital on the rate of growth. The second describes the dataset used in the analysis. The third provides some descriptive statistics on education in the sample of regions under analysis. In the forth section some econometric results on the effects of the educational attainment of the labour force on productivity growth and convergence are presented. A proxy of the allocation of educational skills to technical activities is introduced in the fifth section to test the hypothesis that growth is mainly influenced by the latter. The last section contains conclusions.

HUMAN CAPITAL AND GROWTH: A CONTROVERSIAL RELATIONSHIP

Recently the relationship between human capital and growth has been studied in several papers (Romer, 1990; Barro, 1991, 1996; Mankiw, Romer and Weil, 1992; Levine and Renelt, 1992; Wolff and Gittleman, 1993; Benhabib and Spiegel, 1994; Islam, 1995; Pritchett, 1995) with controversial results.

Barro (1991) and Mankiw, Romer and Weil (1992) analyse the cross-section relationship between the initial endowment of human capital and growth using the enrolment rates to primary and secondary school as a proxy of the human capital input. In both studies a positive and significant correlation has been found between human capital and the rate of growth of income per capita.[1] Using literacy rates as a proxy for human capital Romer (1990) finds an indirect effect on growth through investment. The robustness of these variables has also been confirmed in the sensitivity analysis carried out by Levine and Renelt (1992).

However, the use of the enrolment rates as a proxy of the stock of human capital implies very strong assumptions which raise some doubts on the correct interpretation of the results. The stock must be the steady state one for all the economies in the sample and the rates must be constant across time and countries.[2]

Thanks to the availability of some new data sets developed with different estimation methodologies (Kyriacou, 1991; Barro and Lee, 1993, 1996; Nehru, Swanson and Dubey, 1994) data on educational attainment levels have been introduced in growth regressions. Barro (1996) finds a positive and significant partial correlation between growth and educational attainment (measured by the average years of schooling in primary and secondary school). Benhabib and Spiegel (1994) find a negative and insignificant correlation estimating a standard Cobb–Douglas production function. However, they show that the stock of educated labour force affects positively the rate of growth of total factor productivity by accelerating the internal rate of innovation and the technological catch-up. A negative and insignificant relationship emerges also in the analysis of Pritchett (1995) and Islam (1995).

A more detailed analysis has been carried out by Wolff and Gittleman (1993) who estimate the effects of different levels of educational attainment on the rate of growth. The comparative role of primary, secondary school and higher education in the catch-up process is analysed in a sample of more than 100 countries using data on both enrolment rates and educational attainment. The authors find that, although both enrolment rates and educational attainment levels are significant in the whole sample, the former perform uniformly better than the latter. Moreover, when investment is introduced in the regressions the co-efficients of the educational variables all become insignificant. Their explanation is that education plays an indirect role in the catch-up process: the availability of a more educated work force acts as a stimulus to investment thereby exerting an indirect effect on growth.

An interesting result of their analysis comes from the sample of industrialized countries. Here the educational variables seem to exert no effect on growth and catch-up. Particularly disconcerting is the fact that higher education does not play any role whatsoever. This result is at odds with conventional wisdom which sees scientific knowledge and technical expertise as a strongly influential factor in the catch-up process. This kind of knowledge should be mainly embodied in the share of the work force endowed with higher education.

These findings suggest that higher enrolment rates to primary and secondary school are positively and significantly correlated with higher rates of growth of per capita income but this is seldom true for educational attainment levels. In the latter case the empirical evidence does not corroborate the theoretical hypothesis of a positive and direct effect of human capital (to be more precise: education) on growth.[3]

Different arguments have been proposed to explain these controversial results. In a recent paper Bils and Klenow (1995) argue that the causal relationship is probably inverted, namely growth drives education and not the other way around. Just as faster growth induces more investment in physical capital it could induce people to acquire more education. This explains why enrolment rates are significant in growth regressions while attainment levels are not. The former react quickly to variations in the growth rate; in contrast it takes longer for a significant change in the stock of the educated population to take place.

Another line of criticism questions the representativity of the variables used in the analysis. Education captures just one aspect of human capital complexity since it does not include the experience accumulated on the job (Pritchett, 1995) and differences in school quality (Islam, 1995).

Finally some researchers argue that the cognitive abilities generated by education are not necessarily growth enhancing when applied to redistributive and rentseeking activities instead of socially productive and innovative ones. In his analysis of institutional change North (1990) gives a powerful example of how the institutional structure can deviate knowledge from socially productive uses and stimulate the development of skills which are more suited to redistributive activities. In the sixteenth century successful piracy required profound knowledge about naval warfare, trade routes, armaments and so on, while to be an industrial entrepreneur in the twentieth century implies very different skills.

A similar point is made by Baumol in his analysis of entrepreneurship (Baumol, 1990). He argues that while the supply of entrepreneurs varies among countries, its contribution to growth varies much more because a considerable part of their talent is allocated to unproductive activities like rentseeking and crime instead of production and innovation.[4]

Murphy, Schleifer and Vishny (1991) make an attempt to formalize the problem. In their model when talented people become entrepreneurs they improve technology and productivity grows; when they become rentseekers most of their returns come from the redistribution rather than the production of wealth. As a result, talented people do not address their efforts to improving technology, and the economy stagnates. Testing the model empirically they find that a higher share of engineers is positively and significantly correlated with income per capita growth while the opposite is true for lawyers. Some evidence in this direction comes also from Laband and Sophocleus (1987), Magee, Brock and Young (1989), and Lodde (1995).

This line of research suggests that the poor performance of educational attainment measures in growth regressions may be due to the fact that they do not correctly proxy for the contribution of education to productivity growth. This chapter aims at providing further evidence on this hypothesis thanks to the availability of data on the distribution of the active population of the European regions in different occupations. This allows the construction of a measure of the share of the educated labour force occupied in technical activities. We assume that the adoption and implementation of new technologies, hence the rate of growth of productivity in the regional economies, are mainly affected by this share rather than the whole stock of the educated labour force. This is because technical occupations embody most of the relevant scientific knowledge and technical expertise. The following section describes the data set used in the analysis and explains how this measure has been constructed.

THE DATA SET

While the recent empirical literature on human capital and growth has produced a considerable number of studies, few have focused on industrialized countries.[5] This is probably due to the lack of a sufficient number of observations when national data are used. An analysis at the regional level helps to overcome this problem but raises other difficulties. While some sets of harmonized data are available at the national level (World Bank, Unesco, Barro and Lee, 1996, to quote a few) no harmonization has been done in Europe at the regional level. Starting from 1993 Eurostat provides data classified according to the ISCED classification implemented by UNESCO[6] but they are too recent to be used in growth regressions. Thus an attempt has been made to harmonize census regional data from some European countries by grouping the available classes into three categories which correspond approximately to the Eurostat classification: primary and lower secondary school, upper secondary school and higher education.[7] The variables used in the econometric analysis are the average values in the period 1981–91 of the share of the active population who possess a qualification in primary, secondary or higher education. Since annual observations are not available the series have been calculated as the average value between the starting and final years of the relevant period.[8] Unfortunately the census dates for Germany are very different from the other countries; since 1970 there has been only one census in 1987. Thus mid-point observations instead of average values have been used for this country. The data for UK come from Labour Force Surveys (1981, 1991).

The choice of average values instead of initial ones can be justified on the basis that they are better indicators of the educational input during the period under test. This implies that we are assuming away feedback effects of growth on education but this should not be a serious problem since the period is relatively short. The rationale for this assumption is that the enrolment rates react positively to the expected rate of growth but this is less likely to be the case for the attainment levels since it takes longer for the former to produce significant changes in the latter.

Due to the complex structures of the European national education systems and the differences among them, achieving a reasonable degree of comparability is not an easy task. Depending on the country some types of degrees and diplomas classified within the same category require a different number of years of education. The French and German systems for example are much more complex than the Italian and offer more options to the students. Thus, while in Italy the upper secondary level implies in most cases thirteen years of schooling, in the other two countries the curricula are much more varied. To take these shortcomings into account another proxy of the educational attainment of the active population has been constructed: the average years of schooling. This measure is probably more precise and comparable than the previous ones but, being a global measure, it does not allow analysis of the separate effects of different educational attainment levels on economic growth. Therefore three more variables have been added: the average years of primary, secondary and higher education.

To test the central hypothesis of this chapter a proxy of the allocation of human capital to technical activities has been constructed. The main sources of such information are labour force survey data on the distribution of the active population among different occupations. Eurostat collects EU labour force surveys including information on the professional composition of the active population at the regional level. The database covers the period 1983–95. These data have been harmonized according to the International Standard Classification of Occupations known as ISCO 68 for the period 1983–91 and according to the new classification ISCO 88 thereafter. However the harmonization is not complete; figures at the three-digit level are not comparable because the European countries use different classifications and definitions of specific occupations. Nevertheless they can be used fairly reliably at a more aggregate level.

From this data set an attempt has been made to construct a measure of the share of the active population occupied in scientific and technical activities requiring higher or upper secondary education skills. The classification includes seven main groups: professionals, technical and related workers; administrative and managerial workers; clerical and related workers; sales workers; service workers; agricultural, animal husbandry and forestry workers, fishermen and hunters; production and related workers, transport equipment operators and labourers. The measure has been constructed drawing from the first group, which includes mostly professionals and highly skilled technicians. In particular the following subgroups have been included: physical scientists and related technicians; architects, engineers and related technicians; life scientists and related technicians; statisticians, mathematicians, system analysts and related technicians. In this case average values have also been calculated although the assumption of no feedback effects is much more questionable. To take this problem into account the absence of simultaneity has been tested.

The economic variables used in the analysis are the rate of growth of labour productivity (value added per worker) during the period 1981–91, the initial value of labour productivity and the average share of investment in value added in the same period. The data come from the CRENoS (Centro di Ricerche Economiche Nord Sud) data bank on the European regions and the 'Regio 2' data bank from Eurostat. Value added per worker has been preferred to GDP per capita commonly used in growth regressions. The reason behind this choice is that the former is not affected by differences in unemployment and participation rates across regions which are very wide in the European Union (Paci, 1996). All variables are expressed in purchasing power parity units at constant 1985 prices.

The data set includes 66 regions from five countries: Germany, France, Italy, Belgium and the United Kingdom.[9] The sample is only partially representative of the whole European Union. Northern regions are over-represented with respect to southern ones and this fact is likely to cause a bias in convergence speed estimation. The definition of the regions included varies across countries. For Italy and France the NUTS-2 level has been chosen, while the NUTS-1 level seems more appropriate in the cases of Germany and Belgium.[10] As regards the UK eleven Standard Regions have been considered as units of analysis.

EDUCATION IN THE EUROPEAN REGIONS: SOME DESCRIPTIVE EVIDENCE

Although all regions in the sample belong to the industrialized countries there are considerable differences in the educational qualifications of the active population. Table 10.1 reports standard statistics for the educational variables. As regards total years of schooling the highest value is found in a German region (Hambourg with eleven years) while the lowest belongs to Italy (Basilicata with seven). The widest variation can be found – as expected – in higher education, here again a German region (Berlin) is at the top and an Italian one (Valle d'Aosta) at the bottom. The ratio of the two values is nearly four.

The German active population is in general the most educated. Regarding total years of schooling and higher education all German regions show higher values (between ten and eleven years on average)

Table 10.1 Measures of dispersion of active population educational attainment across the European regions, average years of schooling, 1981–1991

	Primary	Secondary	Higher	Total
Mean	3.122	3.865	1.897	8.884
Median	2.837	3.826	1.659	8.605
Maximum	4.975	6.109	3.496	11.040
Minimum	1.571	2.365	0.868	7.396
Std. dev.	0.843	0.925	0.740	0.852
Skewness	0.547	0.349	0.531	0.904
Kurtosis	2.185	2.193	2.047	2.896

Sources: Population census for Belgium, France, Germany and Italy; Labour Force Survey for the United Kingdom.

than any other in the sample as can be easily seen from Table 10.2. Most of the regions in the sample are concentrated in the third and fourth classes (between eight and nine years of schooling). They belong mainly to France and the UK while the Italian regions are all concentrated in the last three classes. As regards higher education the German regions again show the highest values but comparable levels can be found also in the Paris (Ile de France) and London (South east) regions. Belgium, France and the UK are somewhat in the middle while Italian regions show the lowest values.

Table 10.2 shows also another feature of the educational variables' behaviour. It is possible to recognize national clusters: most of the regions of each country are concentrated in the same or in contiguous classes. This behaviour reflects different institutional aspects of the national education systems. The educational attainment levels of the active population are influenced by several factors such as income per capita, the distribution of earnings or the structure of the labour market which may vary considerably even across regions of the same country; however, they benefit from a common education policy which tends to reduce the range of variation within the boundaries of each country.

The presence of national patterns appears clearly by examining the coefficients of variation (measured by the ratio of the standard deviation to the mean) in Table 10.3. For all levels of education they are much lower within each country than in the whole sample. Leaving aside Belgium for which we have only three observations, Germany shows the most homogeneous educational structure across regions[11] while the

Table 10.2 Distribution of the sample regions among classes of educational attainment: total years of schooling and years of higher education, average values 1981–1991

	Total years of schooling					Years of higher education			
	>10	9–10	8.5–9	8–8.5	< 8	>3	2–3	1–2	<1
Germany	11	0	0	0	0	6	5	0	0
France	0	2	12	7	0	1	4	16	0
United Kingdom	0	0	6	5	0	1	9	1	0
Italy	0	2	4	9	5	0	0	15	5
Belgium	0	3	0	0	0	0	1	2	0

Sources: Population census for Belgium, France, Germany and Italy; Labour Force Survey for the United Kingdom.

Table 10.3 Coefficients of variation of the educational variables within each country and in the whole sample

	Primary	Secondary	Higher	Total
Belgium	12.9	3.4	33.0	1.0
Germany	13.8	7.0	6.7	2.5
France	6.1	6.8	21.1	3.5
United Kingdom	2.5	4.2	13.5	2.6
Italy	7.5	12.3	18.8	5.9
Whole sample	27.1	23.9	38.9	9.6

Sources: Population census for Belgium, France, Germany and Italy; Labour Force Survey for the United Kingdom.

highest dispersion is found in the Italian subset. In general variability increases together with the education level, the only exception being again Germany where values are reversed.

ECONOMETRIC RESULTS

The main purpose of the econometric analysis is to test whether education has contributed significantly to the growth and convergence performance of the regions in the sample and, if this has not happened, to provide a possible explanation. The standard estimated equation is of the form:

$$(1/T) \ln(VA_{it}/VA_{i,t-T}) = b_0 + b_1 \ln(VA_{i,t-T}) + b_2 \ln(EDU_{it,t-T}) + u_{it}$$

where VA_{it} is the final value of value added per worker measured in PPP units at 1985 prices, $VA_{i,t-T}$ is the initial one and $EDU_{it,t-T}$ is the average value of the educational variables during the period 1981–91. We use seven different measures of the educational input: total average years of schooling, average years of primary, secondary and higher education and the shares of the three levels. All variables are in logarithms, the estimation results are reported in Tables 10.4 and 10.5.

If education were a relevant explanatory variable in this process we should expect positive and significant coefficients for the educational variables and a higher convergence speed among the regions of the sample holding education constant. In other words regions with similar

Table 10.4 Convergence in productivity among the European regions: average years of total, primary, secondary and higher education, 1981–1991

	1	2	3	4	5
CONSTANT	0.172	0.176	0.194	0.210	0.168
	(5.57)	(5.85)	(6.85)	(7.00)	(5.83)
LOGVA81	–0.015	–0.018	–0.016	–0.020	–0.015
	(–4.85)**	(–5.42)**	(–5.87)**	(–6.39)**	(–5.15)**
LOGTOTYEARS		0.013			
		(2.14)*			
LOGPRIYEARS			–0.007		
			(–4.01)**		
LOGSECYEARS				0.008	
				(3.72)**	
LOGHIGHYEARS					0.004
					(3.23)**
R^2 adj.	0.26	0.30	0.40	0.38	0.35
F test	23.5	14.7	22.6	21.0	18.7

Notes:
Dependent variable is the average rate of growth of value added per worker 1981–91.
Estimation method OLS.
Number of observations: 66.
t- statistics in parentheses corrected for heteroskedasticity when detected.[12]
**significant at 1 per cent level.
*significant at 5 per cent level.

Table 10.5 Convergence in productivity among the European regions: shares of total, primary, secondary and higher education, average values 1981–1991

	1	2	3	4	5
CONSTANT	0.203	0.227	0.178	0.171	0.159
	(6.75)	(7.42)	(6.33)	(2.52)	(2.93)
LOGVA81	–0.018	–0.020	–0.015	–0.014	–0.013
	(–6.07)**	(–6.61)**	(–5.21)**	(–2.12)*	(–2.48)*
LOGPRI	–0.007				
	(–3.36)**				
LOGSEC		0.007		0.006	
		(4.16)**		(3.67)**	
LOGHIGH			0.004		0.004
			(3.73)**		(2.45)*
LOGINV				–0.002	–0.002
			(–0.61)	(–0.63)	
R^2 adj.	0.36	0.41	0.38	0.21	0.11
F test	19.3	23.4	21.1	5.4	3.15
Number of observations	66	66	66	52	52

Notes:
Dependent variable is the average rate of growth of value added per worker 1981–91.
Estimation method OLS.
t- statistics in parentheses, corrected for heteroskedasticity when detected.
**significant at 1 per cent level.
*significant at 5 per cent level.

educational inputs should converge at a faster rate. At first glance results partially confirm this expectation.

The first equation in Table 10.4 is an estimate of unconditional convergence in the sample. The coefficient of initial value added per worker is negative and significant showing that a process of convergence of this type has taken place during the period being tested although at a slow pace.[13] Introducing the educational variables adds little to the convergence process. In particular the speed of convergence increases holding constant total and secondary years of schooling in regressions 2 and 4 while the effect of higher education in regression 5 is null.

In general the presence of the educational variables raises the explanatory power of the regressions although not dramatically. The effects of the educational variables on the rate of growth of productivity are rather weak, but the coefficients show the expected signs, in particular they are negative for primary education and positive for secondary and higher, and are all significant at the 1 per cent level.[14] The coefficient of total years of education is also significant reinforcing the impression that education plays a role – albeit not a primary one – in the growth and convergence processes.

Results are roughly the same if we use the shares of primary, secondary and higher education in the labour force as shown in Table 10.5. Signs are again as expected and the coefficients of both secondary and higher education are highly significant while the explanatory power is nearly the same as before. In the last two regressions we control for differences in investment rates to test whether the effects of education on growth are direct or indirect as suggested by Romer (1990), Wolff and Grittleman (1993) and Benhabib and Spiegel (1994).

According to these authors education does not affect productivity growth directly, rather it acts as a stimulus or as a complementary factor to investment in physical capital which, in turn, influences the rate of growth. The empirical implication of this hypothesis is that the educational variables should become insignificant when the investment share on output is added to the regressors.[15] This does not happen in our case, since the coefficients of the educational variables are not affected although the coefficient of initial productivity decreases and the overall fit of the regressions worsens substantially.[16]

These results are somewhat at odds with other findings mentioned above on the relationship between educational attainment measures and economic growth in the national industrial economies.[17] Actually this contrast is only apparent, as we shall see below. As already pointed out, the educational qualification of the labour force is influenced by national education policies, therefore it tends to follow a country-specific pattern of behaviour.[18] Thus, the educational measures are likely to capture the effects of some country-specific omitted variables on the growth of productivity. To check this possibility country dummies have been introduced in the regressions.

Table 10.6 shows that the picture changes substantially. The coefficients of all the educational variables are no longer significant and the signs of both primary and secondary education are reversed. The dummy for Italy is significant at the 1 per cent level in all the regressions suggesting that some unknown country-specific factor correlated with the educational variables which influence the rate of growth of productivity is at work.[19]

Further evidence on the stability of the coefficients of the educational variables can be obtained running a recursive estimation of the standard

Table 10.6 Convergence in productivity among the European regions: average years of primary, secondary and higher education, country dummies, 1981–1991

	1	2	3	4	5
CONSTANT	0.147	0.140	0.148	0.142	0.146
	(5.56)	(5.20)	(5.17)	(4.36)	(5.04)
LOGVA81	−0.012	−0.014	−0.013	−0.011	−0.012
	(−4.63)**	(−4.71)**	(−4.70)**	(−3.16)**	(−4.32)**
DUMIT[a]	−0.006	−0.005	−0.007	−0.006	−0.005
	(−6.02)**	(−4.67)**	(−3.65)**	(−3.23)**	(−3.01)**
DUMGE[a]	−0.002	−0.004			−0.003
	(−1.97)*	(−2.24)*			(−2.11)*
LOGTOTYEARS		0.011			
		(1.26)			
LOGPRIYEARS			0.004		
			(1.15)		
LOGSECYEARS				−0.001	
				(−0.26)	
LOGHIGHYEARS					0.002
					(0.93)
R^2 adj.	0.52	0.52	0.50	0.51	0.51
F test	24.1	18.7	22.5	17.8	18.3

Notes:
Dependent variable is the average rate of growth of value added per worker 1981–1991.
Estimation method OLS.
Number of observations: 66.
t- statistics in parentheses corrected for heteroskedasticity when detected.
**significant at 1 per cent level.
*significant at 5 per cent level.
[a]significant dummies only are reported.

equation. In Figures 10.1, 10.2 and 10.3 the recursive coefficients estimates of the average years of total, secondary and higher education are plotted. The signs of the coefficients are very sensitive to changes in the sample. The last 20 observations refer to the Italian regions. It is easy to check that the signs of the three coefficients change from negative to positive when these regions enter the sample.

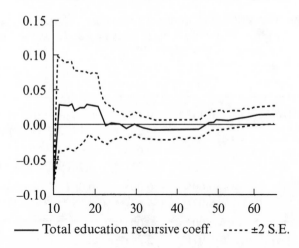

Figure 10.1 *Total average years of education: recursive estimation*

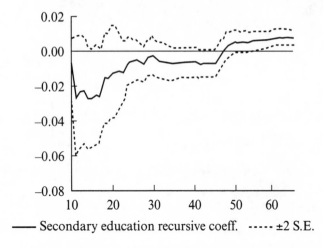

Figure 10.2 *Average years of secondary education: recursive estimation*

EDUCATIONAL SKILLS, ALLOCATION AND GROWTH

How can we interpret such evidence? Some limitations of the analysis must be taken into account: first the sample is not completely represen-tative of the European Union regions since only Italy is included among

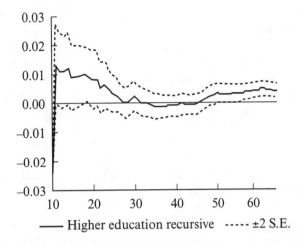

Figure 10.3 Average years of higher education: recursive estimation

the southern countries. Furthermore the timespan is perhaps too short to analyse an essentially long-run relationship. Nevertheless the empirical evidence suggests some considerations. It confirms that in the industrialized countries the role of education as such in the growth and convergence processes is much more controversial than commonly suggested by the theoretical literature. This is probably due to the fact that while in backward economies education may be a fairly good proxy of the human capital input (because it provides basic skills, and their diffusion in the labour force is crucial in terms of growth performance), when growth depends on more specialized and sophisticated skills as in the industralized economies, a generic measure of education is too rough to capture the complex links between human capital and growth.

Disaggregating the educational measure to take into account different levels of education and their separate effects on growth does not change the picture but adds some interesting information and raises further questions. Particularly problematic is the fact that the empirical evidence assigns a marginal or no role to higher education. While literacy or primary education might be crucial skills in low income countries, in industrialized ones, where innovation drives growth, the adoption of new technologies is more and more demanding in terms of educational skills. Scientific and computing skills as well as professional ones play a dominant role in information economies thus implying the primary importance of university education.

If this quite plausible hypothesis is not supported by the empirical evidence one possible explanation is that education as such is not the correct proxy we are searching for to explain the relationship between human capital and growth. In fact not all skills acquired with higher education contribute in the same way to the growth of the economy. This certainly applies to those mentioned above but is not necessarily true for other types of skills which can produce substantial pay-offs at the individual level even when applied to growth-neutral or harmful activities such as rentseeking. This implies that the rate of growth should be affected not by the educational skills of the whole labour force but mainly by those embodied in the share of it occupied in innovative activities. To test this hypothesis we add to the regressors the variable TEC,[20] a measure of the share of the active population allocated to scientific and technical occupations requiring mostly higher or, at least, upper secondary education.

In Table 10.7 the coefficient of the variable TEC is always significant at the 1 per cent level. Its impact on the rate of growth of productivity is not very different from the educational measures, while the speed of convergence increases a little holding it constant. The overall fit of the regression improves too, as can be seen from the value of the R^2 which jumps from 0.26 in the case of unconditional convergence to 0.45. The most important difference, however, is that this is a very robust variable. The coefficient remains strongly significant when country dummies or other variables are added to the regressors.

In regressions 2 and 3 a measure of R&D activity has been introduced,[21] to test whether the latter is a better proxy of the human capital allocated to innovative activities. In regression 2 its coefficient is positive and significant at the 5 per cent level but the impact on productivity growth is rather weak; moreover the explanatory power of the model is very low. Adding TEC to the equation, the coefficient of the R&D variable becomes insignificant suggesting that there is some degree of collinearity between the two variables but the former better explains productivity growth.

For similar reasons we control also for the share of industrial employment. Since most technical skills are concentrated in this sector of the economy the variable TEC may capture structural effects due to the distribution of the labour force among the main sectors of the economy. In this case too the econometric results in regression 4 confirm the robustness of the variable of interest.

To test the robustness of this variable more thoroughly an extreme bounds analysis has been conducted following the approach proposed by Levine and Renelt (1992). Four more Z variables have been included besides those already considered. They are measures of the share of the labour force in agriculture and services, the average rate of growth of labour units and the share of industrial investment on value added. The

Table 10.7 Convergence in productivity among the European regions: share of technical occupations, R&D, share of industrial employment and country dummies, 1981–1991

	1	2	3	4	5
CONSTANT	0.266	0.189	0.299	0.256	0.208
	(10.14)	(2.73)	(4.03)	(8.34)	(6.57)
LOGVA81	–0.021	–0.016	–0.024	–0.020	–0.016
	(–8.55)**	(–2.36)*	(–3.55)**	(–7.22)**	(–5.82)**
LOGTEC	0.010		0.009	0.010	0.006
	(4.30)**		(2.36)*	(5.22)**	(3.10)**
LOGRD		0.001	0.001		
		(2.43)*	(1.33)		
LOGINDEMP				–0.001	
				(–0.07)	
DUMIT[a]					–0.004
					(–4.44)**
DUMGE[a]					0.002
					(2.00)*
R^2 adj.	0.45	0.12	0.21	0.47	0.57
F test	27.9	4.70	5.7	20.2	23.0
Number of observations	66	54	54	66	66

Notes:
Dependent variable is the average rate of growth of value added per worker 1981–1991.
Estimation method OLS.
t- statistics in parentheses corrected for heteroskedasticity when detected.
** significant at 1 per cent level.
* significant at 5 per cent level.
[a] significant dummies only are reported.

results reported in Table 10.8 confirm the robustness of the variable of interest which maintains a positive and significant coefficient both at the higher and lower bound.

A possible objection to these results is that the causal relationship between growth and the active population occupied in technical activities runs the other way around: from growth to technical occupations. While it takes a long time for the share of higher education to adjust to the growth rate, even if the enrolment rates are very responsive to the latter –

Table 10.8 Sensitivity analysis

	Coefficient	S.E.	t-statistic	R^2 adj.	Z variables
High	0.013	0.003	3.96**	0.24	*LOGINDEMP,LOGINV*
Base	0.010	0.002	4.30**	0.45	
Low	0.007	0.003	2.36*	0.40	*LOGRD, DUMMIES*

Notes:
Dependent variable is the average rate of growth of value added per worker 1981–1991.
Estimation method OLS.
Number of observations: 66.
Base equation: $VAGROWTH = b_0 + b_1\ LOGVA81 + b_2\ LOGTEC.$
Variable of interest: *LOGTEC*.
** significant at 1 per cent level.
* significant at 5 per cent level.

because students must first complete their studies then the new cohorts of skilled workers must substitute for the older ones – it could be argued that it is easier to change occupation if pay-offs are higher in those occupations more affected by the growth of the economy, or if the demand of particular skills required by the most dynamic sectors of the economy grows at a faster rate.

To take this possibility into account a Hausman test for simultaneity has been performed on the following simultaneous equations model:

$$(1/T)\ \ln(VA_{it}/VA_{i,t-T}) = a_0 + a_1 \ln(VA_{i,t-T}) + a_2 \ln(TEC_{it,t-T}) + u_{it}$$

$$\ln(TEC_{it,t-T}) = b_0 + b_1 \ln(VA_{i,t-T}) + b_2 \ln(TEC83_{i,t-T}) + b_3$$

$$((1/T)\ \ln(VA_{it}/VA_{i,t-T})) + u_{it}$$

The second equation expresses the variable *TEC* as a function of its initial value (1983), of the initial productivity and of the rate of growth of productivity. The test results are reported in Table 10.9 where the dependent variable is $\ln(TEC_{it,t-T})$, *FITTED* is the series of the fitted values of the dependent variable in the reduced form equation

$$(1/T)\ \ln(VA_{it}/VA_{i,t-T}) = a_0 + a_1 \ln(VA_{i,t-T}) + a_2 \ln(TEC83_{i,t-T}) + v_{it}$$

and *RESIDS* is the error term in the same equation. Since the coefficient of the variable *RESIDS* is not significant the test indicates absence of simultaneity.

Table 10.9 Hausman test for simultaneity

CONSTANT	FITTED	RESIDS	R^2 adj.	F
−3.60	14.94	4.21	0.02	1.54
(18.05)**	(1.67)	(0.52)		

Notes:
Dependent variable is the log of the share of active population occupied in technical activities.
Estimation method OLS.
** significant at 1 per cent level.
* significant at 5 per cent level.

CONCLUDING REMARKS

Since this chapter is not aimed at testing a specific theoretical model the reported results are at best only suggestive. Nevertheless, in our opinion, they confirm that pursuing this line of analysis can shed light on some aspects of the controversial relationship between human capital and economic growth. The main findings can be summarized as follows.

There is no clear evidence of a significant partial correlation between the educational attainment of the labour force and the rate of growth of productivity. When a significant relationship has been found it seems to depend on the fact that the educational variables capture the effects of some country-specific omitted variable on the rate of growth of productivity.

Disaggregating education adds little to the picture. Neither secondary schooling nor higher education has significant effects on the rate of growth once country dummies are included among the regressors. In particular the finding that higher education plays no role in productivity growth and convergence contrasts with the predictions of most theoretical literature on the subject.

The hypothesis tested here to explain these anomalous results is that the allocation of educated labour force to different activities must be taken into account because not all them contribute to the overall growth of the economy. The findings of this chapter give some support to this explanation. They show that a significant and robust correlation exists between the rate of growth of productivity and a measure of the educated labour force occupied in technical activities.

Needless to say this is not the only explanation of why empirical analysis fails to obtain firm conclusions about the contribution of human capital to economic growth. Several arguments have been proposed to explain this anomaly as reported in the first section. What our results suggest is that we should look further into the microeconomics of individual choice of activity because this is a crucial factor underlying the relationship between human capital and growth. Since this choice is very much determined by the structure of incentives and pay-offs in the economy, and these in turn are shaped by institutions we need to bring the latter to the forefront to understand better the complex dynamics of economic development.

NOTES

1. It must be noted anyway that the high R^2 obtained by Mankiw, Romer and Weil depends strongly on the chosen proxy for human capital. They ignore primary education and this substantially affects the variability of the human capital stock measure. Secondary enrolment rates vary by more than primary ones, increasing the disparity within the sample. Following this objection Klenow and Rodriguez (1997) reran the MRW regression obtaining an R^2 value of 0.48 compared to the 0.78 of the original estimation.

2. Pritchett (1995) points out that the justification for including enrolment rates into growth regressions is that they are a proxy for the flow of investment in human capital which is a proxy for the change of the stock of human capital in the labour force. He shows that this assumption is incompatible with the empirical evidence since there is a clear and significant negative correlation between measures of the actual growth of the stock of human capital and initial enrolment rates.

3. This is a puzzling result since the attainment levels can be regarded as a proxy of the educational achievement of the current labour force while the enrolment rates reflect that of the future labour force.

4. According to Baumol the term 'unproductive activities' refers to all activities which do not contribute directly or indirectly to the net output of the economy. In this sense financial activities are productive as well as 'anything that contributes to the output of any good or service desired by consumers, even if that product is not approved of by society' (Baumol, 1990).

5. Jorgenson and Fraumeni (1992) have studied this problem for the United States. Wolff and Gittleman (1993) estimated the effects of educational variables isolating a sample of industrialized countries.

6. More precisely the classes are 0–2, 3 and 5–7 of the ISCED classification which correspond to primary and lower secondary, upper secondary and higher education.

7. The classes have been defined according to the Eurostat classification. 'Primary' includes the active population with no education or no declared degree as well as primary and lower secondary education. The class 'secondary' includes upper secondary schooling, finally 'higher' includes university and other courses at a level higher than upper secondary.

8. In the case of France the closest years have been used (1982 and 1990).

9. The regions in the countries included in the sample are actually 67, however, Corse has been dropped because of missing figures for occupations.

10. For a more detailed explanation of the reasons behind this choice of the regional units see Paci (1996).

11. In spite of the higher political and administrative autonomy of the länder.

12. The White correction method has been used whenever the test is significant at the 1 per cent or 5 per cent level.

13. Here the term convergence is used in a general sense. We are not testing a specific model therefore the negative coefficient of initial productivity may be compatible both with the neoclassical theory of convergence and with the catch-up hypothesis.
14. The negative coefficient of primary education is not obvious. The explanation is that primary education on one side and secondary–higher on the other are complementary variables since the share of active population with no educational qualification is very small. Therefore regions with higher values of primary education exhibit lower ones for the other two variables and vice versa.
15. Unfortunately data on investment rates are not available for the whole sample analysed here, so the United Kingdom and Belgium have been excluded for this reason.
16. Investment rates are never significant in our sample. This is a puzzling result since investment rates are regarded as a very robust regressor in the growth regressions literature (Levine and Renelt, 1992). However it confirms other findings on the European regions' growth (Fagerberg and Verspagen, 1996). No significant correlation has been found between investment and education. Regressing the former on any educational variable gives negative and insignificant coefficients (results are not reported for brevity).
17. The paper by Wolff and Gittleman is an already quoted example. They find insignificant coefficients for all the educational variables in a sample of industrialized countries.
18. The coefficient of variation within each country is much smaller than in the whole sample for all the educational variables; see Table 10.1. There could also be a measurement error which follows national profiles due to problems of comparability among the European national education systems. However, this is more likely to have occurred for the shares of primary, secondary and higher education because these categories are not perfectly suited for taking these differences into account. The other measures based on average years of education are more precise and should be much less influenced by problems of this type. Finally the variable *TOTYEARS* is only marginally affected.
19. Similar results were obtained using the shares of primary, secondary and higher education. They are not reported for brevity.
20. The method adopted for constructing this variable is described in the second section above.
21. It is the share of R&D personnel in business enterprises per 1000 labour force. The source is the databank Regio 2. The available data consist of one annual observation for 1985. As for the investment rates Eurostat does not provide data for the United Kingdom.

REFERENCES

Barro R.J. (1991), 'Economic growth in a cross-section of countries', *Quarterly Journal of Economics*, **106** (2), 407–43.

Barro, R.J. (1996), 'Determinants of economic growth: a cross-country empirical study', NBER Working Paper no. 5698.

Barro, R.J. and J.-W. Lee (1993), 'International comparisons of educational attainment', *Journal of Monetary Economics*, **32**, 363–93.

Barro, R.J. and J.-W. Lee (1996), 'International measures of schooling years and schooling quality', *American Economic Review*, **86**, 218–23.

Baumol, W.J. (1990), 'Entrepreneurship: productive, unproductive and destructive', *Journal of Political Economy*, **98** (5), 893–921.

Benhabib, J. and M.M. Spiegel (1994), 'The role of human capital in economic development: evidence from aggregate cross-country data', *Journal of Monetary Economics*, **34**, 143–73.

Bils, M. and P.J. Klenow (1995), 'Does human capital drive growth or the other way around?', mimeo.

Fagerberg, J. and B. Verspagen (1996), 'Heading for divergence? Regional growth in Europe reconsidered', *Journal of Common Market Studies*, **34** (3), 431–48

Islam, N. (1995), 'Growth empirics: a panel data approach', *Quarterly Journal of Economics*, **110**, 1127–70.

Jorgenson, D.W. and B.M. Fraumeni (1992), 'Investment in education and U.S. economic growth', *Scandinavian Journal of Economics*, Supplement, 51–70.

Klenow, P. and A. Rodriguez-Clare (1997), 'The neoclassical revival in growth economics: has it gone too far?', NBER 1997 Macroeconomics Annual.

Kyriacou, G.A. (1991), 'Level and growth effects of human capital: a cross-country study of the convergence hypothesis', C.V. Starr Center for Applied Economics, Economic Research Reports nos. 91–26.

Laband, D.N. and J.P. Sophocleus (1987), 'The social cost of rent seeking: first estimates', *Economia delle Scelte Pubbliche*, May–August, 127–33.

Levine, R. and D. Renelt (1992), 'A sensitivity analysis of cross country growth regressions', *American Economic Review*, **82** (4), 943–63.

Lodde, S. (1995) 'Allocation of talent and growth in the Italian regions', Contributi di Ricerca CRENoS, 95/3.

Magee, S.P., W.A. Brock and L. Young (1989), *Black Hole Tariffs and Endogenous Policy Theory: Political Economy in General Equilibrium*, Cambridge, Cambridge University Press.

Mankiw, N.G., D. Romer and D.N. Weil (1992), 'A contribution to the empirics of economic growth', *Quarterly Journal of Economics*, **107** (2), 408–37.

Murphy, K.M., A. Shleifer and R.W. Vishny (1991), 'The allocation of talent: implications for growth', *Quarterly Journal of Economics*, **106** (2), 503–30.

Nehru, V., E. Swanson and A. Dubey (1995), 'A new database on human capital stocks in developing and industrial countries: sources, methodology and results', *Journal of Development Economics*, **46** (2), 379–401.

North, D. (1990), *Institutions, Institutional Change and Economic Performance*, Cambridge: Cambridge University Press.

Paci, R. (1996), 'More similar and less equal. Economic growth in the European regions', Contributi di Ricerca Crenos, 96/9.

Pritchett, L. (1995), 'Where has all the education gone?', World Bank working paper no. 1581.

Romer, P. (1990), 'Human capital and growth: theory and evidence', *Carnegie-Rochester Conference Series on Public Policy*, **32**, 251–86.

Wolff, E.N. and M. Gittleman (1993), 'The Role of Education in Productivity Convergence: Does Higher Education Matter?', in A. Szirmai, B. Van Ark and D. Pilat (eds), *Explaining Economic Growth*, Amsterdam: Elsevier.

11. The European Union's regional development programmes: allocation of funds by basic macroeconomic indicators[1]

Gustav Schachter, Carmelina Bevilacqua and Levanto Schachter

The European Union (EU) targets investments and loans at subsidiary regions in order to alleviate spatial disparities, with the intent of achieving greater equity and cohesion. Despite modest convergence in regional incomes per capita in the 1960s, a steadfast core–periphery pattern of inequality has persisted, notwithstanding the adoption of a sequence of national and Union policies and appreciable enlargement of the flows of supposedly palliative resources. The objective of this chapter is to see to what extent the allocations of the EU's regional development funds and official loans have followed simple macroeconomic characteristics of the regions. Because official efforts at securing better spatial balance in the EU's subsidiary economies have not succeeded, alternative allocation criteria may need to be identified.

OVERVIEW OF EU POLICIES AND DISPARITIES

A commitment to a regionally predicated policy was made at the 1972 Conference of the European Council, which issued a call for action to diminish spatial imbalances. To abet intervention, the European Regional Development Fund (ERDF) was created in 1975 and the Social Fund followed in 1989. The adoption of the Single European Act in 1987 took into account the obduracy of interregional divergence; therefore, it directed the Union and the member states to work towards economic cohesion. Resources have thereafter increased: they doubled from ECU 7.2 billion in 1987 to ECU 14.5 billion in 1995.

The Single European Act calls for the European Union to pursue a set of clear objectives:

1. achieve growth and adaptation in regional economies showing structural backwardness, so that they can be fully integrated into the Union area;
2. convert declining, sometimes devastated, industrial regions, by helping them to develop new activities;
3. combat long-term unemployment;
4. integrate young persons into employment patterns, especially for their first jobs; and
5. speed up the adjustment of agricultural production structures and encourage rural development in line with the reform of the common agricultural policy (Bulletin of European Community, 1987, pp. 13–14).

To pursue these five objectives, the Union relies on three structural funds. These are the ERDF, the ESF, and the European Agricultural Guidance and Guarantee Fund (EAGGF). After 1987, and then again after 1989, the scale of regional development resources was increased substantially. In the 1990s the areas eligible for structural funds totalled nearly two-thirds of the EU's territory, where one-half of the EU's population resides. In 1992, when the Treaty of the European Union was signed at Maastricht, a Cohesion Fund was established to help the poorest member states. The European Investment Bank (EIB) accounts for almost 75 per cent of the Union's loans (European Commission, 1987, pp. 15–16). The main recent thrust is to help low-income regions in the poorer countries. Indeed, more than one-half of all structural funds expended during the period 1989 to 1993 have been allocated for regional development. Although before the 1980s most of the funds were dedicated to infrastructure, recent efforts have moved towards improving production capacities and human resource development.

EU structural funds and EIB loans have risen considerably. Between 1975 and 1984 about ECU 1.0 billion was allocated annually for regional development. The annual allocation increased to 5.0 billion between 1984 and 1988 and to ECU 10.0 billion between 1988 and 1993. Plans called for the European Union to spend ECU 25.0 billion annually between 1994 and 1999 for regional development. The European Investment Bank concentrates on financing infrastructure and productive investments. By 1996, the EIB's total loans reached ECU 23.2 billion of which ECU 20.9 billion were placed within the Union; these loans included ECU 13.6 billion (70 per cent) for projects fostering regional development. Between 1989 and 1995 the EIB has made ECU 91.0 billion in loans for projects costing over ECU 210 billion. In 1995, the EIB's loans accounted for 5 per cent of the EU's gross fixed capital formation, but this proportion was higher in the poorer countries: 20 per cent in Portugal and 11 per cent in Spain, Greece and Ireland (EIB, 1975–1998).

Table 11.1 uses 1975 regional per capita GDP, at constant 1985 prices, to divide the EU regions into four illustrative income groups. Taken together these 102 regions form the sample for the study.[2] Broadly

Table 11.1 European regions grouped by GDP per capita, 1975: constant PPP 1985

Group I   Class of int. 16000–12500

Hamburg	Noord-Nederland
Ile de France	Valle d'Aosta
Bruxelles-Brussel	Bremen

Group II   Class of int. 12500–9000

Corse	Nordrhein-Westfalen
Berlin	Liguria
Cataluna	Haute-Normandie
Hovedstadsregionen	Rhone-Alpes
Lombardia	País Vasco
Luxembourg	Picardie
Hessen	Emilia-Romagna
Baden-Wuerttemberg	Madrid
Champagne-Ardenne	Lorraine
Piemonte	Aquitaine
West-Nederland	Franche-Comte
Provence-Alpes-Cote d'Azur	Centre
South East (UK)	

Group III   Class of int 9000–5500

Schleswig-Holstein	Asturias
Bayern	North
Alsace	Baleares
Vlaams Gewest	Poitou-Chartentes
Navarra	Pays de la Loire
Rheinland-Pfals	Bretagne
Friuli-Venezia Giulia	Murcia
Lazio	Cantabria
Aragon	South West (UK)
West Midlands	Umbria
Toscana	Midi-Pyrenees
Saarland	Auvergne
Niedersachsen	Marche
Vest for Storebaelt	Rioja
Nord-Pas-de Calais	Wales

Table 11.1 (continued)

Group III   Class of int 9000–5500

Ost for Storebaelt, Ex. Hov.	Region Wallonne
Basse-Normandie	Languedoc-Roussillon
Scotland	Lastilla-La Mancha
Oost-Neederland	Limousin
Veneto	Attiki
Trentino-al to Adige	Northern Ireland
North West (UK)	Andalucia
Castilla-Leon	Canarias
East Midlands	Abruzzi
Bourgogne	Galicia
Zuid-Nederland	Sardegna
East Anglia	Alentejo
Comunidad Valenciana	Puglia
Yorkshire and Humberside	Calabria
	Campania

Group IV   Class of int. 5500–2000

Basilicata	Voreia Ellada
Ireland	Algarve
Lisboa e Vale do Tejo	Norte
Sicilia	Centro (P)
Molise	Nisia Aigaiou, Kriti
Extermadura	Kentriki Ella

---

speaking, a review of the rankings shows little change over the period 1975 to 1995, the span of time with which we will be concerned. Generally, the northern regions have remained more developed than the southern regions, including Ireland.

Figure 11.1 provides a picture of the regions' income differentiation as of 1995 using fourfold division of Table 11.1. The more lightly shaded central and northern zones with higher incomes stand in contrast to the more darkly shaded third and fourth tier areas of the periphery.

The distribution of funds among the EU's regions is shown in Figure 11.2. Here the more darkly shaded regions receive a larger fraction of EU regional funds and EIB loans as a share of their gross regional products than the more lightly shaded areas. The overlay with Figure 11.1 is apparent. Greece, southern Italy, much of the Iberian peninsula and Ireland, receive proportionately more weighty support for regional investments than the higher income core areas of the EU heartland.

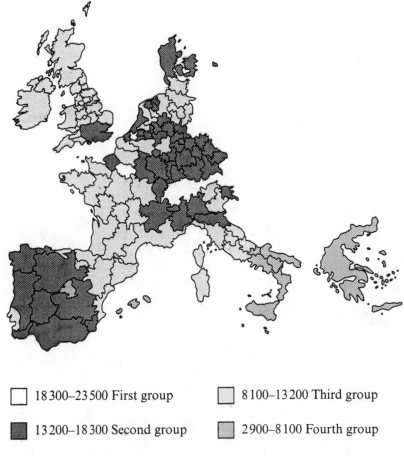

| | 18 300–23 500 First group | | 8 100–13 200 Third group |
| | 13 200–18 300 Second group | | 2 900–8 100 Fourth group |

Figure 11.1 European regions grouped by GDP per capita, 1995: PPP constant 1985 ECU

Table 11.2 provides a succinct overview of the distribution of regional development funds and EIB loans across groups I, II, III and IV, for 1975, 1985 and 1995. In each of the selected years there is a strong pattern for poorer regions to receive larger infusions and, over time, the flows of capital spending have risen. Each group is bench-marked by the member region with the highest ratio of funds and loans to its GDP. For example, in the high income group, in 1975, North Netherlands and Val D'Aosta (Italy) received 0.03 per cent of regional GDP in aid and loans (ERDF funds and EIB loans and global loans), and in 1995 Bremen (Germany) received 1.50 per cent. In the lowest

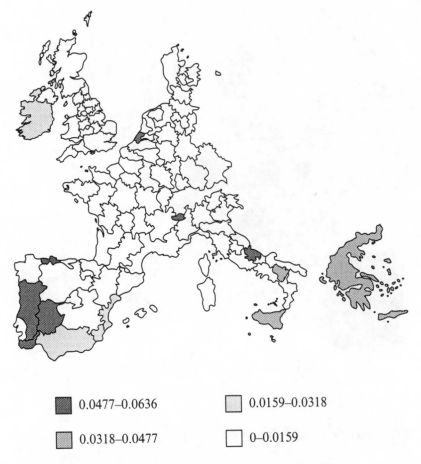

	0.0477–0.0636		0.0159–0.0318
	0.0318–0.0477		0–0.0159

Figure 11.2 Percentage of EU funds over regional GDP, 1995

group of regions, Basilicata (Italy) received 2.57 per cent in 1975, and Nisia-Aigaiou-Kriti (Greece) received 6.35 per cent in 1995.

THE DISTRIBUTION OF FUNDS AND REGIONAL ECONOMIC CONDITIONS

We undertake a simple exercise to determine whether, in total, the disbursement of the EU's regional programme funds and the EIB's loans has conformed to basic regional macroeconomic criteria. As a starting point, we elect to use the region's GDP per capita, unemployment rate

Table 11.2 Highest percentage of regional development funds and EIB loans as a percentage of GDP, 1975–1995

Group	1975		1985		1995	
	Region	% GDP	Region	% GDP	Region	% GDP
I	Nord Nederland Valle d'Aosta	0.03	Valle d'Aosta	1.42	Bremen	1.50
II	Corse	0.37	Hovedstads Regionen	0.79	País Vasco	1.71
III	North UK	1.35	Campania	2.15	Abruzzi	4.87
IV	Basilicata	2.57	Basilicata	6.18	Nisia Aigaiou, Kriti	6.35

Source: EIB (1975–1998) *Bulletins*.

and prior recipient experience in a parsimonious model to ascertain the degree to which allocations have been predicated on such straight-forward measures. In effect, we search for a tacit decision rule guiding EU disbursements. To be sure, additional or more complex indices could be adopted, such as sectoral structure, human-capital quality, or infra-structure adequacy; extensions of the present study along these lines can easily be imagined and pursued. We have chosen simplicity for two rea-sons. First, basic and objective criteria may be easier for technocrats to adopt and defend in the current EU political milieu, which is just emerg-ing to maturity. Second, if our model does explain one-half or more of fund distributions, it is arguable that such expedient simplicity, in the absence of an overarching strategy for success, and carefully tailored studies of individual region's needs and potentials, may be one reason why the massive fund allocations have had little discernible impact on the EU's economic disparities. Clearly, our findings can at most only open the door to much more detailed analyses of the determinants of EU and EIB allocations and of the impact of these interventions on regional conditions.

The data have been compiled mainly from the REGIO series released by Eurostat 1993 and are complete between 1975 and 1990. The EU structural funds and EIB loan data are available from 1975 to 1995. To complete the data set we consulted the Eurostat national accounts, 1970–1995 (EUROSTAT, 1996). The national data have been converted into regional data according to recent studies for the European less-developed regions (Svimez, 1996). Some gaps for regions in countries that joined the Community after 1970 remain. For missing data we approximated values through extrapolation or interpolation using analyses of trends of those variables.

We rely on an ordinary least-squares model using the following variables:

$FUNDS(r,t)$ = ERDF funds loans and EIB funds (ECU) allocated to the   region, normalized by population,

$GDPP(r,t)$ = GDP per capita (ECU) at t–3,

$UNEM(r,t)$ = Unemployment (%) at t–3, and

$PRIOR(r,t)$ = ERDF funds and EIB loans (ECU) at t–1,
              normalized by population,

where r = 102 regions and t = years 1975 to 1995.

The linear model with panel data has been applied without considering the previous subdivision into four groups ranked by GDP per capita, a convention adopted to make the descriptive figures and tables readily intelligible. The logic of the model is self-evident. We assert that EU and EIB decision-makers have, at base, relied on only three indicators in making their regional allocations ($FUNDS$), the dependent variable. The first explanatory variable is per capita regional product ($GDPP$), which is lagged three years, the reasoning being that delays arise in data collection and availability, and in disbursements, so that a given year's outcome is contingent upon conditions three years earlier. The second variable is the region's unemployment rate ($UNEM$), also lagged three years for the same reason. The third variable is the previous year's ERDF funds and EIB loans ($PRIOR$). The rationale here is two-fold. There is inertia in decision-making and regions acquire skill in obtaining new rounds of funding based on learning-by-doing in dealing with the EU and EIB's technocrats. This more-or-less stable symbiosis persists irrespective of whether income levels or unemployment rates change. The hypotheses are (1) the higher is $GDPP$, the lower is $FUNDS$; (2) the higher is $UNEM$, the higher is $FUNDS$; and (3) the higher is $PRIOR$ the higher is $FUNDS$.

Equation (11.1) treats $FUNDS$ as a function of the three explanatory variables, with the following result:

$$FUNDS = 185.39 - 19.45GDPP + 17.70UNEM + 0.75PRIOR$$
$$\quad\;\;(5.69)\quad\;\;(-4.95)\qquad\;(0.94)\qquad\;\;(44.41)\quad(11.1)$$

The adjusted R^2 for equation (11.1) is 0.59 and the numbers in parentheses are t-statistics. In this equation official regional capital flows are inversely related to per capita income and positively associated with prior experience. Unemployment levels do not appear to play a significant role.

Equation (11.2) drops *UNEM* from the right-hand side with little effect:

$$FUNDS = 173.94 - 17.43GDPP + 0.75PRIOR \qquad (11.2)$$
$$(5.76) \qquad (-5.30) \qquad (44.53)$$

Both *GDPP* and *PRIOR* remain significant in explaining EU and EIB allocation patterns. The adjusted $R^2 = 0.59$.

Because a positive correlation exists between *GDPP* and *UNEM*, equation (11.3) substitutes *UNEM* and retains *PRIOR*:

$$FUNDS = 27.20 - 33.46UNEM + 0.77PRIOR \qquad (11.3)$$
$$(4.22) \qquad (-2.10) \qquad (46.84)$$

In (11.3) *PRIOR* retains its very strong effect on annual allotments while *UNEM* is significant. The adjusted $R^2 = 0.57$. Unfortunately, we cannot separate clearly the effects of *GDPP* and *UNEM* on EU decision-makers but it is evident that basic macroeconomic conditions and path dependence shape ongoing outcomes.

DISCUSSION AND CONCLUSION

These results are based on a panel data set covering 102 EU regions and two decades of experience. In line with our expectations, it turns out to be possible to account for almost three-fifths of the variations in EU regional programme investments by looking at relative per capita incomes (or unemployment rates) and prior experience. It is not surprising that comparative income levels matter, in and of themselves, or as proxies for general levels of development, in the decision processes. When juxtaposed with the continuation of persistent regional disparities, we may question whether this decision rule and the distribution profile of funds it generates are having the desired effect of reducing inequality and enhancing cohesion. We take the evidence in the three equations that previous years' official investment levels are a good signal of the current year's allocations to indicate, again, a lack of imagination in the EU's various structural programmes, as they work out in the field. This inertia doubtlessly reflects a degree of political and bureaucratic grid-lock. In addition, regional administrations may have some success at learning-by-doing in dealing with EU and EIB decision-makers so that they can raise and sustain their shares of official investment disbursements, even though *ex post* evidence is ample that the current distributions are having little if any impact on regional convergence.

Because the EU's regional policies are a function of the institutional framework, problems arise. In a sense, the stability of policy decisions is reflective of the weakness of the EU's political structure at this point in the integration process. At all levels (EU, member states, regions), EU regional policies should eventually replace national policies for pursuing integration. The transition from independent states to a political union depends on achieving some convergence among regions but no effective means of making decisions that have high payoffs has been devised to alleviate existing disparities. At present, within the EU and between the EU and member states, rigid rules have been established on deadlines. When an agency does not spend allocated funds by an agreed date, these funds must be returned, so they are often unwisely disbursed. Each project or set of projects is analysed on an *ad hoc* basis with no overall regional or sectoral consideration; that is, there is no evidence of a planning process. Also proponents of projects or programmes are given relatively short notice to devise and submit proposals. So, they often do not have the time or skill adequately to prepare such proposals, which often contain too many generalities and few specifics. Finally, the changeover from a programme framework to a more targeted planning framework has not been fully worked out. In such a framework, the design and execution of policies based on locally relevant investments might have a chance of stimulating catch-up growth rates so that disparities could be lessened.

NOTES

1. Alberta Corona and Domenico Camrada provided research and computational assistance which the authors acknowledge with gratitude.
2. EUROSTAT reports data, which unfortunately are incomplete, for four levels of geographical units: 15 member states (NUTS 0), 64 regions (NUTS 1), 167 administrative regions (NUTS 2) and 824 provinces (NUTS 3). NUTS is an acronym for Nomenclature of Territorial Unit. We have adopted, because of limitations in the data, a mixed set that comprises mostly NUTS 1 and 2 regions, but uses some NUTS 0 and NUTS 3 units.

REFERENCES

Bulletin of the European Community, supplement January 1987 and Supplement July 1974.
European Investment Bank (1975–1998), *Bulletin*.
European Commission (1987), *The Single Act*, Brussels.
EUROSTAT (1978–1987), *Regional Statistics of the Community*, Brussels.
EUROSTAT (1993), *REGIO* (diskette), Brussels.
EUROSTAT (1996), *National Income Accounts*, Brussels.
SVIMEZ (1994–1996), *Rapporto sui Mezzogiorni d'Europa*, Bologna.

PART III

Regional Mosaics in National Contexts

12. Growth and sectoral dynamics in the Italian regions

Raffaele Paci and Francesco Pigliaru

12.1 INTRODUCTION*

This chapter deals with one of the most studied cases of regional inequality. Regional differentials in per capita income and labour productivity in Italy have attracted the attention of economists from all over the world since the 1950s, when Myrdal (1957) used it as an example of cumulative causation (among others, Eckaus, 1961; Chenery, 1962; Lutz, 1962).

The characterizing feature of the Italian case is that all measures of the economic gap between the average Southern region and the rest of the country have shown it to be remarkably persistent. Moreover, we do not yet have a full understanding of what is generating this persistence. The recent renewed attention to regional datasets spurred by the literature on convergence (Barro and Sala-i-Martin, 1995) has further stimulated a long-standing discussion.

First, we provide a comprehensive description of the pattern of regional inequality in Italy. The principal reason for doing this is that a new dataset on the main regional variables for the period 1951–94 was made available recently as the result of a major revision and update of the CRENoS database (see the appendix for more details). In this first part of the chapter we use descriptive statistics and panel regression analysis of the kind widely used in the convergence debate, so that direct comparison with other national cases is possible. In particular, we have added the national business cycle to the standard LSDV model to control for short-term adjustments to transitory deviations from the trend output. We find that a limited convergence process occurred over the years 1951–75 for both per capita income and labour productivity. Afterwards the degree of inequality between Northern and Southern regions increased again. Moreover, the regional distribution of per capita income presents a bimodal polarization where the rich convergence club includes most of the Northern regions, while the poor club consists of a small group of non-Adriatic Southern regions.

Second, we offer our contribution to the debate about the sources of the persistence of a high degree of regional inequality in Italy. We concentrate on sectoral dynamics in order to assess how much of the initially high potential for convergence due to the dualistic structure of the poorer regions has been exploited, by which regions and under what circumstances (regional policy regimes included). We find that dual mechanisms play a role in aggregate convergence as long as the outflows of labour from the low productivity agriculture of the poorer regions are a source of expansion of these regions' industrial sector. Once this migration from agriculture to industry ends in some of these regions, the impact of dualistic mechanisms on convergence weakens significantly. Industrialization, or its failure, still appears to be the key to understanding why some of the lagging regions converge and others do not.

The chapter is organized as follows. A description of the major characteristics of regional dynamics in Italy is given in Section 12.2. In Section 12.3 we present our econometric analysis of the convergence process over the period 1951–94 and in various subperiods. In Section 12.4 we analyse the sectoral dynamics and its interaction with aggregate convergence. Conclusions are given in Section 12.5.

12.2 DISPARITIES AND MOBILITY

The aim of this section is to give a first overview of the stylized facts that have characterized the process of economic growth across the Italian regions in the post-war period. A widely used measure of the degree of dispersion of a distribution is its coefficient of variation (CV). Figure 12.1 reports the CV of per capita income and labour productivity for the 20 Italian regions (see the Appendix for the list). Considering the entire period 1951–94, it results that the dispersion at the beginning of the 1950s was very high, particularly in terms of per capita income, but has declined since. Examining in more detail the evolution over time, the most impressive reduction of the gap took place in a very limited period of time, 1960–75. Then, over the last two decades the degree of regional disparities in Italy does not show any tendency to decline. The CV of both variables exhibits a slowly increasing tendency and this divergence pattern is stronger for the per capita measure.

More hints on the spatial source of the dispersion and on its temporal evolution come from Figure 12.2 which displays the CV *within* the two groups of North–Centre and Southern regions and also *between* them. Looking at labour productivity, it appears that the magnitude and the trend of the differential within the two regions are very similar: a visible

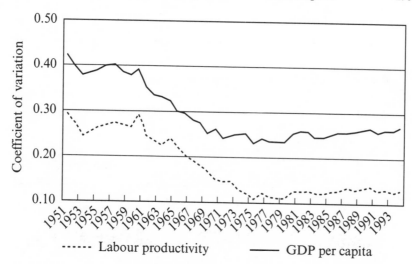

Figure 12.1 Regional dispersion in Italy, 1951–1994

reduction until the end of the 1970s, a very low tendency to grow in the last decade. Consequently, the productivity gap between North and South declined until the mid-1970s and afterwards it slightly increased.

The picture looks quite different if we observe the regional disparities in terms of per capita income. In this case, almost all the reduction in the dispersion of the entire population comes from a process of convergence within the regions of the North–Centre of Italy. The dispersion among these regions was very high at the beginning of the period (CV = 0.35) but afterwards it strongly decreased and it is now stable around a value of 0.09. In contrast, the disparity among the Southern regions was initially lower (0.14) and, despite some fluctuations over the period, it is now back to similar values. As a consequence, the North–South disparity showed a sharp fall in the 1960s and then a low and constant expansion in the last two decades. The conclusion is that the per capita income gap between the North and South of Italy is still there, at the same level it was 40 years ago, since most of the aggregate disparity decline results from an equalizing process within Northern regions.

A corroboration to these findings comes from the analysis of the top and bottom quartiles of the two distributions (Figure 12.3). The evolution of the per capita income index highlights how the overall decrease in the range depends totally on a reduction in the relative strength of the top four regions, all located in the North of Italy, rather than in an improvement of the bottom group of Southern regions. The convergence

A. Labour productivity

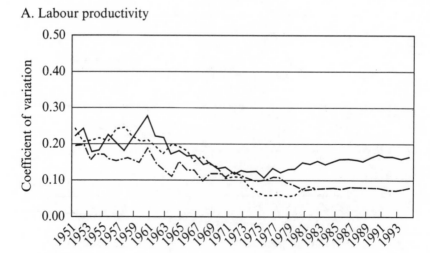

B. Per capita GDP

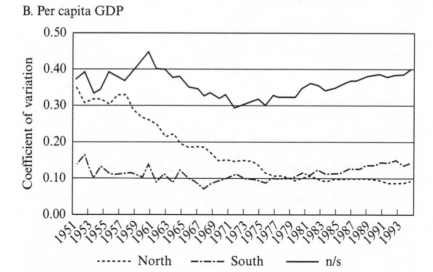

Figure 12.2 Dispersion across groups of Italian regions, 1951–1994

process in terms of labour productivity seems more spatially pervasive since it arises from both extremes of the distribution.

So far it has emerged that regional inequality is still a crucial characteristic of the Italian economic growth. Paci and Saba (1998) have remarked how the Italian regional disparities are the highest among the

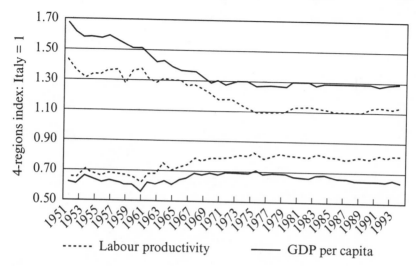

Figure 12.3 Top and bottom quartile index, 1951–1994

European countries in terms of per capita income, while for labour productivity, Italy shows a degree of disparity lower than Spain and Greece. In short, the international comparison highlights the persistence of regional inequality in Italy.

An interesting element to be stressed is that in 1975 the degree of dispersion within the Northern and Southern regions had already declined to a level comparable to those achieved by countries characterized by high factor mobility, such as the United States. The peculiarity of the Italian case seems to reside in the persistence of the abnormally high North–South differentials. We will return to this issue later.

Let us now turn to the analysis of the shape of the distribution of per capita income and labour productivity and its change over time. A first description of this issue is provided in Figure 12.4 through the plot of the relative indices of the two variables in ascending order.[1] Interestingly, the distributions of both per capita output and labour productivity become flatter over time, but their shapes show relevant differences. More precisely, the reduction in the dispersion of per capita income is mainly due to a relative decrease of the first, richest quartile together with growth of the second quartile.[2] At the same time the relative condition of the bottom, poorest quartile has not significantly changed. The convergence process of labour productivity appears more evenly distributed across all groups of regions: the initially more productive regions have reduced their relative strength while the opposite trend has characterized the initially less efficient regions.

A. Labour productivity

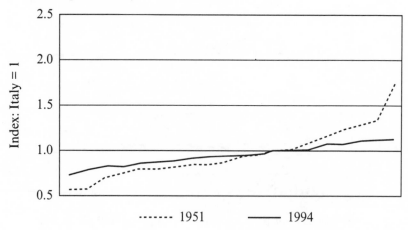

B. Per capita GDP

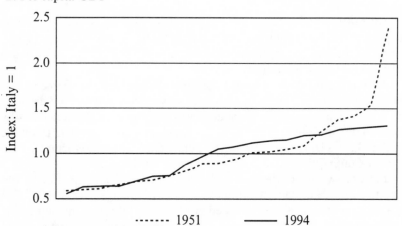

Figure 12.4 The shape of the distribution

One of the hypotheses often put forward in the cross-section growth literature is the existence of different 'convergence clubs'. To investigate directly this issue we have tested whether our two variables, per capita income and labour productivity, are normally distributed. Figure 12.5 reports the deviations from the normal distribution of the observed cumulative probability for 1994. The first result is that the deviations are very limited in the case of labour productivity. This means that the

A. Labour productivity

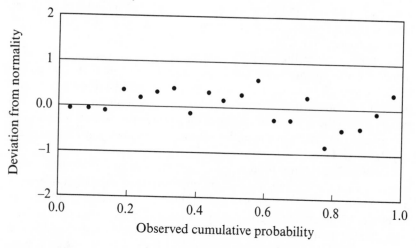

B. GDP per capita

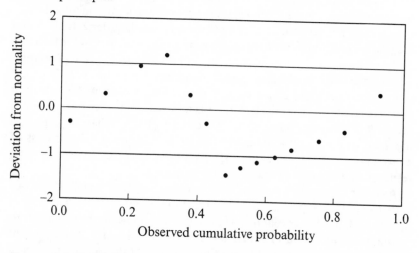

Figure 12.5 Test for normality in the distribution of GDP across the Italian regions, 1994

remaining regional dispersion we have previously documented tends to be normally distributed around the mean. A very different picture emerges when we examine the distribution of per capita income. In this case, the assumption of normality is violated since the distribution exhibits two peaks around the average. This bimodal polarization process highlights the presence of two different convergence clubs in the per capita income distribution across the Italian regions. The first club includes most of the rich Northern regions, while the second is made up of a small group of poor Mezzogiorno regions.

Let now consider the issue of mobility using the distribution dynamics matrices proposed by Quah (1993). For both labour productivity and per capita income, let us take four states characterized by an initially similar number of individuals in each state.[3] Then we compute a transition matrix where the element a_{ij} indicates the average probability of individuals included in state i in the initial year to end in state j in the final year (see Table 12.1).

Considering labour productivity over the entire period 1951–94 it emerges that the Italian regions are characterized by a high degree of mobility. Together with an upward mobility, we can detect downward mobility. As much as 60 per cent of regions with an initial productivity level greater than 110 per cent of the Italian average have shifted down in 1994, some of them even moving below the Italian average. At the same time 50 per cent of the initially less efficient regions have improved their relative positions. As a result of these up and down movements, the distribution of labour productivity ends up with strong polarization around the average. As a matter of fact, 15 out of 20 regions in 1994 are included in the quite narrow range 80–110 per cent relative to the Italian average. The most intensive polarization process occurred over the 1951–75 period when 75 per cent and 57 per cent of the regions moved up from the first and second state, respectively, and also all regions initially in the highest group shifted down. As a result, 90 per cent of the Italian regions were included in the two middle groups in 1975. Afterwards, the process of convergence to the middle range shows a weak tendency to decrease as a result of movements towards the extreme groups.

As regards per capita income, there is a high degree of mobility from one state to another, especially in the upward direction. Notable examples of mobility are the 40 per cent of regions initially included in the second poorest state that moved in 1994 into the next two groups, and the 60 per cent that dropped from the third to the fourth state. Yet the richest group contains all its original members (the entry in the main diagonal is unity). Considering the two subperiods over the years 1951–75 (that is the period of stronger reduction of the income dispersion) the upward mobility of poorer regions is outstanding: 60 per cent and 40 per cent for the first and second groups, respectively. In contrast, over the years 1975–93 the downward shift that occurred in the poorest group (67 per cent) is remarkable. Once more the final distribution of per capita income highlights the presence of two convergence clubs among the Italian regions: a poor club (with

Table 12.1 Distribution dynamics across the Italian regions

A. Labour productivity					B. Per capita income				
1951–1994		Final year			1951–1994		Final year		
Initial year	<80	80–95	95–110	>110	Initial year	<70	70–90	90–110	>110
<80	**0.50**	0.50	0.00	0.00	<70	**0.80**	0.20	0.00	0.00
80–95	0.00	**0.71**	0.29	0.00	70–90	0.20	**0.40**	0.20	0.20
95–110	0.00	0.25	**0.50**	0.25	90–110	0.00	0.00	**0.40**	0.60
>110	0.00	0.00	0.60	**0.40**	>110	0.00	0.00	0.00	**1.00**
Initial distr.	0.20	0.35	0.20	0.25	Initial distr.	0.25	0.25	0.25	0.25
Final distr.	0.10	0.40	0.35	0.15	Final distr.	0.25	0.15	0.15	0.45
1951–1975					1951–1975				
<80	**0.25**	0.75	0.00	0.00	<70	**0.40**	0.60	0.00	0.00
80–95	0.00	**0.43**	0.57	0.00	70–90	0.00	**0.60**	0.40	0.00
95–110	0.00	0.00	**0.75**	0.25	90–110	0.00	0.00	**0.80**	0.20
>110	0.00	0.00	1.00	**0.00**	>110	0.00	0.00	0.00	**1.00**
Initial distr.	0.20	0.35	0.20	0.25	Initial distr.	0.25	0.25	0.25	0.25
Final distr.	0.05	0.30	0.60	0.05	Final distr.	0.10	0.30	0.30	0.30
1975–1994					1975–1994				
<80	**0.00**	1.00	0.00	0.00	<70	**0.50**	0.50	0.00	0.00
80–95	0.33	**0.67**	0.00	0.00	70–90	0.67	**0.33**	0.00	0.00
95–110	0.00	0.25	**0.50**	0.25	90–110	0.00	0.00	**0.50**	0.50
>110	0.00	0.00	0.00	**0.00**	>110	0.00	0.00	0.00	**1.00**
Initial distr.	0.05	0.30	0.60	0.05	Initial distr.	0.10	0.30	0.30	0.30
Final distr.	0.10	0.40	0.35	0.15	Final distr.	0.25	0.15	0.15	0.45

a share of 25 per cent) and a rich one (45 per cent), while the two average states are characterized by very low frequencies.

From the analysis of the transition matrices it thus seems that the process of regional growth in Italy has been characterized by a high degree of mobility with individual regions exhibiting phenomena of catching up and falling behind.[4]

12.3   AGGREGATE CONVERGENCE

In this section we investigate the process of aggregate convergence across the Italian regions. This analysis has been commonly conducted using cross-section regressions (see Barro and Sala-i-Martin, 1995). From the Solow model with Cobb–Douglas technology and exogenous saving rates and technological progress, the unconditional convergence process has been described by the following linear regression equation:

$$\ln y_{it} - \ln y_{it-T}(1/T) = a + b \ln y_{it-T} + u_i \tag{12.1}$$

where y is, alternatively, GDP per capita or per worker.

According to this approach, there is absolute β-convergence if the coefficient $b < 0$; that is, if economies that were poorer at the beginning of the period are growing on average faster than richer ones. The idea of absolute convergence relies on the assumption that the only difference across economies is their initial level of capital per worker. It is common practice to add in equation (12.1) a set of dummy variables to control for unobservable effects that differ among individual cases (for example the level of technology, propensities to save, infrastructures, public policies). This approach leads to the so-called conditional β-convergence. Obviously there are limitations to the number of individuals we can control for, so that we have to rely on the implicit assumption that groups of individuals (regions, countries) are affected in the same way by the left-out variables.[5]

An alternative way to test the existence of the convergence process is by means of panel estimation.[6] The panel formulation has the advantage that it allows us to control for unobservable variables for each individual in our population. As for the timespan to be chosen, equation (12.1) can be interpreted as an approximation of the transitional dynamics of the system around its steady state, so that there are no *a priori* reasons in favour of one particular choice (Islam, 1995). As a consequence, there is no uniformity in the literature about which timespan is more appropriate for convergence analysis (see Islam, 1995 and Evans and Karras, 1996).

In our data set, estimations based on the longest timespan (cross-section data) and on the shortest one (annual panel data) yield very similar results with respect to the few key questions we are considering here (the length of the period characterized by absolute convergence, and the significance of the dummies controlling for groups of regions). In the following, we report the annual panel data estimations. Clearly, the use of annual data poses several problems – see Evans and Karras (1996), Durlauf and Quah (1998) and de la Fuente (1998). One problem is that business cycle fluctuations may create disturbances in the estimates, a point that we will discuss presently.

One way to estimate convergence with a panel of annual data is the following:

$$\ln y_{it} - \ln y_{it-1} = a + b \ln y_{it-1} + d_i + d_t + v_{it} \tag{12.2}$$

where v_{it} is an error term with zero mean which varies across regions and years; d_i are regional effects included to control for region-specific unobservable variables; d_t are time effects that should control for short-term fluctuations common to all regions. In other words the temporal dummies are supposed to capture the effect of the national business cycle. The following analysis confirms this.

We have estimated separately the national business cycle as the residuals of the regression of the Italian growth rate of y_t with respect to a time trend. In Figure 12.6 those residuals are plotted together with the time effects estimated in equation (12.2). As expected, the correlation between the Italian business cycle and the time effects is positive and highly significant for both per capita GDP and labour productivity. Therefore, a more parsimonious and economically meaningful version of (12.2) can be obtained by substituting the 43 time dummies required there with the national business cycle variable (BC).[7] So our final specification of the convergence equation to be estimated over the period 1951–1994 is[8]

$$\ln y_{it} - \ln y_{it-1} = a + b \ln y_{it-1} + d_i + BC_t + v_{it} \tag{12.3}$$

The regression results are reported in Tables 12.2 and 12.3 for labour productivity and per capita income, respectively. For each variable we have estimated the convergence process for the entire period and for two subperiods 1951–75 and 1975–1994.[9] Moreover, for each period, we first report the LSDV results (regression 1), with the business cycle and the regional effects. In regressions 2 and 3 we include two dummy variables, *DS* and *DA*, to test the hypothesis that Southern and Adriatic regions moved towards a common steady state (obviously, in these specifications

A. Per capita GDP

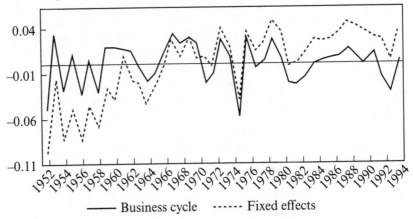

——— Business cycle   ------ Fixed effects

B. Labour productivity

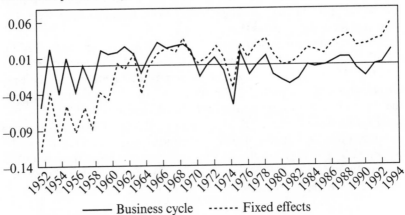

——— Business cycle   ------ Fixed effects

Figure 12.6 National business cycle and temporal fixed effects, 1951–1994

the fixed regional effects are not included).[10] We also report the estimates based on a simple pooling in order to assess the robustness of our results. Regression 4 includes only the initial level of the dependent variable, while in regression 5 the business cycle is added.

Considering labour productivity (Table 12.2), the growth rate appears to be negatively and significantly affected by its lagged levels over the entire period examined. The explanatory power of the model increases considerably only when the business cycle is included. As expected, the national business cycle turns out to be positive, signalling a general increasing trend of the productivity growth rate in Italy. The magnitude of the coefficient of y_{t-1} is quite stable in all the different specifications of the model, showing a speed of the convergence process of 2.3–2.5 per cent per year. The dummy for the Mezzogiorno's regions is negative and significant, which means that the steady-state level for this group of regions is lower than the average. An above-average equilibrium level characterizes the Italian regions belonging to the successful Adriatic belt. The specifications without fixed effects confirm these results, although the explanatory power of the model turns out to be quite small when only the lagged level of labour productivity is included.

Once more the analysis of the growth process over different periods of time allows us to point out crucial differences. Indeed, an absolute convergence process seems to have occurred only in the first period considered, 1951–1975 (regression B.4). Afterwards, the coefficient of the lagged productivity level is not significant (regression C.4). Moreover, the role of the regional fixed effects and geographical dummies is quite negligible in the first period: their inclusion does not alter the value of the convergence coefficient and DS and DA are not even significant. In short, until 1975, regional growth in Italy was characterized by a strong convergence process towards a common steady-state level as was already pointed out in the descriptive analysis of Section 12.2. Afterwards, the last two decades are dominated by local convergence processes: the geographical dummies are remarkably significant (regressions C.2 and C.3). We will try to give some explanations for the mechanisms and causes of these processes in the next section.

Let now turn our analysis to per capita income. As we have already remarked, this variable can yield results which differ from those based on labour productivity whenever participation and unemployment rates are not constant over time and across regions.

The econometric analysis confirms the existence of an unconditional convergence process limited to the 1951–75 period (regression B.4 in Table 12.3), while the coefficient of y_t in the period 1975–94 is not significant (regression C.4). Even in the post-war years, the annual speed of convergence for per capita income (1.4 per cent) is much lower than for productivity. Another difference with respect to labour productivity is that now DS and DA are significant in both subperiods. This result confirms the relevance of local factors (mainly the regional differences in the labour market) which distinguish the growth process of per capita income and thus the tendency towards different convergence clubs.

Table 12.2 Labour productivity convergence across the Italian regions

Periods	Regression	Constant	y_{-1}	BC	Fixed effects	DS	DA	$R^{2adj.}$	F_{test}	DW statistic
A 1951–94 (860 obs)	A.1		−0.024 (−13.32)[a]	0.97 (25.33)[a]	yes			0.53	1009.4	2.22
	A.2	0.28 (15.54)[a]	−0.024 (−13.73)[a]	0.97 (25.45)	no	−0.004 (−1.96)[b]		0.54	334.7	2.20
	A.3	0.27 (15.16)[a]	−0.023 (−13.40)[a]	0.97 (25.50)[a]	no		0.004 (2.19)[b]	0.54	335.4	2.20
	A.4	0.29 (11.89)[a]	−0.025 (−10.51)[a]		no			0.16	159.9	1.93
	A.5	0.28 (15.39)[a]	−0.023 (−13.52)[a]	0.97 (25.39)[a]	no			0.53	494.7	2.19
B 1951–75 (480 obs)	B.1		−0.019 (−5.07)[a]	0.97 (19.42)[a]	yes			0.51	518.4	2.29
	B.2	0.25 (7.13)[a]	−0.021 (−6.01)[a]	0.97 (19.39)[a]	no	0.001 (0.21)		0.50	164.0	2.22
	B.3	0.25 (7.15)[a]	−0.021 (−6.01)[a]	0.97 (19.47)[a]	no		0.005 (1.61)	0.51	167.9	2.23

B.4	0.20 (4.38)[a]	−0.015 (−3.41)[a]		no		0.09	46.6	1.88
B.5	0.26 (7.48)[a]	−0.021 (−6.28)[a]	0.97 (19.40)[a]	no		0.51	247.5	2.22
C 1975–94 (400 obs)								
C.1		−0.053 (−8.22)[a]	0.96 (22.47)[a]	yes		0.61	655.7	2.33
C.2	0.41 (6.46)[a]	−0.036 (−6.09)[a]	0.92 (20.66)[a]	no	−0.008 (−4.12)[a]	0.57	174.8	2.18
C.3	0.27 (4.94)[a]	−0.023 (−4.55)[a]	0.89 (19.88)[a]	no	0.004 (2.91)[a]	0.55	162.9	2.19
C.4	−0.00 (−0.01)	0.002 (0.25)		no		0.03	12.1	1.99
C.5	0.27 (4.93)[a]	−0.023 (−4.50)[a]	0.88 (19.53)[a]	no		0.53	230.2	2.14

Notes:

Dependent variable: GDP per worker, annual growth rate.

y_{-1} = log GDP per worker, one year lag; BC = business cycle in Italy; DS = Dummy South; DA = Dummy Adriatic.

Panel estimation: least squares with cross-section weights.

t-statistics in parentheses. Significance levels: [a]1 per cent, [b]5 per cent.

305

Table 12.3 *Per capita income convergence across the Italian regions*

Periods	Regression	Constant	y_{-1}	BC	Fixed effects	DS	DA	R^2adj.	F_{test}	DW statistic
A 1951–94 (860 obs)	A.1		−0.022 (−12.39)[a]	0.93 (25.96)[a]	yes			0.54	1021.8	2.24
	A.2	0.25 (14.89)[a]	−0.022 (−13.01)[a]	0.92 (25.89)[a]	no	−0.011 (−5.47)[a]		0.54	332.2	2.19
	A.3	0.20 (13.10)[a]	−0.018 (−11.21)[a]	0.93 (25.63)[a]	no		0.005 (3.09)[b]	0.52	313.1	2.16
	A.4	0.21 (10.32)[a]	−0.019 (−8.78)[a]		no			0.12	119.0	2.05
	A.5	0.21 (13.53)[a]	−0.019 (−11.51)[a]	0.93 (25.60)[a]	no			0.52	464.7	2.14
B 1951–75 (480 obs)	B.1		−0.017 (−4.35)[a]	0.91 (19.78)[a]	yes			0.52	535.4	2.32
	B.2	0.24 (7.22)[a]	−0.022 (−6.11)[a]	0.91 (19.70)[a]	no	−0.007 (−2.09)[b]		0.51	168.9	2.24
	B.3	0.18 (6.55)[a]	−0.016 (−5.32)[a]	0.91 (19.80)[a]	no		0.008 (2.77)[a]	0.52	171.5	2.27

B.4	0.16 (4.34)[a]	−0.014 (−3.31)[a]		no		0.07	35.9	2.02
B.5	0.20 (7.19)[a]	−0.018 (−5.85)[a]	0.91 (19.59)[a]	no		0.51	246.9	2.23
C 1975–94 (400 obs)								
C.1		−0.049 (−9.03)[a]	0.95 (24.91)[a]	yes		0.67	824.2	2.21
C.2	0.35 (7.10)[a]	−0.033 (−6.61)[a]	0.94 (23.41)[a]	no	−0.019 (−6.66)[a]	0.63	224.1	2.00
C.3	0.10 (3.11)[a]	−0.008 (−2.46)[a]	0.95 (22.54)[a]	no	0.004 (2.48)[a]	0.60	197.9	1.89
C.4	−0.059 (1.29)	0.004 (−0.87)		no		0.02	8.84	1.81
C.5	0.10 (3.20)[a]	−0.008 (−2.50)[a]	0.95 (22.32)[a]	no		0.59	284.6	1.86

Notes:
Dependent variable: GDP per capita, annual growth rate.
y_{-1} = log GDP per capita, one year lag; BC = business cycle in Italy; DS = Dummy South; DA = Dummy Adriatic.
Panel estimation: least squares with cross-section weights.
t-statistics in parentheses. Significance levels: [a] 1 per cent, [b] 5 per cent.

12.4   SECTORAL DYNAMICS AND CONVERGENCE

As we have seen, absolute convergence in labour productivity was a strong phenomenon up to 1975, then came to a halt. In Section 12.2 we have seen that part of this pattern is due to the fact that a large share of the high initial dispersion of labour productivity across non-Southern regions was eliminated by 1975 (see Figure 12.2, A), so that the potential for convergence within this subgroup had been largely exploited by then. The second component of the slowdown of convergence is of a different nature. The convergence between the Southern regions and the others ends in 1975, when the degree of inequality is still remarkably high compared with those prevailing both in other European nations and in the US (Paci and Saba, 1998; Sum and Fogg, this volume, Chapter 6). Therefore, in the following we concentrate on this second more puzzling component.

Several explanations have been put forward to address it. As Boltho *et al.* (this volume, Chapter 13) show, many explanations focus on the failure of the remarkable effort made by the Italian state to obtain sustainable industrialization of the Southern regions through active regional policies (Sylos Labini 1985; Giannola, 1982; Graziani, 1978).

One feature worth noticing is that, implicitly, this interpretation suggests that the sectoral mix and the mechanisms behind its changes, whether market-driven or policy-induced, are crucial for convergence analysis. This interpretation sheds doubts on the usefulness of aggregative models to identify at least some of the factors generating the observed dynamics of regional productivity differentials. We share these doubts, and think that we can obtain a more complete picture of the troubled history of the Italian regional problem by taking explicitly into account the sectoral dynamics underlying the process. In this section, our specific contribution to this line of research is twofold.

First, we describe a methodology proposed in Paci and Pigliaru (1997) to assess the impact of structural change on regional growth rates, and the main result we obtained by applying it to the Italian data set. Second, we investigate whether industrialization in the Southern regions is indeed important to understand the pattern of the convergence process and the role played by policy to obtain industrialization. To assess such a role, first of all we need to define what market mechanisms were expected to generate an expansion of industry in poorer and mostly agricultural regions and how strong they have been in reality. To proceed along these lines, we use a simple model of the dual economy to obtain testable hypotheses concerning the relationship between sector composition and convergence in a cross-section of economies.

12.4.1 β-Convergence and/or Structural Change

Our first task is to test whether the impact of structural change on regional growth in Italy is compatible with the neoclassical growth model. The two-sector version of Solow's growth model requires, in general, that aggregate growth is the result of a capital-deepening process taking place in *all* sectors of the economy, so that convergence should be detected within each of them. As a consequence, when we use cross-section data to estimate the convergence equation, levels and changes in sectoral weights may help account for growth differentials, but we should still find a significantly negative role played by the variable measuring initial productivity levels.[11]

To test whether the initial productivity level remains significant and negative when structural change is controlled for, Paci and Pigliaru (1997) suggested including a measure of the impact on the aggregate growth rate of sectoral composition and its change for each region in the standard cross-section convergence equation. When we apply this methodology to the case of the Italian regions we find the following. Contrary to the Solovian prediction, the coefficient of the initial value of productivity turns out to be not significant, while sectoral composition and structural change exert the expected positive effect on the convergence process.[12] Sectoral shifts therefore are a crucial factor in explaining the convergence pattern in Italy. Closer inspection of the data suggests that convergence-enhancing structural change was of the type one would expect to take place in dual economies. Indeed, further evidence in Paci and Pigliaru (1997) shows that the Southern regions in 1970 were still characterized by large agricultural weights, and that a fast decline of those weights in favour of the industrial sector took place during the period 1970–75, when aggregate convergence was strong. After that period, this specific mechanism came to a halt and this, not surprisingly, was accompanied by a stalling of the whole convergence process. Taken together, this evidence suggests the usefulness of considering more explicitly the mechanisms of the dual economy in order to test their relevance for the convergence process across Italian regions, their overall strength and their dependence on regional policies.

12.4.2 Convergence and the Dual Economy

Let us start by considering the market mechanisms characterizing a closed neoclassical dual economy (Mas Colell and Razin, 1973). An agricultural good is for consumption only, while the second good, the non-agricultural one, is both a second consumption good and the single investment good in the economy. The savings rate is exogenous as is the proportion of the non-agricultural good used for consumption. Full employment and perfect intersectoral factor mobility are also assumed. Production in both sectors takes place using physical capital and labour, with Cobb–Douglas constant returns to scale technology. In this economy, the sectoral capital–labour ratios turn out to be a constant proportion of the aggregate capital–labour ratio.

The dualistic feature of this system is that differences in the sectoral values of marginal productivity are not instantaneously equalized. Equalization takes time, with workers moving from agriculture, where the lower wage is paid, to the other sector according to a migration rate that is an increasing function of the wage differential. Because migration flows cause the wage gap to diminish, the rate of growth of the non-agricultural labour share is a negative function of the level of the same variable (ρ). As for the dynamics of the aggregate capital–labour ratio k, it is possible to show that:

$$\frac{\dot{k}}{k} = \phi \left(\frac{k}{\rho}\right)^{\beta-1} \qquad (12.4)$$

where ϕ is a positive constant and β is the exponent of capital in the Cobb–Douglas technology. This dual economy converges towards a unique and globally stable steady-state with the values of ρ^* and k^* depending on the parameters of the model (Mas Colell and Razin, 1973).

One interesting feature of this dual economy model is obtained by totally differentiating (12.4) and rearranging terms in order to obtain:

$$\frac{d(\dot{k}/k)}{d\rho} = \omega k^{\beta-1} \rho^{-1} \left(1 - \frac{\dot{k}/k}{\dot{\rho}/\rho}\right) \qquad (12.5)$$

where ω is another positive constant. The sign of (12.5) is positive for small values of ρ, since the growth rate of ρ is higher than that of k. Therefore we have a phase in which capital-deepening occurs at an accelerating rate. As the transition to the steady-state proceeds, the difference between the two growth rates decreases, since $\dot{\rho}/\rho$ decreases and $\dot{k}/k$ increases, and eventually is reversed. Once this is accomplished, $\dot{k}/k$ starts declining.

This result allows us to obtain testable hypotheses about the relationship we should observe in a cross-section of similar economies between the growth rates of labour productivity and the initial levels of the non-agricultural labour share. In general, assuming that technological knowledge is uniform across all economies (on this more below), larger values of ρ exert a negative direct effect on the growth rate of y. Small ρs imply fast growth of the sector which produces the investment good. There is an indirect effect operating through the influence of ρ on capital accumulation, so that when the values of ρ are small enough, $\dot{k}/k$ increases with ρ. These two effects exert opposing influences on productivity growth for the smaller values of ρ, but they exert a common negative influence for the remaining range of the values of ρ. Therefore, as we show in Paci and Pigliaru (1999), a cross-section of similar economies distributed along a common transitional path should generate a relationship between the growth rate of labour productivity and the value of ρ which either takes the inverted-U shape characteristic of capital accumulation, or is monotonically negative.

Before proceeding, a final point about the model should be noticed. The transition to the steady-state is characterized by the fact that for any given value of ρ, the higher are k and y, the lower are the growth rates of these variables (see equation (12.4)). This implies that in our regressions about the relationship between the growth rate of productivity and ρ, we should control for the level of y, the coefficient of which is expected to be negative.

12.4.3 Evidence

Our first step is to find confirmation that the basic mechanism of a dual economy is at work in our case study, so that significant flows of labour migration from agriculture to the non-agricultural sector take place. Moreover, we need to control whether intersectoral migration acquires the pattern postulated by the model, with the growth rate of the non-agricultural share being a decreasing function of its level. A pattern of this type is indeed what we find in our data, as shown in Figure 12.7; the correlation between growth rates and levels is −0.94 for the whole period 1960–94.[13] Moreover, this pattern is remarkably stable. No significant differences were found by dividing the whole period in two subperiods, 1960–75 and 1975–94, with the correlation in both periods constant at −0.94.

Another feature of our dataset is that the non-agricultural share and the level of total labour productivity are strongly correlated (−0.85), as one should expect to be the case in a cross-section with a number of dual economies.

Turning to our econometric evidence, the results of panel data regressions with fixed (regional) effects and temporal dummy variables are shown in Table 12.4.[14] No inverted-U relationships have been detected in our estimations (these results are not reported) so that the relationship between the variable measuring the non-agricultural share and the growth rates was expected to be monotonically negative. This prediction is corroborated by regression 1 for the whole period under investigation. The

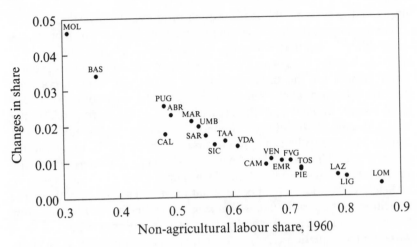

Figure 12.7 Non-agricultural labour share and its changes, 1960–1994

Table 12.4 Productivity growth and sectoral dynamics across the Italian regions, 1960–1994

Regression	NAS_{-1}	y_{-1}	DNAS	Fixed effects	Temporal effects	$R^{2\text{adj.}}$	F_{test}
1	−0.15 (−5.18)[a]			Yes	Yes	0.49	13.1
2	−0.05 (−1.75)[c]	−0.14 (−8.46)[a]		Yes	Yes	0.54	15.6
3	−0.04 (−0.84)	−0.13 (−8.15)[a]	−0.07 (−2.47)[b]	Yes	Yes	0.54	15.5

Notes:
Dependent variable: GDP per worker, annual growth rate.
y_{-1} = log GDP per worker, one year lag.
NAS_{-1} = non-agriculture labour share, one year lag.
$DNAS$ = 1960–75 equals NAS, 1976–94 equals 0.
Panel estimation: least squares dummy variables.
Number of observations: 680.
t-statistics in parentheses. Significance levels: [a]1 per cent, [b]5 per cent, [c]10 per cent.

negative sign is significant at the 1 per cent level in the absence of the lagged value of aggregate labour productivity. When we add the latter, estimates are likely to be affected by the high correlation between the two explanatory variables in our data set; however, we have enough variation unique to each of the two variables to be able to identify the signs of their coefficients, with the coefficient of the sectoral share still bearing the expected negative sign (regression 2). This outcome yields further evidence that the aggregate convergence process is linked to changes in sectoral weights that are consistent with the workings of a dual economy,[15] but this link is rather weak over the whole period.

As for subperiods, we use 1975 as the dividing year since the process of absolute convergence ended then. In regression 3 we tested the stability over time of the coefficient of the non-agricultural sector share, NAS. The dummy-slope DNAS is equal to NAS for the period 1960–75, and to zero for the period 1976–94. The result is that the coefficient is significantly negative in the first subperiod (1960–75), while it is not significant in 1976–94. An explanation for this could be that intersectoral migration ends in the second subperiod, or that its intensity is no longer inversely related with the shares of the non-agricultural sector. As we have already said, such an inverse relationship is stable and significant in both subperiods, so that we rule this first hypothesis out, and conclude that it is not the expansion of the non-agricultural sector *as a whole* in the poorer regions that seems to work in favour of convergence.

A second hypothesis is that the components of the expansion of the non-agricultural sector differ in the two subperiods. One *a priori* factor in favour of this hypothesis is that in the mid-1970s the regional policy focused on mobilizing direct manufacturing investment in the South weakened significantly. If the pattern of industrialization in the South was significantly influenced by this type of policy, and was positive for convergence, this should emerge from the analysis of the two subperiods.[16] Our disaggregated data for the two subperiods corroborate this hypothesis. Figure 12.8 shows the relationship between rates of change and levels of the industrial share in the two subperiods. Contrary to the case of the non-agricultural sector, here the correlation between rates of change and levels is far from constant. It was equal to –0.68 in 1960–75 and dropped to a statistically non-significant –0.27 in 1975–94. This pattern is unique to industry. The other component of the non-agricultural sector, services, shows a relationship between rates of change and levels which is both strong and stable across subperiods (with correlation coefficients equal to –0.82 and –0.83, respectively)

In the case of the industrial sector, one reason behind the low correlation recorded in 1975–94 is that four of the poorer and still little-industrialized regions (Sicily, Sardinia, Calabria, Campania) saw the rate of change of their industrial share turn from positive to negative, while it remained positive for the other four Southern regions (Abruzzo, Molise, Basilicata, Puglia) conventionally considered as being part of the so-called Adriatic belt.

A. 1960–1975

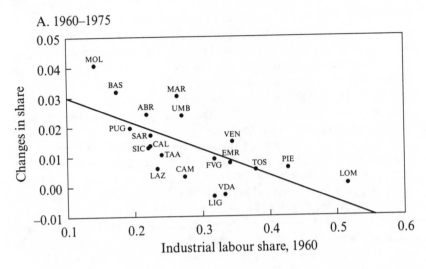

B. 1975–1994

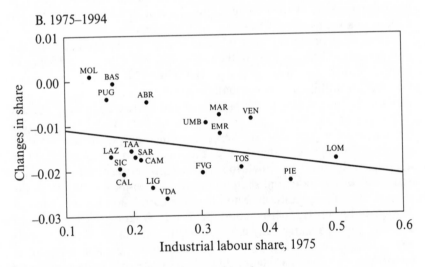

Figure 12.8 Industrial labour share and its changes

Does this different pattern of the process of industrialization in the Southern regions explain part of their growth performances? While we do not offer exhaustive evidence on this important question, some evidence pointing to a positive answer is shown in Figure 12.9, where the straight lines correspond to the averages of the regions' growth rates measured along the axes. Over the period 1960–75 all Southern regions achieved faster than average growth rates of both labour productivity and indus-

A. 1960–1975

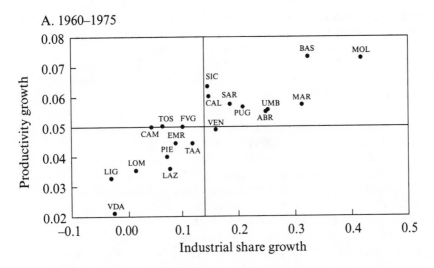

B. 1975–1994

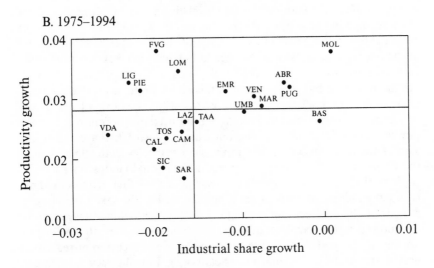

Notes:
Growth rates expressed as annual averages.
Internal line set at the national averages.

Figure 12.9 Growth of aggregate labour productivity and industrial share

trial share (with the partial exception of Campania). Over the period
1975–94 the Southern group is neatly split, with Sicily, Sardinia, Calabria
and Campania experiencing a faster than average decline of their indus-

trial shares accompanied by slower than average productivity growth. In contrast, the remaining Southern regions were characterized by high rates of both industrial expansion and productivity growth.

We sum up our main findings. First, dual mechanisms play a role in aggregate convergence as long as the outflows of labour from the low-productivity agricultural sectors of the poorer regions are a source of expansion of these regions' industrial sectors. Once this migration from agriculture to industry ends in some of these regions, the impact of dualistic mechanisms on convergence weakens significantly.[17]

Second, regional policy is likely to have accelerated industrialization of Southern regions in the initial phases. Starting from the mid-1970s public intervention became much less favourable to industrialization in the Mezzogiorno, both directly and indirectly, as much of the literature on the Mezzogiorno has pointed out (Del Monte and Giannola, 1997). Directly, investment in the South by state-controlled large manufacturing enterprises and funding for financial incentives to private investment diminished dramatically. Indirectly, in the second subperiod public intervention aimed at sustaining income levels in the South allowed a faster than average expansion of the public sector share.[18] Indeed, over the period 1960–75 the pattern of expansion of the non-market service sector in the poorer regions was on average in line with the rest of the country. Interestingly, the second subperiod yields a different picture. In all Southern regions but one (Sardinia), this sector's rate of change is significantly higher than average. In other words, while the flows of labour out of agriculture were initially linked with industrialization in most of the poorer regions, later they were accompanied by faster than average expansion of the non-market services in the same regions – with some of them simultaneously experiencing a decrease in their (small) industrial share.

From the viewpoint of the model used above, the first of these findings is broadly consistent with its main prediction. For the sake of simplicity, models of the dual economy generally assume that all labour exiting the agricultural sector translates into an expansion of industry, the sector producing capital goods. This is the reason why we expect poorer regions to grow faster in the transition to the steady state. In reality, several elements not explicitly included in the model can weaken realization of this predicted outcome. Among them, the existence of non-market sectors, and the influence exerted by policy decisions on their weight, can be important sources of distortions of the sectoral allocation of productive factors. In some circumstances, the role of such sectors in a region's growth performance may be radically different from, and less growth-enhancing than, the one postulated for the industrial sector by the dual model.

Our second finding is likely to raise more fundamental questions. The model predicts that in the absence of distortionary policies market mechanisms should suffice to cause an expansion of industry in the lagging regions. The period in which this phenomenon did occur is also the period of active regional policy. So one possibility is that the specific market mechanisms considered by the model were not enough to trigger industrialization. Again, several reasons can be listed to account for this discrepancy between theory and reality. Among them, we would like to underline the following: although the model discussed in this section assumes uniformity of technology across regions, localized knowledge accumulation may exist and make that assumption inadequate even in the case of regional economies. In particular, if technological knowledge is not continuously uniform across space, we would expect its diffusion mechanisms to cause well-defined spatial patterns within the convergence process.[19] For instance, the existence of one of these patterns might be signalled by the significance of the Adriatic dummy in our regressions in Section 12.3. The presence of localized aspects of technological knowledge may help to explain the different long-run impact of the policies aimed at industrializing the South. One possibility is that these policies were successful in those areas where mechanisms of technology diffusion from Centre–Northern regions were stronger. More generally, industrialization, or its failure, appears to be the key to understanding why some of the lagging regions converge and others do not.

12.5 CONCLUSIONS

In this chapter we have analysed Italian regional growth in the last four decades using several descriptive statistics and panel regression analysis. We have investigated sectoral dynamics in order to assess how much of the initially high potential for convergence due to the dualistic structure of the poorer regions has been exploited, by which regions and under what policy regimes. As far as per capita income is concerned our analysis has shown that a limited convergence process occurred over the years 1951–75; afterwards the degree of inequality between Northern and Southern regions increased again. As a result, the regional distribution of per capita income presents a bimodal polarization where the rich convergence club includes most of the Northern regions, while the poor club consists of a small group of non-Adriatic Southern regions.

For labour productivity, a process of absolute convergence took place across Italian regions up to 1975 and then came to a halt. Such a pattern involves all territorial areas and is caused by two main components. First, the potential for convergence of the initially medium income regions of the Centre–North was largely exploited by the mid-1970s.

Second, part of the Southern regions' large potential for converging was exploited prior to 1975 through a process of sectoral shifts from low- to high-productivity sectors. Since then an important divide has become evident. Four out of eight Southern regions have experienced a relative slowdown of growth and a halt to their processes of convergence, in spite of the fact that they still lagged very significantly behind the Centre–Northern regions; in the other Southern regions convergence did not stop in 1975. A sectoral dimension lies behind this second component. The large weight of a backward agriculture sector characterizing all the Southern regions in the 1950s translated into a sustained process of industrialization and of convergence only in some. For the Southern regions, being (un)successful in convergence coincides with being (un)-successful in expanding the industrial sector. Future research should address the problem of what has prompted the neatly distinct performances of industrialization across groups of regions, how important the mechanisms of technology diffusion have been and what policies have been effective and why.

APPENDIX

In 1997 the Italian Statistical Office (ISTAT) published the new *Regional Accounts* for the period 1980–94 using a more accurate methodology to account for the unofficial sectors of the economy. Similarly, ISTAT reviewed the *National Accounts* for the period 1970–1995. Consequently, CRENoS has updated the database presented in Paci and Saba (1998) embodying the new available information. We have obtained homogeneous series for the entire period 1951–94 by linking the earlier regional data to the new national and regional official ISTAT series. All monetary variables have been calculated in constant values at 1990 prices by means of regional and sectoral deflators. The CRENoS database is available under request.

Primary sources of regional data for the period 1951–1979.

Gross domestic product and value added
- 1951–62, G. Tagliacarne, *Moneta e Credito*, Banca Nazionale del Lavoro, 1961–65
- 1963–69, UNIONCAMERE, *I Conti Economici Regionali*, Milano: Franco Angeli, 1972
- 1970–79, SVIMEZ, *I conti del Centro-Nord e del Mezzogiorno nel ventennio 1970–1989*, Bologna: il Mulino, 1993

Units of labour

* 1951–59, ISTAT, *Occupazione in Italia negli anni 1951–65,* Supplementi straordinari al Bollettino Mensile di Statistica
* 1960–69, ISTAT, *Occupati per attività economica e regione 1960–1970*
* 1970–79, SVIMEZ, *op. cit.*

Deflators

* 1951–59, cost of living index at regional level, ISTAT, *Annuario Statistico Italiano, Bollettino Mensile di Statistica,* 1951–61
* 1960–69, index of consumption prices at the regional level, Padoa Schioppa (1988)
* 1970–79, price index of GDP and value added at the regional and sectoral level, SVIMEZ, *op. cit.*

Regions
The letter in parentheses indicates the inclusion of each region in a group: North–Centre (N), South (S), Adriatic (A).

PIE	Piemonte	(N)	MAR	Marche	(N)(A)
VDA	Valle D'Aosta	(N)	LAZ	Lazio	(N)
LIG	Liguria	(N)	CAM	Campania	(S)
LOM	Lombardia	(N)	ABR	Abruzzo	(S)(A)
TAA	Trentino Alto Adige	(N)	MOL	Molise	(S)(A)
VEN	Veneto	(N)(A)	PUG	Puglia	(S)(A)
FVG	Friuli Venezia Giulia	(N)(A)	BAS	Basilicata	(S)
EMR	Emilia Romagna	(N)(A)	CAL	Calabria	(S)
TOS	Toscana	(N)	SIC	Sicilia	(S)
UMB	Umbria	(N)	SAR	Sardegna	(S)

NOTES

* This paper is part of the CRENoS research project on regional disparities in Italy. We thank John Adams for his valuable comments and suggestions, and Nicola Pusceddu and Andrea Saba for valuable assistance in setting up the new and previous versions of CRENoS data banks, respectively. We gratefully acknowledge financial support from CNR.
1. Both distributions show a high peak for the richest region in 1951; this outlier is the small northern region of Valle d'Aosta.
2. All regions in the first two quartiles are in the North–Centre of Italy. Therefore this result confirms what we have previously remarked, that is the reduction in the overall income dispersion is mainly due to a convergence process among the Northern and Central Italian regions.
3. The choice of the grid points is obviously arbitrary. We have followed the criteria of including a similar number of individuals in each state while leaving the bounded state

with the same width. As a result the grid points (as percentage of the Italian average) are: 70, 90, 110 for per capita income and 80, 95, 110 for labour productivity. We have also tried with different grid points but, although the numeric results are slightly different, the qualitative findings do not change.

4. Examples of individual mobility in the relative distribution are initially wealthy regions that decline (Piemonte), together with initially poor that also decline (Sardegna); moreover there are regions that grow, starting either from medium (Veneto) or very low (Abruzzo) positions.

5. For instance, in the international literature a common way is to group together the African countries or the OECD or the OPEC ones. In cross-region regressions we may assume that regions within the same countries are affected in the same way by the unobservable variables, so that we can control by just including a set of national dummies.

6. A panel model of the convergence process among the Italian regions has been estimated by Di Liberto (1994), Boltho *et al.* (this volume, Chapter 13) and Cellini and Scorcu (1997). The results of these studies are not directly comparable with ours since they used different specifications, periods and data sets.

7. The use of the time dummies instead of *BC* yields results that are qualitatively similar to those presented below.

8. Our estimations are based on a least squares dummy variables (LSDV) model. The fixed effect formulation has been preferred over the random one since we assume that the individual effects are correlated with the exogenous variables. Indeed, this assumption seems quite reasonable since it implies that the unobservable variables, which are reflected by the individual effects, are correlated with the level of GDP per capita (or per worker) in each region. Moreover, since in panel regression we may have problems of both autocorrelation and heteroskedasticity, we have estimated the model with cross-section weights. In this formulation the observations with smaller variances receive a larger weight and thus have greater influence in the computed estimates. However, the standard LSDV model yields results very similar to those presented here.

9. We have identified 1975 as the break year since, as we have remarked in the previous section, in the mid-1970s the process of reduction in the regional dispersion came to a halt.

10. The existence of a specific growth pattern among the Mezzogiorno's region is a well known and widely studied issue in the literature on economic development in Italy. More recently several studies have focused on the positive growth of the so-called 'third Italy' which includes the Italian regions on the Adriatic sea. On this see the original contribution by Bagnasco (1977). The distinction between Adriatic and non-Adriatic regions seems particularly fruitful to analyse the growth differentials among the Southern regions, as we will show in Section 12.4.3.

11. For the exception to this general rule, recall Rybczynski's theorem (Rybczynski, 1955). This theorem deals with the case in which growth in the overall capital–labour ratio is associated with stability of the sectoral ratios. The conditions required by the theorem apply exclusively to the very special case of a small country facing the world market (for a recent use of this feature, see Ventura, 1996), but it is not relevant to the analysis of convergence across a finite number of regional economies.

12. See Table 2 regression 2.2 in Paci and Pigliaru (1997, p. 308).

13. In this section the initial year is 1960 since sectoral data at the regional level are not available for the 1950s.

14. Substituting the temporal dummies with the business cycle variable used in Section 12.3 would not alter substantially the results in Table 12.4.

15. A similar result was found by Paci and Pigliaru (1999) for the regions of the European Union.

16. Using an annual panel for the period 1960–1991, Di Liberto (1999) finds for the whole period that the variable measuring investment in machinery and equipment is significantly positive in convergence regressions. The role of this type of investment in explaining the North–South gap in per capita GDP is analysed by Boltho *et al.*

(Chapter 13, this volume). Finally, Paci and Pusceddu (1994) found a positive influence of the financial incentives made available by the Italian regional policy on the growth process of the Southern regions.
17. This evidence confirms and extends some of the findings about sectoral dynamics and convergence discussed in Paci and Pigliaru (1997a). Moreover, the catching up effect of the sectoral shifts from agriculture to high productivity sectors for the case of the European regions is noted in the contribution by Paci and Pigliaru in this volume (Chapter 8).
18. As for the econometric evidence in previous studies, a number of correlations between growth rates and several measures of the share of public expenditure in GDP have been reported by Di Liberto (1994), and by Paci and Pigliaru (1995). The evidence in this latter paper shows that over the period 1970–89 the convergence process is affected positively by a measure of the stock of public infrastructures and negatively by public consumption.
19. Patterns of this kind have been detected by Quah (1996) for the European regions.

REFERENCES

Bagnasco, A. (1977), *Tre Italie. La problematica territoriale dello sviluppo italiano*, Bologna: il Mulino.

Barro, R. and X. Sala-i-Martin (1995), *Economic Growth*, New York: McGraw-Hill.

Cellini, R. and A. Scorcu (1997), 'How many Italies? What data show about growth and convergence across Italian regions, 1970–91', *Rassegna di lavori dell'ISCO*, **14**, 93–124.

Chenery, H. (1962), *Politiche di sviluppo per l'Italia meridionale*, Milano: Giuffrè.

de la Fuente, A. (1998) 'What kind of regional convergence?', CEPR WP.

Del Monte, A. and A. Giannola (1997), *Istituzioni economiche e Mezzogiorno*, Roma: NIS.

Di Liberto, A. (1994), 'Convergence across Italian regions', *Nota di lavoro*, 68.94, Fondazione Eni Enrico Mattei.

Durlauf, S. and D. Quah (1998), 'The new empirics of economic growth', Centre for Economic Performance Discussion Paper no. 384.

Eckaus, R. (1961), 'The North–South differential in Italian economic development', *Journal of Economic History*, **20**, 285–317.

Evans, P. and G. Karras (1996), 'Do economies converge? Evidence from a panel of US states', *Review of Economics and Statistics*, **78**, 384–8.

Giannola, A. (1982), 'Industrializzazione, dualismo e dipendenza economica del Mezzogiorno negli anni '70', *Economia Italiana*, **4**, 65–90.

Graziani, A. (1978), 'The Mezzogiorno in the Italian economy', *Cambridge Journal of Economics*, **2**, 355–72.

Islam, N. (1995), 'Growth empirics: a panel data approach', *Quarterly Journal of Economics*, **110**, 1127–70.

Lutz, V. (1962) *Italy: A Study in Economic Development*, London: Oxford University Press.

Mas-Colell, A. and A. Razin (1973), 'A model of intersectoral migration and growth', *Oxford Economic Papers*, **25**, 72–9.

Myrdal, G. (1957), *Economic Theory and the Underdeveloped Regions*, London: Duckworth.

Paci, R. and F. Pigliaru (1995), 'Differenziali di crescita nelle regioni italiane: un'analisi *cross-section*', *Rivista di Politica Economica*, **85**, 3–34.

Paci, R. and F. Pigliaru (1997), 'Structural change and convergence: an Italian regional perspective', *Structural Change and Economic Dynamics*, **8**, 297–318.

Paci, R. and F. Pigliaru (1999), 'Is dualism still a source of convergence in Europe?', *Applied Economics*.

Paci, R. and N. Pusceddu (1994), 'Intervento pubblico, industrializzazione e crescita delle regioni del Mezzogiorno', *Studi Economici*, **54**, 67–95.

Paci, R. and A. Saba (1998), 'The empirics of regional economic growth in Italy, 1951–1993', *Rivista Internazionale di Scienze Economiche e Commerciali* (forthcoming).

Quah, D. (1993), 'Galton's fallacy and tests of the convergence hypothesis', *Scandinavian Journal of Economics*, **95**, 427–43.

Quah, D. (1996), 'Regional convergence clusters across Europe', *European Economic Review*, **40**, 951–8.

Rybczynski, T. (1955), 'Factor endowments and relative commodity prices', *Economica*, **22**, 336–41.

Sylos Labini, P. (1985), 'L'evoluzione economica del Mezzogiorno negli ultimi trenta anni', Temi di discussione, Servizio Studi Banca d'Italia, n.46.

Ventura, J. (1996), 'Growth and interdependence', *Quarterly Journal of Economics*, **112**, 57–84.

13. Will East Germany become a new Mezzogiorno?*

Andrea Boltho, Wendy Carlin and Pasquale Scaramozzino[1]

INTRODUCTION

In both popular and academic discussion, the regional economic problems that Germany has encountered since monetary unification in 1990 have often been compared to the North–South problem which Italy has been facing since the monetary unification of 1862. In particular, a number of writers have argued that the process of income convergence between East and West Germany could last an inordinately long time and be very costly, thus resembling the very slow, or possibly absent, convergence between Southern and Northern Italy over the last 130 years (Barro and Sala-i-Martin, 1991; Siebert, 1991; Hughes Hallett and Ma, 1993; Blien, 1994).

That a comparison between the two countries' regional experiences may be warranted is suggested by Table 13.1 which presents early 1990s information on selected economic indicators for the two areas. Both Eastern Germany and Southern Italy show significant gaps *vis-à-vis* the rest of the country in GDP per capita and unemployment levels, though less so in wage levels. Both areas, if in different proportions, also rely very heavily on a net transfer of resources from the central government. Such transfers ensure that consumption standards are relatively uniform across space, but, by the same token, they contribute to, and may even perpetuate, a model of regional dependence. Traditionally, this has been seen as one in which the weak region runs a persistent trade deficit with the rest of the country that allows a divergence between the levels of consumption and of value added per capita. In this area in particular, the seeds of a future Mezzogiorno problem could be sown in East Germany.

These, and other, similarities should not mask the presence of pronounced differences. For one thing, the Mezzogiorno accounts for a much larger share of the Italian economy than does East Germany with

Table 13.1   Selected indicators of the German and Italian regional problems, 1993

	Eastern Germany	Southern Italy
Shares in national totals		
Population	19.3	36.3
GDP	9.9	25.3
Ratios to rest of country		
GDP per capita	0.46	0.60
Consumption per capita	0.64	0.70
Gross fixed capital formation	1.17	0.63
Wage level in industry	0.65	0.90[a]
Unemployment rate	2.1[b]	2.5[c]
Net imports (% of regional GDP)	64.7	13.8

Notes:
[a]   1987.
[b]   Unemployment rate in East 15.0 per cent, in West 7.3 per cent. In addition, hidden unemployment represented some 17 per cent of the total East German labour force as against only 2 per cent in the West.
[c]   Unemployment rate in South 17.7 per cent, in Centre–North 7.0 per cent.

Sources: Statistisches Bundesamt, *Volkswirtschaftliche Gesamtrechnungen*, Fachserie 18, Reihe 1.3, 1995 Hauptbericht, and Sachverständigenrat, *Jahresgutachten, 1995/96* for East Germany; Commission of the European Communities (1993), and SVIMEZ, *Rapporto 1994 sull'Economia del Mezzogiorno*, Bologna: Il Mulino, 1994, for Southern Italy.

respect to West Germany. For another, the former GDR suffered from all the distortions of a command economy and was probably one of the most industrialized countries on earth (the share of manufacturing employment in the labour force was 35 per cent at the end of the 1980s). By contrast, Southern Italy (with a share not much above 11 per cent), lies well below the Italian average. Success for East Germany should thus entail a process of de-industrialization out of a legacy of 'mis-development'. Southern Italy, on the other hand, would seem to require some industrialization out of earlier agricultural 'under-development'.

Nevertheless, there are enough common elements in the two cases to justify a comparative empirical examination. So far this has been eschewed, in spite of the frequent use of the Mezzogiorno analogy in the debate on East German developments. In particular, it would appear important to see whether lessons can be drawn for Germany from the Italian experience of substantial, yet possibly ineffective, government intervention in the South. To this effect, the chapter begins by discussing Southern Italy's apparent failure to converge on the rest of the country in Section 13.1 and some of the reasons for this failure in Section 13.2. Section 13.3 then looks at German experience and policies since unification in the light of Italy's perceived difficulties. The conclusions summarize the main arguments.

13.1 HAS ITALY CONVERGED ?

A simple look at the ratios between GDP per capita in the South and in the rest of Italy (Figure 13.1) shows that the gap, now at some 40 per cent, is nearly as wide as it was in the early 1950s. Barring the period from 1960 to the mid-1970s, there would seem to be very little evidence of convergence. Indeed, since unification, increased divergence has probably occurred. Thus, tentative regional accounts for 1928 show that output per capita in the South was equal to as much as 70 per cent of that in the Centre-North (SVIMEZ, 1954). A careful analysis of the available data for the 1860s suggests that at the time the gap was even smaller, since *vis-à-vis* the North alone: 'a difference in per capita income ... of between 15 and 25 per cent seems plausible' (Eckaus, 1961, p. 300).

Figure 13.1   Southern Italian GDP per capita, 1928–1993 (Centre-North Italy = 100)

This apparent failure of Southern convergence would not have come as a surprise to some of the classic writers on regional problems. Kaldor (1970), in particular, had argued forcefully that processes of cumulative causation could dominate the neoclassical prediction of regional convergence. Similarly, Williamson (1965) had amply documented how, at least in countries at low and intermediate levels of development, regional divergence rather than convergence appeared to be the norm. Theories of endogenous growth would strengthen these conclusions. Recently, however, some writers have reaffirmed the validity of the more complacent neoclassical view by pointing to empirical evidence showing a relentless and all-pervasive movement towards the equalization of regional per capita incomes (Barro and Sala-i-Martin, 1991, 1995).

These authors have studied the process of convergence across the states of the United States (over more than one century), across Japanese prefectures (since 1930) and across regions within Western European countries (since World War II). The empirical regularity which emerges from their findings is that convergence takes place at some 2 per cent per year in almost all the contexts analysed. This is true also for Italy, although the country's convergence rate, at 1.55 per cent per annum, was found to be relatively low (Barro and Sala-i-Martin, 1995, p. 400).

In Solow's (1956) neoclassical growth model, the key to convergence is capital deepening in the presence of diminishing returns to capital. In the absence of barriers to the use of technology, or of systematic differences in preferences across regions, the model predicts that those areas in which the gap between actual and steady-state output per head is greatest will experience faster growth of the capital stock and of per capita incomes. More formally, the transitional dynamics for economy i is:

$$(1/T)\,[\ln(y_{i,t+T}) - \ln(y_{it})] = A_i - [(1 - e^{-\beta T})/T]\,\ln(y_{it}) + u_{i,t,t+T} \qquad (13.1)$$

where y_{it} is output per capita, β is the rate of convergence, A_i is a parameter which depends on the steady-state level of output per head and on the rate of technical progress and $u_{i,t,t+T}$ is a stochastic disturbance. Equation (13.1) implies that the rate of growth of output per capita over the time interval $(t, t+T)$ is inversely related to its initial level.

When estimating equation (13.1), a critical concern is the region-specific intercept coefficient, A_i. Barro and Sala-i-Martin (1991; 1995) posit that the relevant technology and preference parameters are the same across regions, implying that $A_i = A$, $\forall\ i$. Hence, there should be no systematic differences between regional growth rates after controlling for the initial levels of output per head (y_{it}). All regions would experience 'absolute β-convergence', while inclusion in equation (13.1) of variables other than output per capita would result in 'conditional β-convergence'. By contrast, if the intercept coefficients were to be different across regions, convergence would take place only among those regions which share the same coefficient. There would be convergence within, but not between, geographical areas to different steady-state equilibria. Convergence of output per head thus requires the equality of the intercept coefficients across all regions.

Whereas Barro and Sala-i-Martin apply regional data to equation (13.1) as a contribution to the general debate about the empirical support for the neoclassical growth model, this chapter's objectives are more limited. Rather than testing a specific model of growth,[2] this section's main concern with estimating equation (13.1) is to see whether regional gaps have persisted or diminished over time. An estimated positive β coefficient in equation (13.1) is a necessary, but not a sufficient, condition for a lower dispersion of output per capita (Lee, Pesaran and Smith, 1995). By contrast, if the convergence parameter β is negative, the dispersion of output per capita must have necessarily increased (Hart, 1995). Likewise, Canova and Marcet (1995) have proven that 'β-convergence' is a necessary, although not a sufficient, requirement for the reduction of regional inequalities. Hence, failure of β-convergence can be interpreted as evidence of the persistence of such inequalities. In particular, if the intercept coefficients in equation (13.1) are different across groups of regions, there is no convergence to a common steady state. Also, divergence would occur if the estimated parameter β in equation (13.1) turns out to be negative. Thus, while 'absolute β-convergence' does not necessarily imply a reduction in regional inequalities, its failure conclusively means that such inequalities have increased.

Bearing this in mind, Table 13.2 reports estimates of the transitional dynamics parameters, according to equation (13.1), over various sub-periods from 1928 to 1991 for Italy's 20 regions.[3] The most striking feature is that the convergence parameter, β, is wrongly signed for the period 1928–38 and, although it has a modest positive value for 1938–48 and 1950–60, this is not statistically significant. For this earlier period there is no evidence of an inverse relationship between the growth of GDP per capita and its initial level. The area dummies for the Centre and the South attract a negative coefficient that, for the South, is significant over the period 1938–48 suggesting divergence between North and South.

The years 1960 to 1970, on the other hand, show that the rate of convergence, β, is positive, statistically significant and high (some 5 per cent per annum), while the regional dummies are insignificant. Rapid convergence clearly took place in this period. The same, however, is no longer true for the 1970s and 1980s. In the 1970s, β is high but the dummy vari-

Table 13.2 Italy: regressions for per capita output growth, 1928–1991

	1928–38	1938–48	1950–60	1960–70	1970–80	1980–91
Dependent variable: $[\ln(y_{i,t+T})-\ln(y_{it})]/T$						
Constant	−0.0185	0.0396	0.0298*	−0.1854**	−0.2955**	−0.0026
	(0.0435)	(0.0779)	(0.0105)	(0.0441)	(0.0794)	(0.0701)
β	−0.0028	0.0063	0.0051	0.0528**	0.1022*	0.0059
	(0.0053)	(0.0103)	(0.0112)	(0.0135)	(0.0430)	(0.0156)
Centre	−0.0031	−0.0048	−0.0060	−0.0018	−0.0071	0.0029
	(0.0026)	(0.0050)	(0.0055)	(0.0042)	(0.0054)	(0.0037)
South	−0.0066	−0.0180*	−0.0052	−0.0112	−0.0323**	0.0023
	(0.0035)	(0.0071)	(0.0082)	(0.0071)	(0.0099)	(0.0082)
SE	0.0038	0.0070	0.0077	0.0058	0.0076	0.0051
F-stat (d.o.f.)	5.506	5.184	0.401	28.851	6.521	1.562
	(3,14)	(3,14)	(3,16)	(3,16)	(3,16)	(3,16)
w (d.o.f.)	3.516 (2)	6.959 (2)	1.189 (2)	2.913 (2)	11.198 (2)	0.661 (2)
R_2	0.541	0.526	0.070	0.844	0.550	0.227

Notes:
Estimated equation: equation (13.1) in text plus area dummies.
Estimation method: non-linear least squares.
Figures in brackets are standard errors.
w: Wald test on the joint significance of the area dummies, distributed as χ^2 (d.o.f.) under H_o.
*   Significant at 5 per cent.
**   Significant at 1 per cent.
*** Significant at 0.1 per cent.

able for the South is negative and very significant, pointing to a process of convergence within, but not between, South and Centre-North regions.[4] The years 1980–91 see an interruption in both forms of convergence; β is very small and not statistically significant as are the area dummies. When estimated over the whole period 1950–91, the coefficient β is positive and significant (β = 0.0399, SE = 0.0180) but the dummy variable for the South is significantly negative (coefficient = −0.0078, SE = 0.0030).[5]

Overall, the evidence provides little support for the view that Italy has converged. Except for the 1960s, convergence was either absent or limited to the convergence of the Southern regions among themselves. Hence the

'2 per cent rule', or '1.55 per cent rule', suggested by Barro and Sala-i-Martin (1995) does not seem to apply to the Italian case.[6]

13.2   THE ITALIAN FAILURE

The absence of any significant convergence through most of the post-war period came despite a substantial public effort designed to develop the South. Between 1951 and 1990, discretionary intervention in the form of investment incentives and the building of infrastructures averaged some 4 per cent of Southern output and about 1 per cent of Italy's GDP. To this must be added the investment of state-owned corporations that were required to locate up to 80 per cent of their capital formation in the South (Podbielski, 1978). This target was never fully met but the investments made were equal to nearly 3 per cent of regional GDP in the 1960s and 1970s. Finally, the region received a flow of automatic transfers that greatly exceeded its tax payments. Estimates for 1988 suggest that the public sector's net transfer of resources to the South was similar to the area's external deficit, or some 19 per cent of regional GDP (Galli, 1992). Although such figures are well below the recent levels of transfers to East Germany, flows of this size have been kept up for 30 to 40 years.

Despite all this, the North–South gap has remained stubbornly in place. The literature has pointed to a number of reasons for this – an excess of bureaucracy and regulation (Wolleb and Wolleb, 1990), poorer infrastructure (D'Antonio and Vinci, 1992), an inefficient financial system (Faini *et al.*, 1993), insufficient wage gaps (Padoa Schioppa Kostoris, 1993), trade union behaviour (Faini, 1994), and so on. Indeed, writers have increasingly attributed failure to the development effort itself (Trigilia, 1992). Yet, while many of these factors seem plausible, they often fail to explain the evolution of the problem over time. As Figure 13.1 suggests, and as Section 13.1 has shown more precisely, regional differentials closed rapidly in the 1960s only to re-open thereafter. Southern infrastructure, however, did not worsen suddenly after 1970 nor did the efficiency of the region's financial sector. Furthermore, the unit labour cost gap between North and South, after shrinking in the early 1970s, has remained roughly constant since about 1976 (Figure 13.2). Answers need to be provided not only to why the South is still backward today but also to why some convergence occurred over a number of years and then stalled.

The literature suggests that regional convergence may fail for two major reasons. First, the neoclassical assumption of a common steady state across regions of a country may be unwarranted. Different areas may belong to different 'convergence clubs' (Baumol, 1986, p. 1079) for com-

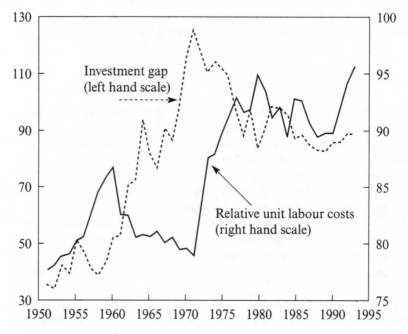

*Figure 13.2 Ratios of Southern Italy's share of investment in machinery
and equipment in GDP and unit labour costs to equivalent
Centre-North Italian figures, 1951–1993*

plex reasons linked to their 'social capability' for growth. This concept
embraces those 'tenacious societal characteristics' that either promote the
'adaptability of education and of industrial and financial organization to
the requirements of modern large-scale technology' (Abramovitz, 1986,
p. 396) or hinder this adaptability through, for example, the pressures of
vested interests. Alternatively, the investment response needed to close the
productivity gap may fail to emerge. In the neoclassical model in which
investment responds to rate of return differentials, failure may be due to
market imperfections that prevent factor endowments from being reflected
in their relative prices. In models of cumulative causation, on the other
hand, investment responds to externalities that may be concentrated in the
richer areas (Krugman and Venables, 1990).

The Role of Investment and Wages

Political unification of a low- and a high-productivity region permits
major deviations of both investment and relative costs from their market-

determined values. Policy can influence the level of investment so as to try to overcome unfavourable agglomeration economies or inadequate social capability. Institutions, on the other hand, such as national wage bargaining or social security systems, can worsen regional competitiveness. This suggests including both investment and relative costs in any explanation of the course of regional differentials. Investment proxies the growth of the capital stock and reflects the policy effort. Competitiveness matters since it plays both a supply and a demand role – low regional costs boost investment and generate net exports. Both, in turn, support employment and reduce dependence on transfers.

Testing this hypothesis involves estimating an equation which links the South to Centre-North ratio of per capita GDP in constant prices (y_m/y_{cn}) to a similar ratio of the two regions' share of investment in machinery and equipment in GDP (*mei*) and to the real exchange rate between the two halves of the country, proxied by the ratio of the two regions' unit labour costs in the industrial sector (*ulc*),[7] as well as to lagged values of the dependent variable. The results, shown in equation (13.2), support the hypothesis that convergence in the 1960s, and lack of convergence both before and after, were importantly influenced by the course of investment and competitiveness (or the real exchange rate), as also illustrated in Figure 13.2:

$$y_m/y_{cn} = 0.267^{**} + 0.017^* mei_{t-1} - 0.127^{**} ulc_{t-1} + 0.348^* (y_m/y_{cn})_{t-1} + 0.368^* (y_m/y_{cn})_{t-2}$$
$$(0.094) \quad (0.008) \qquad (0.042) \qquad (0.161) \qquad\qquad (0.146) \qquad (13.2)$$
$$R^2 = 0.759; \; SE = 0.011; \; LM(1) = 0.896$$
(figures in brackets are standard errors)

In the 1960s, investment in the South was buoyant, productivity growth accelerated and, despite a gradual closing in wage differentials, unit labour costs declined relative to those of the Centre-North. In the first half of the 1970s these trends were reversed largely because of important breaks in regional policies and in the working of the labour market.

At the policy level, a significant retrenchment occurred in the Southern operations of state-owned companies. These had concentrated their activities on the creation of large-scale plants in heavy industry that were hard hit by the oil shock. After 1974, their share of investment in the South was slashed.[8] This shift in policy played a large role in widening the North–South gap, as suggested by equation (13.3) which, with a high degree of statistical significance, links the investment variable (*mei*) that was seen to have been so important in explaining convergence (or its absence) in equation (13.2) to the lagged share of total investment by state-owned companies carried out in the South (*ppss*).[9] Competitiveness was found to be insignificant in this equation, underlining the importance of policy in determining regional investment:

$$mei = 0.097 + 0.460*ppss_{t-1} + 0.724***mei_{t-1} \qquad (13.3)$$
$$(0.060) \quad (0.224) \qquad\quad (0.087)$$

$$R^2 = 0.856; \text{SE} = 0.077; \text{LM}(1) = 0.280$$
(figures in brackets are standard errors)

The shift in investment policy interacted with greater labour market rigidities consequent upon the strikes and wage explosions of the 'Hot Autumn' movement of the late 1960s. This resulted in the abolition of regional wage differentials and added to the rapid erosion of Southern competitiveness illustrated in Figure 13.2. As a consequence, factor mobility was diminished (Attanasio and Padoa Schioppa, 1991) and virtually all links between local labour market conditions and wage negotiations were suppressed (Faini, 1994).

The policy and institutional developments outlined above provide an explanation for the break in convergence that occurred in the 1970s but do not throw much light on why that process had not, by then, become self-sustaining. Nor do they explain the absence, in the subsequent two decades, of new market or policy forces propelling Southern growth.

That the South was unable to build on a decade of convergence may have owed a lot to the nature of the industrial development of the 1960s. As noted above, this had been concentrated on the creation of large-scale plants in state-owned basic and heavy industry. By the time these were hit by the oil shocks, they had failed to generate significant induced effects on employment and investment in other local enterprises. Input–output tables show, for instance, that the sectors that had been stimulated by policies are characterized by a low share of wages and salaries in value added, by weak backward linkage effects and by a high need for inputs (such as energy, transport, marketing, research, or engineering), that come mainly from firms outside the region (Giannola, 1979, 1982).

Transfers and Rentseeking

As for the absence of new growth stimuli, this can be linked, at least in part, to further policy and institutional changes. First, the retrenchment in public investment was offset by a sharp shift towards income maintenance flows and the recruitment of civil servants. By the late 1980s, the government, via salaries and transfers, was generating some 50 per cent of Southern household disposable income[10] and was probably responsible for as much as 60 per cent of resource allocation (Wolleb and Wolleb, 1990). By reinforcing dependence, this is likely to have had detrimental effects on risk-taking and entrepreneurship.

In addition, from the early 1970s, Italy also witnessed a sharp rise in local government expenditure.[11] In part, this reflected a major administrative decentralization to newly created regional bodies and, almost certainly, worsened the quality of public sector intervention. In particular, the devolution of significant spending powers to local government raised the scope for political interference with technical decisions (SVIMEZ, 1993) and for rentseeking activities that are usually easier to pursue at a local, rather than national, level (Olson, 1982). Local politicians were given greater scope for lobbying the central government in order to attract funds to their regions and local entrepreneurs found that the trade-off between business and rentseeking activities had shifted in favour of the latter.

Although this devolution of expenditure applied to the whole country, it is plausible to think that its effects on the scale of lobbying and corruption were more pronounced in the South than in the rest of Italy. After all, as argued by a recent in-depth analysis of Italian regional differences in the area of civic traditions, the Centre and North of the country are 'characterized by a dense network of local associations, by active engagement in community affairs, by egalitarian patterns of politics, by trust and law-abidingness. [In the South] political and social participation [are] organized vertically, not horizontally. Mutual suspicion and corruption [are] regarded as normal. ... Lawlessness [is] expected' (Putnam, 1993, p. 182). The South, in other words, was almost certainly a more fertile ground for the hi-jacking of government expenditures for private gain.

As this account suggests, the changing nature of government intervention in the 1970s and 1980s may have contributed to the reversal of the convergence process. Switching support away from capital formation was clearly detrimental to growth, given the important role of investment in the earlier closing of the GDP gap. Concentrating aid on salaries and transfers strengthened union behaviour inimical to flexibility (Faini, 1994). And administrative devolution, combined with changes in political practices, is likely to have raised the scope for collusion between the administration and the private sector (Sylos-Labini, 1985), encouraging corruption and, at times, providing 'soft' budget constraints to firms with sufficient lobbying strength (Commission of the European Communities, 1993).

Several lessons appear relevant for East Germany. The successes of the 1960s owe much to the simultaneous presence of reasonably flexible labour markets and of reasonably efficient policies (Sarcinelli, 1989).

Investment rose sharply and the area's real exchange rate fell. Intervention was far from perfect. In particular, the emphasis on capital-intensive sectors appears, with the benefit of a hindsight that follows the oil shocks, to have yielded disappointing results. Yet, the focus on investment sharply reduced the productivity gap and, for the first time in the century since unification, some convergence occurred. When one or more of these various factors fell short, however, the gap failed to close. In the 1950s, policy efforts were still limited while rapid Northern growth was strengthening centripetal tendencies. In the 1970s and 1980s, by contrast, labour market flexibility was impaired. In addition, aid had shifted away from investment while administrative reforms were depressing an already low level of social capability by allowing greater interference by politicians, lobbies and even criminal groups in the allocation of public funds.

13.3   GERMAN REUNIFICATION AND CONVERGENCE

As is well known, Germany inherited a massive regional problem upon unification. Early government pronouncements that this problem could be quickly solved soon gave way to more sober assessments (for example, Sachverständigenrat, *Annual Reports*; Sinn and Sinn, 1991; Bryson, 1992). Extrapolating their results from the United States and Western Europe, Barro and Sala-i-Martin suggested, for instance, that 'it would take 35 years for half of the initial East–West gap to be eliminated' (1991, p. 154). To accelerate this process, the country embarked on an historically unprecedented transfer of resources. Italy's experience suggests, however, that this may not be enough to ensure convergence if investment and competitiveness remain low. While consumption standards can be pulled up, GDP per capita may lag behind and dependence could persist. Even a determined investment effort may be insufficient if it is associated with low competitiveness. This raises unemployment by encouraging the premature scrapping of existing capital, stimulating capital–labour substitution on new equipment, and weakening private incentives to invest. Low competitiveness, in other words, perpetuates the need for transfers.

This section examines the prospects for East German convergence in the light of Italy's experience, by looking, first, at the course of investment, second at the problem of regional competitiveness, and finally at the broader issue of the area's social capability for growth.

Investment

The regional development effort, proxied by East Germany's trade deficit and equal to nearly 70 per cent of GDP between 1991 and 1994, has not just allowed rapid growth in incomes and consumption but has also made possible a very high investment share (almost 50 per cent of Eastern GDP versus 20 per cent in the West). Three major instruments have been used to promote investment, for two of which parallels can be found in the Italian experience. As in Italy, the government has invested directly in infrastructure, in view of the strong complementarities between social overhead capital and business investment (Bach *et al.,* 1994; Seitz and Licht, 1995) and, as in Italy, it has provided direct subsidies to capital formation (Lichtblau, 1993). Estimates suggest that roughly half the total investment has been financed by the public sector, through infrastructure spending and subsidies to firms, with private investment on average subsidized by one third (Schmidt, 1996).

In addition, investment has been promoted by the privatization policy. When state-owned firms were sold, an important criterion in the evaluation of competing bids was the ability of the purchaser to provide a commitment to raise the capital stock per worker to the levels found in similar firms in West Germany (Carlin and Mayer, 1992). In this context, a very important difference with Italian experience has been the weight put on the private sector. While in Southern Italy, as late as 1981, nearly 30 per cent of manufacturing employment was still in public sector establishments (Guglielmetti *et al.*, 1994), in East Germany this proportion had fallen from almost 100 per cent in 1989 to virtually zero by 1994 (Carlin and Mayer, 1995). There was also a remarkable shift away from the large-scale plant characteristic of the *Kombinat* of the former GDR. The average establishment size of privately owned firms is now one-third *smaller* than is typical of West Germany (DIW, *Wochenbericht*, No.27, 1996).

The period since unification is too short for a time-series analysis that could assess the contribution of investment to convergence. Cross-section data, however, can shed light on the extent to which rising investments are correlated with the catch-up of East to West German levels of productivity in manufacturing.[12] The available data cover gross value added per employee for 25 two-digit industrial sectors in 1991 to 1994 and corresponding cumulative total investment levels per employee. To test for the significance of the cumulative investment variable two specifications were used, looking respectively at gaps in, and levels of, productivity. In the first, equation (13.4), the dependent variable is the ratio of East to West German productivity in 1994 (π_{eg}/π_{wg}). Three of the

25 industries are clear outliers: the highly capital-intensive sectors of chemicals, non-ferrous metals and pulp and paper processing. Long gestation periods, particularly in the pulp industry,[13] and a complex and slow privatization process in the two other sectors, with a consequent delay in restructuring and investment, account for their anomalous behaviour. Omitting these industries from the regression gives results that provide considerable support to the hypothesis that East German productivity is higher relative to that in the West in those industries in which cumulative investment per employee (*cinv*) has been the highest:

$$\pi_{eg}/\pi_{wg} = 0.377^{***} + 2.189^{*}cinv \qquad (13.4)$$
$$(0.052) \qquad (0.912)$$

$R^2 = 0.218$; SE $= 0.194$ (figures in brackets are standard errors)

A more direct test of whether the level of Eastern productivity in 22 industrial sectors in 1994 was a function of its level in 1991 ($\pi_{eg}94$) and of cumulative investment in the intervening period, shown in equation (13.5), confirms the significant contribution màde by capital formation to productivity:

$$\pi_{eg}94 = 14.461^{*} + 209.510^{**}cinv + 0.928^{*}\pi_{eg}91 \qquad (13.5)$$
$$(5.562) \quad (57.139) \qquad (0.379)$$

$R^2 = 0.613$; SE $= 12.718$ (figures in brackets are standard errors)

As in Italy, investment has spurred productivity growth and convergence but, unlike Italy, East Germany has avoided the narrow sectoral concentration of Italian capital formation.[14] Compared with the West, manufacturing investment is biased towards sectors geared to the domestic market (for example, construction materials and food) and is much weaker in automobiles, while being comparable in mechanical engineering and chemicals. Yet, from the perspective of the economy as a whole, the overall investment effort has been twisted in favour of non-tradable sectors. Whereas total gross fixed capital formation per capita in the East was 45 per cent above that in the West, investment in machinery and equipment in manufacturing was equal in the two regions. The initial effort in infrastructure was, no doubt, indispensable but a good deal more will have to be achieved in private industry to lessen firms' dependence on subsidies to bridge the gap between wages and productivity.

Wage Flexibility and Regional Competitiveness

While subsidies can raise investment projects with low profitability, Italy's experience suggests that competitiveness has a separate influence on convergence. A high real exchange rate implies a narrow export base which constrains the level of output and employment. With net imports still equivalent to some 60 per cent of GDP in 1994, the expansion of the tradable base is crucial for reducing dependence and creating self-sustaining growth. Two institutional changes which came with unification exacerbated the competitiveness problem: the transfers of the Western wage bargaining structures and welfare systems. Wage convergence was thus expected to be very rapid. The 1991 industry–labour agreements foresaw that, in the key engineering sector, Eastern wage rates would achieve parity by early 1994. In fact, convergence has been slower than originally expected. Thus, while negotiated rates in engineering had reached 87 per cent of the West German level at the end of 1994, gross monthly earnings in industry were at only 70 per cent of that level in 1995 (*WSI Mitteilungen*, No.3, 1995; Statistisches Bundesamt, *Tabellen-sammlung zur wirtschaftlichen und sozialen Lage in den neuen Bundesländern*, 4/96).

Survey evidence suggests that there is considerable heterogeneity in wage setting. For the period when most firms were still owned by the privatization agency (the *Treuhandanstalt*), official rates were paid regardless of profitability and local labour market conditions but, as privatization proceeded, a more diversified wage structure has emerged. Large West German or foreign companies typically pay official rates but in small and medium-sized firms owned by East German or by small West German companies, in which modernization is advancing more slowly, wages below official levels are frequent.[15]

The East German labour market is now operating with greater flexibility than the formal structure of wage setting would suggest. Despite the encouraging evidence on productivity convergence, however, manufacturing unit labour costs in 1995 were still nearly 30 per cent higher in the East than in the West (although down from 90 per cent in 1991) – a gap a good deal larger than the 5 per cent differential between the two halves of Italy. This hinders employment since workers with very similar characteristics to those in East Germany can be found just across the border in Poland or in the Czech Republic at only a fraction of East German wages or even of East German unemployment benefits.

Rentseeking and Social Capability

The post-unification mismatch between the paths of income and economic convergence is highlighted by the diverging trends of income and output. By 1995, the average East German household had an income level nearly three-quarters that of the average West German one (over 85 per cent in purchasing power terms), while the economy was producing value added at just over 50 per cent of the West German per capita level (the corresponding figures for Italy are approximately 70 and 60 per cent respectively). Excluding the activities of the privatization agency, net public sector transfers to the East over the period 1991–95 amounted to 4.25 per cent of West German GDP (Deutsche Bundesbank, 1996). Slowly rising tax revenues, in combination with broadly unchanged gross transfers, are expected to lead to some declines in net transfers from 1996.

The sheer magnitude of these figures is bound to raise incentives for the diversion of subsidies into non-productive uses. This, in turn, would slow down convergence and could risk the perpetuation of dependence. The study of Italy helps to bring a perspective to bear on the question of rentseeking behaviour and its relation with development. In particular, it suggests the need to distinguish opportunities for one-off capture of rents from a culture that fosters unproductive activities and that, in Southern Italy, may have had long-standing roots that were apparently not eradicated by post-war growth.

The significance of this analysis for Germany is that history and institutions may be important in determining how far the rentseeking that can arise in a situation of regional dependence becomes embedded in the political and economic culture. Three factors seem relevant for an evaluation of the likelihood of this problem developing: the nature of 'civil society' in the East prior to the division of Germany, the nature of the break in coalitions provided by unification, and the efficiency characteristics of the new or transferred institutions in East Germany through which a rentseeking culture could develop.

An indirect indicator of the social capability of East Germany is its successful earlier industrialization. Figure 13.3 indicates that, including all of Berlin in East Germany, GDP per capita in the East was some 20 per cent higher than in the West between 1913 and 1936. A rough allocation of Berlin's output between East and West still shows an advantage for East Germany in 1936. This historical background sharply distinguishes East Germany from Southern Italy. The prior existence of a flourishing market economy and of successful manufacturing traditions may prove very important in the convergence process.

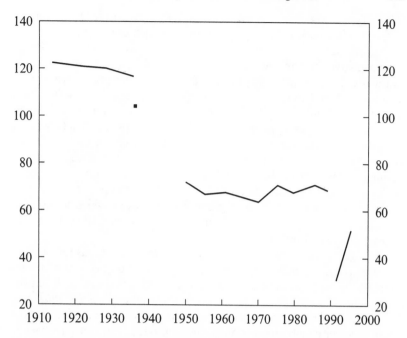

Figure 13.3 East German GDP per capita, 1913–1995 (West Germany = 100)

Unification brought with it sharp institutional changes. The central and regional divisions, or *Bezirk*, of the former GDR were replaced by five *Länder* created from scratch. Although the set-up and the personnel of the lowest level of administration (county and local) were initially left untouched, the new *Länder* embarked on a major territorial and organizational reform of these lower tiers (Wollmann, 1994) resulting in a comprehensive replacement of the élite in the East. While at the *Länder* level this has involved a significant influx of West Germans into top public service positions, at the local level replacement has come from within the East (Wollmann and Berg, 1994). Despite such upheavals, administrative efficiency does not seem to have suffered. Indeed, innovative policy design has been documented in a number of key fields (Wollmann, 1994). A recent study of citizens' attitudes towards local government concludes, on the basis of an econometric analysis of survey evidence, that satisfaction with the East German administration is only some 9 per cent below the equivalent level in the West (Cusack, 1996). The material assembled in Putnam (1993) would strongly suggest that the relative level of dissatisfaction with local government would be much greater in the Italian South.

The foregoing has suggested a number of positive developments: investment has been rising rapidly, some convergence is occurring in manufacturing productivity levels, wage setting is becoming more flexible, administrative reforms seem to have been handled with relative efficiency and a break appears to have taken place with the pre-existing power structure. More broadly, East Germany would seem to be much better placed than Southern Italy in terms of its social capability for convergence to Western levels of per capita GDP. In particular, it has benefited from the wholesale transfer of West Germany's rich institutional framework in the form, for instance, of the industrial relations and vocational training systems, or of the networks of savings, co-operative and development banks. It will take time for these institutions to operate as effectively as in the West but at least the region seems to have avoided many of the institutional weaknesses of Southern Italy. On balance, the emergence of a 'dependence culture' appears unlikely.

These various factors provide a set of necessary conditions for successful convergence. They may, however, not be sufficient unless competitiveness improves further and the size of the tradable sector that eventually emerges is large enough to create 'current account' balance, thereby eliminating dependence on transfers from the West. Competitiveness can be improved either by lowering labour costs or by raising productivity. Cutting wages and social security provisions is clearly very difficult. Ongoing reforms of the German wage negotiation and welfare systems are pointing in the right direction but the process will be slow. The alternative of subsidizing employment, advocated by some observers (Akerlof *et al.*, 1991), seems to have been ruled out. Hence the need to raise productivity by keeping up the investment effort, even if this may not be first best policy.[16]

Even with a more appropriate real exchange rate, East Germany's manufacturing sector may remain too small to eliminate dependence. Employment in manufacturing stood at only 16 per cent of total employment in 1995 as against 27 per cent in West Germany, but only 11 per cent in Southern Italy. Yet, this need not preclude the achievement of a reasonably high level of output per capita. A simple regression, equation (13.6), for Western Europe's regions, linking 1990 GDP per capita, in purchasing power parity terms (y_i), to the share of manufacturing in total employment (nmf_i), and to a dummy variable for the Spanish and Portuguese regions whose productivity is very low (dum_{ep}), confirms the importance of manufacturing for the attainment of high living standards:[17]

$$y_i = 64.289^{***} + 1.487^{***}nmf_i - 24.804^{***}dum_{ep} \qquad (13.6)$$
$$ (4.558) \qquad (0.186) \qquad (3.229)$$

$R^2 = 0.662$; SE $= 12.675$ (figures in brackets are standard errors)

Together with a very similar result for 1985, this would suggest that a 16 per cent manufacturing employment share is compatible with a GDP per capita level of 85 to 90 per cent of the European average, which is well above the 70 to 75 per cent of the Mezzogiorno.

Such a figure would still leave the region below West Germany, but, arguably, more is possible. The area is well endowed with human capital. The presence of urban centres, such as Berlin, Leipzig and Dresden, could attract footloose service activities, lead to agglomeration economies and stimulate the growth of, at least, the surrounding *Länder* of Brandenburg and Saxony. It is striking that the regions that surround the capitals of Europe's three other major economies[18] all enjoy above average GDP per capita levels, yet have shares of manufacturing employment similar to, or below, those of East Germany.

CONCLUSIONS

The process of regional economic convergence within nations raises special features that differentiate it from the more general issue of convergence between countries. Political unification removes a weaker region's external constraint and creates an opportunity for more rapid capital accumulation than the one usually available to sovereign countries for which a closed economy assumption can be justified (Feldstein and Horioka, 1980). In addition, unification brings with it, almost automatically, a measure of per capita income equalization through the operation of a unified tax and social security system. The former factor can be expected to boost supply, the latter demand. Through both, regional convergence could well be more rapid than intra-country convergence, as long as capital and labour mobility are preserved.

Yet, there are forces working in the opposite direction. For one thing, centripetal tendencies can operate via strong scale and agglomeration economies in the richer region. For another, reliance on transfers from the central government brings with it the possibility of persistent dependence of the weaker region on the stronger. Dependence of this kind may foster the diversion of resources to unproductive activities and operate against convergence. In addition, a well-known feature of some political unions, present in both the Italian and German cases, is the extension of wage bargaining institutions and of negotiated wage rates across the country. Since poorer regions are characterized by the existence of a productivity gap, the premature equalization of real product wages weakens their competitiveness. This, in turn, raises unemployment and deters private capital inflows as well as emigration, particularly if social security provisions are generous.

Regional policy can encourage private investment in the poorer region in order to overcome unfavourable externalities and/or the effects of rapid wage equalization. In the absence of high investment, however, the region's real exchange rate will remain 'too high' and transfers could become endemic. Yet, high investment alone may not be sufficient for success. Convergence also requires the prior existence of a social capability for growth which may be impaired by either the historical legacy or by dependence itself.

The Italian experience highlights the empirical relevance of these features of the convergence process. Catch-up in the 1960s was associated with a falling real exchange rate thanks to a relatively flexible labour market and a sustained policy effort focused on investment, while its cessation in the 1970s coincided with a reduction of publicly encouraged investment. At the same time, the reduced sensitivity of wages to regional labour market conditions further impaired Southern competitiveness. The concomitant shift in the focus of policy towards rapidly increasing salary and transfer payments, combined with an increased weight of local government control over spending, created opportunities for the entrenchment of rentseeking and dependence.

East Germany's initial experience showed some of the negative features associated with Italy (for example, rapid wage equalization and huge transfers for income maintenance). Yet, on balance, Germany may have avoided a number of the mistakes made by Italian policymakers. In particular, a rather broad-based investment effort, mainly in private firms, has been initiated while claims for wage parity are being modified and accompanied by the emergence of more realistic forms of bargaining. A relatively efficient process of administrative reform may also prevent the large-scale diversion of massive transfers into rentseeking activities, contrary to what happened in the Mezzogiorno.

It is too early to know whether the leaner and more efficient manufacturing and other tradable sectors which are emerging in the region will prosper sufficiently to eliminate eventually any need for continuing net transfers from the West. Competitiveness is still poor and its improvement requires further investment given that major reductions in labour costs are unlikely. The main danger from a policy standpoint, highlighted by the Italian experience, is that investment support will be withdrawn prematurely. This danger has been heightened, in 1996–97, by the pressure for fiscal consolidation imposed on the government by the Maastricht conditions for European Monetary Union at a time of near recession. Yet, a guardedly optimistic assessment can still be ventured. In part this reflects some of the encouraging recent trends discussed in Section 13.3 above. In part it also reflects a more qualitative judgement based on the two regions' longer-run, and very different, experiences. Much of East Germany has had a tradition of relative prosperity, industry and entrepreneurship; much of the Mezzogiorno has had one of poverty, backward agriculture and lack of civic involvement on the part of its population. In the end, history may matter just as much as the design of economic policies and the working of market forces.

DATA APPENDIX

Italy

National accounts and employment data for the two major territorial divisions (South and Centre-North) for the years 1970–93 come from SVIMEZ, *I conti economici del Centro-nord e del Mezzogiorno nel ventennio 1979–1989*, Bologna: Il Mulino, 1993 and *Rapporto 1994 sull' economia del Mezzogiorno*, Bologna: Il Mulino, 1994. Data for 1951 to 1970 were obtained by linking an earlier series that appears in SVIMEZ, 'La formazione e l'impiego delle risorse e l'occupazione del Mezzogiorno e del Centro-nord dal 1951 al 1983', *Studi Svimez*, No.1, 43–128, 1985. Data on the share of public corporation investment undertaken in the South come from Padoa Schioppa Kostoris (1993) for the years 1960–88 and from various annual SVIMEZ, *Rapporto sull'economia del Mezzogiorno* for 1989–93. Figures for 1957–59 were estimated using data contained in Del Monte, A. (1984), 'The effects of regional policy on the industrial development of the South of Italy', *Mezzogiorno d'Europa*, 4 (4), 563-83.

GDP per capita data for individual regions for the years 1928, 1938 and 1948 come from SVIMEZ, *Statistiche sul Mezzogiorno d'Italia, 1861–1953*, Rome 1954, while data for 1950 and 1960 were found in Molle, Willem, Bas van Holst and Hans Smit, *Regional Disparity and Economic Development in the European Community*, Farnborough: Saxon House, 1980. Annual data for the years 1960–91 come from a data bank constructed by the Fondazione ENI Enrico Mattei in Milan.

Germany

Cross-section value added and employment data for East and West Germany in 1991 and 1993 come from Statistisches Bundesamt, *Fachserie 4*, Reihe 4.3.1–4.3.3. Gross value added at factor prices for East German industries for 1994 was estimated by applying the 1993 turnover/value added ratio to the turnover data in Statistisches Bundesamt, *Fachserie 4*,

Reihe 4.1.1. The 1994 East/West productivity ratio uses 1993 West German data. Investment figures come from *Ifo Schnelldienst*, No.24, 1995. Data unavailability or incompatibility between the productivity and investment series meant that the sectors mineral oil processing, aircraft and spacecraft, and office machinery had to be omitted. The food, drink and tobacco branches were consolidated as were the two parts of the leather industry. Most of the remaining data for East Germany given in the text and in the table come from Statistisches Bundesamt, *Volkswirtschaftliche Gesamtrechnungen* (various issues). 1995 data for both East and West Germany, when available, will follow a different (EU NACE) industry classification.

GDP per capita data for East and West Germany in the years 1913–36 come from *Statistisches Handbuch von Deutschland, 1928–1944*, München: Länderrat des amerikanischen Besatzungsgebiet, 1949. The 1936 estimate dividing East and West Berlin assumes a uniform income per capita for each part of the city. For the years 1936–89, the data come from Maddison, Angus (1995), *Monitoring the World Economy, 1929–1992*, Paris: OECD. According to Maddison, East German growth would appear to be overestimated by these figures. If the growth rate of Czechoslovakia were used instead, East Germany's GDP per capita in 1989 would be 46 per cent of the West German level, rather than 69 per cent. The 1991–95 data come from Statistisches Bundesamt, *Volkswirtschaftliche Gesamtrechnungen*, 1996. Detailed national accounts for East Germany will not be produced from 1995 onwards.

NOTES

*   Reprinted by permission of Academic Press Inc. from *Journal of Comparative Economics*, **24**, 241–64 (1997).

1.   The authors wish to thank, but not implicate, two anonymous referees, Chris Allsopp, Bart van Ark, V. Bhaskar, Thomas Cusack, Ben Fine, Michael Funke, Christopher Gilbert, Andrew Glyn, Jonathan Haskel, Deborah Johnston, Angus Maddison, Romano Piras, Michele Salvati and participants at a CRENoS conference in Cagliari for helpful advice, Dr Delio Miotti of SVIMEZ for the provision of statistics and the Fondazione ENI Enrico Mattei for making available its data bank on the Italian regions.

2.   Indeed, if the objective was to test the neoclassical growth model, then the dependent variable should be productivity and explicit attention should be paid to migration and to capital mobility in the interpretation of the β coefficient (Barro *et al.*, 1995).

3.   The data for the years 1928 to 1948 cover 18, not 20 regions.

4.   Using the equation's results to estimate the steady-state values of Northern and Southern per capita GDP suggests that the latter would not have been much above 50 per cent of the former.

5.   Controlling for the share of agriculture in total value added, as done by Barro and Sala-i-Martin (1991), does not alter any of these findings. The results are not shown separately, but are available from the authors on request.

6. Not dissimilar results for the period since 1963 can also be found in Mauro and Podrecca (1994) and for the post-1970 years in Cellini and Scorcu (1995) and Paci and Pigliaru (1995).
7. Unit labour costs for industry, excluding construction, were obtained by dividing compensation per employee, including social security contributions, by value added per employed worker. The former series applies, therefore, to the corporate sector only; the latter includes both corporate and unincorporated activities.
8. Thus, between 1970–74 and 1975–84, investment by state-owned corporations fell by some 40 per cent in the country as a whole and by more than 60 per cent in the South.
9. Lack of data limits the period covered by this equation to the years 1957–93.
10. As against 36 per cent in 1970; in the Centre-North the increase went only from 31 to 39 per cent.
11. The GDP share of local government expenditure on goods, services and transfers rose moderately between 1951–52 and 1971–72 from some 5 to 7 per cent of GDP, but then almost doubled to roughly 13 per cent of GDP between 1971–72 and 1991–92.
12. Unfortunately, the absence of similar disaggregated regional data for Italy precludes a parallel cross-section analysis.
13. An indication of the lags between investment and production in this industry is provided by the fourfold difference in 1992 between the amount of investment recorded in the official statistics that include only investment in plants actually producing and in the Ifo survey data that include plants under construction.
14. In the 1980s, for instance, Italian state-owned firms were still devoting 35 per cent of their manufacturing investment in the South to steel and chemicals (D'Antonio, 1990).
15. A Deutsches Institut für Wirtschaftsvorschung survey in the Winter of 1993/94 of 5400 firms in industry, including artisan workshops, found that 35 per cent were paying less than the official wage rate and only 5 per cent were paying more (DIW, *Wochenbericht*, No.15, 1994).
16. OECD simulations suggest that in order to achieve full convergence of business sector productivity to West German levels by the year 2005, assuming the continuation of an 85 per cent nominal wage gap and a reduction in subsidies to capital formation, the volume of business investment would have to grow by 8 per cent per annum from 1997. It grew by 23 per cent in 1992, 16 per cent in 1993 and 10 per cent in 1994 (OECD, 1995).
17. Data are available for 91 EU regions in Eurostat, *Regions – Statistical Yearbook*. Twelve regions were omitted in view of their special characteristics; areas including the capital city (the Ile-de-France, Latium and the English South-East), regions that are no more than cities (West Berlin, Bremen and Hamburg) and regions that depend heavily on either tourism (the Balearic Islands, the Méditerranée, Val d'Aosta, Liguria and Trentino-Alto Adige), or on natural gas extraction (the Northern Netherlands).
18. These are the Ile-de-France, Latium and the English South-East.

REFERENCES

Abramovitz, M. (1986), 'Catching up, forging ahead, and falling behind', *Journal of Economic History*, **46** (2), 385–406.

Akerlof, G. A., A.K. Rose, J.L.Yellen and H. Helga (1991), 'East Germany in from the cold: the economic aftermath of currency union', *Brookings Papers on Economic Activity*, No.1, 1–105.

Attanasio, Orazio P. and Fiorella Padoa Schioppa (1991), 'Regional Inequalities, Migration and Mismatch in Italy, 1960–86', in Fiorella Padoa Schioppa (ed.), *Mismatch and Labour Mobility*, Cambridge: Cambridge University Press, pp. 237–320.

Bach, S., M.Gornig, F. Stille and U.Voigt (1994), 'Wechselwirkungen zwischen Infrastrukturaustattung, strukturellem Wandel und Wirtschaftswachstum', Deutsches Institut für Wirtschaftsvorschung, Beiträge zur Strukturvorschung, Heft 151.

Barro, R. J. and X. Sala-i-Martin (1991), 'Convergence across states and regions', *Brookings Papers on Economic Activity*, No.1, 107–82.

Barro, R. J. and X. Sala-i-Martin (1995), *Economic Growth*, New York: McGraw-Hill.

Barro, R. J., N. G. Mankiw and X. Sala-i-Martin (1995), 'Capital mobility in neoclassical models of growth', *American Economic Review*, **85** (1), 103–15.

Baumol, W. J. (1986), 'Productivity growth, convergence, and welfare: what the long-run data show', *American Economic Review*, **76** (5), 1072–85.

Blien, U. (1994), 'Convergence or Mezzogiorno scenario?', mimeo, Institut für Arbeitsmarkt und Berufsforschung, Nürnberg.

Bryson, P. J. (1992), 'The economics of German reunification: a review of the literature', *Journal of Comparative Economics*, **16** (1), 118–49.

Canova, F. and A. Marcet (1995), 'The poor stay poor: non-convergence across countries and regions', CEPR Discussion Paper, No.1265, London.

Carlin, W. and C. Mayer (1992), 'Restructuring enterprises in Eastern Europe', *Economic Policy*, No.15, 311–52.

Carlin, W. and C. Mayer (1995), 'Structure and ownership of East German enterprises', *Journal of the Japanese and International Economies*, **9**, 426–53.

Cellini, R. and A. Scorcu (1995), 'How many Italies? What data show about growth and convergence across Italian regions, 1970–91', mimeo, University of Bologna.

Commission of the European Communities (1993), 'The economic and financial situation in Italy', *Reports and Studies*, No.1, Brussels.

Cusack, T. R. (1996), 'Problem-ridden and conflict-riven: local government in Germany five years after unification', mimeo, Wissenschaftszentrum, Berlin.

D'Antonio, M. (1990), 'Il difficile percorso dell'industria nel Mezzogiorno', *Rivista di politica economica*, **80** (5), 203–52.

D'Antonio, Mariano and Salvatore Vinci (1992), 'L'Economia del Mezzogiorno, Ripresa o Stagnazione?', in Mariano D'Antonio (ed.), *Il Mezzogiorno. Sviluppo o stagnazione?*, Bologna: Il Mulino, pp. 31–52.

Deutsche Bundesbank (1996), 'The debate on public transfers in the wake of German reunification', *Monthly Report*, **48** (10), 17–30.

Eckaus, R. S. (1961), 'The North–South differential in Italian economic development', *Journal of Economic History*, **20** (3), 285–317.

Faini, R. (1994), 'Convergenza economica e ruolo del sindacato nel Mezzogiorno', mimeo, University of Brescia.

Faini, Riccardo, Giampaolo Galli and Curzio Giannini (1993), 'Finance and Development: The Case of Southern Italy', in Alberto Giovannini (ed.), *Finance and Development: Issues and Experience*, Cambridge: Cambridge University Press, pp. 158–217.

Feldstein, M. and C. Horioka (1980), 'Domestic saving and international capital flows', *Economic Journal*, **90** (358), 314–29.

Galli, Giampaolo (1992), 'Bilancia dei Pagamenti e Intermediazione Finanziaria nel Mezzogiorno', in Mariano D'Antonio (ed.), *Il Mezzogiorno. Sviluppo o stagnazione?*, Bologna: Il Mulino, pp. 99–114.

Giannola, Adriano (1979), 'Industria Pubblica e Occupazione', in Augusto Graziani (ed.), *L'economia italiana dal 1945 a oggi*, Bologna: Il Mulino, pp. 314–19.

Giannola, A. (1982), 'The industrialization, dualism and economic dependence of the Mezzogiorno in the 1970s', *Review of Economic Conditions in Italy*, No.1, 67–92.

Guglielmetti, P., D. Miotti and R. Padovani (1994), 'Recenti andamenti dell'occupazione: aspetti territoriali', *Rivista Economica del Mezzogiorno*, **8** (1), 279–306.

Hart, P. E. (1995), 'Galtonian regression across countries and the convergence of productivity', *Oxford Bulletin of Economics and Statistics*, **57** (3), 287–93.

Hughes Hallett, A. J. and Y. Ma (1993), 'East Germany, West Germany, and their Mezzogiorno problem: a parable for European economic integration', *Economic Journal*, **103** (417), 416–28.

Kaldor, N. (1970), 'The case for regional policies', *Scottish Journal of Political Economy*, **17** (3), 337–48.

Krugman, Paul R. and Anthony J. Venables (1990), 'Integration and the Competitiveness of Peripheral Industry', in Christopher Bliss and J.Braga de Macedo (eds), *Unity with Diversity in the European Economy: The Community's Southern Frontier*, Cambridge: Cambridge University Press, pp. 56–75.

Lee, K., H. M. Pesaran and R. Smith (1995), 'Growth and convergence: a multi-country empirical analysis of the Solow growth model', mimeo, University of Cambridge.

Lichtblau, K. (1993), 'Investitionsförderung in den neuen Bundesländern', *IW-Trends*, **20** (3), 17–38.

Mauro, L. and E. Podrecca (1994), 'The case of Italian regions: convergence or dualism ?', *Economic Notes*, **24** (3), 447–72.

Olson, Mancur (1982), *The Rise and Decline of Nations*, New Haven, CT: Yale University Press.

OECD (1995), *OECD Economic Surveys 1994–1995: Germany*, Paris.

Paci, R. and F. Pigliaru (1997), 'Structural change and convergence. An Italian regional perspective', *Structural Change and Economic Dynamics*, **8**, 297–318.

Padoa Schioppa Kostoris, Fiorella (1993), *Italy – the Sheltered Economy*, Oxford: Clarendon Press.

Podbielsky, Gisèle (1978), *Twenty-five Years of Special Action for the Development of Southern Italy*, SVIMEZ, Milan: Giuffrè editore.

Putnam, Robert D. (1993), *Making Democracy Work – Civic Traditions in Modern Italy*, Princeton, NJ: Princeton University Press.

Sarcinelli, M. (1989), 'The Mezzogiorno and the Single European Market: complementary or conflicting aims ?', *Banca Nazionale del Lavoro Quarterly Review*, No.169, 129–64.

Schmidt, K.-D. (1996), 'German unification: a progress report', Kiel Working Paper, No.722, Kiel.

Seitz, H. and G. Licht (1995), 'The impact of public infrastructure capital on regional manufacturing production cost', *Regional Studies*, **29** (3), 231–40.

Siebert, H. (1991), 'German unification: the economics of transition', *Economic Policy*, No.13, 287–340.

Sinn, Gerlinde and Hans-Werner Sinn (1991), *Kaltstart: Volkswirtschaftliche Aspekte der Deutschen Vereinigung*, Tübingen: Mohr.

Solow, R.M. (1956), 'A contribution to the theory of economic growth', *Quarterly Journal of Economics*, **70** (1), 65–94.

SVIMEZ (1954), *Statistiche sul Mezzogiorno d'Italia, 1861–1953*, Rome.

SVIMEZ (1993), *Rapporto sulla Distribuzione Nord-Sud della Spesa Pubblica*, Bologna: Il Mulino.

Sylos-Labini, P. (1985), 'L'evoluzione economica del Mezzogiorno negli ultimi trent'anni', Banca d'Italia – Temi di discussione, No.46, Rome.

Trigilia, Carlo (1992), *Sviluppo senza Autonomia*, Bologna: Il Mulino.

Williamson, J.G. (1965), 'Regional inequality and the process of national development: a description of the patterns', *Economic Development and Cultural Change*, **13** (4) (Part II), 1–84.

Wolleb, Enrico and Guglielmo Wolleb (1990), *Divari Regionali e Dualismo Economico*, Bologna: Il Mulino.

Wollmann, H. (1994), 'The transformation of political and administrative institutions in East Germany between external determinants and "Endogenous Factors"', mimeo, Humboldt University, Berlin.

Wollmann, Helmut and Frank Berg (1994), 'Die ostdeutschen Kommunen: Organisation, Personal, Orientierungs- und Einstellungsmuster im Wandel', in Hiltrud Nassmacher, Oskar Niedermayer and Helmut Wollmann (eds), *Politische Strukturen im Umbruch*, Berlin: Akademie Verlag, pp. 239–73.

14. Regional integration and public investment in Spain

Teresa Garcia-Milà and Ramon Marimon

14.1 INTRODUCTION

During the last thirty years there has been an intense process of convergence of the distribution of average income per capita among the Spanish regions (see Marimon, 1992; Dolado *et al.*, 1994; Mas *et al.*, 1994; Raymond, 1994; Sala-i-Martin, 1993). This is a general phenomenon for countries and regions that are sufficiently developed, and one which has been analysed by Barro and Sala-i-Martin (1991) and (1992). Both within the countries of the European Community and among the Spanish regions, there was an intense process of convergence from the 1950s until the mid-1970s. However, since the mid-1970s – after the oil crisis – growth in Europe has slowed down (see Marimon and Zilibotti, 1998). This decrease in the rate of growth is accompanied by the reduction of migration in Europe and a slowdown in the process of convergence among countries and regions.[1]

Ironically, this slowdown in convergence has coincided with the development of institutions that should promote cohesion among countries (development of the EEC) and among regions (the Autonomous Communities in Spain). Furthermore, in recent years, these institutions have pursued redistributive policies of regional transfers and public investments, and have focused on achieving a lasting reduction of the inequalities between the regions (good examples of this would be the FEDER programme of the EEC, and the public investment policies of both the Spanish central government and the Autonomous Communities).

Does this lack of convergence then indicate that the regional policies pursued have not been effective? That the income policies have had some impact is reflected in the fact that convergence among the Spanish regions is greater in disposable income per capita than in GNP per capita.[2] Nonetheless, from the perspective of regional growth and the integration of Spanish and European regions, purely redistributive policies are not particularly promising. If there is no convergence in per capita GNP, the poorest regions become permanent recipients of transfers and the redistributive policy may distort the efficient allocation of resources – for instance, by discouraging migration.[3]

It is difficult to maintain or justify a regional redistributive policy that is not accompanied by policies aimed at reducing the underlying and primary differences among regions. *A priori* it seems that public investment is the best instrument to implement such a policy. Public capital may play a strategic role in regional development and in promoting long-term equality among the regions. This is a role that it would be difficult for private capital to play, since it does not take into account the global 'externalities' on a particular region. This is the traditional reasoning upon which public investment policies to promote development are normally based. Recent theories of endogenous growth and economic geography provide a set of models in which these ideas may be formalized.

This approach, however, assumes not only that the underlying differences among regions are known, but also that they could be – at least, to a great extent – eliminated by a policy of regional investment, and that there exist appropriate instruments and institutions to carry out such a policy. For instance, if the regional growth differences are due to differences in infrastructures or levels of education, an appropriate investment policy may mitigate these differences, if there is an administrative body which is able to implement it.[4] Furthermore, if the differences are due to differences in sectoral composition and to growth rates which differ across sectors, the efficacy of such an investment policy is less clear. Although such a policy may have a direct effect if it generates employment in certain sectors – for example, in public services and construction – but, as in the case of income policy, if this is the regional investment policy's only effect, it would be very difficult to sustain or justify it, in the long run. Thus, the fundamental question is whether public investment can stimulate the development of a region's private sector.

The objective of this chapter is to shed some light on these problems. In particular, we first study to what extent the differences in the growth rates of employment and production among the regions are due to differences in their sectorial composition and to differences in the growth rates of the sectors, or, if they are more closely related to some intrinsicly regional factors. Second, we analyse the impact of public investment on the different sectors. Here, we specifically study whether public investment has only a direct effect – for example, on public-services and construction – or if it also has an indirect one as a catalyst for the private sector.

There is a literature that estimates the impact of public investment on the production of a country or region. Most of these estimates follow Aschauer (1989) in considering the public sector as a necessary factor of production. Final production Y is assumed to take the form $Y = F(K, G, L)$ where K is private capital, G is public capital (invested by the government) and L is labour. Furthermore, it is normally assumed that production (the function F) has constant returns to scale.

More recently, Mas *et al.* (1994) and García-Fontes and Serra (1993) have estimated the effect of public capital on the production of the Spanish regions (Autonomous Communities) with a similar approach to that of the estimations for the states of the United States that can be found in Munnell (1990), Holtz-Eakin (1994), Garcia-Milà and McGuire (1993) and Garcia-Milà *et al.* (1996). The Spanish case is characterized by a stronger effect of public capital on production than, for example, the American one. Nonetheless, as de la Fuente (1994) has shown, Spain is a good example to see that the redistributive criterion based on the income per capita does not coincide with efficiency in the short run.[5] The four poorest regions in 1990 were: Extremadura, Andalucía, Galicia and Castilla-La Mancha, in that order. The regions with the highest rate of return on public capital were, in decreasing order: Madrid, Catalunya, Baleares and Valencia.[6]

Attempting to assess the efficiency of public investment across regions using a homogeneous production function, however, does not take into account that regions may not only differ with respect to their factor endowments (private and public capital and labour) nor that the different productivities could be due to differences in other factors.[7]

The absence of absolute convergence among regions during the last decade could be explained by 'other factors'. For example, de la Fuente (1994) has measured to what extent differences in income per capita between the Spanish regions are owed to differences in the effection public capital endowments and/or to the differences in education levels.[8] Despite the fact that these factors, particularly education, seem to be significant, a large part of the differences among regions cannot be explained by these factors.

Furthermore, differences in sectoral composition seem to explain, in large part, the differences in growth rates among the regions (see, for instance, Marimon and Zilibotti, 1995). In fact, the coefficient of convergence of the Spanish regions increases significantly when conditioned on this factor (the weight of agriculture) (see Dolado *et al.*, 1994; Mas *et al.*, 1994).[9] That is, the Spanish regions would have converged in income much faster if the importance of agriculture had been the same in all the regions in 1955. As we will show later, this factor continues to be important in explaining the differences between the regions in the last decade. Indeed, as Raymond (1994) has pointed out, the productive structure – in particular, the importance of agriculture – tends to converge (even in the last decade), and this has favoured 'convergence' among regions at an aggregate level.

Given that sectoral factors are important when analysing regional growth, it is necessary to consider them in some detail. Here, we perform two types of statistical analysis of the decomposition in sectoral and regional factors: the classical *shift–share* analysis where we study rates of growth, employment and Gross Value Added for the period 1980–91, and the 'dynamic analysis of dummy variables', which adds a temporal element to the sectoral and regional decomposition. Both approaches show that if a region grows faster in a particular period only because it is specialized in a sector experiencing strong growth, the decomposition will indicate that the sectoral component explains the region's strong growth. Alternatively, if a sector in a region experiences a higher growth rate than the one that the sector registers for the whole reference country (or area), then it is said that there has been a regional effect on the growth of the sector for that region.[10]

Section 14.3 introduces both decomposition methods, having presented the descriptions of the sources and basic statistics in Section 14.2. The results of these analyses are reported in Section 14.4. We obtain that the sectoral component explains to a great extent the evolution of employment, and to a somewhat lesser extent that of production. For example, the dummy variable analysis suggests that 80 per cent of the variance of the annual average rate of growth is explained by the sectoral component. These results are consistent with Marimon and Zilibotti's analysis of the European economies (Marimon and Zilibotti, 1995). Nevertheless, the aggregated regional effects are important as well. In particular, some relatively poor regions such as Andalucía, Extremadura and Castilla-La Mancha show significantly positive regional effects.[11] Since it was in these regions that an active policy of public investments was implemented, one might be tempted to use these results as evidence for the efficiency of the regional policy. However, as we have pointed out, if public investment has a stimulating effect on the economy of a region, this total effect should also be observed in *the regional component of the non-public sectors*.

Once the sectoral and regional effects have been identified, we group them into subsectors that could be identified as being private or semi-public in order to study the effect of public investment in these subgroups. We analyse these sectoral effects at the level of disaggregation permitted by the regional accounts.[12] In particular, we distinguish three main sectors: (i) *semi-public*, which includes public services, construction and energy; (ii) *private* which consists of the private services and manufacturing; and (iii) *agriculture*. To study the importance of regional effects, we focus our attention on private services and manufacturing. The effects on the *semi-public* sector, as we have already indicated, are considered to be direct effects.

Following Marimon and Zilibotti (1995), we calibrated the evolution of employment in the corresponding 'virtual' Autonomous Communities. That is, for each region (or a sector of a region) we generated the employment series that this region would have experienced if the different sectors had grown at the average rate over all Autonomous Communities, starting from the initial distribution of employment in the region in 1980. By comparing the evolution of this 'virtual' employment with the 'actual' one, one can obtain a clear picture of the relative performance of the different sectors in the Autonomous Communities (see Section 14.4).

The existing studies on the Spanish economy tend to conclude that there are important regional effects (see, for example, Esteban, 1994), and as we have already said, this is specially true for regions where there has been a great deal of public investment. Section 14.5 analyses the relationship between such public investment efforts and the disaggregated results of Section 14.4. In Section 14.6 we study the convergence of the productivity rates of the different sectors. These results suggest a very different picture that could be summarized as follows:

The positive regional effects recorded in less-developed regions (Andalucía, Extremadura and Castilla La-Mancha) are mainly effects on the semi-public sector. For example, the 'regional effect' on aggregate employment in Andalucia is tied exclusively to a well above-average increase of employment in the construction sector. As a whole, the subsectors of this sector, especially construction and public services, are the ones which exhibit a tendency toward convergence of their productivity rates. In these regions, the regional effect is particularly intense in the second half of the decade, coinciding with a period of expansion of the Spanish economy and the great amount of public investment in these regions. Although public investment is positively correlated with the 'regional effect' of the semi-public sector, it does not seem to induce a 'regional effect' on the private sector. Murcia is the only region where the investment policies of the public sector have corresponded to a positive regional effect on the evolution of employment in manufacturing and in the private services.

14.2 BASIC STATISTICS ON THE EVOLUTION OF EMPLOYMENT AND GROSS VALUE ADDED

In 1980, the Spanish regions were a heterogeneous group, as a consequence of a long historical evolution of differentiation between a predominantly rural Spain and a more industrialized and service-oriented Spain with dynamic urban centres. Despite the strong growth of the

Spanish economy in the second half of the 1980s and the transformations – for instance, in sectoral composition – experienced by many regions, this heterogeneity still exists in the period studied, 1980–1991. For example, the standard deviation of the income per capita (at the purchasing power parity) is 14.3 in 1980 and 14.9 in 1991. However, both the disparity among the regions and its persistence, are phenomena that Spain shares with other European countries (see, for example Giovanetti and Marimon, 1995). In this section, we make a preliminary approximation to the evolution of the employment and production of the Autonomous Communities, while taking into account the changes in the sectoral composition. Our study is based on data on employment and gross value-added (GVA) at market prices for the period 1980–91, obtained from the Spanish Regional Accounts. The sectoral disaggregation comprises six sectors: agriculture, energy, manufacturing, construction, retailing and non-retailing services.

Tables 14.1 and 14.2 show the average annual rates of growth for the period studied. The first interesting observation, one which largely motivated this chapter, is the existence of important differences in the rates of growth of the Autonomous Communities, both in terms of employment and of production.

For the employment variable, the average annual rates (last column) show significant differences in the evolution of employment for the whole period considered. Thus, while employment in Murcia grows by nearly 30 per cent during the twelve years of our sample, employment in Asturias decreases by more than 7 per cent. As we will show at a disaggregated level, these figures reflect the vitality of the economy in Murcia and the depression in Asturias.

Similar differences can be observed in the evolution of the GVA, which generally corresponds to that of employment. If we order the Autonomous Communities by their employment and GVA growth rates, there are only four cases, with notable differences, which are reflected in the extreme values of the productivity growth rate, as can be seen in Table 14.3. The most characteristic case is Extremadura, which displays the highest productivity growth rate during the period studied. The sectors that induce this result are energy and construction, both with above-average employment and GVA growth rates, and with substantial improvements in productivity.[13] On the contrary, Valencia shows the lowest rate of growth in productivity. Again, the construction sector of this region drives this result, with a growth rate of productivity which is well above average.

Sectoral differences in the rates of growth are important both in employment and GVA, with some sectors shrinking very quickly, that is,

Table 14.1 Employment: annual growth rate (%), average 1980–1991

	Agriculture	Energy	Industry	Con-struction	Retail services	Non-retail services	Total
ESP	−4.41	−0.84	−0.24	2.56	2.34	3.80	1.01
AND	−3.39	0.13	−0.39	8.59	2.45	3.35	1.58
ARA	−5.14	−1.92	0.51	2.74	2.15	4.08	0.89
AST	−6.09	−2.44	−2.68	2.00	1.33	4.31	−0.69
BAL	−10.41	1.80	0.59	2.26	3.09	5.31	1.81
CAN	−6.90	0.59	0.71	0.29	2.66	3.14	1.08
CTB	−7.59	−0.67	−1.64	1.47	1.19	3.84	−0.68
C-L	−5.08	−0.84	−0.17	1.47	2.21	5.10	0.34
C-M	−4.69	−2.68	0.46	3.32	2.38	4.71	0.74
CAT	−4.48	−1.36	−0.09	1.45	1.88	3.79	1.06
VAL	−4.03	1.31	0.56	2.40	2.85	3.90	1.54
EXT	−4.47	3.30	−1.76	7.16	1.87	4.30	0.67
GAL	−3.55	−1.02	−0.10	−0.30	2.09	4.45	−0.18
MAD	−2.22	2.01	−0.21	1.27	2.57	3.42	2.02
MUR	−2.72	−0.63	0.99	3.01	4.16	4.68	2.22
NAV	−5.44	0.00	0.90	1.91	1.64	1.95	0.77
PV	−7.86	−0.56	−1.96	1.41	2.05	2.64	0.05
RIO	−5.56	−2.01	0.47	1.12	3.09	4.37	0.82

Note: ESP – Spain; AND – Andalucia; ARA – Aragon; AST – Asturias; BAL – Baleares; CAN – Canarias; CTB – Cantabria; C-L – Castella-Leon; C-M – Castella-La Mancha; CAT – Catalunya; VAL – Comunidad Valenciana; EXT – Extremadura; GAL – Galicia; MAD – Madrid; MUR – Murcia; NAV – Navarra; PV – País Vasco; RIO – Rioja.

agriculture, and others growing steadily, such as the service sectors, in particular public services and construction. The sectoral GVA growth rates have a structure similar to those of employment in all sectors except for energy, which experienced a spectacular increase in production while employment decreased. This is clearly reflected in a productivity growth rate of 6.27 per cent, by far the largest of this period, as can be seen in Table 14.3.

Table 14.2 Real GVA (basis 1980): annual growth rate (%), average
1980–1991

	Agriculture	Energy	Industry	Con-struction	Retail services	Non-retail services	Total
ESP	−2.33	5.38	0.25	4.02	3.65	4.62	2.74
AND	−0.92	5.68	0.59	8.89	3.73	4.52	3.45
ARA	−5.00	3.33	2.48	2.88	3.45	4.73	2.65
AST	−2.81	3.37	−2.31	3.39	2.85	5.28	1.72
BAL	−5.65	11.87	0.15	4.84	4.55	7.36	4.30
CAN	−2.63	2.25	4.27	6.10	2.85	3.63	3.06
CTB	−1.13	14.21	−1.59	3.69	2.76	4.63	1.61
C-L	−4.03	1.72	−0.06	3.19	3.18	5.09	1.89
C-M	−3.40	7.16	2.14	4.62	3.86	5.78	3.16
CAT	−3.54	6.43	0.06	3.06	3.84	5.47	2.61
VAL	−3.50	8.13	0.73	1.45	3.61	4.46	2.60
EXT	−1.86	13.15	−1.46	9.86	3.20	5.12	3.82
GAL	−1.68	2.41	0.63	3.10	2.90	5.21	2.22
MAD	−6.52	7.57	0.80	1.71	4.22	3.90	3.27
MUR	3.47	0.83	0.48	6.99	3.45	6.56	3.34
NAV	−3.53	5.88	1.38	3.83	3.68	0.86	2.09
PV	−2.54	7.97	−1.66	3.29	3.12	3.07	1.52
RIO	0.15	6.20	0.73	2.17	3.40	5.62	2.18

Note: ESP – Spain; AND – Andalucia; ARA – Aragon; AST – Asturias; BAL – Baleares;
CAN – Canarias; CTB – Cantabria; C-L – Castella-Leon; C-M – Castella-La Mancha;
CAT – Catalunya; VAL – Comunitad Valenciana; EXT – Extremadura; GAL – Galicia;
MAD – Madrid; MUR – Murcia; NAV – Navarra; PV – País Vasco; RIO – Rioja.

This sectoral diversity of the Autonomous Communities is illustrated in
Tables 14.4 and 14.5, which show the sectoral national and regional composition of employment for 1980 and 1991, respectively. Tables 14.6 and
14.7 show the same information for the GVA. At a national level, the
main feature is the decline in the relative importance of agriculture, and
to a lesser extent, that of manufacturing, giving way to an increase in the
importance of services, both private, and public.

Table 14.3 Productivity: annual growth rate (%), average 1980–1991

	Agriculture	Energy	Industry	Con-struction	Retail services	Non-retail services	Total
ESP	2.18	6.27	0.48	1.43	1.28	0.79	1.71
AND	2.56	5.54	0.98	0.27	1.24	1.13	1.84
ARA	0.15	5.35	1.96	0.13	1.27	0.63	1.74
AST	3.50	5.96	0.38	1.36	1.50	0.93	2.43
BAL	5.32	9.88	−0.43	2.53	1.41	1.94	2.45
CAN	4.58	1.65	3.53	5.79	0.19	0.48	1.96
CTB	6.99	14.99	0.05	2.19	1.55	0.76	2.31
C-L	1.10	2.58	0.11	1.70	0.95	−0.01	1.55
C-M	1.35	10.12	1.68	1.26	1.45	1.02	2.40
CAT	0.98	7.90	0.14	1.59	1.92	1.61	1.53
VAL	0.55	6.73	0.17	−0.93	0.73	0.54	1.04
EXT	2.73	9.54	0.30	2.52	1.31	0.79	3.13
GAL	1.94	3.47	0.73	3.41	0.79	0.73	2.41
MAD	−4.39	5.44	1.01	0.44	1.61	0.46	1.23
MUR	6.36	1.46	−0.51	3.86	−0.69	1.80	1.10
NAV	2.02	5.88	0.48	1.88	2.01	−1.07	1.31
PV	5.78	8.57	0.30	1.85	1.04	0.42	1.47
RIO	6.05	8.38	0.26	1.04	0.30	1.20	1.36

Note: ESP – Spain; AND – Andalucia; ARA – Aragon; AST – Asturias; BAL – Baleares; CAN – Canarias; CTB – Cantabria; C-L – Castella-Leon; C-M – Castella-La Mancha; CAT – Catalunya; VAL – Comunitad Valenciana; EXT – Extremadura; GAL – Galicia; MAD – Madrid; MUR – Murcia; NAV – Navarra; PV – País Vasco; RIO – Rioja.

The regions continue to exhibit important differences in their sectoral compositions. Taking as a point of reference employment in 1980, about 40 per cent of the employed population of Galicia and Extremadura work in agriculture, while this figure is only 1.5 per cent in Madrid or 6.5 per cent in Catalunya and the País Vasco. Differences of a similar magnitude are observed for the manufacturing sector: Canarias and Extremadura record figures of less than 10 per cent, while the País Vasco

Table 14.4 Employment: sectoral composition (%), 1980

	Agriculture	Energy	Industry	Con-struction	Retail services	Non-retail services	Total
ESP	18.32	1.27	24.00	8.33	34.04	14.03
AND	24.12	0.84	15.65	5.31	35.60	18.18
ARA	20.59	1.93	25.37	7.36	31.29	13.45
AST	25.77	8.94	19.57	6.91	27.48	11.32
BAL	13.88	1.05	14.42	12.10	48.59	9.96
CAN	18.53	1.16	7.30	11.92	45.14	15.95
CTB	24.88	0.75	25.90	7.11	29.19	12.17
C-L	31.27	2.26	17.77	8.62	27.94	12.15
C-M	29.91	1.23	20.28	9.14	27.26	12.19
CAT	6.51	1.00	35.34	9.06	37.77	10.32
VAL	14.30	0.46	29.94	8.40	34.42	12.49
EXT	36.65	0.50	10.67	6.89	29.52	15.77
GAL	41.59	0.97	13.97	9.54	24.02	9.92
MAD	1.50	0.73	22.91	9.77	42.62	22.47
MUR	21.64	1.09	22.84	8.93	31.37	14.13
NAV	12.73	0.44	35.03	7.32	30.38	14.10
PV	6.60	0.92	43.02	6.09	30.64	12.72
RIO	21.39	0.54	34.85	7.49	23.78	11.94

Note: ESP – Spain; AND – Andalucia; ARA – Aragon; AST – Asturias; BAL – Baleares; CAN – Canarias; CTB – Cantabria; C-L – Castella-Leon; C-M – Castella-La Mancha; CAT – Catalunya; VAL – Comunitad Valenciana; EXT – Extremadura; GAL – Galicia; MAD – Madrid; MUR – Murcia; NAV – Navarra; PV – País Vasco; RIO – Rioja.

share is 40 per cent. Differences in the remaining sectors are not as pronounced, although they are significant, as can be seen from Table 14.4.

Despite the sectoral changes in Spain as a whole during the last decade, differences among regions are, in general, preserved. Figures 14.1 and 14.2 show the evolution of the coefficients of variation of the percentage share of employment and GVA for each sector across

Table 14.5 Employment: sectoral composition (%), 1991

	Agriculture	Energy	Industry	Con-struction	Retail services	Non-retail services	Total
ESP	9.98	1.04	20.94	9.85	39.28		18.92
AND	13.89	0.72	12.63	11.68	39.11		21.98
ARA	10.45	1.42	23.34	8.99	35.87		18.94
AST	13.93	7.36	15.67	9.28	34.31		19.44
BAL	3.40	1.05	12.63	12.70	55.77		14.46
CAN	7.50	1.10	7.02	10.94	53.54		19.90
CTB	11.27	0.76	23.29	9.00	35.83		19.86
C-L	16.98	1.98	16.81	9.76	34.24		20.23
C-M	16.25	0.84	19.65	12.08	32.54		18.65
CAT	3.50	0.77	31.17	9.45	41.28		13.83
VAL	7.68	0.45	26.91	9.22	39.66		16.09
EXT	20.59	0.66	8.16	13.69	33.62		23.28
GAL	28.52	0.88	14.09	9.42	30.76		16.33
MAD	0.94	0.73	17.97	9.01	45.23		26.13
MUR	12.55	0.80	19.99	9.73	38.59		18.34
NAV	6.33	0.40	35.53	8.29	33.42		16.03
PV	2.67	0.86	34.43	7.07	38.11		16.85
RIO	10.43	0.40	33.57	7.75	30.39		17.48

Note: ESP – Spain; AND – Andalucia; ARA – Aragon; AST – Asturias; BAL – Baleares; CAN – Canarias; CTB – Cantabria; C-L – Castella-Leon; C-M – Castella-La Mancha; CAT – Catalunya; VAL – Comunitad Valenciana; EXT – Extremadura; GAL – Galicia; MAD – Madrid; MUR – Murcia; NAV – Navarra; PV – País Vasco; RIO – Rioja.

regions, with respect to the total. For employment, the divergences, very pronounced for the energy sector, and smaller for construction and services, hardly change, except for agriculture, where they increase slightly. The sectoral share of the GVA does not show a great degree of convergence either, but the differences are reduced for the energy sector, and become slightly less pronounced for construction and services.

Table 14.6 GVA: sectoral composition (%), 1980

	Agriculture	Energy	Industry	Con-struction	Retail services	Non-retail services	Total
ESP	7.42	4.56	26.56	8.69	41.37		11.40
AND	12.82	4.34	19.31	7.70	41.46		14.38
ARA	11.30	4.43	24.62	9.22	38.54		11.89
AST	5.71	9.33	29.72	9.38	35.70		10.16
BAL	4.37	1.34	11.47	9.82	64.33		8.67
CAN	7.24	6.47	7.03	8.44	55.85		14.97
CTB	7.32	0.55	35.10	7.15	39.65		10.23
C-L	13.79	6.92	24.54	8.45	33.33		12.97
C-M	19.41	8.77	19.90	8.51	32.05		11.35
CAT	3.50	3.53	36.01	8.46	41.34		7.16
VAL	6.40	2.87	28.05	9.27	43.73		9.69
EXT	19.43	4.35	11.48	7.84	38.11		18.79
GAL	13.61	8.85	20.42	10.51	35.72		10.88
MAD	0.58	1.64	22.15	10.93	49.37		15.32
MUR	8.97	13.41	19.69	7.68	39.59		10.65
NAV	7.83	1.23	37.06	6.80	33.01		14.07
PV	2.95	5.28	44.15	5.53	33.57		8.52
RIO	10.34	1.47	44.28	6.44	28.98		8.49

Note: ESP – Spain; AND – Andalucia; ARA – Aragon; AST – Asturias; BAL – Baleares; CAN – Canarias; CTB – Cantabria; C-L – Castella-Leon; C-M – Castella-La Mancha; CAT – Catalunya; VAL – Comunitad Valenciana; EXT – Extremadura; GAL – Galicia; MAD – Madrid; MUR – Murcia; NAV – Navarra; PV – País Vasco; RIO – Rioja.

The diversity in the sectoral composition and the very different evolution of the sectors – for example, agriculture and services – during the period analysed, suggests that both sectoral and regional factors have played an important role in determining the heterogeneous growth expe-

Table 14.7 GVA: sectoral composition (%), 1991

	Agriculture	Energy	Industry	Con- struction	Retail services	Non- retail services	Total
ESP	4.25	6.03	20.27	9.97	45.57		13.91
AND	7.98	5.48	14.19	13.52	42.72		16.11
ARA	4.82	4.76	24.18	9.45	41.96		14.82
AST	3.46	11.13	19.05	11.22	40.30		14.83
BAL	1.45	2.89	7.34	10.39	66.01		11.92
CAN	3.88	5.94	8.00	11.62	54.65		15.91
CTB	5.42	1.97	24.69	8.93	44.86		14.12
C-L	7.14	6.79	19.84	9.72	38.28		18.23
C-M	9.42	13.32	17.84	9.93	34.52		14.96
CAT	1.77	5.28	27.28	8.88	47.11		9.68
VAL	3.26	5.11	22.92	8.19	48.71		11.81
EXT	10.47	11.20	6.47	14.60	35.70		21.56
GAL	8.88	9.04	17.19	11.55	38.40		14.95
MAD	0.19	2.57	16.97	9.25	54.63		16.38
MUR	9.09	10.23	14.46	11.25	40.04		14.93
NAV	4.20	1.84	34.33	8.19	39.13		12.32
PV	1.88	10.40	31.12	6.69	39.85		10.06
RIO	8.29	2.24	37.81	6.43	33.02		12.21

Note: ESP – Spain; AND – Andalucia; ARA – Aragon; AST – Asturias; BAL – Baleares; CAN – Canarias; CTB – Cantabria; C-L – Castella-Leon; C-M – Castella-La Mancha; CAT – Catalunya; VAL – Comunitad Valenciana; EXT – Extremadura; GAL – Galicia; MAD – Madrid; MUR – Murcia; NAV – Navarra; PV – País Vasco; RIO – Rioja.

rienced by the Autonomous Communities in this period. To analyse the weights of and the interrelation between these factors, we perform a decomposition analysis. A short description of the methodologies used is given in the next section.

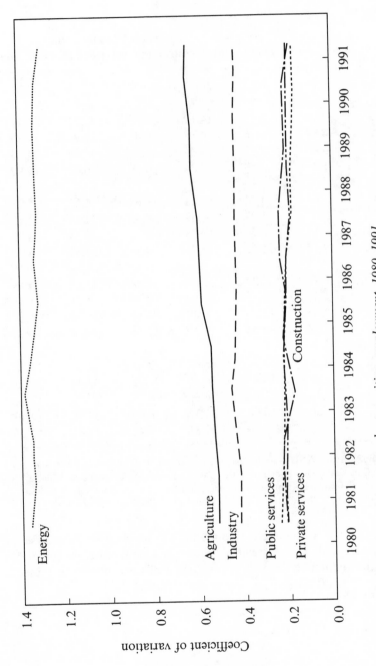

Figure 14.1 Convergence in σ: sectoral composition, employment, 1980–1991

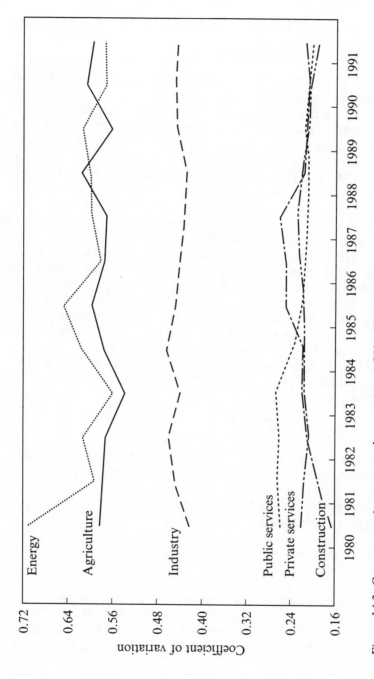

Figure 14.2 Convergence in σ: sectoral composition, GVA, 1980–1991

363

14.3   MODELS OF DECOMPOSITION

In this section we briefly present the methods of decomposition employed.

14.3.1   The *Shift–Share* Analysis

If we apply the classical *shift–share* analysis to the Spanish Autonomous Communities, we can decompose the growth of a certain Autonomous Community in terms of employment or GVA into three different components: (1) the growth related to the rate of growth of the reference area, in our case Spain, (that is, the expected growth of the region if it grows at the same rate as the reference area); this we will call the *national* component; (2) the growth that could be explained by applying the rates of growth of the different sectors at the national level to the sectoral composition of the Autonomous Communities (the growth differential that is explained by the specialization of the region in sectors that are more or less dynamic at the national level); this we will call the *sectoral* component; (3) the growth related to the differences in the rates of growth of specific sectors within the region with respect to the performance of the sectors at a national level (this part is explained by the degree of dynamism of the whole region relative to the national average); this we will call the competitive or *regional* component. To facilitate a better understanding of these concepts, we formalize these definitions.

Let us call $E(i, r, t)$ the employment in industry i, region r in year t. Then, we can define the rate of growth of employment in industry i, region r during the period from t to T as:

$$g(i, r, t - T) = \frac{E(i, r, T) - E(i, r, t)}{E(i, r, t)}$$

Furthermore, we may define $g(i, \cdot, t - T)$ as the rate of growth of sector i at a national level, and $g(\cdot, \cdot, t - T)$, the rate of growth of all the sectors at a national level.

The employment growth rate in industry i, region r during the period $t - T$ can be decomposed as follows:

$$g(i, r, t - T) = g(\cdot, \cdot, t - T) + [g(i, \cdot, t - T) - g(\cdot, \cdot, t - T)] \\ + [g(i, r, t - T) - g(i, \cdot, t - T)]$$

The first term on the right-hand side is the national growth rate, the second term represents the differential growth of the sector relative to all the sectors as a whole and at a national level, and the last term represents the difference between the performance of a sector in this particular region and in the whole country. Applying this decomposition to the employment in each sector and region in the starting year, we obtain the growth rate of employment in a region and sector as the sum of the three components, *national*, *sectoral* and *regional* in the *shift–share* terminology. Aggregating all the sectors we obtain a similar decomposition for the total growth of employment of the region, with the interpretation given at the beginning of this section.[14]

14.3.2 Dynamic Decomposition

The *shift–share* decomposition covers only the period of analysis as a whole, and it does not capture the possible differences in performance in each individual year included in the sample. However, the period analysed is not homogeneous: it covers both a period of recession in the first half of the decade, and one of strong expansion beginning in 1985–86. In this section we propose a decomposition of the growth rate of employment that adds a time factor to the sectoral and regional components. The estimated statistical model with dummy variables is in line with those proposed by Stockman (1988) and Costello (1993), and follows closely Marimon and Zilibotti (1995).

We specify the model as follows:

$$g(i, r, t) = m(i, r) + f(i, t) + n(r, t) + u(i, r, t)$$
$$i = 1, ..., I; r = 1, ..., R; t = 1, ..., T$$

where

- $g(i, r, t)$ represents the growth rate of employment in sector i, region r, for period t;
- $m(i, r)$ is a time invariant effect which is specific to sector 1 and region r;
- $f(i, t)$ is the effect specific to sector i and time t, common to all the regions;
- $n(r, t)$ is the interaction between the regional, and the temporal effect, for all sectors;
- $u(i, r, t)$ is an idiosyncratic disturbance term which is assumed to be orthogonal to all other effects.

The model is estimated by defining dummy variables for each combination of characteristics, and the values of $m(i, r)$, $f(i, r)$ and $n(i, t)$ are obtained by multiplying the estimated coefficient by the corresponding dummy variable. The model defined in this way shows perfect multicolinearity, and thus we need to introduce $R + T + I - 1$ independent restrictions that allow for its identification.

In general, we impose restrictions of exclusion, choosing a region and a year as a reference, as in Stockman (1988) and Costello (1993). However, we believe, as in Marimon and Zilibotti (1995), that this is not the best normalization for the problem we are analysing since, depending on the region chosen, the results may be very different. Following the criteria of these latter authors, we impose the following normalization:

$$- \sum_{r=1}^{R} m\,(i, r) = 0, \quad i = 1, ..., I$$

$$- \sum_{t=1}^{T} n\,(r, t) = 0, \quad r = 1, ..., R$$

$$- \sum_{r=1}^{R} n\,(r, t) = 0, \quad t = 1, ..., T$$

which constitutes a set of $I + R + T$ restrictions, of which all but one are independent.

This normalization provides an economic interpretation of the estimated coefficients, and also permits us to compare the average values across time of some components to those obtained by the *shift–share* analysis.

1. $m(i, r)$ is the long-term effect of sector i in region r expressed as a deviation with respect to the average over all regions. This component may be identified with the regional effect in the *shift–share* analysis, except that in this last approach the deviation is not relative to the simple average of the Autonomous Communities, but relative to the weighted regional average, where the weights are determined by the growth rate of sector i at the national level.
2. $f(i, t)$ represents the average growth rate over all the Autonomous Communities in the sector i at time t. Its average across time is equivalent to the sum of the national and sectoral components of the *shift–share* analysis, aside from possible differences between weighted and non-weighted averages, as mentioned above.
3. $n(r, t)$ represents the innovations that affect all the sectors of region r in year t, as deviations from the average with respect to each year and each region. In this particular case, there are no equivalent terms in the *shift–share* analysis, since we imposed the restriction that the average over time equals zero.

If we define $c(i, r, t) = m(i, r, t) + n(r, t)$, we can identify this as the dynamic regional component, which will coincide with the term $m(i, r, t)$ in the long term, since $n(r, t)$ is zero by construction. In this way, the growth rate $g(i, r, t)$ is decomposed into a *sectoral component* $f(i, t)$, a *regional component* $c(i, r, t)$, and the idiosyncratic residual.

14.4   RESULTS

14.4.1   Relative Importance of the Sectoral and Regional Components

One of the questions posed by the literature has been to what extent the sectoral component may explain deviations with respect to the average, or whether the regional component is the principal factor in explaining interregional differences. This question is important because, on the one hand, it may help to understand the differences in performance of the different economic areas of a country and, on the other, its answer may suggest different economic policies at a general or regional level.

If the sectoral composition is important for understanding the differences among Autonomous Communities, regional policies should contribute to modifying the regions' productive structure and to developing those sectors which are most promising. However, if the dominant explanation is that some regions are *per se* more dynamic in all sectors, and that other regions have below-average economic activity levels in all sectors, the regional policies should be aimed at improving the production, trade and general economic conditions of these poorest regions.

To illustrate the relative importance of the sectoral and regional components in the evolution of the Autonomous Communities, here we present some statistics that summarize the contribution of each component.

From the results of the *shift–share* decomposition, we have constructed a measure of the forecast error of employment growth in each Autonomous Community when one of the components is used and the other is excluded. Thus, for the sectoral component we compute $\sum_r((total - national - sectoral)^2)$ and for the regional $\sum_r((total - national - regional)^2)$. The first one is approximately half of the second one (53 per cent), indicating that the sectoral component explains a greater part of the observed variation in employment growth.

For the variable GVA, however, the relative importance between the sectoral and regional components is inverted, as it is the squared sum of the forecast errors of the sectoral component which is more than twice the value obtained for the regional component, thus making the latter a better predictor. It should be kept in mind, however, that both the sectoral and the regional components are small shares of the national one, and that their contribution is smaller than for the employment variable.

The results obtained from these statistics summarize what is also reflected in the more detailed analysis of the next section. For the employment variable the deviations with respect to the national average are larger, and the sectoral component is at least as important as the regional one. For the GVA the deviations are less important, and they could be explained to a great extent by the regional component, even though the sectoral component is still relevant.

The results obtained from the dummy variable analysis when considering both the dynamic and the long-term performance suggest again that the sectoral component plays a crucial role in explaining the variance of the employment growth rate. We obtain this conclusion from the decomposition of the variance of the employment growth rate.

First, we analyse the long-run performance, that is, the annual average growth rate, almost 80 per cent of which is explained by the sectoral effect $m(i, r)$, while hardly 20 per cent is explained by the regional component $\bar{f}(i)$ as can be seen in Table 14.8.

Table 14.9 shows the results for the analysis of short-run fluctuations. In this case 47 per cent of the total variation is explained by the sectoral and regional components together, but once again the sectoral component contributes more strongly, explaining by itself almost 35 per cent.

All of these findings seem to indicate that the sectoral composition of the Autonomous Communities plays an important role in the different evolution of the regions.

Table 14.8 Analysis of the long-run variation

	Var. $\bar{g}(i, r, \cdot)$ explained by	Correlations	
		$\bar{g}(i, r, \cdot)$	$f(i, \cdot)$
$\bar{g}(i, r, \cdot)$	1.000	1.000	
$\bar{f}(r, \cdot)$	0.799	0.894	1.000
$m(i, r)$	0.201	0.449	−0.000

Table 14.9 Analysis of the short-run variation

	Var. $g(i, r, t)$ explained by	Correlations	
		$g(i, r, t)$	$f(i, t)$
$g(i, r, t)$	1.000	1.000	
$f(r, t)$	0.349	0.590	1.000
$c(i, r, t)$	0.121	0.347	0.000

14.4.2 Analysis of the Regions

As we have already shown, the evolution of employment is largely explained by its sectoral composition. This can also be observed when we analyse the regions in more detail, employing the *shift–share* analysis (Figures 14.3 and 14.4). Thus, those Autonomous Communities for which the sectoral factor is negative (Galicia, Extremadura, Castilla-Leon, Castilla-La Mancha, Asturias, and to a lesser extent, La Rioja and Cantabria) present an above-average share of employment in the agricultural sector, and a below-average share in the service sector, the sectors with least and greatest dynamism (respectively) in this period. The cases in which the sectoral composition favours growth, Madrid above all, Canarias, Baleares, and to a lesser extent Catalunya, are characterized by the opposite situation to the one described earlier, that is, a relatively low share of employment in agriculture, and a strong concentration in construction and services.

Similar results are obtained when analysing the importance of the sectoral component for the evolution of production (Figures 14.5 and 14.6). The greatest divergence between the results obtained for employment and for GVA is detected when the sectoral effects have a negative sign. While Castilla-La Mancha, La Plioja, Cantabria, and to a lesser extent Castina-Leon present again negative values (together with Navarra and the País Vasco), the sectoral effects on GVA growth are not significant for the cases of Galicia, Asturias and Extremadura. These latter regions are characterized by a very low productivity in the agricultural sector, coupled with a large share of employed population engaged in agricultural, as is the case in Galicia and Asturias, and/or a very productive energy sector with a much greater share in GVA than in employment, as is the case in Galicia and Extremadura.

Nonetheless, the regional effects are significant and especially important if we want to assess the differential performance of the regions. To analyse this, we use two methods of decomposition. In particular, using dynamic decomposition, we construct what Marimon and Zilibotti (1995) define as 'virtual' economies. This involves constructing for each region the path that employment would have followed if the growth of each sector each year had been at the national average for that year. That is, taking as the initial value for each region and sector the level of employment in 1980, a virtual economy is obtained by adding the corresponding values of $f(i, t)$.[15] The difference between the observed value and the 'virtual' one yields the regional component for each year. Its average over time for each Autonomous Community is equivalent to the regional component of the *shift–share* analysis.

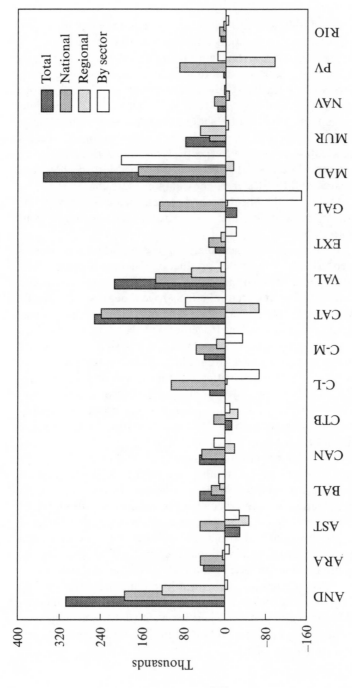

Note: AND – Andalucia; ARA – Aragon; AST – Asturias; BAL – Baleares; CAN – Canarias; CTB – Cantabria; C-L – Castella-Leon; C-M – Castella-La Mancha; CAT – Catalunya; VAL – Comunitad Valenciana; EXT – Extremadura; GAL – Galicia; MAD – Madrid; MUR – Murcia; NAV – Navarra; PV – Pais Vasco; RIO – Rioja.

Figure 14.3 Shift share: employment growth, 1980–1991 (thousands)

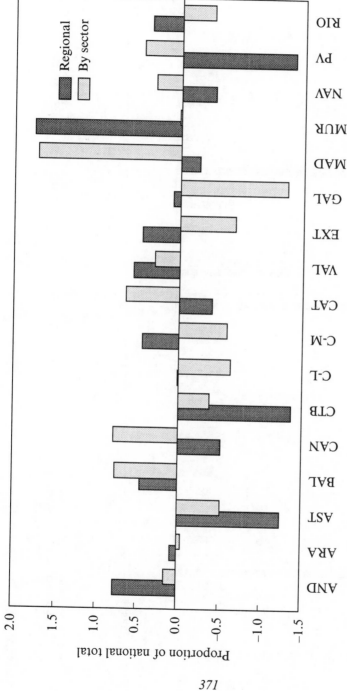

Note: AND – Andalucia; ARA – Aragon; AST – Asturias; BAL – Baleares; CAN – Canarias; CTB – Cantabria; C-L – Castella-Leon; C-M – Castella-La Mancha; CAT – Catalunya; VAL – Comunitad Valenciana; EXT – Extremadura; GAL – Galicia; MAD – Madrid; MUR – Murcia; NAV – Navarra; PV – Pais Vasco; RIO – Rioja.

Figure 14.4 Shift share: employment growth, 1980–1991 (proportion of national total)

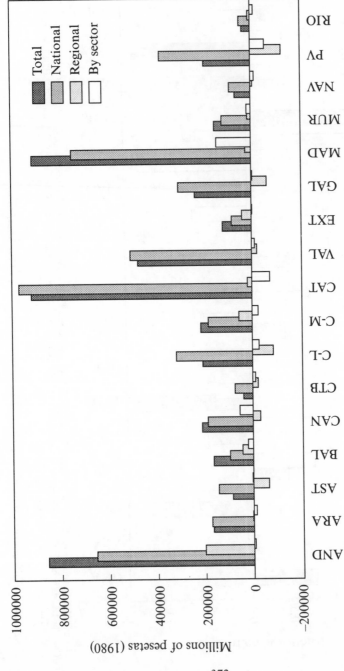

Note: AND – Andalucia; ARA – Aragon; AST – Asturias; BAL – Baleares; CAN – Canarias; CTB – Cantabria; C-L – Castella-Leon; C-M – Castella-La Mancha; CAT – Catalunya; VAL – Comunitad Valenciana; EXT – Extremadura; GAL – Galicia; MAD – Madrid; MUR – Murcia; NAV – Navarra; PV – Pais Vasco; RIO – Rioja.

Figure 14.5 Shift share: GVA growth, 1980–1991 (millions of pesetas, 1980)

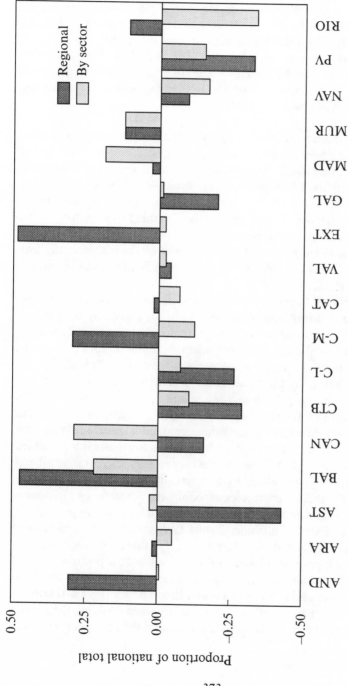

Note: AND – Andalucia; ARA – Aragon; AST – Asturias; BAL – Baleares; CAN – Canarias; CTB – Cantabria; C-L – Castella-Leon; C-M – Castella-La Mancha; CAT – Catalunya; VAL – Comunitad Valenciana; EXT – Extremadura; GAL – Galicia; MAD – Madrid; MUR – Murcia; NAV – Navarra; PV – País Vasco; RIO – Rioja.

Figure 14.6 Shift share: GVA growth, 1980–1991 (proportion of national total)

373

Figures 14.7 (aggregate data) and 14.8 (a–q) (sectoral data) present the 'virtual' and 'real' economies for each Autonomous Community. We observe that, with the exception of Galicia, regions whose actual economies outperformed their virtual ones over the entire period analysed are those with positive regional effects in the *shift–share* analysis.[16] From the analysis of Figures 14.7 and 14.8 (a–q) we may group the Autonomous Communities according to their regional performance and dynamics of development.

1. Three northern regions show very significant negative regional effects, both in employment and production: Asturias, Cantabria and the País Vasco. On one hand, Asturias and Cantabria exhibit similar aggregated (Figure 14.7) and sectoral dynamics (Figures 14.8(c) and 14.8(f)), especially in the differential performance of their actual economies relative to their virtual ones for the private sectors (manufacturing and private services) after 1985. On the other hand, in the País Vasco (Figure 14.8(p)) this divergence of the real economy from the virtual one after 1985 is due to the manufacturing sector, and also to public services.

2. Among those Autonomous Communities with a positive regional component, Murcia and Baleares show an especially pronounced dynamism in all sectors, including the private ones. For Murcia, the favourable evolution of employment in many sectors (see Figure 14.8(n)) allows this region to outperform the average. Indeed, this positive evolution in the later years is mainly a result of the performance of the private sector's manufacturing and services. The performance of Baleares is similar (Figure 14.8(d)), but the regional effect is very important in explaining production growth (Figure 14.6) in most of the sectors (except for manufacturing and agriculture; Tables 14.2 and 14.3). These are the only regions where it is possible to speak of a 'regional effect' as an externality that acts as a catalyst to most of the productive sectors, especially the private ones. (To a lesser extent, Valencia and La Rioja may also be included in this group.)

3. Andalucía, Extremadura and Castilla-La Mancha form a well- defined group, characterized by relative poverty (these are, together with Galicia, the poorest regions in this period), with a positive regional component which is clearly related to the performance of the *semi-public* sector: public services, construction and energy. Furthermore, this positive regional effect is particularly intense during the second half of the 1980s. In Andalucia it is clearly the construction sector

which is responsible for boosting the growth of employment above the 'virtual' level, especially after 1986. In Extremadura, the three *semi-public* service sectors all contribute to this effect, with this positive effect partly offset by a negative regional effect in the manufacturing sector during the second half of the decade. In Castilla-La Mancha, many sectors contribute, among them agriculture, and in the later years of the sample manufacturing, although public services play a clear catalysing role.

We also would like to stress that for this group, except for Extremadura, employment in the manufacturing sector has performed at the average over the regions (which also applies for the remaining of the poorest regions, Galicia). This result is similar to that obtained by Marimon and Zilibotti (1995) when comparing the evolution of manufacturing employment in Spain to that in the rest of Europe.

An alternative way of analysing the regional performance is to identify those Autonomous Communities with employment and/or GVA growth either above or below average, and to look at how sectoral and regional components explain these deviations.

Murcia, Madrid, Baleares and Andalucía[17] present the best results for employment as well as for GVA for this sample. For Andalucía the regional component is clearly the dominant factor, while for Madrid the sectoral component clearly dominates. In Baleares and Murcia, however, the growth differential is explained by a combination of the two.

The worst results of the period are those of Asturias, Cantabria, País Vasco and Castilla-Leon for both employment and GVA, and Galicia, but only for employment. In general, the regional component plays a more important role than the sectoral one in explaining the differences in performance. In Galicia, however, the large agricultural sector – in recession – is responsible for the negative evolution of employment.

This last result appears to contradict the fact that the evolution of employment was largely explained by sectoral composition. This apparent contradiction disappears when the positive regional effects of the poorest regions are taken into account, which are predominantly agricultural. That is, even though we could not state that in Andalucía, Extremadura and Castilla-La Mancha the 'regional effect' worked like an externality that stimulated most of the productive sectors, especially the private ones, it is true that their 'regional effects' partly offset the negative effects of their sectoral composition.

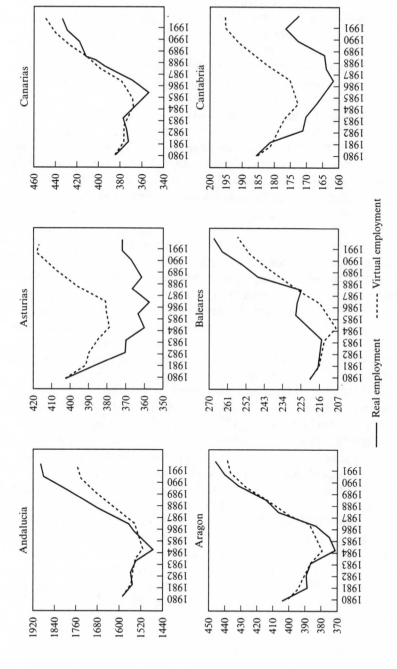

Figure 14.7 Total real and virtual regional employment, 1980–1991 (thousands)

——— Real employment ----- Virtual employment

376

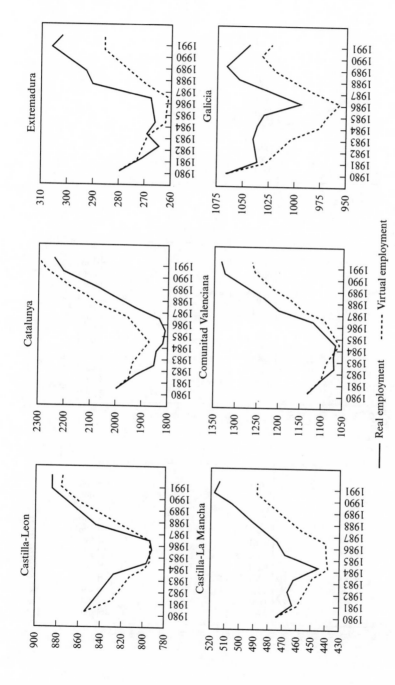

Figure 14.7 (continued)

377

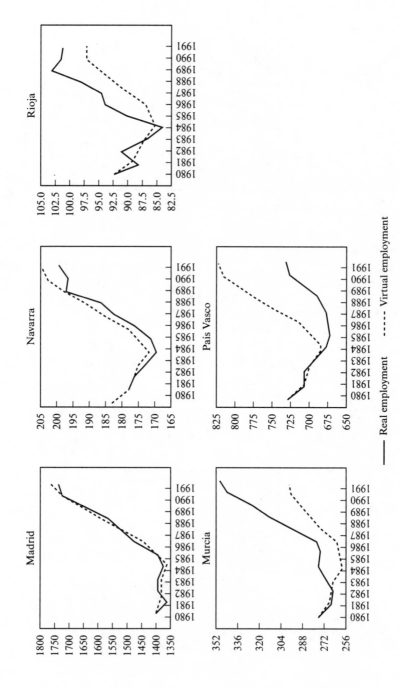

Figure 14.7 (continued)

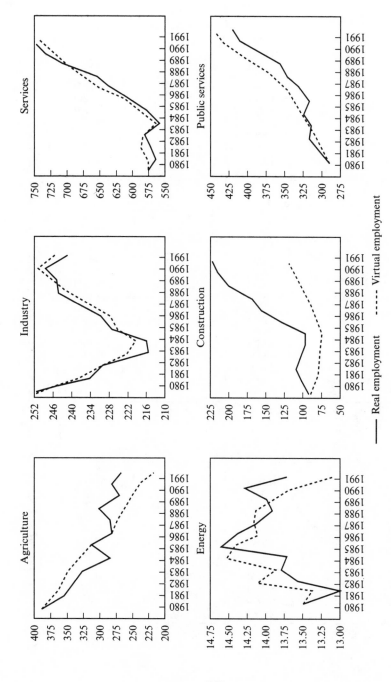

Figure 14.8(a) Real and virtual regional employment by industry, 1980–1991, Andalucia (thousands)

—— Real employment   ------ Virtual employment

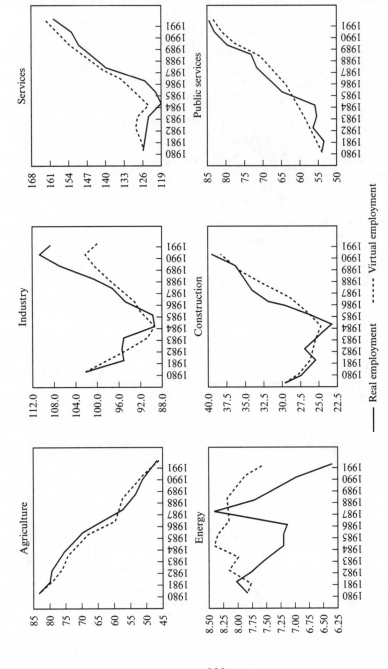

Figure 14.8(b) Real and virtual regional employment by industry, 1980–1991, Aragon (thousands)

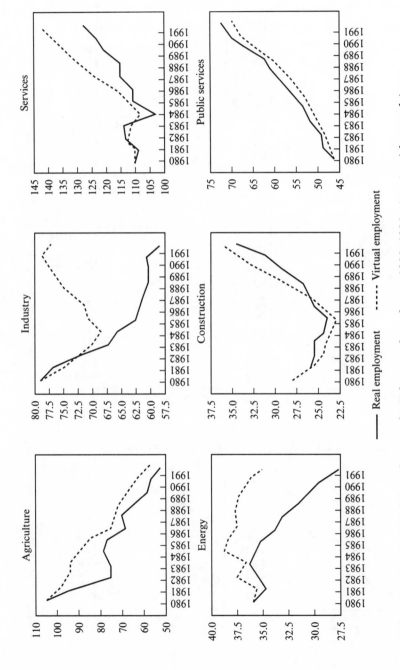

Figure 14.8(c) Real and virtual regional employment by industry, 1980–1991, Asturias (thousands)

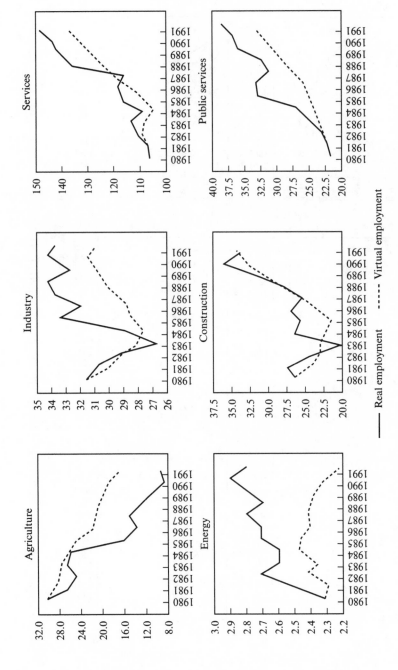

Figure 14.8(d) Real and virtual regional employment by industry, 1980–1991, Baleares (thousands)

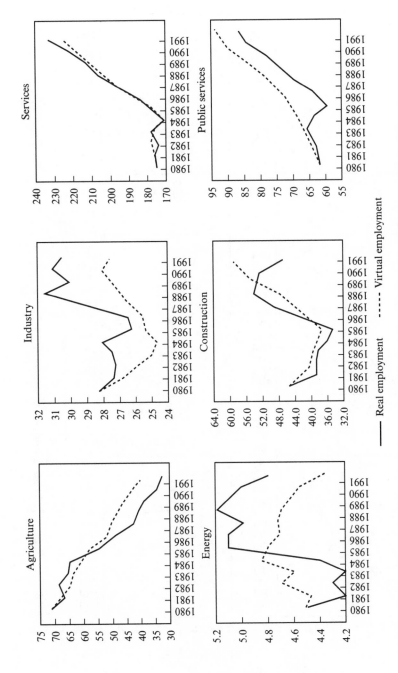

Figure 14.8(e) Real and virtual regional employment by industry, 1980–1991, Canarias (thousands)

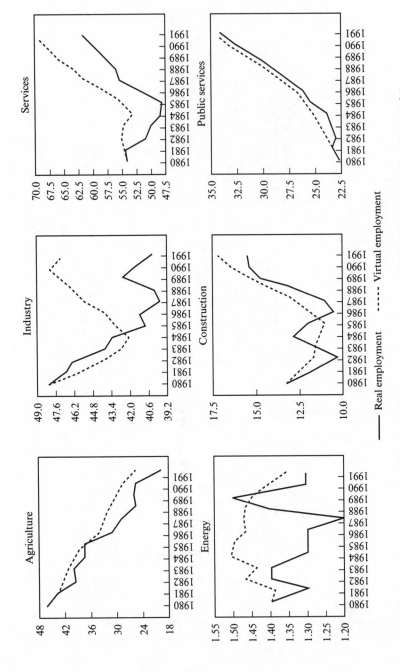

Figure 14.8(f) Real and virtual regional employment by industry, 1980–1991, Cantabria (thousands)

— Real employment   ---- Virtual employment

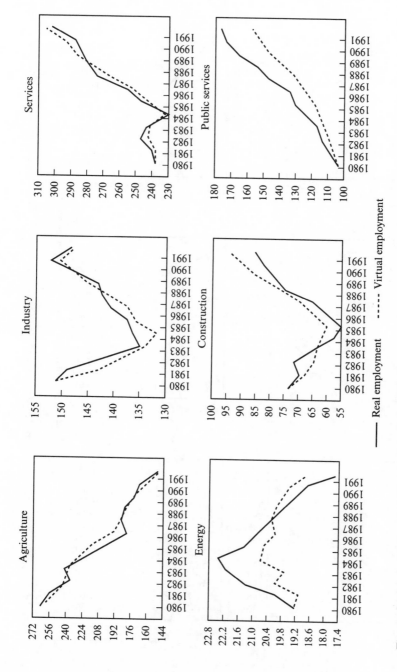

Figure 14.8(g) Real and virtual regional employment by industry, 1980–1991, Castilla-Leon (thousands)

— Real employment   ----- Virtual employment

385

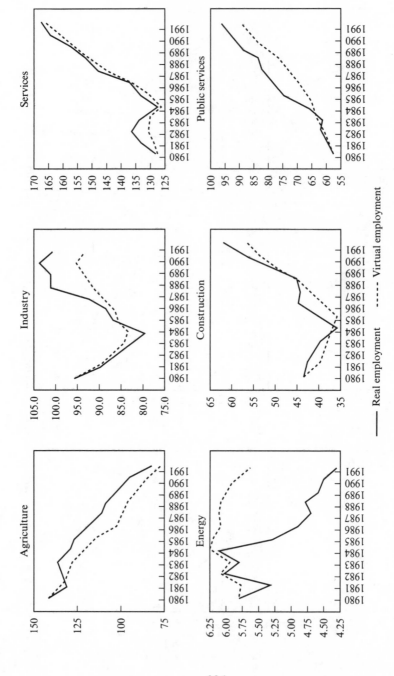

Figure 14.8(h) Real and virtual regional employment by industry, 1980–1991, Castilla-La Mancha (thousands)

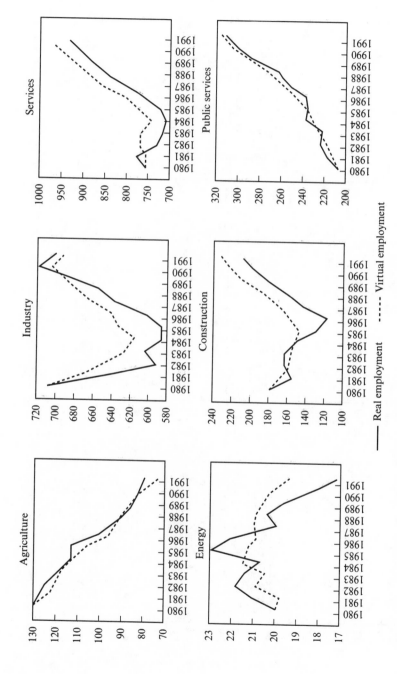

Figure 14.8(i) Real and virtual regional employment by industry, 1980–1991, Catalunya (thousands)

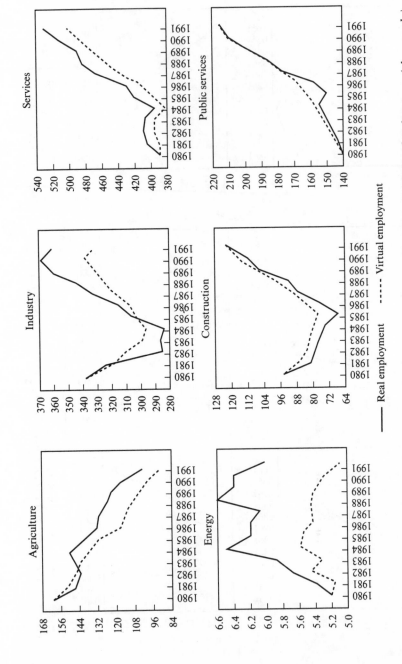

Figure 14.8(j) Real and virtual regional employment by industry, 1980–1991, Comunidad Valenciana (thousands)

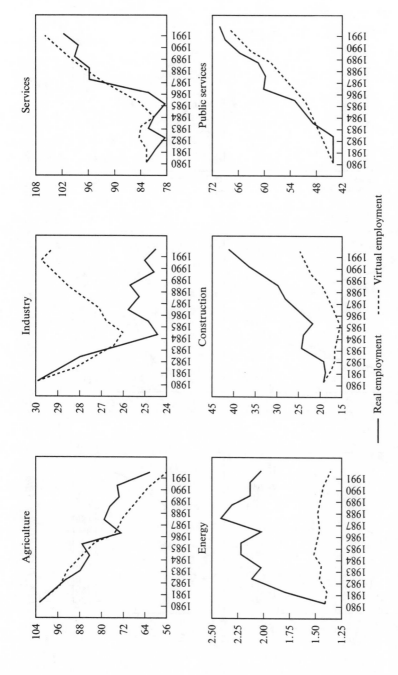

Figure 14.8(k) Real and virtual regional employment by industry, 1980–1991, Extremadura (thousands)

— Real employment   ----- Virtual employment

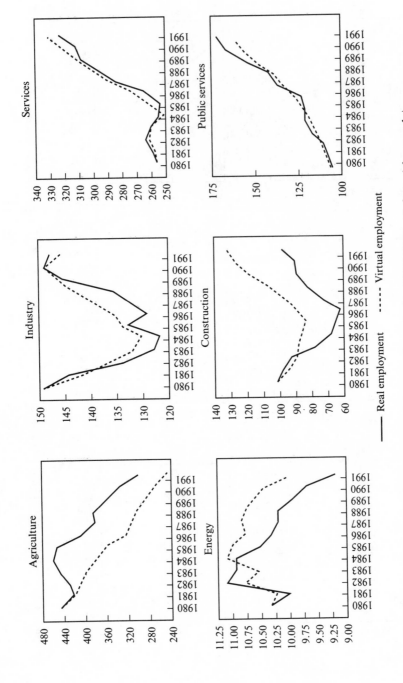

Figure 14.8(1) Real and virtual regional employment by industry, 1980–1991, Galicia (thousands)

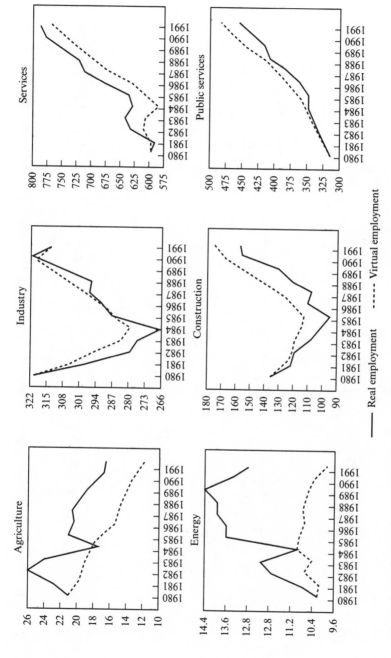

Figure 14.8(m) Real and virtual regional employment by industry, 1980–1991, Madrid (thousands)

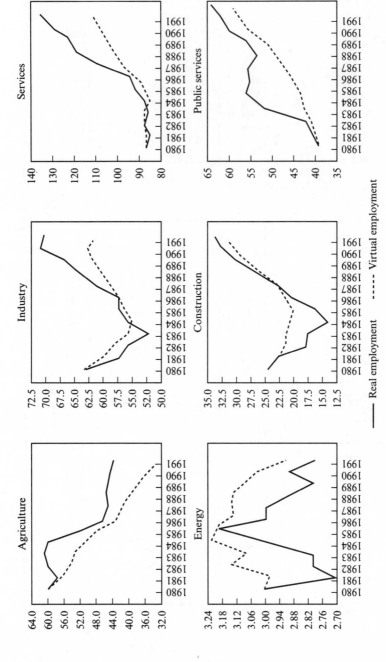

Figure 14.8(n) Real and virtual regional employment by industry, 1980–1991, Murcia (thousands)

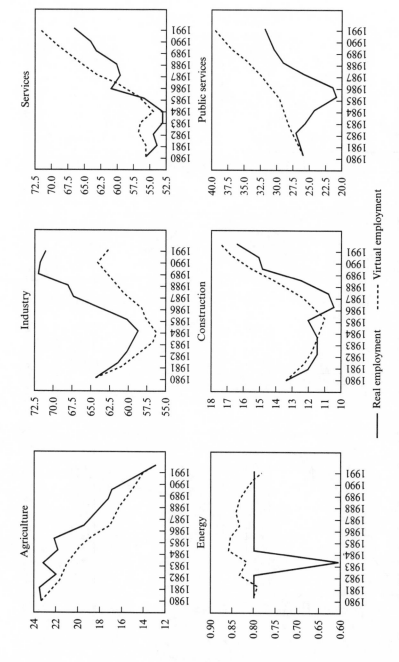

Figure 14.8(o) Real and virtual regional employment by industry, 1980–1991, Navarra (thousands)

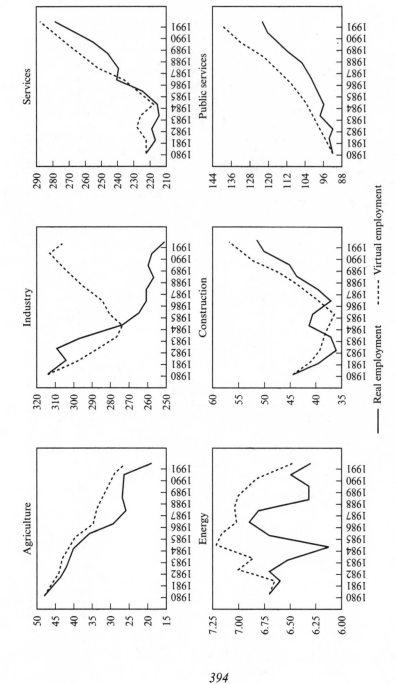

Figure 14.8(p) Real and virtual regional employment by industry, 1980–1991, País Vasco (thousands)

—— Real employment   ----- Virtual employment

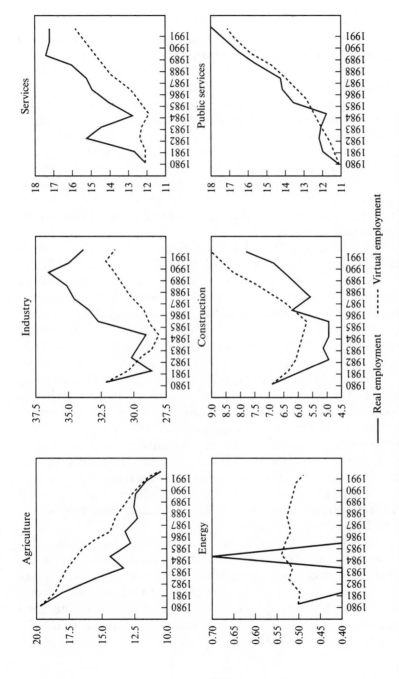

Figure 14.8(q) Real and virtual regional employment by industry, 1980–1991, Rioja (thousands)

— Real employment   ----- Virtual employment

14.5   REGIONAL EFFECTS AND PUBLIC INVESTMENT

The period studied is characterized by an important public investment policy, part of which was clearly oriented toward regional redistribution. Figure 14.9 illustrates this investment effort (particularly pronounced in the second half of the 1980s) which coincides with the recuperation of the Spanish economy.[18] This redistributive character is seen in Figure 14.10, which shows a negative relationship between GVA per capita in 1980 and public investment per unit of product in the period studied. In fact, this negative relationship is even more pronounced for 1985–91, corresponding to the period of greater investment and economic activity. Although eleven years is a rather short period to evaluate the effects of a policy of regional development, it is long enough to be able to find some evidence of the positive effects of public investment in stimulating the regional economy growth.

As we have already indicated, this stimulus does not refer to the direct effect of public investment, which would be particularly reflected in an increase of the economic activity of *semi-public* sectors (public services, construction and energy), but to the new economic activity generated in sectors dominated by private initiative, that we group under the name *private sector*, which henceforth will be used to refer to private services and manufacturing.[19] As a whole, these two sectors present very different performances. While employment in the *semi-public* sector grows by 41 per cent, it increases by less than half this figure in the private one, namely by 16 per cent. Therefore, we are interested in analysing how these differences are transmitted to the Autonomous Communities and in studying the role of public investment in the unequal evolution of these sectors.

In the previous section, we observed how different regions reported very different performances of their *semi-public* and private sectors. Figures 14.11 and 14.12 make this difference more explicit. The proportion of the regional total is the same as the one observed in Figures 14.4 and 14.6, but now we focus on identifying the relative importance of the *semi-public* and private sectors.[20]

Figures 14.11 and 14.12 confirm the above aggregation. The Autonomous Communities with a positive and significant regional effect on employment can be divided into two groups: the first one includes Murcia, Baleares, Valencia and La Rioja, where the positive regional component comes predominantly from the private sector and the regional effect of the *semi-public* sector has little importance; the second is formed by Andalucía, Castilla-La Mancha and Extremadura where the *semi-public*

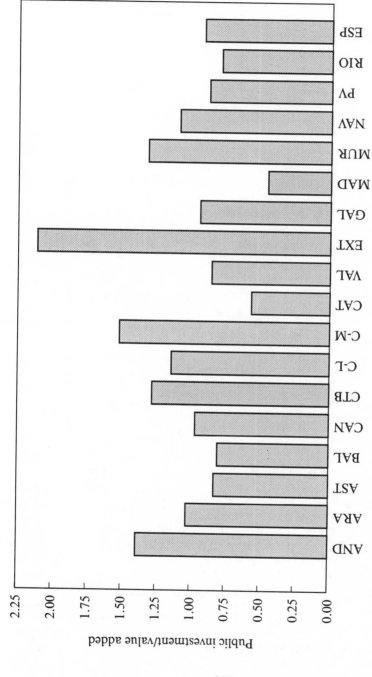

Note: AND – Andalucia; ARA – Aragon; AST – Asturias; BAL – Baleares; CAN – Canarias; CTB – Cantabria; C-L – Castella-Leom; C-M – Castella-La Mancha; CAT – Catalunya; VAL – Comunitad Valenciana; EXT – Extremadura; GAL – Galicia; MAD – Madrid; MUR – Murcia; NAV – Navarra; PV – Pais Vasco; RIO – Rioja; ESP – Spain

Figure 14.9 Public investment, 1980–1991 (per unit of GVA, 1980)

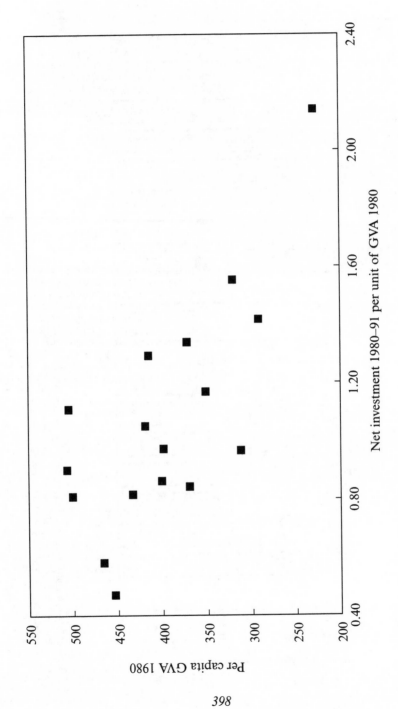

Figure 14.10 Public investment, GVA

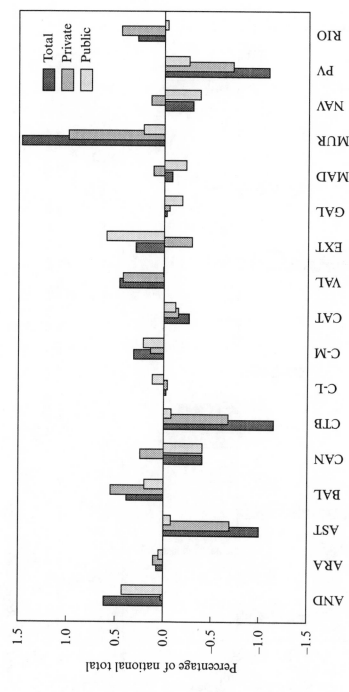

Note: AND – Andalucia; ARA – Aragon; AST – Asturias; BAL – Baleares; CAN – Canarias; CTB – Cantabria; C-L – Castella-Leom; C-M – Castella-La Mancha; CAT – Catalunya; VAL – Comunidad Valenciana; EXT – Extremadura; GAL – Galicia; MAD – Madrid; MUR – Murcia; NAV – Navarra; PV – País Vasco; RIO – Rioja; ESP – Spain

Figure 14.11 Regional effect, employment

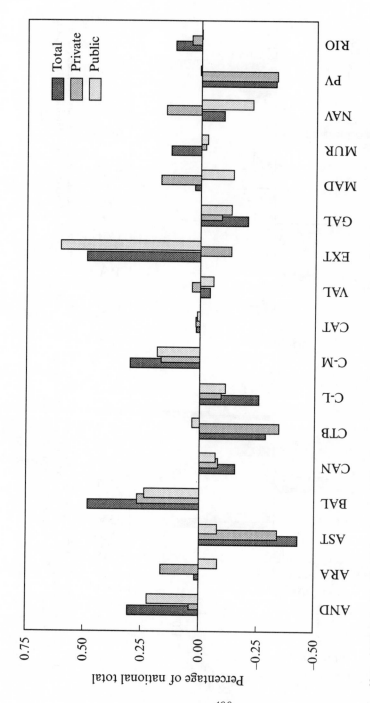

Note: AND – Andalucia; ARA – Aragon; AST – Asturias; BAL – Baleares; CAN – Canarias; CTB – Cantabria; C-L – Castella-Leom; C-M – Castella-La Mancha; CAT – Catalunya; VAL – Comunitad Valenciana; EXT – Extremadura; GAL – Galicia; MAD – Madrid; MUR – Murcia; NAV – Navarra; PV – País Vasco; RIO – Rioja; ESP – Spain

Figure 14.12 Regional effect, GVA

sector explains most of the positive regional effect. We would like again to point out that the strongly negative regional effects of Asturias, Cantabria and País Vasco are basically due to the negative effects of the private sector, which means that the *semi-public* sector has at least not had a negative effect on employment (except, perhaps, for Canarias and Navarra).

The regional effects on GVA growth (Figure 14.12) are even stronger than in the previous analysis. Andalucía, Extremadura, and to a lesser extent, Castilla-La Mancha are the regions with a positive regional effect induced by the *semi-public* sector. Murcia and La Rioja also report a positive regional effect, but here agriculture is the sector with the largest share in this effect. In Baleares, the important positive regional component is due in equal measure to the private and *semi-public* sectors. In contrast to the effects on employment, the *semi-public* sector in Baleares makes an important contribution to some of the negative regional effects.

When taking the positive regional effects on employment and income into consideration jointly, Andalucía, Castilla-La Mancha and Extremadura seem to be the regions where the positive regional effects are induced by the *semi-public* sector. As shown in Figure 14.9, the largest investment effort by the public sector has been concentrated in these regions. The performance of these regions suggests that the effect of public investment is mainly a direct one. To study this hypothesis in more detail, we computed the correlations across the Autonomous Communities between public investment and the regional components.[21] Correlations are shown in Table 14.10.

As is apparent from Table 14.10, public investment has not had a significant effect on the contribution of the private sector to the growth differential among the regions. However, one can observe a clear relationship between public investment and the regional effect of the *semi-public* sector, in particular the regional effect of GVA.

These results seem to confirm the hypothesis that public investment is not sufficient to generate additional economic activity in a region, and that the economic improvements are directly linked with the activity derived from the public intervention itself. If the objective of the regional

Table 14.10 Correlation between public investment and regional effects

	Employment	GVA
Total	0.139	0.342
Private	0.088	−0.036
Semi-public	0.243	0.613

public investment policy was to stimulate the private investment in some regions, this goal has not been reached. However, as we have already pointed out, public investment, by virtue of its direct effect on the *semi-public* sector has surely contributed to mitigating the decline of some predominantly agricultural regions (possibly providing services that improve the welfare of the population). This also means that it may have contributed to reducing migration. If these had been the objectives pursued, then our analysis would have yield a more positive result.

14.6 CONVERGENCE

The goal of an active interregional redistribution policy based on transfers and public investments is to reduce the disparities among regions. To the extent that this policy was effective, its results should include a reduction of the initial differences. A certain 'natural' process of convergence may exist even in the absence of an active regional policy. This 'natural' convergence process is due to the existence of decreasing returns to scale and has been explained by Barro and Sala-i-Martín (1991). During the period considered, there was an active regional policy, but little convergence among the Autonomous Communities.[22] Figure 14.13 shows the *convergence in* σ (that is, the coefficient of variation among the regions of the corresponding variable) of the income per capita. Divergence increases from 1980 to 1981 and there is a moderate tendency toward convergence during the period 1981–91.

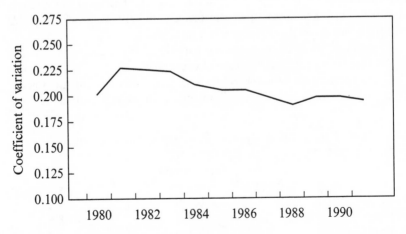

Figure 14.13 Convergence in σ: per capita GVA

If we take into account the *convergence in β* (that is, the tendency of the poorest regions to grow faster), we obtain similar conclusions. As can be seen in the first part of Table 14.11, non-linear least squares estimates of the convergence parameter β for GVA per capita yield a value around 1 per cent and not statistically significant for the period 1980–91, and a value near the familiar 2 per cent and significant for 1981–91.

In an integrated economy with factor mobility, productivities should converge. But if for any reason labour is not perfectly mobile (for example, people prefer to live in their own region or the information channels about the job opportunities are not well developed), an efficient regional policy should be able to equalize these rates. Figures 14.14 and 14.15

Table 14.11 Convergence in β

	a	$β$	R^2	s.e.
GVA per capita				
1980–91	0.083	0.011	0.12	0.0060
	(2.05)	(1.38)		
1981–91	0.152	0.024	0.34	0.0075
	(3.29)	(2.44)		
Productivity (1980–91)				
Total	0.187	0.027	0.53	0.0041
	(4.54)	(3.51)		
Agriculture	0.140	0.020	0.05	0.0284
	(1.15)	(0.83)		
Energy	0.227	0.022	0.22	0.0294
	(2.88)	(1.84)		
Industry	0.002	–0.001	0.00	0.0100
	(0.02)	(–0.05)		
Construction	0.432	0.093	0.52	0.0110
	(4.21)	(2.32)		
Private services	0.09	0.011	0.05	0.0067
	(0.96)	(0.79)		
Public services	0.246	0.043	0.35	0.0058
	(2.92)	(2.21)		

Notes:
t-statistics in parenthesis.
The estimated equation is as follows:
$(1/T)\log(y_{r,t}/y_{r,t-T}) = a - [(1 - e^{βT})(1/T)\log(y_{r,t-T})] + ε_r$. where $y_{r,t}$ represents, either GVA per capita or productivity by sectors.

show the convergence in σ of the labour productivity rates by sectors.
Total productivity exhibits a certain tendency to converge (CVT), but its
sectoral decomposition shows that the subsectors of the *semi-public*
sector, in particular construction and public services, are those which
show a tendency towards convergence.

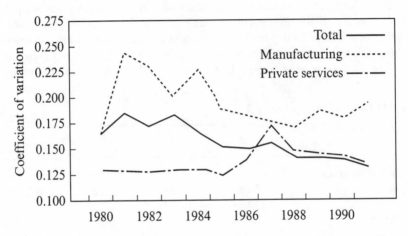

*Figure 14.14   Convergence in σ: productivity, total, manufacturing and
        private services*

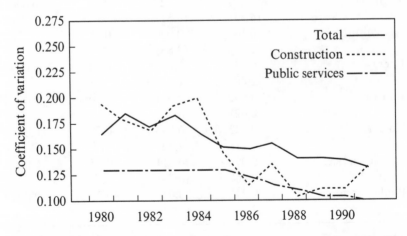

*Figure 14.15   Convergence in σ: productivity, total, construction and public
        services*

The second half of Table 14.11 shows the estimates of the *convergence in β* for the productivity of each sector. Total productivity presents a *convergence in β* of almost 3 per cent, but not all sectors contribute equally. Neither agriculture nor the two sectors classified as private (manufacturing and retailing services) show a significant coefficient, and in some cases it is even negative. The three remaining sectors, grouped under *semi-public*, yield an estimate for *β* which is significant (for the energy sector, it is only significant at 10 per cent) and greater than 2 per cent. Construction stands out for its high rate of convergence, close to 9 per cent, while that of non-retailing services is also above-average, with a value around 4 per cent. Results for convergence in *β* once again point mainly to the *semi-public* sector as exhibiting a tendency toward convergence.

These convergence results confirm that the public investment policy, with a direct effect in the *semi-public* subsectors, contributes to the convergence of the Autonomous Communities during the period 1980–91. However, this convergence among Autonomous Communities does not affect the private sector (manufacturing and private services) where, for example, differences in productivity persist. Therefore, some questions arise: to what extent has public investment, by discouraging migration, contributed toward maintaining the differences in productivity rates? To what extent has it, by improving infrastructure, helped to prevent a larger divergence?

14.7 CONCLUSIONS

Using statistical methods of decomposition, we have analysed the importance of the sectoral and regional effects on the growth of Spanish regions during the period 1980–91. This period is characterized by scant convergence among the regions that contrasts with the active public investment policy oriented toward favouring regional integration. In addition to characterizing the evolution of employment at a regional level, the purpose of this chapter has been to study to what extent the public investment policy has induced important 'regional effects' for the less developed regions.

Our results for the evolution of employment at the regional level in Spain concur with the results obtained by Marimon and Zilibotti (1995) for the evolution of employment at the national level in Europe. In particular, the sectoral effects are the major determinants of this performance. On the order of 80 per cent of the long-term variation of employment is due to its sectoral composition. Furthermore, as is the case with Spain relative to the rest of Europe, the low creation of employment in some relatively poorer regions (for instance, Castilla-La Mancha) is not due to poor performance in the manufacturing sector, but rather to the destruction of employment in agriculture in these regions. As in (post-1974) the rest of Europe, this weight of sectoral composition was translated into persistence of the differences in regional employment growth rates, which are exceptionally low in traditionally agricultural regions.

These regional differences have been partly mitigated by the growth of employment in construction and public services in the relatively poorer regions such as Andalucía, Extremadura and Castilla-La Mancha. This has led to some convergence of employment rates among Spanish regions during a period where the employment rate in Spain did not converge to that of the EEC.[23]

In other words, our study on employment in the Autonomous Communities and other studies on employment in Europe raise the same questions. Why has there not been a greater degree of adjustment through wages? Why has there not been a greater degree of adjustment by migration?[24] We have neither focused on these particular aspects of employment, nor have we tried to provide an answer to these questions. Nevertheless, the sectoral analysis shows that the *semi-public* sector (public services, construction and energy) has played a role as an *absorption mechanism* for the surplus of agricultural workers. The persistence of low rates of employment also shows the limitations of such a mechanism as a generator of net employment. Furthermore, if neither manufacturing nor private services are able to absorb the rest, it does not seem that the *semi-public* sector is able to absorb the volume of unemployment that still exists either.

Our analysis has also permitted us to group the Autonomous Communities by their performance in employment and production growth. Some regions are very similar with respect to their regional and/or sectoral effects, especially concerning whether this regional effect is a *direct effect* on the *semi-public* sector only or whether it is a *global effect* on all sectors With regard to the sectoral effect, as was to be expected, the share of agricultural employment determines which regions have positive and negative sectoral effects. More interesting, although quantitatively less important, are the regional effects. Thus, we can distinguish the following groups of regions:

(i)   Asturias, Cantabria and the País Vasco exhibit a negative regional effect, especially pronounced for the manufacturing sector.

(ii) Murcia and Baleares exhibit a positive regional effect for most sectors (Valencia and La Rioja show similar but weaker results).

(iii) Andalucía, Extremadura and Castilla-La Mancha display a positive regional effect, but one which is limited to the semi-public sector.

This grouping is a useful point of reference for evaluating the impact of regional public investment. In the period from 1980 to 1991, the regions where there has been the most public investment (per unit of GVA in 1980, see Figure 14.8) were, in descending order: Extremadura, Castilla-La Mancha, Andalucía and Murcia. The first three of these regions were also the poorest (in terms of income per capita) at the beginning of the period. That is, public investment, of a clearly redistributive nature, has had a positive effect on the three poorest Spanish regions. However, this effect has been directly on the *semi-public* sector, and no stimulating effect on manufacturing or private services was detected.[25] Furthermore, the investment policy in Murcia has been accompanied by well above-average growth of most of the productive sectors, which makes this region (the sixth in the poverty ranking of 1980) the one where public investment seems to have generated positive 'externalities' for the region as a whole.

Murcia is an exception, however, so when the correlation between public investment and the different regional components is computed, there is a significant relationship only to the *semi-public* component (especially in terms of GVA). Indeed, only in the *semi-public* sector did we find a tendency towards convergence in the productivity rates. At the end of the period, and despite the notable effort of integration represented by the development of the Autonomous Communities, disparity among the private regional sectors continues to exist.

APPENDIX: COMPARISON BETWEEN THE DUMMY VARIABLE AND THE *SHIFT–SHARE* MODELS

The best way to compare the two methods of decomposition utilized in this chapter is to derive them explicitly. Hence, this appendix is devoted to presenting this simple exercise in algebra. Following the notation used throughout the paper, $g(i, r, t)$ denotes the growth rate of employment of sector i in the region r at year t, while $g(i, r, t-T)$ expresses the growth rate for the period $t - T$. Given the sectors, $i = i, \ldots, I$, regions, $r = 1, \ldots, R$ and a period, $t = 1, \ldots T$, $\bar{g}(i, \cdot, t)$ denotes the average regional rate, that is: $\bar{g}(i, \cdot, t) = \frac{1}{R}\sum_{r=1}^{R} g(i, r, t)$. This average rate normally differs from the growth rate of sector i at year t ($g(i, \cdot, t)$), because in this latter rate the regions are weighted according to the relative weight of the sector in that particular region, that is: $g(i, \cdot, t) = \sum_{r=1}^{R} \alpha(i, r, t)g(i, r, t)$, where $\alpha(i, r, t)$ is the fraction of the employment of industry i located in region r at the beginning of the year (period) t; $\sum_{r=1}^{R} \alpha(i, r, t) = 1$.

The growth rates may be decomposed as follows:

$$
\begin{aligned}
g(i, r, t) &= [g(i, r, t) - \bar{g}(i, \cdot, t)] + \bar{g}(i, \cdot, t) \\
&\equiv h(i, r, t) + f(i, t) \\
&= [h(i, r, t) - \bar{h}(i, r, \cdot)] + \bar{h}(i, r, \cdot) + f(i, t) \\
&\equiv d(i, r, t) + m(i, r) + f(i, t) \\
&= [d(i, r, t) - \bar{d}(\cdot, r, t)] + \bar{d}(\cdot, r, t) + m(i, r) + f(i, t) \\
&\equiv u(i, r, t) + n(r, t) + m(i, r) + f(i, t)
\end{aligned}
$$

It is easy to see that this decomposition satisfies, by construction, the following restrictions:

$$
\begin{aligned}
\sum_{r=1}^{R} m(i, r) = 0 \quad & i = 1, \ldots, I \\
\sum_{r=1}^{R} n(r, t) = 0 \quad & t = 1, \ldots, T \\
\sum_{t=1}^{T} n(r, t) = 0 \quad & r = 1, \ldots, R
\end{aligned}
$$

If we define dummy variables for each combination of characteristics and estimate the model imposing the above zero-sum restrictions, we obtain the values of $m(i, r), f(i, r)$ and $n(i, t)$ as the product of the coefficients estimated with their corresponding dummy variables, with the 'idiosyncratic' component $u(i, r, t)$ as the orthogonal residual given by:

$$
u(i, r, t) = g(i, r, t) - [n(r, t) + m(i, r) + f(i, t)]
$$

To study the regional factor, it is useful to aggregate as follows:

$$
\begin{aligned}
c(i, r, t) &= g(i, r, t) - [u(i, r, t) + f(i, t)] \\
&= m(i, r) + n(r, t)
\end{aligned}
$$

That is,

$$
\begin{aligned}
g(i, r, t) &= f(i, t) + m(i, r) + n(r, t) + u(i, r, t) \\
&= f(i, t) + c(i, r, t) + u(i, r, t)
\end{aligned}
$$

Thus, the growth rate $g(i, r, t)$ is 'explained' by a *sectoral* component $f(i, t)$, and by a *regional* component $c(i, r, t)$. The 'virtual' economies correspond to the evolution of an economy at the rates $f(i, t)$ beginning from the initial distribution of employment.

We can use this dynamic decomposition to isolate the long-run effects. Thus, the average annual growth rate of a sector i in a region r is given by

$$\bar{g}(i, r, \cdot) = \bar{f}(i, \cdot) + \bar{m}(i, r) + \bar{n}(r, \cdot) + \bar{u}(i, r, \cdot)$$

$$= \bar{f}(i, \cdot) + \bar{c}(i, r) + \bar{u}(i, r, \cdot)$$

$$= \bar{f}(i, \cdot) + m(i, r) + 0$$

Hence, we can rewrite this equation for the period $t - T$ as

$$g(i, r, t - T) = f(i, t - T) + m(i, r, T - t) + n(r, t - T)$$

where $n(r, t - T)$ equals zero because in estimating the equation we have imposed the condition that its average over time was zero.

The growth rate for the whole period can in turn be decomposed as follows:

$$g(i, r, t - T) = [g(i, r, t - T) - \bar{g}(i, \cdot, t - T)] + \bar{g}(r, \cdot, t - T)$$

$$\equiv h(i, r, t - T) + f(i, t - T)$$

$$= [h(i, r, t - T) - \bar{h}(\cdot, r, t - T)] + \bar{h}(\cdot, r, t - T) + f(i, t - T)$$

$$\equiv m(i, r, t - T) + n(r, t - T) + f(i, t - T)$$

$$= m(i, r, t - T) + n(r, t - T) + [f(i, t - T)$$

$$- \bar{f}(\cdot, t - T)] + \bar{f}(\cdot, t - T)$$

$$\equiv m(i, r, t - T) + n(r, t - T) + s(i, t - T) + a(t - T)$$

In this case, the decomposition satisfies, by construction, the following restrictions:

$$\sum_{r=1}^{R} n(r, t - T) = 0$$

$$\sum_{i=1}^{I} s(i, t - T) = 0$$

If we estimate this equation with a constant term, $s(t - t)$, and dummy variables for the regions, $n(r, t - T)$, and for the sectors, $s(i, t - T)$, imposing the above restrictions, we obtain the idiosyncratic term $m(i, r, t - T)$ as an orthogonal residual.

Thus, we have decomposed the growth rate for each region and sector into a *national* component $a(t - T)$, a *sectoral* component $s(i, t - T)$ and a *regional* component $c(i, r, t - T) = m(i, r, t - T) + n(i, r, t - T)$. This decomposition is identical to the one of the classical *shift–share* analysis, even though its results are somewhat different since the latter analysis employs weighted average growth rates, while the former one uses simple average rates. Thus, from the *shift–share* decomposition introduced in Section 14.3.1

$$g(i, r, t-T) = g(\,\cdot\,,\,\cdot\,, t-T) + [g(i,\,\cdot\,, t-T) - g(\cdot,\,\cdot\,, t-T)]$$
$$+ [g(i, r, t-T) - g(i,\,\cdot\,, t-T)]$$

We can establish the following relationship:

$$g(i, r, t-T) = a(t-T) + s(i, t-T)$$
$$+ [n(r, t-T) + m(i, r, t-T)]$$
$$g(i, r, t-T) = \bar{g}(\cdot,\,\cdot\,,\,\cdot\,) + [\bar{g}(i,\,\cdot\,, t-T) - \bar{g}(\cdot,\,\cdot\,, t-T)]$$
$$+ [g(i, r, t-T) - \bar{g}(i,\,\cdot\,, t-T)]$$

The major difference between these two approaches lies in the fact that the different growth rates used in the *shift–share* analysis are *weighted*, while those used in the dummy variable analysis are *simple* averages. While it is straightforward to perform *shift–share* analysis using simple average rates, there is not a general agreement on how to perform the dummy variable analysis using weighted averages. Furthermore, we have to keep in mind that regional effects are also affected by the use of weighted averages. To analyse the robustness of our results and make more obvious the companion of our analysis with others (most of them, of the *shift–share* type), we considered it better to keep our analysis comparable.

NOTES

1. Here we explicitly refer to 'convergence in σ', that is, the decrease in the variability of the average income per capita among regions. However, this slowdown in convergence appears also when measured as 'convergence in β', which states that countries (regions) which are relatively poorer grow relatively faster. Different convergence criteria also yield similar results (see, for instance, Esteban, 1994).
2. On the one hand, estimates by the FIES Foundation for 1993 indicate that for Extremadura, the poorest Spanish region, the deviation from the average over all Autonomous Communities for GNP per capita is –34 per cent, but only –21.6 per cent for the average disposable income per capita. On the other hand, Baleares, the richest region, deviates 42.1 per cent in GNP per capita and 27.7 per cent in disposable income per capita (see Raymond, 1994).
3. There is some evidence that migration is being discouraged. For example, the convergence is even stronger with respect to disposable income per 'employee', corresponding to the fact that the poorest regions have lower employment rates (see Raymond, 1994). As in Europe, and in contrast to the US, variations in the productivity among regions do not induce migration (Decressin and Fatàs, 1994; Jimeno and Bentolila, 1995). In fact, our study points out that the differences in productivity among regions are important and that they persist throughout the period studied (see also Esteban, 1994).

4. This institutional factor should not be discounted. For example, Putnam (1993) shows how the different regional Italian administrative entities – which have similar responsibilities and capabilities – have very different levels of efficiency. Putnam claims that these differences are explained by differing levels of 'strength of the civil society' in the Italian regions (something which is very strongly correlated with the level of development of the region).

5. Together with the income criterion, de la Fuente has also considered a *need* criterion, based on an estimation of the differences in effective capital endowments. It is difficult to justify a regional policy based on this 'egalitarian' principle that does not take into account the differential effect of public investment in the different structures of production.

6. Assuming a Cobb–Douglas regional production function and that regions only differ in their effective public capital endowments, differences in productivity correspond to differences in the ratio of GNP to effective public capital endowment (Y/G) (see de la Fuente, 1994). De la Fuente's ranking seems to capture primarily the effect included in the numerator, that is, that the differences in production are greater than those of the public capital endowment.

7. Estimates of the production functions referred to above normally assume that the functional form is $\log(Y) = a + \alpha_k \log(K) + \alpha_g \log(G) + \alpha_l \log(L)$; $\alpha_k + \alpha_g + \alpha_l = 1$; some specifications estimate a value of the parameter a for each region that captures the intrinsic regional characteristics which also affect the productivity of the factors. Another way of considering the regional differences is to assume that a is a function of other factors such as educational level, quality of the infrastructure, legal system, and so on. This is the 'conditional convergence' approach (see, for example, Sala-i-Martin, 1994).

8. Under the assumption of a homogeneous function, this estimation is made assuming that the effect is the same. Differences in the educational levels and in public capital help to explain income differences.

9. Convergence in β, that is, the convergence of the different economies to their respective stationary states.

10. An important difference between the two decomposition methods, apart from the dynamics, lies in the fact that the *shift–share* analysis uses weighted averages – that is, the rate of growth of a sector in Spain – while the dummy variables analysis employs non-weighted averages – that is, the rate of growth of a sector in all the Autonomous Communities. Therefore, if we made the two types of analysis, we could test the robustness of our results relative to possible aggregation effects.

11. This grouping is the same with both of the applied methodologies.

12. Since 1986, the Regional Accounts disaggregate the manufacturing and retailing services sectors into sub-sectors, but they do not provide more information about construction (public or private contracts) or the composition of non-retailing services.

13. As we will show later, these sectors, classified together with construction as *semi-public*, will play an important role as paths of incidence of public investment.

14. The *shift–share* decomposition used in this paper is the one first proposed by Dunn (1960), not the modified one (Dunn, 1980). Applying either definition does not change the results aggregated by sectors, which are the figures we present here. The additional decomposition of the regional component into differential and allocative components, suggested by Esteban (1972) does not add any relevant information in our sample.

15. The matrices of $f(i, t)$, as well as those of $m(i, t)$ and $n(r, t)$ can be found in Tables 14.12, 14.13 and 14.14, respectively. In Table 14.12 one can observe how the manufacturing, construction and private service sectors are most clearly pro-cyclical, as the difference in the performance of the construction sector differs notably in the first and second halves of the decade. Table 14.13 contains information similar to that contained in Table 14.1, although in the present case the values are differences with respect to the average. Finally, Table 14.14 captures how the cycle has affected each Autonomous Community, reflecting certain temporal disparities in the respective fluctuations.

Table 14.12 Employment: cyclical sectoral effects, $f(i, t)$

	Agriculture	Energy	Industry	Construction	Retail services	Non-retail services
1981	−0.05452	−0.00785	−0.05358	−0.07795	0.00331	0.02964
1982	−0.03517	0.05304	−0.03380	−0.05040	0.01674	0.02435
1983	−0.01798	−0.02265	−0.03563	−0.01495	−0.00485	0.03207
1984	−0.04410	0.05069	−0.01369	−0.03231	−0.03448	0.02462
1985	−0.05879	−0.00734	0.02805	−0.02325	0.03576	0.03155
1986	−0.10497	−0.02090	0.01231	0.07451	0.04363	0.03737
1987	−0.02847	0.00344	0.02961	0.07948	0.05859	0.05258
1988	−0.03895	−0.00285	0.02421	0.08949	0.03752	0.04761
1989	−0.05373	−0.01480	0.02081	0.10152	0.03836	0.06741
1990	−0.05735	−0.02116	0.01950	0.07077	0.02739	0.04918
1991	−0.10419	−0.04340	−0.02316	0.04649	0.03150	0.03052
Prom.	−0.05438	−0.00307	−0.00231	0.02395	0.02304	0.03881

Table 14.13 Employment: long-run regional effects, $m(i,r)$

	Agriculture	Energy	Industry	Construction	Retail services	Non-retail services
AND	0.01987	0.00441	−0.00156	0.05847	0.00118	−0.00587
ARA	0.00160	−0.01634	0.00740	0.00312	−0.00177	0.00118
AST	−0.00846	−0.02167	−0.02485	−0.00412	−0.00979	0.00339
BAL	−0.05557	0.02095	0.00814	−0.00163	0.00741	0.01295
CAN	−0.01712	0.00894	0.00941	−0.02104	0.00323	−0.00793
CTB	−0.02450	−0.00367	−0.01423	−0.00934	−0.01126	−0.00115
C-L	0.00224	−0.00536	0.00061	−0.00933	−0.00120	0.01093
C-M	0.00634	−0.02413	0.00684	0.00875	0.00046	0.00725
CAT	0.00860	−0.01064	0.00145	−0.00956	−0.00440	−0.00157
VAL	0.01321	0.01608	0.00785	−0.00024	0.00509	−0.00057
EXT	0.00865	0.03550	−0.01543	0.04521	−0.00451	0.00325
GAL	0.01827	−0.00720	0.00126	−0.02694	−0.00238	0.00473
MAD	0.03191	0.02300	0.00018	−0.01136	0.00234	−0.00513
MUR	0.02679	−0.00320	0.01216	0.00574	0.01773	0.00688
NAV	−0.00150	0.00307	0.01122	−0.00503	−0.00677	−0.01951
PV	−0.02751	−0.00253	−0.01745	−0.00990	−0.00273	−0.01275
RIO	−0.00282	−0.01721	0.00700	−0.01280	0.00737	0.00392

Note: AND – Andalucia; ARA – Aragon; AST – Asturias; BAL – Baleares; CAN –
Canarias; CTB – Cantabria; C-L – Castella-Leon; C-M – Castella-La Mancha; CAT –
Catalunya; VAL – Comunitad Valenciana; EXT – Extremadura; GAL – Galicia; MAD –
Madrid; MUR – Murcia; NAV – Navarra; PV – País Vasco; RIO – Rioja.

Table 14.14 *Employment: cyclical regional effects, n(r,t)*

	1981	1982	1983	1984	1985	1986	1987	1988	1989	1990	1991
AND	0.00561	0.00821	-0.02167	-0.04324	0.02577	0.01728	0.00829	0.00407	-0.00862	0.01654	-0.01225
ARA	-0.00677	-0.00427	0.00714	-0.03031	0.00029	0.02291	0.04218	-0.02252	-0.00796	-0.00784	0.00715
AST	0.00503	-0.02133	0.02522	-0.00084	0.01064	-0.00661	-0.00087	-0.02844	-0.00815	0.00906	0.01629
BAL	0.02339	-0.00550	-0.01336	0.06817	-0.01433	-0.02473	-0.01970	0.01143	-0.00998	-0.00802	0.01549
CAN	-0.02124	0.01802	0.01136	-0.00123	-0.02244	0.03428	0.01094	0.02395	-0.03038	-0.01131	-0.01195
CTB	-0.00485	-0.02447	0.03346	0.00962	-0.00303	-0.03208	-0.02237	0.02231	0.04808	-0.00920	-0.01747
C-L	0.02584	0.01325	-0.00280	-0.02075	-0.01344	0.00265	0.01504	-0.00154	-0.01214	-0.00211	-0.00400
C-M	-0.00380	0.02543	-0.00987	-0.01434	0.03457	0.00161	-0.02600	-0.00357	-0.00585	0.00642	-0.00460
CAT	0.00541	0.00043	0.00124	-0.01247	-0.00536	-0.02809	0.00141	0.00646	0.00934	0.00627	0.01536
VAL	-0.01235	-0.01751	0.01068	0.01504	-0.02099	0.01354	0.01784	0.00011	0.00288	-0.00231	-0.00693
EXT	0.03525	0.00326	0.02828	-0.00145	-0.01621	-0.00840	0.04126	-0.03043	-0.03050	-0.00055	-0.02051
GAL	0.00763	0.01139	-0.01231	-0.00895	-0.00719	-0.02582	0.02110	0.01261	0.00469	-0.01060	0.00745
MAD	0.01468	0.03693	-0.01880	-0.08734	0.06362	0.02552	-0.01846	-0.01026	-0.00483	0.00120	-0.00226
MUR	-0.02953	-0.02994	0.01828	-0.00242	0.00935	0.00017	-0.00460	0.01172	0.00211	0.01869	0.00617
NAV	0.00387	-0.00778	-0.04555	0.03873	-0.00161	-0.02076	0.00436	0.01186	0.02744	-0.02686	0.01630
PV	-0.00206	-0.00276	0.01309	0.01041	0.01231	-0.03061	-0.02369	0.00410	0.00907	0.02686	-0.02143
RIO	-0.04612	-0.00336	-0.02439	0.08137	-0.05195	0.05914	-0.04673	0.01100	0.01480	-0.01095	0.01719

Note: AND – Andalucia; ARA – Aragon; AST – Asturias; BAL – Baleares; CAN – Canarias; CTB – Cantabria; C-L – Castella-Leon; C-M – Castella-La Mancha; CAT – Catalunya; VAL – Comunitad Valenciana; EXT – Extremadura; GAL – Galicia; MAD – Madrid; MUR – Murcia; NAV – Navarra; PV – País Vasco; RIO – Rioja.

413

16. The case of Galicia is an exception because its 'real' economy has outperformed its 'virtual' one every year, but the *shift–share* regional effect, even though small in size, is negative. This divergence appears because the growth rate of the agricultural sector obtained as a simple average among the Autonomous Communities (–5.44 per cent) is significantly lower than the weighted one (–4.41 per cent) due to the fact that regions with a high share in employment in the agricultural sector, such as Galicia, have an above-average growth rate in this sector. In the dummy variable model, the positive deviation of the agricultural sector in Galicia relative to the average is much greater than in the *shift–share* analysis. Therefore, given the importance of agriculture in this region, this difference transforms the negative sign (indeed, almost zero) of the *shift–share* analysis to a positive one in the dummy variable dynamic analysis.

17. As we have already mentioned, the disparities between employment and GVA in Valencia and Extremadura are reflected in the extreme performance of their productivities.

18. We have constructed the data on public investment from the series of net stock of capital of the Public Administrations elaborated by the IVIE.

19. Here, we do not include agriculture because even though public investment policy may aim to stimulate this sector, this does not mean that it was oriented to generate agricultural employment.

20. The difference between the regional total and the two components plotted in these figures correspond to the agrarian sector, not included in the two large sectors.

21. The correlated variables were constructed as follows. Public investment is

$$\frac{KPU_{1991} - KPU_{1980}}{VBA_{1980}}$$

where *KPU* is the net stock of capital of the Public Administrations. The total regional effect is *REG/SUM*, where *REG = REGPR + REGPU + REGA* is the regional effect, which can be decomposed in three sectors ('private', '*semi-public*' and agriculture) and *SUM* is the total variation of employment during the period. The 'private' effect is *REGPR/SUM* and the '*semi-public*' sector effect is given by *REGPU/SUM*.

22. Using data of the Autonomous Communities for 1955–91, Mas *et al.* (1994) reported clear convergence for the period 1960–79, but an absence of convergence for 1980–91. For a similar period, 1955–89 and using data for the Spanish provinces, Dolado *et al.* (1994), also found that the level of convergence is higher in the first part of the period, and although in the period 1964–77 there is no convergence among provinces, there is among Autonomous Communities.

23. The standard deviation among the Autonomous Communities (employed/total population) changes from 12.98 per cent to 9.38 per cent between 1981 and 1990 (see de la Fuente, 1994). In the same period, the employment rate in Spain changed from 48 per cent to 48.4 per cent, while the EEC rate increased from 60.2 per cent to 61 per cent (source, OECD).

24. Jimeno and Bentolila (1995) show how the shares of Spanish regional participation and migration rates are due to employment shocks.

25. In Castilla-La Mancha one can observe a positive regional effect at the end of the period (see Figure 14.12) which may have contributed towards this region surpassing Galicia at the end of the period, in terms of income per capita. As a matter of fact, Castilla-La Mancha and Murcia are the two Autonomous Communities where employment rates grew fastest in this period.

REFERENCES

Aschauer, D. (1989), 'Is public expenditure productive?', *Journal of Monetary Economics*, **23**, 177–200.

Barro, R. and X. Sala-i-Martin (1991), 'Convergence across states and regions', *Brookings Papers on Economic Activity*, **1**, 107–82.

Barro, R. and X. Sala-i-Martin (1992), 'Convergence', *Journal of Political Economy*, **100**, 223–51.

Costello, D. (1993), 'A cross-country, cross-industry comparison of productivity growth', *Journal of Political Economy*, **101** (2), 207–22.

de la Fuente, A. (1994), 'Desigualdad regional en España, 1981–90: fuentes y evolución', in *Crecimiento y Convergencia Regional en España y Europe, Vol. II*, Instituto de Análisis Económico, CSIC, Barcelona.

de la Fuente, A. (1994), 'Capital público y productividad', in *Crecimiento y Convergencia Regional en España y Europa, Vol. II*, Instituto de Análisis Económico, CSIC, Barcelona.

de la Fuente, A. (1994), 'Inversión pública y desigualdad regional en España, 1981–90', in *Crecimiento y Convergencia Regional en España y Europa, Vol. II*, Instituto de Análisis Económics, CSIC, Barcelona.

Decressin, J and A. Fatàs (1994), 'Regional labour dynamics in Europe and implications for EMU', mimeo, INSEAD, Paris.

Dolado, J.J., J.M. González-Páramo and J.M. Roldán (1994), 'Convergencia económica las provincias Españolas: evidencia empírica (1955–1989)', *Moneda y Crédito*, **198**, 81–120.

Edgar, S. Dunn (1960), 'A statistical and analytical technique for regional analysis', *Papers and Proceedings of the Regional Science Association*, Vol. 6.

Edgar, S. Dunn (1980), *The Development of the U.S. Urban Systems*, Baltimore: Johns Hopkins University Press.

Esteban, J.M. (1972), 'A reinterpretation of shift-share analysis', *Regional Science and Urban Economics*, Vol. 2.

Esteban, J.M. (1994), 'La Desigualdad Interregional en Europa y España: Descripción y Análisis', in *Crecimiento y Convergencia Regional en España y Europa, Vol. II*, Instituto de Análisis Económico, CSIC, Barcelona.

García-Fontes, W. and D. Serra (1993), 'Capital Público, Infraestructurea y Crecimiento', in *Crecimiento y Convergencia Regional en España y Europa, Vol. II*, Instituto de Análisis Económico, CSIC, Barcelona.

Garcia-Milà, T. and T.J. McGuire (1993), 'The contribution of publicly provided inputs to states' economies', *Regional Science and Urban Economics*, **22**, 229–41.

Garcia-Milà, T., T.J. McGuire and R. Porter (1996), 'The effect of public capital in state-level production functions reconsidered', *Review of Economics and Statistics*, **78**, 177–80.

Giovannetti, G. and R. Marimon (1995), 'Una Unión Monetaria para una Europa heterogénea', mimeo, European University Institute.

Holtz-Eakin, D. (1994), 'Public-sector capital and the productivity puzzle', *Review of Economics and Statistics*, **76**, 12–21.

Jimeno, J.F. and S. Bentolila (1995), 'Regional unemployment persistence (Spain, 1976–1993)', mimeo, FEDEA, Madrid.

Marimon, R. (1992), 'L'emergència i el creixement de les regions', *Revista Económica*, **96**, Banca Catalana, Barcelona.

Marimon, R. and F. Zilibotti (1995), 'Porqué Hay más Desempleo en España que en Europa? La España 'Real' *vs.* la España 'Virtual'', in R. Marimón (ed.), *La Economía Española en und Europa Diversa: Empleo, Integración Regional y Unión Monetaria*, Barcelona: Antoni Bosch.

Marimon, R. and F. Zilibotti (1998), 'Actual versus virtual employment in Europe. Is Spain different?', *European Economic Review*, **42**, 123–53.

Mas, M., J. Maudos, F. Pérez and E. Uriel (1994), 'Disparidades regionales y convergencia en las Comunidades Autónomas', *Revista de Economía Aplicada*, **II.4**, 129–48.

Mas, M., J. Maudos, F. Pérez and E. Uriel (1994), 'Capital público y productividad de las regiones Españolas', *Moneda y Crédito*, **198**, 163–92.

Munnell, A.H. (1990), 'How Does Public Infrastructure Affect Regional Economic Performance?', in A.H. Munnell (ed.), *Is there a Shortfall in Public Capital Investment?*, Federal Reserve of Boston.

Putman, R.D. (1993), *Making Democracy Work*, Princeton, NJ: Princeton University Press.

Raymond, J.L. (1994), 'La distribución regional del PIB per cápita y su evolución en el tiempo: un análisis de la hypótesis de convergencia', *Revista Asturiana de Economía*, **1**, 69–91.

Sala-i-Martin, X. (1993), 'The wealth of regions', mimeo, Yale University.

Sala-i-Martin, X. (1994), *Apuntes de Crecimiento Económico*, Barcelona: Antoni Bosch.

Stockman, A. (1988), 'Sectoral and national aggregate disturbances to industrial output in seven European countries', *Journal of Monetary Economics*, **21**, 387–409.

15. An assessment of regional risk sharing in Italy and the United Kingdom

Luca Dedola, Stefano Usai and Marco Vannini

15.1 INTRODUCTION*

The basic idea of risk sharing is the cross-sectional counterpart of the permanent income hypothesis (Cochrane, 1991). Economic agents (and governments) pursue the insurance of consumption expenditures against income fluctuations due to shocks of different persistence. Within a competitive equilibrium, full consumption smoothing can be achieved when financial markets are complete, but it can also obtain with incomplete financial markets, even without institutions implementing optimal policies, under special assumptions concerning either the working of the security markets or the homogeneity of agents. The main theoretical implication of perfect risk sharing is that individual consumption should not vary in response to idiosyncratic income shocks. At the aggregate level, for example regions within a country or nations if one takes an international perspective, under certain assumptions Pareto-efficient risk sharing implies that changes in consumption across regions (nations) are perfectly correlated.

The most recent empirical literature on risk sharing (Asdrubali *et al.*, 1996; Atkeson and Bayoumi, 1993; Canova and Ravn, 1996; Obstfeld, 1989, 1994; Townsend, 1995; van Wincoop, 1995) has focused mainly on two issues, namely the degree of risk sharing achieved internationally (or within states or villages) and the decomposition of the observed amount of income and consumption smoothing into various channels.

The general area of risk sharing and consumption smoothing has received a great deal of attention for a number of reasons. It has been stressed in particular that society can gain from improved insurance not only because individuals will face reduced consumption uncertainty but also because of several growth-enhancing effects. As argued by

Townsend (1995, p. 84), lack of insurance can reinforce low levels of income, consumption and savings for certain groups, or can contribute to inequality in society as a whole. In both cases, within an endogenous growth framework, one can establish positive links with the rate of growth of the economy, as in Greenwood and Jovanovic (1990) and Persson and Tabellini (1996a, b). Moreover, as suggested by Murdoch (1995, p. 104), when individuals are unable to borrow or insure, they will increasingly mitigate risk via income smoothing, choosing, for instance, safer production techniques or showing reluctance in adopting new technologies and taking advantages of new economic opportunities.

One further reason behind the current wave of research into risk sharing is the fact that many countries are considering entering economic and monetary unions. It is then natural to ask what amount of risk sharing they can hope to achieve by looking at various case studies. The evidence gathered so far refers mainly to the United States and OECD (see for instance Atkeson and Bayoumi, 1993; Asdrubali *et al.*, 1996; Canova and Ravn, 1996; Sorensen and Yosha, 1998), and provinces of Canada (Bayoumi and McDonald, 1994) and Japan (van Wincoop, 1995). To our knowledge, little has been done (Bayoumi and Rose, 1993; Scorcu, 1998; Dedola *et al.*, 1997; Pellegrini, 1997) on the amount of interregional risk sharing in EU countries.

The analysis in this chapter tries to complement the existing evidence by looking more closely at the degree of interregional risk sharing within Italy and the United Kingdom. We choose to focus on these two countries in view of the well known differences between their financial systems and other distinctive characteristics, like the policy regime, that seem relevant to the issue of consumption insurance and the study of the channels through which it takes place. At the same time, these two countries are comparable in terms of population and economic performances.

For most of the period under investigation they experienced very different political regimes: Thatcherism in the United Kingdom and a sequence of activist governments in Italy.[1] So while in the United Kingdom the State was retreating from the economy, in Italy, with few exceptions, it was expanding. Moreover, up to the late 1980s both the size and the efficiency of the financial system were still significantly greater in the United Kingdom than in Italy. As of 1988, the share of total gross value-added held by the credit and insurance sector, at market prices, was 4.45 per cent in Italy and 16.21 per cent in the United Kingdom. Likewise, only 1.73 per cent of total employment was concentrated in this sector in Italy, whereas it was up to 3.86 per cent in the United Kingdom. At the end of 1989, per branch inhabitants, assets and deposits[2] were equal, respectively, to 2956, ECU 115.31 and ECU 78.51 in the United Kingdom and 3528, ECU 56.26 and ECU 29.64 in Italy: a clear indication that in the latter country the banking system was far from saturation. Also, until 1990, when a new law opened the possibility of transforming public sector banks into joint-stock corporations, most Italian credit institutions were heavily controlled by the State and in some cases 'they were used as instruments of policy-inspired distribution channels with a clear impact on the allocation of credit for the whole economy' (CEC, 1993, p. 141).[3] The contrast between the stock markets of the two countries is even more remarkable: at the end of 1990, the stock market capitalization of shares relative to GDP in Italy was 12.9 per cent (the lowest in the EC), whereas the same indicator for the United Kingdom was 79 per cent (the highest in the EC). Similarly, the Milan Stock Exchange represented 7.3 per cent of total EC stock market capitalization of shares, whereas the London Stock Exchange ranked first in Europe with 40.5 per cent. Finally, one obvious yet striking difference between the two countries, and indeed between Italy and all its European counterparts, is the extent and persistence of regional disparities. Thus, in many respects, it seems appropriate to consider these two countries as polar extremes.

We begin by looking at the extent of risk sharing across the regions of Italy and the United Kingdom and compare our findings to those provided by van Wincoop (1995) for Japanese prefectures and OECD countries. We also test the perfect risk-sharing hypothesis by running a regression for each of the regions considered along the lines of Obstfeld (1994), and further elaborate this point by estimating cointegrating relationships between regional consumption and both aggregate consumption and regional income. Then, following Asdrubali *et al.* (1996), we assess the relative importance of central government and market institutions in achieving risk sharing within these two countries. More precisely, we measure the contribution to regional risk sharing stemming from (a) cross-ownership of productive assets, holdings of government bonds or other forms of financial assets, such as bank deposits,[4] (b) taxes and transfers by the government, (c) portfolio adjustments by agents through lending and borrowing on credit markets or through intertemporal consumption smoothing. Finally, we examine whether the smoothing patterns of regions in the United Kingdom and in Italy vary according to the persistence of shocks.

On the first count, we find that the extent of consumption insurance enjoyed by both Italian and British regions is substantially larger than previous studies have usually found among the US states or internationally. On the second count, we ascertain that the relative importance of the three channels of interregional risk sharing in both countries is significantly different and that the share of each source varies with the persistence of the risks which have to be insured. In particular, risk sharing in Italy, thanks mainly to direct and indirect government actions, appears to be almost perfect even for low-frequency fluctuations.

15.2 THE THEORY OF RISK SHARING AND ITS EMPIRICAL IMPLICATIONS

15.2.1 A Formal Characterization of Risk Sharing

Risk sharing can be the result of both market and institutional features. Complete financial markets may not only allocate funds optimally across their uses and spur growth this way (for example Greenwood and Smith, 1994), but also, as a by-product, allow agents to smooth consumption across states of nature. Institutions too may provide insurance against shocks, raising income and consumption levels and enhancing growth. Two channels that have been discussed in the literature are the reduction of income smoothing (Murdoch, 1995) and of inequality (Persson and Tabellini, 1996a, b). Other authors, however, have pointed out that under some circumstances improved consumption insurance can entail a lower rate of growth (Deveraux and Smith, 1994; Deveraux and Makoto, 1997).

Following Canova and Ravn (1996) and Ubide (1994), a simple way of deriving the theoretical results about risk sharing is to start off by solving a Pareto planner's problem for the aggregate (that is, the world or the national) economy, and to ignore the decentralization mechanism that may achieve the planner's allocation.

As is customary, the planner seeks to maximize a weighted average of the lifetime utility of the K regional representative agents subject to an aggregate resource constraint. Following Obstfeld and Rogoff (1996, Appendix 5C.2) denote by h_t the history of the aggregate economy at date t, which determines the state of nature as of t and which is a list of the realizations of all possible states for every period before t. Correspondingly, $\pi(h_t/h_1)$ is the conditional probability that the economy's history as of date t turns out to be h_t, given what has happened through date 1. The set $H_t(h_1)$ is defined to consist of all continuations of h_1 through date t.

The planner then solves the following problem:

$$\max_{c_i} \sum_{i=1}^{K} \theta_i \sum_t \beta^t \{ \sum_{h_t \in H_t(h_1)} \pi(h_t|h_1) U[c_i(h_t)] \} \tag{15.1}$$

$$s.t. \sum_{i=1}^{K} \phi_i c_i(h_t) = \sum_{i=1}^{K} \phi_i y_i(h_t)$$

where c_i and y_i are consumption and income of region i respectively, θ_i is the weight attached by the planner to the individual region, and ϕ_i represents its output share. The optimality conditions are:

$$\frac{U'(c_i(h_t))}{U'(c_j(h_t))} = \frac{\theta_i/\phi_i}{\theta_j/\phi_j} \tag{15.2}$$

Then, the aggregate output is distributed among the K representative agents in such a way that the weighted marginal utilities are equalized across all regions in every state of the world.

Taking natural logarithms we have that for every regional representative agent:

$$\log[U'(c_i(h_t))] - \log[U'(c_a(h_t))] = A_i \tag{15.3}$$

where the subscript a denotes the average aggregate marginal utility, and $A_i = \log(\theta_i/\phi_i) - \log(\theta_j/\phi_j)$. In words, the (log of) marginal utility of region i should be proportional to the (log of) average marginal utility of aggregate consumption. To give empirical content to this result, we have to assume a functional form for the momentary utility. Accordingly, we assume the standard time separable CRRA (constant relative risk aversion) utility function (which is also consistent with balanced growth).[5] The previous equation then becomes:

$$-\sigma_i \log(c_i) + \sigma_a \log(c_a) = A_i \tag{15.4}$$

From this equation one can develop many tests on consumption insurance across countries and regions (Obstfeld, 1994).

15.2.2 Time Series and Cross-Sectional Implications

As we noted earlier, the theory of consumption smoothing has several strong empirical predictions, though a set of ancillary assumptions (for example, the functional form of the utility function) has to be postulated in order to make them testable. A great deal of studies have looked at how those predictions fare in the data from different perspectives. Obviously the easiest statement to investigate (and to reject) is the perfect correlation of (the marginal utility of) consumption across countries (or regions). In the context of increasingly more sophisticated RBC models, a host of studies have shown, by means of simulation methods, that actual consumption correlation is lower than the one implied by this class of models, even allowing for incomplete markets (Baxter and Crucini, 1993), non-tradables (Stockman and Tesar, 1995) and uninsurable risk (van Wincoop, 1995).

Other authors took a different route, by devising statistical tests of the risk-sharing propositions. Within this group, the works by Obstfeld (1994), Canova and Ravn (1996) and Lewis (1996) have tested directly for the presence of complete consumption insurance, deriving the empirical counterparts of the theory either from the (expected) equalization of (the marginal utilities of) consumption, or from the proportionality of local consumption to global income (consumption) and the insensibility to local income. Whereas Bayoumi and McDonald (1994), Atkeson and Bayoumi (1993) and Bayoumi (1995) put more emphasis on capital mobility and the degree of financial markets integration, deriving their tests from the empirical literature on the optimal intertemporal profile of consumption, mainly from the expected equalization of interest rates.

One issue common to all papers is how to deal with the non-stationarity and likely cointegration of income and consumption time series and its implications for the test results. Most studies take first differences to achieve data stationarity. However, as stressed by Vahid and Engle (1993), the existence of a common trend (implied by the permanent income hypothesis, the intertemporal counterpart of consumption smoothing) makes this practice prone to omitted-variable problems.[6] We tackle this problem in two ways: on one hand, as in Canova and Ravn (1996), we use different filtering procedures, namely FOD (first order differences), HP (Hodrick and Prescott) and LT (linearly detrended). On the other hand, we directly address in several ways the potential cointegration among the variables. This led us to test for a further implication of perfect risk sharing, that is, that regional consumption should be cointegrated with aggregate consumption. It is obvious that this may entail permanent redistribution of income among regions with different trends in output, possibly through centralized redistribution arrangements as a national fiscal system.[7]

More precisely, in order to assess the degree of risk sharing at different frequencies across British and Italian regions, we carried out three different and complementary tests.

Taking first differences of equation (15.4) we can express the growth rate of individual consumption as a linear function of the aggregate consumption growth rate; the former should perfectly comove with the latter in response to a common shock and should be absolutely independent of any idiosyncratic shocks. Hence, following Obstfeld (1994) we tested the hypothesis of perfect risk sharing in Italy and the UK by estimating the following equation:

$$\Delta c_{it} = \alpha + \beta \Delta c_{at} + \gamma \Delta y_{it} + u_t \qquad (15.5)$$

The perfect risk-sharing hypothesis has the following and obvious parameter implications, $\gamma = 0$ and $\beta = 1$. However, as pointed out by Bayoumi and McDonald (1994), this test cannot distinguish between failure of perfect risk sharing across regions and failure of the representative consumer within the ith region to optimally smooth consumption across time, since both facts entail excess sensitivity to local income (growth). In order to overcome this problem, they augment the above specification with global income and suggest testing perfect capital mobility through the joint insignificance of all parameters but the constant, while the significance of the regional income coefficient measures only deviations from rational behaviour. This procedure was applied to Italian data by Scorcu (1996), whose findings are broadly consistent with ours.

In order to shed some light on the long-run aspects of risk sharing, but also as a robustness check for our findings under the other two methodologies against a potential omitted variable bias, we tested for cointegration among regional consumption and both aggregate consumption and regional income. Equation (15.4) clearly implies that consumption of region j, if integrated of order one, that is, I(1), should be cointegrated with consumption of all other regions and with aggregate consumption. Moreover, when risk aversion coefficients are the same, the cointegrating vector in the latter case is $(1,-1)$.[8] We tested this hypothesis by means of unit root tests especially developed by Oh (1996) to exploit the structure of panel data. This approach is particularly useful in our case, since the UK series are not very long, so that the usual individual time-series tests (for example the augmented Dickey–Fuller test) are likely to have very low power. Next we tried to assess the role of regional income, much in the spirit of the above Obstfeldt test. We estimated equation (15.5) with pooled OLS in levels, allowing for individual fixed effects. Subsequently we applied, as before, panel unit roots test to the residuals from this regression. As the last check, we reran the Obstfeldt regressions on differenced data for each region adding the variables in levels, that is, in error correction form.

Finally, as in Asdrubali *et al.* (1996), we obtained as a by-product of the decomposition of risk sharing another test of the perfect insurance proposition for panel data. Bayoumi (1995) provides a nice interpretation of this procedure along the following lines. Under the assumption of perfect capital mobility, individual maximization of utility by infinitely-lived representative agents under an intertemporal budget constraint yields the usual Euler equation:

$$E_t[U'(c_{t+1})/U'(c_t)] = \beta(1+r_t) \qquad (15.6)$$

where β is the common subjective discount factor and r_t is the real interest rate.

Under the standard assumptions for the utility function (see Section 15.2.1) and taking logarithms and first differences (see Bayoumi, 1995, pp. 3–4), the growth rate of consumption for region i could be written as:

$$\Delta c_{it} = \sigma \log \beta + \sigma \log(1+r_t) + \varepsilon_t \qquad (15.7)$$

Again it is clear that when interest rates are equalized across regions, the growth rate of consumption of region i should perfectly comove with region j, and should not depend on idiosyncratic (that is, region-specific) shocks. As pointed out by Bayoumi (1995), the error term in the above equation is the sum of two disturbances, a common one and a specific one that reflects the change in the regional permanent income. The test proposed by Bayoumi (1995) is then the following one:

$$\Delta c_{it} = \alpha + \sum_{j=2}^{T} \delta_j d_j + \gamma \Delta y_{it} + u_t \qquad (15.8)$$

where the d_j are time dummy variables, equal to one when $j=t$ and zero otherwise. The coefficient on regional income γ measures to what degree the idiosyncratic shocks to regional output affect consumption, while the time dummies account for the degree to which consumption follows the full insurance path, since their coefficients are estimated in a panel and are common across regions. We also restricted γ, the coefficient on regional income, to be equal across regions, as in Asdrubali *et al.* (1996) and in one regression in Bayoumi (see Table 3 in Bayoumi, 1995).

15.3 SOME EVIDENCE ON REGIONAL RISK SHARING IN ITALY AND THE UNITED KINGDOM

The scope for interregional risk sharing in Italy and in the United Kingdom can be inferred from Table 15.1, which presents data on the regional and national gross product variability in the two countries.

Table 15.1 Variability of gross regional product growth rates in Italy (1961–1994) and the United Kingdom (1976–1994)

Variance		Variance	
Piemonte	0.00096	North	0.00065
Valle d' Aosta	0.00150	Yorkshire	0.00089
Lombardia	0.00058	East Midlands	0.00076
Trentino	0.00073	East Anglia	0.00099
Veneto	0.00054	South East	0.00130
Friuli	0.00080	South West	0.00071
Liguria	0.00087	West Midlands	0.00145
Emilia	0.00081	North West	0.00114
Toscana	0.00066	Wales	0.00139
Umbria	0.00089	Scotland	0.00062
Marche	0.00078	Northern Ireland	0.00065
Lazio	0.00042	**United Kingdom**	**0.00099**
Abruzzo	0.00136		
Molise	0.00137		
Campania	0.00059		
Puglia	0.00124		
Basilicata	0.00411		
Calabria	0.00258		
Sicilia	0.00131		
Sardegna	0.00093		
Italy	**0.00052**		

Source: Calculations use ISTAT for Italy, and Regional Trends (HMSO) for the United Kingdom.

Especially for Italy, it is clear that the variability of national output is always smaller than the variability of regional product. In particular, in the case of Basilicata, the former is one twelfth of the latter. The evidence for the United Kingdom is less sharp. Regional variability is smaller than national variability in six out of eleven cases.[9]

Another piece of indirect evidence on consumption smoothing in Italy can be detected from Tables 15.2 and 15.3 which display the correlation coefficients of consumption growth rates and gross domestic product growth rates respectively. This comparison is now standard in the international real business cycle literature. The most striking feature is that in

Table 15.2 Correlation coefficients for consumption growth rates in the Italian regions, 1961–1994

	PIE	VDA	LOM	TAA	VEN	FVG	LIG	EMR	TOS	UMB	MAR	LAZ	ABR	MOL	CAM	PUG	BAS	CAL	SIC	SAR
Piemonte	1.00	0.81	0.93	0.83	0.87	0.88	0.94	0.91	0.80	0.85	0.82	0.89	0.85	0.75	0.84	0.88	0.85	0.84	0.88	0.78
Valle d'Aosta		1.00	0.73	0.78	0.79	0.69	0.85	0.80	0.65	0.73	0.75	0.71	0.71	0.60	0.69	0.66	0.67	0.66	0.71	0.57
Lombardia			1.00	0.77	0.87	0.84	0.90	0.87	0.82	0.85	0.84	0.81	0.83	0.81	0.83	0.88	0.87	0.85	0.86	0.81
Trentino				1.00	0.74	0.75	0.80	0.79	0.65	0.80	0.74	0.68	0.73	0.74	0.71	0.72	0.74	0.77	0.74	0.64
Veneto					1.00	0.90	0.93	0.94	0.86	0.90	0.92	0.73	0.90	0.82	0.90	0.86	0.92	0.89	0.92	0.88
Friuli						1.00	0.89	0.94	0.87	0.88	0.87	0.76	0.86	0.83	0.89	0.87	0.91	0.87	0.87	0.85
Liguria							1.00	0.95	0.86	0.85	0.90	0.86	0.88	0.72	0.87	0.84	0.86	0.83	0.86	0.79
Emilia								1.00	0.86	0.90	0.93	0.82	0.89	0.83	0.92	0.85	0.93	0.90	0.91	0.87
Toscana									1.00	0.83	0.81	0.77	0.79	0.73	0.87	0.84	0.84	0.79	0.83	0.82
Umbria										1.00	0.87	0.71	0.89	0.87	0.86	0.85	0.88	0.88	0.88	0.86
Marche											1.00	0.68	0.85	0.85	0.92	0.80	0.90	0.89	0.90	0.89
Lazio												1.00	0.72	0.52	0.78	0.78	0.73	0.66	0.73	0.68
Abruzzo													1.00	0.77	0.87	0.89	0.89	0.87	0.88	0.82
Molise														1.00	0.80	0.77	0.90	0.90	0.86	0.84
Campania															1.00	0.87	0.92	0.89	0.93	0.90
Puglia																1.00	0.88	0.81	0.85	0.85
Basilicata																	1.00	0.94	0.93	0.91
Calabria																		1.00	0.93	0.90
Sicilia																			1.00	0.91
Sardegna																				1.00

Source: Calculations using ISTAT.

426

Table 15.3 Correlation coefficients for gross domestic product growth rates in the Italian regions, 1961–1994

	PIE	VDA	LOM	TAA	VEN	FVG	LIG	EMR	TOS	UMB	MAR	LAZ	ABR	MOL	CAM	PUG	BAS	CAL	SIC	SAR
Piemonte	1.00	0.62	0.92	0.75	0.79	0.78	0.71	0.80	0.71	0.63	0.73	0.74	0.61	0.47	0.63	0.57	0.32	0.24	0.32	0.41
Valle d'Aosta		1.00	0.66	0.45	0.37	0.48	0.74	0.53	0.39	0.55	0.41	0.50	0.29	0.29	0.24	0.13	0.27	0.29	0.14	0.03
Lombardia			1.00	0.66	0.79	0.79	0.78	0.78	0.74	0.65	0.66	0.74	0.55	0.43	0.59	0.42	0.20	0.23	0.29	0.37
Trentino				1.00	0.75	0.73	0.65	0.77	0.55	0.61	0.72	0.59	0.67	0.48	0.70	0.51	0.57	0.23	0.48	0.50
Veneto					1.00	0.83	0.65	0.87	0.82	0.64	0.73	0.60	0.54	0.41	0.71	0.47	0.24	0.13	0.40	0.49
Friuli						1.00	0.75	0.85	0.69	0.62	0.66	0.64	0.53	0.42	0.64	0.48	0.22	0.16	0.37	0.52
Liguria							1.00	0.70	0.62	0.67	0.49	0.67	0.50	0.51	0.50	0.39	0.32	0.21	0.31	0.32
Emilia								1.00	0.77	0.75	0.77	0.59	0.62	0.55	0.63	0.51	0.33	0.19	0.38	0.41
Toscana									1.00	0.73	0.75	0.58	0.63	0.54	0.79	0.54	0.28	0.30	0.57	0.54
Umbria										1.00	0.69	0.56	0.67	0.70	0.70	0.63	0.45	0.34	0.50	0.45
Marche											1.00	0.54	0.70	0.59	0.77	0.62	0.56	0.45	0.65	0.56
Lazio												1.00	0.59	0.42	0.52	0.46	0.30	0.21	0.40	0.52
Abruzzo													1.00	0.67	0.71	0.71	0.71	0.37	0.66	0.63
Molise														1.00	0.57	0.74	0.65	0.47	0.61	0.46
Campania															1.00	0.69	0.51	0.45	0.70	0.71
Puglia																1.00	0.54	0.42	0.56	0.61
Basilicata																	1.00	0.58	0.74	0.54
Calabria																		1.00	0.62	0.49
Sicilia																			1.00	0.78
Sardegna																				1.00

Source: Calculations using ISTAT.

general consumption is more correlated than income across Italian regions. Many simulated models would predict this result, but the usual finding in the empirical literature mentioned earlier is that such a correlation pattern does not hold at the international level (Backus *et al.*, 1992), that is why this phenomenon has become known as the international consumption correlation puzzle. The same does not hold true for the regions of the United Kingdom (Tables 15.4 and 15.5): for many of them income turns out to be more correlated than consumption.

Table 15.6 presents some evidence concerning the consumption puzzle regarding Japan's prefectures and OECD countries. They do not look too different in the (imperfect) degree of consumption insurance and capital mobility that can be achieved at different frequencies. It is very tempting to compare the degree of risk sharing across and within nations as a way of gauging the degree of market imperfections and the weight of uninsurable risk on one hand, and the role of institutions such as federal governments on the other hand. Indeed, it is often the case that regions of the same country have very integrated financial markets and share some redistribution mechanism. However, as pointed out by Obstfeld (1994) with incomplete markets regional studies can disguise the real degree of insurance achievable, overstating the role of uninsurable (for example because of moral hazard or debtor's sovereignty problems) country-specific shocks. Moreover, the existence of a large economic role played by governments and of a high degree of good tradability across regions within a country could also suggest the same wrong conclusion. In order to overcome these drawbacks and to fully take advantage of regional studies, it is crucial to be able to distinguish both quantitatively and qualitatively the different channels through which consumption insurance takes place. But before turning to this decomposition let us have a closer look at global risk sharing.

15.3.1   Global Risk Sharing

Here we focus on the tests discussed in the previous section concerning the general implications of risk sharing. We begin with the test used by Obstfeld (1994) and then apply panel and cointegration tecniques to control for omitted-variable bias and to study some long-run implications of the hypothesis. The data set consists of annual observations, taken from ISTAT (Italy) and HMSO (UK) official statistical accounts, on per capita regional consumption and production for the twenty regions of Italy and the eleven regions of the United Kingdom. The sample period runs from 1960 to 1994 for Italy and from 1976 to 1994 for the United Kingdom.

Table 15.4 *Correlation coefficients for consumption growth rates in the British regions, 1976–1994*

	NO	YH	EM	EA	SE	SW	WM	NW	WA	SC	NI
North	1.00	0.83	0.71	0.83	0.82	0.64	0.77	0.89	0.75	0.79	0.79
Yorkshire		1.00	0.74	0.80	0.86	0.59	0.82	0.88	0.74	0.88	0.63
East Midlands			1.00	0.76	0.80	0.59	0.91	0.86	0.67	0.83	0.69
East Anglia				1.00	0.88	0.68	0.83	0.84	0.85	0.80	0.82
South East					1.00	0.79	0.83	0.91	0.77	0.86	0.66
South West						1.00	0.60	0.79	0.71	0.57	0.43
West Midlands							1.00	0.91	0.71	0.85	0.77
North West								1.00	0.76	0.86	0.73
Wales									1.00	0.69	0.59
Scotland										1.00	0.70
Northern Ireland											1.00

Source: Calculations using Regional Trends (HMSO).

Table 15.5 *Correlation coefficients for gross domestic product growth rates in the British regions, 1976–1994*

	NO	YH	EM	EA	SE	SW	WM	NW	WA	SC	NI
North	1.00	0.83	0.87	0.66	0.82	0.84	0.82	0.83	0.75	0.83	0.66
Yorkshire		1.00	0.93	0.82	0.86	0.92	0.92	0.95	0.86	0.82	0.83
East Midlands			1.00	0.84	0.84	0.90	0.87	0.89	0.81	0.76	0.81
East Anglia				1.00	0.62	0.78	0.74	0.81	0.64	0.58	0.72
South East					1.00	0.92	0.90	0.92	0.86	0.88	0.75
South West						1.00	0.91	0.94	0.92	0.91	0.83
West Midlands							1.00	0.95	0.86	0.91	0.80
North West								1.00	0.86	0.85	0.79
Wales									1.00	0.86	0.82
Scotland										1.00	0.77
Northern Ireland											1.00

Source: Calculations using Regional Trends (HMSO).

As is apparent from Tables 15.7 and 15.8, the degree of consumption insurance in both countries is, on the whole, considerable. In particular, for the UK, the F-test is never rejected at the 1 per cent level and it fails only twice (Wales and Northern Ireland) at the 5 per cent level. This

Table 15.6 Data moments for Japanese prefectures, OECD countries, Italian and British regions

	Japan (1975–88)	OECD (1970–89)	Italy (1961–94)	United Kingdom (1976–94)
Time series moments				
corr (c_i,c_j)	0.46	0.46	0.77	0.82
corr (y_i,y_j)	0.42	0.43	0.55	0.94
corr (c_i,y_i)	0.37	0.81	0.59	0.83
Cross-sectional moments				
st.dev. (gc_i)	8.69		2.34	3.45
st.dev. (gy_i)	13.71	10.79	3.29	3.15
corr (gc_i,gy_i)	0.32	0.67	0.66	0.69
corr (corr (c_i,c_j), corr (y_i,y_j))	0.00	0.75	0.32	0.18
corr (st.dev. (c_i), st.dev. (y_i))	–0.28	0.74	0.89	–0.37

reflects income coefficients that are in general not significant and consumption coefficients usually close to one. It is interesting to note that for Wales, the rejection seems to depend more on the low coefficient for aggregate consumption (only 0.75), since γ is not significantly different from zero, whereas for Ulster both parameters are also individually significant and very different from what was expected, with γ larger than β.

The picture is somewhat less clear-cut for Italy, where we reject the null three times at the 1 per cent level (Lazio, Abruzzo and Basilicata) and four times at the 5 per cent level (Trentino Alto Adige, Molise, Sicilia and Sardegna). The coefficients are more sharply estimated than for the United Kingdom, and in general the βs fall slightly short of one, while the γs are very often significant. In particular, for the regions rejecting the hypothesis of perfect risk sharing at the 1 per cent level, regional income is highly significant except for Basilicata, whose coefficient on aggregate consumption is fairly greater than 1. This might be an indication of high dependence on aggregate income innovations due to large government transfers. Lazio is a particularly puzzling case, since its consumption growth is equally accounted for by both aggregate consumption and regional production shocks.

The first section of Table 15.9 presents the results of carrying out, as suggested by Oh (1996), the augmented Dickey–Fuller test for unit roots by means of pooled OLS on the 'residuals' obtained imposing the (1,–1) cointegrating vector on consumption data. It is apparent that, regardless

Table 15.7 Obstfeld test for Italy, 1961–1994

	$\Delta c_{it} = \alpha + \beta \Delta c_{at} + \gamma \Delta y_{it}$		
	β	γ	$P(F\text{-test})\ H_0\colon \beta=1, \gamma=0$
Piemonte	0.89	0.04	0.3
	(0.08)	(0.05)	
Valle d'Aosta	0.89	0.13	0.3
	(0.17)	(0.09)	
Lombardia	0.80	0.15	0.1
	(0.09)	(0.08)	
Trentino	0.64	0.20	0.034
	(0.13)	(0.1)	
Veneto	0.88	0.14	0.1
	(0.07)	(0.06)	
Friuli	0.93	0.08	0.0
	(0.1)	(0.07)	
Liguria	1.03	0.05	0.4
	(0.08)	(0.06)	
Emilia	0.92	0.08	0.3
	(0.07)	(0.05)	
Toscana	0.75	0.22	0.1
	(0.14)	(0.11)	
Umbria	0.98	–0.03	0.7
	(0.13)	(0.08)	
Marche	1.02	0.03	0.7
	(0.12)	(0.09)	
Lazio	0.50	0.40	0.0001*
	(0.1)	(0.1)	
Abruzzo	0.89	0.22	0.0007*
	(0.1)	(0.06)	
Molise	0.94	0.19	0.04
	(0.17)	(0.07)	
Campania	0.91	0.13	0.3
	(0.11)	(0.09)	
Puglia	0.86	0.13	0.2
	(0.15)	(0.08)	
Basilicata	1.16	0.04	0.008*
	(0.08)	(0.03)	
Calabria	0.97	0.08	0.1
	(0.1)	(0.04)	
Sicilia	1.17	0.03	0.4
	(0.11)	(0.06)	
Sardegna	0.80	0.18	0.4
	(0.1)	(0.07)	

Notes: Standard errors in parentheses, *5 per cent rejection of H_0, **1 per cent rejection of H_0.
Source: Estimates using ISTAT.

Table 15.8 Obstfeld test for the United Kingdom, 1976–1994

	$\Delta c_{it} = \alpha + \beta \Delta c_{at} + \gamma \Delta y_{it}$		
	β	γ	$P(F\text{-test})\ H_0\colon \beta=1,\ \gamma=0$
North	1.33	–0.4	0.25
	(0.2)	(0.24)	
Yorkshire	0.95	0.04	0.95
	(0.19)	(0.19)	
East Midlands	0.99	–0.07	0.86
	(0.22)	(0.24)	
East Anglia	0.97	0.15	0.50
	(0.14)	(0.14)	
South East	1.13	–0.1	0.69
	(0.15)	(0.12)	
South West	0.78	0.14	0.64
	(0.28)	(0.34)	
West Midlands	1.02	0.14	0.19
	(0.17)	(0.13)	
North West	1.23	–0.17	0.20
	(0.12)	(0.11)	
Wales	0.72	–0.07	0.023*
	(0.25)	(0.2)	
Scotland	0.94	0.19	0.50
	(0.15)	(0.18)	
Northern Ireland	0.62	0.72	0.019*
	(0.19)	(0.22)	

Notes: Standard errors in parentheses, *5 per cent rejection of H_0, **1 per cent rejection of H_0.
Source: Estimates using Regional Trends (HMSO).

of the lag structure, we could never reject the null hypothesis of a unit root, that is, of no cointegration: long-run risk pooling seems to be out of the reach of both Italian and British consumers. The last columns depict the results from the same test applied to the residuals from the following pooled OLS regression in levels

$$c_{it} = \alpha_i + \beta c_{at} + \gamma y_{it} + \varepsilon_{it}$$

where α_i is an individual fixed effect. With the inclusion of the regional income the residuals become stationary. Thus we have additional confirmation of the imperfect long-run risk sharing: the low-frequency evolution

Table 15.9 Stationarity of residuals from cointegrating relations

	Cointegrating vector (1,−1)		Cointegrating vector estimated by pooled OLS	
	Lagged coefficient	*t*-value	Lagged coefficient	*t*-value
Italy (1961–94)				
1 lag	−0.009	−3.81	−0.12	−9.00**
2 lags	−0.006	−2.60	−0.10	−7.32*
3 lags	−0.003	−1.36	−0.09	−6.31
4 lags	−0.003	−1.17	−0.08	−5.67
United Kingdom (1976–94)				
1 lag	−0.019	−1.26	−0.36	−7.15**
2 lags	−0.007	−0.47	−0.34	−5.97*
3 lags	−0.006	−0.36	−0.44	−7.29**
4 lags	−0.006	−0.40	−0.45	−6.21**

Notes:
* Rejection of unit root at 5 per cent level.
** Rejection of unit root at 1 per cent level.

Source: Estimates using ISTAT and Regional Trends (HMSO).

of local consumption cannot be accounted for without considering the long-run dynamics of local income. Moreover, as pointed out by Canova and Ravn (1996), this fact provides indirect evidence of lack of convergence in per capita income across the regions in our data set, a result that other authors (see Paci and Pigliaru, 1997 and references therein) reached for Italian regions with a different methodology.

Finally we ran an error correction (Engel and Granger, 1987) version of the Obstfeld regression, that is, one augmented with the variables in levels; Tables 15.10 and 15.11 report the results for Italy and the UK, respectively. The first thing to notice is that, as should be expected given the not very long span of data, level variables do not appear to be very significant for the regions of the United Kingdom, while Italian regions show that long-run relations may be important in understanding the extent of risk sharing they enjoy. Hence, our previous findings for the UK are broadly confirmed, with the levels significant only for the regions for which we rejected the perfect risk sharing proposition, Wales again at the 1 per cent level and East Midlands at the 5 per cent level. Strikingly, the two regions show fairly strong evidence of a (1,−1) cointegrating vector between regional and aggregate consumption and of no cointegration

Table 15.10 Error correction model for Italy, 1961–1994

	Long-run relation: $\alpha_1 c_j = \alpha_2 y_j + \alpha_3 c_a$					$P(F\text{-test})\ H_0$:
	β	γ	α_1	α_2	α_3	$\beta=1, \gamma=0$
Piemonte	0.99	−0.02	0.6**	−0.003	0.57**	0.79
	(0.11)	(0.06)	(0.14)	(0.06)	(0.13)	
Valle d'Aosta	0.89	0.14	0.15	0.058	0.14	0.56
	(0.28)	(0.14)	(0.1)	(0.15)	(0.15)	
Lombardia	0.75	0.27	0.17**	0.15*	0.03	0.004**
	(0.12)	(0.08)	(0.06)	(0.06)	(0.05)	
Trentino	0.63	0.25	0.21	0.21	0.019	0.11
	(0.19)	(0.13)	(0.11)	(0.15)	(0.11)	
Veneto	0.84	0.12	0.25	−0.08	0.34*	0.20
	(0.1)	(0.07)	(0.13)	(0.09)	(0.015)	
Friuli	0.87	0.11	0.34*	0.11	0.23	0.37
	(0.12)	(0.08)	(0.14)	(0.11)	(0.12)	
Liguria	1.22	−0.06	0.22**	−0.11	0.31**	0.07
	(0.1)	(0.06)	(0.08)	(0.07)	(0.09)	
Emilia	0.97	0.06	0.02	0.004	0.2*	0.48
	(0.1)	(0.06)	(0.16)	(0.08)	(0.1)	
Toscana	0.83	0.04	0.47**	−0.18	0.61**	0.44
	(0.16)	(0.12)	(0.17)	(0.11)	(0.2)	
Umbria	0.94	−0.08	0.41**	−0.09	0.52**	0.16
	(0.13)	(0.08)	(0.13)	(0.07)	(0.17)	
Marche	1.07	0.02	0.74**	0.17*	0.65**	0.61
	(0.13)	(0.1)	(0.2)	(0.06)	(0.18)	
Lazio	0.62	0.33	0.55**	0.32**	0.26**	0.001 **
	(0.12)	(0.1)	(0.11)	(0.11)	(0.06)	
Abruzzio	0.70	0.25	0.22	0.19**	0.03	0.0007 **
	(0.12)	(0.07)	(0.13)	(0.06)	(0.12)	
Molise	0.85	0.21	0.45**	0.07*	0.41**	0.03 *
	(0.17)	(0.09)	(0.09)	(0.08)	(0.11)	
Campania	0.76	0.22	0.3*	0.22	0.12	0.053
	(0.12)	(0.09)	(0.12)	(0.11)	(0.07)	
Puglia	0.77	0.04	0.19	0.05	0.14	0.18
	(0.14)	(0.09)	(0.14)	(0.08)	(0.09)	
Basilicata	0.99	0.08	0.58**	0.12**	0.5**	0.0013 **
	(0.07)	(0.03)	(0.1)	(0.03)	(0.09)	
Calabria	0.99	0.02	0.47**	−0.06*	0.57**	0.92
	(0.1)	(0.05)	(0.1)	(0.03)	(0.12)	
Sicilia	0.96	0.08	0.25	0.05	0.22	0.43
	(0.11)	(0.07)	(0.15)	(0.04)	(0.13)	
Sardegna	0.84	0.15	0.2*	−0.05	0.25**	0.09
	(0.11)	(0.07)	(0.9)	(0.03)	(0.09)	

Notes: Standard errors in parentheses, * 5 per cent rejection of H_0, ** 1 per cent rejection of H_0.

Source: Estimates using ISTAT.

Table 15.11 *Error correction model for the United Kingdom, 1976–1994*

	β	γ	α_1	α_2	α_3	$P(F\text{-test})\ H_0:$ $\beta=1, \gamma=0$
				Long-run relation: $\alpha_1 c_j = \alpha_2 y_j + \alpha_3 c_a$		
North	1.28	−0.32	0.03	0.17	0.25	0.41
	(0.22)	(0.26)	(0.21)	(0.2)	(0.24)	
Yorkshire	0.96	0.06	0.01	−0.04	0.28	0.97
	(0.25)	(0.25)	(0.25)	(0.19)	(0.24)	
East Midlands	0.94	−0.37	0.84**	−0.38	1.21**	0.02*
	(0.2)	(0.24)	(0.23)	(0.22)	−36.00	
East Anglia	0.92	0.25	0.02	0.18	0.09	0.21
	(0.18)	(0.16)	(0.26)	(0.21)	(0.29)	
South East	1.00	−0.05	0.02	−0.48**	0.67**	0.76
	(0.21)	(0.18)	(0.14)	(0.15)	(0.25)	
South West	1.26	−0.48	0.00	−1.08*	1.16*	0.54
	(0.41)	(0.48)	(0.19)	(0.43)	(0.49)	
West Midlands	0.94	0.15	0.02	0.2*	0.14	0.75
	(0.23)	(0.21)	(0.38)	(0.09)	(0.31)	
North West	1.26	−0.22	0.48*	0.01	0.49	0.20
	(0.14)	(0.13)	(0.24)	(0.09)	(0.28)	
Wales	0.93	−0.23	0.64**	0.02	0.59*	0.008**
	(0.28)	(0.24)	(0.23)	(0.11)	(0.24)	
Scotland	0.80	0.31	0.03	0.11	0.3	0.51
	(0.22)	(0.26)	(0.25)	(0.14)	(0.28)	
Northern Ireland	0.57	0.39	0.04	0.65	−0.06	0.48
	(0.36)	(0.43)	(0.33)	(0.35)	(0.23)	

Notes:
Standard errors in parentheses.
*5 per cent significance level.
**1 per cent significance level.

Source: Estimates using Regional Trends (HMSO).

between regional consumption and production. The picture is somewhat different for Italian regions: on the one hand the number of regions for which the hypothesis of perfect risk sharing is rejected drops to five, of which four at the 1 per cent level, with Lombardia joining Basilicata, Lazio and Abruzzo, and instead Trentino, Sicilia and Sardegna passing the test now. The striking feature is that for all the regions that fail the test, with the exception of Abruzzo, regional consumption and income are cointegrated, indicating imperfect risk pooling even in the long run. Moreover, ten out of twenty regions show strong signs of cointegration between regional and national consumption, while for six of them regional income enters the long-run relation significantly.

15.3.2 Channels of Regional Risk Sharing

The methodology put forward by Asdrubali *et al.* (1996) in order to estimate how risk sharing is allocated among different channels is based on the decomposition of the cross-sectional variance of gross regional product. We said earlier that risk sharing can take place thanks to three different channels, (a) cross-ownership of productive assets, holdings of government bonds or other forms of financial assets, such as bank deposits, (b) taxes and transfers by government, (c) portfolio adjustments by agents through lending and borrowing on credit markets or through intertemporal consumption smoothing.[10] The former two channels provide ex-ante insurance while the latter one provides ex-post insurance. Also, unlike the case of taxes and transfers, the smoothing achieved through the capital and credit channels is based on market transactions.

The available data allow us to test the relative importance of the three aforementioned channels for the period 1983–1992 for Italy and 1979–1994 for the United Kingdom.

Methodology
The estimation methodology is based on the decomposition of the period-by-period cross-sectional variance in gross regional product, starting from the following identity:

$$grp^i = \frac{grp^i}{ri^i} \; \frac{ri^i}{rdi^i} \; \frac{rdi^i}{con^i} \; con^i \tag{15.9}$$

where i identifies the region and grp, ri, rdi and con denote per capita gross regional product, regional income, regional disposable income and aggregate consumption. (See the appendix for further details on data.)

If we take logs, multiply both sides by log grp and take expectations we obtain the following expression:

$$\begin{aligned} \text{var} (\log grp) = {} & \text{cov} (\log grp, \log grp - \log ri) \\ & + \text{cov} (\log grp, \log ri - \log rdi) \\ & + \text{cov} (\log grp, \log rdi - \log con) \\ & + \text{cov} (\log grp, \log con) \end{aligned} \tag{15.10}$$

By dividing both sides by the variance of log grp we get:

$$1 = \beta_K + \beta_G + \beta_C + \beta_U \tag{15.11}$$

where the βs are the OLS coefficient derived from the following set of panel regressions:

$$\log grp_t^i - \log ri_t^{ii} = \alpha_{K,t} + \beta_K \log grp_t^i + u_{K,t}^i \qquad (15.12)$$

$$\log ri_t^{ii} - \log rdi_t^{ii} = \alpha_{G,t} + \beta_G \log grp_t^i + u_{G,t}^i \qquad (15.13)$$

$$\log rdi_t^{ii} - \log con_t^i = \alpha_{C,t} + \beta_C \log grp_t^i + u_{C,t}^i \qquad (15.14)$$

$$\log con_t^i = \alpha_{U,t} + \beta_U \log grp_t^i + u_{U,t}^i \qquad (15.15)$$

The αs are time fixed effects, β_K, β_G, β_C are to be interpreted as the incremental percentage amount of smoothing achieved through the channels outlined above, corresponding to (a) capital markets; (b) government fiscal policies; (c) credit markets or intertemporal consumption substitution; β_U represents the amount of gross regional product variability which is not smoothed.

In order to investigate how the relative weights of these channels vary with the nature of the fluctuations, we filter the data by three methods.[11] In particular, FOD are used to test for short cycle insurance, HP filtered series for intermediate frequencies and DT series for low frequencies. We expect the role of the first channel to increase and that of the third to decrease with the persistence of shocks. For, as anticipated above, highly persistent shocks can be insured ex ante (via the capital market) but not ex post (via the credit market) since those agents who wish to borrow are unlikely to repay. As for the role of the government, this depends on the type of redistributive policies which are currently at work.

Since regional data show different variability levels we avoid the problem of heteroskedasticity by using generalized least squares (GLS) which impose cross-section weights; no sign of autocorrelation is detected.

The Italian case

Table 15.12 summarizes the results for Italy. We see that they vary according to the filtering method. Starting from the first order difference estimation, almost two thirds (64 per cent) of risk sharing is achieved via the first channel. Since the other two channels exhaust the residual part, risk sharing is perfect. The fact that a considerable amount of risk sharing takes place through the first channel, over a period in which labour mobility came to a halt, is an indication that the cross-ownership of capital and holdings of financial assets must have played a substantial role.[12]

Table 15.12 GLS estimates of income and consumption smoothing among Italian regions, 1983–1992

	First order difference detrended data short run	Hodrick–Prescott detrended data medium run	Linearly detrended data long run
Capital markets	63.5	73.4	74.7
	(11.5)	(13.8)	(11.5)
Government policy	20.1	19.6	20.5
	(3.9)	(4.0)	(4.2)
Consumption smoothing	20.3	16.4	16.7
	(3.2)	(2.5)	(2.5)
Not smoothed	0.0	0.0	0.0
	(0.3)	(0.2)	(2.7)

Notes:
Percentage of shocks to gross regional product absorbed at each level of income smoothing by each channel.
t-statistics are in parentheses.

Source: Estimates using ISTAT.

This finding, however, calls for further investigations, in light of the major role played within this channel by interest payments on public debt and the saving behaviour of Italian households.[13] In particular, it must be stressed that as a result of the persistent high levels of public debt, during the period under study the bond market in Italy was much more important than the share market and served basically the purpose of raising resources for the public sector.[14] It is also worth noting, incidentally, that in Italy even checking accounts bear some interest. The fiscal and redistributive policy by the government is responsible for 20 per cent of risk sharing, which is greater than the percentage of smoothing (13 per cent) accomplished by the federal government in the United States. Finally, consumption smoothing accounts for the remaining 20 per cent.

Similar results obtain under the two alternative filtering methods. The role of capital market increases with the length of the risks to be insured going from 63.5 per cent (FOD) to 73.4 per cent (HP) and finally to 74.7 per cent (DT). The opposite occurs for credit markets, whose total smoothing share goes from around 20 per cent to 16 per cent. The role of the national government remains stable around 20 per cent, and so is the amount of unsmoothed risk sharing, which equals zero. The fact that the role of credit markets declines with the persistence of shocks is not surprising. Shocks with long duration are difficult to smooth ex post by borrowing in the credit market given that the debt is likely either to be repaid after a long time or to be defected. As a result, we find that government fiscal policies, both in Italy and in the United States (see Table 15.15 derived from Asdrubali *et al.*, 1996 and Sala-i-Martin and Sachs, 1992), favour regions suffering from persistent adverse shocks, and that agents exposed to such shocks prefer to insure themselves on capital markets in advance, anticipating the difficulties of doing it later through the credit market.

Given that the fraction of risk sharing attributed to the first channel is higher in Italy than in both the United States and the United Kingdom, we looked for further evidence on this aspect. Accordingly, we perform a test suggested by Atkeson and Bayoumi (1993), who applied it to Europe and the United States, which allows one to evaluate the role of capital markets in providing insulation from regional fluctuations through geographic diversification of investments. In particular such a test assesses the extent of interregional portfolio diversification by apportioning the fluctuations of regional capital income into three types of changes. The first type is related to consumers who derive the bulk of their income from capital and invest nationally (these are defined as capitalists); the second type refers to consumers who derive their income mostly from labour but invest nationally too (named workers); the third type concerns consumers (called local investors) who, for informational reasons, invest mainly locally. Formally, denoting these three types of individuals with subscripts 1, 2 and 3, we can write:

$$\Delta I^1_{Ki} = \Delta I_{Kn}$$
$$\Delta I^2_{Ki} = \beta \Delta I_{Li}$$
$$\Delta I^3_{Ki} = \Delta P_{Ki} \tag{15.16}$$

where I_{Ki} and I_{Kn} represents per capita income from capital respectively in region i and at the national level, I_{Li} and P_{Ki} are per capita labour income and capital product in region i. Assuming that all types of agents receive a constant proportion of total capital income λ^{1i}, λ^{2i} and $(1 - \lambda^{1i} - \lambda^{2i})$, we can estimate the following equation using a GLS weighted least squares estimator for panel data:

$$\Delta I_{Kit} = \alpha_i + \lambda^1 \Delta I_{Knt} + \beta \lambda^2 \Delta I_{Lit} + (1 - \lambda^1 - \lambda^2) \Delta P_{Kit} \tag{15.17}$$

The results displayed in Table 15.13 show that the most important changes in regional capital income are due to changes in national capital

Table 15.13   GLS estimates of Italian regional private sector capital income, 1983–1992

	Coefficient
National capital income	0.75
	(24.62)
Labour income	0.07
	(4.73)
Capital production	–0.03
	(–2.21)
Adjusted *R*-squared	0.80

Note: *t*-statistics in parentheses.

Source: Estimates using ISTAT.

income. This should be interpreted as an indication that fluctuations in personal income from capital are not associated with region-specific shocks. Italian capitalists (that is, savers) look for steady and predictable income stream associated with a balanced portfolio choice. The other two influences are rather small. It should be noted, however, that the sign of the coefficient on the change in personal labour income is unexpected. We expected a negative sign, implying a negative correlation between capital income and labour income, given that workers should insure themselves against movements in their local labour income by choosing a portfolio of national assets.

The fact that portfolios are rather similar across Italy should come as no surprise, in as much as a relevant share of savings still consists of treasury bills. More importantly, investment decisions are usually delegated to intermediaries that invest nationally and internationally according to standardized practices.

The British case
The GLS estimation results for the United Kingdom case are presented in Table 15.14. Again, we immediately note that perfect risk sharing obtains in the short run over the period 1979–1994. But the role of the three channels is very different compared to Italy and the United States (see Table 15.15). As a matter of fact, the amount of smoothing attributable to market transactions, represented by the first and the third channel, is around 100 per cent. Their relative importance is almost the same, 48 per cent for the

Table 15.14 GLS estimates of income and consumption smoothing among British regions, 1978–1994

	First order difference detrended data short run	Hodrick–Prescott detrended data medium run	Linearly detrended data long run
Capital markets	48.1	4.42	40.4
	(8.1)	(7.8)	(7.4)
Government policy	−5.6	0.0	0.0
	(−1.7)	−(0.8)	(0.3)
Consumption smoothing	56.2	41.2	26.8
	(5.1)	(3.8)	(2.8)
Not smoothed	−0.6	10.6	25.3
	(−0.1)	(1.1)	(2.7)

Notes:
Percentage of shocks to gross regional product absorbed at each level of income smoothing by each channel.
t-statistics are in parentheses.

Source: Estimates using Regional Trends (HMSO).

Table 15.15 GLS estimates of income and consumption smoothing among the United States, 1963–1990

	First order difference* detrended data	Persistence of shocks** Low	Persistence of shocks** High
Capital markets	39	33	46
	(3)	(3)	(4)
Government policy	13	11	16
	(1)	(1)	(1)
Consumption smoothing	23	33	14
	(6)	(7)	(7)
Not smoothed	25	24	24
	(6)	(7)	(7)

Notes:
*Percentage of shocks to gsp absorbed at each level of income smoothing by each channel.
**Percentage of shocks to gsp absorbed at each level of smoothing for states with low and high (top third) persistence of shocks.
Standard errors in parenthesis.

Source: Asdrubali, Sorensen and Yosha (1996).

former and 56 per cent for the latter. The government, in contrast, plays no role (β_S is negative and not significant).[15]

This result parallels that of Bayoumi and Rose (1993) who show, using a different procedure, that capital market integration among British regions is complete. This is mainly due to cross-ownership of capital (thanks also to a large and well-developed stock market), cross-patterns of earning retentions and efficient credit markets.

Unlike the Italian case, notably risk sharing in the United Kingdom becomes less perfect in the transition from medium to long term.[16] The amount of gross product variation which is left unsmoothed equals 10 per cent (not significant) for medium-term risks and becomes 25 per cent (significant) for more persistent shocks. This implies that either consumption patterns tend to diverge or that the more permanent components of domestic consumption respond to fluctuations in domestic variables. This phenomenon is strongly connected to the declining role of the credit market which plunges from 56 per cent with FOD to 27 per cent with DT (via 41 per cent with HP). At the same time it is remarkable that while in Italy and in the United States (see Table 15.15 and Sala-i-Martin and Sachs, 1992) long-run shocks are smoothed through taxes and transfers by the central government this is not the case for the United Kingdom, where fiscal policies seem to play no role in consumption smoothing irrespective of the type of shock considered.

15.4   SOME CONCLUDING REMARKS AND POLICY IMPLICATIONS

We have assessed both to what extent and through which channels risk sharing took place among the regions of Italy and the United Kingdom. Empirical works in this area, with few exceptions, have focused mainly on risk sharing among countries or within a federation of states like the US. Here, we consider the regions of two countries with very different financial systems and policy regimes over most of the sample period.

The econometric evidence that we gathered suggests that the regions of both countries exhibit a considerable degree of risk sharing but, according to the unit root tests and the cointegration analyses, this result does not carry over to the long run.

The role played by the various channels of risk sharing changes according to one country's institutional arrangements and policy regimes. In particular in Italy a considerable amount of smoothing occurs thanks to capital markets (about 70 per cent), while government and consumption smoothing account for about the same share of smoothing (around

20 per cent). Such a hierarchy is almost independent of persistency even though it should be noticed that the capital market role increases while the consumption smoothing role decreases with persistency. In the United Kingdom, in contrast, we find that government does not play any role in insuring for production fluctuations and the whole of consumption smoothing (at least in the short run) is obtained thanks to market transactions (48 per cent via capital market and 56 per cent via consumption smoothing). However, such a pattern changes dramatically when shocks to be insured are more persistent. We find that the credit market is able to insure only about 25 per cent of long-run shocks and that the vacuum left by the credit market is not covered by the state. As a consequence, in the United Kingdom there is less risk sharing in the long run (the quota of unsmoothed consumption is around 25 per cent).

Such evidence suggests that in Italy, in contrast to the United Kingdom, persistent shocks have been insured. In other words, semi-permanent redistributive policies, directly and indirectly connected to government actions, have been at work over the years. More analysis is needed to investigate how such policies have affected not only consumption smoothing but, more generally, economic agents' incentive patterns, for instance with respect to their decision to move and to invest across regions.

APPENDIX

The main sources of data and the methodology for constructing the various measures of smoothing are as follows.

Italy

Gross Regional Product. We use the CRENoS database on gross regional product at market price deflated by using regional price indexes (for more details see Paci and Saba, 1997).

Regional Income. It is defined as the sum of earnings and distributed profits of residents of the region and corresponds to what would have been available for consumption without the government intervention. It is obtained from the newly available ISTAT data on regional accounts – which provide data on Gross Operating Income, wages for independent and dependent workers, the balance of interest payments and other capital returns. It is to be noted that interest payments include returns on state bonds.

Regional Disposable Income. Defined as regional income plus government production, expenditure and transfers at the regional level minus total taxes raised at the regional level. This is obtained as the sum of Regional Income (obtained above) and the balance of current and capital accounts of the Public Administration at the regional level as provided by ISTAT.

Regional Consumption. It consists of consumption by families, public administration and other non-profit organizations at the regional level.

Great Britain

Gross Regional Product. We use data provided by HMSO – Regional Trends, various years – on gross regional product at market price.

Regional Income. It is defined as the sum of earnings and distributed profits of residents of the region and corresponds to what would have been available for consumption without government intervention.

Regional Disposable Income. Defined as regional income plus transfers at the regional level minus total taxes raised at the regional level.

Regional Consumption. It consists of the consumption by families.

NOTES

*   We thank for their valuable comments, without implicating them, Guido Pellegrini, Francesco Pigliaru, Antonello Scorcu, Oved Yosha and participants at the CRENoS Conference on Growth and Convergence. We also thank CRENoS for providing us with the data set on Italian regions. The views expressed here are those of the authors alone, and not of any institution with which they are affiliated

1.   In 1970 the public debt to GDP ratios of the two countries were fairly different: 80 per cent in the United Kingdom and 38 per cent in Italy; by the end of 1991 Italy's ratio jumped to 101.7 whereas in the United Kingdom it remained below 45 per cent. Over the same period the ratio of government net borrowing to GDP in Italy has been consistently higher (exceeding 10 per cent since 1981) than the corresponding figures for the United Kingdom (which reached a maximum of 4.5 per cent in 1975).

2.   The population indicator regards all banks, whereas the assets and deposits ratios refer to commercial banks (see CEC, 1993).

3.   For an econometric analysis of the links between the development of the financial system and growth in Italy see Usai and Vannini (1995).

4.   It should be stressed that what enters this channel are the net flows of dividends, interest and rental income payments across regional borders plus any labour income earned outside the region of residence. In the literature on risk sharing, insurance through this channel is referred to in several, occasionally misleading, ways, for example, capital market smoothing or factor income smoothing.

5.   We also ignore non-traded goods, since it is plausible that they are less of a problem in regional risk sharing. We could also have assumed separability in leisure and other non-traded goods.

6. Bayoumi and his coauthors (1993, 1994, 1995) solve this problem by estimating their equations with GMM and by including among the instruments the savings ratio.
7. It should be stressed that even with different output growth rates across regions or nations, (perfect) capital mobility would ultimately imply convergence of growth rates of consumption in a broad class of growth models (Rebelo, 1992).
8. We directly estimated with pooled OLS, allowing for heterogeneity in the intercepts, the cointegrating vector between regional and aggregate consumption, finding that is basically the one we assumed.
9. Note, however, that for i.i.d. random variables the variance of their average is always lower than the variance of one of them. In general, whether this result holds for dependent random variables, rests on their covariance pattern.
10. It should be noted that, due to lack of data, we are unable to consider other potentially important channels, such as labour mobility and public goods. As for labour mobility, however, it is likely that labour movements due to idiosyncratic shocks take some time and should not affect our measurement; as for public goods, unlike Asdrubali *et al.* (1996), we manage to take account of central government expenditures for production at the regional level, which should mitigate this problem (see the appendix for more details on the data).
11. Asdrubali *et al.* (1996) use just first differences variables.
12. This result is confirmed in a parallel analysis by Pellegrino (1997) who finds that more than 80 per cent of risk sharing is due to the net flow of factor income. The difference between our results and Pellegrino's (who does not find any role for government policy) is due to a different specification of the second channel which, in our analysis, includes the public administration balance of accounts.
13. For a comprehensive analysis of households and government saving behaviour in Italy see Ando, Guiso and Visco (1994) who provide a detailed picture based on microeconomic panel data.
14. At the end of the 1990s (see CEC, 1993) the capitalization of the Italian bond market represented 13.7 per cent of the EC market, whereas London was about 12.5 per cent, Paris 11.6 per cent, Amsterdam 4.1 per cent and Madrid 1.3 per cent. Only Germany, with 22.8 per cent, had a greater fraction of the EC market. But unlike its main European counterparts, Italy's total market capitalization was almost entirely represented by public sector bonds (more than 99 per cent).
15. It should be remembered that the available data for the United Kingdom are not perfectly homogenous with Italian ones given that consumption series do not include government expenditure at the regional level and that we do not manage to correct disposable income data in order to take into account the public administration regional budget. It should nevertheless be noted that the role for regional administration in the United Kingdom is rather modest.
16. Similar results are found by Canova and Ravn (1996) in the international context.

REFERENCES

Ando, A, L. Guiso and I. Visco (1994), *Saving and the Accumulation of Wealth, Essays on Italian Household and Government Saving Behaviour*, Cambridge: Cambridge University Press.

Asdrubali, P., B.E. Sorensen and O. Yosha (1996), 'Channels of interstate risk-sharing: United States 1963–1990', *Quarterly Journal of Economics*, November, 1081–110.

Atkeson, A. and T. Bayoumi (1993), 'Do private capital markets insure regional risk? Evidence from the United States and Europe', *Open Economies Review*, **4**, 303–24.

Backus, D.E., P.J. Kehoe and F.E. Kydland (1992), 'International business cycle', *Journal of Political Economy*, **100**(4), 745–75.

Barro, R. and X. Sala-i-Martin (1993), 'Convergence across states and regions', *Brookings Papers on Economic Activity*, **1**, 107–58.

Baxter, M. and M. Crucini (1993), 'Explaining saving–investment correlations', *American Economic Review*, **83**(3), 416–36.

Bayoumi, T. (1995), 'Explaining consumption: a simple test of alternative hypothesis', CEPR Discussion Paper No. 1289.

Bayoumi, T. and R. McDonald (1994), 'On the optimality of consumption across Canadian provinces', CEPR Discussion Paper No. 1030.

Bayoumi, T. and A.K. Rose (1993), 'Domestic savings and intra-national capital flows', *European Economic Review*, **37**, 1197–202.

Canova, F. and M. O. Ravn (1996), 'International consumption risk sharing', *International Economic Review*, **37**, 573–601.

Cochrane, J.H. (1991), 'A simple test of consumption insurance', *Journal of Political Economy*, **99**, 957–76.

Commission of the European Communities (1993), 'The economic and financial situation in Italy', *European Economy Report and Studies*, Vol 1.

Dedola, L., S. Usai and M. Vannini (1997), 'Channels of regional risk sharing in Italy and the UK', Quaderni di ricerca del DEIS, University of Sassari.

Deveraux, M.B. and G.W. Smith (1994), 'International risk sharing and economic growth', *International Economic Review*, **35**(3), 535–50.

Deveraux, M.B. and S. Makoto (1997), 'Growth and risk sharing with incomplete assets markets', *Journal of International Economics*, **42**(3–4), 453–81.

Engle, R.F. and C.W.J. Granger (1987), 'Cointegration and error correction: representation, estimation and testing', *Econometrica*, **22**(2), 251–76.

Greenwood, J. and B. Jovanovic (1990), 'Financial development, growth and distribution of income', *Journal of Political Economy*, **98**, 1076–107.

Greenwood, J. and B. Smith (1994), 'Financial markets in development and the development of financial markets', mimeo, University of Rochester.

ISTAT (1997), *Conti Economici Regionali delle Amministrazioni Pubbliche e delle Famiglie*, serie Argomenti, ISTAT, Rome.

Lewis, K.K. (1996), 'What can explain the apparent lack of international consumption risk sharing?', *Journal of Political Economy*, **104**(2), 267–97.

Murdoch, J. (1995), 'Income smoothing and consumption smoothing', *Journal of Economic Perspectives*, **9**(3), 103–14.

Obstfeld, M. (1989), 'How Integrated are World Capital Markets? Some New Tests', in G. Calvo *et al.* (eds), *Debt, Stabilisation and Development: Essays in the Memory of Carlos Diaz Alejandro*, Oxford: Basil Blackwell.

Obstfeld, M. (1994), 'Risk taking, global diversification and growth', *American Economic Review*, **84**, 1310–30.

Obstfeld, M. and K. Rogoff (1996), *Foundations of International Macroeconomics*, Cambridge, MA: MIT Press.

Oh, W. (1996), 'Essays in nonlinearity of business cycles, cointegration and structural change', PhD, Texas A&M University.

Paci R. and F. Pigliaru (1997), 'Structural change and convergence: an Italian regional perspective', *Structural Change and Economic Dynamics*, **8**, 297–318.

Paci, R. and A. Saba (1998), 'The empirics of regional economic growth in Italy, 1951–1993', *Rivista Internazionale di Scienze Economiche e Commerciali*, **45**, 515–42.

Pellegrini, G. (1997), 'Lo stato come assicurazione contro il rischio di fluttuazioni del reddito e del consumo regionale: liesperienza italiana (1983–1992)', paper presented at the XVIII Italian conference on Regional Science, 8–11 October 1997, Siracusa.

Persson, T. and G. Tabellini (1996a), 'Federal fiscal constitutions – risk sharing and moral hazard', *Econometrica*, **64**(3), 623–46

Persson, T. and G. Tabellini (1996b), 'Federal fiscal constitutions: risk sharing and redistribution', *Journal of Political Economy*, **104**(5), 979–1009.

Rebelo, S. (1992), 'Growth in open economies', *Carnegie Rochester Conference Series on Public Policy*, **36**, 5–46.

Sala-i-Martin, X. and J. Sachs (1992), 'Fiscal Federalism and Optimal Currency Areas: Evidence for Europe from the United States', in M.B. Canzeroni, V. Grilli and P.R. Masson (eds), *Establishing a Central Bank: Issues in Europe and Lessons from the US*, Cambridge: Cambridge University Press, 195–219.

Scorcu, A. E. (1998), 'Consumption risk-sharing in Italy', *Applied Economics*, **30**, 407–14.

Sorensen, B.E. and O. Yosha (1997), 'International risk sharing and European monetary unification', *Journal of International Economics*, **45**, 211–38.

Stockman, A.C. and L.L. Tesar (1995), 'Tastes and technologies in a two-country model of the business cycle: explaining international comovements', *American Economic Review*, **85**, 168–85.

Townsend, R.M. (1995), 'Consumption insurance: an evaluation of risk-bearing systems in low-income economies', *Journal of Economic Perspectives*, **9**(3), 83–102.

Ubide, Angel J. (1994), 'Is there consumption risk sharing in the EEC?', EUI Working Paper ECO No. 94/37.

Usai, S. and M. Vannini (1995), 'Financial development and economic growth. Evidence from a panel of Italian regions', *Contributi di Ricerca Crenos*, University of Cagliari.

Vahid, F. and R.F. Engle (1993), 'Common trends and common cycles', *Journal of Applied Econometrics*, **8**, 341–60.

van Wincoop, E. (1995), 'Regional risk sharing', *European Economic Review*, **37**, 1545–67.

16. Economic growth and regional convergence in a sustainable space-economy

Jeroen C.J.M. van den Bergh and Peter Nijkamp

16.1 ENDOGENOUS SPATIAL GROWTH: PROLOGUE

The analysis of spatial growth disparities has a long history in regional economics. The theoretical and empirical research on this issue offers different viewpoints, sometimes based on a neoclassical paradigm with a clear emphasis on labour supply, capital and technological progress, sometimes based on a post-Keynesian approach with particular emphasis on base activities as the generator of export (and hence output) growth in a region. Nevertheless, the neoclassical growth model, based on a standard production function with flexible factor prices and exogenous technical change, has become rather popular in the past decades (see Armstrong and Taylor, 1994). Assuming free factor mobility, with capital more mobile than labour, it is likely that low-wage regions will experience the fastest output growth, since capital will move into these areas faster than labour will move out.

However, the assumption of a fixed technology in spatial-economic dynamics is rather restrictive, and has been severely criticized in both the technological innovation literature and the economic growth literature. In recent years, in particular the 'endogenous growth' school starting with Romer (1986) and Lucas (1988) has made path-breaking attempts to include technical progress as part of an economic system's behaviour. In this context, Romer (1994) states: 'The phrase "endogenous growth" embraces a diverse body of theoretical and empirical work that emerged in the 1980s. This work distinguishes itself from neoclassical growth by emphasizing that economic growth is an endogenous outcome of an economic system, not the result of forces that impinge from outside' (p. 3). An avalanche of contributions to endogenous growth theory has been published in past years (see for example Barro and Sala-i-Martin, 1995).

The regional economic implications of the endogenous growth theory have so far received less attention. Recent reviews and extensions can be found in Nijkamp and Poot (1993, 1997a, 1997b). In the latter contributions the endogeneity of technological innovation and its implication for spatial disparity in a multiregional system has been analysed. In addition, due attention was given to limits to spatial growth caused by thresholds in existing infrastructure capacity or by environmental sustainability conditions, as well as to endogenous strategies to alleviate these barriers.

The present chapter aims to present a modelling experiment in the spirit of endogenous growth theory. It takes for granted an open multiregional system, with different input endowments and environmental quality conditions. Research and Development (R&D) is then conceived of as an endogenous driving force for improving environmental quality through the production of innovative pollution abatement technology. The openness of the spatial system concerned implies that not only commodity trade may take place, but also dispersion of environmental pollution and diffusion of new knowledge on environmental technologies. The resulting model is rather complex in nature and cannot be solved analytically. Hence, we had to resort to simulation experiments in order to investigate the steady-state properties of the spatial environmental–economic system under consideration.

The chapter is organized as follows. Section 16.2 gives a concise sketch of some recent contributions and issues regarding (spatial-) economic growth and environmental sustainability. In Section 16.3 a model is presented that utilizes a two-region system, with trading economies, regional environments and a global environment. The spatial-economic effects of growth, environmental policy, technology investment and technology diffusion are all considered in this model. This model combines elements of equilibrium trade theory, economic growth theory and environmental economics. Next, Section 16.4 presents various results of scenario analysis based on numerical simulation exercises performed with the above mentioned model. Section 16.5 offers some concluding remarks.

16.2 GROWTH AND SUSTAINABILITY IN SPACE

The relationship between environmental quality and economic growth is a topic which has attracted a lot of interest and generated much debate among economic growth theorists. For instance, neoclassical economic growth theory has frequently been applied to issues of renewable resource limits, long-run pollution effects and sometimes even to a combination of these recent contributions (Tahvonen and Kuuluvainen, 1991, 1993). Analyses of this flavour have focused on the role of substitution between man-made capital and natural resources materials in production, technological improvements in materials efficiency of production, and backstop technologies (Dasgupta and Heal, 1979). In this context, the issue of sustainability has also explicitly been treated, although so far there is no unanimous agreement on its theoretical interpretations (Toman *et al.*, 1994). Conservation-preservationist's and exploitationist's views are linked to the distinction between strong and weak sustainability (Pearce and Turner, 1990), with the Hartwick rule of investing resource rents in man-made capital as an extreme case of the latter (Hartwick, 1977).

It is noteworthy that recently modern growth theory has also been applied to environmental issues and sustainability (Gradus and Smulders, 1993; Bovenberg and Smulders, 1994; Ricker, 1997; Smulders, 1994). The focus of most of these contributions is on endogenous technology and knowledge formation, and especially on the influence of pollution and of preferences on technology choice. Alternative approaches to the relationship between technology, growth and environment have stressed the need to adopt an evolutionary economic perspective (Faber and Proops, 1990; Erdman, 1993). While economists have been much concerned with the trade-off between economic (Pareto) efficiency and environmental sustainability, several other approaches focus on controllability (Perrings, 1991) and stability, the latter often based on ecological theory or ecological metaphors (Holling, 1986, 1994). Common and Perrings (1992) provide an interesting and systematic comparison of various lines of thought in this context. Thus, there is an increasing interest in the complex relationship between growth and sustainability.

The issues of regional and urban sustainability have attracted relatively little attention, except maybe in the context of urban systems (Breheny, 1992; Nijkamp and Perrels, 1994). It is, however, increasingly recognised that there is an interwoven connection between regional production and consumption patterns and environmental quality at various geographical levels. In recent years this has led to a clear focus on spatial sustainable development (Giaoutzi and Nijkamp, 1994; van den Bergh, 1996; Maxwell and Costanza, 1994).

One analytical approach is to consider a region as an open system, in terms of both economic and environmental processes (van den Bergh and Nijkamp, 1991). The other approach is to deal with multiregional systems. Regional economics provides a rich perspective for theory formation and application regarding multi-regional dynamics (Andersson and Kuenne, 1986). Spatial price equilibrium theory offers one approach (see Verhoef and van den Bergh, 1996). More complex, but also theoretically more refined, are spatial general equilibrium models (Roson, 1994; van den Bergh *et al.*, 1996). Incorporating dynamics in such models is, however, a very difficult task (cf. Musu, 1994). Finally, game-theoretic models may be used to deal with specific questions of environmental policy coordination (van der Ploeg and De Zeeuw, 1992). Thus, there is a wide spectrum of analytical approaches to the issue of sustainable development in an open economic system (see also Nordhaus, 1990, 1993).

In the context of open economic systems, in recent years much attention has been given to the cost-effectiveness and efficiency of environmental policies with spatially discriminating impacts. For example, some countries argue that it might be more beneficial from a global environmental perspective to invest in abatement technology in more polluting and less developed countries than in their own country. Another example concerns the plans of Dutch electricity companies to invest in tropical rain forest in Latin America in order to compensate for the emission of CO_2. Thus, there are many trade-offs to be made in a complex and open spatial system.

The relationship between environmental quality and spatial economic processes is extremely important, but has until now not received very much focused attention from either regional or environmental economics. A general introduction is provided by Siebert (1985, 1996). The lessons for environmental policy-makers from the existing – mainly theoretical – literature on the environment include mainly corrections on Pigouvian charges and taxation. These corrections are motivated by endogenous location, imperfect markets, international trade power, international coordination of policy (for national, transboundary and global problems) and long-term sustainability (Anderson and Blackhurst, 1992; Markusen *et al.*, 1993). These extensions go in different directions. In the case of imperfect markets, trade power and endogenous locations, the standard Pigouvian tax should be corrected downwards. In the case of transport related externalities, endogenous technology and sustainability, a tighter policy is needed.

An integrated treatment of these issues has not received a great deal of attention so far. In the context of a static spatial equilibrium model the link between environmental regulation, trade, transport and spatial economic structure is addressed by Verhoef and van den Bergh (1996). They derive policy rules under first- and second-best optimality conditions, the latter case relating to a transport tax regime which compensates for disoptimal production taxes in regions that have not implemented an optimal environmental policy.

The analysis framework adopted in our paper starts from the conception that spatial sustainability is a complex issue which can only be dealt with to its full extent in a multi-regional setting. Developing a spatial analysis in a continuous – rather than a discrete – space may also be useful, but requires different and more tedious modelling efforts, and would furthermore be less suitable for treating economic growth issues. It might be more adequate to cover issues related to non-point resource pollution (Russel and Shogren, 1993; Dosi and Tomasi, 1994). In a discrete multi-regional setting, the following relevant situations of spatial sustainability can be envisaged:

i.   imports of region A may cause unsustainable patterns in their own region A;
ii. imports of region A may cause unsustainable patterns in region B via trade;
iii. exports of region A may cause unsustainable patterns in their own region A;
iv. exports of region A may cause unsustainable patterns in region B via trade;
v.   environmental sustainability of region A is linked to that of region B via the spillovers from the global environment.

Situation (ii) may in fact be referred to as 'importing sustainability at the cost of unsustainability elsewhere'. Situations (iii) and (iv) may be denoted as 'exporting unsustainability'. Finally, case (v) in combination with the dependence of regional production on regional environmental quality allows one to study the issue of spatial (interregional) environmental externalities in a broad sense. We will now present the main structure of our model.

16.3   A MODEL FOR A TWO-REGION ECONOMIC–ENVIRONMENTAL SYSTEM

16.3.1   Introduction

Our model aims to map out the evolution of an open system of two regions, with environmental and economic spillovers, while using elements from endogenous growth theory. We will – without loss of generality – present a simple illustrative model of two interactive regions. The emphasis in the model is on environmental decay, and less on resource depletion (in other words, we assume a situation of renewable resource). The model incorporates six components:

- there are production and consumption processes in the regional economies, and there is trade connecting them;
- growth originates from man-made production factors and is reflected in the output of the regional economies;
- regional environmental processes interact through the global environment, and are a link between generation and reception of environmental externalities;
- technology allows for more efficient use of material resources in production;
- there is diffusion of technology from region 1 to region 2 (that is, diffusion in know-how);
- regional welfare is a composite indicator made up of regional consumption, and regional and global environmental quality.

The different parts of the model are presented below (i denotes region i; $i=1,2$). The model is not a spatial price equilibrium model; this would make the specification unnecessarily complicated, at least from the viewpoint of the spatial interactions of a sustainable growth model with endogenous R&D. The functional specifications and numerical values adopted here are mainly illustrative in nature. Without loss of generality, we have in the various equations already inserted the parameter values used for our simulation experiments. A list of definitions of variables is contained in the Annex.

16.3.2 Production

We assume a two-region economy, where the physical-environmental conditions of each region are distinctly different, so that product specialization takes place (that is, a heterogeneous open spatial system with distinct regions which are economically different). In this Ricardian economy the specification of production relationships is then straightforward. Each region uses two distinct regional inputs to produce output Q_i. The regional environment is supposed to act as one input (E_i), while the other input is a composite factor, namely an aggregate of capital and labour (K_i). The latter assumption is only made for the sake of simplicity, but is not strictly necessary.

$$Q_1 = 0.3K_1^{a1}E_1^{b1} \tag{16.1}$$

and

$$Q_2 = 0.3K_2^{a2}E_2^{b2} \tag{16.2}$$

This means that the environment of a region – through its resource base – acts as an input augmenting factor (through productivity rise). It is further assumed that the commodities represented by Q_i ($i = 1,2$) are different. This is formalized in the model by including consumption of each i ($i = 1,2$) in the welfare functions of each region. As a result, trade will develop between the two regions. Clearly, the assumption of strict specialization may easily be relaxed, but we are mainly interested in the sustainability aspects and less in the trade aspects of our model.

In order to allow for endogenous formation of trade patterns, regional production prices (P_i) are determined per unit of output, based on the costs of the two inputs. The cost of the input factor (capital and labour) is assumed to act as a numéraire and set equal to one, while the cost of resource materials (R_i) is determined by fixed depletion costs augmented with environmental taxes, denoted by t_i. The latter assumes implicitly that an increasing exhaustion of natural resource materials is unpriced, so that we are essentially dealing with renewable resources. This leads to the following price equation:

$$P_i = (K_i + t_i R_i)/\text{MAX}(1,Q_i) \qquad (16.3)$$

In the case of resource depletion, we might introduce a higher resource price, induced by taxation. However, endogenous price formation is not considered here. The MAX function is not essential and is merely included to ensure that the denominator is not equal to zero and prices are bounded from above, so that infinite values of P_i are avoided.

16.3.3   Consumption and Trade

Next, we will address the consumption and trade issues. In order to derive trade and consumption patterns, the following assumptions are made:

(i)   Markets do clear; in other words, production in each region is equal to total demand, comprising domestic consumption C_{ii}, export C_{ji} ($i \neq j$), investments I_i and research and development $I_{\text{R\&D},i}$. In order to analyse interesting contrast patterns, we assume here that only region 1 invests in R&D. C_{ii} denotes the domestic consumption of commodity i (that is, produced in region i), while C_{ij} is the import by region i of commodity j (that is, produced in region j ($i \neq j$)). It is clear that in this simplified economic world there is trade in consumption, not in investment goods (that is, each region produces its own investments). Then we have the following equations:

$$Q_1 = C_{11} + C_{21} + I_1 + I_{R\&D,1} \qquad (16.4)$$

and

$$Q_2 = C_{22} + C_{12} + I_2 \qquad (16.5)$$

(ii) Total trade flows in opposite directions are assumed to be balanced:[1]

$$P_1 C_{21} = P_2 C_{12} \qquad (16.6)$$

(iii) It is also assumed that there is a fixed import coefficient, in the sense that there is a balanced fixed relationship between the domestic consumption in region 1 and its imports (this would implicitly mean an equilibrium price regime). Consequently, the coefficient o_1 reflects then the degree of economic closeness of region 1:

$$C_{11}/C_{12} = o_1 \qquad (16.7)$$

A large value of o_1 means then a more closed system, while a small value means a very open system; clearly, a value of 1 means that imports equal domestic consumption. In our simulation experiments we have mainly used a value of 2.

Rewriting (16.4)–(16.7) gives the following reduced submodel for consumption and trade variables:

$$C_{12} = P_1 (Q_1 - I_1 - I_{R\&D,1})/(o_1 P_1 + P_2) \qquad (16.8)$$

$$C_{11} = o_1 C_{12} \qquad (16.9)$$

$$C_{21} = P_2 C_{12}/P_1 \qquad (16.10)$$

$$C_{22} = Q_2 - I_2 - C_{12} \qquad (16.11)$$

16.3.4 Technology

We will now address the impact of technology. The stock of technological knowledge (T) in region 1 is improved by net investments in research and development ($I_{R\&D,1}$), in the following straightforward way.

$$dT/dt = I_{R\&D,1}, \text{ with } T(0) = 0. \qquad (16.12)$$

The fruits of R&D manifest themselves as technological progress which is assumed to reach region 2 through a diffusion (T_d) with a time delay of 4 periods, where d_d is a dummy variable with a default value equal to 0 (see Section 16.4).

$$T_d(t) = d_d\, T(t-4),\ \text{with}\ T_d(s) = 0,\ s = 1,2,3 \qquad (16.13)$$

We assume that region 1 produces its technology because of its economic and environmental potential benefits. Of course, one might also assume that environmental taxes are used to subsidize new environmental technology, but this is not considered here. The development of technology allows for more efficient resource use in production (hence causing less pollution) which is assumed to have the following upper limits (with decreasing returns to scale):

$$R_1 = 0.585\,(Q_1^{0.8})\,((T + 100)/(4\,T + 100)) \qquad (16.14)$$

$$R_2 = 0.585\,Q_2^{0.8}\,((T_d + 100)/(4\,T_d + 100)) \qquad (16.15)$$

It should be noted that our interest is mainly in the environmental implications, and less in resource depletion. Hence, we do not analyse here any further the stock of resources.

16.3.5   Growth

Growth in both regions occurs via investment in the capital and labour stock K. Depreciation D takes place as a fixed proportion of the existing stock:

$$\mathrm{d}K_i/\mathrm{d}_t = I_i - D_i(K_i),\ \text{with}\ K_i(0) = 100 \qquad (16.16)$$

Investment is considered a regional activity, and is restricted from above by regional production. When not limited, investment is at least equal to depreciation (D_i), in which case the stock of input factors remains constant. In the scenarios studied in the following section we will assume a balanced growth path with a net growth rate g, whose value is set equal to 3 per cent. The operator function MIN will ensure that this growth rate is identical to the *ex post* growth rate, as long as sufficient output is produced, that is:

$$I_i = \mathrm{MIN}(Q_i,\, D_i + g* K_i),\ \text{with}\ K_i(0)=100 \qquad (16.17)$$

Since we are more interested in the distributional issues of sustainability, the above simplified assumption of a fixed net investment growth seems tentatively warranted.

16.3.6 Environment

Our interest is in particular in the spatial dimensions of environmental quality. Environmental quality E_i in each region i follows a dynamic path which can be described by a logistic growth curve. We assume that within certain limits no irreversible environmental decay will take place, so that recovery is possible. The carrying capacity (C_c) is set equal to 180. The intrinsic recovery (growth) rate of the renewable environment $(r(.))$ is positively related to a global environment index (E_{glob}). Resource use and extraction in region i (R_i) causes the environmental quality in the region to decline.

$$dE_i/dt = r(E_{glob})*(1-E_i/C_c) - R_i, \; E_i(0) = 100 \qquad (16.18)$$

$$r(E_{glob}) = MIN(E_{glob}/C_c,1)*0.2 \qquad (16.19)$$

The E_{glob} index represents the quality of the global environment, which is obtained by summing additive and multiplicative aggregation functions of the regional environmental indicators:

$$E_{glob} = (E_1*E_2)^{0.5} + 0.5 *(E_1 + E_2) \qquad (16.20)$$

In other words, even if only one region has a low environmental quality, this has severe implications for the global environment. However, only when both regions collapse in terms of environmental sustainability, the global environment will do so.

16.3.7 Welfare

Finally, we focus on the evaluation of regional performances. We will not use an optimization approach, but for our comparative analysis of different economic scenarios we will use a regional welfare criterion. In our study, welfare is calculated for each region, based on the consumption of both commodities, regional environmental quality and the state of the global environment.

$$W_i = C_{i1}^{0.6}*C_{i2}^{0.6}*E_i^{0.4}*E_{glob}^{0.2} \qquad (16.21)$$

Thus, our model is not an optimizing model in a strict sense. It compares different economic and environmental states of the regions by using a social welfare criterion. For an optimization model using Pontryagin's principle for the same problems we refer to Inoue (1996).

This concludes the presentation of the model equations. Since it is an impossible task to derive relevant analytical properties of this model, we have to resort to simulation experiments. In the next section simulation results are presented and discussed based on the above simplified model specification.

16.4   SIMULATION RESULTS FOR THE SPATIAL SUSTAINABLE GROWTH MODEL

The simulation experiments in this section in particular investigate the implications of different economic and environmental scenarios. The above model allows for a great number of scenarios to be designed and studied. The main distinctions are: uniform vs. non-uniform regions, presence or absence of environmental technology and presence or absence of innovation diffusion mechanisms. Each of these represents then specific combinations of values for all parameter and initial state variables. Recognizing this large diversity of choices, the following six core scenarios are considered in detail:

1.   A symmetric economic system, that is, identical production functions for both regional economies: $a_i=b_i=0.5$ ($i=1,2$).

   1(a)   *Ex ante* net growth equals 3 per cent: $g=0.03$.

   1(b)   As 1(a) and with positive R&D for environmental technology: $I_{R\&D,1}=5$.

   1(c)   As 1(a) and with environmental taxation: $t_1 = 20$.

2.   An asymmetric economic system: $a_1=b_2=0.2$, $b_1=a_2=0.8$.

   2(a)   *Ex ante* net growth equals 3%: $g=0.03$.

   2(b)   As 2(a) and with positive R&D for environmental technology: $I_{R\&D,1}=5$.

   2(c)   As 2(a) and with technology diffusion: $d_d =1$.

Ad 1(a)   Plain Growth in a Homogeneous World

The simulation results of this baseline scenario, using the Stella software, are given in Figures 16.1 and 16.2. From Figure 16.1 one can see the homogeneity of the regions under the assumption of identical patterns of input factors (K_i) and production ($Prod_i$). The *ex ante* growth rate of 3 per cent of actors initially translates into an identical *ex post* growth, but after time period 18 production starts to decrease until it becomes zero.

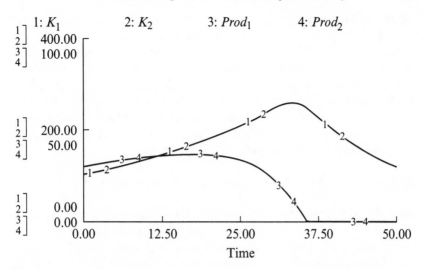

Figure 16.1 Scenario 1(a): composite input factors (K_i*) and production (*$Q_i = Prod_i$*)*

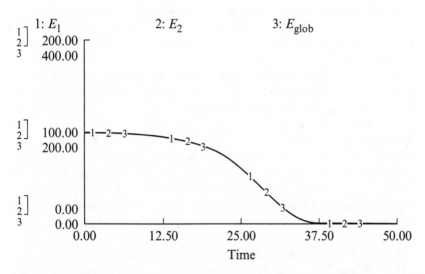

Figure 16.2 Scenario 1(a): regional and global environmental quality (E_i* and *E_{glob}*)*

When production is very low, investment (I_i) decreases until it becomes zero, and the stock of input factors starts to decrease. Note that the increase in capital does not translate into an increase of production. The reason for this is that the environmental input in production, as a result of resource extraction, decreases in quality. This is shown in Figure 16.2 where, again, the homogeneity of the regions can be seen from the identical patterns for regional environmental quality, implying the same pattern for the global environment. The homogeneity also implies, of course, that the trade and consumption patterns are symmetric.

Ad 1(b)   Environmental Technology in a Homogeneous World

With fixed investment in environmental technology in region 1 $(I_{R\&D,1})$, interregional differential impacts emerge in our spatial economic system (see Figures 16.3–16.7). Comparing Figure 16.3 with Figure 16.1 shows that this strategy has positive impacts on the production in both regions, although clearly less so in region 2. Considering Figure 16.4, one can observe that the environmental quality in region 1 is improved relative to the initial position, whereas it is deteriorating in region 2. The global environment is also better off than under scenario 1(a) and even improves initially. A comparison between Figures 16.2 and 16.4 shows that temporarily the environment in region 2 is better off as well. Because of the technology strategy in region 1, its initial welfare is lower than in region 2, as is shown in Figure 16.5. However, after time period 12 the positions are reversed, and a maximum difference is reached in time period 38. Finally, Figure 16.6 shows that the trade pattern is asymmetric and much more irregular now. Domestic consumption of commodity 2 (C_{22}) is decreasing from time 0 onward, and is substituted by importing commodity 1 (C_{21}). This is the consequence of changes in relative prices of the commodities, as shown in Figure 16.7. In region 1 the domestic consumption of commodity 1 (C_{11}) can increase because of the favourable development of environmental quality, while the moderately increasing import of commodity 2 (C_{12}) is the net result of the sharp increase of purchasing power of region 1 and the increase in the relative price of commodity 2.

Finally, it should be noted that the scenario results presented so far are largely doomsday results, which stem largely from the assumption that environmentally disruptive activities created by the capital and labour stock increase exponentially, while the resource-saving input investments increase linearly (cf. Meadows *et al.*, 1972, 1992). The question is now whether such a trend can be curbed. This will be studied next.

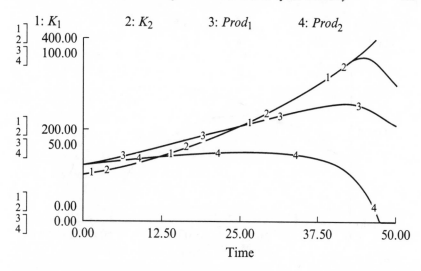

Figure 16.3   Scenario 1(b): composite input factors (K_i*) and production
(*$Q_i = \text{Prod}_i$*)*

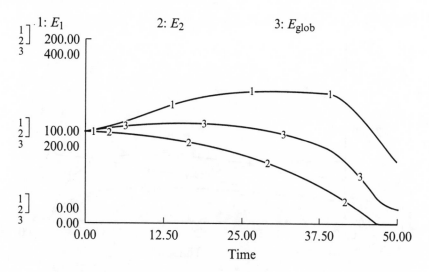

Figure 16.4   Scenario 1(b): regional and global environmental quality (E_i
and E_{glob}*)*

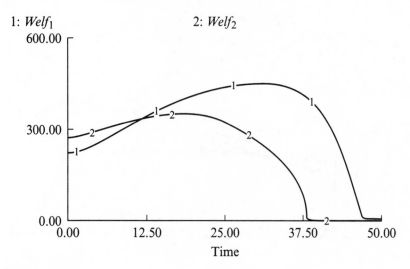

*Figure 16.5 Scenario 1(b): regional welfare indexes·(*Welf$_i$*)*

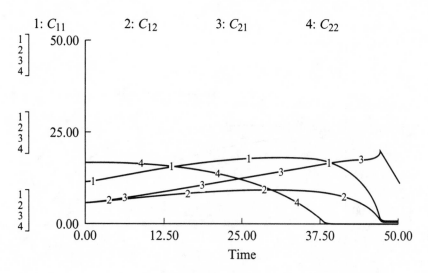

*Figure 16.6 Scenario 1(b): consumption (*C$_{ii}$ *and* C$_{ij}$*) and trade (*C$_{ij}$*)*

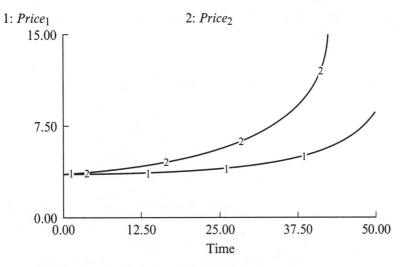

*Figure 16.7 Scenario 1(b): prices of regional outputs (*Price$_i$)*

Ad 1(c)   Environmental Policy in a Homogeneous World

The introduction of an environmental tax (t_1) on the use of natural resource materials in production in region 1 means that the relative prices of commodities are affected (Figure 16.8). However, since in our simplified model this does not affect the resource efficiency of materials inputs and since there is no alternative way of producing, the dynamic effects are missing. The only effect here will be a shift of income and welfare, via changes in trade. This is all based, of course, on implicit assumptions regarding the international markets, in particular the absence of substitutes for commodity 1. Therefore, we will now turn to more interesting, asymmetric cases.

Ad 2(a)   Plain Growth in a Heterogeneous World

In the baseline scenario 2(a) and the following two scenarios, the starting point is a heterogeneous system of regions with regard to the production structure. This is reflected by the patterns in Figure 16.9, where region 1 is less able to increase its production than region 2. Therefore, it uses less resources and causes less environmental damage, and can sustain its local environment longer than region 2. This is reflected by relative prices in Figure 16.10, where initially region 2 has a price advantage, since it can produce more with a certain endowment of natural resources, but the unsustainability of this region is reflected by the sharp increase through the price curve of region 1.

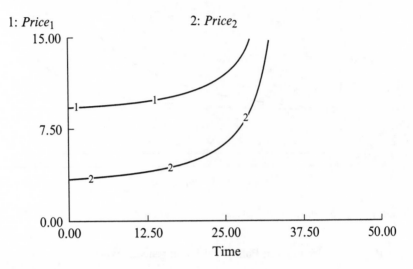

*Figure 16.8 Scenario 1(c): prices of regional outputs (*Price$_i$*)*

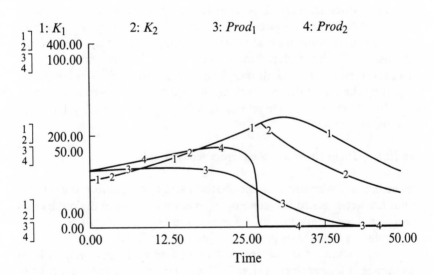

*Figure 16.9 Scenario 2(a): composite input factors (*K$_i$*) and production*
$(Q_i = $Prod$_i)$

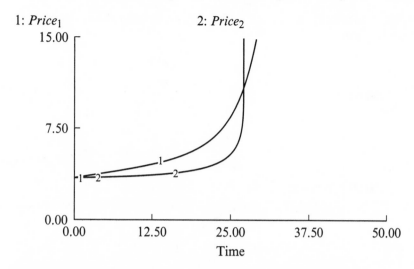

*Figure 16.10 Scenario 2(a): prices of regional outputs (*Price$_i$*)*

Ad 2(b)   Environmental Technology in a Heterogeneous World

This scenario is chosen as a benchmark for comparison with scenario 2(c). In this case, as in scenario 1(b), technological progress, related to natural resource materials efficiency in production, causes an improvement toward a more sustainable development, not only in region 1 but also in region 2, via the global environmental effect, and via trade. The comparison between scenarios 2(b) and 2(c) is discussed below.

Ad 2(c)   Technology Diffusion in a Heterogeneous World

Here the enhancement of sustainability in region 2 is not only occurring via the mechanism outlined above, but also via diffusion of technology. Region 2 is supposed to catch up, with a four-year delay, with the technology of region 1. In Figure 16.11 the difference between the two scenarios for the environmental quality in region 2 is shown. Resource materials can now increasingly more efficiently be used in region 2 as well. The differential effect over time on the global environment is shown in Figure 16.12, and for region 1's environment in Figure 16.13. Finally, the welfare indicators for both regions show that in scenario 2(b) region 1 ends up with higher welfare; under scenario 2(c) region 2 always has higher welfare. This can be explained by the fact that it profits from the diffusion of technology, without having to pay for it, in contrast to region

1, where the beneficial effect is without delay, but also at the cost of sacrificing scarce output.

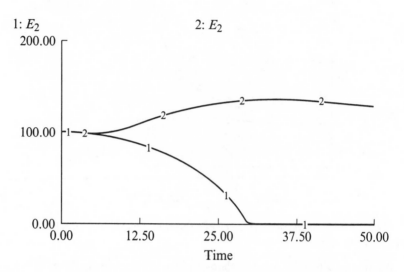

Figure 16.11   Comparison of environmental quality in region 2 (E₂) under different scenarios: 1=scenario 2(b) and 2=scenario 2(c)

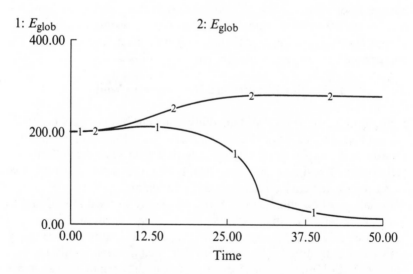

Figure 16.12   Comparison of global environmental quality (E_glob) under different scenarios: 1=scenario 2(b) and 2=scenario 2(c)

The last results offer also an interesting policy scope (see Arrow *et al.*, 1995). Clearly, it may be interesting for a region to adopt a passive attitude *vis-à-vis* environmental abatement investments. First, it may pay off to wait until via a diffusion process these new technologies become available either at zero prices or at competitive prices on the international market. And second, since via the global environment also the 'active' region is suffering from the pollution of the latecomer, it may be forced to subsidize environmental technology in the passive region in order to survive itself. These are interesting free rider problems as a result of spatial openness via the global environmental (see also Klaasen, 1995).

The results here are merely illustrative of the type of questions to be addressed in the context of spatial sustainable economic development, based on the use of formal modelling procedures. The aim was, rather than to show doomsday or optimistic scenarios – which can never be tested anyway – to show the impact of spatial disaggregation and trade in the context of economic growth, given technological progress and diffusion, and environmental taxation. Many issues have not been dealt with yet, but can easily be included here. Furthermore, the evaluation of the different outcomes is a separate task, in which one can play around with different objectives, for instance, allowing for concern for future generations, or adopting a planner's perspective, concerned with maximization

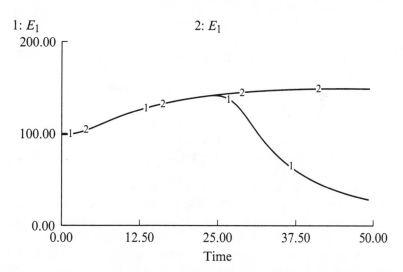

Figure 16.13 Comparison of environmental quality in region 1 (E_1) under different scenarios: 1 = scenario 2(b) and 2 = scenario 2(c)

of some social welfare function, including externalities. One has to notice, however, that the problem of choosing a social evaluation criterion is even more complicated here than in a non-spatial setting, caused by the fact that one has then to undertake also an aggregation of regional welfare variables.

16.5   CONCLUDING REMARKS

The question of optimal sustainable growth is a complicated one. Following the intriguing view of Solow in the 1970s, when he claimed that '...we must find the largest constant consumption per head which can be maintained forever with account taken of the finiteness of the pool of exhaustible resources and of the fact that we can not consume capital that isn't there' (Solow, 1974, p. 35), it is increasingly recognized that there is no straightforward remedy to achieve sustainable growth. Our model has made some provisional attempts which led to interesting findings, but is certainly not yet a mature and policy-relevant approach. Several limitations have to be mentioned, which are often implicit in other studies:

- the weak demand responses in terms of substitution reaction to relative commodity prices, both domestically and for international trade;
- the lack of shifts in investment behaviour as a result of changes in factor input productivity;
- the exogenous nature of eco-taxes in the model, without being influenced by resource productivity;
- the lack of a government sector collecting and redistributing environmental taxes;
- the lack of input mobility between the regions;
- the unpriced nature of R&D and technology diffusion;
- the lack of international policy trade-offs in open economic systems.

Future work may focus on theoretical generalizations, increasing the realistic mapping of environmental and spatial processes, by investigating the heterogeneity of regions, policy coordination issues and conflicts among multiple regions. Increasing environmental realism may mean that resource and pollution issues are disaggregated as well as integrated, or alternatively, that peculiar ecological dynamics such as those arising from species interactions or complex ecosystems are included. More attention for spatial processes can involve explicit treatment of the link between trade, transport and environment. Dealing with heterogeneity of regions can involve specific treatment of the unique production structure, the growth capacity, natural resource endowments, environmental resilience, preferences, human capital or technology. Furthermore, policy coordination is a very important topic, at the level of both sub-national regions and countries. So far, much empirical work in this context has mainly been done in regard to the problem of acid rain (Alcamo *et al.*, 1990). Recent developments in EU environmental policies demonstrate clearly the various dilemma's at regional, national and EU levels, in combination with global sustainable development issues. It goes without saying that still a long research trajectory is necessary to fully understand all conditions for spatial sustainable development.

NOTE

1   Note that combining equations (16.4) and (16.6) leads to the identity: $P_1 * Q_1 = P_1 * C_{11} + P_2 * C_{12} + P_1 * I_1 + P_1 * I_{R\&D,1}$. This may be regarded as a balanced budget relation (income = outlays) for region 1. An analogous result holds for region 2.

ANNEX   LIST OF VARIABLES (*i* denotes region, *i* = 1, 2)

Stock variables

K_i = factors input in production (capital, labour)
T = accumulated research and development
E_i = indicator of state of the environment in region i

Flow variables

Q_i = production
P_i = price of produced goods in region i
I_i = investment in K_i
$I_{R\&D, 1}$ = research and development outlays in region 1
T_d = diffusion of technology from region 1 to 2
C_{ij} = consumption of commodity j in region i
R_i = resource materials use in production
E_{glob} = global environmental indicator
W_i = welfare in region i

Parameters

a,b = production function elasticities (region 1)
c,d = production function elasticities (region 2)

C_c = carrying capacity of the regional environments
g = *ex ante* net growth rate of actors
o_1 = trade indicator for openness region 1
t_i = environmental taxation

Functions
$D_i(K_i)$ = depreciation of capital dependent on the capital stock
r = intrinsic regeneration rate of regional environments
MAX(,) = function which generates the maximum of two inputs
MIN(,) = function which generates the minimum of two inputs

REFERENCES

Alcamo, J., R. Shaw and L. Hordijk (eds) (1990), *The Rains Model of Acidification: Science and Strategies in Europe*, Dordrecht: Kluwer Academic Publishers.
Andersson, Å.E. and R.E. Kuenne (1986) 'Regional Economic Dynamics', in P. Nijkamp (ed.), *Handbook of Regional and Urban Economics*, Vol. 1, Amsterdam: North-Holland, pp. 201–53.
Anderson, K. and R. Blackburst (eds) (1992), *The Greening of World Trade Issues*, New York: Harvester Wheatsheaf.
Armstrong, H. and J. Taylor (1994), *Regional Economics and Policy*, London: Harvester Wheatsheaf.
Arrow, K.J., R.H. Mnookin, L. Ross, Al. Twesky and R. Wilson (eds) (1995), *Barriers to Conflict Resolution*, New York: W.W. Norton & Co.
Barro, R.J. and X. Sala-i-Martin (1995), *Economic Growth*, New York: McGraw-Hill.
Bergh, J.C.J.M. van den and P. Nijkamp (1991), 'A general dynamic economic–ecological model for regional sustainable development', *Journal of Environmental Systems*, **20**, 89–214.
Bergh, J.C.J.M. van den, P. Nijkamp and P. Rietveld (eds) (1996), *Recent Advances in Spatial Equilibrium Modelling: Methodology and Applications*, Berlin: Springer-Verlag.
Bergh, J.C.J.M. van den (1996), *Ecological Economics and Sustainable Development*, Cheltenham: Edward Elgar.
Bovenberg, A.L. and S.A. Smulders (1994), 'Environmental policy in a two-sector endogenous growth model', in proceedings of workshop on Quantitative Economics and Environmental Policy, OCFEB, Erasmus University, Rotterdam.
Breheny, M.J. (1992), *Sustainable Development and Urban Form*, European Research in Regional Science, Vol. 2, London: Pion.
Common, M. and C. Perrings (1992), 'Towards an ecological economics of sustainability', *Ecological Economics*, **6**, 7–34.
Dasgupta, P.S. and G.M. Heal (1979), *Economic Theory and Exhaustible Resources*, Cambridge: Cambridge University Press.

Dosi, C. and T. Tomasi (eds) (1994), *Nonpoint Source Pollution Regulation: Issues and Analysis*, Dordecht: Kluwer Academic Publishers.

Erdman, G. (1993), 'Evolutionary Economics as an Approach to Environmental Problems', in H. Giersch (ed.), *Economic Progress and Environmental Concerns*, Berlin: Springer-Verlag, pp. 213–38.

Faber, M. and J.L.R. Proops (1990), *Evolution, Time, Production and the Environment*, Heidelberg: Springer-Verlag.

Giaoutzi, M. and P. Nijkamp (1994), *Decision Support Modes for Regional Sustainable Development*, Aldershot: Avebury.

Gradus, R. and S.A. Smulders (1993), 'The trade-off between environmental care and longterm growth: pollution in three proto-type growth models', *Journal of Economics*, **58**, 25–52.

Hartwick, J.M. (1977), 'Intergenerational equity and the investing of rents from exhaustible resources', *American Economic Review*, **67**, 972–4.

Holling, C.S. (1986), 'The Resilience of Terrestrial Ecosystems: Local Surprise and Global Change', in W.C. Clark and R.E. Munn (eds), *Sustainable Development of the Biosphere*, Cambridge: Cambridge University Press.

Holling, C.S. (1994), 'New Science and New Investments for a Sustainable Biosphere', in A.M. Jansson, M. Hammer, C. Folke and R. Costanza (eds), *Investing in Natural Capital: The Ecological Economics Approach to Sustainability*, Washington DC: Island Press.

Inoue, T. (1996), 'On optimal environmental policies for sustainable growth in a two-country model', discussion paper, University of Nagoya.

Klaasen, G. (1995), 'Trading sulfur emission reduction commitments in Europe: a theoretical and empirical analysis', PhD dissertation, IIASA, Laxenburg.

Lucas, R.E. (1988), 'On the mechanics of economic development', *Journal of Monetary Economics*, **22**, 3–42.

Markusen, J. R., E.R. Morey and N. D. Olewiler (1993), 'Environmental policy when market structure and plant locations are endogenous', *Journal of Environmental Economics and Management*, **24**, 69–86.

Maxwell, T. and R. Costanza (1994), 'Spatial ecosystem modeling in a distributed computational environment', in J.C.J.M. van den Bergh and J. van der Straaten (eds), *Toward Sustainable Development: Concepts, Methods and Policy*, Washington DC: Island Press, pp. 111–38.

Meadows, D.H., D.L. Meadows, J. Randers and W.W. Behrens III (1972), *The Limits to Growth*, New York: Universe Books.

Meadows, D.H., D.L. Meadows and J. Randers (1992), *Beyond the Limits: Confronting Global Collapse; Envisioning a Sustainable Future*, Post Mills: Chelsea Green Publishing Co.

Musi, I. (1994), 'On sustainable endogenous growth', *Feem Note di Laroro*, no.11/94.

Nijkamp, P. and J. Poot (1993), 'Endogenous technological change, innovation diffusion and transitional dynamics in a nonlinear growth model', *Australian Economic Papers*, December, 191–213.

Nijkamp, P. and A. Perrels (1994), *Sustainable Cities in Europe*, London: Earthscan.

Nijkamp, P. and J. Poot (1997a), 'Endogenous Technological Change, Long Run Growth and Regional Interdependence: A Survey', in C.S. Bertuglia, S. Lombardo and P. Nijkamp (eds), *Innovative Behaviour in Space and Time*, Berlin: Springer-Verlag, pp. 213–38.

Nijkamp, P. and J. Poot (1998), 'Spatial perspectives on new theories of economic growth', *Annals of Regional Science*, **32**, 7–37.

Nordhaus', W.D. (1990), 'To slow or not to slow: The economics of the greenhouse effect', *Economic Journal*, **101**, 920–37.

Nordhaus, W.D. (1993), 'How Much Should we Invest in Preserving our Current Climate', in H. Giersch (ed.), *Economic Progress and Environmental Concerns*, Berlin: Springer-Verlag.

Pearce, D.W. and R.K. Turner (1990), *Economics of Natural Resources and the Environment*, New York: Harvester Wheatsheaf.

Perrings, C. (1991), 'Ecological sustainability and environmental control', *Structural Change and Economic Dynamics*, **2**, 275–95.

Ploeg, F. van der and A.J. de Zeeuw (1992), 'International aspects of pollution control', *Environmental and Resource Economics*, **2**, 117–39.

Ricker, M. (1997), 'Limits to economic growth as shown by a computable general equilibrium model', *Ecological Economics*, **21**(2), 141–58.

Romer, P.M. (1986), 'Increasing returns and long-run growth', *Journal of Political Economy*, **94**, 1002–37.

Romer, P.M. (1994), 'The origins of endogenous growth', *Journal of Economic Perspectives*, **8**(1), 3–22.

Roson, R. (ed.) (1994), 'Transportation and General Equilibrium Models', proceedings of an international workshop', Venice.

Russell, C.S. and J.F. Shogren (eds) (1993), *Theory, Modeling and Experience in the Management of Non-Point Source Pollution*, Dordrecht: Kluwer Academic Publishers.

Siebert, H. (1985), 'Spatial Aspects of Environmental Economics', in A.V. Kneese and J.L. Sweeney (eds), *Handbook of Natural Resource and Energy Economics*, Vol. 1–3, Amsterdam: North-Holland.

Siebert, H. (1996), *Economics of the Environment: Theory and Policy*, 2nd edn, Berlin: Springer-Verlag.

Smulders, S.A. (1994), 'Growth, market structure and the environment: essays on the theory of endogenous economic growth', PhD dissertation, Tilburg University (KUB), Tilburg.

Solow, R.M. (1974), 'Intergenerational equity and exhaustible resources', *Review of Economic Studies*, Symposium Issue, 29–45.

Tahvonen, O. and J. Kuuluvainen (1991), 'Optimal growth with renewable resources and pollution', *European Economic Review*, **35**, 650–61.

Tahvonen, O. and J. Kuuluvainen (1993), 'Economic growth, pollution and renewable resources', *Journal of Environmental Economics and Management*, **24**, 101–18.

Toman, M.A., J. Pezzey and J. Krautkraemer (1994), 'Neoclassical Economic Growth Theory and Sustainability', in D. Bromley (ed.), *Handbook of Environmental Economics*, Oxford: Blackwell, pp. 139–65.

Verhoef, E.T. and J.C.J.M. van den Bergh (1996), 'A Spatial Price Equilibrium Model for Environmental Policy Analysis of Mobile and Immobile Sources of Pollution', in J.C.J.M. van den Bergh, P. Nijkamp and P. Rietveld (eds), *Recent Advances in Spatial Equilibrium Modelling*, Berlin: Springer-Verlag, pp. 201–20.

Index